ALSO BY JAMES W. LOEWEN

Lies Across America: What Our Historic Sites Get Wrong

Lies My Teacher Told Me About Christopher Columbus

The Mississippi Chinese: Between Black and White

Mississippi: Conflict and Change (with Charles Sallis et al.)

Rethinking Our Past: Recognizing Facts, Fiction, and Lies in American History

Social Science in the Courtroom

Sundown Towns:
A Hidden Dimension of American Racism

LIES
MY TEACHER
TOLD ME

EVERYTHING YOUR AMERICAN
HISTORY TEXTBOOK GOT WRONG

James W. Loewen

A Touchstone Book

Published by Simon & Schuster

New York London Toronto Sydney

ILLUSTRATION AND TEXT CREDITS
15, Smithsonian Institution; 44, Lee Boltin; 49, 58, Library of Congress; 59, New York
Public Library; 109, Library of Congress; 112, Smithsonian Institution; 115, Library of
Congress; 119, D. W. Meinig/Yale University Press; 120, Library of Congress; 129, Division of Parks, Recreation, and Historic Sites, Georgia Department of Natural Resources;
133, Amway Environmental Foundation; 169, Scott Nearing; 187, Collection of architectural toys and games, Canadian Centre for Architecture/Centre Canadien d'Architecture,
Montréal, acquired with the support of Bell Québec; 202, Mississippi Department of
Archives and History; 205, Andrea Ades Vasquez, American Social History Project;
210, Miller Brewing Co.; 219 ("What Did You Learn in School Today?" by Tom Paxton),
© 1962, 1990 Cherry Lane Music Publ. Co., all rights reserved, used by permission;
223, Bettmann/Corbis; 246, 247, 248, AP/Wide World Photos; 249 (left) Ronald L.
Haeberle/Life magazine © Time Warner, (right) Bettmann/Corbis; 251, Fred Ward/
Black Star; 272, Walter Reed Army Medical Center; 277, Mother Jones; 283, Boy Scouts of
America; 310, The Norman Rockwell Agency.

Touchstone
A Division of Simon & Schuster, Inc.
1230 Avenue of the Americas
New York, NY 10020

This Touchstone trade paperback edition October 2007

TOUCHSTONE and colophon are registered trademarks of Simon & Schuster, Inc.

For information about special discounts for bulk purchases, please contact Simon &
Schuster Special Sales at 1-800-456-6798 or business@simonandschuster.com

Designed by Mary Austin Speaker

Manufactured in the United States of America

20   19   18   17   16   15   14   13   12   11

Library of Congress Cataloging-in-Publication Data is available.

ISBN-13: 978-0-7432-9628-1
ISBN-10:   0-7432-9628-1

Dedicated to all American history teachers
who teach against their textbooks
(and their ranks are growing)

ACKNOWLEDGMENTS

TO THE FIRST EDITION

THE PEOPLE LISTED BELOW in alphabetical order talked with me, commented on chapters, suggested sources, corrected my mistakes, or provided other moral or material aid. I thank them very much. They are: Ken Ames, Charles Arnaude, Stephen Aron, James Baker, Jose Barreiro, Carol Berkin, Sanford Berman, Robert Bieder, Bill Bigelow, Michael Blakey, Linda Brew, Tim Brookes, Josh Brown, Lonnie Bunch, Vernon Burton, Claire Cuddy, Richard N. Current, Pete Daniel, Kevin Dann, Martha Day, Margo Del Vecchio, Susan Dixon, Ariel Dorfman, Mary Dyer, Shirley Engel, Bill Evans, John Fadden, Patrick Ferguson, Paul Finkelman, Frances FitzGerald, William Fitzhugh, John Franklin, Michael Frisch, Mel Gabler, James Gardiner, John Garraty, Elise Guyette, Mary E. Haas, Patrick Hagopian, William Haviland, Gordon Henderson, Mark Hilgendorf, Richard Hill, Mark Hirsch, Dean Hoge, Jo Hoge, Jeanne Houck, Frederick Hoxie, David Hutchinson, Carolyn Jackson, Clifton H. Johnson, Elizabeth Judge, Stuart Kaufman, David Kelley, Roger Kennedy, Paul Kleppner, J. Morgan Kousser, Gary Kulik, Jill Laramie, Ken Lawrence, Mary Lehman, Steve Lewin, Garet Livermore, Lucy Loewen, Nick Loewen, Barbara M. Loste, Mark Lytle, John Marciano, J. Dan Marshall, Juan Mauro, Edith Mayo, James McPherson, Dennis Meadows, Donella Meadows, Dennis Medina, Betty Meggars, Milton Meltzer, Deborah Menkart, Donna Morgenstern, Nanepashemet, Janet Noble, Roger Norland, Jeff Nygaard, Jim O'Brien, Wardell Payne, Mark Pendergrast, Larry Pizer, Bernice Reagon, Ellen Reeves, Joe Reidy, Roy Rozensweig, Harry Rubenstein, Faith Davis Ruffins, John Salter, Saul Schniderman,

Barry Schwartz, John Anthony Scott, Louis Segal, Ruth Selig, Betty Sharpe, Brian Sherman, David Shiman, Beatrice Siegel, Barbara Clark Smith, Luther Spoehr, Jerold Starr, Mark Stoler, Bill Sturtevant, Lonn Taylor, Linda Tucker, Harriet Tyson, Ivan Van Sertima, Herman Viola, Virgil J. Vogel, Debbie Warner, Barbara Woods, Nancy Wright, and John Yewell.

Three institutions helped materially. The Smithsonian Institution awarded me two senior postdoctoral fellowships. Members of its staff provided lively intellectual stimulation, as did my fellow fellows at the National Museum of American History. Interns at the Smithsonian from the University of Michigan, Johns Hopkins, and especially Portland State University chased down errant facts. The flexible University of Vermont allowed me to go on leave to work on this book, including a sabbatical leave in 1993. Finally, The New Press, André Schiffrin, and especially my editor, Diane Wachtell, provided consistent encouragement and intelligent criticism.

TO THE SECOND EDITION

AS I ENDURED THE MORAL and intellectual torture of subjecting myself to six new high school American history textbooks in 2006–07, the following assisted in important ways: Cindy King, David Luchs, Susan Luchs, Natalie Martin, Jyothi Natarajan, the Life Cycle Institute and Department of Sociology at Catholic University of America, and Joey the guide dog in training. Many of the folks thanked for their assistance with the first edition—including those at The New Press—also helped this time. So did Amanda Patten at Simon & Schuster.

CONTENTS

INTRODUCTION

TO THE SECOND EDITION

I really like your book, Lies My Teacher Told Me. *I've been using it to heckle my history teacher from the back of the room.* —HIGH SCHOOL STUDENT[1]

I just wanted to let you know that I don't consider Lies My Teacher Told Me *outdated; I really don't see much improvement in textbooks at all!*
—HIGH SCHOOL TEACHER, SHERWOOD, AR[2]

I was expecting some liberal bullshit, but I thought it was right on.
—WORKER, BAYER PHARMACEUTICALS, BERKELEY, CA[3]

R EADERS NEW TO *Lies My Teacher Told Me* should go straight to page one. This introduction tells old friends (and enemies?) how this edition differs from the first and why it came to be. Since it came to be largely because reader response to the first edition was so positive, the introduction seems self-congratulatory to me—another reason to skip it. *Lies My Teacher Told Me* does take readers on a voyage of discovery through our past, however, and some readers may want to learn of the reactions of fellow passengers.

From the first day, readers made *Lies* a success. As its name implies, The New Press was a small fledgling publisher without an advertising budget; word of mouth caused *Lies* to sell. The book first created a stir on the West Coast. "Although the book is considered controversial by some, libraries in Alameda County [California] can't keep it on their shelves," reported an article at California State University at Hayward. A high school student wrote to the editor of the *San Francisco Examiner:* "I was a poor (D-plus) student in history until I read *People's History of the United States* and *Lies My Teacher Told Me.* After reading those two books, my GPA in history rose to 3.8 and stayed there. If you truly want students to take an interest in American history, then stop lying to them."[4] An early review in the *San Francisco Chronicle* called *Lies* "an extremely convincing plea for truth in education," and my book spent several weeks on the Bay Area bestseller list in 1995.[5]

Independent bookstores—the kind whose owners and clerks read books and whose customers ask them for recommendations—spread the buzz across North America. "Turns American history upside down," wrote "Joan" of Toronto in 1995 in a column called "Best New Books Recommended by Leading Independent Bookstores." "A landmark book," she went on, "a must read, not only for teachers of history and those who write it, but for any thinking individual."[6] *The Nation*, a national magazine, said that *Lies* "contains so much history that it ends up functioning not just as a critique but also as a kind of counter-textbook that retells the story of the American past." Soon *Lies* reached the bestseller lists in Boston; Burlington, Vermont; and other cities. It was also a bestseller for the History and Quality Paperback Book Clubs. In paperback, *Lies* has gone through more than thirty printings at Simon & Schuster. From the launch of Amazon.com, *Lies* has been the sales leader in its category (historiography). So far as I can tell, *Lies* is the bestselling book by a living sociologist.[7] Counting all editions, including Recorded Books, sales of the first edition totaled about a million copies.

I wrote *Lies My Teacher Told Me* partly because I believed that Americans took great interest in their past but had been bored to tears by their high school American history courses. Readers' reactions confirmed this belief. Their responses were not only wide, but deep. "My history classes in high school, I found, were not important to me or my life," e-mailed one reader from the San Francisco area, because they "did not make it relevant to what was happening today." Some adult readers had always blamed themselves for their lack of interest in high school history. "For all these years (I am forty-nine), I have had the opinion that I don't like history," wrote a woman from Utah, "when in truth, what I don't like is illogic, or inconsistency. Thank you for your work. You have changed my life."

Many readers found the book to be a life-changing experience. A forklift operator in Ohio, a forty-seven-year-old housewife in Denver, a "do-gooder" in upstate New York were inspired to finish college or graduate school and change careers by reading this book. "Words cannot describe how much your book has changed me," wrote a woman from New York City. "It's like seeing everything through new eyes. The eyes of truth as I like to call it." While readers repeat adjectives like "shocked," "stunned," and "disillusioned," many have also found *Lies* to be uplifting.

To be sure, not every reaction was positive. Although one reader "never could decide whether you were a Socialist or a Republican," others thought they could and that *Lies* suffers from a leftward bias. "Marxist/hippie/socialist/ anti-American/anti-Christian" commented one reader at Amazon.com, who would be shocked to learn my real feelings about capitalism. "What a piece of racist trash," said an anonymous postcard from El Paso. "Take your sour mind to Africa where you can adjust *that* history."

That was, of course, a white response—a *very* white response. Very different has been the reaction from "Indian country." A reader who I infer is part-Indian wrote:

> Your book *Lies My Teacher Told Me*, and especially the chapter "Red Eyes," has had an unprecedented effect on how I view the world. I have never felt inclined to write a letter of approval for anything I've read before. Your description of the Indian experience in the United States and, more importantly, the concept of a syncretic American society has subtly, but powerfully, changed my understanding of my country, and, in fact, my own ancestry.

If, as *Lies My Teacher Told Me* shows, history is the least-liked subject in American high schools, it is positively abhorred in Indian country. There it is the record of five centuries of defeat. Yet, properly understood, American history is not a record of Native incompetence but of survival and perseverance. From speaking before Native audiences in six states, I have come to understand to what extent false history holds Native Americans down. I now believe that only when they accurately understand their past—including their recent past—will young American Indians find the social and intellectual power to make history in the twenty-first century. That understanding must include the concept of syncretism—blending elements from two different cultures to come up with something new. Syncretism is how cultures typically change and survive, and all Americans need to understand that Native American cultures, too, must change to survive. Natives as well as non-Natives often labor under the misapprehension that "real" Indian culture was those practices that existed before white contact. Actually, real Indian culture is still being produced—by sculptors like Nalenik Temela (page 133), musicians like Keith Secola, and American Indian parents everywhere.

Lies has also enjoyed huge success among African Americans. In the fall of 2004, for example, it reached number three on the bestseller list of Essence magazine and was the only book on that list by a nonblack author. "My students, who are all African Americans, were immensely enthused and energized by your book," wrote a sociology professor at Hampton University. A Missouri native wrote that he found Lies My Teacher Told Me and Lies Across America "incredibly empowering" and planned "to buy an extra copy of both books and leave them in the barbershop I patronize in downtown St. Louis. I figure if one or two kids read it, it will make a huge difference for generations to come."

Working-class groups and labor historians have also enjoyed Lies. "Thanks again for your scholarship and solidarity in helping show the side of the story that best reflects the roots of the other 90 percent who aren't wealthy," wrote a nonwealthy reader in 2004. Programs in gay and lesbian studies and women's studies have also invited me to speak, even though Lies My Teacher Told Me— unlike its successor Lies Across America—contains no explicit treatment of sexual identity or preference or gender issues.[8] Prisoners respond positively, too: a Wisconsin inmate, for example, wrote, "My congratulations to you for the courage you had to have to write such a book that goes against the grain." Hardly least, "regular" white folks—even males—like my book, too, perhaps because I take obvious satisfaction in and give credit to those white men from Bartolomé de Las Casas through Robert Flournoy to Mississippi judge Orma Smith who have fought for justice for all of us.

If Lies My Teacher Told Me has made such an impact, why this new edition? Especially when the book, as of 2007, was selling better than ever, averaging nearly two thousand copies per week?

Back in 2003, writing from Walnut Creek, California, a devoted reader convinced me of the need for a new edition. "I think many people believe that your book describes problems that USED TO exist in school textbooks, not as current problems," she e-mailed me. "My own anecdotal experience with my own kids' school textbooks is that many of your original findings remain valid. An updated edition would make it harder for people to minimize your book's truth by characterizing it as dated." Questions from audiences over the years taught me that despite my debunking of automatic progress in Chapter 11, many readers still believe in the myth, even as applied to the textbook publishing industry. The problems I noted with high school history books were so galling that these readers *want* to believe—and therefore *do* believe—that the books must have improved. Unfortunately, we cannot assume progress. Whether history textbooks have improved is an empirical question. It can only be answered with data. And it is an interesting question, especially to me, because it subsumes another query: Did my book make any difference?

So I spent much of 2006–07 pondering six new U.S. history textbooks. I did find them improved in a few regards—especially in their treatment of Christopher Columbus and the ensuing Columbian Exchange. I also found them worse or unchanged in many other regards—but that is the subject of the rest of the book. It's safe to conclude that *Lies* didn't influence textbook publishers very much. This did not surprise me, because fifteen years earlier, Frances FitzGerald's critique of textbooks, *America Revised*, was also a bestseller, but it, too, made little impact on the industry.

However, *Lies* did reach and move teachers. Doing so is important, because one teacher can reach a hundred students, and another hundred next year. Teachers were a central audience I had in mind as I wrote *Lies*. What have they made of it?

Sadly, a few teachers rejected *Lies* unread, concluding from its title that I am one more teacher-basher. The book itself never bashes teachers. As a former college professor who in a typical semester appeared before students for nine hours a week, I have great respect for K–12 teachers. Many work in classrooms for as many as thirty-five hours a week; on top of that they must assign, read, and comment on homework, prepare and grade exams, and develop next week's lesson plans. When are they supposed to find time to research what they teach in American history? During their unpaid summers and weekends? Moreover, I realize that a sizable proportion—I used to estimate 25 to 30 percent, but the number is growing—of high school American history teachers are serious about their subject. They study it themselves and get their students involved in doing history and critiquing their textbooks. In speeches to teacher groups, I used to begin by acknowledging all the foregoing, trying to persuade them to venture beyond the book's title.[9] Moreover, there is a certain tension between the title and the subtitle, "Everything Your American History Textbook Got Wrong." If teachers merely rely on their textbooks, however, and try to get students to "learn" them, and if the textbooks are as bad as the next eleven chapters suggest, then teachers are complicit in miseducating their charges about our past.

In central Illinois, a teacher provided an example of what to do about bad textbooks. In autumn 2003, treating the early years of the republic, she told her sixth graders in passing that most presidents before Lincoln were slave owners. Her students were outraged—not with the presidents, but with her, for lying to them. "That's not true," they protested, "or it would be in the book!" They pointed out that the book devoted many pages to Washington, Jefferson, Madison, Jackson, and other early presidents, pages that said not one word about their owning slaves. "Maybe I'm wrong, then," she replied, suggesting that they check her facts. Each chose a president and found out about him. When they regrouped, they were outraged at their textbook for denying them this information. They wrote letters to the putative author and the publisher. The author never replied, which did not surprise me—as we shall see, many authors never wrote "their" textbooks, especially in their later editions. Some are even deceased. The students did get a reply from a spokesperson at the publisher. "We are always glad to get feedback on our product," it went, or boilerplate to that effect. Then it suggested, "If you will look at pages 501–506, you will find substantial treatment of the Civil Rights Movement." The students looked at each other blankly: how did this relate to their complaint?

Such a critique is a win-win action for students. Either they improve the textbook for the next generation of students, or they learn that a vacuum resides at the intellectual center of the textbook establishment. Either way, they become critical readers for the rest of the academic year.

The story of these sixth graders shows that we underestimate children at our peril. Teachers who have gotten students as young as fourth grade to challenge textbooks and do original research have found that they exceeded expectations. A fifth-grade teacher in far southwestern Virginia wrote me that at the start of the year his students say they hate history. "Within two weeks, all or most love history." He gets them involved with:

> primary source documents such as newspaper accounts and actual photos of freedmen being lynched. This is tough on the kids sometimes but they handle it well. They get an attitude about evil and vow to keep it from happening. They no longer think that video games with people getting blown up are funny. They even start to check out books on history and read them and get away from the sanitized vanilla yogurt in the textbooks and shoot for a five-alarm chili type of history. They love history that has "the good stuff" in it. And then they are promoted and go back to the textbook!

Which creates a problem. They raise hell with the next teacher! They become politically active within the middle school. They look like they will become good citizens.

Surely good citizens are what we want—but what do we mean by a "good citizen"? Educators first required American history as a high school subject as part of a nationalist flag-waving campaign around 1900. Its nationalistic genesis has always interfered with its basic mission: to prepare students to do their job *as Americans*.

Again, what exactly is our job as Americans? Surely it is *to bring into being the America of the future.* What should characterize that nation? How should it balance civil liberties and surveillance against potential terrorists? Should it allow gay marriage? What should its energy policies be, as the world's finite supply of oil begins to impact upon us? To participate in these discussions and influence these debates, good citizens need to be able to evaluate the claims that our leaders and would-be leaders make. They must read critically, winnow fact from fraud, and seek to understand causes and results in the past. These skills must stand at the center of any competent history course.

These are *not* skills that American history textbooks foster—even the recent ones. Nor do courses based on them. Why then do teachers put up with such books? The answer: they make their busy lives easier. The teachers' edition of *Holt American Nation*, to take one example, begins with twenty-two pages of ads making this point. One page touts its "Management System." It contrasts two photographs. One shows a teacher struggling to carry a textbook, several other books, some overhead projections, a binder of lecture notes, and miscellaneous papers, the other a teacher smiling as she slips a single CD into her purse. "Everything you need is on one disk!" trumpets the ad, including "editable lesson plans," "classroom presentations" containing lecture notes suitable for projection, and an "easy-to-use test generator." No longer do teachers need to make their own lesson plans or construct their own tests, and if they run out of things to say in the classroom, the disk also contains previews of the teaching resources and movies that Holt offers as ancillary materials. Many of these supplements, including a series of CNN videos, are more valuable education tools than the textbook itself. The problem is that the purpose of all the ancillaries is to get teachers to adopt Holt's textbook. Then, since the textbook runs to 1,240 pages—and all too many teachers assign them all—students are unlikely to have time to do anything with any of these additional materials.

Sometimes help comes from the top down. Many school systems have grown displeased with the low student morale in these textbook-driven history courses. As a matter of school-board policy, at least two systems require any teacher in social studies or history to read my book. Homeschoolers have also found their way to *Lies My Teacher Told Me*. Wrote David Stanton, editor of a resource catalog for homeschoolers, "I read it cover to cover (including the footnotes), found it hard to put down, and was sad when it ended."

Students have also taken matters into their own hands. A fourteen-year-old in Mount Vernon, South Dakota, going into the ninth grade, had already read *Lies My Teacher Told Me* and *Lies Across America*. "These are EXCELLENT books!" she wrote. "After reading them, I spread them around the school to different teachers. All were shocked and, due to this, are changing their teaching methods." John Jennings, a high school student somewhere in cyberspace, wrote that he and a group of his friends "have read your book *Lies My Teacher Told Me* and it has opened our eyes to the true history behind our country, positive and negative." He went on to add that he is "signed up to take American History next semester . . . and we are using one of the twelve textbooks you reviewed, so I can't wait to attempt to start discussions in class concerning issues discussed in your book and use your book as a reference." A North Carolina dad wrote, "My daughter uses *Lies My Teacher Told Me* as a guerrilla text in her grade eleven Advanced Placement U.S. History, and loves it—although the teacher isn't always as pleased." My favorite e-mail of all came in from a lad somewhere at AOL.com: "Dear Mr. Loewen, I really like your book, *Lies My Teacher Told Me*. I've been using it to heckle my history teacher from the back of the room." My friends all like it, too, he went on. "If I could get a group price on it from the publisher, I could sell it in the corridors of my high school." I got him the group price, and since then, several teachers—perhaps including his—have told me that my book, in the hands of precocious pupils, made their lives miserable until they got their own copy, which jarred them out of their textbook rut. So there is also hope from the bottom up.

Best of all has been the response in the "aftermarket"—adults who have turned to *Lies* because they sensed something remiss about their boring high school history courses. Many find it a book to share. "I read it twice and then it made the round of friends who were stubborn about returning it, but I finally got it back and now I'm reading it again," wrote a security guard in California. "After completing each successive chapter, I always felt that I had to comment to a friend about what I just learned," wrote a graduate-student-to-be in education. "I have been sharing your information with every teacher I can get to stand still for five minutes," wrote a teacher's aide in Montana. "This is a book that you buy two of," wrote a professor in New Hampshire, "one to read and keep, and one to lend or give away." A reader in Sherman Oaks, California, said, "It is more than just interesting: it is life-enriching. I will give copies as gifts . . . for years to come." Some readers get them cheap: they join the Quality Paperback Book Club to obtain four copies of *Lies* for a dollar each, give them to four friends, quit the club, then join again to get four more.[10]

I hope you find this new edition of *Lies* as useful as the first in getting people to question what they think they know about American history. If you do, share it with others. No doubt the publisher would like to sell everyone you know a copy, but I'm happiest when *Lies* gets multiple readers. I'm also happy to get readers' reactions—positive or negative[11]—to my work. You can reach me through my website, uvm.edu/~jloewen/, or jloewen@uvm.edu.

INTRODUCTION

SOMETHING HAS GONE VERY WRONG

It would be better not to know so many things than to know so many things that are not so. —JOSH BILLINGS[1]

American history is longer, larger, more various, more beautiful, and more terrible than anything anyone has ever said about it. —JAMES BALDWIN[2]

Concealment of the historical truth is a crime against the people.
—GEN. PETRO G. GRIGORENKO, SAMIZDAT LETTER
TO A HISTORY JOURNAL, c. 1975, USSR[3]

Those who don't remember the past are condemned to repeat the eleventh grade.
—JAMES W. LOEWEN

HIGH SCHOOL STUDENTS hate history. When they list their favorite subjects, history invariably comes in last. Students consider history "the most irrelevant" of twenty-one subjects commonly taught in high school. *Bor-r-ring* is the adjective they apply to it. When students can, they avoid it, even though most students get higher grades in history than in math, science, or English.[4] Even when they are forced to take classes in history, they repress what they learn, so every year or two another study decries what our seventeen-year-olds don't know.[5]

Even male children of affluent white families think that history as taught in high school is "too neat and rosy."[6] African American, Native American, and Latino students view history with a special dislike. They also learn history especially poorly. Students of color do only slightly worse than white students in mathematics. If you'll pardon my grammar, nonwhite students do more worse in English and most worse in history.[7] Something intriguing is going on here: surely history is not more difficult for minorities than trigonometry or Faulkner. Students don't even know they are alienated, only that they "don't *like* social studies" or "aren't any good at history." In college, most students of color give history departments a wide berth.

Many history teachers perceive the low morale in their classrooms. If they have a lot of time, light domestic responsibilities, sufficient resources, and a flexible principal, some teachers respond by abandoning the overstuffed textbooks and reinventing their American history courses. All too many teachers grow disheartened and settle for less. At least dimly aware that their students are not requiting their own love of history, these teachers withdraw some of their energy from their courses. Gradually they end up going through the motions, staying ahead of their students in the textbooks, covering only material that will appear on the next test.

College teachers in most disciplines are happy when their students have had significant exposure to the subject before college. Not teachers in history. History professors in college routinely put down high school history courses. A colleague of mine calls his survey of American history "Iconoclasm I and II," because he sees his job as disabusing his charges of what they learned in high school to make room for more accurate information. In no other field does this happen. Mathematics professors, for instance, know that non-Euclidean geometry is rarely taught in high school, but they don't assume that Euclidean geometry was *mistaught*. Professors of English literature don't presume that *Romeo and Juliet* was misunderstood in high school. Indeed, history is the only field in which the more courses students take, the stupider they become.

Perhaps I do not need to convince you that American history is important. More than any other topic, it is about *us*. Whether one deems our present society wondrous or awful or both, history reveals how we arrived at this point. Understanding our past is central to our ability to understand ourselves and the world around us. We need to know our history, and according to sociologist C. Wright Mills, we know we do.[8]

Outside of school, Americans show great interest in history. Historical novels, whether by Gore Vidal (*Lincoln, Burr*, et al.) or Dana Fuller Ross (*Idaho!, Utah!, Nebraska!, Oregon!, Missouri!*, and on! and on!) often become bestsellers. The National Museum of American History is one of the three big draws of the Smithsonian Institution. The series *The Civil War* attracted new audiences to public television. Movies based on historical incidents or themes are a continuing source of fascination, from *Birth of a Nation* through *Gone With the Wind* to *Dances with Wolves*, *JFK*, and *Saving Private Ryan*. Not history itself but traditional American history courses turn students off.

Our situation is this: American history is full of fantastic and important stories. These stories have the power to spellbind audiences, even audiences of difficult seventh graders. These same stories show what America has been about and are directly relevant to our present society. American audiences, even young ones, need and want to know about their national past. Yet they sleep through the classes that present it.

What has gone wrong?

We begin to get a handle on this question by noting that textbooks dominate American history courses more than they do any other subject. When I first came across that finding in the educational research literature, I was dumbfounded. I would have guessed almost anything else—plane geometry, for instance. After all, it would be hard for students to interview elderly residents of their community about plane geometry, or to learn about it from library books or old newspaper files or the thousands of photographs and documents at the Library of Congress website. All these resources—and more—are relevant to American history. Yet it is in history classrooms, not geometry, where students spend more time reading from their textbooks, answering the fifty-five boring questions at the end of each chapter, going over those answers aloud, and so on.[9]

Between the glossy covers, American history textbooks are full of information—overly full. These books are huge. The specimens in my original collection of a dozen of the most popular textbooks averaged four and a half pounds in weight and 888 pages in length. To my astonishment, during the last twelve years they grew even larger. In 2006 I surveyed six new books. (Owing to publisher consolidation, there no longer are twelve.) Three are new editions of "legacy textbooks," descended from books originally published half a century ago; three are "new new" books.[10] These six new books average 1,150 pages and almost six pounds! I never imagined they would get bigger. I had thought—hoped?—that the profusion of resources on the Web would make it obvious that these behemoths are obsolete. The Web did not exist when the earlier batch of textbooks came into being. In those days, for history textbooks to be huge made some sense: students in Bogue Chitto, Mississippi, say, or Beaver Dam, Wisconsin, had few resources in American history other than their textbooks. No longer: today every school that has a phone line is connected to the Web.

There students can browse hundreds of thousands of primary sources including newspaper articles, the census, historic photographs, and original documents, as well as secondary interpretations from scholars, citizens, other students, and rascals and liars. No longer is there any need to supply students with nine months' reading between the covers of one book, written or collected by a single set of authors.

The new books are so huge that they may endanger their readers. Each of the 1,104 pages in *The American Journey* is wider and taller than any page in the twelve already enormous high school textbooks in my original sample. Surely at 5.6 pounds, *Journey* is the heaviest book ever assigned to middle-school children in the history of American education. (At more than $84, it may also be the most expensive.) A new nonprofit organization, Backpack Safety America, has formed, spurred by chiropractors and other health care professionals. Its mission is "to reduce the weight of textbooks and backpacks." In the meantime, pending that accomplishment, chiropractors are visiting schools teaching proper posture and lifting techniques.[11]

Publishers, too, realize that the books look formidably large, so they try to disguise their total page count by creative pagination. *Journey*, for example, has 1,104 pages but manages to come in under a thousand by using separate numbering for thirty-two pages at the front of the book and seventy-two pages at the end. Students aren't fooled. They know these are by far the heaviest volumes to lug home, the largest to hold in the lap, and the hardest to get excited about.

Editors also realize how daunting these books appear to the poor children who must read them, so they provide elaborate introductions and enticements, beginning with the table of contents. For *The Americans*, for example, a 1,358-page textbook from McDougal Littell weighing in at almost seven pounds, the table of contents runs twenty-two pages. It is profusely illustrated and has little colored banners with titles like "Geography Spotlight," "Daily Life," and "Historical Spotlight." Right after it comes a three-page layout, "Themes in History" and "Themes in Geography." Then come hints on how to read the complex, disjointed thirty- to forty-page chapters. "Each chapter begins with a two-page chapter opener," it says. "Study the chapter opener to help you get ready to read."

"Oh, no," groan students. "Nothing good will come of this." They know that no one has to tell them how to get ready to read a Harry Potter book or any other book that is readable. Something different is going on here.

Unfortunately, having a still bigger book only spurs conscientious teachers to spend even more time making sure students read it and deal with its hundreds of minute questions and tasks. This makes history courses even more boring. Publishers then try to make their books more interesting by inserting various special aids to give them eye appeal. But these gimmicks have just the opposite effect. Many are completely useless, except to the marketing department. Consider the little colored banners in the table of contents of *The Americans*. No student would ever need to have a list of the "Geography Spotlights" in this book. One spotlight happens to be "The Panama Canal," but the student seeking information on the canal would find it by looking in the index in the back, not by surmising that it might be a Geography Spotlight, then finding that list within the twenty-two pages of contents in the front, and then scanning it to see if *Panama Canal* appears. The only possible use for these bannered lists is for the sales rep to point to when trying to get a school district to adopt the book.

The books are huge so that no publisher will lose an adoption because a book has left out a detail of concern to a particular geographical area or group. Textbook authors seem compelled to include a paragraph about every U.S. president, even William Henry Harrison and Millard Fillmore. Then there are the review pages at the end of each chapter. *The Americans*, to take one example, highlights 840 "Main Ideas Within Its Main Text." In addition, the text contains 310 "Skill Builders," 890 "Terms and Names," 466 "Critical Thinking" questions, and still other projects within its chapters. And that's not counting the hundreds of terms and questions in the two-page reviews that follow each chapter. At year's end, no student can remember 840 main ideas, not to mention 890 terms and countless other factoids. So students and teachers fall back on one main idea: to memorize the terms for the test on that chapter, then forget them to clear the synapses for the next chapter. No wonder so many high school graduates cannot remember in which century the Civil War was fought![12]

Students are right: the books are boring.[13] The stories that history textbooks tell are predictable; every problem has already been solved or is about to be solved. Textbooks exclude conflict or real suspense. They leave out anything that might reflect badly upon our national character. When they try for drama, they achieve only melodrama, because readers know that everything will turn out fine in the end. "Despite setbacks, the United States overcame these challenges," in the words of one textbook. Most authors of history textbooks don't even try for melodrama. Instead, they write in a tone that if heard aloud might be described as "mumbling lecturer." No wonder students lose interest.

Authors almost never use the present to illuminate the past. They might ask students to consider gender roles in contemporary society as a means of prompting students to think about what women did and did not achieve in the suffrage movement or the more recent women's movement. They might ask students to prepare household budgets for the families of a janitor and a stockbroker as a means of prompting thinking about labor unions and social classes in the past and present. They might, but they don't. The present is not a source of information for writers of history textbooks.

Conversely, textbooks seldom use the past to illuminate the present. They portray the past as a simpleminded morality play. "Be a good citizen" is the message that textbooks extract from the past. "You have a proud heritage. Be all that you can be. After all, look at what the United States has accomplished." While there is nothing wrong with optimism, it can become something of a burden for students of color, children of working-class parents, girls who notice the dearth of female historical figures, or members of any group that has not achieved socioeconomic success. The optimistic approach prevents any understanding of failure other than blaming the victim. No wonder children of color are alienated. After a thousand pages, bland optimism gets pretty offputting for everyone.

Textbooks in American history stand in sharp contrast to other teaching materials. Why are history textbooks so bad? Nationalism is one of the culprits. Textbooks are often muddled by the conflicting desires to promote inquiry and to indoctrinate blind patriotism. "Take a look in your history book, and you'll see why we should be proud" goes an anthem often sung by high school glee clubs. But we need not even look inside.[14] The titles themselves tell the story: *The Great Republic, The American Pageant, Land of Promise, Triumph of the American Nation.*[15] Such titles differ from the titles of all other textbooks students read in high school or college. Chemistry books, for example, are called *Chemistry* or *Principles of Chemistry*, not *Triumph of the Molecule*. And you can tell history textbooks just from their covers, graced as they are with American flags, bald eagles, the Washington Monument.

None of the facts is remembered, because they are presented simply as one damn thing after another. While textbook authors tend to include most of the trees and all too many twigs, they neglect to give readers even a glimpse of what they might find memorable: the forests. Textbooks stifle meaning by suppressing causation. Students exit history textbooks without having developed the ability to think coherently about social life.

Even though the books bulge with detail, even though the courses are so busy they rarely reach 1960, our teachers and our textbooks still leave out most of what we need to know about the American past. And despite their emphasis on facts, some of the factoids they present are flatly wrong or unverifiable. Errors often go uncorrected, partly because the history profession does not bother to review high school textbooks. In sum, startling errors of omission and distortion mar American histories. History can be imagined as a pyramid. At its base are the millions of primary sources—the plantation records, city directories, census data, speeches, songs, photographs, newspaper articles, diaries, and letters that document times past. Based on these primary materials, historians write secondary works—books and articles on subjects ranging from deafness on Martha's Vineyard to Grant's tactics at Vicksburg. Historians produce hundreds of these works every year, many of them splendid. In theory, a few historians, working individually or in teams, then synthesize the secondary literature into tertiary works—textbooks covering all phases of U.S. history.

In practice, however, it doesn't happen that way. Instead, history textbooks are clones of each other. The first thing editors do when recruiting new authors is to send them a half-dozen examples of the competition. Often a textbook is written not by the authors whose names grace its cover, but by minions deep in the bowels of the publisher's offices. When historians do write textbooks, they risk snickers from their colleagues—tinged with envy, but snickers nonetheless: "Why are you devoting time to pedagogy rather than original research?"

The result is not happy for textbook scholarship. Many history textbooks list up-to-the-minute secondary sources in their bibliographies, yet the narratives remain totally traditional—unaffected by recent research.[16]

What would we think of a course in poetry in which students never read a poem? The editor's voice in an English literature textbook might be as dull as the voice in a history textbook, but at least in the English textbook the voice stills when the book presents original works of literature. The omniscient narrator's voice of history textbooks insulates students from the raw materials of history. Rarely do authors quote speeches, songs, diaries, or letters. Students need not be protected from this material. They can just as well read one paragraph from William Jennings Bryan's "Cross of Gold" speech as read *American Adventures'* two paragraphs *about* it.

Textbooks also keep students in the dark about the nature of history. History is furious debate informed by evidence and reason. Textbooks encourage students to believe that history is facts to be learned. "We have not avoided controversial issues," announces one set of textbook authors; "instead, we have tried to offer reasoned judgments" on them—thus removing the controversy! Because textbooks employ such a godlike tone, it never occurs to most students to question them. "In retrospect I ask myself, why *didn't* I think to ask, for example, who *were* the original inhabitants of the Americas, what was *their* life like, and how did it change when Columbus arrived," wrote a student of mine in 1991. "However, back then everything was presented as if it were the full picture," she continued, "so I never thought to doubt that it was."

As a result of all this, most high school seniors are hamstrung in their efforts to analyze controversial issues in our society. (I know because I encounter these students the next year as college freshmen.) We've got to do better. Five-sixths of all Americans never take a course in American history beyond high school. What our citizens "learn" in high school forms much of what they know about our past.

This book includes eleven chapters of amazing stories—some wonderful, some ghastly—in American history, including a new chapter on our two Iraq wars and the continuing "war on terrorism." Arranged in roughly chronological order, these chapters do not relate mere details but events and processes with important consequences. Yet most textbooks leave out or distort these events and processes. I know, because for twenty years I have been lugging around eighteen textbooks, taking them seriously as works of history and ideology, studying what they say and don't say, and trying to figure out why. I chose these eighteen as representing the range of textbooks available for American history courses.[17] These books, which are listed (with full citations) in the Appendix, have been my window into the world of what high school students carry home, read, memorize, and forget. In addition, I have spent many hours observing high school history classes in Mississippi, Vermont, and the Washington, D.C., metropolitan area, and more hours talking with high school history teachers.

Chapter 12 analyzes the process of textbook creation and adoption in an attempt to explain what causes textbooks to be as bad as they are. I must confess an interest here: I once co-wrote a history textbook. *Mississippi: Conflict and Change* was the first revisionist state history textbook in America. Although the book won the Lillian Smith Award for "best nonfiction about the South" in 1975, Mississippi rejected it for use in public schools. In turn, three local school systems, my coauthor, and I sued the state textbook board. In April 1980 *Loewen et al. v. Turnipseed et al.* resulted in a sweeping victory on the basis of the First and Fourteenth Amendments. The experience taught me firsthand more than most writers or publishers would ever want to know about the textbook adoption process. I also learned that not all the blame can be laid at the doorstep of the adoption agencies.

Chapter 13 looks at the effects of using standard American history textbooks. It shows that the books actually make students stupid. Finally, an afterword cites distortions and omissions undiscussed in earlier chapters and recommends ways that teachers can teach and students can learn American history more honestly. It is offered as an inoculation program of sorts against the future lies we are otherwise sure to encounter.

As a sociologist, I am reminded constantly of the power of the past. Although each of us comes into the world *de novo,* we are not really new creatures. We arrive into a social slot, born not only to a family but also a religion, community, and, of course, a nation and a culture. Sociologists understand the power of social structure and culture to shape not only our path through the world but also our understanding of that path and that world. Yet we often have to expend much energy trying to get students to see the influence on their lives of the social structure and culture they inherit. Not understanding their past renders many Americans incapable of thinking effectively about our present and future. If our journey together through this book will make the realities of our past more apparent, then this "most irrelevant" subject—American history—might become more relevant to you. At least, that's my hope.

I.

HANDICAPPED BY HISTORY

THE PROCESS OF HERO-MAKING

What passes for identity in America is a series of myths about one's heroic ancestors.
                                                                    —JAMES BALDWIN[1]

One is astonished in the study of history at the recurrence of the idea that evil must be forgotten, distorted, skimmed over. We must not remember that Daniel Webster got drunk but only remember that he was a splendid constitutional lawyer. We must forget that George Washington was a slave owner . . . and simply remember the things we regard as creditable and inspiring. The difficulty, of course, with this philosophy is that history loses its value as an incentive and example; it paints perfect men and noble nations, but it does not tell the truth.   —W.E.B. DUBOIS[2]

By idolizing those whom we honor, we do a disservice both to them and to ourselves. . . . We fail to recognize that we could go and do likewise.
                                                                    —CHARLES V. WILLIE[3]

T HIS CHAPTER is about heroification, a degenerative process (much like calcification) that makes people over into heroes. Through this process, our educational media turn flesh-and-blood individuals into pious, perfect creatures without conflicts, pain, credibility, or human interest.

Many American history textbooks are studded with biographical vignettes of the very famous (*Land of Promise* devotes a box to each president) and the famous (*The Challenge of Freedom* provides "Did You Know?" boxes about Elizabeth Blackwell, the first woman to graduate from medical school in the United States, and Lorraine Hansberry, author of *A Raisin in the Sun*, among many others). In themselves, vignettes are not a bad idea. They instruct by human example. They show diverse ways that people can make a difference. They allow textbooks to give space to characters such as Blackwell and Hansberry, who relieve what would otherwise be a monolithic parade of white male political leaders. Biographical vignettes also provoke reflection as to our purpose in teaching history: Is Chester A. Arthur more deserving of space than, say, Frank Lloyd Wright? Who influences us more today—Wright, who invented the carport and transformed domestic architectural spaces, or Arthur, who, um, signed the first Civil Service Act? Whose rise to prominence provides more drama—Blackwell's or George H. W. Bush's (the latter born with a silver Senate seat in his mouth[4])? The choices are debatable, but surely textbooks should include some people based not only on what they achieved but also on the distance they traversed to achieve it.

We could go on to third- and fourth-guess the list of heroes in textbook pantheons. My concern here, however, is not who gets chosen, but rather what happens to the heroes when they are introduced into our history textbooks and our classrooms. Two twentieth-century Americans provide case studies of heroification: Woodrow Wilson and Helen Keller. Wilson was unarguably an important president, and he receives extensive textbook coverage. Keller, on the other hand, was a "little person" who pushed through no legislation, changed the course of no scientific discipline, declared no war. Only one of all the history textbooks I surveyed includes her photograph. Most books don't even mention her. But teachers love to talk about Keller and often show audiovisual materials or recommend biographies that present her life as exemplary. All this attention ensures that students retain something about both of these historical figures, but they may be no better off for it. Heroification so distorts the lives of Keller and Wilson (and many others) that we cannot think straight about them.

Teachers have held up Helen Keller, the blind and deaf girl who overcame her physical handicaps, as an inspiration to generations of schoolchildren. Every fifth grader knows the scene in which Anne Sullivan spells *water* into young Helen's hand at the pump. At least a dozen movies and filmstrips have been made on Keller's life. Each yields its version of the same cliché. A McGraw-Hill educational film concludes: "The gift of Helen Keller and Anne Sullivan to the world is to constantly remind us of the wonder of the world around us and how much we owe those who taught us what it means, for there is no person that is unworthy or incapable of being helped, and the greatest service any person can make us is to help another reach true potential."[5]

To draw such a bland maxim from the life of Helen Keller, historians and filmmakers have disregarded her actual biography and left out the lessons she specifically asked us to learn from it. Keller, who struggled so valiantly to learn to speak, has been made mute by history. The result is that we really don't know much about her.

Over the past twenty years, I have asked hundreds of college students who Helen Keller was and what she did. All know that she was a blind and deaf girl. Most remember that she was befriended by a teacher, Anne Sullivan, and learned to read and write and even to speak. Some can recall rather minute details of Keller's early life: that she lived in Alabama, that she was unruly and without manners before Sullivan came along, and so forth. A few know that Keller graduated from college. But about what happened next, about the whole of her adult life, they are ignorant. A few students venture that Keller became a "public figure" or a "humanitarian," perhaps on behalf of the blind or deaf. "She wrote, didn't she?" or "she spoke"—conjectures without content. Keller, who was born in 1880, graduated from Radcliffe in 1904 and died in 1968. To ignore the sixty-four years of her adult life or to encapsulate them with the single word *humanitarian* is to lie by omission.

The truth is that Helen Keller was a radical socialist. She joined the Social-

Always a voice for the voiceless, Helen Keller championed women's suffrage. Her position at the head of this 1912 demonstration shows her celebrity status as well as her commitment to the cause. The shields are all from western states, where women were already voting.

ist Party of Massachusetts in 1909. She had become a social radical even before she graduated from Radcliffe, and *not*, she emphasized, because of any teachings available there. After the Russian Revolution, she sang the praises of the new communist nation: "In the East a new star is risen! With pain and anguish the old order has given birth to the new, and behold in the East a man-child is born! Onward, comrades, all together! Onward to the campfires of Russia! Onward to the coming dawn!" [6] Keller hung a red flag over the desk in her study. Gradually she moved to the left of the Socialist Party and became a Wobbly, a member of the Industrial Workers of the World (IWW), the syndicalist union persecuted by Woodrow Wilson.

Keller's commitment to socialism stemmed from her experience as a disabled person and from her sympathy for others with handicaps. She began by working to simplify the alphabet for the blind, but soon came to realize that to deal solely with blindness was to treat symptom, not cause. Through research she learned that blindness was not distributed randomly throughout the population but was concentrated in the lower class. Men who were poor might be blinded in industrial accidents or by inadequate medical care; poor women who became prostitutes faced the additional danger of syphilitic blindness. Thus Keller learned how the social class system controls people's opportunities in life, sometimes determining even whether they can see. Keller's research was not just book learning: "I have visited sweatshops, factories, crowded slums. If I could not see it, I could smell it." [7]

At the time Keller became a socialist, she was one of the most famous women on the planet. She soon became the most notorious. Her conversion to socialism caused a new storm of publicity—this time outraged. Newspapers that had extolled her courage and intelligence now emphasized her handicap. Columnists charged that she had no independent sensory input and was in thrall to those who fed her information. Typical was the editor of the *Brooklyn Eagle,* who wrote that Keller's "mistakes spring out of the manifest limitations of her development."

Keller recalled having met this editor: "At that time the compliments he paid me were so generous that I blush to remember them. But now that I have come out for socialism he reminds me and the public that I am blind and deaf and especially liable to error. I must have shrunk in intelligence during the years since I met him." She went on, "Oh, ridiculous *Brooklyn Eagle!* Socially blind and deaf, it defends an intolerable system, a system that is the cause of much of the physical blindness and deafness which we are trying to prevent." [8]

Keller, who devoted much of her later life to raising funds for the American Foundation for the Blind, never wavered in her belief that our society needed radical change. Having herself fought so hard to speak, she helped found the American Civil Liberties Union to fight for the free speech of others. She sent $100 to the NAACP with a letter of support that appeared in its magazine *The Crisis*—a radical act for a white person from Alabama in the 1920s. She supported Eugene V. Debs, the Socialist candidate, in each of his campaigns for the presidency. She composed essays on the women's movement, on politics, on economics. Near the end of her life, she wrote to Elizabeth Gurley Flynn, leader of the American Communist Party, who was then languishing in jail, a victim of the McCarthy era: "Loving birthday greetings, dear Elizabeth Flynn! May the sense of serving mankind bring strength and peace into your brave heart!"[9]

One may not agree with Helen Keller's positions. Her praise of the USSR now seems naïve, embarrassing, to some even treasonous. But she *was* a radical—a fact few Americans know, because our schooling and our mass media left it out.[10]

What we did not learn about Woodrow Wilson is even more remarkable.

Among the progressive-era reforms with which students often credit Woodrow Wilson is women's suffrage. Although women did receive the right to vote during Wilson's administration, the president was at first unsympathetic. He had suffragists arrested; his wife detested them. Public pressure, aroused by hunger strikes and other actions of the movement, convinced Wilson that to oppose women's suffrage was politically unwise. Textbooks typically fail to show the interrelationship between the hero and the people. By giving the credit to the hero, authors tell less than half of the story.

When I ask my college students to tell me what they recall about President Wilson, they respond with enthusiasm. They say that Wilson led our country reluctantly into World War I and after the war led the struggle nationally and internationally to establish the League of Nations. They associate Wilson with progressive causes like women's suffrage. A handful of students recall the Wilson administration's Palmer raids against left-wing unions. But my students seldom know or speak about two antidemocratic policies that Wilson carried out: his racial segregation of the federal government and his military interventions in foreign countries.

Under Wilson, the United States intervened in Latin America more often than at any other time in our history. We landed troops in Mexico in 1914, Haiti in 1915, the Dominican Republic in 1916, Mexico again in 1916 (and nine more times before the end of Wilson's presidency), Cuba in 1917, and Panama in 1918. Throughout his administration Wilson maintained forces in Nicaragua, using them to determine Nicaragua's president and to force passage of a treaty preferential to the United States.

In 1917 Woodrow Wilson took on a major power when he started sending secret monetary aid to the "White" side of the Russian civil war. In the summer of 1918 he authorized a naval blockade of the Soviet Union and sent expeditionary forces to Murmansk, Archangel, and Vladivostok to help overthrow the Russian Revolution. With the blessing of Britain and France, and in a joint command with Japanese soldiers, American forces penetrated westward from Vladivostok to Lake Baikal, supporting Czech and White Russian forces that had declared an anticommunist government headquartered at Omsk. After briefly maintaining front lines as far west as the Volga, the White Russian forces disintegrated by the end of 1919, and our troops finally left Vladivostok on April 1, 1920.[11]

Few Americans who were not alive at the time know anything about our "unknown war with Russia," to quote the title of Robert Maddox's book on this fiasco. Not one of the twelve American history textbooks in my original sample even mentioned it. Two of the six new books do; Boorstin and Kelley, for example, write: "The United States, hoping to keep stores of munitions from falling into German hands when Bolshevik Russia quit fighting, contributed some 5,000 troops to an Allied invasion of northern Russia at Archangel. Wilson likewise sent nearly 10,000 troops to Siberia as part of an Allied expedition." It is possible, although surely difficult, for an American student to infer from that passage that Wilson was intervening in Russia's civil war.

Russian textbooks, on the other hand, give the episode considerable coverage. According to Maddox: "The immediate effect of the intervention was to prolong a bloody civil war, thereby costing thousands of additional lives and wreaking enormous destruction on an already battered society. And there were longer-range implications. Bolshevik leaders had clear proof . . . that the Western powers meant to destroy the Soviet government if given the chance." [12]

This aggression fueled the suspicions that motivated the Soviets during the Cold War, and until its breakup the Soviet Union continued to claim damages for the invasion.

Wilson's invasions of Latin America are better known than his Russian adventure. Textbooks do cover some of them, and it is fascinating to watch textbook authors attempt to justify these episodes. Any accurate portrayal of the invasions could not possibly show Wilson or the United States in a favorable light. With hindsight we know that Wilson's interventions in Cuba, the Dominican Republic, Haiti, and Nicaragua set the stage for the dictators Batista, Trujillo, the Duvaliers, and the Somozas, whose legacies still reverberate. [13] Even in the 1910s, most of the invasions were unpopular in this country and provoked a torrent of criticism abroad. By the mid-1920s, Wilson's successors reversed his policies in Latin America. The authors of history textbooks know this, for a chapter or two after Wilson they laud our "Good Neighbor Policy," the renunciation of force in Latin America by Presidents Coolidge and Hoover, which was extended by Franklin D. Roosevelt.

Textbooks might (but don't) call Wilson's Latin American actions a "Bad Neighbor Policy" by comparison. Instead, faced with unpleasantries, textbooks—old and new—wriggle to get the hero off the hook, as in this example from the old *Challenge of Freedom*: "President Wilson wanted the United States to build friendships with the countries of Latin America. However, he found this difficult. . . ." Several textbooks blame the invasions on the countries invaded: "Wilson recoiled from an aggressive foreign policy," states the new *American Pageant*. "Political turmoil in Haiti soon forced Wilson to eat some of his anti-imperialist words. . . . Wilson reluctantly dispatched marines to protect American lives and property." This passage is sheer invention. Unlike his secretary of the navy, who later complained that what Wilson "forced [me] to do in Haiti was a bitter pill for me," no documentary evidence suggests that Wilson suffered any such qualms about dispatching troops to the Caribbean. [14]

Every textbook I surveyed mentions Wilson's 1914 invasion of Mexico, but they posit that the interventions were not Wilson's fault. "Cries for intervention burst from the lips of American jingoes," according to *Pageant* in 2006. "Yet President Wilson stood firm against demands to step in." Soon Wilson *did* order troops to Mexico, of course, even before Congress gave him authority to do so. Walter Karp has shown that this view of a reluctant Wilson again contradicts the facts—the invasion was Wilson's idea from the start, and it upset Congress as well as the American people.[15] Wilson's intervention was so outrageous that leaders of both sides of Mexico's ongoing civil war demanded that the U.S. forces leave; the pressure of public opinion in the United States and around the world finally influenced Wilson to recall the troops.

Textbook authors commonly use another device when describing our Mexican adventures: they identify Wilson as ordering our forces to withdraw, but nobody is specified as having ordered them in! Imparting information in a passive voice helps to insulate historical figures from their own unheroic or unethical deeds.

Some books go beyond omitting the actor and leave out the act itself. Half of the textbooks do not even mention Wilson's takeover of Haiti. After U.S. marines invaded the country in 1915, they forced the Haitian legislature to select our preferred candidate as president. When Haiti refused to declare war on Germany after the United States did, we dissolved the Haitian legislature. Then the United States supervised a pseudo-referendum to approve a new Haitian constitution, less democratic than the constitution it replaced; the referendum passed by a hilarious 98,225 to 768. As Piero Gleijesus has noted, "It is not that Wilson failed in his earnest efforts to bring democracy to these little countries. He never tried. He intervened to impose hegemony, not democracy."[16] The United States also attacked Haiti's proud tradition of individual ownership of small tracts of land, which dated back to the Haitian Revolution, in favor of the establishment of large plantations. American troops forced peasants in shackles to work on road construction crews. In 1919 Haitian citizens rose up and resisted U.S. occupation troops in a guerrilla war that cost more than three thousand lives, most of them Haitian. Students who read *Pathways to the Present* learn this about Wilson's intervention in Haiti: "In Haiti, the United States stepped in to restore stability after a series of revolutions left the country weak and unstable. Wilson . . . sent in American troops in 1915. United States marines occupied Haiti until 1934." These bland sentences veil what we did, about which George Barnett, a U.S. marine general, complained to his commander in Haiti: "Practically indiscriminate killing of natives has gone on for some time." Barnett termed this violent episode "the most startling thing of its kind that has ever taken place in the Marine Corps." [17]

During the first two decades of this century, the United States effectively made colonies of Nicaragua, Cuba, the Dominican Republic, Haiti, and several other countries. Nor, as we have seen, did Wilson limit his interventions to our hemisphere. His reaction to the Russian Revolution solidified the alignment of the United States with Europe's colonial powers. His was the first administration to be obsessed with the specter of communism, abroad and at home. Wilson was blunt about it. In Billings, Montana, stumping the West to seek support for the League of Nations, he warned, "There are apostles of Lenin in our own midst. I can not imagine what it means to be an apostle of Lenin. It means to be an apostle of the night, of chaos, of disorder." [18] Even after the White Russian alternative collapsed, Wilson refused to extend diplomatic recognition to the Soviet Union. He participated in barring Russia from the peace negotiations after World War I and helped oust Béla Kun, the communist leader who had risen to power in Hungary. Wilson's sentiment for self-determination and democracy never had a chance against his three bedrock "ism"s: colonialism, racism, and anticommunism. A young Ho Chi Minh appealed to Woodrow Wilson at Versailles for self-determination for Vietnam, but Ho had all three strikes against him. Wilson refused to listen, and France retained control of Indochina.[19] It seems that Wilson regarded self-determination as all right for, say, Belgium, but not for the likes of Latin America or Southeast Asia.

At home, Wilson's racial policies disgraced the office he held. His Republican predecessors had routinely appointed blacks to important offices, including those of port collector for New Orleans and the District of Columbia and register of the treasury. Presidents sometimes appointed African Americans as postmasters, particularly in southern towns with large black populations. African Americans took part in the Republican Party's national conventions and enjoyed some access to the White House. Woodrow Wilson, for whom many African Americans voted in 1912, changed all that. A Southerner, Wilson had been president of Princeton, the only major northern university that flatly refused to admit blacks. He was an outspoken white supremacist—his wife was even worse—and told "darky" stories in cabinet meetings. His administration submitted an extensive legislative program intended to curtail the civil rights of African Americans, but Congress would not pass it. Unfazed, Wilson used his power as chief executive to segregate the federal government. He appointed

Southern whites to offices traditionally reserved for blacks. His administration used the excuse of anticommunism to surveil and undermine black newspapers, organizations, and union leaders. He segregated the navy, which had not previously been segregated, relegating African Americans to kitchen and boiler work. Wilson personally vetoed a clause on racial equality in the Covenant of the League of Nations. The one occasion on which Wilson met with African American leaders in the White House ended in a fiasco as the president virtually threw the visitors out of his office. Wilson's legacy was extensive: he effectively closed the Democratic Party to African Americans for another two decades, and parts of the federal government remained segregated into the 1950s and beyond.[20] In 1916 the Colored Advisory Committee of the Republican National Committee issued a statement on Wilson that, though partisan, was accurate: "No sooner had the Democratic Administration come into power than Mr. Wilson and his advisors entered upon a policy to eliminate all colored citizens from representation in the Federal Government."[21]

Of all the history textbooks I reviewed, eight never even mention this "black mark" on Wilson's presidency. Only four accurately describe Wilson's racial policies. *Land of Promise*, back in 1983, did the best job:

> Woodrow Wilson's administration was openly hostile to black people. Wilson was an outspoken white supremacist who believed that black people were inferior. During his campaign for the presidency, Wilson promised to press for civil rights. But once in office he forgot his promises. Instead, Wilson ordered that white and black workers in federal government jobs be segregated from one another. This was the first time such segregation had existed since Reconstruction! When black federal employees in Southern cities protested the order, Wilson had the protesters fired. In November, 1914, a black delegation asked the President to reverse his policies. Wilson was rude and hostile and refused their demands.

Most of the textbooks that do treat Wilson's racism give it only a sentence or two. Some take pains to separate Wilson from the practice: "Wilson allowed his Cabinet officers to extend the Jim Crow practice of separating the races in federal offices" is the entire treatment in *Pathways to the Present*. Omitting or absolving Wilson's racism goes beyond concealing a character blemish. It is overtly racist. No black person could ever consider Woodrow Wilson a hero. Textbooks that present him as a hero are written from a white perspective. The cover-up denies all students the chance to learn something important about the interrelationship between the leader and the led. White Americans engaged in a new burst of racial violence during and immediately after Wilson's presidency. The tone set by the administration was one cause. Another was the release of America's first epic motion picture.[22]

The filmmaker D. W. Griffith quoted Wilson's two-volume history of the United States, now notorious for its racist view of Reconstruction, in his infamous masterpiece *The Clansman*, a paean to the Ku Klux Klan for its role in putting down "black-dominated" Republican state governments during Reconstruction. Griffith based the movie on a book by Wilson's former classmate, Thomas Dixon, whose obsession with race was "unrivaled until *Mein Kampf*," according to historian Wyn Wade. At a private White House showing, Wilson saw the movie, now retitled *Birth of a Nation*, and returned Griffith's compliment: "It is like writing history with lightning, and my only regret is that it is all so true." Griffith would go on to use this quotation in successfully defending his film against NAACP charges that it was racially inflammatory.[23]

This landmark of American cinema was not only the best technical production of its time but also probably the most racist major movie of all time. Dixon intended "to revolutionize northern sentiment by a presentation of history that would transform every man in my audience into a good Democrat! . . . And make no mistake about it—we are doing just that."[24] Dixon did not overstate by much. Spurred by *Birth of a Nation*, William Simmons of Georgia reestablished the Ku Klux Klan. The racism seeping down from the White House encouraged this Klan, distinguishing it from its Reconstruction predecessor, which President Grant had succeeded in virtually eliminating in one state (South Carolina) and discouraging nationally for a time. The new KKK quickly became a national phenomenon. It grew to dominate the Democratic Party in many Southern states, as well as in Indiana, Oklahoma, and Oregon. Klan spectacles in the 1920s in towns from Montpelier, Vermont, to West Frankfort, Illinois, to Medford, Oregon, were the largest public gatherings in their history, before or since. During Wilson's second term, a wave of antiblack race riots swept the country. Whites lynched blacks as far north as Duluth.[25]

Americans need to learn from the Wilson era, that there is a connection between racist presidential leadership and like-minded public response. To accomplish such education, however, textbooks would have to make plain the relationship between cause and effect, between hero and followers. Instead, they reflexively ascribe noble intentions to the hero and invoke "the people" to excuse questionable actions and policies. According to *Triumph of the American Nation:* "As President, Wilson seemed to agree with most white Americans that segregation was in the best interests of black as well as white Americans."

Wilson was not only antiblack; he was also far and away our most nativist president, repeatedly questioning the loyalty of those he called "hyphenated Americans." "Any man who carries a hyphen about with him," said Wilson, "carries a dagger that he is ready to plunge into the vitals of this Republic whenever he gets ready."[26] The American people responded to Wilson's lead with a wave of repression of white ethnic groups; again, most textbooks blame the people, not Wilson. *The American Tradition* admits that "President Wilson set up" the Creel Committee on Public Information, which saturated the United States with propaganda linking Germans to barbarism. But *Tradition* hastens to shield Wilson from the ensuing domestic fallout: "Although President Wilson had been careful in his war message to state that most Americans of German descent were 'true and loyal citizens,' the anti-German propaganda often caused them suffering."

Wilson displayed little regard for the rights of anyone whose opinions differed from his own. But textbooks take pains to insulate him from wrongdoing. "Congress," not Wilson, is credited with having passed the Espionage Act of June 1917 and the Sedition Act of the following year, probably the most serious attacks on the civil liberties of Americans since the short-lived Alien and Sedition Acts of 1798. In fact, Wilson tried to strengthen the Espionage Act with a provision giving broad censorship powers directly to the president. Moreover, with Wilson's approval, his postmaster general used his new censorship powers to suppress all mail that was socialist, anti-British, pro-Irish, or that in any other way might, in his view, have threatened the war effort. Robert Goldstein served three years in prison for producing *The Spirit of '76,* a film about the Revolutionary War that depicted the British, who were now our allies, unfavorably.[27] Textbook authors suggest that wartime pressures excuse Wilson's suppression of civil liberties, but in 1920, when World War I was long over, Wilson vetoed a bill that would have abolished the Espionage and Sedition acts.[28] Textbook authors blame the anticommunist and anti–labor union witch hunts of Wilson's second term on his illness and on an attorney general run amok. No evidence supports this view. Indeed, Attorney General Palmer asked Wilson in his last days as president to pardon Eugene V. Debs, who was serving time for a speech attributing World War I to economic interests and denouncing the

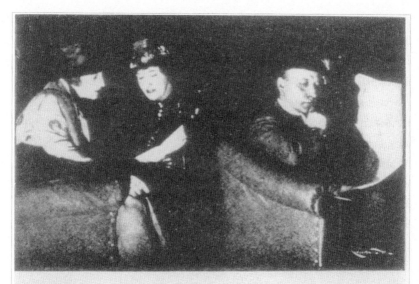

Spies *and* Lies

German agents are everywhere, eager to gather scraps of news about our men, our ships, our munitions. It is still possible to get such information through to Germany, where thousands of these fragments—often individually harmless—are patiently pieced together into a whole which spells death to American soldiers and danger to American homes.

But while the enemy is most industrious in trying to collect information, and his systems elaborate, he is *not* superhuman—indeed he is often very stupid, and would fail to get what he wants were it not deliberately handed to him by the carelessness of loyal Americans.

Do not discuss in public, or with strangers, any news of troop and transport movements, or bits of gossip as to our military preparations, which come into your possession.

Do not permit your friends in service to tell you—or write you—"inside" facts about where they are, what they are doing and seeing.

Do not become a tool of the Hun by passing on the malicious, disheartening rumors which he so eagerly sows. Remember he asks no better service than to have you spread his lies of disasters to our soldiers and sailors, gross scandals in the Red Cross, cruelties, neglect and wholesale executions in our camps, drunkenness and vice in the Expeditionary Force, and other tales certain to disturb American patriots and to bring anxiety and grief to American parents.

And do not wait until you catch someone putting a bomb under a factory. Report the man who spreads pessimistic stories, divulges—or seeks—confidential military information, cries for peace, or belittles our efforts to win the war.

Send the names of such persons, even if they are in uniform, to the Department of Justice, Washington. Give all the details you can, with names of witnesses if possible—show the Hun that we can beat him at his own game of collecting scattered information and putting it to work. The fact that you made the report will not become public.

You are in contact with the enemy *today*, just as truly as if you faced him across No Man's Land. In your hands are two powerful weapons with which to meet him—discretion and vigilance. *Use them.*

COMMITTEE ON PUBLIC INFORMATION
8 JACKSON PLACE, WASHINGTON, D. C.

Contributed through Division of Advertising  United States Gov't Comm. on Public Information

Creel Committee Advertising in the "Saturday Evening Post"

To oppose America's participation in World War I, or even to be pessimistic about it, was dangerous. The Creel Committee asked all Americans to "report the man who . . . cries for peace, or belittles our efforts to win the war." Send their names to the Justice Department in Washington, it exhorted. After World War I, the Wilson administration's attacks on civil liberties increased, now with anticommunism as the excuse. Neither before nor since these campaigns has the United States come closer to being a police state.

Espionage Act as undemocratic.[29] The president replied, "Never!" and Debs languished in prison until Warren Harding pardoned him.[30] *The American Way* adopts perhaps the most innovative approach to absolving Wilson of wrongdoing: *Way* simply moves the "red scare" to the 1920s, after Wilson had left office!

Because heroification prevents textbooks from showing Wilson's shortcomings, textbooks are hard-pressed to explain the results of the 1920 election. James Cox, the Democratic candidate who was Wilson's would-be successor, was crushed by the nonentity Warren G. Harding, who never even campaigned. In the biggest landslide in the history of American presidential politics, Harding got almost 64 percent of the major-party votes. The people were "tired," textbooks suggest, and just wanted a "return to normalcy." The possibility that the electorate knew what it was doing in rejecting Wilson never occurs to our authors.[31] It occurred to Helen Keller, however. She called Wilson "the greatest individual disappointment the world has ever known!"

It isn't only high school history courses that heroify Wilson. Those few textbooks that do discuss Wilson's racism and other shortcomings, such as *Land of Promise*, have to battle uphill, for they struggle against the archetypal Woodrow Wilson commemorated in so many history museums, public television documentaries, and historical novels.

For twenty-five years now, Michael Frisch has been conducting an experiment in social archetypes at the State University of New York at Buffalo. He asks his first-year college students for "the first ten names that you think of" in American history before the Civil War. When Frisch found that his students listed the same political and military figures year after year, replicating the privileged positions afforded them in high school textbooks, he added the proviso, "excluding presidents, generals, statesmen, etc." Frisch still gets a stable list, but one less predictable on the basis of history textbooks. Most years, Betsy Ross has led the list. (Paul Revere usually comes in second.)

What is interesting about this choice is that Betsy Ross never did anything. Frisch notes that she played "no role whatsoever in the actual creation of any actual first flag." Ross came to prominence around 1876, when some of her descendants, seeking to create a tourist attraction in Philadelphia, largely invented the myth of the first flag. With justice, high school textbooks universally ignore Betsy Ross; not one high school textbook lists her in its index.[32] So how and why does her story get transmitted? Frisch offers a hilarious explanation: If George Washington is the Father of Our Country, then Betsy Ross is our

Blessed Virgin Mary! Frisch describes the pageants reenacted (or did we only imagine them?) in our elementary school years: "Washington [the god] calls on the humble seamstress Betsy Ross in her tiny home and asks her if she will make the nation's flag, to his design. And Betsy promptly brings forth—from her lap!—the nation itself, and the promise of freedom and natural rights for all mankind."[33]

I think Frisch is onto something, but maybe he is merely on something. Whether or not one buys his explanation, Betsy Ross's ranking among students surely proves the power of the social archetype. In the case of Woodrow Wilson, textbooks actually participate in creating the social archetype. Wilson is portrayed as "good," "idealist," "for self-determination, not colonial intervention," "foiled by an isolationist Senate," and "ahead of his time." We name institutions after him, from the Woodrow Wilson Center at the Ronald Reagan Building in Washington, D.C., to Woodrow Wilson Junior High School in Decatur, Illinois, where I misspent my adolescence. If a fifth face were to be chiseled into Mount Rushmore, many Americans would propose that it should be Wilson's.[34] Against such archetypal goodness, even the unusually forthright treatment of Wilson's racism in *Land of Promise* cannot but fail to stick in students' minds.

Curators of history museums know that their visitors bring archetypes in with them. Some curators consciously design exhibits to confront these archetypes when they are inaccurate. Textbook authors, teachers, and moviemakers

This statue of George Washington, now in the Smithsonian Institution, exemplifies the manner in which textbooks would portray every American hero: ten feet tall, blemish-free, with the body of a Greek god.

would better fulfill their educational mission if they also taught against inaccurate archetypes. Surely Woodrow Wilson does not need their flattering omissions, after all. His progressive legislative accomplishments in just his first two years, including tariff reform, an income tax, the Federal Reserve Act, and the Workingmen's Compensation Act, are almost unparalleled. Wilson's speeches on behalf of self-determination stirred the world, even if his actions did not live up to his words.

Why do textbooks promote wartless stereotypes? The authors' omissions and errors can hardly be accidental. The producers of the filmstrips, movies, and other educational materials on Helen Keller surely know she was a socialist; no one can read Keller's writings without becoming aware of her political and social philosophy. At least one textbook author, Thomas Bailey, senior author of *The American Pageant*, clearly knew of the 1918 U.S. invasion of Russia, for he wrote in a different venue in 1973, "American troops shot it out with Russian armed forces on Russian soil in two theatres from 1918 to 1920."[35] Probably several other authors knew of it, too. Wilson's racism is also well known to professional historians. Why don't they let the public in on these matters?

Heroification itself supplies a first answer. Socialism is repugnant to most Americans. So are racism and colonialism. Michael Kammen suggests that authors selectively omit blemishes to make certain historical figures sympathetic to as many people as possible.[36] The textbook critic Norma Gabler testified that textbooks should "present our nation's patriots in a way that would honor and respect them"; in her eyes, admitting Keller's socialism and Wilson's racism would hardly do that.[37] In the early 1920s the American Legion said that authors of textbooks "are at fault in placing before immature pupils the blunders, foibles and frailties of prominent heroes and patriots of our Nation."[38] The Legion would hardly be able to fault today's history textbooks on this count.

Perhaps we can go further. I began with Helen Keller because omitting the last sixty-four years of her life exemplifies the sort of culture-serving distortion that will be discussed later in this book. We teach Keller as an ideal, not a real person, to inspire our young people to emulate her. Keller becomes a mythic figure, the "woman who overcame"—but for *what?* There is no content! Just look what *she* accomplished, we're exhorted—yet we haven't a clue as to what that really was.

Keller did not want to be frozen in childhood. She herself stressed that the meaning of her life lay in what she did once she overcame her disability. Certainly she was not the first deaf-blind child on record as learning to speak; that honor goes perhaps to Ragnhild Käta, a Norwegian girl whose achievement inspired Keller. Nor was she the first deaf-blind American to learn to read and write; that was Laura Bridgman, who taught the manual alphabet to Anne Sullivan so Sullivan could teach it to Keller. In 1929, when she was nearing fifty, Keller wrote a second volume of autobiography, *Midstream*, that described her social philosophy in some detail. She wrote about visiting mill towns, mining towns, and packing towns where workers were on strike. She intended that we learn of these experiences and of the conclusions to which they led her. Consistent with our American ideology of individualism, the truncated version of Helen Keller's story sanitizes a hero, leaving only the virtues of self-help and hard work. Keller herself, while scarcely opposing hard work, explicitly rejected this ideology.

> I had once believed that we were all masters of our fate—that we could mould our lives into any form we pleased. . . . I had overcome deafness and blindness sufficiently to be happy, and I supposed that anyone could come out victorious if he threw himself valiantly into life's struggle. But as I went more and more about the country I learned that I had spoken with assurance on a subject I knew little about. I forgot that I owed my success partly to the advantages of my birth and environment. . . . Now, however, I learned that the power to rise in the world is not within the reach of everyone.[39]

Textbooks don't want to touch this idea. "There are three great taboos in textbook publishing," an editor at one of the biggest houses told me, "sex, religion, and social class." While I had been able to guess the first two, the third floored me. Sociologists know the importance of social class, after all. Reviewing American history textbooks convinced me that this editor was right, however. The notion that opportunity might be unequal in America, that not everyone has "the power to rise in the world," is anathema to textbook authors, and to many teachers as well. Educators would much rather present Keller as a bland source of encouragement and inspiration to our young—if she can do it, you can do it! So they leave out her adult life and make her entire existence over into a vague "up by the bootstraps" operation. In the process, they make this passionate fighter for the poor into something she never was in life: boring.

Woodrow Wilson gets similarly whitewashed. Although some history textbooks disclose more than others about the seamy underside of Wilson's presidency, all eighteen books reviewed share a common tone: respectful, patriotic, even adulatory. Ironically, Wilson was widely despised in the 1920s. Only after World War II did he come to be viewed kindly by policy makers and historians. Our postwar bipartisan foreign policy, one of far-reaching interventions sheathed in humanitarian explanations, was "shaped decisively by the ideology and the international program developed by the Wilson Administration," according to Gordon Levin Jr.[40] Textbook authors are thus motivated to underplay or excuse Wilson's foreign interventions, many of which were counterproductive blunders, as well as other unsatisfactory aspects of his administration.

A host of other reasons—pressure from the "ruling class," pressure from textbook adoption committees, the wish to avoid ambiguities, a desire to shield children from harm or conflict, the perceived need to control children and avoid classroom disharmony, pressure to provide answers—may help explain why textbooks omit troublesome facts. A certain etiquette coerces us all into speaking in respectful tones about the past, especially when we're passing on Our Heritage to our young. Could it be that we don't *want* to think badly of Woodrow Wilson? We seem to feel that a person like Helen Keller can be an inspiration only so long as she remains uncontroversial, one-dimensional. We don't want complicated icons. "People do not like to think. If one thinks, one must reach conclusions," Helen Keller pointed out. "Conclusions are not always pleasant."[41] Most of us automatically shy away from conflict, and understandably so. We particularly seek to avoid conflict in the classroom. One reason is habit: we are so accustomed to blandness that the textbook or teacher who brings real intellectual controversy into the classroom can strike us as a violation of polite rhetoric, of classroom norms. We are supposed to speak well of the deceased, after all. Probably we are supposed to maintain the same attitude of awe, reverence, and respect when we read about our national heroes as when we visit our National Cathedral and view the final resting places of Helen Keller and Woodrow Wilson, as close physically in death as they were distant ideologically in life.

Whatever the causes, the results of heroification are potentially crippling to students. Helen Keller is not the only person this approach treats like a child. Denying students the human-ness of Keller, Wilson, and others keeps students in intellectual immaturity. It perpetuates what might be called a Disney version of history. Disney's Hall of Presidents similarly presents our leaders as heroic statesmen, not imperfect human beings.[42] Our children end up without realistic role models to inspire them. Students also develop no understanding of causality in history. Our nation's thirteen separate forays into Nicaragua, for instance, are surely worth knowing about as we attempt to understand why that country embraced a communist government in the 1980s. Textbooks should show history as contingent, affected by the power of ideas and individuals. Instead, they present history as a "done deal."

Do textbooks, educational videos, and American history courses achieve the results they seek with regard to our heroes? Surely textbook authors want us to think well of the historical figures they treat with such sympathy. And, on a superficial level at least, we do. Almost no recent high school graduates have anything "bad" to say about either Keller or Wilson. But are these two considered heroes? I have asked hundreds of (mostly white) college students on the first day of class to tell me who their heroes in American history are. As a rule, they do not pick Helen Keller, Woodrow Wilson, Christopher Columbus, Miles Standish or anyone else in Plymouth, John Smith or anyone else in Virginia, Abraham Lincoln, or indeed anyone else in American history whom the textbooks implore them to choose.[43] Our post-Watergate students view all such "establishment" heroes cynically. They're bor-r-ring.

Some students choose "none"—that is, they say they have no heroes in American history. Other students display the characteristically American sympathy for the underdog by choosing African Americans: Martin Luther King Jr., Malcolm X, perhaps Rosa Parks, Harriet Tubman, or Frederick Douglass. Or they choose men and women from other countries: Gandhi, Mother Teresa, or Nelson Mandela.

In one sense this is a healthy development. Surely we want students to be skeptical. Probably we want them to challenge being told whom to believe in. But replying "none" is too glib, too nihilistic, for my taste. It is, however, an understandable response to heroification. For when textbook authors leave out the warts, the problems, the unfortunate character traits, and the mistaken ideas, they reduce heroes from dramatic men and women to melodramatic stick figures. Their inner struggles disappear and they become goody-goody, not merely good.

Students poke fun at the goody-goodiest of them all by telling Helen Keller jokes. In so doing, schoolchildren are not poking cruel fun at a disabled person, they are deflating a pretentious symbol that is too good to be real. Nonetheless, our loss of Helen Keller as anything but a source of jokes is distressing. Knowing the reality of her quite amazing life might empower not only deaf or blind students, but any schoolgirl, and perhaps boys as well. For like other peoples around the world, we Americans need heroes. Statements such as "If Martin Luther King were alive, he'd . . ." suggest one function of historical figures in our contemporary society. Most of us tend to think well of ourselves when we have acted as we imagine our heroes might have done. Who our heroes are and whether they are presented in a way that makes them lifelike, hence usable as role models, could have a significant bearing on our conduct in the world.

We now turn to our first hero, Christopher Columbus. "Care should be taken to vindicate great names from pernicious erudition," wrote Washington Irving, defending heroification.[44] Irving's three-volume biography of Columbus, published in 1828, still influences what high school teachers and textbooks say about the Great Navigator. Therefore, it will come as no surprise that heroification has stolen from us the important facets of his life, leaving only melodramatic minutiae.

2.

1493

THE TRUE IMPORTANCE OF CHRISTOPHER COLUMBUS

Columbus is above all the figure with whom the Modern Age—the age by which we may delineate these past 500 years—properly begins, and in his character as in his exploits we are given an extraordinary insight into the patterns that shaped the age at its start and still for the most part shape it today. —KIRKPATRICK SALE[1]

As a subject for research, the possibility of African discovery of America has never been a tempting one for American historians. In a sense, we choose our own history, or more accurately, we select those vistas of history for our examinations which promise us the greatest satisfaction, and we have had little appetite to explore the possibility that our founding father was a black man. —SAMUEL D. MARBLE[2]

History is the polemics of the victor. —WILLIAM F. BUCKLEY JR.

What we committed in the Indies stands out among the most unpardonable offenses ever committed against God and mankind and this trade [in American Indian slaves] as one of the most unjust, evil, and cruel among them.

—BARTOLOMÉ DE LAS CASAS[3]

In fourteen hundred and ninety-three, Columbus stole all he could see.

—TRADITIONAL VERSE, UPDATED

IN FOURTEEN HUNDRED AND NINETY-TWO, Christopher Columbus sailed in from the blue. American history books present Columbus pretty much without precedent, and they portray him as America's first great hero. In so canonizing him, they reflect our national culture. Indeed, now that Presidents' Day has combined Washington's and Lincoln's birthdays, Columbus is one of only two people the United States honors by name in a national holiday. The one date that every schoolchild remembers is 1492, and sure enough, every textbook I surveyed includes it. But most of them leave out virtually everything that is important to know about Columbus and the European exploration of the Americas. Meanwhile, they make up all kinds of details to tell a better story and to humanize Columbus so readers will identify with him.

Columbus, like Christ, was so pivotal that historians use him to divide the past into epochs, making the Americas before 1492 "pre-Columbian." American history textbooks recognize Columbus's importance by granting him an average of a thousand words—three pages including a picture and a map—a lot of space, considering all the material these books must cover. Their heroic collective account goes something like this:

> Born in Genoa, Italy, of humble parents, Christopher Columbus grew up to become an experienced seafarer. He sailed the Atlantic as far as Iceland and West Africa. His adventures convinced him that the world must be round. Therefore the fabled riches of the East—spices, silk, and gold— could be had by sailing west, superseding the overland route through the Middle East, which the Turks had closed off to commerce.
>
> To get funding for his enterprise, Columbus beseeched monarch after monarch in western Europe. After at first being dismissed by Ferdinand and Isabella of Spain, Columbus finally got his chance when Queen Isabella decided to underwrite a modest expedition.
>
> Columbus outfitted three pitifully small ships, the *Niña*, the *Pinta*, and the *Santa Maria*, and set forth from Spain. The journey was difficult. The ships sailed west into the unknown Atlantic for more than two months. The crew almost mutinied and threatened to throw Columbus overboard. Finally they reached the West Indies on October 12, 1492.
>
> Although Columbus made three more voyages to America, he never really knew he had discovered a New World. He died in obscurity, unappreciated and penniless. Yet without his daring American history would have been very different, for in a sense Columbus made it all possible.

Unfortunately, almost everything in this traditional account is either wrong or unverifiable. The authors of history textbooks have taken us on a trip of their own, away from the facts of history, into the realm of myth. They and we have been duped by an outrageous concoction of lies, half-truths, truths, and omissions that is in large part traceable to the first half of the nineteenth century.

The textbooks' first mistake is to underplay previous explorers. People from other continents had reached the Americas many times before 1492. Even if Columbus had never sailed, other Europeans would have soon reached the Americas. Indeed, Europeans may already have been fishing off Newfoundland in the 1480s.[4] In a sense Columbus's voyage was not the first but the last "discovery" of the Americas. It was epoch-making because of the way in which Europe responded. Columbus's importance is therefore primarily attributable to changing conditions in Europe, not to his having reached a "new" continent.

American history textbooks seem to understand the need to cover social changes in Europe in the years leading up to 1492. They point out that history passed the Vikings by and devote several pages to the reasons Europe was ready this time "to take advantage of the discovery" of America, as one textbook puts it. Unfortunately, none of the textbooks provides substantive analysis of the major changes that prompted the new response.

Most of the books I examined begin the Columbus story with Marco Polo and the Crusades. Here is their composite account of what was happening in Europe:

> "Life in Europe was slow paced." "Curiosity about the rest of the world was at a low point." Then, "many changes took place in Europe during the 500 years before Columbus's discovery of the Americas in 1492." "People's horizons gradually widened, and they became more curious about the world beyond their own localities." "Europe was stirring with new ideas. Many Europeans were filled with burning curiosity. They were living in a period called the Renaissance." "The Renaissance encouraged people to regard themselves as individuals." "What started Europeans thinking new thoughts and dreaming new dreams? A series of wars called the Crusades were partly responsible." "The Crusaders acquired a taste for the exotic delights of Asia." "The desire for more trade quickly spread." "The old trade routes to Asia had always been very difficult."

The accounts resemble each other closely. Sometimes different textbooks even use the same phrases. Overall, the level of scholarship is discouragingly low, perhaps because their authors are more at home in American history than European history. They don't seem to know that the Renaissance was syncretic. That is, Italians combined ideas from India (via the Turks), Greece (preserved by

Muslim scholars), Arabs, and other cultures to form something new. Authors also provide no real causal explanations for the age of European conquest. Instead, they argue for Europe's greatness in transparently psychological terms—"people grew more curious." Such arguments make sociologists smile: we know that nobody measured the curiosity level in Spain in 1492 or can with authority compare it to the curiosity level in, say, Norway or Iceland in 1005.

Several textbooks claim that Europe was becoming richer and that the new wealth led to more trade. Actually, as the historian Angus Calder has pointed out, "Europe was smaller and poorer in the fifteenth century than it had been in the thirteenth," owing in part to the bubonic plague.[5]

Some teachers still teach what their predecessors taught me fifty years ago: that Europe needed spices to disguise the taste of bad meat, but the bad Turks cut off the spice trade. Three books in my original sample—*The American Tradition, Land of Promise,* and *The American Way*—repeated this falsehood. In the words of *Land of Promise,* "Then, after 1453, when Constantinople fell to the Turks, trade with the East all but stopped." But A. H. Lybyer disproved this statement in 1915! Turkey had nothing to do with the development of new routes to the Indies. On the contrary, the Turks had every reason to keep the old Eastern Mediterranean route open, since they made money from it.[6]

In 1957 Jacques Barzun and Henry Graff published a book that has become a standard treatise for graduate students of history, *The Modern Researcher,* in which they pointed out how since 1915, textbooks have perpetuated this particular error. Probably several of the half-dozen authors of the offending textbooks encountered *The Modern Researcher* in graduate school. Somehow the information did not stick. This may be because blaming Turks fits with the West's archetypal conviction that followers of Islam are likely to behave irrationally or nastily. In proposing that Congress declare Columbus Day a national holiday in 1963, Rep. Roland Libonati put it this way: "His Christian faith gave to him a religious incentive to thwart the piratical activities of the Turkish marauders preying upon the trading ships of the Christian world." Of course, recent developments, most especially the terrorist attacks of September 11, 2001, reinforce this archetype of a threatening Islam. College students today are therefore astonished to learn that Turks and Moors allowed Jews and Christians freedom of worship at a time when European Christians tortured or expelled Jews and Muslims. Not a single textbook tells that the Portuguese fleet in 1507 blocked the Red Sea and Persian Gulf to stop trade along the old route, because Portugal controlled the new route, around Africa.[7]

Most textbooks note the increase in international trade and commerce, and some relate the rise of nation-states under monarchies. Otherwise, they do a poor job of describing the changes in Europe that led to the Age of Exploration. Some textbooks even invoke the Protestant Reformation, although it didn't begin until twenty-five years *after* 1492.

What is going on here? We must pay attention to what the textbooks are telling us and what they are not telling us. The changes in Europe not only prompted Columbus's voyages and the probable contemporaneous trips to America by Portuguese, Basque, and Bristol fishermen, but they also paved the way for Europe's domination of the world for the next five hundred years. Except for the invention of agriculture, this was probably the most consequential development in human history. Our history books ought to discuss seriously what happened and why, instead of supplying vague, nearly circular pronouncements such as this from *The American Tradition:* "Interest in practical matters and the world outside Europe led to advances in shipbuilding and navigation."

Perhaps foremost among the significant factors the textbooks leave out are advances in military technology. Around 1400, European rulers began to commission ever bigger guns and learned to mount them on ships. Europe's incessant wars gave rise to this arms race, which also ushered in refinements in archery, drill, and siege warfare. Eventually China, the Ottoman Empire, and other nations in Asia and Africa would fall prey to European arms. In 1493, the Americas began to succumb.[8]

We live with this arms race still. But the West's advantage in military technology over the rest of the world, jealously maintained from the 1400s on, remains very much contested. Just as the thirteen British colonies tried to outlaw the sale of guns to Native Americans,[9] the United States now tries to outlaw the sale of nuclear technology to Third World countries. A key point of George W. Bush's foreign policy has been to deny nuclear weapons and other "weapons of mass destruction" to Iraq, Iran, and North Korea and keep them out of the hands of terrorists like al-Qaeda. Since money is to be made in the arms trade, however, and since all nations need military allies, the arms trade with non-Western nations persists. The Western advantage in military technology is still a burning issue. Nonetheless, not a single textbook mentions arms as a cause of European world domination.

In the years before Columbus's voyages, Europe also expanded the use of new forms of social technology—bureaucracy, double-entry bookkeeping, and mechanical printing. Bureaucracy, which today has negative connotations, was actually a practical innovation that allowed rulers and merchants to manage far-flung enterprises efficiently. So did double-entry bookkeeping, based on the decimal system, which Europeans first picked up from Arab traders. The printing press and increased literacy allowed news of Columbus's findings to travel across Europe much farther and faster than news of the Vikings' expeditions.

A third important development was ideological or even theological: amassing wealth and dominating other people came to be positively valued as the key means of winning esteem on earth and salvation in the hereafter. As Columbus put it, "Gold is most excellent; gold constitutes treasure; and he who has it does all he wants in the world, and can even lift souls up to Paradise." [10] In 1005 the Vikings intended only to settle Vineland, their name for New England and the maritime provinces of Canada. By 1493 Columbus planned to plunder Haiti. [11] The sources are perfectly clear about Columbus's motivation: in 1495, for instance, Michele de Cuneo wrote about accompanying Columbus on his 1494 expedition into the interior of Haiti: "After we had rested for several days in our settlement, it seemed to the Lord Admiral that it was time to put into execution his desire to search for gold, which was the main reason he had started on so great a voyage full of so many dangers." [12] Columbus was no greedier than the Spanish, or later the English and French. But most textbooks downplay the pursuit of wealth as a motive for coming to the Americas when they describe Columbus and later explorers and colonists. Even the Pilgrims left Europe partly to make money, but you would never know it from our textbooks. Their authors apparently believe that to have America explored and colonized for economic gain is somehow undignified.

A fourth factor affecting Europe's readiness to embrace a "new" continent was the particular nature of European Christianity. Europeans believed in a transportable, proselytizing religion that rationalized conquest. (Followers of Islam share this characteristic.) Typically, after "discovering" an island and encountering a tribe of American Indians new to them, the Spaniards would read aloud (in Spanish) what came to be called "the Requirement." Here is one version:

> I implore you to recognize the Church as a lady and in the name of the Pope take the King as lord of this land and obey his mandates. If you do not do it, I tell you that with the help of God I will enter powerfully against you all. I will make war everywhere and every way that I can. I will subject you to the yoke and obedience to the Church and to his majesty. I

will take your women and children and make them slaves. . . . The deaths and injuries that you will receive from here on will be your own fault and not that of his majesty nor of the gentlemen that accompany me.[13]

Having thus satisfied their consciences by offering the Native Americans a chance to convert to Christianity, the Spaniards then felt free to do whatever they wanted with the people they had just "discovered."

A fifth development that caused Europe's reaction to Columbus's reports about Haiti to differ radically from reactions to earlier expeditions was Europe's recent success in taking over and exploiting various island societies. On Malta, Sardinia, the Canary Islands, and, later, in Ireland, Europeans learned that conquest of this sort was a route to wealth. As described below, textbooks now do tell about a sixth factor: the diseases Europeans brought with them that aided their conquest. New and more deadly forms of smallpox, influenza, and bubonic plague had arisen in Europe since the Vikings had sailed.[14]

Why don't textbooks mention arms as a facilitator of exploration and domination? Why do they omit most of the foregoing factors? If crude factors such as military power or religiously sanctioned greed are perceived as reflecting badly on us, who exactly is "us"? Who are the textbooks written for (and by)? Plainly, descendants of the Europeans.

High school students don't usually think about the rise of Europe to world domination. It is rarely presented as a question. It seems natural, a given, not something that needs to be explained. Deep down, our culture encourages us to imagine that we are richer and more powerful because we're smarter. (It's interesting to speculate as to who, exactly, is this "we.") Of course, there are no studies showing Americans to be more intelligent than, say, Iraqis. Quite the contrary: Jared Diamond begins his recent bestseller *Guns, Germs, and Steel* by introducing a friend of his, a New Guinea tribesman, who Diamond thinks is at least as smart as Diamond, even though his culture must be considered "primitive." Still, since textbooks don't identify or encourage us to think about the real causes, "we're smarter" festers as a possibility. Also left festering is the notion that "it's natural" for one group to dominate another.[15] While history brims with examples of national domination, it also is full of counterexamples. The way American history textbooks treat Columbus reinforces the tendency not to think about the process of domination. The traditional picture of Columbus landing on the American shore shows him dominating immediately, and this is based on fact: Columbus claimed everything he saw right off the boat. When textbooks celebrate this process, they imply that taking the land and dominating the natives were inevitable, if not natural. This is unfortunate, because Columbus's voyages constitute a splendid teachable moment. As official missions of a nation-state, they exemplify the new Europe. Merchants and rulers collaborated to finance and authorize them. The second expedition was heavily armed. Columbus carefully documented the voyages, including directions, currents, shoals, and descriptions of the residents as ripe for subjugation. Thanks to the printing press, detailed news of Haiti and later conquests spread swiftly. Columbus had personal experience of the Atlantic islands recently taken over by Portugal and Spain, as well as with the slave trade in West Africa. Most important, his purpose from the beginning was not mere exploration or even trade, but conquest and exploitation, for which he used religion as a rationale.[16] If textbooks included these facts, they might induce students to think intelligently about why the West dominates the world today.

The textbooks concede that Columbus did not start from scratch. Every textbook account of the European exploration of the Americas begins with Prince Henry the Navigator, of Portugal, between 1415 and 1460. Henry is portrayed as discovering Madeira and the Azores and sending out ships to circumnavigate Africa for the first time. The textbook authors seem unaware that ancient Phoenicians and Egyptians sailed at least as far as Ireland and England, reached Madeira and the Azores, traded with the aboriginal inhabitants of the Canary Islands, and sailed all the way around Africa before 600 BC. Instead, the textbooks credit Bartolomeu Dias with being the first to round the Cape of Good Hope at the southern tip of Africa in 1488. Omitting the accomplishments of the Phoenicians is ironic, because it was Prince Henry's knowledge of their feats that inspired him to replicate them.[17] But this information clashes with another social archetype: our culture views modern technology as a European development. So the Phoenicians' feats do not conform to the textbooks' overall story line about how white Europeans taught the rest of the world how to do things. None of the textbooks credits the Muslims with preserving Greek wisdom, enhancing it with ideas from China, India, and Africa, and then passing on the resulting knowledge to Europe via Spain and Italy. Instead, they show Henry inventing navigation and imply that before Europe there was nothing, at least nothing modern. Several books tell how "the Portuguese designed a new kind of sailing ship—the caravel," in the words of Boorstin and Kelley.

In fact, Henry's work was based mostly on ideas that were known to the ancient Egyptians and Phoenicians and had been developed further in Arabia,

North Africa, and China. Even the word the Portuguese applied to their new ships, *caravel,* derived from the Egyptian *caravos.*[18] Cultures do not evolve in a vacuum; diffusion of ideas is perhaps the most important cause of cultural development. Contact with other cultures often triggers a cultural flowering. Anthropologists call this *syncretism:* combining ideas from two or more cultures to form something new. Children in elementary school learn that Persian and Mediterranean civilizations flowered in antiquity owing to their location on trade routes. Here with Henry at the dawn of European world domination, textbooks have a golden opportunity to apply this same idea of cultural diffusion to Europe. They squander it. Not only did Henry have to develop new instruments, according to *The American Way,* but "people didn't know how to build seagoing ships, either."[19] Students are left without a clue as to how aborigines ever reached Australia, Polynesians reached Madagascar, or prehistoric peoples reached the Canaries. By "people" *Way* means, of course, Europeans—a textbook example of Eurocentrism.

These books are expressions of what the anthropologist Stephen Jett calls "the doctrine of the discovery of America by Columbus."[20] Table I provides a chronological list of expeditions that may have reached the Americas before Columbus, with comments on the quality of the evidence for each as of 2006.[21] While the list is long, it is still probably incomplete. A map found in Turkey dated 1513 and said to be based on material from the library of Alexander the Great includes coastline details of South America and Antarctica. Ancient Roman and Carthaginian coins keep turning up all over the Americas, causing some archaeologists to conclude that Roman seafarers visited the Americas more than once.[22] Native Americans also crossed the Atlantic: anthropologists conjecture that Native Americans voyaged east millennia ago from Canada to Scandinavia or Scotland. Two American Indians shipwrecked in Holland around 60 BC became major curiosities in Europe.[23]

The evidence for each of these journeys offers fascinating glimpses into the societies and cultures that existed on both sides of the Atlantic and in Asia before 1492. They also reveal controversies among those who study the distant past. If textbooks allowed for controversy, they could show students which claims rest on strong evidence, which on softer ground. As they challenged students to make their own decisions as to what probably happened, they would also be introducing students to the various methods and forms of evidence—oral history, written records, cultural similarities, linguistic changes, human genetics, pottery, archaeological dating, plant migrations—that researchers use to

TABLE I. EXPLORERS OF AMERICA

YEAR	FROM	TO	QUALITY OF EVIDENCE
70,000? B.C.–12,000? B.C.	Siberia	Alaska	High: the survivors peopled the Americas.
6000? B.C.–1500? B.C.	Indonesia *(or other direction)*	South America	Moderate: similarities in blowguns, papermaking, etc.
5000? B.C.	Japan	Ecuador	Moderate: similar pottery, fishing styles.
10,000? B.C.–600? B.C.	Siberia	Canada, New Mexico	High: Navajos and Crees resemble each other culturally, differ from other Indians.
9000? B.C.– to present	Siberia	Alaska	High: continuing contact by Inuits across Bering Sea.
1000 B.C.	China	Central America	Low: Chinese legend; cultural similarities.
1000 B.C.–AD 300	Afro-Phoenicia	Central America	Moderate: Negroid and Caucasoid likenesses in sculpture and ceramics, Arab history, etc.
500 B.C.	Phoenicia, Celtic Britain	New England, perhaps elsewhere	Low: megaliths, possible similarities in script and language.
A.D. 600	Ireland, via Iceland	Newfoundland? West Indies?	Low: legends of St. Brendan, written c. A.D. 850, confirmed by Norse sagas.
1000–1350	Greenland, Iceland	Labrador, Baffin Land, Newfoundland, Nova Scotia, possibly Cape Cod and further south	High: oral sagas, confirmed by archaeology on Newfoundland.

YEAR	FROM	TO	QUALITY OF EVIDENCE
1304?–1424?	*Polynesia*	*Chile*	*Moderate: chicken bones precede Spanish; similar fishhooks.*
1311?–1460?	*West Africa*	*Haiti, Panama, possibly Brazil*	*Moderate: Portuguese sources in West Africa, Columbus on Haiti, Balboa in Panama.*
c. 1460	*Portugal*	*Newfoundland? Brazil?*	*Low: inference from Portuguese sources and actions.*
1375?–1491	*Basque Spain*	*Newfoundland coast*	*Low: cryptic historical sources.*
1481–91	*Bristol, England*	*Newfoundland coast*	*Low: cryptic historical sources.*
1492	*Spain*	*Caribbean, including Haiti*	*High: historical sources.*

derive knowledge about the distant past. Unfortunately, textbooks seem locked into a rhetoric of certainty. James West Davidson and Mark H. Lytle, coauthors of the textbook *The United States—A History of the Republic*, have also written *After the Fact*, a book for college history majors in which they emphasize that history is not a set of facts but a series of arguments, issues, and controversies.[24] Davidson and Lytle's high school textbook, however, like its competitors, presents history as answers, not questions.

New evidence that emerges, as archaeologists, historians, and biologists compare American cultures and life forms with cultures and life forms in Africa, Europe, and Asia, may confirm or disprove these arrivals. Keeping up with such evidence is a lot of work. To tell about earlier explorers, textbook authors would have to familiarize themselves with sources such as those cited in the three preceding notes. It's easier just to retell the old familiar Columbus story.

Most of the textbooks I studied at least mention the expeditions of the

Norse. These daring sailors reached America in a series of voyages across the North Atlantic, establishing communities on the Faeroe Islands, Iceland, and Greenland. The Norse colony on Greenland lasted five hundred years (982–c. 1500), as long as the European settlement of the Americas until now. From Greenland a series of expeditions, some planned, some accidental, reached various parts of North America, including Baffin Land, Labrador, Newfoundland, and possibly New England.

Most textbooks that mention the Viking expeditions minimize them. *Land of Promise* writes, "They merely touched the shore briefly, and sailed away." Perhaps the authors of *Promise* did not know that, around 1005, Thorfinn and Gudrid Karlsefni led a party of 65 or 165 or 265 homesteaders (the old Norse sagas vary), with livestock and supplies, to settle Vineland. They lasted two years; Gudrid gave birth to a son. Then conflict with Native Americans caused them to give up. This trip was no isolated incident: Norse were still exporting wood from Labrador to Greenland 350 years later. Some archaeologists and historians believe that the Norse got as far down the coast as North Carolina. The Norse discoveries remained known in western Europe for centuries and were never forgotten in Scandinavia. Columbus surely learned of Greenland and probably also of North America if he visited Iceland in 1477 as he claimed to have done.[25]

It may be fair to say that the Vikings' voyages had little lasting effect on the fate of the world. Should textbooks therefore leave them out? Is impact on the present the sole reason for including an event or fact? It cannot be, of course, or our history books would shrink to twenty-page pamphlets. We include the Norse voyages, not for their ostensible geopolitical significance, but because including them gives a more complete picture of the past. Moreover, if textbooks would only intelligently compare the Norse voyages to Columbus's second voyage, they would help students understand the changes that took place in Europe between 1000 and 1493. As we shall see, Columbus's second voyage was ten times larger than the Norse attempts at settlement. The new European ability to mobilize was in part responsible for Columbus's voyages taking on their awesome significance.

Although seafarers from Africa and Asia may also have made it to the Americas, they never make it into history textbooks. The best known are the voyages of the Phoenicians, probably launched from Morocco or West Africa but ultimately deriving from Egypt, that are said to have reached the Atlantic coast of Mexico in about 750 B.C. Organic material associated with colossal heads of basalt that stand along the eastern coast of Mexico has been dated to at least 750 B.C. The stone heads may be realistic portraits of West Africans, perhaps part of the Phoenician group, according to anthropologist Ivan Van Sertima, who has done much to bring these images into popular consciousness.[26] The first non-native person to describe these heads, Jose Melgar, concluded in 1862, "[T]here had doubtless been blacks in this region." Perhaps around the same time, natives elsewhere in Mexico created small ceramic and stone sculptures of what seem to be Caucasoid and Negroid faces. As Alexander von Wuthenau, who collected many such terra-cotta statues, put it, "It is contradictory to elementary logic and to all artistic experience that an Indian could depict in a masterly way the head of a Negro or of a white person without missing a single racial characteristic, unless he had seen such a person."[27] Some scholars have dismissed the Caucasoid images as "stylized" Indian heads and question their antiquity, since most were purchased, rather than found by archaeologists who could date them from their surroundings. Mayan specialists claim that the "Negroid faces" may represent jaguars or human babies. Some point out that natives found near the sites today have broad noses and thick lips, but of course, if Africans had come to the area, in antiquity or as part of the slave trade after 1492, that would hardly be surprising.[28] Van Sertima and others have adduced additional bits of evidence, including similarities in looms and other cultural elements, and information in Arab historical sources about extensive ocean navigation by Africans and Phoenicians in the eighth century BC.[29]

What is the importance today of these possible African and Phoenician predecessors of Columbus? Like the Vikings, they provide a fascinating story, one that can hold high school students on the edge of their seats. We might also realize another kind of importance by contemplating the particular meaning of Columbus Day. Italian Americans infer something positive about their "national character" from the exploits of their ethnic ancestors. The American sociologist George Homans once quipped, explaining why he had written on his own ancestors in East Anglia, rather than on some larger group elsewhere: "They may be humans, but not Homans!" Similarly, Scandinavians and Scandinavian Americans have always believed the Norse sagas about the Vikings, even when most historians did not, and finally confirmed them by conducting archaeological research in Newfoundland.

If Columbus is especially relevant to western Europeans and the Vikings to Scandinavians, what is the meaning to African Americans of the pre-Columbian voyagers from Africa? After visiting the von Wuthenau museum in Mexico City,

Rock heads nine feet tall face the ocean in south-eastern Mexico. Archaeologists call them *Olmec heads* after their name for the Indians who carved them. According to an archaeologist who helped uncover them, the faces are "amazingly Negroid." Today some archaeologists believe that the mouth lines resemble jaguarlike expressions Mayan children still make. Others think the statues are of "fat babies" or Indian kings or resemble sculptures in Southeast Asia.

the Afro-Carib scholar Tiho Narva wrote, "With his unique collection surrounding me, I had an eerie feeling that veils obscuring the past had been torn asunder. . . . Somehow, upon leaving the museum I suddenly felt that I could walk taller for the rest of my days."[30] Van Sertima's book has been reprinted more than twenty times, and he is lionized by black undergraduates across America. Rap music groups chant "but we already had been there" in verses about Columbus.[31] Obviously, African Americans want to see positive images of "themselves" in American history. So do we all.

As with the Norse, including the Phoenicians and Africans gives a more complete and complex picture of the past, showing that navigation and exploration did not begin with Europe in the 1400s. Like the Norse, the Phoenicians and Africans illustrate human possibility, in this case black possibility, or, more accurately, the prowess of a multiracial society.[32] Unlike the Norse, the Africans and Phoenicians seem to have made a permanent impact on the Americas. The huge stone statues in Mexico imply as much. It took enormous effort to quarry these basalt blocks, each weighing ten to forty tons, move them from quarries seventy-five miles away, and sculpt them into heads six to ten feet tall. Wherever they were from, the human models for these heads were important people, people to be worshiped or obeyed or at least remembered.[33] However, most archaeologists think they were Mayan, so including the Afro-Phoenicians must be done as a mere possibility—an ongoing controversy.

Of all the textbooks I surveyed, only two even mention the possibility of African or Phoenician exploration. *The American Adventure* simply poses two questions: "What similarities are there between the great monuments of the Maya and those of ancient Egypt?" and "Might windblown sailors from Asia, Europe, Africa, or the South Pacific have mingled with the earlier inhabitants of the New World?" The textbook supplies no relevant information and even claims "You should be able to deal with these questions without doing research." Nonsense. Most classrooms will simply ignore the questions.[34] *The United States—A History of the Republic* mentions pre-Columbian expeditions only to assure us that we need not concern ourselves with them: "None of these Europeans, Africans, or Asians left lasting traces of their presence in the Americas, nor did they develop any lasting relationships with the first Americans."

American history textbooks promote the belief that most important developments in world history are traceable to Europe. To grant too much human potential to pre-Columbian Africans might jar European American sensibilities. As Samuel Marble put it, "The possibility of African discovery of America has never been a tempting one for American historians."[35] Teachers and curricula that present African history and African Americans in a positive light are often condemned for being Afrocentric. White historians insist that the case for the Afro-Phoenicians has not been proven; we must not distort history to improve black children's self-image, they say. They are right that the case hasn't been proven, but textbooks should include the Afro-Phoenicians as a possibility, a controversy.

Standard history textbooks and courses discriminate against students who have been educated by rap songs or by Van Sertima. Imagine an eleventh-grade classroom in American history in early fall. The text is *Life and Liberty;* students are reading Chapter 2, "Exploration and Colonization." What happens when an African American girl shoots up her hand to challenge the statement "Not until 1497 to 1499 did the Portuguese explorer Vasco da Gama sail around Africa"? From rap songs the girl has learned that Phoenicians beat da Gama by more than two thousand years. Does the teacher take time to research the question and find that the student is right, the textbook wrong? More likely, s/he puts down the student's knowledge: "Rap songs aren't appropriate in a history class!" Or s/he humors the child: "Yes, but that was long ago and didn't lead to anything. Vasco da Gama's discovery is the important one." These responses allow the class to move "forward" to the next topic. They also contain some truth: the Phoenician circumnavigation didn't lead to any new trade routes or national alliances, because the Phoenicians were already trading with India through the Red Sea and the Persian Gulf. Textbooks don't name Vasco da Gama because something came from his "discovery," however. They name him because he was white. Two pages later, *Life and Liberty* tells us that Hernando de

Soto "discovered [the] Mississippi River." Of course, it had been discovered and named *Mississippi* by ancestors of the American Indians who were soon to chase de Soto down it. Textbooks portray de Soto in armor, not showing that by the time he reached the river, his men and women had lost almost all their clothing in a fire set by Natives in Alabama and were wearing replacements woven from reeds. De Soto's "discovery" had no larger significance and led to no trade or white settlement.[36] His was merely the first white face to gaze upon the Mississippi. That's why most American history textbooks include him. From Erik the Red to Peary at the North Pole to the first man on the moon, we celebrate most discoverers because they were first and because they were white, not because of events that flowed or did not flow from their accomplishments. My hypothetical teacher subtly changed the ground rules for da Gama, but they changed right back for de Soto. In this way students learn that black feats are not considered important while white ones are.[37]

Comparing two other possible pre-Columbian expeditions, from the west coasts of Africa and Ireland, provides an interesting vantage point from which to consider this debate. When Columbus reached Haiti, he found the Arawaks in possession of some spear points made of "guanine." The Arawaks said they got them from black traders who had come from the south and east. Guanine proved to be an alloy of gold, silver, and copper, identical to the gold alloy preferred by West Africans, who also called it "guanine." Islamic historians have recorded stories of voyages west from Mali in West Africa around 1311, during the reign of Mansa Bakari II. From time to time in the fourteenth and fifteenth centuries, shipwrecked African vessels—remnants, perhaps, of transatlantic trade—washed up on Cape Verde. From contacts in West Africa, the Portuguese heard that African traders were visiting Brazil in the mid-1400s; this knowledge may have influenced Portugal to insist on moving the pope's "line of demarcation" farther west in the Treaty of Tordesillas (1494).[38] Traces of diseases common in Africa have been detected in pre-Columbian corpses in Brazil. Columbus's son Ferdinand, who accompanied the admiral on his third voyage, reports that people they met or heard about in eastern Honduras "are almost black in color, ugly in aspect," probably Africans. The first Europeans to reach Panama—Balboa and company—reported seeing black slaves in an Indian town. The Indians said they had captured them from a nearby black community. Oral history from Afro-Mexicans contains tales of pre-Columbian crossings from West Africa. In all, then, data from diverse sources suggest the possibility of pre-Columbian voyages from West Africa to America.[39]

In contrast, the evidence for an Irish trip to America comes from only one side of the Atlantic. Irish legends written in the ninth or tenth century tell of "an abbot and seventeen monks who journeyed to the 'promised land of the saints' during a seven-year sojourn in a leather boat" centuries earlier. The stories include details that are literally fabulous: each Easter the priest and his crew supposedly conducted Mass on the back of a whale. They visited a "pillar of crystal" (perhaps an iceberg) and an "island of fire." We cannot simply dismiss these legends, however. When the Norse first reached Iceland, Irish monks were living on the island, whose volcanoes could have provided the "island of fire."[40]

How do American history textbooks treat these two sets of legendary voyagers? Five of the twelve textbooks in my original sample admitted the possibility of an Irish expedition. *Challenge of Freedom* gave the fullest account:

> Some people believe that . . . Irish missionaries may have sailed to the Americas hundreds of years before the first voyages of Columbus. According to Irish legends, Irish monks sailed the Atlantic Ocean in order to bring Christianity to the people they met. One Irish legend in particular tells about a land southwest of the Azores. This land was supposedly discovered by St. Brendan, an Irish missionary, about 500 AD.

Not one textbook—old or new—mentions the West Africans, however.

While leaving out Columbus's predecessors, American history books continue to make mistakes when they get to the last "discoverer." They present cut-and-dried answers, mostly glorifying Columbus, always avoiding uncertainty or controversy. Often their errors seem to be copied from other textbooks. Let me repeat the collective Columbus story they tell, this time italicizing everything in it that we have solid reason to believe is true.

> Born in Genoa, of humble parents, *Christopher Columbus grew up to become an experienced seafarer, venturing as far as Iceland and West Africa.* His adventures convinced him that the world must be round and that the fabled riches of the East—spices and gold—could be had by sailing west, superseding the overland routes, which the Turks had closed off to commerce. *To get funding for his enterprise, he beseeched monarch after monarch in Western Europe.* After at first being dismissed by Ferdinand and Isabella of Spain, Columbus finally got his chance when *Isabella decided to underwrite a modest expedition. Columbus outfitted three* pitifully small *ships, the Niña, the Pinta, and the Santa Maria, and set forth from*

Spain. After an arduous journey of more than two months, during which his mutinous crew almost threw him overboard, Columbus discovered the West Indies on October 12, 1492. Unfortunately, although he made three more voyages to America, he never knew he had discovered a New World. Columbus died in obscurity, unappreciated and penniless. Yet without his daring American history would have been very different, for in a sense he made it all possible.

As you can see, textbooks get the date right, and the names of the ships. Most of the rest that they tell us is untrustworthy. Many aspects of Columbus's life remain a mystery. He claimed to be from Genoa, Italy, and there is evidence that he was. There is also evidence that he wasn't: Columbus didn't seem to be able to write in Italian, even when writing to people in Genoa. Some historians believe he was Jewish, a converso or convert to Christianity, probably from Spain. (Spain was pressuring its Jews to convert or leave the country.) He may have been a Genoese Jew. Still other historians claim he was from Corsica, Portugal, or elsewhere.[41]

What about Columbus's class background? One textbook tells us he was poor, "the son of a poor Genoese weaver," while another assures us he was rich, "the son of a prosperous wool-weaver." Each book is certain, but people who have spent years studying Columbus say we cannot be sure.

We do not even know for certain where Columbus thought he was going. Evidence suggests he was seeking Japan, India, and Indonesia; other evidence indicates he was trying to reach "new" lands to the west. Historians have asserted each viewpoint for centuries. Because "India was known for its great wealth," Las Casas points out, it was in Columbus's interest "to induce the monarchs, always doubtful about his enterprise, to believe him when he said he was setting out in search of a western route to India."[42] After reviewing the evidence, Columbus's recent biographer Kirkpatrick Sale concluded "we will likely never know for sure." Sale noted that such a conclusion is "not very satisfactory for those who demand certainty in their historical tales."[43] Predictably, all our textbooks are of this type: all "know" he was seeking Japan and the East Indies. Thus authors keep their readers from realizing that historians do not know all the answers, hence history is not just a process of memorizing them.

The extent to which textbooks sometimes disagree, particularly when each seems so certain of what it declares, can be pretty scary. What was the weather like during Columbus's 1492 trip? According to *Land of Promise*, his ships were "storm-battered"; but *American Adventures* says they enjoyed "peaceful seas." How long was the voyage? "After more than two months at sea," according to *The*

Challenge of Freedom, the crews saw land; but *The American Adventure* says the voyage lasted "nearly a month." What were the Americas like when Columbus arrived? "Thickly peopled" in one book, quoting Columbus; "thinly spread," according to another.

To make a better myth, American culture has perpetuated the idea that Columbus was boldly forging ahead while everyone else, even his own crew, imagined the world was flat. The 1991 edition of *The American Pageant* is the only textbook that still repeated this hoax. "The superstitious sailors . . . grew increasingly mutinous," according to *Pageant,* because they were "fearful of sailing over the edge of the world." In truth, few people on both sides of the Atlantic believed in 1492 that the world was flat. Most Europeans and Native Americans knew the world to be round. It looks round. It casts a circular shadow on the moon. Sailors see its roundness when ships disappear over the horizon, hull first, then sails.

Washington Irving wins credit for popularizing the flat-earth fable in 1828. In his bestselling biography of Columbus, Irving described Columbus's supposed defense of his round-earth theory before the flat-earth savants at Salamanca University. Irving himself surely knew the story to be fiction.[44] He probably thought it added a nice dramatic flourish and would do no harm. But it does. It invites us to believe that the "primitives" of the world, admittedly including pre-Columbian Europeans, had only a crude understanding of the planet they lived on, until aided by a forward-thinking European. It also turns Columbus into a man of science who corrected our faulty geography.

Most textbooks include a portrait of Columbus. These head-and-shoulder pictures have no value whatsoever as historical documents, because not one of the countless images we have of the man was painted in his lifetime. To make the point that these images are inauthentic, the Library of Congress sells this T-shirt featuring six different Columbus faces.

Intense debunking of the flat-earth legend, especially in 1992, the Columbus quincentenary, has made an impact. By 1994, even *Pageant* had removed its flat-earth language. Now the "superstitious sailors . . . grew increasingly mutinous" merely because they were "fearful of sailing into the oceanic unknown." Unfortunately, teachers who themselves learned the flat-earth story will never infer from that modestly revised sentence that it was wrong.[45] Boorstin and Kelley confront the legend more directly than other textbooks but again with wholly ineffectual words: "In Columbus's time all educated people and most

C. Columbus solicits funds for a promising project. Spain, 1489.

Without project funding, the world might still be flat.

American culture perpetuates the image of Columbus boldly forging ahead while everyone else imagined the world was flat. A character in the movie *Star Trek V*, for instance, repeats the Washington Irving lie: "The people of your world once believed the earth to be flat; Columbus proved it was round." Every October, Madison Avenue makes use of the flat-earth theme. This ad seeks clients for daring and courageous stockbrokers! With images like these in our culture, history textbooks need to disabuse students of the flat-earth myth.

sailors believed that the earth was a sphere." To be sure, the sentence quietly notes that not everyone believed in flat-earth geography. But it still implies that the round-earth idea was unusual. Not only students but also teachers read textbooks like Boorstin and Kelley without challenging their belief that Columbus proved the world round. Thus many teachers still implicitly relay to their students the flat-earth legend.

Even the death of Columbus has been changed to make a better story. Having Columbus come to a tragic end—sick, poor, and ignorant of his great accomplishment—adds melodramatic interest. "Columbus's discoveries were not immediately appreciated by the Spanish government," according to *The American Adventure.* "He died in neglect in 1506." "He finally reaped only misfortune and disgrace," conclude Boorstin and Kelley. They add that he "died still believing that he had sailed to the coast of Asia." In fact, Spain "immediately appreciated" Columbus's "discoveries," which is why they immediately outfitted him for a much larger second voyage. In 1499 Columbus "reaped" a major gold strike on Haiti. He and his successors then forced hundreds of thousands of Natives to mine the gold for them. Money from the Americas continued to flow in to Columbus in Spain, perhaps not what he felt he deserved, but enough to keep all wolves far from his door. Columbus died well-off and left his heirs well-endowed, even with the title, "Admiral of the Ocean Sea," now carried by his eighteenth-generation descendant. Moreover, Columbus's own journal shows clearly that he knew he had reached a "new" continent.[46]

Some of the details the textbook authors pile on are harmless, I suppose, such as the fabrications about Isabella's sending a messenger galloping after Columbus and pawning her jewels to pay for the expedition.[47] All of the enhancements humanize Columbus, however, and magnify his greatness, to induce readers to identify with him. Here is a passage from *Land of Promise:*

> It is October, 1492. Three small, storm-battered ships are lost at sea, sailing into an unknown ocean. A frightened crew has been threatening to throw their stubborn captain overboard, turn the ships around, and make for the safety of familiar shores.
>
> Then a miracle: The sailors see some green branches floating on the water. Land birds fly overhead. From high in the ship's rigging the lookout cries, "Land, land ahead!" Fears turn to joy. Soon the grateful captain wades ashore and gives thanks to God.

As Columbus cruised the coast of Venezuela on his third voyage, he passed the Orinoco River. "I have come to believe that this is a mighty continent, which was hitherto unknown," he wrote. "I am greatly supported in this view by reason of this great river and by this sea which is fresh." Columbus knew that no mere island could sustain such a large flow of water. When he returned home, he added a continent to the islands in his coat of arms. Its presence at the bottom of the lower left quadrant visually rebukes the authors of American history textbooks.

Now, really. *Niña, Pinta,* and *Santa Maria* were not "storm-battered." To make a better myth, the textbook authors want the voyage to seem harder than it was, so they invent bad weather. Columbus's own journal reveals that the three ships enjoyed lovely sailing. Seas were so calm that for days at a time sailors were able to converse from one ship to another. Indeed, the only time they experienced even moderately high seas was on the last day, when they knew they were near land.

To make a better myth, to make the trip seem longer than it was, most of the textbooks overlook Columbus's stopover in the Canary Islands. The voyage across the unknown Atlantic took one month, not two.

To make a better myth, the textbooks describe Columbus's ships as tiny and inefficient, when actually "these three vessels were fully suited to his purpose," as naval author Pietro Barozzi has pointed out.[48]

To make a better myth, several textbooks exaggerate the crew's complaints into a near-mutiny. The primary sources differ. Some claim the sailors threatened to go back home if they didn't reach land soon. Other sources claim that Columbus lost heart and that the captains of the other two ships persuaded him to keep on. Still other sources suggest that the three leaders met and agreed to continue on for a few more days and then reassess the situation. After studying the matter, Columbus's biographer Samuel Eliot Morison reduced the complaints to mere griping: "They were all getting on each other's nerves, as happens even nowadays."[49] So much for the crew's threat to throw Columbus overboard.

Such exaggeration is not entirely harmless. Another archetype lurks below the surface: that those who direct social enterprises are more intelligent than those nearer the bottom. Bill Bigelow, a high school history teacher, has pointed out that "the sailors are stupid, superstitious, cowardly, and sometimes scheming. Columbus, on the other hand, is brave, wise, and godly." These portrayals amount to an "anti–working class pro-boss polemic." [50] Indeed, even in 2006, *Pageant* still characterizes the sailors as "a motley crew," even though they now grasp that the world is round.

False entries in the log of *Santa Maria* are interpreted to form another piece of the myth. "Columbus was a true leader," says *A History of the United States*. "He altered the records of distances they had covered so the crew would not think they had gone too far from home." Salvador de Madariaga has persuasively argued that to believe this, we would have to think the others on the voyage were fools. Columbus had "no special method, available only to him, whereby distances sailed could be more accurately reckoned than by the other pilots and masters." Indeed, Columbus was less experienced as a navigator than the Pinzon brothers, who captained *Niña* and *Pinta*.[51] During the return voyage, Columbus confided in his journal the real reason for the false log entries: he wanted to keep the route to the Indies secret.[52]

To make a better myth, our textbooks find space for many other humanizing particulars. They have the lookout cry *"Tierra!"* or "Land!" Most of them tell us that Columbus's first act after going ashore was "thanking God for leading them safely across the sea"—even though the surviving summary of Columbus's own journal states only that "before them all, he took possession of the island, as in fact he did, for the King and Queen, his Sovereigns." [53] Many of the textbooks tell of Columbus's three later voyages to the Americas, but most do not find space to tell us how Columbus treated the lands and the people he "discovered."

Christopher Columbus introduced two phenomena that revolutionized race relations and transformed the modern world: the taking of land, wealth, and labor from indigenous people in the Western Hemisphere, leading to their near extermination, and the transatlantic slave trade, which created a racial underclass.

Columbus's initial impression of the Arawaks, who inhabited most of the islands in the Caribbean, was quite favorable. He wrote in his journal on October 13, 1492: "At daybreak great multitudes of men came to the shore, all young and of fine shapes, and very handsome. Their hair was not curly but loose and coarse like horse-hair. All have foreheads much broader than any people I had hitherto seen. Their eyes are large and very beautiful. They are not black, but the color of the inhabitants of the Canaries." (This reference to the Canaries was ominous, for Spain was then in the process of exterminating the aboriginal people of those islands.) Columbus went on to describe the Arawaks' canoes, "some large enough to contain 40 or 45 men." Finally, he got down to business: "I was very attentive to them, and strove to learn if they had any gold. Seeing some of them with little bits of metal hanging at their noses, I gathered from them by signs that by going southward or steering round the island in that direction, there would be found a king who possessed great cups full of gold." At dawn the next day, Columbus sailed to the other side of the island, probably one of the Bahamas, and saw two or three villages. He ended his description of them with these menacing words: "I could conquer the whole of them with fifty men and govern them as I pleased." [54]

On his first voyage, Columbus kidnapped some ten to twenty-five American Indians and took them back with him to Spain.[55] Only seven or eight arrived alive, but along with the parrots, gold trinkets, and other exotica, they caused quite a stir in Seville. Ferdinand and Isabella provided Columbus with seventeen ships, twelve hundred to fifteen hundred men, cannons, crossbows, guns, cavalry, and attack dogs for a second voyage.

One way to visualize what happened next is with the help of the famous science fiction story *War of the Worlds*. H. G. Wells intended his tale of earthlings' encounter with technologically advanced aliens as an allegory. His frightened British commoners (New Jerseyites in Orson Welles's famed radio adaptation) were analogous to the "primitive" peoples of the Canaries or America, and his terrifying aliens represented the technologically advanced Europeans. As we identify with the helpless earthlings, Wells wanted us also to sympathize with the natives on Haiti in 1493, or on Australia in 1788, or in the upper Amazon jungle today.[56]

When Columbus and his men returned to Haiti in 1493, they demanded food, gold, spun cotton—whatever the Natives had that they wanted, including sex with their women. To ensure cooperation, Columbus used punishment by example. When an Indian committed even a minor offense, the Spanish cut off his ears or nose. Disfigured, the person was sent back to his village as living evidence of the brutality the Spaniards were capable of.

After a while, the Natives had had enough. At first their resistance was mostly passive. They refused to plant food for the Spanish to take. They abandoned towns near the Spanish settlements. Finally, the Arawaks fought back. Their sticks and stones were no more effective against the armed and clothed Spanish, however, than the earthlings' rifles against the aliens' death rays in *War of the Worlds*.

The attempts at resistance gave Columbus an excuse to make war. On March 24, 1495, he set out to conquer the Arawaks. Bartolomé de Las Casas described the force Columbus assembled to put down the rebellion.

> Since the Admiral perceived that daily the people of the land were taking up arms, ridiculous weapons in reality . . . he hastened to proceed to the country and disperse and subdue, by force of arms, the people of the entire island . . . For this he chose 200 foot soldiers and 20 cavalry, with many crossbows and small cannon, lances, and swords, and a still more terrible weapon against the Indians, in addition to the horses: this was 20 hunting dogs, who were turned loose and immediately tore the Indians apart.[57]

Naturally, the Spanish won. According to Kirkpatrick Sale, who quotes Ferdinand Columbus's biography of his father: "The soldiers mowed down dozens with point-blank volleys, loosed the dogs to rip open limbs and bellies, chased fleeing Indians into the bush to skewer them on sword and pike, and 'with God's aid soon gained a complete victory, killing many Indians and capturing others who were also killed.' "[58]

Having as yet found no fields of gold, Columbus had to return some kind of dividend to Spain. In 1495 the Spanish on Haiti initiated a great slave raid. They rounded up fifteen hundred Arawaks, then selected the five hundred best specimens (of whom two hundred would die en route to Spain). Another five hundred were chosen as slaves for the Spaniards staying on the island. The rest were released. A Spanish eyewitness described the event: "Among them were many women who had infants at the breast. They, in order the better to escape us, since they were afraid we would turn to catch them again, left their infants anywhere on the ground and started to flee like desperate people; and some fled so far that they were removed from our settlement of Isabela seven or eight days beyond mountains and across huge rivers; wherefore from now on scarcely any will be had."[59] Columbus was excited. "In the name of the Holy Trinity, we can send from here all the slaves and brazil-wood which could be sold," he wrote to Ferdinand and Isabella in 1496. "In Castile, Portugal, Aragon . . . and the Canary Islands they need many slaves, and I do not think they get enough from Guinea." He viewed the Indian death rate optimistically: "Although they die now, they will not always die. The Negroes and Canary Islanders died at first." [60]

In the words of Hans Koning, "There now began a reign of terror in Hispaniola." Spaniards hunted American Indians for sport and murdered them for dog food. Columbus, upset because he could not locate the gold he was certain was on the island, set up a tribute system. Ferdinand Columbus described how it worked:

> [The Indians] all promised to pay tribute to the Catholic Sovereigns every three months, as follows: In the Cibao, where the gold mines were, every person of 14 years of age or upward was to pay a large hawk's bell of gold dust; all others were each to pay 25 pounds of cotton. Whenever an Indian delivered his tribute, he was to receive a brass or copper token which he must wear about his neck as proof that he had made his payment. Any Indian found without such a token was to be punished. [61]

With a fresh token, a Native was safe for three months, much of which time would be devoted to collecting more gold. Columbus's son neglected to mention how the Spanish punished those whose tokens had expired: they cut off their hands. [62]

All of these gruesome facts are available in primary-source material—letters by Columbus and by other members of his expeditions—and in the work of Las Casas, the first great historian of the Americas, who relied on primary materials and helped preserve them. I have quoted a few primary sources in this chapter. Most textbooks make no use of primary sources. A few incorporate brief extracts that have been carefully selected or edited to reveal nothing unseemly about the Great Navigator. *American Journey*, for example, quotes the passage I include above, about the Arawaks being "handsome," but stops at that point. Nothing about how Columbus could conquer them "with fifty men and govern them as I pleased." [63]

The tribute system eventually broke down because what it demanded was impossible. To replace it, Columbus installed the *encomienda* system, in which he granted or "commended" entire Indian villages to individual colonists or groups of colonists. Since it was not called slavery, this forced-labor system escaped the moral censure that slavery received. Following Columbus's example, Spain made the *encomienda* system official policy on Haiti in 1502; other conquistadors subsequently introduced it to Mexico, Peru, and Florida.[64]

The tribute and *encomienda* systems caused incredible depopulation. On Haiti the colonists made the Arawaks mine gold for them, raise Spanish food, and even carry them everywhere they went. They couldn't stand it. Pedro de Cordoba wrote in a letter to King Ferdinand in 1517, "As a result of the sufferings and hard labor they endured, the Indians choose and have chosen suicide. Occasionally a hundred have committed mass suicide. The women, exhausted by labor, have shunned conception and childbirth. . . . Many, when pregnant, have taken something to abort and have aborted. Others after delivery have killed their children with their own hands, so as not to leave them in such oppressive slavery."[65]

Beyond acts of individual cruelty, the Spanish disrupted the Native ecosystem and culture. Forcing Indians to work in mines rather than in their gardens led to widespread malnutrition. The intrusion of rabbits and livestock caused further ecological disaster. Diseases new to the Americans played a huge role, including swine flu, probably carried by pigs that Columbus brought to Haiti on his second voyage in 1493.[66] Some of the Arawaks tried fleeing to Cuba, but the Spanish soon followed them there. Estimates of Haiti's pre-Columbian population range as high as eight million people. When Christopher Columbus returned to Spain, he left his brother Bartholomew in charge of the island. Bartholomew took a census of Indian adults in 1496 and came up with 1.1 million. The Spanish did not count children under fourteen and could not count Arawaks who had escaped in the mountains. Kirkpatrick Sale estimates that a more accurate total would probably be in the neighborhood of three million. "By 1516," according to Benjamin Keen, "thanks to the sinister Indian slave trade and labor policies initiated by Columbus, only some 12,000 remained." Las Casas tells us that fewer than two hundred full-blooded Haitian Indians were alive in 1542. By 1555, they were all gone.[67]

Thus nasty details like cutting off hands have somewhat greater historical importance than nice touches like *"Tierra!"* Columbus not only sent the first slaves across the Atlantic, he probably sent more slaves—about five thousand—than any other individual. To her credit, Queen Isabella opposed outright enslavement and returned some American Indians to the Carribbean. But other nations rushed to emulate Columbus. In 1501 the Portuguese began to de-

American History reproduces *Columbus Landing in the Bahamas,* the first of eight huge "historical" paintings in the rotunda of the U.S. Capitol (above). The 1847 painting by John Vanderlyn illustrates the heroic treatment of Columbus in most textbooks. An alternative representation of Columbus's enterprise might be Theodore de Bry's woodcut, created around 1588 (opposite). De Bry based this engraving on accounts of Indians who impaled themselves, drank poison, jumped off cliffs, hanged themselves, and killed their children. The artist squeezed all of these fatal deeds into one picture! De Bry's images became important historical documents in their own right. Accompanied by Las Casas's writings, they circulated throughout sixteenth-century Europe and gave rise to the "Black Legend" of Spanish cruelty, which other European countries used to denounce Spain's colonialism, mostly out of envy. No textbook includes any visual representation of the activities of Columbus and his men that is other than glorious.

populate Labrador, transporting the now extinct Beothuk Indians to Europe and Cape Verde as slaves. After the English established beachheads on the Atlantic coast of North America, they encouraged coastal tribes to capture and sell members of more distant tribes. Charleston, South Carolina, became a major port of exporting American Indian slaves. The Pilgrims and Puritans sold the survivors of the Pequot War into slavery in Bermuda in 1637. The French shipped virtually the entire Natchez nation in chains to the West Indies in 1731.[68]

A particularly repellent aspect of the slave trade was sexual. As soon as the 1493 expedition got to the Caribbean, before it even reached Haiti, Columbus was rewarding his lieutenants with native women to rape.[69] On Haiti, sex slaves were one more perquisite that the Spaniards enjoyed. Columbus wrote a friend in 1500, "A hundred *castellanoes* are as easily obtained for a woman as for a farm,

and it is very general and there are plenty of dealers who go about looking for girls; those from nine to ten are now in demand." [70]

The slave trade and the new diseases destroyed whole American Indian nations. Enslaved Indians died. To replace the dying Haitians, the Spanish imported tens of thousands more Indians from the Bahamas, which "are now deserted," in the words of the Spanish historian Peter Martyr, reporting in 1516.[71] Packed in below deck, with hatchways closed to prevent their escape, so many slaves died on the trip that "a ship without a compass, chart, or guide, but only following the trail of dead Indians who had been thrown from the ships could find its way from the Bahamas to Hispaniola,"[72] lamented Las Casas. Puerto Rico and Cuba were next.

Because the Indians died, Indian slavery then led to the massive slave trade the other way across the Atlantic, from Africa. This trade also began on Haiti, initiated by Columbus's son in 1505. Predictably, Haiti then became the site of the first large-scale slave revolt, when blacks and American Indians banded together in 1519. The uprising lasted more than a decade and was finally brought to an end by the Spanish in the 1530s.[73]

One of the new textbooks, *The Americans*, reveals the conflict on Haiti. This book also quotes Las Casas to show how Haiti was only the beginning: "This tactic begun here [will soon] spread throughout these Indies and will end when there are no more land or people to subjugate and destroy in this part of the world." One of my original twelve, *The American Adventure*, associated Columbus with slavery. One old book and one new one let it go with the phrase "Columbus proved to be a far better admiral than governor" or its equivalent. The other books, old and new, mostly adore him.

Clearly most textbooks are not about teaching the history of Columbus. Their enterprise seems to be Building Character. They therefore treat Columbus as an origin myth: He was good and so are we.[74] In 1989 President George H. W. Bush invoked Columbus as a role model for the nation: "Christopher Columbus not only opened the door to a New World, but also set an example for us all by showing what monumental feats can be accomplished through perseverance and faith."[75] The columnist Jeffrey Hart went even further: "To denigrate Columbus is to denigrate what is worthy in human history and in us all."[76] Textbook authors who are pushing Columbus to build character obviously have no interest in telling what he did with the Americas once he reached them—even though that's half of the story, and perhaps the more important half.

As Kirkpatrick Sale poetically sums up, Columbus's "second voyage marks the first extended encounter of European and Indian societies, the clash of cultures that was to echo down through five centuries."[77] The authors of *The Americans* have read Sale, for they write, "[Haiti] signaled the start of a cultural clash that would continue for the next five centuries." These are not mere details about Haiti between 1493 and 1500 that the other textbooks omit or gloss over. They are facts crucial to understanding American and European history. Captain John Smith, for example, used Columbus as a role model in proposing a get-tough policy for the Virginia Indians in 1624: "The manner how to suppress them is so often related and approved, I omit it here: And you have twenty examples of how the Spaniards got the West Indies, and forced the treacherous and rebellious infidels to do all manner of drudgery work and slavery for them, themselves living like soldiers upon the fruits of their labors."[78] The methods unleashed by Columbus are, in fact, the larger part of his legacy. After all, they worked. The island was so well pacified that Spanish convicts, given a second chance on Haiti, could "go anywhere, take any woman or girl, take anything, and have the Indians carry him on their backs as if they were mules."[79] In 1499, when Columbus finally found gold on Haiti in significant amounts, Spain became the envy of Europe. After 1500, Portugal, France, Holland, and England joined in conquering the Americas. These nations were at least as brutal as Spain. The English, for example, unlike the Spanish, did not colonize by making use of Native labor but simply forced the Indians out of the way. Many American Indians fled English colonies to Spanish territories (Florida, Mexico) in search of more humane treatment.

Columbus's voyages caused almost as much change in Europe as in the Americas. Crops, animals, ideas, and diseases began to cross the oceans regularly. Perhaps the most far-reaching impact of Columbus's findings was on European Christianity. In 1492 all of Europe was in the grip of the Catholic Church. As the *Encyclopedia Larousse* puts it, before America, "Europe was virtually incapable of self-criticism." [80] After America, Europe's religious uniformity was ruptured. For how were these new peoples to be explained? They were not mentioned in the Bible. American Indians simply did not fit within orthodox Christianity's explanation of the moral universe. Moreover, unlike the Muslims, who might be written off as "damned infidels," American Indians had not rejected Christianity, they had just never encountered it. Were they doomed to hell? Even the animals of America posed a religious challenge. According to the Bible, at the dawn of creation all animals lived in the Garden of Eden. Later, two of each species entered Noah's ark and ended up on Mt. Ararat. Since Eden and Mt. Ararat were both in the Middle East, where could these new American species have come from? Such questions shook orthodox Catholicism and contributed to the Protestant Reformation, which began in 1517.[81]

Politically, nations like the Arawaks—without monarchs, without much hierarchy—stunned Europeans. In 1516 Thomas More's *Utopia*, probably based on an account of the Incan empire in Peru, challenged European social organization by suggesting a radically different and superior alternative. Other social philosophers seized upon American Indians as living examples of Europe's primordial past, which is what John Locke meant by the phrase "In the beginning, all the world was America." Depending upon their political persuasion, some Europeans glorified American Indian nations as examples of simpler, better societies from which European civilization had devolved, while others maligned them as primitive and underdeveloped. In either case, from Montaigne, Montesquieu, and Rousseau down to Marx and Engels, European philosophers' concepts of the good society were transformed by ideas from America.[82]

America fascinated the masses as well as the elite. In *The Tempest*, Shakespeare noted this universal curiosity: "They will not give a doit to relieve a lambe beggar, they will lay out ten to see a dead Indian." [83] Europe's fascination with the Americas was directly responsible, in fact, for a rise in European self-consciousness. From the beginning America was perceived as an "opposite" to

Europe in ways that even Africa never had been. In a sense, there was no "Europe" before 1492. People were simply Tuscan, French, and the like. Now Europeans began to see similarities among themselves, at least as contrasted with Native Americans. For that matter, there were no "white" people in Europe before 1492. With the transatlantic slave trade, first Indian, then African, Europeans increasingly saw "white" as a race and race as an important human characteristic.[84]

Columbus's own writings reflect this increasing racism. When Columbus was selling Queen Isabella on the wonders of the Americas, the Indians were "well built" and "of quick intelligence." "They have very good customs," he wrote, "and the king maintains a very marvelous state, of a style so orderly that it is a pleasure to see it, and they have good memories and they wish to see everything and ask what it is and for what it is used." Later, when Columbus was justifying his wars and his enslavement of the Natives, they became "cruel" and "stupid," "a people warlike and numerous, whose customs and religion are very different from ours."

It is always useful to think badly about people one has exploited or plans to exploit. Modifying one's opinions to bring them into line with one's actions or planned actions is the most common outcome of the process known as "cognitive dissonance," according to social psychologist Leon Festinger. No one likes to think of himself or herself as a bad person. To treat badly another person whom we consider a reasonable human being creates a tension between act and attitude that demands resolution. We cannot erase what we have done, and to alter our future behavior may not be in our interest. To change our attitude is easier.[85]

Columbus gives us the first recorded example of cognitive dissonance in the Americas, for although the Natives may have changed from hospitable to angry, they could hardly have evolved from intelligent to stupid so quickly. The change had to be in Columbus.

The Americas affected more than the mind. African and Eurasian stomachs were also affected. Almost half of all major crops now grown throughout the world originally came from the Americas. According to Alfred Crosby Jr., adding corn to African diets caused the population to grow, which helped fuel the African slave trade to the Americas. Adding potatoes to European diets caused the population to explode in the sixteenth and seventeenth centuries, which in turn helped fuel the European emigration to the Americas and Australia. Crops from America also played a key role in the ascendancy of England, Germany, and, finally, Russia; the rise of these northern nations shifted the power base of Europe away from the Mediterranean.[86]

Shortly after ships from Columbus's second voyage returned to Europe, syphilis began to plague Spain and Italy. There is likely a causal connection. On the other hand, more than two hundred drugs derive from plants whose pharmacological uses were discovered by American Indians.[87]

Economically, exploiting the Americas transformed Europe, enriching first Spain, then, through trade and piracy, other nations. Columbus's gold finds on Haiti were soon dwarfed by discoveries of gold and silver in Mexico and the Andes. European religious and political leaders quickly amassed so much gold that they applied gold leaf to the ceilings of their churches and palaces, erected golden statues in the corners, and strung vines of golden grapes between them. Marx and Engels held that this wealth "gave to commerce, to navigation, to industry an impulse never before known." Some writers credit it with the rise of capitalism and eventually the industrial revolution. Capitalism was probably already under way, but at the least, American riches played a major role in the transformation. Gold and silver from America replaced land as the basis for wealth and status, increasing the power of the new merchant class that would soon dominate the world.[88] Where Muslim nations had once rivaled Europe, the new wealth undermined Islamic power. American gold and silver fueled a 400 percent inflation that eroded the economies of most non-European countries and helped Europe to develop a global market system. Africa suffered: the trans-Saharan trade collapsed, because the Americas supplied more gold and silver than the Gold Coast ever could. African traders now had only one commodity that Europe wanted: slaves. In anthropologist Jack Weatherford's words, "Africans thus became victims of the discovery of America as surely as did the American Indians."[89]

These vast changes were given the term "the Columbian exchange" in 1972 by Alfred W. Crosby Jr., in his book of that title. In the 1990s the term caught on, owing to the quincentenary. Not one textbook in my original sample told of these geopolitical implications of Columbus's encounter with the Americas, but gradually the concept seeped into American history textbooks. Today most books credit American Indians with having developed important crops. Authors also recognize that Europeans (and Africans) brought diseases as well as livestock to the Americas. The two-way flow of ideas, however, still goes unnoticed, especially from west to east.

Instead, Eurocentrism blinds textbook authors to contributions *to* Europe, whether from Arab astronomers, African navigators, or American Indian social structure. By operating within this limited viewpoint, our history textbooks never invite us to think about what happened to reduce mainland Indian societies, whose wealth and cities awed the Spanish, to the impoverished peasantry they are today. They also rob us of the chance to appreciate how important American Indian ideas have been in the formation of the modern world. Thus, they keep students from understanding what caused the world to develop as it has—including why Europe (and its extensions: the United States, Canada, etc.) won.

Some people have attacked the portrait of Columbus presented here as too negative. But I am not proposing that we should begin courses of American history by crying that Columbus was *bad* and so are we. Textbooks should show that neither morality nor immorality can simply be conferred upon us by history. Merely being part of the United States, without regard to our own acts and ideas, does not make us moral or immoral beings. History is more complicated than that.

Again we must pause to consider: Who are "we"? Columbus is not a hero in Mexico, even though Mexico is much more Spanish in culture than the United States and might be expected to take pride in this hero of Spanish history. Why not? Because Mexico is also much more Indian than the United States, and Mexicans perceive Columbus as white and European. "No sensible Indian person," wrote George P. Horse Capture, "can celebrate the arrival of Columbus." [90] Cherishing Columbus is a characteristic of white history, not American history.

Columbus's conquest of Haiti can be seen as an amazing feat of courage and imagination by the first of many brave empire builders. It can also be understood as a bloody atrocity that left a legacy of genocide and slavery that endures in some degree to this day. Both views of Columbus are valid; indeed, Columbus's importance in history owes precisely to his being both a heroic navigator and a great plunderer. If Columbus were only the former, he would merely rival Leif Eriksson. Columbus's actions exemplify both meanings of the word *exploit*—a remarkable deed and also a taking advantage of. The worshipful biographical vignettes of Columbus provided by most of our textbooks serve to indoctrinate students into a mindless endorsement of colonialism that is strikingly inappropriate in today's postcolonial era. In the words of the historian Michael Wallace, the Columbus myth "allows us to accept the contemporary division of the world into developed and underdeveloped spheres as natural and given, rather than a historical product issuing from a process that began with Columbus's first voyage."[91]

We understand Columbus and all European explorers and settlers more clearly if we treat 1492 as a meeting of three cultures (Africa was soon involved), rather than a discovery by one, and several of the new books do this. The term *New World* is itself part of the problem, for people had lived in the Americas for thousands of years. The Americas were new only to Europeans. *Discover* is another part of the problem, for how can one person discover what another already knows and owns? Textbook authors are struggling with this issue, trying to move beyond colonialized history and Eurocentric language. Boorstin and Kelley begin their first chapter with the sentence, "The discovery of America"—by which they mean Columbus's—"was the world's greatest surprise." Five pages later, the authors try to take back the word: "It was only for the people of Europe that America had to be 'discovered.' Millions of Native Americans were already here!" Taking back words is ineffectual, however. Boorstin and Kelley's whole approach is to portray whites discovering nonwhites rather than a mutual multicultural encounter. Indeed, they are so Eurocentric that they don't even notice they left out "the people of Africa and Asia" from their sentence of people who had yet to "discover" America.

The point isn't idle. Words are important—they can influence, and in some cases rationalize, policy. In 1823 Chief Justice John Marshall of the U.S. Supreme Court decreed that Cherokees had certain rights to their land in Georgia by dint of their "occupancy" but that whites had superior rights owing to their "discovery." How American Indians managed to occupy Georgia without having previously discovered it Marshall neglected to explain.[92]

The process of exploration has itself typically been multiracial and multicultural. African pilots helped Prince Henry's ship captains learn their way down the coast of Africa.[93] On Christmas Day 1492, Columbus needed help. *Santa Maria* ran aground off Haiti. Columbus sent for help to the nearest Arawak town, and "all the people of the town" responded, "with very big and many canoes." "They cleared the decks in a very short time," Columbus continued, and the chief "caused all our goods to be placed together near the palace, until some houses that he gave us where all might be put and guarded had been emptied."[94] On his final voyage Columbus shipwrecked on Jamaica, and the Arawaks there kept him and his crew of more than a hundred alive for a whole year until Spaniards from Haiti rescued them.

So it has continued. William Erasmus, a Canadian Indian, pointed out,

"Explorers you call great men were helpless. They were like lost children, and it was our people who took care of them."[95] Native Americans cured Cartier's men of scurvy near Montreal in 1535. They repaired Francis Drake's *Golden Hind* in California so he could complete his round-the-world voyage in 1579. Lewis and Clark's expedition to the Pacific Northwest was made possible by tribe after tribe of American Indians, with help from two Shoshone guides, Sacagawea and Toby, who served as interpreters. When Admiral Peary discovered the North Pole, the first person there was probably neither the European American Peary nor the African American Matthew Henson, his assistant, but their four Inuit guides, men and women on whom the entire expedition relied.[96] Our histories fail to mention such assistance. They portray proud Western conquerors bestriding the world like the Colossus at Rhodes.

So long as our textbooks hide from us the roles that people of color have played in exploration, from at least 6000 BC to the twentieth century, they encourage us to look to Europe and its extensions as the seat of all knowledge and intelligence. So long as they say "discover," they imply that whites are the only people who really matter. So long as they simply celebrate Columbus, rather than teach both sides of his exploit, they encourage us to identify with white Western exploitation rather than study it.

The passage in the left-hand column of the opposing page is one of the many legends that hang about Columbus like barnacles—"myths, all without substance."[97] The passage in the right-hand column is part of a contemporaneous account of an Arawak cacique (leader) who had fled from Haiti to Cuba.

The reader will have already guessed that the passage on the left comes from an American history textbook, in this case *American Adventures*. Since the incident probably never happened, including it in a textbook is hard to defend. One way to understand its inclusion is by examining what it does in the narrative. The incident is melodramatic. It creates a mild air of suspense, even though we can be sure, of course, that everything will turn out all right in the end. Surely the passage encourages identification with Columbus's enterprise, makes Columbus the underdog—riding a mule, shabby of cloak—and thus places us on his side.

The passage on the right was recorded by Las Casas, who apparently learned it from Arawaks on Cuba. Unlike the mule story, the cacique's story teaches important facts: that the Spanish sought gold, that they killed Indians, that Indians fled and resisted. (Indeed, after futile attempts at armed resistance on Cuba, this cacique fled "into the brambles." Weeks later, when the Spanish cap-

A man riding a mule moved slowly down a dusty road in Spain. He wore an old and shabby cloak over his shoulders. Though his face seemed young, his red hair was already turning white. It was early in the year 1492 and Christopher Columbus was leaving Spain.

Twice the Spanish king and queen had refused his request for ships. He had wasted five years of his life trying to get their approval. Now he was going to France. Perhaps the French king would give him the ships he needed.

Columbus heard a clattering sound. He turned and looked up the road. A horse and rider came racing toward him. The rider handed him a message, and Columbus turned his mule around. The message was from the Spanish king and queen, ordering him to return. Columbus would get his ships.

Learning that Spaniards were coming, one day [the cacique] gathered all his people together to remind them of the persecutions that the Spanish had inflicted on the people of Hispaniola:

"Do you know why they persecute us?"

They replied: "They do it because they are cruel and bad."

"I will tell you why they do it," the cacique stated, "and it is this—because they have a lord whom they love very much, and I will show him to you."

He held up a small basket made from palms full of gold, and he said, "Here is their lord, whom they serve and adore. . . . To have this lord, they make us suffer, for him they persecute us, for him they have killed our parents, brothers, all our people. . . . Let us not hide this lord from the Christians in any place, for even if we should hide it in our intestines, they would get it out of us; therefore let us throw it in this river, under the water, and they will not know where it is."

Whereupon they threw the gold into the river.[98]

tured him, they burned him alive.) Nonetheless, no history textbook includes the cacique's story or anything like it. Doing so might enable us to identify with the Natives' side. By avoiding the names and stories of individual Arawaks and omitting their points of view, authors "otherize" the Indians. Readers need not concern themselves with the Indians' ghastly fate, for American Indians never appear as recognizable human beings. Textbooks themselves, it seems, practice cognitive dissonance.

Excluding the passage on the right, including the passage on the left, excluding the probably true, including the improbable, amounts to colonialist history. This is the Columbus story that has dominated American history books. All around the globe, however, the nations that were "discovered," conquered, "civilized," and colonized by European powers are now independent, at least politically. Europeans and European Americans no longer dictate to them as master to native and therefore need to stop thinking of themselves as superior, morally and technologically. A new and more accurate history of Columbus—provided to students by just one of these textbooks (*The Americans*)—could assist this transformation.

Of course, this new history must not judge Columbus by standards from our own time. In 1493 the world had not decided, for instance, that slavery was wrong. Some American Indian nations enslaved other Indians. Africans enslaved other Africans. Europeans enslaved other Europeans. To attack Columbus for doing what everyone else did would be unreasonable.

However, some Spaniards of the time—Bartolomé de Las Casas, for example—opposed the slavery, land-grabbing, and forced labor that Columbus introduced on Haiti. Las Casas began as an adventurer and became a plantation owner. Then he switched sides, freed his Natives, became a priest, and fought desperately for humane treatment of the Indians. When Columbus and other Europeans argued that American Indians were inferior, Las Casas pointed out that Indians were sentient and rational human beings, just like anyone else. When other historians tried to overlook or defend the Indian slave trade, begun by Columbus, Las Casas denounced it as "among the most unpardonable offenses ever committed against God and mankind." He helped prompt Spain to enact laws against American Indian slavery.[99] Although these laws came too late to help the Arawaks and were often disregarded, they did help some Indians survive. Centuries after his death, Las Casas was still influencing history: Simon Bolívar used Las Casas's writings to justify the revolutions between 1810 and 1830 that liberated Latin America from Spanish domination.

When history textbooks leave out the Arawaks, they offend Native Americans. When they omit the possibility of African and Phoenician precursors to Columbus, they offend African Americans. When they glamorize explorers such as de Soto just because they were white, our histories offend all people of color. When they leave out Las Casas, they omit an interesting idealist with whom we all might identify. When they glorify Columbus, our textbooks prod us toward identifying with the oppressor. When textbook authors omit the causes and process of European world domination, they offer us a history whose purpose must be to keep us unaware of the important questions. Perhaps worst of all, when textbooks paint simplistic portraits of a pious, heroic Columbus, they provide feel-good history that bores everyone.

3.

THE TRUTH ABOUT THE FIRST THANKSGIVING

Considering that virtually none of the standard fare surrounding Thanksgiving contains an ounce of authenticity, historical accuracy, or cross-cultural perception, why is it so apparently ingrained? Is it necessary to the American psyche to perpetually exploit and debase its victims in order to justify its history?   —MICHAEL DORRIS[1]

European explorers and invaders discovered an inhabited land. Had it been pristine wilderness then, it would possibly be so still, for neither the technology nor the social organization of Europe in the 16th and 17th centuries had the capacity to maintain, of its own resources, outpost colonies thousands of miles from home.

—FRANCIS JENNINGS[2]

The Europeans were able to conquer America not because of their military genius, or their religious motivation, or their ambition, or their greed. They conquered it by waging unpremeditated biological warfare.   —HOWARD SIMPSON[3]

It is painful to advert to these things. But our forefathers, though wise, pious, and sincere, were nevertheless, in respect to Christian charity, under a cloud; and, in history, truth should be held sacred, at whatever cost . . . especially against the narrow and futile patriotism, which, instead of pressing forward in pursuit of truth, takes pride in walking backwards to cover the slightest nakedness of our forefathers.

—COL. THOMAS ASPINWALL[4]

OVER THE LAST FEW YEARS, I have asked hundreds of college students, "When was the country we now know as the United States first settled?" This is a generous way of phrasing the question; surely "we now know as" implies that the original settlement antedated the founding of the United States. I initially believed—certainly I had hoped—that students would suggest 30,000 BC or some other pre-Columbian date.

They did not. Their consensus answer was "1620."

Obviously, my students' heads have been filled with America's origin myth, the story of the first Thanksgiving. Textbooks are among the retailers of this primal legend.

Part of the problem is the word *settle*. "Settlers" were white, a student once pointed out to me. "Indians" didn't settle. Students are not the only people misled by *settle*. The film that introduces visitors to Plimoth Plantation tells how "they went about the work of civilizing a hostile wilderness." One Thanksgiving weekend I listened as a guide at the Statue of Liberty talked about European immigrants "populating a wild East Coast." As we shall see, however, if American Indians hadn't already settled New England, Europeans would have had a much tougher job of it.

Starting the story of America's settlement with the Pilgrims leaves out not only American Indians but also the Spanish. The first non-Native settlers in "the country we now know as the United States" were African slaves left in South Carolina in 1526 by Spaniards who abandoned a settlement attempt. In 1565 the Spanish massacred the French Protestants who had settled briefly near present-day Jacksonville, Florida, and established their own fort at St. Augustine. Between 1565 and 1568 Spaniards explored the Carolinas, building several forts that were then burned by the Indians. Some later Spanish settlers may have been our first pilgrims, seeking regions new to them to secure religious liberty: these were probably Spanish Jews, who settled in New Mexico in the late 1500s.[5] Few Americans know that one-third of the United States, from San Francisco to Arkansas to Natchez to Florida, has been Spanish longer than it has been "American," and that Hispanic Americans lived here before the first ancestor of the Daughters of the American Revolution ever left England. Moreover, Spanish culture left an indelible mark on the American West. The Spanish introduced horses, cattle, sheep, pigs, and the basic elements of cowboy culture, including its vocabulary: *mustang, bronco, rodeo, lariat,* and so on.[6] Horses that escaped from the Spanish and propagated triggered the rapid flowering of a new culture among the Plains Indians. "How refreshing it would be," wrote James Axtell, "to find a textbook that began on the West Coast before treating the traditional eastern colonies."

Why don't they? Perhaps because most textbook authors are WASPs (White Anglo-Saxon Protestants). The forty-six authors of the eighteen texts I surveyed ranged from Bauer and Berkin to Williams and Wood, but only two were

Spanish-surnamed: Linda Ann DeLeon, an author of *Challenge of Freedom*, and J. Klor de Alva, an author of *The Americans*. Surely it is no coincidence that the books by these last two offer by far the fullest accounts of early Spanish settlements in "what is now the United States," including mention of the missions the Spanish set up from the Carolinas to the Gulf of Mexico and from San Diego to San Francisco.[7] Within our lifetimes, the school-age population of the United States is destined to become majority minority, with Hispanic, African, Asian, and Native Americans totalling more than 51 percent. At that point, probably after much hand-wringing and tooth-gnashing, the history books will give more attention to our Hispanic past—which they always should have done. Meanwhile, the *Spanish* are seen as intruders, while the *British* are seen as settlers.[8]

Beginning the story in 1620 also omits the Dutch, who were living in what is now Albany by 1614. Indeed, should English be required for proper settling, 1620 is not even the date of the first permanent *English* settlement, for in 1607, the London Company sent settlers to Jamestown, Virginia.

No matter. The *mythic* origin of "the country we now know as the United States" is at Plymouth Rock, and the year is 1620. Here is a representative account from *The American Tradition*:

> After some exploring, the Pilgrims chose the land around Plymouth Harbor for their settlement. Unfortunately, they had arrived in December and were not prepared for the New England winter. However, they were aided by friendly Indians, who gave them food and showed them how to grow corn. When warm weather came, the colonists planted, fished, hunted, and prepared themselves for the next winter. After harvesting their first crop, they and their Indian friends celebrated the first Thanksgiving.[9]

My students also remember that the Pilgrims had been persecuted in England for their religious beliefs, so they had moved to Holland. They sailed on the *Mayflower* to America and wrote the Mayflower Compact, the forerunner to our Constitution, according to my students. Times were rough, until they met Squanto, who taught them how to put a small fish as fertilizer in each little corn hill, ensuring a bountiful harvest. But when I ask my students about the plague, they just stare back at me. "What plague? The Black Plague?" No, I sigh, that was three centuries earlier.

The Black Plague does provide a useful introduction, however. William Langer has written that the Black (or bubonic) Plague "was undoubtedly the worst disaster that has ever befallen mankind."[10] In the years 1348 through 1350, it killed perhaps 30 percent of the population of Europe. Catastrophic as that was, the disease itself comprised only part of the horror. According to Langer, "Almost everyone, in that medieval time, interpreted the plague as a punishment by God for human sins." Thinking the day of judgment was imminent, farmers did not plant crops. Many people gave themselves over to alcohol. Civil and economic disruption may have caused as much death as the disease itself. The entire culture of Europe was affected: fear, death, and guilt became prime artistic motifs. Milder plagues—typhus, syphilis, and influenza, as well as bubonic—continued to ravage Europe until the end of the seventeenth century.[11]

The warmer parts of Europe, Asia, and Africa have historically been the breeding ground for most human illnesses. Humans evolved in tropical regions; tropical diseases evolved alongside them. People moved to cooler climates only with the aid of cultural inventions—clothing, shelter, and fire—that helped maintain warm temperatures around their bodies. Microbes that live outside their human hosts during part of their life cycle had trouble coping with northern Europe and Asia.[12] When people migrated to the Americas across the newly drained Bering Strait, if the archaeological consensus is correct, the changes in climate and physical circumstance threatened even those hardy parasites that had survived the earlier slow migration northward from Africa. These first immigrants entered the Americas through a frigid decontamination chamber. The first settlers in the Western Hemisphere thus probably arrived in a healthier condition than most people on earth have enjoyed before or since. Many of the diseases that had long shadowed them simply could not survive the journey.[13]

Neither did some animals. People in the Western Hemisphere had no cows, pigs, horses, sheep, goats, or chickens before the arrival of Europeans and Africans after 1492. Many diseases—from anthrax to tuberculosis, cholera to streptococcus, ringworm to various poxes—are passed back and forth between humans and livestock. Since early inhabitants of the Western Hemisphere had no livestock, they caught no diseases from them.[14]

Europe and Asia were also made unhealthy by a subtler factor: social density. Organisms that cause disease need a constant supply of new hosts for their own survival. This requirement is nowhere clearer than in the case of smallpox, which cannot survive outside a living human body. But in its enthusiasm, the organism often kills its host. Thus the pestilence creates its own predicament: it requires new victims at regular intervals. The various influenza viruses must likewise move on, for if their victims survive, they enjoy a period of immunity lasting at least a few weeks, and sometimes a lifetime.[15] Small-scale societies like the Paiute Indians of Nevada, living in isolated nuclear and extended families, could and did suffer post-Columbian smallpox epidemics, transmitted to them by more urban neighbors, but they could not sustain such an organism over time.[16] Even residents of villages did not experience sufficient social density. Villagers might encounter three hundred people each day, but these would usually be the same three hundred people. Coming into repeated contact with the same few others does not have the same consequences as meeting new people, either for human culture or for culturing microbes.

Some areas in the Americas did have high social density.[17] Incan roads connected towns from northern Ecuador to Chile.[18] Fifteen hundred to two thousand years ago the population of Cahokia, Illinois, numbered about forty thousand. Trade linked the Great Lakes to Florida, the Rockies to what is now New England.[19] We are therefore not dealing with isolated bands of "primitive" peoples. Nonetheless, most of the Western Hemisphere lacked the social density found in much of Europe, Africa, and Asia. And nowhere in the Western Hemisphere were there sinkholes of sickness like London or Cairo, with raw sewage running in the streets.

The scarcity of disease in the Americas was also partly attributable to the basic hygiene practiced by the region's inhabitants. Residents of northern Europe and England rarely bathed, believing it unhealthy, and rarely removed all of their clothing at one time, believing it immodest. The Pilgrims smelled bad to the Indians. Squanto "tried, without success, to teach them to bathe," according to Feenie Ziner, his biographer.[20]

For all these reasons, the inhabitants of North and South America (like Australian aborigines and the peoples of the far-flung Pacific islands) were "a remarkably healthy race"[21] before Columbus. Ironically, their very health proved their undoing, for they had built up no resistance, genetically or through childhood diseases, to the microbes that Europeans and Africans would bring to them.

In 1617, just before the Pilgrims landed, a pandemic swept southern New England. For decades, English and French fishermen had fished off the Massachusetts coast. After filling their hulls with cod, they would go ashore to lay in firewood and fresh water and perhaps capture a few American Indians to sell into slavery in Europe. It is likely that these fishermen transmitted some illness to the people they met.[22] The plague that ensued made the Black Death pale by comparison. Some historians think the disease was the bubonic plague; others suggest that it was viral hepatitis, smallpox, chicken pox, or influenza.

Within three years the plague wiped out between 90 to 96 percent of the inhabitants of coastal New England. Native societies lay devastated. Only "the twentieth person is scarce left alive," wrote Robert Cushman, an English eyewitness, recording a death rate unknown in all previous human experience.[23] Unable to cope with so many corpses, the survivors abandoned their villages and fled, often to a neighboring tribe. Because they carried the infestation with them, American Indians died who had never encountered a white person. Howard Simpson describes the horrific scenes that the Pilgrims saw: "Villages lay in ruins because there was no one to tend them. The ground was strewn with the skulls and the bones of thousands of Indians who had died and none was left to bury them."[24]

The biggest single change in the treatment of Native Americans is the inclusion of this illustration in most of the new textbooks. The first edition of *Lies My Teacher Told Me* decried the absence of any treatment of the repeated epi-

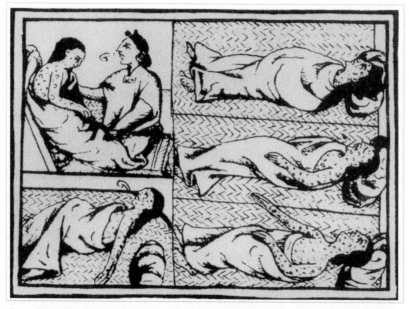

These Aztec drawings depicting smallpox, coupled with the words of William Bradford, convey something of the horror of the epidemic around Plymouth: "A sorer disease cannot befall [the Indians], they fear it more than the plague. For usually they that have this disease have them in abundance, and for want of bedding and linen and other helps they fall into a lamentable condition as they lie on their hard mats, the pox breaking and mattering and running one into another, their skin cleaving by reason thereof to the mats they lie on. When they turn them, a whole side will flay off at once as it were, and they will be all of a gore blood, most fearful to behold. And then being very sore, what with cold and other distempers, they die like rotten sheep." Quoted in Simpson, *Invisible Armies*, 8.

demics that ravaged Native populations. No book included this illustration or any other representation of disease.

During the next fifteen years, additional epidemics, most of which we know to have been smallpox, struck repeatedly. European Americans also contracted smallpox and the other maladies, to be sure, but they usually recovered, including, in a later century, the "heavily pockmarked George Washington." Native Americans usually died. The impact of the epidemics on the two cultures was profound. The English Separatists, already seeing their lives as part of a divinely inspired morality play, found it easy to infer that God was on their side. John Winthrop, governor of the Massachusetts Bay Colony, called the plague "miraculous." In 1634 he wrote to a friend in England: "But for the natives in these parts, God hath so pursued them, as for 300 miles space the greatest part of them are swept away by the smallpox which still continues among them. So as God hath thereby cleared our title to this place, those who remain in these parts, being in all not 50, have put themselves under our protection. . . ."[25] God, the Original Real Estate Agent!

Many Natives likewise inferred that their god had abandoned them. Robert Cushman reported that "those that are left, have their courage much abated, and their countenance is dejected, and they seem as a people affrighted." After a smallpox epidemic the Cherokee "despaired so much that they lost confidence in their gods and the priests destroyed the sacred objects of the tribe."[26] After all, neither American Indians nor Pilgrims had access to the germ theory of disease. Native healers could supply no cure; their medicines and herbs offered no relief. Their religion provided no explanation. That of the whites did. Like the Europeans three centuries before them, many American Indians surrendered to alcohol, converted to Christianity, or simply killed themselves.[27]

These epidemics probably constituted the most important geopolitical event of the early seventeenth century. Their net result was that the English, for their first fifty years in New England, would face no real Indian challenge. Indeed, the plague helped prompt the legendarily warm reception Plymouth enjoyed from the Wampanoags. Massasoit, the Wampanoag leader, was eager to ally with the Pilgrims because the plague had so weakened his villages that he feared the Narragansetts to the west.[28] When a land conflict did develop between new settlers and old at Saugus in 1631, "God ended the controversy by sending the small pox amongst the Indians," in the words of the Puritan minister Increase Mather. "Whole towns of them were swept away, in some of them not so much as one Soul escaping the Destruction."[29] By the time the Native populations of New England had replenished themselves to some degree, it was too late to expel the intruders.

Today, as we compare European technology with that of the "primitive" American Indians, we may conclude that European conquest of America was inevitable, but it did not appear so at the time. Historian Karen Kupperman speculates:

> The technology and culture of Indians on America's east coast were genuine rivals to those of the English, and the eventual outcome of the rivalry was not at first clear. . . . One can only speculate what the outcome of the rivalry would have been if the impact of European diseases on the American population had not been so devastating. If colonists had not been able to occupy lands already cleared by Indian farmers who had vanished, colonization would have proceeded much more slowly. If Indian culture had not been devastated by the physical and psychological assaults it had suffered, colonization might not have proceeded at all.[30]

After all, Native Americans had driven off Samuel de Champlain when he had tried to settle in Massachusetts in 1606. The following year, Abenakis had helped expel the first Plymouth Company settlement from Maine.[31] Alfred Crosby has speculated that the Norse might have succeeded in colonizing Newfoundland and Labrador if they had not had the bad luck to emigrate from Greenland and Iceland, distant from European disease centers.[32] But this is "what if" history. The New England plagues were no "if." They continued west, racing in advance of the line of culture contact.

Everywhere in America, the first European explorers encountered many more Indians than did their successors. A century and a half after Hernando de Soto traveled the southeastern United States, French explorers there found the population less than a quarter of what it had been when de Soto had passed through, with attendant catastrophic effects on Native culture and social organization.[33] Likewise, on their famous 1804–06 expedition, Lewis and Clark encountered far more Natives in Oregon than lived there a mere twenty years later.[34]

Henry Dobyns has put together a heartbreaking list of ninety-three epidemics among Native Americans between 1520 and 1918. He has recorded forty-one eruptions of smallpox, four of bubonic plague, seventeen of measles and ten of influenza (both often deadly among Native Americans), and twenty-five of tuberculosis, diphtheria, typhus, cholera, and other diseases. Many of these outbreaks reached truly pandemic proportions, beginning in Florida or Mexico and stopping only when they reached the Pacific and Arctic oceans.[35] Disease played the same crucial role in Mexico and Peru as it did in Massachusetts. How did the Spanish manage to conquer what is now Mexico City? "When the Christians were exhausted from war, God saw fit to send the Indians smallpox, and there was a great pestilence in the city." When the Spanish marched into Tenochtitlan, there were so many bodies that they had to walk on them. Most of the Spaniards were immune to the disease, and that fact itself helped to crush Aztec morale.[36]

The pestilence continues today. Miners and loggers recently introduced European diseases to the Yanomamos of northern Brazil and southern Venezuela, killing a fourth of their total population in 1991 alone. Charles Darwin, writing in 1839, put it almost poetically: "Wherever the European had trod, death seems to pursue the aboriginal."[37]

Europeans were never able to "settle" China, India, Indonesia, Japan, or much of Africa, because too many people already lived there. The crucial role played by the plagues in the Americas can be inferred from two simple population estimates: William McNeill reckons the population of the Americas at one hundred million in 1492, while William Langer suggests that Europe had only about seventy million people when Columbus set forth.[38] The Europeans' advantages in military and social technology might have enabled them to dominate the Americas, as they eventually dominated China, India, Indonesia, and Africa, but not to "settle" the hemisphere. For that, the plague was required. Thus, apart from the European (and African) invasion itself, the pestilence is surely the most important event in the history of America.

The first epidemics wreaked havoc, not only with American Indian societies, but also with estimates of pre-Columbian Native American population. The result has been continuing controversy among historians and anthropologists. In 1840 George Catlin estimated aboriginal numbers in the United States and Canada at the time of white contact to be perhaps fourteen million. He believed only two million still survived. By 1880, owing to warfare and deculturation as well as illness, Native numbers had dropped to 250,000, a decline of 98 percent.[39] In 1921 James Mooney asserted that only one million Native Americans had lived in what is now the United States in 1492. Mooney's estimate was accepted until the 1960s and 1970s, even though the arguments supporting it, based largely on inference rather than evidence, were not convincing. Colin McEvedy provided an example of the argument:

> The high rollers, of course, claim that native numbers had been reduced to these low levels [between one million and two million] by epidemics of smallpox, measles, and other diseases introduced from Europe—and indeed they could have been. But there is no record of any continental [European] population being cut back by the sort of percentages needed to get from twenty million to two or one million. Even the Black Death reduced the population of Europe by only a third.[40]

Note that McEvedy has ignored both the data and also the reasoning about illness summarized above, relying on what amounts to common sense to disprove both. Indeed, he contended, "No good can come of affronting common sense." But pre-Pilgrim American epidemiology is not a field of everyday knowledge in which "common sense" can be allowed to substitute for years of relevant research. By "common sense" what McEvedy really meant was tradition, and this tradition is Eurocentric. Our archetypes of the "virgin continent" and its corollary, the "primitive tribe," subtly influenced estimates of Native population: scholars who viewed Native American cultures as primitive reduced their estimates of precontact populations to match the stereotype. The tiny Mooney estimate thus "made sense"—resonated with the archetype. Never mind that the land was, in reality, not a virgin wilderness but recently widowed.[41]

The very death rates that some historians and geographers now find hard to believe, the Pilgrims knew to be true. For example, William Bradford described how the Dutch, rivals of Plymouth, traveled to an Indian village in Connecticut to trade. "But their enterprise failed, for it pleased God to afflict these Indians with such a deadly sickness, that out of 1,000, over 950 of them died, and many of them lay rotting above ground for want of burial. . . ."[42] This is precisely the 95 percent mortality that McEvedy rejected. On the opposite coast, the Native population of California sank from three hundred thousand in 1769 (by which time it had already been cut in half by various Spanish-borne diseases) to thirty thousand a century later, owing mainly to the gold rush, which brought "disease, starvation, homicide, and a declining birthrate."[43]

For a century after Catlin, historians and anthropologists "overlooked" the evidence offered by the Pilgrims and other early chroniclers. Beginning with

P. M. Ashburn in 1947, however, research has established more accurate estimates based on careful continent-wide compilations of small-scale studies of first contact and on evidence of early plagues. Most current estimates of the precontact population of the United States and Canada range from ten to twenty million.[44]

None of my original twelve textbooks, most of which were published in the 1980s, lets its readers in on the furious debate of the 1960s and early 1970s, telling how and why estimates changed. Instead, they simply stated numbers—very different numbers. "As many as ten million," *American Adventures* proposed. "There were only about 1,000,000 North American Indians," opined *The American Tradition*. "Scattered across the North American continent were about 500 different groups, many of them nomadic." Like other Americans who have not studied the literature, the authors of these textbooks were still under the thrall of the "virgin land" and "primitive tribe" archetypes; their most common American Indian population estimate was the discredited figure of one million, which five textbooks supplied. Only two provided estimates of ten to twelve million, in the range supported by contemporary scholarship. Two hedged their bets by suggesting one to twelve million, which might reasonably prompt classroom discussion of why estimates are so vague. Three omitted the subject altogether. The new books are even worse: none of them even raises the subject of population estimates.

The problem is not so much the estimates as the attitude. Presenting a controversy seems somehow radical. It invites students to come to their own conclusions. Textbook authors don't let that happen. They see their job as presenting "facts" for children to "learn," not encouraging them to think for themselves. Such an approach keeps students ignorant of the reasoning, arguments, and weighing of evidence that go into social science.

About the plagues, my twelve original textbooks told even less. Only three of them even mentioned Indian disease as a factor at Plymouth or anywhere in New England.[45] Today, most new textbooks do include "Old World" diseases as part of the Columbian Exchange. It's about time! After all, in colonial times, everyone knew about the plague. Even before the *Mayflower* sailed, King James of England gave thanks to "Almighty God in his great goodness and bounty towards us" for sending "this wonderful plague among the salvages [*sic*]."[46] Two hundred years later the oldest American history in my collection— J. W. Barber's *Interesting Events in the History of the United States*, published in 1829—still recalled the plague:

A few years before the arrival of the Plymouth settlers, a very mortal sickness raged with great violence among the Indians inhabiting the eastern parts of New England. "Whole towns were depopulated. The living were not able to bury the dead; and their bodies were found lying above ground, many years after. The Massachusetts Indians are said to have been reduced from 30,000 to 300 fighting men. In 1633, the small pox swept off great numbers."[47]

Unfortunately, the Pilgrims' arrival in Massachusetts poses another historical controversy that textbook authors take pains to duck. The textbooks say the Pilgrims intended to go to Virginia, where there existed an English settlement already. However, "the first land they sighted was Cape Cod, well north of their target," explains *The American Journey*. "Because it was November and winter was fast approaching, the colonists decided to drop anchor in Cape Cod Bay." Winter's onset cannot have been the reason, however, for the weather would be much milder in Virginia than Massachusetts. Moreover, the Pilgrims spent six full weeks—until December 26—scouting around Cape Cod looking for the best spot. How did the Pilgrims wind up in Massachusetts in the first place, when they set out for Virginia? "Violent storms blew their ship off course," according to some textbooks; others blame an "error in navigation." Both explanations may be wrong. Some historians believe the Dutch bribed the captain of the *Mayflower* to sail north so the Pilgrims would not settle near New Amsterdam. Others hold that the Pilgrims went to Cape Cod on purpose.[48]

Bear in mind that the Pilgrims numbered only about 35 of the 102 settlers aboard the *Mayflower*; the rest were ordinary folk seeking their fortunes in the new Virginia colony. Historian George Willison has argued that the Pilgrim leaders, wanting to be far from Anglican control, never planned to settle in Virginia. They had debated the relative merits of Guiana, in South America, versus the Massachusetts coast, and, according to Willison, they intended a hijacking.

Certainly the Pilgrims already knew quite a bit about what Massachusetts could offer them, from the fine fishing along Cape Cod to that "wonderful plague," which offered an unusual opportunity for English settlement. According to some historians, Squanto, a Wampanoag from the village of Patuxet, Massachusetts, had provided Ferdinando Gorges, a leader of the Plymouth Company in England, with a detailed description of the area. Gorges may even have sent Squanto and Capt. Thomas Dermer as advance men to wait for the Pilgrims, although Dermer sailed away when the Pilgrims were delayed in England. In any event, the Pilgrims were familiar with the area's topography. Recently published maps that Samuel de Champlain had drawn when he had toured the area in 1605 supplemented the information that had been passed on by sixteenth-century explorers. John Smith had studied the region and named it "New England" in 1614, and he even offered to guide the Pilgrim leaders. They rejected his services as too expensive and carried his guidebook along instead.[49]

These considerations prompt me to believe that the Pilgrim leaders probably ended up in Massachusetts on purpose. But evidence for any conclusion is soft. Some historians believe Gorges took credit for landing in Massachusetts after the fact. Indeed, the *Mayflower* may have had no specific destination. Readers might be fascinated if textbook authors presented two or more of the various possibilities, but, as usual, exposing students to historical controversy is taboo. Each textbook picks just one reason and presents it as fact.

Only one of all the textbooks I surveyed adheres to the hijacking possibility. "The New England landing came as a rude surprise for the bedraggled and tired [non-Pilgrim] majority on board the *Mayflower*," says *Land of Promise*. "[They] had joined the expedition seeking economic opportunity in the Virginia tobacco plantations." Obviously, these passengers were not happy at hav-

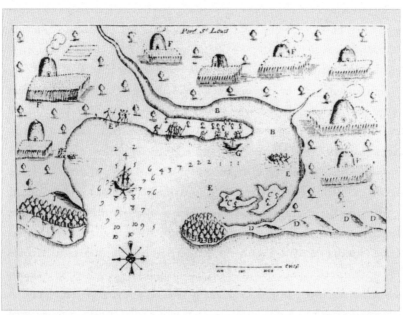

Among the Pilgrims' sources of information about New England were probably the maps of Samuel de Champlain, including this chart of Patuxet (Plymouth) when it was still an Indian village, before the plague of 1617.

ing been taken elsewhere, especially to a shore with no prior English settlement to join. "Rumors of mutiny spread quickly." *Promise* then ties this unrest to the Mayflower Compact, giving its readers a fresh interpretation of why the colonists adopted the agreement and why it was so democratic: "To avoid rebellion, the Pilgrim leaders made a remarkable concession to the other colonists. They issued a call for every male on board, regardless of religion or economic status, to join in the creation of a 'civil body politic.'" The compact achieved its purpose: the majority acquiesced.

Actually, the hijacking hypothesis does not show the Pilgrims in such a bad light. The compact provided a graceful solution to an awkward problem. Although hijacking and false representation doubtless were felonies then as now, the colony did survive with a lower death rate than Virginia, so no permanent harm was done. The whole story places the Pilgrims in a somewhat dishonorable light, however, which may explain why only one textbook selects it.

The "navigation error" story lacks plausibility: the one parameter of ocean travel that sailors could and did measure accurately in that era was latitude—distance north or south from the equator. The "storms" excuse is perhaps still less plausible, for if a storm blew them off course, when the weather cleared they could have turned southward again, sailing out to sea to bypass any shoals. They had plenty of food and beer, after all.[50] But storms and pilot error leave the Pilgrims pure of heart, which may explain why most textbooks choose one of the two.

Regardless of motive, the Mayflower Compact provided a democratic basis for the Plymouth colony. Since the framers of our Constitution in fact paid the compact little heed, however, it hardly deserves the attention textbook authors lavish on it. But textbook authors clearly want to package the Pilgrims as a pious and moral band who laid the antecedents of our democratic traditions. Nowhere is this motive more embarrassingly obvious than in John Garraty's *American History*. "So far as any record shows, this was the first time in human history that a group of people consciously created a government where none had existed before." Here Garraty paraphrases a Forefathers' Day speech, delivered in Plymouth in 1802, in which John Adams celebrated "the only instance in human history of that positive, original social compact." George Willison has dryly noted that Adams was "blinking several salient facts—above all, the circumstances that prompted the compact, which was plainly an instrument of minority rule."[51] Of course, Garraty's paraphrase also exposes his ignorance of the Republic of Iceland, the Iroquois Confederacy, and countless other polities antedating 1620. Such an account simply invites students to become ethnocentric.

In their pious treatment of the Pilgrims, history textbooks introduce the archetype of American exceptionalism—the notion that the United States is different from—and better than—all other nations on the planet. How is America exceptional? Well, we're exceptionally *good*, for one thing. As Woodrow Wilson put it, "America is the only idealistic nation in the world." [52] And we're exceptionally strong and hardy, too: as we face the future, in the words of *The American Pageant*, "the world's oldest republic had an extraordinary tradition of resilience and resourcefulness to draw on." (Never mind that tiny San Marino may have formed as a republic in AD 301, Iceland became a republic in 930, and Switzerland around 1300.) These stellar qualities are evident from the "beginning," here at Plymouth Rock, according to our textbooks. The Pilgrims "were equipped," Boorstin and Kelley inform us, "with just the right combination of hopes and fears, optimism and pessimism, self-confidence and humility to be successful settlers. And this was one of the most fortunate coincidences in our history." Such a happy portrait of the Pilgrims can be painted only by omitting the facts about the plague, the possible hijacking, and their Indian relations.

To highlight that happy picture, textbooks underplay Jamestown and the sixteenth-century Spanish settlements in favor of Plymouth Rock as the archetypal birthplace of the United States. Virginia, according to T. H. Breen, "ill-served later historians in search of the mythic origins of American culture." [53] Historians could hardly tout Virginia as moral in intent, for, in the words of the first history of Virginia written by a Virginian: "The chief Design of all Parties concern'd was to fetch away the Treasure from thence, aiming more at sudden Gain, than to form any regular Colony." [54] The Virginians' relations with American Indians were particularly unsavory: in contrast to Squanto, a volunteer, the English in Virginia took Indian prisoners and forced them to teach colonists how to farm. [55] In 1623 the English indulged in the first use of chemical warfare in the colonies when negotiating a treaty with tribes near the Potomac River, headed by Chiskiack. The English offered a toast "symbolizing eternal friendship," whereupon the chief, his family, advisors, and two hundred followers dropped dead of poison. [56] Besides, the early Virginians engaged in bickering, sloth, even cannibalism. They spent their early days digging random holes in the ground, haplessly looking for gold instead of planting crops. Soon they were starving and digging up putrid Native corpses to eat or renting themselves out to American Indian families as servants—hardly the heroic founders that a great nation requires.[57]

Textbooks indeed cover the Virginia colony, and they at least mention the Spanish settlements, but they still devote 50 percent more space to Massachusetts. As a result, and owing also to Thanksgiving, of course, students are much more likely to remember the Pilgrims as our founders.[58] They are then embarrassed when I remind them of Virginia and the Spanish, for when prompted, students do recall having heard of both. But neither our culture nor our textbooks give Virginia the same archetypal status as Massachusetts. That is why almost all my students know the name of the Pilgrims' ship, while almost no students remember the names of the three ships that brought the English to Jamestown. (For the next time you're on *Jeopardy!* they were *Susan Constant*, *Discovery*, and *Godspeed*.)

Despite having ended up many miles from other European enclaves, the Pilgrims hardly "started from scratch" in a "wilderness." Throughout southern New England, Native Americans had repeatedly burned the underbrush, creating a parklike environment. After landing at Provincetown, the Pilgrims assembled a boat for exploring and began looking around for their new home. They chose Plymouth because of its beautiful cleared fields, recently planted in corn, and its useful harbor and "brook of fresh water." It was a lovely site for a town. Indeed, until the plague, it had been a town, for "New Plimoth" was none other than Squanto's village of Patuxet. The invaders followed a pattern: throughout the hemisphere Europeans pitched camp right in the middle of Native populations—Cuzco, Mexico City, Natchez, Chicago. Throughout New England, colonists appropriated American Indian cornfields for their initial settlements, avoiding the backbreaking labor of clearing the land of forest and rock.[59] (This explains why, to this day, the names of so many towns throughout the region—Marshfield, Springfield, Deerfield—end in *field*.) "Errand into the wilderness" may have made a lively sermon title in 1650, a popular book title in 1950, and an archetypal textbook phrase in 2000, but it was never accurate. The new settlers encountered no wilderness: "In this bay wherein we live," one colonist noted in 1622, "in former time hath lived about two thousand Indians."[60]

Moreover, not all the Native inhabitants had perished, and the survivors now facilitated English settlement. The Pilgrims began receiving Indian assistance on their second full day in Massachusetts. A colonist's journal tells of sailors discovering two American Indian houses:

Having their guns and hearing nobody, they entered the houses and found the people were gone. The sailors took some things but didn't dare stay. . . . We had meant to have left some beads and other things in the houses as a sign of peace and to show we meant to trade with them. But we didn't do it because we left in such haste. But as soon as we can meet with the Indians, we will pay them well for what we took.

It wasn't only houses that the Pilgrims robbed. Our eyewitness resumes his story:

We marched to the place we called Cornhill, where we had found the corn before. At another place we had seen before, we dug and found some more corn, two or three baskets full, and a bag of beans. . . . In all we had about ten bushels, which will be enough for seed. It was with God's help that we found this corn, for how else could we have done it, without meeting some Indians who might trouble us.

From the start, the Pilgrims thanked God, not the American Indians, for assistance that the latter had (inadvertently) provided—setting a pattern for later thanksgivings. Our journalist continues:

The next morning, we found a place like a grave. We decided to dig it up. We found first a mat, and under that a fine bow. . . . We also found bowls, trays, dishes, and things like that. We took several of the prettiest things to carry away with us, and covered the body up again.[61]

A place "like a grave"!

Although Karen Kupperman says the Pilgrims continued to rob graves for years,[62] more help came from a live Indian, Squanto. Here my students return to familiar turf, for they have all learned the Squanto legend. *Land of Promise* provides a typical account:

Squanto had learned their language, he explained, from English fishermen who ventured into the New England waters each summer. Squanto taught the Pilgrims how to plant corn, squash, and pumpkins. Would the small band of settlers have survived without Squanto's help? We cannot say. But by the fall of 1621, colonists and Indians could sit down to several days of feast and thanksgiving to God (later celebrated as the first Thanksgiving).

What do most books leave out about Squanto? First, how he learned English. According to Ferdinando Gorges, around 1605 an English captain stole Squanto, who was then still a boy, along with four Penobscots and took them to England. There Squanto spent nine years, three in the employ of Gorges. At length, Gorges helped Squanto arrange passage back to Massachusetts. Some historians doubt that Squanto was among the five Indians stolen in 1605.[63] All sources agree, however, that in 1614 an English slave raider seized Squanto and two-dozen fellow Indians and sold them into slavery in Málaga, Spain. What happened next makes Ulysses look like a homebody. Squanto escaped from slavery, escaped from Spain, and made his way back to England. After trying to get home via Newfoundland, in 1619 he talked Thomas Dermer into taking him along on his next trip to Cape Cod.

It happens that Squanto's fabulous odyssey provides a "hook" into the plague story, a hook that our textbooks choose not to use. For now Squanto set foot again on Massachusetts soil and walked to his home village of Patuxet, only to make the horrifying discovery that "he was the sole member of his village still alive. All the others had perished in the epidemic two years before."[64] No wonder Squanto threw in his lot with the Pilgrims.

Now *that* is a story worth telling! Compare the pallid account in *Land of Promise*: "He had learned their language from English fishermen."[65]

As translator, ambassador, and technical advisor, Squanto was essential to the survival of Plymouth in its first two years. Like other Europeans in America, the Pilgrims had no idea what to eat or how to raise or find food until American Indians showed them. William Bradford called Squanto "a special instrument sent of God for their good beyond their expectation. He directed them how to set their corn, where to take fish, and to procure other commodities, and was also their pilot to bring them to unknown places for their profit." Squanto was not the Pilgrims' only aide: in the summer of 1621 Massasoit sent another Indian, Hobomok, to live among the Pilgrims for several years as guide and ambassador.[66]

"Their profit" was the primary reason most *Mayflower* colonists made the trip. As Robert Moore has pointed out, "Textbooks neglect to analyze the profit motive underlying much of our history."[67] Profit, too, came from American In-

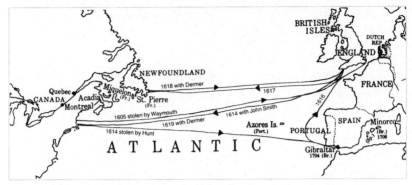

Squanto's travels acquainted him with more of the world than any Pilgrim encountered. He had crossed the Atlantic perhaps six times, twice as an English captive, and had lived in Maine, Newfoundland, Spain, and England, as well as Massachusetts.

dians, by way of the fur trade, without which Plymouth would never have paid for itself. Hobomok helped Plymouth set up fur-trading posts at the mouth of the Penobscot and Kennebec rivers in Maine; in Aptucxet, Massachusetts; and in Windsor, Connecticut.[68] Europeans had neither the skill nor the desire to "go boldly where none dared go before." They went to the Indians.[69]

All this brings us to Thanksgiving. Throughout the nation every fall, elementary-school children reenact a little morality play, *The First Thanksgiving*, as our national origin myth, complete with Pilgrim hats made out of construction paper and Indian braves with feathers in their hair. Thanksgiving is the occasion on which we give thanks to God as a nation for the blessings that He [*sic*] hath bestowed upon us. More than any other celebration, more even than such overtly patriotic holidays as Independence Day and Memorial Day, Thanksgiving celebrates our ethnocentrism. We have seen, for example, how King James and the early Pilgrim leaders gave thanks for the plague, which proved to them that God was on their side. The archetypes associated with Thanksgiving—God on our side, civilization wrested from wilderness, order from disorder, through hard work and good Pilgrim character traits—continue to radiate from our history textbooks. Many decades ago, in an analysis of how American history was taught in the 1920s, Bessie Pierce pointed out the political uses to which Thanksgiving is put: "For these unexcelled blessings, the pupil is urged to follow in the footsteps of his forbears, to offer unquestioning obedience to the law of the land, and to carry on the work begun."[70]

Thanksgiving dinner is a ritual, with all the characteristics that Mircea Eliade assigns to the ritual observances of origin myths:

1. It constitutes the history of the acts of the founders, the Supernaturals.
2. It is considered to be true.
3. It tells how an institution came into existence.
4. In performing the ritual associated with the myth, one "experiences knowledge of the origin" and claims one's patriarchy.
5. Thus one "lives" the myth, as a religion.[71]

My Random House dictionary lists as its main heading for the Plymouth colonists not *Pilgrims* but *Pilgrim Fathers*. Until recently, the Library of Congress similarly cataloged its holdings for Plymouth under *Pilgrim Fathers*, and of course *fathers* was capitalized, meaning "fathers of our country," not of Pilgrim children. Thanksgiving has thus moved from history into the field of religion, "civil religion," as Robert Bellah has called it. To Bellah, civil religions hold society together. Plymouth Rock achieved iconographic status around 1880, when some enterprising residents of the town rejoined its two pieces on the waterfront and built a Greek templet around it. The templet became a shrine, the Mayflower Compact became a sacret text, and our textbooks began to play the same function as the Anglican Book of Common Prayer, teaching us the meaning behind the civil rite of Thanksgiving.[72]

The religious character of Pilgrim history shines forth in an introduction by Valerian Paget to William Bradford's famous chronicle *Of Plimoth Plantation*:

> The eyes of Europe were upon this little English handful of unconscious heroes and saints, taking courage from them step by step. For their children's children the same ideals of Freedom burned so clear and strong that . . . the little episode we have just been contemplating, resulted in the birth of the United States of America, and, above all, of the establishment of the humanitarian ideals it typifies, and for which the Pilgrims offered their sacrifice upon the altar of the Sonship of Man.[73]

In this invocation, the Pilgrims supply not only the origin of the United States, but also the inspiration for democracy in Europe and perhaps for all goodness in the world today! I suspect that the original colonists, Separatists and Anglicans alike, would have been amused.

The civil ritual we practice marginalizes Native Americans. Our archetypal image of the first Thanksgiving portrays the groaning boards in the woods, with the Pilgrims in their starched Sunday best next to their almost naked Indian guests. As a holiday greeting card puts it, "*I* is for the Indians we invited to share our food." The silliness of all this reaches its zenith in the handouts that schoolchildren have carried home for decades, complete with captions such as, "They served pumpkins and turkeys and corn and squash. The Indians had never seen such a feast!" When Native American novelist Michael Dorris's son brought home this "information" from his New Hampshire elementary school, Dorris pointed out that "the *Pilgrims* had literally never seen 'such a feast,' since all foods mentioned are exclusively indigenous to the Americas and had been provided *by* [or with the aid of] the local tribe."[74]

This notion that "we" advanced peoples provided for the Natives, exactly the converse of the truth, is not benign. It reemerges time and again in our history to complicate race relations. For example, we are told that white plantation owners furnished food and medical care for their slaves, yet every shred of food, shelter, and clothing on the plantations was raised, built, woven, or paid for by black labor. Today Americans believe as part of our political understanding of the world that we are the most generous nation on earth in terms of foreign aid, overlooking the fact that the net dollar flow from almost every Third World nation runs *toward* the United States.

The true history of Thanksgiving reveals embarrassing facts. The Pilgrims did not introduce the tradition; Eastern Indians had observed autumnal harvest celebrations for centuries. Although George Washington did set aside days for national thanksgiving, our modern celebrations date back only to 1863. During the Civil War, when the Union needed all the patriotism that such an observance might muster, Abraham Lincoln proclaimed Thanksgiving a national holiday. The Pilgrims had nothing to do with it; not until the 1890s did they even get included in the tradition. For that matter, they were not commonly known as "the Pilgrims" until the 1870s.[75]

The ideological meaning American history has ascribed to Thanksgiving compounds the embarrassment. The Thanksgiving legend makes Americans ethnocentric. After all, if our culture has God on its side, why should we consider other cultures seriously? This ethnocentrism intensified in the middle of the last century. In *Race and Manifest Destiny*, Reginald Horsman has shown how the idea of "God on our side" was used to legitimize the open expression of Anglo-Saxon superiority vis-à-vis Mexicans, Native Americans, peoples of the Pacific, Jews, and even Catholics.[76] Today, when textbooks promote this ethnocentrism with their Pilgrim stories, they leave students less able to learn from and deal with people from other cultures.

On occasion, we pay a more direct cost: censorship. In 1970, for example, the Massachusetts Department of Commerce asked the Wampanoags to select a speaker to mark the 350th anniversary of the Pilgrims' landing. Frank James "was selected, but first he had to show a copy of his speech to the white people in charge of the ceremony. When they saw what he had written, they would not allow him to read it."[77] James had written:

> Today is a time of celebrating for you . . . but it is not a time of celebrating for me. It is with heavy heart that I look back upon what happened to my People. . . . The Pilgrims had hardly explored the shores of Cape Cod four days before they had robbed the graves of my ancestors, and stolen their corn, wheat, and beans. . . . Massasoit, the great leader of the Wampanoag, knew these facts; yet he and his People welcomed and befriended the settlers . . . little knowing that . . . before 50 years were to pass, the Wampanoags . . . and other Indians living near the settlers would be killed by their guns or dead from diseases that we caught from them. . . . Although our way of life is almost gone and our language is almost extinct, we the Wampanoags still walk the lands of Massachusetts. . . . What has happened cannot be changed, but today we work toward a better America, a more Indian America where people and nature once again are important.[78]

What the Massachusetts Department of Commerce censored was not some incendiary falsehood but historical truth. Nothing James would have said, had he been allowed to speak, was false, excepting the word *wheat*. Most of our textbooks also omit the facts about grave robbing, Indian enslavement, and so on, even though they were common knowledge in colonial New England. Thus our popular history of the Pilgrims has not been a process of gaining perspective but of deliberate forgetting. Instead of these important facts, textbooks supply the feel-good minutiae of Squanto's helpfulness, his name, the fish in the corn-hills, sometimes even the menu and the number of American Indians who attended the prototypical first Thanksgiving.

I have focused here on untoward detail only because our histories have suppressed everything awkward for so long. The Pilgrims' courage in setting forth in the late fall to make their way on a continent new to them remains unsurpassed. In their first year the Pilgrims, like the American Indians, suffered from diseases, including scurvy and pneumonia; half of them died. It was not immoral of the Pilgrims to have taken over Patuxet. They did not cause the plague and were as baffled as to its origin as the stricken Indian villagers. Massasoit was happy that the Pilgrims were using the bay, for the Patuxet, being dead, had no more need for the site. Pilgrim-Indian relations started reasonably positively. The newcomers did eventually pay the Wampanoags for the corn they had dug up and taken. Plymouth, unlike many other colonies, usually paid Indians for the land it took. In some instances Europeans settled in Indian towns because Natives had *invited* them, as protection against another tribe or a nearby competing European power.[79] In sum, U.S. history is no more violent and oppressive than the history of England, Russia, Indonesia, or Burundi—but neither is it exceptionally less violent.

The antidote to feel-good history is not feel-bad history but honest and inclusive history. If textbook authors feel compelled to give moral instruction, the way origin myths have always done, they could accomplish this aim by allowing students to learn both the "good" and the "bad" sides of the Pilgrim tale. Conflict would then become part of the story, and students might discover that the knowledge they gain has implications for their lives today. Correctly taught, the issues of the era of the first Thanksgiving could help Americans grow more thoughtful and more tolerant, rather than more ethnocentric. Ironically, Plymouth, Massachusetts, the place where the myth began, now provides a model. Native Americans and non-Native allies did not take the suppression of Frank James's speech in 1970 lying down. That year and every November since, they have organized a counter-parade—"the National Day of Mourning"— that directly negates the traditional Thanksgiving celebration. After years of conflict, Plymouth agreed to allow both parades and also paid for two new historical markers telling the Wampanoag's side of the story.

Textbooks need to learn from Plymouth. Origin myths do not come cheaply. To glorify the Pilgrims is dangerous. The genial omissions and the invented details with which our textbooks retail the Pilgrim archetype are close cousins of the overt censorship practiced by the Massachusetts Department of Commerce in denying Frank James the right to speak. Surely, in history, "truth should be held sacred, at whatever cost."

4.

RED EYES

To understand the making of Anglo-America is impossible without close and sustained attention to its indigenous predecessors, allies, and nemeses. —JAMES AXTELL [1]

The invaders also anticipated, correctly, that other Europeans would question the morality of their enterprise. They therefore [prepared] . . . quantities of propaganda to overpower their own countrymen's scruples. The propaganda gradually took standard form as an ideology with conventional assumptions and semantics. We live with it still. —FRANCIS JENNINGS [2]

Memory says, "I did that." Pride replies, "I could not have done that." Eventually, memory yields. —FRIEDRICH NIETZSCHE [3]

There is not one Indian in the whole of this country who does not cringe in anguish and frustration because of these textbooks. There is not one Indian child who has not come home in shame and tears. —RUPERT COSTO [4]

Old myths never die—they just become embedded in the textbooks. —THOMAS BAILEY [5]

HISTORICALLY, AMERICAN INDIANS have been the most lied-about subset of our population. That's why Michael Dorris said that, in learning about Native Americans, "One does not start from point zero, but from minus ten." [6] High school students start below zero because of their textbooks, which unapologetically present Native Americans through white eyes. Today's textbooks should do better, especially since what historians call Indian history (though really it is interracial) has flowered since the 1970s, and the information on which new textbooks might be based currently rests on library shelves.

Textbooks' treatment of Native peoples has improved in recent years. In 1961 the bestselling *Rise of the American Nation* contained ten illustrations featuring Native people, alone or with whites (of 268 illustrations); most of these pictures focused on the themes of primitive life and savage warfare. Twenty-five years later, the retitled *Triumph of the American Nation* contained fifteen illustrations of American Indians; more important, no longer were Native Americans depicted as one-dimensional primitives. Rather, they were people who participated in struggles to preserve their identities and their land. Included were Metacomet (King Philip), Crispus Attucks (first casualty of the Revolution, who was also part black in ancestry), Sequoyah (who invented the Cherokee alphabet), and Navajo code-talkers in World War II. In 2003, the successor, *Holt American Nation*, had forty-three illustrations of American Indians. Some other textbooks published after 2000 continue this trend of giving more attention to Native Americans. *The Americans* stands out for its honest coverage of some of the events this chapter will treat, and *American Journey*, the middle-school textbook, is close behind.

Nevertheless, the authors of American history textbooks still "need a crash course in cultural relativism and ethnic sensitivity," as James Axtell put it in 1987. Even *The Americans*, the best of these books, devotes its first two pages to a reproduction of Benjamin West's 1771 painting, *Penn's Treaty with the Indians*. Painted almost a century after the event, West followed the usual convention of

depicting fully clothed Europeans—even with hats, scarves, and coats—presenting trade goods to nearly naked Americans. In reality, of course, no two groups of people have ever been dressed so differently at one spot on the earth's surface on the same day. The artist didn't really try to portray reality. He meant to show "primitive" (American Indian) and "civilized" (European).

Axtell also criticizes textbooks for still using such terms as *half-breed*, *massacre*, and *war-whooping*.[7] Reserving milder terms such as *frontier initiative* and *settlers* for whites is equally biased. If we cast off our

A nearly naked American Indian shakes William Penn's hand, sculpted in sandstone in the United States Capitol. Having been in Philadelphia in August, I can report that if this negotiation occurred then, Penn was near death through heat exhaustion. Having also been in Philadelphia after Thanksgiving, I can report that if this negotiation took place in winter, the Natives were suffering from frostbite.

American-ness and imagine we come from, say, Botswana, this typical sentence (from *The American Journey*) appears quite jarring: "In 1637 war broke out in Connecticut between settlers and the Pequot people." Surely the Pequots, having lived in villages in Connecticut probably for thousands of years, are "settlers." The English were newcomers, having been there for at most three years; traders set up camp in Windsor in 1634. Replacing *settlers* by *whites* makes for a more accurate but "unsettling" sentence. *Invaders* is more accurate still, and still more unsettling.

Even worse are the authors' overall interpretations, which continue to be shackled by the "conventional assumptions and semantics" that have "explained" Indian-white relations for centuries, according to Axtell. Textbook authors still write history to comfort descendants of the "settlers."

Our journey into a more accurate history of American Indian peoples and their relations with European and African invaders cannot be a happy excursion. Native Americans are not and must not be props in a sort of theme park of the past, where we go to have a good time and see exotic cultures. "What we have done to the peoples who were living in North America" is, according to anthropologist Sol Tax, "our Original Sin."[8] If we look Indian history squarely in the eye, we are going to get red eyes. This is our past, however, and we must acknowledge it. It is time for textbooks to send white children home, if not with red eyes, at least with thought-provoking questions.

Most of today's textbooks at least try to be accurate about American Indian cultures. Thirteen of the eighteen textbooks I surveyed begin by devoting more than five pages to precontact Native societies.[9] From the start, however, American Indian societies pose a problem for textbooks.[10] Their authors are consumers, not practitioners, of archaeology, ethnobotany, linguistics, physical anthropology, folklore studies, cultural anthropology, ethnohistory, and other related disciplines. Scholars in these fields can tell us much, albeit tentatively, about what happened in the Americas before Europeans and Africans arrived. Unfortunately, the authors of history textbooks treat archaeology et al. as dead disciplines to be mined for answers. These fields study dead people, to be sure, but they are alive with controversy. Every year headlines appear about charcoal possibly forty thousand years old found in cooking fires in Brazil, new dates for an archaeological dig in Pennsylvania, or more speculative claims that some new human remain, artifact, or idea hails from China, Europe, or Africa. In 2007 came evidence that a comet may have exploded in the earth's atmosphere thirteen thousand years ago, setting much of North America on fire. Possibly the resulting firestorm killed off the larger mammals, like horses and mastodons, and decimated the human population.[11]

"Possibly," however, does not fit with textbook style, which is to present definitive answers. Only *The American Adventure* admits uncertainty: "This page may be out of date by the time it is read." *Adventure* goes on to present competing claims that humans have been in the Americas for twelve thousand, twenty-one thousand, and forty thousand years. As a result, although *Adventure* is one of the oldest of all the textbooks I surveyed, its pre-Columbian pages have not gone out of date.[12] Most other textbooks retain their usual authoritative tone. Regarding the date of the first human settlement of the Americas, estimates vary from twelve thousand years before the present to more than seventy thousand BP.[13] Some scientists believe that the original settlers came in successive waves over thousands of years; genetic similarities convince others that most Natives descended from a single small band.[14] Most textbook authors simply choose one date and present it as undisputed fact. Some newer books add "probably," as in: people "probably followed the animal herds," from *Holt American Nation*. But then, like the others, they supply one date for students to memorize.

Authors need to go further. Walking across Beringia (the isthmus across the Bering Strait) is only a hypothesis. They ought to give other theories, including boats, a hearing. They would not have to do all the work themselves, either, but could set students loose on the Web and in the library, arming them and their teachers with ideas about what to look for and how to assess reputed new findings. The school year might then begin with a debate among students who have chosen different dates and routes—each marshaling evidence from glottochronology (dating linguistic changes), genetics, archaeology, and other disciplines to bolster their conclusion. Students would be excited. They would realize, at the start, that history still remains to be done—that it is not just an inert body of facts to be memorized.

We can see the absence of intellectual excitement from the beginning. How did people get here? Every book says something like this, from Boorstin and Kelley:

> So much of the earth's water had frozen into ice that it lowered the level of the sea in the Bering Strait. Then as they tracked wild game they could walk across the 56 miles from Siberia to Alaska. Without knowing it, they had discovered two large continents that were completely empty of people but were full of wild game. . . . In the thousands of years afterwards many other groups followed. These small bands spread all across North and South America.

Actually, while most scholars still accept a "Beringia" crossing, archaeological evidence is slim, and more and more archaeologists believe boat crossings, accidental or purposeful, may have been the method. After all, people got to Australia at least forty thousand years ago, and no matter how much ice piled up on land during the Ice Age, you could never walk to Australia, across the deep ocean divide known as Wallace's Line. Of course, archaeologists have unearthed no evidence of boats anywhere in the world dating back more than ten thousand years. But then, no artifacts survive from so long ago other than stone tools, and no humans were ever so primitive as to fashion stone boats. Absence of evidence is not evidence of absence.[15]

Textbook writers like Beringia, I believe, because it fits their overall story line of unrelenting progress. The people themselves are pictured as primitive savages, vaguely Neanderthalian. This archetype—not very bright, enmeshed in wars with nature and other humans—probably underlies authors' certainty that they must have walked. Unlike us, the original Americans didn't have to be intelligent—they just had to walk.[16] And they certainly weren't bright, for "without knowing it, they had discovered two large continents." This is a startling assertion. Somehow our authors, writing at least eleven thousand years after the fact, know what these first settlers thought—or, rather, know that they did *not* think they had reached new continents. John Garraty's *American History* makes the same claim: "They did not know that they were exploring a new continent." Now, *continent* means "a large land mass, surrounded by water." How could humans confront the vastness of Canada—itself larger than Australia—and *not* know they were exploring a large land mass? These first settlers must have been stunningly stupid.[17]

The depiction of mental dullness persists as Garraty tells of "the wanderers" who "moved slowly southward and to the east. . . . Many thousand years passed before they had spread over all of North and South America." Actually, many archaeologists believe that people reached most parts of the Americas within a thousand years, far too rapidly to allow easy archaeological determination of the direction and timing of their migration. Archaeological finds do not grow older as we move northwest through the Yukon and across Alaska.[18] Moreover, even if the first Americans did arrive on foot, they were just as surely explorers as Columbus.

Garraty drones on, continuing to imply that the first settlers were rather dim: "None of the groups made much progress in developing simple machines or substituting mechanical or even animal power for their own muscle power." But this was not the Americans' "fault." No "animal power" was available. For that matter, in Europe and Asia before 1769, most "simple machines" depended on horses, oxen, water buffalo, mules, or cattle—beasts unknown in the Americas. In *Guns, Germs, and Steel*, Jared Diamond suggests that the availability of at least some of these animals for domestication was a critical factor in developing not only machines but also the division of labor we call "civilization."[19]

All of the textbooks are locked into the old savage-to-barbaric-to-civilized school of anthropology dating back to L. H. Morgan and Karl Marx around 1875. Their authors may well have encountered such thinking in anthropology courses when they were undergraduates; it is no longer taught today, however. Garraty exemplifies the evolutionary stereotype: "Those who planted seeds and cultivated the land instead of merely hunting and gathering food were more secure and comfortable." Apparently he has not encountered the "affluent primitive" theory, which persuaded anthropologists some forty years ago that gatherer-hunters lived quite comfortably. *American History* then makes an even sillier mistake: "These agricultural people were mostly peaceful, though they could fight fiercely to protect their fields. The hunters and wanderers, on the other hand, were quite warlike because their need to move about brought them frequently into conflict with other groups." Here Garraty conflates *civil* and *civilization*. Decades ago, most anthropologists challenged this outmoded continuum, determining that hunters and gatherers were relatively peaceful, compared to agriculturalists, and that modern societies were more warlike still. We have only to remember the history of the twentieth century to see at once that violence can increase with civilization.

Most textbooks do confer civilization on some Natives—the Aztecs, Incas, and Mayans—based on the premise, embraced by the Spanish conquistadors themselves, that wealth equals civilization. In the words of *The American Adventure*: "Unlike the noncivilized peoples of the Caribbean, the Aztec were rich and prosperous." Boorstin and Kelley cannot easily concede even that much. After devoting a page to the advanced civilizations of the Mayans, Incas, and Aztecs, Boorstin and Kelley proceed to put them down: "Unlike the peoples of Europe, they had not built ships to cross the oceans. They had not reached out to the world. In their isolation they found it hard to learn new ways. When the Spanish came, it seemed that the Incas, the Mayas and the Aztecs had ceased to progress. They were ripe for conquest."

Among other things, that paragraph is simply bad history. In fact, the rate of change was accelerating in the Western Hemisphere before the Spanish came. The Incas had taken less than the previous century to assemble their huge empire. The Aztecs had come to dominate central Mexico by alliance and force still more recently.

To Boorstin and Kelley, the Natives to the north in what is now the United States lagged even further behind the "unprogressive" Aztecs, Mayans, and Incas. Of course, if Boorstin and Kelley had looked around the world in 1392, they would have seen no such decisive differences between American and European cultures. This is a secular form of predestination: historians observe that peoples were conquered and come up with reasons why that was right. In sociology we call this "blaming the victim." The authors of *The American Pageant* take the same approach:

> Unlike the Europeans, who would soon arrive with the presumption that humans had dominion over the earth and with the technologies to alter the very face of the land, the Native Americans had neither the desire nor the means to manipulate nature aggressively. . . . They were so thinly spread across the continent that vast areas were virtually untouched by a human presence. In the fateful year 1492, probably no more than 4 million Native Americans padded through the whispering, primeval forests and paddled across the sparkling virgin waters of North America. They were blissfully unaware that the historic isolation of the Americas was about to end forever.

This passage exemplifies the unfortunate results when publishers try to keep a legacy text in print forever. These clichés about Native Americans were known to be false in 1956, when Bailey wrote the first edition of this seemingly ageless text. Chapter 3 shows what is wrong with this wilderness scenario. For one thing, the numbers are all wrong. In the central valley of Mexico alone lived about twenty-five million people. In the rest of North America lived perhaps twenty million more. Furthermore, the image of the moccasined Indian "padding" through the virgin forest won't do; a majority of Native Americans in what is now the United States farmed. *Pageant* originated more than half a century ago and is now in its thirteenth printing. In 1956, it may have been written by its "author," Thomas Bailey. Who wrote the current edition is anyone's guess.

In the late 1990s, someone—certainly not Bailey, long deceased, and probably not either of the other two listed authors—realized that the book needed to mention the Columbian Exchange and the post-1492 epidemics that decimated American Indians. As a result, a later page tells of these staggering population declines, without acknowledging the contradiction between that passage and this one. Thomas Bailey's own book thus proves him right: "Old myths never die—they just become embedded in the textbooks." Boorstin and Kelley are even less competent; they still omit the Columbian Exchange entirely.

Even the best textbooks cannot resist contrasting "primitive" Americans with modern Europeans. Part of the problem is that the books are really comparing rural America to urban Europe—Massachusetts to London. Comparing Tenochtitlan (now Mexico City) to rural Scotland might produce a very different impression, for when Cortés arrived, Tenochtitlan was a city of one hundred thousand to three hundred thousand, whose central market was so busy and noisy "that it could be heard more than four miles away," according to Bernal Díaz, who accompanied Cortés.[20] It would be even better if authors could forsake the entire primitive-to-civilized continuum altogether. After all, from the perspective of the average inhabitant, life may have been just as "advanced" and far more pleasant in Massachusetts or Scotland as in Aztec Mexico or London.

For a long time Native Americans have been rebuking textbook authors for reserving the adjective *civilized* for European cultures. In 1927 an organization of Native leaders called the Grand Council Fire of American Indians criticized textbooks as "unjust to the life of our people." They went on to ask, "What is civilization? Its marks are a noble religion and philosophy, original arts, stirring music, rich story and legend. We had these. Then we were not savages, but a civilized race."[21]

Even an appreciative treatment of Native cultures reinforces ethnocentrism so long as it does not challenge the primitive-to-civilized continuum. This continuum inevitably conflates the meaning of *civilized* in everyday conversation— "refined or enlightened"—with "having a complex division of labor," the only definition that anthropologists defend. When we consider the continuum carefully, it immediately becomes problematic. Was the Third Reich civilized, for instance? Most anthropologists would answer yes. In what ways do we prefer the civilized Third Reich to the more primitive Arawak society that Columbus encountered? If we refuse to label the Third Reich civilized, are we not using the term to mean "polite, refined"? If so, we must consider the Arawaks civilized, and we must also consider Columbus and his Spaniards primitive, if not savage. Ironically, societies characterized by a complex division of labor are often marked by inequality and support large specialized armies. Precisely these "civilized" societies are likely to resort to savage violence in their attempts to conquer "primitive" societies.[22]

Thoughtless use of the terms *civilized* and *civilization* blocks any real inquiry into the worldview or the social structure of the "uncivilized" person or society. In 1990 President George H. W. Bush condemned Iraq's invasion of Kuwait with the words, "The entire civilized world is against Iraq"—an irony, in that Iraq's Tigris and Euphrates valleys are the earliest known seat of civilization.

The three new "from scratch" textbooks in my sample of new histories do a somewhat better job than the legacy texts. They recognize diversity among Native societies. They tell about the League of Five Nations among the Iroquois in the Northeast, potlatches among the Northwestern coastal Indians, cliff dwellings in the Southwest, and caste divisions among the Natchez in the Southeast. In the process of presenting ten or twenty different cultures in six or eight pages, however, textbooks can hardly reach a high level of sophistication. So they seize upon the unusual. No matter that the Choctaws were more numerous and played a much larger role in American history than the Natchez— they were also more ordinary. Students will not find among the Native Americans portrayed in their history textbooks many "regular folks" with whom they might identify.

After contact with Europeans and Africans, American Indian societies changed rapidly. Native Americans took into their cultures not only guns, blankets, and kettles, but also new foods, ways of building houses, and ideas from Christianity. Most American history textbooks emphasize the changes in only one group, the Plains Indians. The rapid efflorescence of this colorful culture after the Spaniards introduced the horse to the American West supplies an exhilarating example of syncretism—blending elements of two different cultures to create something new.[23] The transformation in the Plains cultures, however, was only the tip of the cultural-change iceberg. An even more profound metamorphosis occurred as Europeans linked Native peoples to the developing world economy. This process continues to affect formerly independent cultures to this day. In the early 1970s, for example, Lapps in Norway replaced their sled dogs with snowmobiles, only to find themselves vulnerable to Arab oil embargoes.[24] In the 1990s many Native American groups gained not only wealth but also new respect from their non-Native neighbors when their new casinos and hotels connected them to the world economy. This connecting seems inevitable, hence perhaps is neither to be praised nor decried—but it should not be ignored, because it is crucial to understanding how Europeans took over America.

In Atlantic North America, members of Indian nations possessed a variety of sophisticated skills, from the ability to weave watertight baskets to an understanding of how certain plants can be used to reduce pain. At first, Native Americans traded corn, beaver, fish, sassafras, and other goods with the French, Dutch, and English, in return for axes, blankets, cloth, beads, and kettles. Soon, however, Europeans persuaded Natives to specialize in the fur and slave trades. Native Americans were better hunters and trappers than Europeans, and with the guns the Europeans sold them, they became better still. Other Native skills began to atrophy. Why spend hours making a watertight basket when in one-tenth the time you could trap enough beavers to trade for a kettle? Even agriculture, which the Native Americans had shown to the Europeans, declined, because it became easier to trade for food than to grow it. Everyone acted in rational self-interest in joining such a system—that is, Native Americans were not mere victims—because everyone's standard of living improved, at least in theory.

Some of the rapid changes in eastern Indian societies exemplify syncretism. When the Iroquois combined European guns and Native American tactics to smash the Hurons, they controlled their own culture and chose which elements of European culture to incorporate, which to modify, which to ignore. Native Americans learned how to repair guns, cast bullets, build stronger forts, and fight to annihilate.[25] Native Americans also became well known as linguists, often speaking two European languages (French, English, Dutch, Russian, or Spanish) and at least two American Indian languages. English colonists sometimes used Natives as interpreters when dealing with the Spanish or French, not just with other Native American nations.

These developments were not all matters of happy economics and voluntary syncretic cultural transformation, however. Natives were operating under a military and cultural threat, and they knew it. They quickly deduced that European guns were more efficient than their bows and arrows. Europeans soon realized that trade goods could be used to win and maintain political alliances with American Indian nations. To deal with the new threat and because whites "demanded institutions reflective of their own with which to relate," many Native groups strengthened their tribal governments.[26] Chiefs acquired power they had never had before. These governments often ruled unprecedentedly broad areas, because the heightened warfare and the plagues had wiped out smaller tribes or caused them to merge with larger ones for protection. Large nations became ethnic melting pots, taking in whites and blacks as well as other Indians. New confederations and nations developed, such as the Creeks, Seminoles, and Lumbees.[27] The tribes also became more male-dominated, in imitation of Europeans or because of the expanded importance of war skills in their cultures.[28]

Tribes that were closest to the Europeans got guns first, guns that could be trained on interior peoples who had not yet acquired any. Suddenly some nations had a great military advantage over others. The result was an escalation of Indian warfare. Native nations had engaged in conflict before Europeans came, of course. Tribes rarely fought to the finish, however. Some tribes did not want to take over the lands belonging to other nations, partly because each had its own sacred sites. For a nation to exterminate its neighbors was difficult anyway, since all enjoyed roughly the same level of military technology. Now all this changed. European powers deliberately increased the level of warfare by playing one Native nation off another. The Spanish, for example, used a divide-and-conquer strategy to defeat the Aztecs in Mexico. In Scotland and Ireland, the English had played tribes against one another to extend British rule. Now they did the same in North America.[29]

Ran away from his Master Nathanael Holbrook of Sherburn, on Wednesday the 19th of Sept last, an Indian Lad of about 18 Years of Age, named John Pittarne; He is pretty well sett and of a guilty Countenance and has short Hair; He had on a grey Coat with Pewter Buttons, Leather Breeches, an old tow Shirt, grey Stockings, good Shoes, and a Felt Hat.

Whoever shall take up the said Servant, and convey him to his Master in Sherburn, shall have Forty Shillings Reward and all necessary Charges paid. We hear the said Servant intended to change his Name and his Clothes.

Like African slaves, Indian slaves escaped when they could. This notice comes from the *Boston Weekly News-Letter* for October 4, 1739.

For many tribes the motive for the increased combat was the enslavement of other Natives to sell to the Europeans for more guns and kettles. As northern tribes specialized in fur, certain southern tribes specialized in people. Some Native Americans had enslaved each other long before Europeans arrived. Now Europeans vastly expanded Indian slavery.[30] I had expected to find in our textbooks the cliché that Native Americans did not make good slaves, but only two books, *Triumph of the American Nation* and *The American Tradition*, say even that. *American History* buries a sentence, "A few Indians were enslaved," in its discussion of the African slave trade. Otherwise, the textbooks are silent on the subject of the Native American slave trade in what is now the United States—except for one surprising standout. *The American Pageant* contains a paragraph that tells how the Carolina colonists enlisted the coastal Savannah Indians to bring them slaves from the interior, making "manacled Indians . . . among the young colony's major exports." *Pageant* goes on to tell how Indian captives wound up enslaved in the West Indies and New England.[31]

Europeans' enslavement of Native Americans has a long history. Ponce de Leon went to Florida not really to seek the mythical fountain of youth; his main business was to seek gold and capture slaves for Hispaniola.[32] In New England, Indian slavery led directly to African slavery: the first blacks imported there, in 1638, were brought from the West Indies in exchange for Native Americans from Connecticut.[33] On the eve of the New York City slave rebellion of 1712, in which Native and African slaves united, about one resident in four was enslaved and one slave in four was American Indian. A 1730 census of South Kingston, Rhode Island, showed 935 whites, 333 African slaves, and 223 Native American slaves.[34]

As *Pageant* (alone) implies, the center of Native American slavery, like African American slavery, was South Carolina. Its population in 1708 included 3,960 free whites, 4,100 African slaves, 1,400 Indian slaves, and 120 indentured servants, presumably white. These numbers do not reflect the magnitude of Native slavery, however, because they omit the export trade. From Carolina, as from New England, colonists sent enslaved American Indians (who might escape) to the West Indies (where they could never escape), in exchange for enslaved Africans. Charleston shipped more than ten thousand Natives in chains to the West Indies in one year.[35] Farther west, so many Pawnee Indians were sold to whites that *Pawnee* became the name applied in the plains to all slaves, whether they were of Indian or African origin.[36] On the West Coast, Pierson Reading, a manager of John Sutter's huge grant of Indian land in central California, extolled the easy life he led in 1844: "The Indians of California make as obedient and humble slaves as the Negro in the south." In the Southwest, whites enslaved Navajos and Apaches right up to the middle of the Civil War.[37]

Intensified warfare and the slave trade rendered stable settlements no longer safe, helping to de-agriculturize Native Americans. To avoid being targets for capture, American Indians abandoned their cornfields and their villages and began to live in smaller settlements from which they could more easily escape to the woods. Ultimately, they had to trade with Europeans even for food.[38] As Europeans learned from Natives what to grow and how to grow it, they became less dependent upon Indians and Indian technology, while American Indians became more dependent upon Europeans and European technology.[39] Thus, what worked for the Native Americans in the short run worked against them in the long. In the long run, it was Indians who were enslaved, Indians who died, Indian technology that was lost, Indian cultures that fell apart. By the time the pitiful remnant of the Massachuset tribe converted to Christianity and joined the Puritans' "praying Indian towns," they did so in response to an invading culture that told them their religion was wrong and Christianity was right. This process exemplifies what anthropologists call *cultural imperialism*. Even the proud Plains Indians, whose syncretic culture combined horses and guns from the Spanish with Native art, religion, and hunting styles, showed the effects of cultural imperialism: the Sioux word for white man, *wasichu*, means "one who has everything good."[40]

The textbook *Life and Liberty* is distinguished by its graphic presentation of change in Native societies. It confronts students with this provocative pair of illustrations and asks, "Which shows Indian life before Europeans arrived and which shows Indian life after? What evidence tells you the date?" Thus *Life and Liberty* helps students understand that Europeans did not "civilize" or "settle" "roaming" Indians, but had the opposite impact.

To be anthropologically literate about culture contact, students should be familiar with the terms *syncretism* and *cultural imperialism*, or at least the concepts they denote. None of the textbooks I studied mentions either term, and most of them tell little about the process of cultural change, again except for the Plains Indian horse culture, which, as a consequence, comes across as unique. Even the best of the new textbooks are short on analysis. They don't treat the crucial importance of incorporation into the global economy, which helps to explain why sometimes Europeans traded and coexisted with Natives and other times merely attacked them. Nor do they tell how contact worked to de-skill Native Americans.

Just as American societies changed when they encountered whites, so European societies changed when they encountered Natives. Textbooks completely miss this side of the mutual accommodation and acculturation process.[41] Instead, their view of white-Indian relations is dominated by the archetype of the frontier line. Textbooks present the process as a moving line of white (and black) settlement—American Indians on one side, whites (and blacks) on the other. Pocahontas and Squanto aside, the Natives and Europeans don't meet much in textbook history, except as whites remove Indians farther west. In reality, whites and Native Americans in what is now the United States worked together, sometimes lived together, and quarreled with each other for 325 years, from the first permanent Spanish settlement in 1565 to the end of Sioux and Apache autonomy around 1890.

The term *frontier* hardly does justice to this process, for it implies a line or boundary. Contact, not separation, was the rule. *Frontier* also locates the observer somewhere in the urban East, from which the frontier is "out there." Textbook authors seem not to have encountered the trick question, "Which came first, civilization or the wilderness?" The answer is civilization, for only the "civilized" mind could define the world of Native farmers, fishers, and gatherers and hunters, coexisting with forests, crops, and animals, as a "wilderness." Calling the area beyond secure European control *frontier* or *wilderness* makes it subtly alien. Such a viewpoint is intrinsically Eurocentric and marginalizes the actions of nonurban people, both Native and non-Native.[42]

The band of interaction was amazingly multicultural. In 1635 "sixteen different languages could be heard among the settlers in New Amsterdam," languages from North America, Africa, and Europe.[43] In 1794, when the zone of contact had reached the eastern Midwest, a single northern Ohio town, "the Glaize," was made up of hundreds of Shawnee, Miami, and Delaware Indians;

British and French traders and artisans; several Nanticokes, Cherokees, and Iroquois; a few African American and white American captives; and whites who had married into or been adopted by Indian families. The Glaize was truly multicultural in its holidays, observing Mardi Gras, St. Patrick's Day, the birthday of the British queen, and American Indian celebrations.[44] In 1835, when the contact area was near the West Coast, John Sutter, with permission of the Mexican authorities, recruited Native Americans to raise his wheat crop; operate a distillery, a hat factory, and a blanket company; and build a fort (now Sacramento). Procuring uniforms from Russian traders and officers from Europe, Sutter organized a two-hundred-man Indian army, clothed in tsarist uniforms and commanded in German![45]

Our history textbooks still obliterate the interracial, multicultural nature of frontier life. Boorstin and Kelley tell us, "A focus of community life was the fort built by John Sutter," but they never mention that the "community" was largely American Indians. *American History* devotes almost a page to Sutter's Fort without ever hinting that Native Americans were anything other than enemies: "Gradually he built a fortified town, which he called *Sutter's Fort.* The entire place was surrounded by a thick wall 18 feet high (about 6 meters) topped with cannon for protection against unfriendly Indians." No reader would infer from that account that friendly Indians *built* the fort.

Historian Gary Nash tells us that interculturation took place from the start in Virginia, "facilitated by the fact that some Indians lived among the English as day laborers, while a number of settlers fled to Indian villages rather than endure the rigors of life among the autocratic English."[46] Indeed, many white and black newcomers chose to live an American Indian lifestyle. In his *Letters from an American Farmer*, Michel Guillaume Jean de Crévecoeur wrote, "There must be in the Indians' social bond something singularly captivating, and far superior to be boasted of among us; for thousands of Europeans are Indians, and we have no examples of even one of those Aborigines having from choice become Europeans."[47] Crévecoeur overstated his case: as we know from Squanto's example, some Natives chose to live among whites from the beginning. The migration was mostly the other way, however. As Benjamin Franklin put it, "No European who has tasted Savage Life can afterwards bear to live in our societies."[48]

Europeans were always trying to stop the outflow. Hernando de Soto had to post guards to keep his men and women from defecting to Native societies. The Pilgrims so feared Indianization that they made it a crime for men to wear long hair. "People who did run away to the Indians might expect very extreme punishments, even up to the death penalty," Karen Kupperman tells us, if caught by whites.[49] Nonetheless, right up to the end of independent Native nationhood in 1890, whites continued to defect, and whites who lived an Indian lifestyle, such as Daniel Boone, became cultural heroes in white society.

Communist Eastern Europe erected an Iron Curtain to stop its outflow but could never explain why, if communist societies were the most progressive on earth, they had to prevent people from defecting. American colonial embarrassment similarly went straight to the heart of their ideology, also an ideology of progress. Textbooks in Eastern Europe and the United States have handled the problem in the same way: by omitting the facts. Not one American history textbook mentions the attraction of Native societies to European Americans and African Americans.

African Americans frequently fled to American Indian societies to escape bondage. What did whites find so alluring? According to Benjamin Franklin, "All their government is by Counsel of the Sages. There is no Force; there are no Prisons, no officers to compel Obedience, or inflict Punishment." Probably foremost, the lack of hierarchy in the Native societies in the eastern United States attracted the admiration of European observers.[50] Frontiersmen were taken with the extent to which Native Americans enjoyed freedom as individuals. Women were also accorded more status and power in most Native societies than in white societies of the time, which white women noted with envy in captivity narratives. Although leadership was substantially hereditary in some nations, most American Indian societies north of Mexico were much more democratic than Spain, France, or even England in the seventeenth and eighteenth centuries. "There is not a Man in the Ministry of the Five Nations, who has gain'd his Office, otherwise than by Merit," waxed Lt. Gov. Cadwallader Colden of New York in 1727. "Their Authority is only the Esteem of the People, and ceases the Moment that Esteem is lost." Colden applied to the Iroquois terms redolent of "the natural rights of mankind": "Here we see the natural Origin of all Power and Authority among a free People."[51]

Indeed, Native American ideas are partly responsible for our democratic institutions. We have seen how Native ideas of liberty, fraternity, and equality found their way to Europe to influence social philosophers such as Thomas More, Locke, Montaigne, Montesquieu, and Rousseau. These European thinkers then influenced Americans such as Franklin, Jefferson, and Madison.[52] In recent years historians have debated whether American Indian ideas may also have influenced our democracy more directly. Through 150 years of colonial

After Col. Henry Bouquet defeated the Ohio Indians at Bushy Run in 1763, he demanded the release of all white captives. Most of them, especially the children, had to be "bound hand and foot" and forcibly returned to white society. Meanwhile, the Native prisoners "went back to their defeated relations with great signs of joy," in the words of the anthropologist Frederick Turner (in *Beyond Geography*, 245). Turner rightly calls these scenes "infamous and embarrassing."

contact, the Iroquois League stood before the colonies as an object lesson in how to govern a large domain democratically. The terms used by Lt. Gov. Colden find an echo in our Declaration of Independence fifty years later.

In the 1740s the Iroquois wearied of dealing with several often bickering English colonies and suggested that the colonies form a union similar to the league. In 1754 Benjamin Franklin, who had spent much time among the Iroquois observing their deliberations, pleaded with colonial leaders to consider his Albany Plan of Union: "It would be a strange thing if six nations of ignorant savages should be capable of forming a scheme for such a union and be able to execute it in such a manner as that it has subsisted ages and appears insoluble; and yet that a like union should be impracticable for ten or a dozen English colonies."[53]

The colonies rejected the plan. But it was a forerunner of the Articles of

As a symbol of the new United States, Americans chose the eagle clutching a bundle of arrows. They knew that both the eagle and the arrows were symbols of the Iroquois League. Although one arrow is easily broken, no one can break six (or thirteen) at once.

Confederation and the Constitution. Both the Continental Congress and the Constitutional Convention referred openly to Iroquois ideas and imagery. In 1775 Congress formulated a speech to the Iroquois, signed by John Hancock, that quoted Iroquois advice from 1744. "The Six Nations are a wise people," Congress wrote, "let us harken to their council and teach our children to follow it." [54]

John Mohawk has argued that American Indians are directly or indirectly responsible for the public-meeting tradition, free speech, democracy, and "all those things which got attached to the Bill of Rights." Without the Native example, "do you really believe that all those ideas would have found birth among a people who had spent a millennium butchering other people because of intolerance of questions of religion?" [55] Mohawk may have overstated the case for Native democracy, since heredity played a major role in officeholding in many American Indian societies. His case is strengthened, however, by the fact that wherever Europeans went in the Americas, they projected monarchs ("King Philip") or other undemocratic leaders onto Native societies. To some degree, this projecting was done out of European self-interest, so they could claim to have purchased tribal land as a result of dealing with one person or faction. The practice also betrayed habitual European thought: Europeans could not believe that nations did *not* have such rulers, since that was the only form of government they knew.

For a hundred years after our Revolution, Americans credited Native Americans as a source of their democratic institutions. Revolutionary-era cartoonists used images of American Indians to represent the colonies against Britain. Virginia's patriot rifle companies wore Indian clothes and moccasins as they fought the redcoats. When colonists took action to oppose unjust authority, as in the Boston Tea Party or the antirent protests against Dutch plantations in the Hudson River valley during the 1840s, they chose to dress as American Indians, not to blame Indians for the demonstrations but to appropriate a symbol identified with liberty.[56]

Of course, Dutch traditions influenced Plymouth as well as New York. So did English common law and the Magna Carta. American democracy seems to be another example of syncretism, combining ideas from Europe and Native America. The degree of Native influence is hard to specify, since that influence came through several sources. Textbooks might present it as a soft hypothesis rather than hard fact. But they should not leave it out. In all the textbooks I surveyed, discussion of any intellectual influence of Native Americans on European Americans was limited to a single caption in one book, *Discovering American History*, beneath a wampum belt paired with Benjamin Franklin's famous cartoon of a divided, hence dying snake. "Franklin's Albany Plan might have been inspired by the Iroquois League" is the caption. "The wampum belt expresses the unity of tribes achieved through the League. Compare it with Franklin's cartoon." The other books are silent.

But, then, textbooks leave out most contributions of Native Americans to American culture. Our regional cuisines—the dishes that make American food distinctive—often combine Indian with European and African elements. Examples range from New England pork and beans to New Orleans gumbo to Texas chili.[57] Mutual acculturation between Native and African Americans— owed to shared experience in slavery as well as escapes by blacks to Native communities—accounts for soul food being part Indian, from corn bread and grits to greens and hush puppies.[58] Native place names dot our landscape, from Okefenokee to Alaska. Native farming methods were not "primitive." Farmers in some tribes drew two or three times as much nourishment from the soil as we do.[59] Place names, too, show intellectual interchange. Whites had to be asking Indians, "Where am I?" "What is this place called?" "What is that animal?" "What is the name of that mountain?"

Although textbooks "appreciate" Native cultures, the possibility of real interculturation, especially in matters of the intellect, is foreign to them. This is a shame, for authors thereby ignore much of what has made America distinctive from Europe. In a travel narrative, Peter Kalm wrote in 1750, "The French, English, Germans, Dutch, and other Europeans, who have lived for several years in distant provinces, near and among the Indians, grow so like them in their behavior and thought that they can only be distinguished by the difference of their color."[60] In the famous essay, "The Frontier in American History," Frederick Jackson Turner told how the frontier masters the European, "strips off the garments of civilization," and requires him to be an Indian in thought as well as dress. "Before long he has gone to planting Indian corn and plowing with a sharp stick." Gradually he builds something new, "but the outcome is not the old Europe." It is syncretic; it is American.[61]

Acknowledging how aboriginal we are culturally—how the United States and Europe, too, have been influenced by Native American as well as European

In the nineteenth century, Americans knew of Native American contributions to medicine. Sixty percent of all medicines patented in the century were distributed bearing Indian images, including Kickapoo Indian Cough Cure, Kickapoo Indian Sagwa, and Kickapoo Indian Oil. In this century, America has repressed the image of Indian as healer.

ideas—would require significant textbook rewriting. If we recognized American Indians as important intellectual antecedents of our political structure, we would have to acknowledge that acculturation has been a *two*-way street, and we might have to reassess the assumption of primitive Indian culture that legitimizes the entire conquest.[62] In 1970 the Indian Historian Press produced a critique of our histories, *Textbooks and the American Indian*. One of the press's yardsticks for evaluating books was the question, "Does the textbook describe the religions, philosophies, and contributions to thought of the American Indian?"[63] Unfortunately, the answer must still be no.

Consider how textbooks treat Native religions as a unitary whole. *The American Way* describes Native American religion in these words: "These Native Americans [in the Southeast] believed that nature was filled with spirits. Each form of life, such as plants and animals, had a spirit. Earth and air held spirits too. People were never alone. They shared their lives with the spirits of nature." *Way* is trying to show respect for Native American religion, but it doesn't work. Stated flatly like this, the beliefs seem like make-believe, not the sophisticated theology of a higher civilization. Let us try a similarly succinct summary of the beliefs of many Christians today: "These Americans believed that one great male god ruled the world. Sometimes they divided him into three parts, which they called father, son, and holy ghost. They ate crackers and wine or grape juice, believing that they were eating the son's body and drinking his blood. If they believed strongly enough, they would live on forever after they died." Textbooks *never* describe Christianity this way. It's offensive. Believers would immediately argue that such a depiction fails to convey the symbolic meaning or the spiritual satisfaction of communion.

Textbooks could present American Indian religions from a perspective that takes them seriously as attractive and persuasive belief systems.[64] The anthropologist Frederick Turner has pointed out that when whites remark upon the fact that Indians perceive a spirit in every animal or rock, they are simultaneously admitting their own loss of a deep spiritual relationship with the earth. Native Americans are "part of the total living universe," wrote Turner; "spiritual health is to be had only by accepting this condition and by attempting to live in accordance with it." Turner contends that this life view is healthier than European alternatives: "Ours is a shockingly dead view of creation. We ourselves are the only things in the universe to which we grant an authentic vitality, and because of this we are not fully alive."[65] Thus, Turner shows that taking

Native American religions seriously might require reexamination of the Judeo-Christian tradition. No textbook would suggest such a controversial idea.

Similarly, textbooks give readers no clue as to what the zone of contact was like from the Native side. They emphasize Native Americans such as Squanto and Pocahontas, who sided with the invaders. And they invert the terms, picturing white aggressors as "settlers" and often showing Native settlers as aggressors. "The United States Department of Interior had tried to give each tribe both land and money," says *The American Way*, describing the U.S. policy of forcing tribes to cede most of their land and retreat to reservations. Whites were baffled by Native ingratitude at being "offered" this land, *Way* claims: "White Americans could not understand the Indians. To them, owning land was a dream come true." In reality, whites of the time were hardly baffled. Even Gen. Philip Sheridan—who is notorious for having said, "The only good Indian is a dead Indian"—understood. "We took away their country and their means of support, and it was for this and against this they made war," he wrote. "Could anyone expect less?"[66] The textbooks have turned history upside down.

Let us try a right-side-up view. "After King Philip's War, there was continuous conflict at the edge of New England. In Vermont the settlers worried about savages scalping them." This description is accurate, provided the reader understands that the settlers were Native American, the scalpers white. Even the best of our American history books fail to show the climate of white actions within which Native Americans on the border of white control had to live. It was so bad, and Natives had so little recourse, that the Catawbas in North Carolina "fled in every direction" in 1786 when a solitary white man rode into their village unannounced. And the Catawbas were a friendly tribe![67]

From the opposite coast, here is a story that might help make such dispersal understandable: "An old white settler told his son who was writing about life on the Oregon frontier about an incident he recalled from the cowboys and Indians days. Some cowboys came upon Indian families without their men present. The cowboys gave pursuit, planning to rape the squaws, as was the custom. One woman, however, pushed sand into her vagina to thwart her pursuers."[68] The act of resistance is what made the incident memorable. Otherwise, it was entirely ordinary. Such ordinariness is what our textbooks leave out. They do not challenge our archetypal Laura Ingalls Wilder picture of peaceful white settlers suffering occasional attacks by brutal Indians. If they did, the fact that so many tribes resorted to war, even after 1815 when resistance was clearly doomed, would become understandable.

Indian Massacre at Wilkes-Barre shows a motif common in nineteenth-century lithographs: Indians invading the sanctity of the white settlers' homes. Actually, whites were invading Indian lands and often Indian homes, but pictures such as this, not the reality, remain the archetype.

Our history is full of wars with Native American nations. "For almost two hundred years," notes David Horowitz, "almost continuous warfare raged on the American continent, its conflict more threatening than any the nation was to face again." American Indian warfare absorbed 80 percent of the entire federal budget during George Washington's administration and dogged his successors for a century as a major issue and expense. Yet most of my original twelve textbooks barely mentioned the topic. *The American Pageant* still offers a table of "Total Costs and Number of Battle Deaths of Major U.S. Wars" that completely omits Indian wars. *Pageant* includes the Spanish-American War, according it a toll of 385 battle deaths, but leaves out the Ohio War of 1790–95, which cost 630 dead and missing U.S. troops in a single battle, the Battle of Wabash River.[69]

At least today's textbooks no longer blame the Natives for all the violence, as did most textbooks written before the civil rights movement. Historians used to say, "Civilized war is the kind *we* fight against *them*, whereas savage war is the atrocious kind that they fight against us."[70] Not one of the eighteen history books I examined portrays Natives as savages. The authors of the newer books are careful to admit brutality on both sides. Some mention the massacres of defenseless Native Americans at Sand Creek and Wounded Knee. Like much of our "knowledge" about Native Americans, the "savage" stereotype derived not only from old textbooks but also from our popular culture—particularly from Western movies and novels, such as the popular "Wagons West" series by Dana Fuller Ross. These paperbacks, which have sold hundreds of thousands of copies, claim boldly, "The general outlines of history have been faithfully followed." Titled with state names, the novels' covers warn that "marauding Indian bands are spreading murder and mayhem among terror-stricken settlers."[71] In the Hollywood West, wagon trains were invariably encircled by savage Indian hordes. Native Americans rode round and round the "settlers," while John Wayne picked them off from behind wagon wheels and boxes. Hollywood borrowed the haplessly circling Indians from Buffalo Bill Cody's Wild West Show, where they had to ride in a circle, presenting a broadside target, because they were in a circus tent!

In the real West, among 250,000 whites and blacks who journeyed across the Plains between 1840 and 1860, only 362 pioneers (and 426 Native Americans) died in all the recorded battles between the two groups. Much more common, American Indians gave the new settlers directions, showed them water holes, sold them food and horses, bought cloth and guns, and served as guides and interpreters.[72] These activities are rarely depicted in movies, novels, or our textbooks. Inhaling the misinformation of the popular culture, students have no idea that Natives considered European warfare far more savage than their own.

Most new textbooks do tell about New England's first Indian war, the Pequot War of 1636–37, which provides a case study of the intensified warfare Europeans brought to America. Allied with the Narragansetts, traditional enemies of the Pequots, the colonists attacked at dawn. Surrounding the Pequot village, whose inhabitants were mostly women, children, and old men, the English set it on fire and shot those who tried to escape the flames. William Bradford described the scene: "It was a fearful sight to see them thus frying in the fire and the streams of blood quenching the same, and horrible was the stink and scent thereof; but the victory seemed a sweet sacrifice, and they gave praise thereof to God, who had wrought so wonderfully for them."[73] The slaughter shocked the Narragansetts, who had wanted merely to subjugate the Pequots, not exterminate them. The Narragansetts reproached the English for their style of warfare, crying, "It is naught, it is naught, because it is too furious, and slays too many men." In turn, Capt. John Underhill scoffed, saying that the Narragansett style of fighting was "more for pastime, than to conquer and subdue enemies." Underhill's analysis of the role of warfare in Narragansett society was correct, and might accurately be applied to other tribes as well. Through the centuries, whites frequently accused their Native allies of not fighting hard enough. The Puritans tried to erase the Pequots even from memory, passing a law making it a crime to say the word *Pequot*. Bradford concluded proudly, "The rest are scattered, and the Indians in all quarters are so terrified that they are afraid to give them sanctuary."[74] None of these quotations entered our older textbooks, which devoted just one and a quarter sentences to this war on average. While no new book quotes Bradford—they don't often quote anyone!—they do tell how the English colonists destroyed the Pequots. Perhaps as a result, future college students, unlike mine, will no longer come up with *savage* when asked for five adjectives that apply to Indians.

Today's textbooks also give considerable attention to perhaps the most violent Indian war of all, King Philip's War. This war began in 1675, when white New Englanders executed three Wampanoag Indians and the Wampanoags attacked. One reason for the end of peace was that the fur trade, which had linked Natives and Europeans economically, was winding down in Massachusetts.[75] *Pathways to the Present* presents students with the Native side of this conflict by quoting a Native leader, Miantonomo: "Our fathers had plenty of deer and skins, our plains were full of deer, as also our woods, and of turkeys, and our coves full of fish and fowl. But these English having gotten our land, they with scythes cut down the grass, and with axes fell the trees; their cows and horses eat the grass, and their hogs spoil our clam banks, and we shall be starved." *The Americans* also quotes Miantonomo, and several other recent books do a decent job explaining King Philip's War, which is important, because this was no minor war. "Of some 90 Puritan towns, 52 had been attacked and 12 destroyed," according to Nash. "At the end of the war several thousand English and perhaps twice as many Indians lay dead."[76] King Philip's War cost more American lives in combat, Anglo and Native, in absolute terms than the French and Indian War, the Revolution, the War of 1812, the Mexican War, or the Spanish-American War. In proportion to population, casualties were greater than in any other American war.[77]

War with American Indians started in New Mexico, in 1598, when residents of Acoma pueblo killed thirteen Spanish conquistadors who were trying to take over their town.[78] It spread to the Southeast where, "because of fierce and implacable Indian resistance, the Spanish were unable to colonize Florida for over a hundred years."[79] Except for a few minor skirmishes, it ceased in

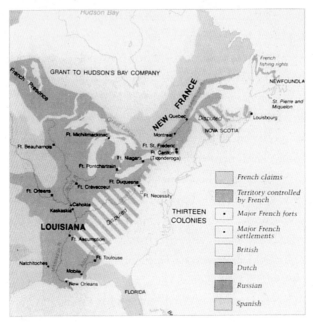

Most textbook maps, like that above, show "French Territory," "British Territory," "Spanish Territory," and sometimes "Disputed Territory," with no mention of Indians at all. In maps that include Indian nations, such as the map opposite from D. W. Meinig, *The Shaping of America* (New Haven: Yale University Press, 1986), 1: 209, the function of Indians as buffers between the colonial powers is graphically evident.

1890 with the massacre at Wounded Knee. Our histories can hardly describe each war, because there were so many. But precisely because there were so many, to minimize Indian wars misrepresents our history.

We must also admit the Indian-ness of some of our other wars. From 1600 to 1754 Europe was often at war, including three world wars—the War of the League of Augsburg (1689–97), known in the United States as King William's War; the War of the Spanish Succession (1702–13), known here as Queen Anne's War; and the War of the Austrian Succession (1744–48), known here as King George's War. In North America the major European powers, England, France, and Spain, buffered from each other by Indian land, fought mainly through their Indian allies. Native Americans inadvertently provided a gift of relative peace to the colonies by absorbing the shock of combat themselves.

Another world war, the Seven Years War (1754–63), in the United States called the French and Indian War, was also fought in North America mostly by Native Americans on both sides. Native Americans not only fought in the American Revolution but were its first cause, for the Proclamation of 1763,

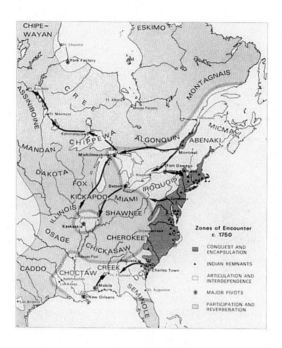

which placated Native American nations by forbidding the colonies from making land grants beyond the Appalachian continental divide, enraged many colonists. They saw themselves as paying to support a British army that only obstructed them from seizing Indian lands on the western frontier. After hostilities with Britain broke out, however, the fledgling United Colonies in 1775 were initially more concerned about relations with Indian nations than with Europe, so they sent Benjamin Franklin first to the Iroquois, then to France.[80] Native Americans also played a large role in the War of 1812 and participated as well in the Mexican War and the Civil War.[81] In each war Natives fought mostly against other Natives. In each, the larger number aligned against the colonies, later the United States, correctly perceiving that, for geopolitical reasons, opponents of the United States offered them better chances of being accorded human rights and retaining their land.

Even in describing the French and Indian War, some textbooks leave out the Indians! One of the worst defeats American Indians ever inflicted on white forces was the rout of General Braddock in 1755 in Pennsylvania. Braddock had 1,460 men, including eight Indian scouts and a detachment of Virginia militia under George Washington. Six hundred to 1,000 Native Americans and 290 French soldiers opposed them, but you would never guess any Indians were there from *The American Tradition:* "On July 9, as they were approaching the fort,

Above is one of many old lithographs that show American Indians attacking Braddock. Some textbooks today make the Indians invisible. Below is the image from *The Americans* in 2007 titled "The British general Edward Braddock met defeat and death near Fort Duquesne in 1755." No one could infer that Natives had anything to do with his defeat from this image.

the French launched an ambush. Braddock's force was surrounded and defeated. The red-coated British soldiers, unaccustomed to fighting in the wilderness [*sic*], suffered over 900 casualties. Braddock, mortally wounded, murmured as he died, 'We shall know better how to deal with them another time.'" *Tradition* thus renders Braddock's last words meaningless, for "them" refers not to the French but to Native Americans.

In our Revolution, most of the Iroquois Confederacy sided with the British and attacked white Americans in New York and northern Pennsylvania. In

1778 the United States suffered a major defeat when several hundred Tories and Senecas routed 400 militia and regulars at Forty Fort, Pennsylvania, killing 340. After the Revolution, although Britain gave up, its Native American allies did not. Our insistence on treating the Indians as if we had defeated them led to the Ohio War of 1790–95 and later to the War of 1812.

The never-ending source of dispute was land. To explain this constant conflict, half of the textbooks I examined, including several current ones, rely on the cliché that Native Americans held some premodern understanding of land ownership. When students learn from *American Journey*, for example, that the Dutch "bought Manhattan from the Manhates people for a small amount of beads and other goods," presumably they are supposed to smile indulgently. What a bargain! What foolish Indians, not to recognize the potential of the island! Not one book points out that the Dutch paid the *wrong tribe* for Manhattan. Doubtless the Canarsees, native to Brooklyn, were quite pleased with the deal which, just for the record, probably didn't involve beads at all, but more than $2,400 worth of metal kettles, steel knives and axes, guns, and blankets, in today's dollars. The Weckquaesgeeks, who lived on Manhattan and really owned it, weren't so happy. For years afterward they warred sporadically with the Dutch. Perhaps the most famous street in America, Wall Street, was named for the wall the Dutch built to protect New Amsterdam from the Weckquaesgeeks, evidence that the Dutch hardly imagined they had bought Manhattan from its real owners. But our history books leave out this part of the story. The authors of one book, *American Pageant*, may actually know that the Dutch paid the wrong tribe. The way they phrase it, however—the Dutch bought "Manhattan Island from the Indians (who did not actually 'own' it) for virtually worthless trinkets"—again merely invites readers to infer that Native Americans did not believe in land ownership and could not bargain intelligently.[82]

Europeans were forever paying the wrong tribe or paying a small faction within a much larger nation. Often they didn't really care; they merely sought justification for theft. Such fraudulent transactions might even have worked in their favor, for they frequently set one tribe or faction against another. The biggest single purchase from the wrong tribe took place in 1803. All the textbooks tell how Jefferson "doubled the size of the United States by buying Louisiana from France." Not one points out that it was not France's land to sell—it was Indian land. The French never consulted with the Native owners before selling; most Native Americans never even *knew* of the sale. Indeed, France did not really sell Louisiana for $15 million. France merely sold *its claim* to the territory.

The United States was still paying Native American tribes for Louisiana throughout the nineteenth century. We were also fighting them for it: the *Army Almanac* lists more than fifty Indian wars in the Louisiana Purchase from 1819 to 1890. To treat France as the seller, as all our textbooks do, is Eurocentric. Equally Eurocentric are the maps textbooks use to show the Lewis and Clark expedition. Even the newest maps still blandly label huge expanses "Spanish Territory," "British Territory," and "French Territory," making Native Americans invisible and implying that the United States bought vacant land from the French. Although the Mandans hosted the expedition during the winter of 1804–05 and the Clatsops did so the next winter, even these tribes drop out. Apparently Lewis and Clark did it all on their own.

Some recent textbooks still chide Natives for not understanding that when they sold their land, they transferred not only the agricultural rights, but also the rights to the property's game, fish, and sheer enjoyment. "To Native Americans, no one owned the land—it was there for everyone to use," in the words of *The Americans*. Nonsense! American Indians and Europeans had about the same views of land ownership, although Natives did not think that *individuals* could buy or sell, only whole villages. Authors seem unaware that most land sales before the twentieth century, including sales among whites, transferred primarily the rights to farm, mine, and otherwise develop the land, not the right to bar passage across it. Undeveloped private land was considered public and accessible to all, within limits of good conduct.[83] Moreover, tribal negotiators typically made sure that deeds and treaties specifically reserved hunting, fishing, gathering, and traveling rights to Native Americans.[84]

Most textbooks do state that conflict over land was the root cause of our Indian wars. *Pathways to the Present*, for example, begins its discussion of the War of 1812 by telling how Tecumseh met with Gov. William Henry Harrison of Indiana Territory to complain about whites encroaching upon Indian land. Other recent textbooks likewise emphasize conflict with the Indians, who were seen as backed by the British, as the key cause of this dispute. All along the boundary, from Vermont to the Georgia Piedmont, white Americans wanted to push the boundary of white settlement ever farther into Indian country. This is a significant change for the better; earlier textbooks simply repeated the pretext offered by the Madison administration—Britain's refusal to show proper respect to American ships and seamen—even though it made no sense. After all, Britain's maritime laws caused no war until the frontier states sent War Hawks—

senators and representatives who promised military action to expand the boundaries of the United States—to Congress in 1810. Whites along the frontier wanted the war, and along the frontier most of the war was fought, beginning in November 1811 when Harrison replied to Tecumseh's complaint by attacking the Shawnees and allied tribes at the Battle of Tippecanoe. The United States fought five of the seven major land battles of the War of 1812 primarily against Native Americans.[85]

All but two textbooks miss the key result of the war. Some authors actually cite the "Star Spangled Banner" as the main outcome! Others claim that the war left "a feeling of pride as a nation" or "helped Americans to win European respect." *The American Adventure* excels, pointing out, "The American Indians were the only real losers in the war." *Triumph of the American Nation* expresses the same sentiments, but euphemistically: "After 1815 the American people began the exciting task of occupying the western lands." All the other books miss the key outcome: in return for our leaving Canada alone, Great Britain gave up its alliances with American Indian nations in what would become the United States. Without war materiel and other aid from European allies, future Indian wars were transformed from major international conflicts to domestic mopping-up operations. This result was central to the course of Indian-U.S. relations for the remainder of the century. Thus Indian wars after 1815, while they cost thousands of lives on both sides, would never again amount to a serious threat to the United States.[86] Although Native Americans won many battles in subsequent wars, there was never the slightest doubt over who would win in the end.

Another result of the War of 1812 was the loss of part of our history. As historian Bruce Johansen put it, "A century of learning [from Native Americans] was coming to a close. A century and more of forgetting—of calling history into service to rationalize conquest—was beginning."[87] After 1815 American Indians could no longer play what sociologists call the role of conflict partner—an important other who must be taken into account—so Americans forgot that Natives had ever been significant in our history. Even terminology changed: until 1815 the word *Americans* had generally been used to refer to Native Americans; after 1815 it meant European Americans.[88]

Ironically, several textbooks that omit King Philip's War and the Native American role in the War of 1812 focus instead on such minor Plains wars as Geronimo's Apache War of 1885–86, which involved maybe forty Apache fighters.[89] The Plains wars fit the post-1815 story line of the textbooks, since they pitted white settlers against semi-nomadic Indians. The Plains Indians are the Native Americans textbooks love to mourn: authors can lament their passing while considering it inevitable, hence untroubling.

The textbooks also fail to show how the continuous Indian wars have reverberated through our culture. Carleton Beals has written that "our acquiescence in Indian dispossession has molded the American character."[90] As soon as Natives were no longer conflict partners, their image deteriorated in the minds of many whites. Kupperman has shown how this process unfolded in Virginia after the Indian defeat in the 1640s: "It was the ultimate powerlessness of the Indians, not their racial inferiority, which made it possible to see them as people without rights."[91] Natives who had been "ingenious," "industrious," and "quick of apprehension" in 1610 now became "sloathfull and idle, vitious, melancholy, [and] slovenly." This is another example of the process of cognitive dissonance. Like Christopher Columbus, George Washington changed his attitudes toward Indians. Washington held positive views of Native Americans early in his life, but after unleashing attacks upon them in the Revolutionary War and the Ohio War in 1790, he would come to denounce them as "animals of prey."[92]

This process of rationalization became unofficial national policy after the War of 1812. In 1845 William Gilmore Simms wrote, "Our blinding prejudices . . . have been fostered as necessary to justify the reckless and unsparing hand with which we have smitten [American Indians] in their habitations and expelled them from their country." In 1871 Francis A. Walker, Commissioner of Indian Affairs, considered American Indians *beneath* morality: "When dealing with savage men, as with savage beasts, no question of national honor can arise." Whatever action the United States cared to take "is solely a question of expediency."[93] Thus, cognitive dissonance destroyed our national idealism. From 1815 on, instead of spreading democracy, we exported the ideology of white supremacy. Gradually we sought American hegemony over Mexico, the Philippines, much of the Caribbean basin, and, indirectly, over other nations. Although European nations professed to be shocked by our actions on the western frontier, before long they were emulating us. Britain exterminated the Tasmanian aborigines; Germany pursued total war against the Herrero of Namibia. Most western nations have yet to face this history. Ironically, Adolf Hitler displayed more knowledge of how we treated Native Americans than American high schoolers today who rely on their textbooks. Hitler admired our concentration camps for American Indians in the west and according to

John Toland, his biographer, "often praised to his inner circle the efficiency of America's extermination—by starvation and uneven combat" as the model for his extermination of Jews and Gypsies (Rom people).[94]

Were there alternatives to this history of war? Of course, there were. Indeed, France, Russia, and Spain all pursued different alternatives in the Americas. Since the alternatives to war remain roads largely not taken in the United States, however, they are tricky topics for historians. As Edward Carr noted, "History is, by and large, a record of what people did, not of what they failed to do."[95] On the other hand, making the present seem inevitable robs history of all its life and much of its meaning. History is contingent upon the actions of people. "The duty of the historian," Gordon Craig has reminded us, "is to restore to the past the options it once had." Craig also pointed out that this is an appropriate way to teach history and to make it memorable.[96] White Americans chose among real alternatives and were often divided among themselves. At various points in our history, our anti-Indian policies might have gone another way. For example, one reason the War of 1812 was so unpopular in New England was that New Englanders saw it as a naked attempt by slave owners to appropriate Indian land.

Peaceful coexistence of whites and Native Americans presents itself as perhaps the most obvious alternative to war, but was it really possible? In thinking about this question, we must take care not to compare a static Indian culture to changing modern culture. We have seen the rapid changes in independent Native cultures—giving up farming in response to European military actions, the flowering of multilingualism, development of more formal hierarchies, the entire Plains Indian culture. Such changes would no doubt have continued. Thus we are not talking about bow-and-arrow hunters living side by side with computerized urbanites.

We should keep in mind that the thousands of white and black Americans who joined American Indian societies must have believed that coexistence was possible. From the start, however, white conduct hindered peaceful coexistence. A thousand little encroachments eventually made it impossible for American Indians to farm near whites. Around Plymouth, the Indians leased their grazing land but retained their planting grounds. Too late they found that this did not keep colonists from letting their livestock roam free to ruin the crops. When Native Americans protested, they usually found that colonial courts excluded their testimony. On the other hand, "the Indian who dared to kill an Englishman's marauding animals was promptly hauled into a hostile court."[97]

The precedent established on the Atlantic coast—that American Indians were not citizens of the Europeans' state and lacked legal rights—prevented peaceful white-Indian coexistence throughout the colonies and later the United States. Even in Indian Territory, supposedly under Native control, whether Indians were charged with offenses on white land or whites on Indian land, trial had to be held in a white court in Missouri or Arkansas, miles away.[98]

Since many whites had a material interest in dispossessing American Indians of their land, and since European and African populations grew ever larger while plagues continued to reduce the Native population, plainly the United States was going to rule. In this sense war only prolonged the inevitable. Another alternative to war would have been an express commitment to racial harmony: a predominantly European but nonracist United States that did not differentiate racially between Indians and non-Indians.[99] U.S. history provides several examples of relatively nonracist enclaves. Sociologists call them *triracial isolates* because their heritage is white, black, and red, as it were. For centuries these communities occupied swamps and other undesirable lands, wanting mostly to be left alone. The Revolutionary War hero Crispus Attucks, an escaped slave of Wampanoag, European, and African ancestry, was a member of such an enclave. The Lumbee Indians in North Carolina comprise the largest of these groups. Other triracial isolates include the Wampanoags in Massachusetts, the Seminoles in Florida, and smaller bands from Louisiana to Maine.[100]

The first English settlement in North America, Roanoke Island in 1585, probably did not die out but was absorbed into the nearby Croatoan Indians, "thereby achieving a harmonious biracial society that always eluded colonial planters," in the words of historian J. F. Fausz. Eventually the English and Croatoans may have become part of the Lumbees. The English never learned the outcome of the "Lost Colony," however. Frederick Turner has suggested that they did not want to think about the possibility that English settlers had survived by merging with Native Americans. Instead, Fausz tells us, "tales of the 'Lost Colony' came to epitomize the treacherous nature of hostile Indians and served as the mythopoetic 'bloody shirt' for justifying aggressions against the Powhatan years later." Triracial isolates have generally won only contempt from their white neighbors, which is why they have chosen rural isolation. Our textbooks isolate them, too: none mentions the term or the peoples.[101]

A related possibility for Natives, Europeans, and Africans was intermarriage. Alliance through marriage is a common way for two societies to deal with each other, and Indians in the United States repeatedly suggested such a policy.[102]

Spanish men married Native women in California and New Mexico and converted them to Spanish ways. French fur traders married Native women in Canada and Illinois and converted to Native ways. Not the English. Textbooks might usefully pass on to students the old cliché—the French penetrated Indian societies, the Spanish acculturated them, and the English expelled them—for it offers a largely accurate summary of European-Indian relationships.[103] In New England and Virginia, English colonists quickly moved to forbid interracial marriage.[104] Pocahontas stands as the first and almost the last Native to be accepted into British-American society, which we may therefore call "white society," through marriage. After her, most interracial couples found greater acceptance in Native society. There their children often became chiefs, because their bicultural background was an asset in the complex world the tribes now had to navigate.[105] In Anglo society "half-breeds" were not valued but stigmatized.

Another alternative to war was the creation of an American Indian state within the United States. In 1778, when the Delaware Indians proposed that Native Americans be admitted to the union as a separate state, Congress refused even to consider the idea.[106] In the 1840s, Indian Territory sought the right enjoyed by other territories to send representatives to Congress, but white Southerners stopped them.[107] The Confederacy won the backing of most Native Americans in Indian Territory, however, by promising to admit the territory as a state if the South won the Civil War. After the war Native Americans proposed the same arrangement to the United States. Again the United States said no, but eventually admitted Indian Territory as the white-dominated state of Oklahoma—ironically, the name means [land for] red people in Choctaw.

Our textbooks pay no attention to any of these possibilities. Instead, they dwell on another road not taken: total one-way acculturation to white society. The overall story line most American history textbooks tell about American Indians is this: We tried to Europeanize them; they wouldn't or couldn't do it; so we dispossessed them. While more sympathetic than the account in earlier textbooks, this account falls into the trap of repeating as history the propaganda used by policy makers in the nineteenth century as a rationale for removal—that Native Americans stood in the way of progress. The only real difference is the tone. Back when white Americans were doing the dispossessing, justifications were shrill. They denounced Native cultures as primitive, savage, and nomadic. Often writers invoked the hand or blessings of God, said to favor those who "did more" with the land.[108] Now that the dispossessing is done, our histories since 1980 can see more virtue in the conquered

When they stress Natives' alleged unwillingness to acculturate, American histories slip into the story line of the official seal of the Massachusetts Bay Colony. "Come Over and Help Us" is white settler propaganda, which grew into an archetype of well-meaning Europeans and tragically different Indians.

cultures. But they still pictured American Indians as tragically different, unable or unwilling to acculturate.

The trouble is, it wasn't like that. The problem was not Native failure to acculturate. In reality, many European Americans did not really want Indians to acculturate. It wasn't in their interest. At times this was obvious, as when the Massachusetts legislature in 1789 passed a law prohibiting teaching Native Americans how to read and write "under penalty of death."[109] President Thomas Jefferson told a delegation of Cherokees in 1808, "Let me entreat you therefore, on the lands now given [sic] you to begin every man a farm, let him enclose it, cultivate it, build a warm house on it, and when he dies let it belong to his wife and children after him."[110] In reality, the Cherokees already were farmers who were visiting Jefferson precisely to ask the president to assign their lands to them in severalty (as individual farms) and to make them citizens.[111] Jefferson put them off. *The American Way* asks students, "Why were the Indians moved further west?" Its teachers' edition provides the answer: "They were moved so the settlers could use the land for growing crops." We might add this catechism: "What were the Indians doing on the land?" "They were growing crops!" When Jefferson spoke to the Cherokees, whites had been burning Native houses and cornfields for 186 years, beginning in Virginia in 1622.

A census taken among the Cherokee in Georgia in 1825 (reported in Vogel, ed., *This Country Was Ours,* 289) showed that they owned "33 grist mills, 13 saw mills, 1 powder mill, 69 blacksmith shops, 2 tan yards, 762 looms, 2,486 spinning wheels, 172 wagons, 2,923 plows, 7,683 horses, 22,531 black cattle, 46,732 swine, and 2,566 sheep." Some Cherokees were wealthy planters, including Joseph Vann, who cultivated three hundred acres, operated a ferry, steamboat, mill, and tavern, and owned this mansion. It aroused the envy of the sheriff and other whites in Murray County, who evicted Vann in 1834 and appropriated the house for themselves, according to Lela Latch Lloyd.

No matter how thoroughly Native Americans acculturated, they could not succeed in white society. Whites would not let them. "Indians were always regarded as aliens, and were rarely allowed to live within white society except on its periphery," according to Nash.[112] Native Americans who amassed property, owned European-style homes, perhaps operated sawmills, merely became the first targets of white thugs who coveted their land and improvements. In time of war the position of assimilated Indians grew particularly desperate. Consider Pennsylvania. During the French and Indian War the Susquehannas, living peaceably in white towns, were hatcheted by their neighbors, who then collected bounties from authorities who weren't careful whose scalp they were paying for, so long as it was Indian. Through the centuries and across the country, this pattern recurred. In 1860, for instance, California ranchers killed 185 of the 800

Wiyots, a tribe allied with the whites, because they were angered by *other* tribes' cattle raids.[113]

The new textbooks do a splendid job telling how the "Five Civilized Tribes"—Choctaws, Chickasaws, Cherokees, Creeks, and Seminoles—acculturated successfully, but were exiled to Oklahoma anyway. Nevertheless, authors never let these settled Indians interfere with the traditional story line. Forgetting how whites forced Natives to roam, forgetting just who taught the Pilgrims to farm in the first place, our culture and our textbooks still stereotype Native Americans as roaming primitive hunting folk, hence unfortunate victims of progress. As Boorstin and Kelley put it, "North of Mexico, most of the people lived in wandering tribes and led a simple life. North American Indians were mainly hunters and gatherers of wild food. An exceptional few—in Arizona and New Mexico—settled in one place and became farmers."

Ironically, to Native eyes, Europeans were the nomads. As Chief Seattle put it in 1855, "To us the ashes of our ancestors are sacred and their resting place is hallowed ground. You wander far from the graves of your ancestors and seemingly without regret." In contrast, Indian "roaming" consisted mainly of moving from summer homes to winter homes and back again.[114]

One way to understand why acculturation couldn't work for most Natives is to imagine that the United States allowed lawless discrimination against all people whose last name starts with the letter *L*. How long would *we* last? The first non-L people who wanted our homes or jobs could force us out, and we would be without resources. People around us would then blame us L people for being vagrants. That is what happened to Native Americans. In Massachusetts, colonists were constantly tempted to pick quarrels with Indian families because the result was likely to be acquiring their land.[115] In Oregon, 240 years later, the process continued. Ten thousand whites had moved onto the Nez Percé reservation by 1862, so a senator from Oregon suggested that the United States should remove the nation. Senator William Fessenden of Maine pointed out the problem: "There is no difficulty, I take it, in Oregon in keeping men off the lands that are owned by white men. But when the possessor happens to be an Indian, the question is changed altogether."[116] Without legal rights, acculturation cannot succeed. Inmuttooyahlatlat, known to whites as Chief Joseph, said this eloquently: "We ask that the same law shall work alike on all men. If an Indian breaks the law, punish him by the law. If a white man breaks the law, punish him also. Let me be a free man—free to travel, free to stop, free to work, free to trade where I choose, free to talk and think and act for myself."[117]

It was not to be. Most courts simply refused to hear testimony from Native Americans against whites. After noting how non-Indians could rise through the ranks of Native societies, anthropologist Peter Farb summed up the possibilities in white society: "At almost no time in the history of the United States, though, were the Indians afforded similar opportunities for voluntary assimilation."[118] The acculturated Native simply stood out as a target.

The authors of history textbooks occasionally announce their intentions in writing. In the teachers' edition of *The American Way*, for instance, Nancy Bauer states: "It is the goal of this book that its readers will understand America, be proud of its strengths, be pleased in its determination to improve, and welcome the opportunity to join as active citizens in *The American Way*." That the author could not possibly pay reasonable attention to Indian history follows logically. It is understandable that textbook authors might write history in such a way that descendants of the "settlers" can feel good about themselves by feeling good about the past. Feeling good is a human need, but it imposes a burden that history cannot bear without becoming simpleminded. Casting Indian history as a tragedy because Native Americans could not or would not acculturate is feel-good history for whites. By downplaying Indian wars, textbooks help us forget that we wrested the continent from Native Americans. Today's college students, when asked to compile a list of U.S. wars, never think to include Indian wars, individually or as a whole. The Indian-white wars that dominated our history from 1622 to 1815 and were of considerable importance until 1890 have mostly disappeared from our national memory.

The answer to minimizing the Indian wars is not maximizing them. Telling Indian history as a parade of white villains might be feel-good history for those who want to wallow in the inference that America or whites are bad. What happened is more complex than that, however, so the history we tell must be more complex. Textbooks are beginning to reveal some of the divisions among whites that lent considerable vitality to the alternatives to war. Several tell of Roger Williams of Salem, who in the 1630s challenged Massachusetts to renounce its royal patent to the land, asserting, "The natives are the true owners of it," unless they sold it. (The Puritans renounced Williams, and he fled to Rhode Island.)[119] Most authors now mention Helen Hunt Jackson, who in 1881 paid to provide copies of her famous indictment of our Native American policies, *A Century of Dishonor*, to every member of Congress.[120] All recent textbooks tell how Andrew Jackson and John Marshall waged a titanic struggle over Georgia's attempt to subjugate the Cherokees. Chief Justice Marshall found for the Cherokees, whereupon President Jackson ignored the Court, reputedly with the words, "John Marshall has made his decision; now let him enforce it!" But no textbook brings any suspense to the issue as one of the dominant questions throughout our first century as a nation. None tells how several Christian denominations—Quakers, Shakers, Moravians, some Presbyterians—and a faction of the Whig Party mobilized public opinion on behalf of fair play for the Native Americans.[121] By ignoring the Whigs, textbooks make the Cherokee removal seem inevitable, another example of unacculturated aborigines helpless in the way of progress.

Native Americans would have textbooks note that, despite all the wars, the plagues, the pressures against their cultures, American Indians still survive, physically and culturally, and still have government-to-government relations with the United States. As recently as 1984, a survey of American history textbooks complained that "contemporary issues important to Native peoples were entirely excluded."[122] The books I examined did better. The American Indian Movement (AIM) spurred three major Indian takeovers in the early 1970s: Alcatraz Island in San Francisco Bay, the Bureau of Indian Affairs in Washington, D.C., and Wounded Knee, South Dakota. Most new textbooks competently explain the causes and results of all three.

Anti-Indian racism eased considerably during the twentieth century. Taking advantage of their special status as "dependent domestic nations," as decreed by Chief Justice Marshall long ago, many tribes developed gaming establishments and hotels to build a solid relationship with the global economy. Ironically, the very fact that the United States is beginning to let Natives acculturate successfully, albeit on Anglo terms, poses a new threat to Native coexistence. Poverty and discrimination long helped to isolate American Indians. If they can now get good jobs, as some can, buy new vehicles and satellite televisions, as some have, and commute to the city for part of their life, as some do, it is much harder to maintain the intangible values that make up the core of Indian cultures.[123] Only one textbook—one of the oldest I studied—raises the key question now facing Native Americans: Can distinctively Indian cultures survive? *Discovering American History* treats this issue in an exemplary way, inviting students to experience the dilemma through the words of Native American teenagers. Newer textbooks cannot raise this issue because they remain locked into non-Indian sources and a non-Indian interpretive framework. Textbooks still define Native Americans in opposition to civilization and still conceive of Indian cultures in what anthropologists call the ethnographic present—frozen at the time

Perhaps Native Americans can break through the dilemma of acculturation and become modern and Indian. Certainly their artists have accomplished this. Only since the 1930s have Inuit artists in Canada been carving soapstone, a material that in the previous century their ancestors used for making pots. This sculpture, *Dancing to My Spirit*, by Nalenik Temela, is a beautiful example of syncretism.

of white contact. When textbooks show sympathy for "the tragic struggle of American Indians to maintain their way of life," they exemplify this myopia. Native Americans never had "a" way of life; they had many. American Indians would not have maintained those ways unchanged over the last five hundred years, even without European and African immigration. Indians have long struggled to change their ways of life. That autonomy we took from them. Even today we divide Native American leadership into "progressives" who want to acculturate and "traditionals" who want to "remain Indian." Textbook authors do not put other Americans into this straitjacket. We non-Indians choose what we want from the past or from other cultures. We jettisoned our medical practices of the 1780s while retaining the Constitution. But Native American medical practitioners who abandon their traditional ways to embrace pasteurization from France and antibiotics from England are seen as compromising their Indian-ness. We can alter our modes of transportation or housing while remaining "American." Indians cannot and stay "Indian" in our eyes.

Improved histories might increase the chances for syncretism on both sides of our ideological frontier. If we knew the extent to which American Indian ideas have shaped American culture, the United States might recognize Native

American societies as cultural assets from which we could continue to learn. At present, none of our textbooks hints at this possibility; even the more enlightened ones merely champion better treatment for Indians while stopping short of suggesting that our society might still benefit from American Indian ideas.

Even if no Natives remained among us, however, it would still be important for us to understand the alternatives foregone, to remember the wars, and to learn the unvarnished truths about white-Indian relations. Indian history is the antidote to the pious ethnocentrism of American exceptionalism, the notion that European Americans are God's chosen people. Indian history reveals that the United States and its predecessor British colonies have wrought great harm in the world. We must not forget this—not to wallow in our wrongdoing, but to understand and to learn, that we might not wreak harm again. We must temper our national pride with critical self-knowledge, suggests historian Christopher Vecsey: "The study of our contact with Indians, the envisioning of our dark American selves, can instill such a strengthening doubt." [124] History through red eyes offers our children a deeper understanding than comes from encountering the past as a story of inevitable triumph by the good guys.

5.

"GONE WITH THE WIND"

THE INVISIBILITY OF RACISM
IN AMERICAN HISTORY TEXTBOOKS

History, despite its wrenching pain,
Cannot be unlived, and if faced
With courage, need not be lived again.
                                    —MAYA ANGELOU[1]

The black-white rift stands at the very center of American history. It is the great chal-
lenge to which all our deepest aspirations to freedom must rise. If we forget that—
if we forget the great stain of slavery that stands at the heart of our country, our
history, our experiment—we forget who we are, and we make the great rift deeper and
wider.   —KEN BURNS[2]

We have got to the place where we cannot use our experiences during and after the Civil
War for the uplift and enlightenment of mankind.   —W.E.B. DUBOIS[3]

More Americans have learned the story of the South during the years of the Civil War
and Reconstruction from Margaret Mitchell's Gone With the Wind *than from all*
of the learned volumes on this period.

                    —WARREN BECK AND MYLES CLOWERS[4]

WHEN WAS THE COUNTRY we now know as the United States first settled? If we forget the lesson of the last chapter for the moment—that Native Americans settled—the best answer might be 1526. In the summer of that year, five hundred Spaniards and one hundred black slaves founded a town perhaps near the mouth of the Pee Dee River in present-day South Carolina. Disease and disputes with nearby Indians caused many deaths in the early months of the settlement. In November the slaves rebelled, killed some of their masters, and escaped to the Indians. By then only 150 Spaniards survived; they retreated to Haiti. The ex-slaves remained behind and probably merged with nearby Indian nations.[5]

This is cocktail-party trivia, I suppose. American history textbooks cannot be faulted for not mentioning that the first non-Native settlers in the United States were black. Educationally, however, the incident has its uses. It shows that Africans (is it too early to call them African Americans?) rebelled against slavery from the first. It points to the important subject of three-way race relations—Indian-African-European—which most textbooks completely omit.[6] It teaches that slavery cannot readily survive without secure borders. And, symbolically, it illustrates that African Americans, and the attendant subject of black-white race relations, were part of American history from the first European attempts to settle.

Perhaps the most pervasive theme in our history is the domination of black America by white America. Race is the sharpest and deepest division in American life. Issues of black-white relations propelled the Whig Party to collapse, prompted the formation of the Republican Party, and caused the Democratic Party to label itself the "white man's party" for almost a century. One of the first times Congress ever overrode a presidential veto was for the 1866 Civil Rights Act, passed by Republicans over the wishes of Andrew Johnson. Senators mounted the longest filibuster in U.S. history, more than 534 hours, to oppose the 1964 Civil Rights bill. Thomas Byrne Edsall has shown how race prompted the sweeping political realignment of 1964–72, in which the white South went from a Democratic bastion to a Republican stronghold.[7] Race still affects politics; George W. Bush won just 11 percent of the black vote but 57 percent of the white vote in 2004.

Almost no genre of our popular culture goes untouched by race. From the 1850s through the 1930s, except perhaps during the Civil War and Reconstruction, minstrel shows, which derived in a perverse way from plantation slavery, were the dominant form of popular entertainment in America. During most of that period *Uncle Tom's Cabin* was our longest-running play, mounted in thousands of productions. America's first epic motion picture, *Birth of a Nation*; first talkie, *The Jazz Singer*; and biggest blockbuster ever, *Gone With the Wind*, were substantially about race relations. The most popular radio show of all time was *Amos 'n' Andy*, two white men posing as humorously incompetent African Americans.[8] The most popular television miniseries ever was *Roots*, which changed our culture by setting off an explosion of interest in genealogy and ethnic background. In music, race relations provide the underlying thematic material for many of our spirituals, blues numbers, reggae songs, and rap pieces.

The struggle over racial slavery may be the predominant theme in American history. Until the end of the nineteenth century, cotton—planted, cultivated, harvested, and ginned mostly by slaves—was by far our most important export.[9] Our graceful antebellum homes, in the North as well as in the South, were built largely by slaves or from profits derived from the slave and cotton trades. Black-white relations became the central issue in the Civil War, which killed almost as many Americans as died in all our other wars combined. Black-white relations were the principal focus of Reconstruction after the Civil War; America's failure to allow African Americans equal rights led eventually to the struggle for civil rights a century later.

The subject also pops up where we least suspect it—at the Alamo, throughout the Seminole Wars, even in the expulsion of the Mormons from Missouri.[10] Studs Terkel is right: race *is* our "American obsession."[11] Since those first Africans and Spaniards landed on the Carolina shore in 1526, our society has repeatedly been torn apart and sometimes bound together by this issue of black-white relations.

Over the years white America has told itself varying stories about the enslavement of blacks. In each of the last two centuries America's most popular novel was set in slavery—*Uncle Tom's Cabin* by Harriet Beecher Stowe and *Gone With the Wind* by Margaret Mitchell. The two books tell very different stories: *Uncle Tom's Cabin* presents slavery as an evil to be opposed, while *Gone With the Wind* suggests that slavery was an ideal social structure whose passing is to be lamented. Until the civil rights movement, American history textbooks in this century pretty much agreed with Mitchell. In 1959 my high school textbook presented slavery as not such a bad thing. If bondage was a burden for African Americans, well, slaves were a burden on Ole Massa and Ole Miss, too. Besides, slaves were reasonably happy and well fed. Such arguments constitute the "magnolia myth," according to which slavery was a social structure of harmony and grace that did no real harm to anyone, white or black. A famous 1950 textbook by Samuel Eliot Morison and Henry Steele Commager actually said, "As for Sambo, whose wrongs moved the abolitionists to wrath and tears, there is some reason to believe that he suffered less than any other class in the South from its 'peculiar institution.' "[12] *Peculiar institution* meant slavery, of course, and Morison and Commager here provided a picture of it that came straight from *Gone With the Wind.*

This is not what textbooks say today. Since the civil rights movement, textbooks have returned part of the way toward Stowe's devastating indictment of the institution. The discussion in *American History* begins with a passage that describes the living conditions of slaves in positive terms: "They were usually given adequate food, clothing, and shelter." But the author immediately goes on to point out, "Slaves had absolutely no *rights*. It was not simply that they could not vote or own property. Their owners had complete control over their lives." He concludes, "Slavery was almost literally inhuman." *American Adventures* tells us, "Slavery led to despair, and despair sometimes led black people to take their own lives. Or in some cases it led them to revolt against white slaveholders." *Life and Liberty* takes a flatter view: "Historians do not agree on how severely slaves were treated"; the book goes on to note that whipping was common in some places, unheard of on other plantations. *Life and Liberty* ends its section on slave life, however, by quoting the titles of spirituals—"All My Trials, Lord, Soon Be Over"—and by citing the inhumane details of slave laws. No one could read any of these three books and think well of slavery. Indeed, most textbooks I studied portray slavery as intolerable to the slave.[13]

Today's textbooks also show how slavery increasingly dominated our political life in the first half of the nineteenth century. They tell that the cotton gin made slavery more profitable.[14] They tell how in the 1830s Southern states and the federal government pushed the Indians out of vast stretches of Mississippi, Alabama, and Georgia, and slavery expanded. And they tell that in the decades between 1830 and 1860, slavery's ideological demands grew shriller, more overtly racist. No longer was it enough for planters and slave traders to apologize for slavery as a necessary evil. Now they came to view slavery as a "positive value to the slaves themselves," in the words of *Triumph of the American Nation*. This ideological extremism was matched by harsher new laws and customs. "Talk of freeing the slaves became more and more dangerous in the South," in the words of *The United States—A History of the Republic*. Merely to *receive* literature advocating abolition became a felony in some slaveholding states. Southern states passed new ordinances interfering with the rights of masters to free their slaves. The legal position of already free African Americans became ever more precarious, even in the North, as white Southerners prevailed on the federal government to make it harder to restrict slavery anywhere in the nation.[15]

Meanwhile, many Northern whites, as well as some who lived below the Mason-Dixon Line, grew increasingly unhappy, disgusted that their nation had lost its idealism.[16] The debate over slavery loomed ever larger, touching every subject. In 1848 Thomas Hart Benton, a senator from Missouri, likened the ubiquity of the issue to a biblical plague: "You could not look upon the table but there were frogs. You could not sit down at the banquet table but there were frogs. You could not go to the bridal couch and lift the sheets but there were frogs. We can see nothing, touch nothing, have no measures proposed, without having this pestilence thrust before us." [17]

Slavery was the underlying reason that South Carolina, followed by ten other states, left the Union. In 1860, leaders of the state were perfectly clear about why they were seceding. On Christmas Eve, they signed a "Declaration of the Immediate Causes Which Induce and Justify the Secession of South Carolina from the Federal Union." Their first grievance was "that fourteen of the States have deliberately refused, for years past, to fulfill their constitutional obligations," specifically this clause, which they quote: "No person held to service or labour in one State, under the laws thereof, escaping into another, shall, in consequence of any law or regulation therein, be discharged from such service or labour, but shall be delivered up . . ." This is of course the Fugitive Slave Clause, under whose authority Congress had passed the Fugitive Slave Act of 1850, which South Carolina of course approved. This measure required officers of the law and even private citizens in free states to participate in capturing and returning African Americans when whites claimed them to be their slaves. This made the free states complicit with slavery. They wriggled around, trying to avoid full compliance. Pennsylvania, for example, passed a law recognizing the supremacy of the federal act but pointing out that Pennsylvanians still had the right to determine pay for their officers of the law, and they refused to pay for time spent capturing and returning alleged slaves. South Carolina attacked such displays of states' rights:

> But an increasing hostility on the part of the non-slaveholding States to the institution of slavery, has led to a disregard of their obligations. . . . The States of Maine, New Hampshire, Vermont, Massachusetts, Connecticut, Rhode Island, New York, Pennsylvania, Illinois, Indiana, Michigan, Wisconsin and Iowa, have enacted laws which either nullify the Acts of Congress or render useless any attempt to execute them.

Thus South Carolina *opposed* states' rights when claimed by free states. This is understandable. Historically, whatever faction has been out of power in America has pushed for states' rights. White Southerners dominated the executive and judicial branches of the federal government throughout the 1850s—and through the Democratic Party, the legislative branch as well—so of course they opposed states' rights. Slave owners were delighted when Supreme Court Chief Justice Taney decided in 1857 that throughout the nation, irrespective of the wishes of state or territorial governments, blacks had no rights that whites must respect. Slave owners pushed President Buchanan to use federal power to legitimize slaveholding in Kansas the next year. Only after they lost control of the executive branch in the 1860 election did slave owners begin to suggest limiting federal power.

South Carolina's leaders went on to condemn New York for denying "even the right of transit for a slave" and other Northern states for letting African Americans vote. Before the Civil War, these matters were states' rights. Nevertheless, South Carolina claimed the right to determine whether New York could prohibit slavery within New York or Vermont could define citizenship in Vermont. Carolinians also contested the rights of residents of other states even to *think* differently about their peculiar institution, giving as another reason for secession that Northerners "have denounced as sinful the institution of slavery." In short, slavery permeates the document from start to finish. Of course, the election of Lincoln provided the trigger, but the abiding purpose of secession was to protect, maintain, and enhance slavery. Nor was South Carolina unusual; other states used similar language when they seceded.

Despite this clear evidence, before 1970 many textbooks held that almost anything *but* slavery—differences over tariffs and internal improvements, the conflict between agrarian South and industrial North, and especially "states' rights"—led to secession. This was a form of Southern apologetics.[18] Never was there any excuse for such bad scholarship, and in the aftermath of the civil rights movement most textbook authors came to agree with Abraham Lincoln in his Second Inaugural "that [slavery] was somehow the cause of the war." As *The United States—A History of the Republic* put it in 1981, "At the center of the conflict was slavery, the issue that would not go away."

To my surprise, our newest history textbooks have backtracked on this issue. *American Journey* states, for example:

> Southerners justified secession with the theory of **states' rights**. The states, they argued, had voluntarily chosen to enter the Union. They defined the Constitution as a contract among the independent states. Now because

the national government had violated that contract—by refusing to enforce the Fugitive Slave Act and by denying the Southern states equal rights in the territories—the states were justified in leaving the Union.

As we have seen, the national government had not refused to enforce the Fugitive Slave Act, and states, Northern or Southern, have no "rights in the territories," being separate from them, so this paragraph confuses more than it explains. Several other recent textbooks are equally confusing. *Pathways to the Present* provides a box comparing "The Aims of the South" to "The Aims of the North." It quotes a House Resolution of July 25, 1861, to show that the United States was fighting "to preserve the Union," which was accurate at that point in the war. (Ending slavery was not a war aim until 1863.) But its quote for Southern war aims, drawn from Jefferson Davis's inaugural address, says only, "We have vainly endeavored to secure tranquility and obtain respect for the rights which we were entitled." *What* rights? Why did the South secede? *Pathways* is silent. Boorstin and Kelley never discuss why the South seceded at all, other than citing the trigger provided by the election of Lincoln. Why not simply quote South Carolina's "Declaration"? After all, South Carolina wrote it precisely to "justify secession."[19]

Except for backsliding on slavery's role underlying secession, most textbooks now handle the topic with depth and understanding. Why did they improve? To ask this is to engage in "historiography"—looking at the writing of history. Who wrote this textbook? Of what background? To what audience? When? Before the 1960s, publishers had been in thrall to the white South. In the 1920s, Florida and other Southern states passed laws requiring "Securing a Correct History of the U.S., Including a True and Correct History of the Confederacy."[20] Many states required textbooks to call the Civil War "the War between the States," as if no single nation had existed that secession had rent apart. (I cannot find evidence that anyone called it "the War between the States" while it was going on.)

In the fifteen years between 1955 and 1970, however, the civil rights movement destroyed segregation as a formal system in America. The movement did not succeed in transforming American race relations, but it did help African Americans win more power. Today many school boards, curricular committees, and high school history departments include African Americans or white Americans who have cast off the ideology of white supremacy. Thus *when* an account is written influences *what* is written. Contemporary textbooks can now devote more space to the topic of slavery and can use that space to give a more accurate portrayal.[21]

Americans seem perpetually startled at slavery. Children are shocked to learn that George Washington and Thomas Jefferson owned slaves. Interpreters at Colonial Williamsburg say that many visitors are surprised to learn that slavery existed there—in the heart of plantation Virginia! Very few adults today realize that our society has been slave much longer than it has been free. Even fewer know that slavery was important in the North, too, until after the Revolutionary War. The first colony to legalize slavery was not Virginia but Massachusetts. In 1720, of New York City's population of seven thousand, sixteen hundred were African Americans, most of them slaves. Wall Street was the marketplace where owners could hire out their slaves by the day or week.[22]

Most textbooks downplay slavery in the North, however, so slavery seems to be a sectional rather than national problem. Indeed, even the expanded coverage of slavery comes across as an unfortunate but minor blemish, compared to the overall story line of our textbooks. James Oliver Horton has pointed out that "the black experience cannot be fully illuminated without bringing a new perspective to the study of American history."[23] Textbook authors have failed to present any new perspective. Instead, they shoehorn their improved and more accurate portrait of slavery into the old "progress as usual" story line. In this saga, the United States is always intrinsically and increasingly democratic, and slaveholding is merely a temporary aberration, not part of the big picture. Ironically, the very success of the civil rights movement allows authors to imply that the problem of black-white race relations has now been solved, at least formally. This enables textbooks to discuss slavery without departing from their customarily optimistic tone.

While textbooks now show the horror of slavery and its impact on black America, they remain largely silent regarding the impact of slavery on white America, North or South. Textbooks have trouble acknowledging that anything might be wrong with white Americans or with the United States as a whole. Perhaps telling realistically what slavery was like for slaves is the easy part. After all, slavery as an institution is dead. We have progressed beyond it, so we can acknowledge its evils. Even the Museum of the Confederacy in Richmond mounted an exhibit on slavery that did not romanticize the institution.[24] Without explaining slavery's relevance to the present, however, its extensive coverage is like extensive coverage of the Hawley-Smoot Tariff—just more facts for hapless eleventh graders to memorize.

Slavery's twin legacies to the present are the social and economic inferiority it conferred upon blacks and the cultural racism it instilled in whites. Both continue to haunt our society. Therefore, treating slavery's enduring legacy is necessarily controversial. Unlike slavery, racism is not over yet.

To function adequately in civic life in our troubled times, students must learn what causes racism. Although it is a complicated historical issue, racism in the Western world stems primarily from two related historical processes: taking land from and destroying indigenous peoples and enslaving Africans to work that land. To teach this relationship, textbooks would have to show students the dynamic interplay between slavery as a socioeconomic system and racism as an idea system. Sociologists call these the *social structure* and the *superstructure*. Slavery existed in many societies and periods before and after the African slave trade. Made possible by Europe's advantages in military and social technology, the slavery started by Europeans in the fifteenth century was different, because it became the enslavement of one *race* by another. Increasingly, whites viewed the enslavement of whites as illegitimate, while the enslavement of Africans became acceptable. Unlike earlier slaveries, children of African American slaves would be slaves forever and could never achieve freedom through intermarriage with the owning class. The rationale for this differential treatment was racism. As Montesquieu, the French social philosopher who had such a profound influence on American democracy, ironically observed in 1748: "It is impossible for us to suppose these creatures to be men, because, allowing them to be men, a suspicion would follow that we ourselves are not Christian." [25] Here Montesquieu presages cognitive dissonance by showing how "we" molded our ideas (about blacks) to rationalize our actions.

Historians have chronicled the rise of racism in the West. Before the 1450s, Europeans considered Africans exotic but not necessarily inferior. As more and more nations joined the slave trade, Europeans came to characterize Africans as stupid, backward, and uncivilized. Amnesia set in; Europe gradually found it convenient to forget that Moors from Africa had brought to Spain and Italy much of the learning that led to the Renaissance. Europeans had known that Timbuktu, with its renowned university and library, was a center of learning. Now, forgetting Timbuktu, Europe and European Americans perceived Africa as the "dark continent." [26] By the 1850s many white Americans, including some

Northerners, claimed that black people were so hopelessly inferior that slavery was a proper form of education for them; it also removed them physically from the alleged barbarism of the "dark continent."

The superstructure of racism has long outlived the social structure of slavery that generated it. The following passage from Margaret Mitchell's *Gone With the Wind*, written in the 1930s, shows racism alive and well in that decade. The narrator is interpreting Reconstruction:

> The former field hands found themselves suddenly elevated to the seats of the mighty. There they conducted themselves as creatures of small intelligence might naturally be expected to do. Like monkeys or small children turned loose among treasured objects whose value is beyond their comprehension, they ran wild—either from perverse pleasure in destruction or simply because of their ignorance.[27]

White supremacy permeates Mitchell's romantic bestseller. Yet in 1988, when the American Library Association asked library patrons to name the best book in the library, *Gone With the Wind* won an actual majority against all other books ever published![28]

The very essence of what we have inherited from slavery is the idea that it is appropriate, even "natural," for whites to be on top, blacks on the bottom. In its core our culture tells us—tells all of us, including African Americans—that Europe's domination of the world came about because Europeans were smarter. In their core, many whites and some people of color believe this. White supremacy is not only a residue of slavery, to be sure. Developments in American history since slavery ended have maintained it. Nine of the eighteen textbooks do list *racism* (or *racial discrimination*, *race prejudice*, etc.) in their indexes, but in several, the word never appears in the text. *Racism* is merely the indexer's handle for paragraphs on slavery, segregation, and the like. Only one book, *Pathways to the Present*, defines the term.[29]

Worse yet, only three textbooks discuss what might have caused racism (or racial prejudice, etc.). The closest any of the textbooks comes to explaining the connection between slavery and racism is this single sentence from *The American Pageant*, after telling how slave owners "increasingly lived in a state of imagined siege": "Their fears bolstered an intoxicating theory of biological racial superiority. . . ." *The American Tradition* includes a similar but much vaguer sentence: "In defense of their 'peculiar institution,' southerners became more and more determined to maintain their own way of life," but such a statement hardly suffices to show today's students the origin of racism in our society—it doesn't even use the word. *The American Adventure* offers by far the longest treatment: "[African Americans] looked different from members of white ethnic groups. The color of their skin made assimilation difficult. For this reason they remained outsiders." Here *Adventure* has retreated from history to lay psychology. Unfortunately for its argument, skin color in itself does not explain racism. Jane Elliot's famous experiments in Iowa classrooms have shown that children can quickly develop discriminatory behavior and prejudiced beliefs based on eye color. Conversely, the leadership positions that African Americans frequently reached among American Indian nations from Ecuador to the Arctic show that people do not automatically discriminate against others on the basis of skin color.[30]

Events and processes in American history, from the time of slavery to the present, are what explain racism. Except for the half sentence quoted above from *Pageant*, however, not one textbook connects history and racism. Half-formed and uninformed notions rush in to fill the analytic vacuum textbooks thus leave. *Adventure*'s three sentences imply that it is natural to exclude people whose skin color is different. White students may conclude that *all* societies are racist, perhaps by nature, so racism is all right. Black students may conclude that all whites are racist, perhaps by nature, so to be antiwhite is all right. The elementary thinking in *Adventure*'s three sentences is all too apparent. Yet this is the *most substantial* treatment of the causes of racism among all the textbooks I examined, old or new. Six pages titled "Segregation and Discrimination" in *We Americans* tell about lynching (but include no illustration), segregation laws, and harsh racial etiquette, but say nothing about their causes.

Instead of analyzing racism, textbooks still subtly exemplify it. Consider a late passage (page 1,083!) in *Holt American Nation* extolling the value of DNA testing: "Since Jefferson had no sons, scientists compared DNA from male-line descendants of Jefferson's paternal grandfather with DNA from descendants of Eston Hemings, Sally Hemings's youngest son. They found a match. Since the chances of a match were less than one percent, Jefferson very likely was Eston Hemings's father." *Holt* fails to notice that the last five words of the paragraph contradict the first five. Jefferson *did* have at least one son, Eston Hemings. Changing *had no sons* to *acknowledged no sons* would fix the paragraph; surely the awkwardness was overlooked because Jefferson had no *white* sons, hence no "real" sons.

In omitting racism or treating it so poorly, history textbooks shirk a critical responsibility. Not all whites are or have been racist. Moreover, levels of racism have changed over time.[31] If textbooks were to explain this, they would give students some perspective on what caused racism in the past, what perpetuates it today, and how it might be reduced in the future.

Although textbook authors no longer sugarcoat how slavery affected African Americans, they minimize white complicity in it. They present slavery virtually as uncaused, a tragedy, rather than a wrong perpetrated by some people on others. Some books maintain the fiction that planters did the work on the plantations. "There was always much work to be done," according to *Triumph of the American Nation*, "for a cotton grower also raised most of the food eaten by his family and slaves." Although managing a business worth hundreds of thousands of dollars was surely time-consuming, the truth as to who did most of the work on the plantation is surely captured more accurately by this quotation from a Mississippi planter lamenting his situation after the war: "I never did a day's work in my life, and don't know how to begin. You see me in these coarse old clothes; well, I never wore coarse clothes in my life before the war."[32]

The emotion generated by textbook descriptions of slavery is sadness, not anger. For there's no one to be angry *at.* Somehow we ended up with four million slaves in America but no owners. This is part of a pattern in our textbooks: anything bad in American history happened anonymously. Everyone named in our history made a positive contribution (except John Brown, as the next chapter shows). Or as Frances FitzGerald put it when she analyzed textbooks in 1979, "In all history, there is no known case of anyone's creating a problem for anyone else."[33]

Certainly the Founding Fathers never created one. "Popular modern depictions of Washington and Jefferson," historian David Lowenthal points out, "are utterly at variance with their lives as eighteenth-century slave-holding planters."[34] Textbooks play their part by minimizing slavery in the lives of the founders. As with Woodrow Wilson, Helen Keller, and Christopher Columbus, authors cannot bear to reveal anything bad about our heroes. In 2003 an Illinois teacher told her sixth graders that most presidents before Lincoln were slave owners. Her students were outraged—not with the presidents, but with her, for lying to them. "That's not true," they protested, "or it would be in the book!" They pointed out that their textbook devoted many pages to Washington, Jefferson, Madison, Jackson, and other early presidents, pages that said not one word about their owning slaves. Of course, she wasn't wrong, and we shall learn of her creative response to her students in the last chapter of this book.

In real life the Founding Fathers and their wives wrestled with slavery. Textbooks canonize Patrick Henry for his "Give me liberty or give me death" speech. Not one tells us that eight months after delivering the speech he ordered "diligent patrols" to keep Virginia slaves from accepting the British offer of freedom to those who would join their side. Henry wrestled with the contradiction, exclaiming, "Would anyone believe I am the master of slaves of my own purchase!"[35] Almost no one would today, because only two of all the textbooks I examined, *Land of Promise* and *The American Adventure*, even mention the inconsistency.[36] Henry's understanding of the discrepancy between his words and his deeds never led him to act differently, to his slaves' sorrow. Throughout the Revolutionary period he added slaves to his holdings, and even at his death, unlike some other Virginia planters, he freed not a one. Nevertheless, *Triumph of the American Nation* quotes Henry calling slavery "as repugnant to humanity as it is inconsistent with the Bible and destructive of liberty," without ever mentioning that he held slaves. *American Adventures* devotes three whole pages to Henry, constructing a fictitious melodrama in which his father worries, "How would he ever earn a living?" *Adventures* then tells how Henry failed at storekeeping, "tried to make a living by raising tobacco," "started another store," "had three children as well as a wife to support," "knew he had to make a living in *some* way," "so he decided to become a lawyer." The student who reads this chapter and later learns that Henry grew wealthy from the work of scores of slaves has a right to feel hoodwinked. None of the new textbooks does any better.

Even more embarrassing is the case of Founding Father Thomas Jefferson. American history textbooks use several tactics to harmonize the contradiction between Jefferson's assertion that everyone has an equal right to "Life, Liberty, and the pursuit of Happiness" and his enslavement of 175 human beings at the time he wrote those words. Jefferson's slaveholding affected almost everything he did, from his opposition to internal improvements to his foreign policy.[37] Nonetheless, half of the books in my earlier sample never noted that Jefferson owned slaves. *Life and Liberty* offered a half-page minibiography of Jefferson, revealing that he was "shy," "stammered," and "always worked hard at what he did." Elsewhere *Life and Liberty* noted all manner of minutiae about him, such as his refusal to wear a wig, that he walked rather than rode in his inaugural parade—but said nothing about Jefferson and slavery.

All recent textbooks mention that Jefferson owned slaves, but that is all they do—mention it, almost always in a subordinate clause. Here is *The Americans'* entire treatment: "Despite his elite background and ownership of slaves, he was a strong ally of the small farmer and average citizen." *American Journey* is similarly concise: "He had proclaimed in the Declaration of Independence that 'all men were created equal'—but he was a slaveowner." *Pathways to the Present* grants six words to Jefferson's complicity with the institution. They follow four paragraphs of praise about him, including his opposition to the practice: "In his time, Jefferson's commitment to equality among white men, as well as his opposition to slavery, were brave and radical ideas. Today, Jefferson remains a puzzle for historians: the author of some of the most eloquent words ever written about human freedom was himself the owner of slaves." Actually, by 1820 Jefferson had become an ardent advocate of the expansion of slavery to the western territories. And he never let his ambivalence about slavery affect his private life. Jefferson was an average owner who had his slaves whipped and sold into the Deep South as examples, to induce other slaves to obey. By 1822 Jefferson owned 267 slaves. During his long life, of hundreds of different slaves he owned, he freed only three, and five more at his death—all blood relatives of his.[38]

Another textbook tactic to minimize Jefferson's slaveholding is to admit it but emphasize that others did no better. "Jefferson revealed himself as a man of his times," states *Land of Promise*. Well, what were those times? Certainly most white Americans in the 1770s were racist. Race relations were in flux, however, owing to the Revolutionary War and to its underlying ideology about the rights of mankind that Jefferson, among others, did so much to spread. Five thousand black soldiers fought alongside whites in the Continental Army, "with courage and skill," according to *Triumph of the American Nation*. In reality, of course, some fought "with courage and skill," like some white recruits, and some failed to fire their guns and ran off, like some white recruits.[39] But because these men fought in integrated units for the most part and received equal pay, their existence in itself helped decrease white racism.[40]

Moreover, the American Revolution is one of those moments in our history when the power of ideas made a real difference. "In contending for the birthright of freedom," said a captain in the army, "we have learned to feel for the bondage of others."[41] Abigail Adams wrote her husband in 1774 to ask how we could "fight ourselves for what we are daily robbing and plundering from those who have as good a right to freedom as we have."[42] The contradiction between his words and his slave owning embarrassed Patrick Henry, who offered only a lame excuse—"I am drawn along by the general inconvenience of living here without them"—and admitted, "I will not, I cannot justify it."[43] Other options were available to planters. Some, including George Washington, valued consistency more than Henry or Jefferson and freed their slaves outright or at least in their wills. Other slave owners freed their male slaves to fight in the colonial army, collecting a bounty for each one who enlisted. In the first two decades after the Revolution, the number of free blacks in Virginia soared tenfold, from two thousand in 1780 to twenty thousand in 1800. Most Northern states did away with slavery altogether. Thus, Thomas Jefferson lagged behind many whites of his times in the actions he took with regard to slavery.[44]

Manumission gradually flagged, however, because most of the white Southerners who, like Jefferson, kept their slaves, grew rich. Their neighbors thought well of them, as people often do of those richer than themselves. To a degree the ideology of the upper class became the ideology of the whole society, and as the Revolution receded, that ideology increasingly justified slavery. Jefferson spent much of his slave-earned wealth on his mansion at Monticello and on books that he later donated to the University of Virginia; these expenditures became part of his hallowed patrimony, giving history yet another reason to remember him kindly.[45]

Other views are possible, however. In 1829, three years after Jefferson's death, David Walker, a black Bostonian, warned members of his race that they should remember Jefferson as their greatest enemy. "Mr. Jefferson's remarks respecting us have sunk deep into the hearts of millions of whites, and never will be removed this side of eternity."[46] For the next hundred years, the open white supremacy of the Democratic Party, Jefferson's political legacy to the nation, would bear out the truth of Walker's warning.

Textbooks are in good company: the Jefferson Memorial, too, whitewashes its subject. The third panel on its marble walls is a hodgepodge of quotations from widely different periods in Jefferson's life whose effect is to create the impression that Thomas Jefferson was very nearly an abolitionist. In their original contexts, the same quotations reveal a Jefferson conflicted about slavery—at times its harsh critic, more often its apologist. Perhaps asking a marble memorial to tell the truth is demanding too much. Should history textbooks similarly be a shrine, however? Should they encourage students to worship Jefferson? Or should they help students understand him, wrestle with the problems he wrestled with, grasp his accomplishments, and also acknowledge his failures?

The idealistic spark in our Revolution, which caused Patrick Henry such verbal discomfort, at first made the United States a proponent of democracy around the world. However, slavery and its concomitant ideas, which legitimated hierarchy and dominance, sapped our Revolutionary idealism. Most textbooks never hint at this clash of ideas, let alone at its impact on our foreign policy.

After the Revolution, many Americans expected our example would inspire other peoples. It did. Our young nation got its first chance to help in the 1790s, when Haiti revolted against France. Whether a president owned slaves seems to have determined his policy toward the second independent nation in the hemisphere. George Washington did, so his administration loaned hundreds of thousands of dollars to the French planters in Haiti to help them suppress their slaves. John Adams did not, and his administration gave considerable support to the Haitians. Jefferson's presidency marked a general retreat from the idealism of the Revolution. Like other slave owners, Jefferson preferred a Napoleonic colony to a black republic in the Caribbean. In 1801 he reversed U.S. policy toward Haiti and secretly gave France the go-ahead to reconquer the island. In so doing, the United States not only betrayed its heritage, but also acted against its own self-interest. For if France had indeed been able to retake Haiti, Napoleon would have maintained his dream of an American empire. The United States would have been hemmed in by France to its west, Britain to its north, and Spain to its south.[47] But planters in the United States were scared by the Haitian Revolution. They thought it might inspire slave revolts here (which it did). When Haiti won despite our flip-flop, the United States would not even extend it diplomatic recognition, lest its ambassador inflame our slaves "by exhibiting in his own person an example of successful revolt," in the words of a Georgia senator.[48] Nine of the eighteen textbooks mention how Haitian resistance led France to sell us its claim to Louisiana, but none tells of our flip-flop.

Racial slavery also affected our policy toward the next countries in the Americas to revolt, Spain's colonies. Haiti's example inspired them to seek independence, and the Haitian government gave Simon Bolívar direct aid. Our statesmen were ambivalent, eager to help boot a European power out of the hemisphere but worried by the racially mixed rebels doing the booting. Some planters wanted our government to replace Spain as the colonial power, especially in Cuba. Jefferson suggested annexing Cuba. Fifty years later, diplomats in the Franklin Pierce administration signed the Ostend Manifesto, which proposed that the United States buy or take the island from Spain. Slave owners, still obsessed with Haiti as a role model, thus hoped to prevent Cuba's becoming a second Haiti, with "flames [that might] extend to our own neighboring shores," in the words of the Manifesto.[49] In short, slavery prompted the United States to have imperialist designs on Latin America rather than visions of democratic liberation for the region.

Slavery affected our foreign policy in still other ways. The first requirement of a slave society is secure borders. We do not like to think of the United States as a police state, a nation like East Germany that people had to escape from, but the slaveholding states were just that. Indeed, after the Fugitive Slave Act of 1850, which made it easy for whites to kidnap and sell free blacks into slavery, thousands of free African Americans realized they could not be safe even in Northern states and fled to Canada, Mexico, and Haiti.[50] The *Dred Scott* decision in 1857, which declared "A Negro had no rights a white man was bound to respect," confirmed their fears. Slaveholders dominated our foreign policy until the Civil War. They were always concerned about our Indian borders and made sure that treaties with Native nations stipulated that Indians surrender all African Americans and return any runaways.[51]

U.S. territorial expansion between 1787 and 1855 was owed in large part to slavers' influence. The largest pressure group behind the War of 1812 was slaveholders who coveted Indian and Spanish land and wanted to drive Indian societies farther away from the slaveholding states to prevent slave escapes. Even though Spain played no real role in that war, in the aftermath we took Florida from Spain because slaveholders demanded we do so. Indeed, Andrew Jackson attacked a Seminole fort in Florida in 1816 precisely because it harbored hundreds of runaway slaves, thus initiating the First Seminole War.[52]

The Seminoles did not exist as a tribe or nation before the arrival of Europeans and Africans. They were a triracial isolate composed of Creek Indians, remnants of smaller tribes, runaway slaves, and whites who preferred to live in Indian society. The word *Seminole* is itself a corruption of the Spanish *cimarron* (corrupted to *maroons* on Jamaica), a word that came to mean runaway slaves.[53] The Seminoles' refusal to surrender their African American members led to the First and Second Seminole Wars (1816–18, 1835–42). Whites attacked not because they wanted the Everglades, which had no economic value to the United States in the nineteenth century, but to eliminate a refuge for runaway slaves. The Second Seminole War was the longest and costliest war the United States ever fought against Indians.[54] The college textbook *America: Past and Present* tells why we fought it, putting the war in the context of slave revolts:

The most sustained and successful effort of slaves to win their freedom by force of arms took place in Florida between 1835 and 1842 when hundreds of black fugitives fought in the Second Seminole War alongside the Indians who had given them a haven. The Seminoles were resisting removal to Oklahoma, but for the blacks who took part, the war was a struggle for their own freedom, and the treaty that ended it allowed most of them to accompany their Indian allies to the trans-Mississippi West.

Five of the six new textbooks do mention this war, but only *Pathways to the Present* verges on telling that ex-slaves were the real reason for it.

Slavery was also perhaps the key factor in the Texas War (1835–36). The freedom for which Davy Crockett, James Bowie, and the rest fought at the Alamo was the freedom to own slaves. As soon as Anglos set up the Republic of Texas, its legislature ordered all free black people out of the Republic.[55] Our next major war, the Mexican War (1846–48), was again driven chiefly by Southern planters wanting to push the borders of the nearest free land farther from the slave states.

Probably the clearest index of how slavery affected U.S. foreign policy is provided by the Civil War, for between 1861 and 1865 we had two foreign policies, the Union's and the Confederacy's. The Union recognized Haiti and shared considerable ideological compatibility with postrevolutionary Mexico. The Confederacy threatened to invade Mexico and then welcomed Louis Napoleon's takeover of it as a French colony, because that removed Mexico as a standard-bearer of freedom and a refuge for runaway slaves.[56] Confederate diplomats also had their eyes on Cuba, had they won the Civil War.

For our first seventy years as a nation, then, slavery made our foreign policy more sympathetic with imperialism than with self-determination. Textbooks cannot show the influence of slavery on our foreign policy if they are unwilling to talk about ideas like racism that might make whites look bad. When textbook authors turn their attention to domestic policy, racism remains similarly invisible. Thus, although textbooks devote a great deal of attention to Stephen A. Douglas, the most important leader of the Democratic Party at mid-century, they suppress his racism. Recall that Douglas had bulldozed what came to be called the Kansas-Nebraska Act through Congress in 1854. Douglas himself, a senator from Illinois and seeker of the presidency, was neither for nor against slavery. He mainly wanted the United States to organize territorial governments in Kansas and Nebraska, until then Indian land, because he was connected with interests that wanted to run a railroad through the territory.[57] He needed Southern votes. During most of the 1840s and 1850s, Southern planters controlled the Supreme Court, the presidency, and at least one house of Congress. Emboldened by their power while worried about their decreasing share of the nation's white population, slave owners agreed to support the new territories only if Douglas included in the bill a clause opening them to slavery. Douglas capitulated and incorporated what he called "popular sovereignty" in the bill. This meant Kansas could go slave if it chose to, even though it lay north of the Missouri Compromise line, set up in 1820 to separate slavery from freedom. So, for that matter, could Nebraska. The result was civil war in Kansas.

While textbooks do not treat Stephen Douglas as a major hero like Christopher Columbus or Woodrow Wilson, they do discuss him with sympathy. In 1858 Douglas ran for reelection against Abraham Lincoln in a contest that presaged the ideologies that would dominate the two major parties for the next three decades.[58] Accordingly, textbooks give the debates an extraordinary amount of space: an average of seven paragraphs and two pictures.[59] Authors of my earlier sample of textbooks used this space as if they were writing for GQ. *American History* gave the debates sixteen paragraphs; here are two of them:

> Even without his tall "stovepipe" hat, the six-feet, six-inch [the author has added two inches] Lincoln towered over the Little Giant. He wore a formal black suit, usually rumpled and always too short for his long arms and legs. Douglas was what we would call a flashy dresser. He wore shirts with ruffles, fancy embroidered vests, a broad felt hat. He had a rapid-fire way of speaking that contrasted with Lincoln's slow, deliberate style. . . .
>
> Lincoln's voice was high pitched, Douglas's deep. Both had to have powerful lungs to make themselves heard over street noises and the bustle of the crowds. They had no public address systems to help them.

So we learn that Douglas was a flashy dresser and spoke powerfully—but where are his ideas? What did he say? All twelve textbooks in my original sample provided just three sentence fragments from Douglas himself. Here is every word of his they provided: "forever divided into free and slave states, as our fathers made it," "thinks the Negro is his brother," and "for a day or an hour." Just twenty-four words in twelve books! While celebrating the "Little Giant" for his "powerful speech" or "splendid oratory," nine textbooks silenced him completely.

Two of the six new textbooks supply at least a longer sentence fragment by

Douglas: "Slavery cannot exist a day or an hour anywhere, unless it is supported by local police regulations"—Douglas's so-called Freeport doctrine. *Holt American Nation* provides a longer quotation. While *Pathways to the Present* doesn't quote a word, it does summarize: "Douglas supported popular sovereignty on issues including slavery." Thus four recent textbooks do tell that the debates had something to do with slavery. They need to go further. Douglas's position was not so vague. The debates were largely about race and the position African Americans should eventually hold in our society. That is why Paul Angle chose the title *Created Equal?* for his centennial edition of the debates.[60] On July 9, 1858, in Chicago, Douglas made his position clear, as he did repeatedly throughout that summer:

> In my opinion this government of ours is founded on the white basis. It was made by the white man, for the benefit of the white man, to be administered by white men. . . .
>
> I am opposed to taking any step that recognizes the Negro man or the Indian as the equal of the white man. I am opposed to giving him a voice in the administration of the government. I would extend to the Negro, and the Indian, and to all dependent races every right, every privilege, and every immunity consistent with the safety and welfare of the white races; but equality they never should have, either political or social, or in any other respect whatever.
>
> My friends, you see that the issues are distinctly drawn.[61]

Textbook readers *cannot* see that the issues are distinctly drawn, however, because even the newest textbooks give no hint of Douglas's racism. Only one book among all eighteen, *American History*, quotes Douglas on race: "Lincoln 'thinks the Negro is his brother,' the Little Giant sneered." These six words in one book, now out of print, among eighteen textbooks, hardly do justice to Douglas on race.

Why do textbooks censor Douglas? Since they devote paragraphs to his wardrobe, it cannot be for lack of space. To be sure, textbook authors rarely quote anyone. But more particularly, the heroification process seems to be operating again. Douglas's words on race might make us think badly of him. So let's leave them out.

Compared to Douglas, Lincoln was an idealistic equalitarian, but in southern Illinois, arguing with Douglas, he, too, expressed white supremacist ideas.

Thus, at the debate in Charleston he said, "I am not, nor ever have been in favor of bringing about the social and political equality of the white and black races [applause]—that I am not nor ever have been in favor of making voters or jurors of Negroes." Most textbook authors protect us from a racist Lincoln. By so doing, they diminish students' capacity to recognize racism as a force in American life. For if Lincoln could be racist, then so might the rest of us be. And if Lincoln could transcend racism, as he did on occasion, then so might the rest of us.

During the Civil War, Northern Democrats countered the Republican charge that they favored rebellion by professing to be the "white man's party." They protested the government's emancipation of slaves in the District of Columbia and its diplomatic recognition of Haiti. They claimed Republicans had "nothing except 'nigger on the brain.'" They were enraged when the U.S. army accepted African American recruits. And they made race a paramount factor in their campaigns.

In those days before television, parties held coordinated rallies. On the last Saturday before the election, Democratic senators might address crowds in each major city; local officeholders would hold forth in smaller towns. Each of these rallies featured music. Hundreds of thousands of songbooks were printed so the party faithful might sing the same songs coast to coast. A favorite in 1864 was sung to the tune of "Yankee Doodle Dandy":

THE NEW NATIONAL ANTHEM
"NIGGER DOODLE DANDY"

Yankee Doodle is no more,
Sunk his name and station;
Nigger Doodle takes his place,
And favors amalgamation.
CHORUS: *Nigger Doodle's all the go,*
Ebony shins and bandy,
"Loyal" people all must bow
To Nigger Doodle dandy.
The white breed is under par
It lacks the rich a-romy,
Give us something black as tar,
Give us "Old Dahomey."

CHORUS: *Nigger Doodle's all the go, &c.*
Blubber lips are killing sweet,
And kinky heads are splendid;
And oh, it makes such bully feet
To have the heels extended.
CHORUS: *Nigger Doodle's all the go, &c.*

I have shared these lyrics with hundreds of college students and scores of high school history teachers. To get audiences to take the words seriously, I usually try to lead them in a sing-along. Often even all-white groups refuse. They are shocked by what they read. Nothing in their high school history textbooks hinted that national politics was ever like this.

Partly because many party members and leaders did not identify with the war effort, when the United States won, Democrats emerged as the minority party. Republicans controlled Reconstruction. Like slavery, Reconstruction is a subject on which textbooks have improved since the civil rights movement. The earliest accounts, written even before Reconstruction ended, portrayed Republican state governments struggling to govern fairly but confronted with immense problems, not the least being violent resistance from racist ex-Confederates. Textbooks written between about 1890 and the 1960s, however, painted an unappealing portrait of oppressive Republican rule in the postwar period, a picture that we might call the Confederate myth of Reconstruction. For years black families kept the truth about Reconstruction alive. The aging slaves whose stories were recorded by WPA writers in the 1930s remained proud of blacks' roles during Reconstruction. Some still remembered the names of African Americans elected to office sixty years earlier. "I know folks think the books tell the truth," said an eighty-eight-year-old former slave, "but they shore don't." [62] As those who knew Reconstruction from personal experience died off, however, even in the black community the textbook view took over.

My most memorable encounter with the Confederate myth of Reconstruction came during a discussion with seventeen first-year students at Tougaloo College, a predominantly black school in Mississippi, one afternoon in January 1970. I was about to launch into a unit on Reconstruction, and I needed to find out what the students already knew. "What was Reconstruction?" I asked. "What images come to your mind about that era?" The class consensus: Reconstruction was the time when African Americans took over the governing of the Southern states, including Mississippi. But they were too soon out of slavery, so they messed up and reigned corruptly, and whites had to take back control of the state governments.

I sat stunned. So many major misconceptions glared from that statement that it was hard to know where to begin a rebuttal. African Americans never took over the Southern states. All governors were white, and almost all legislatures had white majorities throughout Reconstruction. African Americans did not "mess up"; indeed, Mississippi enjoyed less corrupt government during Reconstruction than in the decades immediately afterward. "Whites" did not take back control of the state governments; rather, *some* white Democrats used force and fraud to wrest control from biracial Republican coalitions.

For young African Americans to believe such a hurtful myth about their past seemed tragic. It invited them to doubt their own capability, since their race had "messed up" in its one appearance on American history's center stage. It also invited them to conclude that it is only right that whites be always in control. Yet my students had merely learned what their textbooks had taught them. Like almost all Americans who finished high school before the 1970s, they had encountered the Confederate myth of Reconstruction in their American history classes. I, too, learned it from my college history textbook. John F. Kennedy and his ghostwriter retold it in their portrait of L.Q.C. Lamar in *Profiles in Courage*, which won the Pulitzer Prize.

Compared to the 1960s, today's textbooks have vastly improved their treatments of Reconstruction. All but four of the eighteen textbooks I surveyed paint a very different picture of Reconstruction from *Gone With the Wind*.[63] No longer do histories claim that federal troops controlled Southern society for a decade or more. Now they point out that military rule ended by 1868 in all but three states. No longer do they say that allowing African American men to vote set loose an orgy of looting and corruption. The 1961 edition of *Triumph of the American Nation* condemned Republican rule in the South: "Many of the 'carpetbag' governments were inefficient, wasteful, and corrupt." In stark contrast, the 1986 edition explains that "The southern reconstruction legislatures started many needed and long overdue public improvements . . . strengthened public education . . . spread the tax burden more equitably . . . [and] introduced overdue reforms in local government and the judicial system." Among the newest textbooks, only Boorstin and Kelley still calls Congressional Reconstruction a "vindictive act that turned the states into conquered provinces."

Like their treatment of slavery, most textbooks' new view of Reconstruction represents a sea change, past due, much closer to what the original sources for the period reveal, and much less dominated by white supremacy. The improvements have continued since the first edition of *Lies* appeared in 1995. Textbooks of the 1980s and early 1990s inadvertently still took a white supremacist viewpoint. Their rhetoric made African Americans rather than whites the "problem" and assumed that the major issue of Reconstruction was how to integrate African Americans into the system, economically and politically. "Slavery was over," said *The American Way*. "But the South was ruined and the Blacks had to be brought into a working society." Blacks were already working, of course. One wonders what the author thinks they had been doing in slavery![64] Similarly, according to *Triumph of the American Nation*, Reconstruction "meant solving the problem of bringing black Americans into the mainstream of national life." *Triumph* supplied an instructive example of the myth of lazy, helpless black folk: "When white planters abandoned their plantations on islands off the coast of South Carolina, black people there were left helpless and destitute." In reality, these black people enlisted in Union armies, operated the plantations themselves, and made raids into the interior to free slaves on mainland plantations.

Today's textbooks show African Americans striving to better themselves. But authors still soft-pedal the key problem during Reconstruction, white vio-

This illustration of armed whites raiding a black neighborhood in Memphis, Tennessee, in the 1866 riot, exemplifies white-black violence during and after Reconstruction. Forty African Americans died in this riot; whites burned down every black school and church in the city.

lence. The figures are astounding. The victors of the Civil War executed but one Confederate officeholder, Henry Wirz, notorious commandant of Andersonville prison, while the losers murdered hundreds of officeholders and other Unionists, white and black.[65] In Hinds County, Mississippi, alone, whites killed an average of one African American a day, many of them servicemen, dur-

Although the narratives in textbooks have improved, some of the pictures have not. Seven of the eighteen textbooks feature this cartoon, "The Solid South" represented as a delicate white woman. She is weighed down by Grant and armaments stuffed into a carpetbag, propped up by bluecoated soldiers of occupation. Two new textbooks do ask students to interpret the cartoon. The new edition of *Pageant* merely refers to "the carpetbags and bayonets of the Grant administration" as though they were fact. The other four textbooks merely use the drawing to illustrate Reconstruction: "The South's heavy burden," captions *Triumph of the American Nation*.

ing Confederate Reconstruction—the period from 1865 to 1867 when ex-Confederates ran the governments of most Southern states. In Louisiana in the summer and fall of 1868, white Democrats killed 1,081 persons, mostly African Americans and white Republicans.[66] In one judicial district in North Carolina, a Republican judge counted 700 beatings and 12 murders.[67] Moreover, violence was only the most visible component of a broader pattern of white resistance to black progress.

Attacking education was an important element of the white supremacists' program. "The opposition to Negro education made itself felt everywhere in a combination not to allow the freedmen any room or building in which a school might be taught," said Gen. O. O. Howard, head of the Freedmen's Bureau. "In 1865, 1866, and 1867 mobs of the baser classes at intervals and in all parts of the South occasionally burned school buildings and churches used as schools, flogged teachers or drove them away, and in a number of instances murdered them."[68]

Almost all textbooks include at least a paragraph on white violence during Reconstruction. Most tell how that violence, coupled with failure by the United States to implement civil rights laws, played a major role in ending Republican state governments in the South, thus ending Reconstruction. But, overall, textbook treatments of Reconstruction still miss the point: the problem of Reconstruction was integrating *Confederates*, not African Americans, into the new order. As soon as the federal government stopped addressing the problem of racist whites, Reconstruction ended. Since textbooks find it hard to say anything really damaging about white people, their treatments of why Reconstruction failed still lack clarity.

Into the 1990s, American history textbooks still presented the end of Reconstruction as a failure of African Americans. *Triumph* in 1990 explained, "Other northerners grew weary of the problems of black southerners and less willing to help them learn their new roles as citizens." *The American Adventure* echoed: "Millions of ex-slaves could not be converted in ten years into literate voters, or successful politicians, farmers, and businessmen." Actually, black voters voted more wisely than most white voters. To vote Republican during Reconstruction was in their clear interest, and most African Americans did, but some were willing to vote for those white Democrats who made sincere efforts to win their support. Meanwhile, increasing numbers of white Southerners blindly voted for white Democrats simply because they stood for white supremacy.

Because I, too, "learned" that African Americans were the unsolved problem of Reconstruction, reading Gunnar Myrdal's *An American Dilemma* was an eye-opening experience for me. Myrdal introduced his 1944 book by describing the change in viewpoint he was forced to make as he conducted his research.

> When the present investigator started his inquiry, the preconception was that it had to be focused on the Negro people. . . . But as he proceeded in his studies into the Negro problem, it became increasingly evident that little, if anything, could be scientifically explained in terms of the peculiarities of the Negroes themselves. . . . The Negro problem is predominantly a white . . . problem.[69]

This is precisely the understanding many nonblacks still need to achieve. It goes against our culture. As one college student said to me, "You'll never believe all the stuff I learned in high school about Reconstruction—like, it wasn't so bad, it set up school systems. Then I saw *Gone With the Wind* and learned the truth about Reconstruction!" What is identified as the problem determines the frame of rhetoric and solutions sought. Myrdal's insight, to focus on whites, is critical to understanding Reconstruction. Textbooks still fail to counter the Confederate myth of Reconstruction, so well portrayed in *Gone With the Wind*, with an analysis that has equal power.

Focusing on white racism is even more central to understanding the period Rayford Logan called "the nadir of American race relations": the years between 1890 and 1940 when African Americans were put back into second-class citizenship.[70] During this time white Americans, North and South, joined hands to restrict black civil and economic rights. Unfortunately, most Americans do not even know the term, and not one of the textbooks I examined used it. Instead, they break the period into various eras, most of them inaccurate as well as inconsequential, such as Gay Nineties or Roaring Twenties. During the Gay Nineties, for example, the United States suffered its second-worst depression ever, as well as the Pullman and Homestead strikes and other major labor disputes. Thus "Gay Nineties" leads logically to the query, "Gay for whom?"

Although none uses the term, most textbooks do provide some twigs about the nadir, while failing to provide an overview of the forest. The finest overall coverage, in *American History*, summarizes the period in a section entitled "The Long Night Begins": "After the Compromise of 1877 the white citizens of the North turned their backs on the black citizens of the South. Gradually the southern states broke their promise to treat blacks fairly. Step by step they deprived them of the right to vote and reduced them to the status of second-class citizens." *American History* then spells out the techniques—restrictions on voting, segregation in public places, and lynchings—which Southern whites used to maintain white supremacy.

Triumph of the American Nation, on the other hand, sums up in these bland words: "Reconstruction left many major problems unsolved and created new and equally urgent problems. This was true even though many forces in the North and the South continued working to reconcile the two sections." These sentences are so vague as to be content-free. Frances FitzGerald used an earlier version of this passage to attack what she called the "problems" approach to American history. "These 'problems' seem to crop up everywhere," she deadpanned. "History in these texts is a mass of problems."[71] Five hundred pages later in *Triumph*, when the authors reach the civil rights movement, race relations again becomes a "problem." The authors make no connection between the failure of the United States to guarantee black civil rights in 1877 and the need for a civil rights movement a century later. Nothing ever causes anything. Things just happen.

In fact, during Reconstruction and the nadir, a battle raged for the soul of the Southern white racist and in a way for that of the whole nation. There is a parallel in the reconstruction of Germany after World War II, a battle for the soul of the German people, a battle that Nazism lost (we hope). But in the United States, as *American History* tells, racism won. Between 1890 and 1907 every Southern and border state "legally" disenfranchised the vast majority of its African American voters. Lynchings rose to an all-time high. In 1896 the Supreme Court upheld segregation in *Plessy v. Ferguson.*

Unfortunately, the textbooks mostly misunderstand segregation. Therefore, they misread *Brown*, the 1954 Supreme Court decision that would begin to undo segregation. "The problem, however," in the words of *American Journey*, "was that the facilities were separate but in no way equal." *The Americans* concurs: "Without exception, the facilities reserved for whites were superior to those reserved for nonwhites." While it was true that "separate" rarely meant "equal," that was never the crux of the matter. As the Supreme Court said in *Brown*, "[Some] Negro and white schools involved have been equalized or are being equalized, with respect to buildings, curricula, qualifications and salaries of teachers, and other 'tangible' factors. Our decision, therefore, cannot turn on merely a comparison of these tangible factors."

Only Boorstin and Kelley gets *Brown* right: "The problem, of course, was that there really could never be such a thing as 'separate but equal' facilities for the two races. When any race was kept apart from another, it was deprived of its equality—which meant its right to be treated like all other citizens." Textbooks need to offer the sociological definition of segregation: a system of racial etiquette that keeps the oppressed group separate from the oppressor when both are doing equal tasks, like learning the multiplication tables, but allows intimate closeness when the tasks are hierarchical, like cooking or cleaning for white employers. The rationale of segregation thus implies that the oppressed are a pariah people. "Unclean!" was the caste message of every "colored" water fountain, waiting room, and courtroom Bible. "Inferior" was the implication of every school that excluded blacks (and often Mexicans, Native Americans, and "Orientals"). This ideology was born in slavery and remained alive to rationalize the second-class citizenship imposed on African Americans after Reconstruction. This stigma is why separate could never mean equal, even when black facilities might be newer or physically superior. Elements of this stigma survive to harm the self-image of some African Americans today, which helps explain why Caribbean blacks who immigrate to the United States often outperform black Americans.[72]

During the nadir, segregation increased everywhere. Jackie Robinson was *not* the first black player in major league baseball. Blacks had played in the major leagues in the nineteenth century, but by 1889 whites had forced them out. In 1911 the Kentucky Derby eliminated black jockeys after they won fifteen of the first twenty-eight derbies.[73] Particularly in the South, whites attacked the richest and most successful African Americans, just as they had the most acculturated Native Americans, so upward mobility offered no way out for blacks but only made them more of a target. In the North as well as in the South, whites forced African Americans from skilled occupations and even unskilled jobs such as postal carriers.[74] Eventually our system of segregation spread to South Africa, to Bermuda, and even to European-controlled enclaves in China and India.

Once Northerners did nothing to stop what came to be called the "Mississippi plan"—that state's 1890 Constitution that "legally" (but in defiance of the Fourteenth and Fifteenth Amendments) removed African Americans from citizenship—they became complicit with it. All other Southern states and places as far away as Oklahoma followed suit by 1907, and the nation acquiesced. American popular culture evolved to rationalize whites' retraction of civil and political rights from African Americans. The Bronx Zoo exhibited an

African behind bars, like a gorilla.[75] Theatrical productions of *Uncle Tom's Cabin* played throughout the nadir, but since the novel's indictment of slavery was no longer congenial to an increasingly racist white society, rewrites changed Uncle Tom from a martyr who gave his life to protect his people into a sentimental dope who was loyal to kindly masters. In the black community, *Uncle Tom* eventually came to mean an African American without integrity who sells out his people's interests. In the 1880s and 1890s, minstrel shows featuring bumbling, mislocuting whites in blackface grew wildly popular from New England to California. By presenting heavily caricatured images of African Americans who were happy on the plantation and lost and incompetent off it, these shows demeaned black ability. Minstrel songs such as "Carry Me Back to Old Virginny," "Old Black Joe," and "My Old Kentucky Home" told whites that Harriet Beecher Stowe got *Uncle Tom's Cabin* all wrong: blacks really liked slavery. Second-class citizenship was appropriate for such a sorry people.[76]

Textbooks now abandoned their idealistic presentations of Reconstruction in favor of the Confederate myth, for if blacks were inferior, then the historical period in which they enjoyed equal rights must have been dominated by wrong-thinking Americans, surely motivated by private gain. Vaudeville continued the minstrel show portrayals of silly, lying, chicken-stealing black idiots. So did early silent movies. Some movies made even more serious charges against Afri-

These cartoons by Thomas Nast mirror the revival of racism in the North. Left, *And Not This Man?* from *Harper's Weekly*, August 5, 1865, provides evidence of Nast's idealism in the early days after the Civil War. Nine years later, as Reconstruction was beginning to wind down, Nast's images of African Americans reflected the increasing racism of the times. Opposite is *Colored Rule in a Reconstructed (?) State*, from the same journal, March 14, 1874. Such idiotic legislators could obviously be discounted as the white North contemplated giving up on black civil rights.

can Americans: D. W. Griffith's racist epic *Birth of a Nation* showed them obsessed with interracial sex and debased by corrupt white carpetbaggers.

In politics, the white electorate had become so racist by 1892 that the Democratic candidate, Grover Cleveland, won the White House partly by tarring Republicans with their attempts to guarantee civil rights to African Americans, thereby conjuring fears of "Negro domination" in Northern as well as Southern white minds. From the Civil War to the end of the century, not a single Democrat in Congress, representing the North or the South, ever voted in favor of any civil rights legislation. The Supreme Court was worse: its segregationist decisions from 1896 (*Plessy*) through at least 1927 (*Rice v. Gong Lum,* which barred Chinese from white schools) told the nation that whites were the master race. We have seen how Woodrow Wilson won the presidency in 1912 and proceeded to segregate the federal government. Aided by *Birth of a Nation,* which opened in 1915, the Ku Klux Klan rose to its zenith, boasting more than four million members. For a time the KKK openly dominated the state governments of Georgia, Indiana, Oklahoma, and Oregon, and it probably inducted President Warren G. Harding as a member in a White House ceremony. During the Wilson and Harding administrations, perhaps one hundred race riots took

Not only industrial jobs but even moving services were reserved for whites in some cities.

place, more than in any other period since Reconstruction. White mobs killed African Americans across the United States. Some of these events, like the 1919 Chicago riot, are well-known. Others, such as the 1921 riot in Tulsa, Oklahoma, in which whites dropped dynamite from airplanes onto a black ghetto, killing more than seventy-five people and destroying more than eleven hundred homes, have completely vanished from our history books.[77]

It is almost unimaginable how racist the United States became during the nadir. From Myakka City, Florida, to Medford, Oregon, whites attacked their black neighbors, driving them out and leaving the towns all-white. Communities with no black populations passed ordinances or resolved informally to threaten African American newcomers with death if they remained overnight. Thus were created thousands of "sundown towns"—probably a majority of all incorporated communities in Illinois, Indiana, Oregon, and several other Northern states. Sundown towns ranged in size from DeLand, Illinois, population 500, to Appleton, Wisconsin, 57,000, and Warren, Michigan, almost 200,000. Many suburbs kept out Jews; in the West many towns excluded Chinese, Mexican, or Native Americans. Entire areas—most of the Ozarks, the Cumberlands, the Upper Peninsula of Michigan—became almost devoid of African Americans. Within metropolitan areas, whites pushed blacks into what now became known as "black neighborhoods" as cities grew increasingly segregated residentially![78]

African Americans were excluded from juries throughout the South and in many places in the North, which usually meant they could forget about legal redress even for obvious wrongs like assault, theft, or arson by whites. Lynchings offer evidence of how defenseless blacks were, for the defining characteristic of a lynching is that the murder takes place in public, so everyone knows who did it, yet the crime goes unpunished. During the nadir, lynchings took place as far north as Duluth. Once again, as *Dred Scott* had proclaimed in 1857, "a Negro had no rights a white man was bound to respect." Every time African Americans interacted with European Americans, no matter how insignificant the contact, they had to be aware of how they presented themselves, lest they give offense by looking someone in the eye, forgetting to say "sir," or otherwise stepping out of "their place." Always, the threat of overwhelming force lay just beneath the surface.[79]

The nadir left African Americans in a dilemma. An "exodus" to form new black communities in the West did not lead to real freedom. Migration north led only to segregated urban ghettoes. Concentrating on Booker T. Washington's plan for economic improvement while forgoing civil and political rights could not work, because economic gains could not be maintained without civil and political rights.[80] "Back to Africa" was not practicable.

Many African Americans lost hope; family instability and crime increased. This period of American life, not slavery, marked the beginning of what some social scientists have called the "tangle of pathology" in African American society.[81] Indeed, some historians date low black morale to even later periods, such as the great migration to Northern cities (1918–70), the Depression (1929–39), or changes in urban life and occupational structure after World War II. This tangle was the result, not the cause, of the segregation and discrimination African Americans faced. Black jockeys and mail carriers were shut out, not because they were inadequate, but because they succeeded.

Recent textbooks point out more trees in the nadir forest. From *The American Way* students learn that "By the early 1900s, [white workers] had convinced most labor unions not to admit Blacks." *The Americans* tells that "African Americans found themselves forced into segregated neighborhoods" in the North. Boorstin and Kelley lets Woodrow Wilson off the hook for his administration's extreme racism but does blame Attorney General A. Mitchell Palmer for inciting "excitable citizens" to "vent their fears and their hates against any Americans who seemed 'different,'" including "blacks, Jews, and Catholics." Several books tell about lynchings, although none includes a picture. Three new textbooks mention the riot in Springfield, Illinois, in 1908, in which whites drove out two-thirds of the black population, trying to make Springfield a sundown town. All of the newer texts mention the rise of the "second" Ku Klux Klan.

On the other hand, ten textbooks imply or state that Jackie Robinson was "the first African American to play major league baseball," in the words of *American Journey*, even though he wasn't. Students never learn that blacks played in the major leagues until the nadir, so the usual textbook story line—generally uninterrupted progress to the present—stays in place. None of the books that treat the Springfield riot tells that its aim was to drive out the entire black population of the city. No textbook even mentions sundown towns. *The Americans* notes that the Progressives "did little" for African Americans, which hardly does justice to the movement that removed black aldermen from city councils across the nation by enacting at-large voting. Current authors do emphasize that African Americans were not mere victims but did respond to the new oppression that surrounded them. In the process, however, *Journey* goes too far. "African Americans rose to the challenge of achieving equality," it assures us; subsequent subheadings are "Equality for African Americans" and "Other Successes." No nadir here! And none of the textbooks that do more-or-less recognize the nadir ever analyzes the causes of the worsening.

Textbook authors would not have to invent their descriptions of the nadir from scratch. African Americans have left a rich and bitter legacy from the period. Students who encounter Richard Wright's narrative of his childhood in *Black Boy*, read Ida B. Wells's description of a lynching in *The Red Record*, or sing aloud Big Bill Broonzy's "If You're Black, Get Back!" cannot but understand the plight of a people envisioning a narrowing of their options. No book can convey the depths of the black experience without including material from the oppressed group. Yet not one textbook in my original sample let African Americans speak for themselves about the conditions they faced.

It is also crucial that students realize that the discrimination confronting African Americans during the nadir (and afterward) was national, not just Southern. Few textbooks point this out. Therefore, most of my first-year college students have no idea that in many locales until after World War II, the North, too, was segregated: that blacks could not buy houses in communities around Minneapolis, could not work in the construction trades in Philadelphia, would not be hired as department store clerks in Chicago, and so on. As late as the 1990s and 2000s, some Northern suburbs still effectively barred

African Americans. So did hundreds of independent run-down towns more than half a century after the *Brown* decision.

Even *The American Adventure* forgets its own good coverage of the nadir and elsewhere offers this simplistic view of the period: "The years 1880–1910 seemed full of contradictions. . . . During Reconstruction many people tried hard to help the black people in the South. Then, for years, most white Americans paid little attention to the blacks. Little by little, however, there grew a new concern for them." The trouble is, many white high school graduates share this worldview. Even if white concern for blacks has been only sporadic, they would argue, why haven't African Americans shaped up in the hundred-plus years since

Lynch mobs often posed for the camera. They showed no fear of being identified because they knew no white jury would convict them. *Mississippi: Conflict and Change,* a revisionist state history textbook I co-wrote, was rejected by the Mississippi State Textbook Board partly because it included this photograph. At the trial that ensued, a rating committee member stated that material like this would make it hard for a teacher to control her students, especially a "white lady teacher" in a predominantly black class. At this point the judge took over the questioning. "Didn't lynchings happen in Mississippi?" he asked. Yes, admitted the rating committee member, but it was all so long ago, why dwell on it now? "It is a history book, isn't it?" asked the judge, who eventually ruled in the book's favor. None of the eighteen textbooks in my sample includes a picture of a lynching. I hasten to reassure that no classroom riots resulted from our book or this photograph.

Reconstruction ended? After all, immigrant groups didn't have everything handed to them on a platter, either.

It is true that some immigrant groups faced harsh discrimination, from the NO IRISH NEED APPLY signs in Boston to the lynching of Italian Americans in New Orleans to the pogroms against Chinese work camps in California. Some white suburban communities in the North shut out Jews and Catholics until recent years. Nonetheless, the segregation and physical violence aimed at African Americans has been of a higher order of magnitude. If African Americans in the nadir had experienced only white indifference, as *The American Adventure* implies, rather than overt violent resistance, they could have continued to win Kentucky Derbies, deliver mail, and even buy houses in white neighborhoods. Their problem was not black failure or white indifference—it was white racism.

Although formal racial discrimination grows increasingly rare, as young Americans grow up, they cannot avoid coming up against the rift of race relations. They will encounter predominantly black athletic teams cheered by predominantly white cheerleaders on television, self-segregated dining rooms on college campuses, and arguments about affirmative action in the workplace. More than any other social variable (except sex), race will determine whom they marry. Most of their friendship networks will remain segregated by race, and most churches, lodges, and other social organizations will be overwhelmingly either black or nonblack. The ethnic incidents and race riots of tomorrow will provoke still more agonizing debate.

Since the nadir, the climate of race relations has improved, owing especially to the civil rights movement. But massive racial disparities remain, inequalities that can only be briefly summarized here. In 2000, African American and Native American median family incomes averaged only 62 percent of white family income; Hispanics averaged about 64 percent as much as whites. Money can be used to buy many things in our society, from higher SAT scores to the ability to swim, and African American, Hispanic, and Native American families lag in their access to all those things. Ultimately, money buys life itself, in the form of better nutrition and health care and freedom from danger and stress. It should therefore come as no surprise that in 2000, African Americans and Native Americans had median life expectancies at birth that were six years shorter than whites'.

On average, African Americans still have worse housing, lower scores on IQ tests, and higher percentages of young men in jail. The sneaking suspicion that African Americans might be inferior goes unchallenged in the hearts of some blacks and many whites. It is all too easy to blame the victim and conclude that people of color are themselves responsible for being on the bottom. Without causal historical analysis, these racial disparities are impossible to explain.

When textbooks make racism invisible in American history, they obstruct our already poor ability to see it in the present. The closest they come to analysis is to present a vague feeling of optimism: in race relations, as in everything, our society is constantly getting better. We used to have slavery; now we don't. We used to have lynchings; now we don't. Baseball used to be all white; now it isn't. The notion of progress suffuses textbook treatments of black-white relations, implying that race relations have somehow steadily improved on their own. This cheery optimism only compounds the problem, because whites can infer that racism is over. "The U.S. has done more than any other nation in history to provide equal rights for all," *The American Tradition* assures us. Of course, its authors have not seriously considered the levels of human rights in the Netherlands, Lesotho, or Canada today, or in Choctaw society in 1800, because they don't mean their declaration as a serious statement of comparative history—it is just ethnocentric cheerleading.

High school students "have a gloomy view of the state of race relations in America today," according to nationwide polls. Students of all racial backgrounds brood about the subject.[82] Another poll reveals that for the first time in this century, young white adults have less tolerant attitudes toward black Americans than those over thirty. One reason is that "the under-30 generation is pathetically ignorant of recent American history."[83] Too young to have experienced or watched the civil rights movement as it happened, these young people have no understanding of the past and present workings of racism in American society.

Educators justify teaching history because it gives us perspective on the present. If there is one issue in the present to which authors should relate the history they tell, the issue is racism. But as long as history textbooks make white racism invisible in the twentieth century, neither they nor the students who use them will be able to analyze race relations intelligently in the twenty-first.

6.

JOHN BROWN AND ABRAHAM LINCOLN

THE INVISIBILITY OF ANTIRACISM IN AMERICAN HISTORY TEXTBOOKS

It is not only radical or currently unfashionable ideas that the texts leave out—it is all ideas, including those of their heroes. —FRANCES FITZGERALD[1]

You may dispose of me very easily. I am nearly disposed of now. But this question is still to be settled—this Negro question, I mean; the end of that is not yet.

—JOHN BROWN, 1859[2]

I am here to plead his cause with you. I plead not for his life, but for his character—his immortal life; and so it becomes your cause wholly, and is not his in the least.

—HENRY DAVID THOREAU, "A PLEA FOR CAPTAIN JOHN BROWN," 1859[3]

We shall need all the anti-slavery feeling in the country, and more; you can go home and try to bring the people to your views, and you may say anything you like about me, if that will help. . . . When the hour comes for dealing with slavery, I trust I will be willing to do my duty though it cost my life.

—ABRAHAM LINCOLN TO ABOLITIONIST UNITARIAN MINISTERS, 1862[4]

PERHAPS THE MOST telling criticism Frances FitzGerald made in her 1979 survey of American history textbooks, *America Revised*, was that they leave out ideas. As presented by textbooks of the 1970s, "American political life was completely mindless," she observed.[5]

Why would textbook authors avoid even those ideas with which they agree?

Taking ideas seriously does not fit with the rhetorical style of textbooks, which presents events so as to make them seem foreordained along a line of constant progress. Including ideas would make history contingent: things could go either way, and have on occasion. The "right" people, armed with the "right" ideas, have not always won. When they didn't, the authors would be in the embarrassing position of having to disapprove of an outcome in the past. Including ideas would introduce uncertainty. This is not textbook style. Textbooks unfold history without real drama or suspense, only melodrama.

On the subject of race relations, John Brown's statement that "this question is still to be settled" seems almost as relevant today, and almost as ominous, as when he spoke in 1859. The opposite of racism is antiracism, of course, or what we might call racial idealism or equalitarianism, and it is still not clear whether it will prevail. In this struggle, our history textbooks offer little help. Just as they underplay white racism, they also neglect racial idealism. In so doing, they deprive students of potential role models to call upon as they try to bridge the new fault lines that will spread out in the future from the great rift in our past.

Since ideas and ideologies played an especially important role in the Civil War era, American history textbooks give a singularly inchoate view of that struggle. Just as textbooks treat slavery without racism, they treat abolitionism without much idealism.[6] Consider the most radical white abolitionist of them all, John Brown.

The treatment of Brown, like the treatment of slavery and Reconstruction, has changed in American history textbooks. From 1890 to about 1970, John Brown was insane. Before 1890 he was perfectly sane, and after 1970 he has slowly been regaining his sanity. Before reviewing six more textbooks in 2006–07, I had imagined that they would maintain this trend, portraying Brown's actions so as to render them at least intelligible if not intelligent. In their treatment of Brown, however, the new textbooks don't differ much from those of the 1980s, so I shall discuss them all together. Since Brown himself did not change after his death—except to molder more—his mental health in our textbooks provides an inadvertent index of the level of white racism in our society. Perhaps our new textbooks suggest that race relations circa 2007 are not much better than circa 1987.

In the eighteen textbooks I reviewed, Brown makes two appearances: Pottawatomie, Kansas, and Harpers Ferry, Virginia. Recall that the 1854 Kansas-Nebraska Act tried to resolve the question of slavery through "popular sovereignty." The practical result of leaving the slavery decision to whoever settled in Kansas was an ideologically motivated settlement craze. Northerners rushed to live and farm in Kansas Territory and make it "free soil." Fewer Southern planters moved to Kansas with their slaves, but slave owners from Missouri repeatedly crossed the Missouri River to vote in territorial elections and to establish a reign of terror to drive out the free-soil farmers. In May 1856 hundreds of pro-slavery "border ruffians," as they came to be called, raided the free-soil town of Lawrence, Kansas, killing two people, burning down the hotel, and destroying two printing presses. An older textbook, *The American Tradition*, describes Brown's action at Pottawatomie flatly: "In retaliation, a militant abolitionist named John Brown led a midnight attack on the proslavery settlement of Pottawatomie. Five people were killed by Brown and his followers." The 2006 edition of *The American Pageant* provides a much fuller account, but one that is far from neutral.

> The fanatical figure of John Brown now stalked upon the Kansas battlefield. Spare, gray-bearded, and iron-willed, he was obsessively dedicated to the abolitionist cause. The power of his glittering gray eyes was such, so he claimed, that his stare could force a dog or cat to slink out of a room. Becoming involved in dubious dealings, including horse stealing, he moved to Kansas from Ohio with a part of his large family. Brooding over the recent attack on Lawrence, "Old Brown" of Osawatomie led a band of his followers to Pottawatomie Creek in May 1856. There they literally hacked to pieces five surprised men, presumed to be proslaveryites. This fiendish butchery besmirched the free-soil cause and brought vicious retaliation from the proslavery forces.

Pageant's prose is typical of books written during the nadir of race relations, 1890–1940 (when most white Americans, including historians, felt that blacks should not have equal rights), and comes as something of a shock at the beginning of the twenty-first century. In this rendering, those who fought for black equality had to be wrongheaded.

Indeed, the first edition of this textbook came out in 1956, long before the changes wrought by the civil rights movement had any chance to percolate through our culture and influence the writing of our history textbooks. The choice of language—from "fanatical figure" and "dubious dealings" to "fiendish butchery"—is hardly objective. One man's "stalk" is another's "walk." Bias is also evident in the choice of details included and omitted. The account throughout makes Northerners the initial aggressors, omitting mention of the earlier murders by pro-slavery Southerners. Actually, free-staters, being in the majority, had tried to win Kansas democratically and legally; it was pro-slavery forces who had used terror and threats to try to control the state. No reader of *Pageant* would guess that pro-slavery men had recently killed five free-state settlers, including the two slain in the Lawrence raid. Nor had Brown moved to Kansas "with his large family"; rather, he had moved to the Adirondacks, hoping his sons would join him there, but five sons and their families instead went to Kansas, hoping to farm in peace. They then asked their father for aid when threatened by their pro-slavery neighbors. Other errors include "presumed to be proslaveryites" (they were), and "literally hacked to pieces" (they weren't).[7]

Of all eighteen textbooks, another of the new books, *Pathways to the Present*, is the most sympathetic to Brown but never goes beyond neutrality. It compactly describes Brown's Harpers Ferry raid:

> On October 16, 1859, the former Kansas raider John Brown and a small group of men attacked the federal arsenal at Harpers Ferry, Virginia. . . . Brown and his followers hoped to seize the weapons and give them to enslaved people to start a slave uprising.
>
> United States troops under the command of Colonel Robert E. Lee cornered and defeated Brown's men. Convicted of treason, Brown was sentenced to be hanged. Just before his execution, he wrote a note that would prove to be all too accurate: "I John Brown am now quite certain that the crimes of this guilty land will never be purged away, but with blood."

Eight other books, new and older, are negative, although they don't imply that he was crazy. The other nine are openly hostile. Several textbooks, including four of the six recent ones, emphasize the claim that no slaves actually joined Brown. Boorstin and Kelley makes the point at length: "The party forcibly 'freed' about 30 slaves. Taking these reluctant people with them, Brown and his men retreated to the arsenal. Ironically, the first person to die in the affair—killed by John Brown and his men—was an already-free black gunned down by these 'liberators.' "

The United Daughters of the Confederacy (UDC) would love these accounts, because they can be taken to imply that African Americans had no interest in freedom. The UDC erected a monument in Harpers Ferry to Haywood

Shepherd, the free black man referred to by Boorstin and Kelley. At its dedication in 1931, they claimed he was "representative of Negroes of the neighborhood, who would not take part." But this is bad history. Hannah Geffert and Jean Libby have shown that Brown drew considerable support from enslaved African Americans around Harpers Ferry. His men armed the thirty mentioned by Boorstin and Kelley, including some who came from nearby plantations that the raiders never visited.[8] These newly freed men then stopped the eastbound passenger train, guarded it, helped the raiders find other slave owners, and probably killed an armed white resident of the town who refused to halt when challenged. (After the raid the state indicted eleven of them for these actions.) Well after the raid, local African Americans continued the resistance to slavery that Brown's raid had triggered: Libby notes that many slaves from the area were listed as "fugitive" in the 1860 census, and "the barns of all of the jurors of John Brown's trial were burned—a time-honored signal of revolution."[9] Thus, the UDC interpretation that textbooks supply, implying that the slaves themselves were not sympathetic to the cause of abolition, is simply inaccurate.

Four textbooks still linger in the former era when Brown's actions proved him mad. "John Brown was almost certainly insane," opines *American History. The American Way* tells a whopper: "[L]ater Brown was proved to be mentally ill." The 2006 *American Pageant*, like its predecessor, characterizes Brown as "deranged," "gaunt," "grim," and "terrible," says that "thirteen of his near relatives were regarded as insane, including his mother and grandmother," and terms the Harpers Ferry raid a "mad exploit." Other books finesse the sanity issue by calling Brown merely "fanatical." Not one author, old or new, has any sympathy for the man or takes any pleasure in his ideals and actions.

For the benefit of readers who, like me, grew up reading that Brown was at least fanatic if not crazed, let's consider the evidence. To be sure, some of Brown's lawyers and relatives, hoping to save his neck, suggested an insanity defense. But no one who knew Brown thought him crazy. He favorably impressed people who spoke with him after his capture, including his jailer and even reporters writing for Democratic newspapers, which supported slavery. Governor Wise of Virginia called him "a man of clear head" after Brown got the better of him in an informal interview. "They are themselves mistaken who take him to be a madman," Governor Wise said. In his message to the Virginia legislature he said Brown showed "quick and clear perception," "rational premises and consecutive reasoning," "composure and self-possession."[10]

After 1890, textbook authors inferred Brown's madness from his plan,

At left is John Brown as he appeared in 1858. He looked like a middle-aged businessman—which he was. He grew a beard later that year, partly as a modest attempt to disguise himself after becoming wanted for helping eleven African Americans escape slavery in Missouri. Few Americans recognize this portrait. At right is John Brown as he looked in 1937 to John Steuart Curry, who painted a version of his portrait on the walls of the Kansas State Capitol. This Brown is gaunt and deranged, which he had become in our culture by 1937. Astoundingly, at the start of the new millennium, *American Journey* chose a variant of this painting as its only portrait of Brown. Many Americans can name this man.

which admittedly was far-fetched. Never mind that John Brown himself presciently told Frederick Douglass that the venture would make a stunning impact even if it failed. Nor that his twenty-odd followers can hardly all be considered crazed, too.[11] Rather, we must recognize that the insanity with which historians have charged John Brown was never psychological. It was ideological. Brown's actions made no sense to textbook writers between 1890 and about 1970. To make no sense is to be crazy.

Clearly, Brown's contemporaries did not consider him insane. Brown's ideological influence in the month before his hanging, and continuing after his death, was immense. He moved the boundary of acceptable thoughts and deeds regarding slavery. Before Harpers Ferry, to be an abolitionist was not quite acceptable, even in the North. Just talking about freeing slaves—advocating immediate emancipation—was behavior at the outer limit of the ideological continuum. By engaging in armed action, including murder, John Brown made mere verbal abolitionism seem much less radical.

After an initial shock wave of revulsion against Brown, in the North as well as in the South, Americans were fascinated to hear what he had to say. In his 1859 trial John Brown captured the attention of the nation like no other abolitionist or slave owner before or since. He knew it: "My whole life before had not afforded me one half the opportunity to plead for the right." [12] In his speech to the court on November 2, just before the judge sentenced him to die, Brown argued, "Had I so interfered in behalf of the rich, the powerful, it would have been all right." He referred to the Bible, which he saw in the courtroom, "which teaches me that all things whatsoever I would that men should do to me, I should do even so to them. It teaches me further, to remember them that are in bonds as bound with them. I endeavored to act up to that instruction." Brown went on to claim the high moral ground: "I believe that to have interfered as I have done, as I have always freely admitted I have done, in behalf of His despised poor, I did no wrong but right." Although he objected that his impending death penalty was unjust, he accepted it and pointed to graver injustices: "Now, if it is deemed necessary that I should forfeit my life for the furtherance of the ends of justice, and mingle my blood further with the blood of my children and with the blood of millions in this slave country whose rights are disregarded by wicked, cruel, and unjust enactments, I say, let it be done." [13]

Brown's willingness to go to the gallows for what he thought was right had a moral force of its own. "It seems as if no man had ever died in America before, for in order to die you must first have lived," Henry David Thoreau observed in a eulogy in Boston. "These men, in teaching us how to die, have at the same time taught us how to live." Thoreau went on to compare Brown with Jesus of Nazareth, who had faced a similar death at the hands of the state. [14]

During the rest of November, Brown provided the nation graceful instruction in how to face death. In Larchmont, New York, George Templeton Strong wrote in his diary, "One's faith in anything is terribly shaken by anybody who is ready to go to the gallows condemning and denouncing it." [15] Brown's letters to his family and friends softened his image, showed his human side, and prompted an outpouring of sympathy for his children and soon-to-be widow, if not for Brown himself. His letters to supporters and remarks to journalists, widely circulated, formed a continuing indictment of slavery. We see his charisma in this letter from "a conservative Christian"—so the author signed it—written to Brown in jail: "While I cannot approve of all your acts, I stand in awe of your position since your capture, and dare not oppose you lest I be found fighting against God; for you speak as one having authority, and seem to be strengthened from on high." [16] When Virginia executed John Brown on December 2, making him the first American since the founding of the nation to be hanged as a traitor, church bells mourned in cities throughout the North. Louisa May Alcott, William Dean Howells, Herman Melville, John Greenleaf Whittier, and Walt Whitman were among the poets who responded to the event. "The gaze of Europe is fixed at this moment on America," wrote Victor Hugo from France. Hanging Brown, Hugo predicted, "will open a latent fissure that will finally split the Union asunder. The punishment of John Brown may consolidate slavery in Virginia, but it will certainly shatter the American Democracy. You preserve your shame but you kill your glory." [17]

Brown remained controversial after his death. Republican congressmen kept their distance from his felonious acts. Nevertheless, Southern slave owners were appalled at the show of Northern sympathy for Brown and resolved to maintain slavery by any means necessary, including quitting the Union if they lost the next election. Brown's charisma in the North, meanwhile, was not spent but only increased owing to what many came to view as his martyrdom. As the war came, as thousands of Americans found themselves making the same commitment to face death that John Brown had made, the force of his example took on new relevance. That's why soldiers marched into battle singing "John Brown's Body." Two years later, church congregations sang Julia Ward Howe's new words to the song: "As He died to make men holy, let us die to make men free"—and the identification of John Brown and Jesus Christ took another turn. The next year saw the 54th Massachusetts Colored Regiment parading through Boston to the tune, en route to its heroic destiny with death in South Carolina, while William Lloyd Garrison surveyed the cheering bystanders from a balcony, his hand resting on a bust of John Brown. In February 1865 another Massachusetts colored regiment marched to the tune through the streets of Charleston, South Carolina. [18]

That was the high point of old John Brown. At the turn of the century, as Southern and border states disfranchised African Americans, as lynchings proliferated, as blackface minstrel shows came to dominate American popular culture, white America abandoned the last shards of its racial idealism. A history published in 1923 makes plain the connection to Brown's insanity: "The farther we get away from the excitement of 1859 the more we are disposed to consider this extraordinary man the victim of mental delusions." [19] Not until the civil rights movement of the 1960s was white America freed from enough of its racism to accept that a white person did not have to be crazy to die for black equality. In a sense, the murders of Mickey Schwerner and Andrew

Goodman in Mississippi, James Reeb and Viola Liuzzo in Alabama, and various other white civil rights workers in various other Southern states during the 1960s liberated textbook writers to see sanity again in John Brown. *Rise of the American Nation*, written in 1961, calls the Harpers Ferry plan "a wild idea, certain to fail," while in *Triumph of the American Nation*, published in 1986, the plan becomes "a bold idea, but almost certain to fail." [20]

Frequently in American history the ideological needs of white racists and black nationalists coincide. So it was with their views of John Brown. During the heyday of the Black Power movement, I listened to speaker after speaker in a Mississippi forum denounce whites. "They are your enemies," thundered one black militant. "Not one white person has ever had the best interests of black people at heart." John Brown sprang to my mind, but the speaker anticipated my objection: "You might say John Brown did, but remember, he was crazy." John Brown might provide a defense against such global attacks on whites, but, unfortunately, American history textbooks have erased him as a usable character.

No black person who met John Brown thought him crazy. Many black leaders of the day—Martin Delaney, Henry Highland Garnet, Frederick Douglass, Harriet Tubman, and others—knew and respected Brown. Only illness kept Tubman from joining him at Harpers Ferry. The day of his execution black-owned businesses closed in mourning across the North. Frederick Douglass called Brown "one of the greatest heroes known to American fame." [21] A black college deliberately chose to locate at Harpers Ferry, and in 1918 its alumni dedicated a memorial stone to Brown and his men "to commemorate their heroism." The stone stated, in part, "That this nation might have a new birth of freedom, that slavery should be removed forever from American soil, John Brown and his 21 men gave their lives."

Quite possibly textbooks should not portray this murderer as a hero, although other murderers, from Christopher Columbus to Nat Turner, get the heroic treatment. However, the flat prose that textbooks use for Brown is not really neutral. Textbook authors' withdrawal of sympathy from Brown is perceptible; their tone in presenting him is different from the tone they employ for almost everyone else. We see this, for instance, in their treatment of his religious beliefs. John Brown was a serious Christian, well read in the Bible, who took its moral commands to heart. Yet every recent textbook except *Pathways to the Present* does not credit Brown with religiosity but instead blames him for it. [22] "Brown believed that God had called on him to fight slavery," *The Americans* says twice.

But Brown never believed God commanded him in the sense of giving him instructions; rather, he thought deeply about the moral meaning of Christianity and decided that slavery was incompatible with it. Boorstin and Kelley calls Brown "the self-proclaimed antislavery messiah." But Brown never thought of himself as a messiah. On the contrary, he tried to get Frederick Douglass or Harriet Tubman to join him, believing enslaved African Americans would be much more likely to follow them than him.

By way of comparison, consider Nat Turner, who in 1831 led the most important slave revolt since the United States became a nation. John Brown and Nat Turner both killed whites in cold blood. Both were religious, but, unlike Brown, Turner did see visions and hear voices. In most textbooks, Turner has become something of a hero. Several textbooks call Turner "deeply religious" or "a gifted preacher." None calls him "a religious fanatic." They reserve that term for Brown. The closest any textbook comes to suggesting that Turner might have been crazy is this passage from *American History:* "Historians still argue about whether or not Turner was insane." But the author immediately goes on to qualify: "The point is that nearly every slave hated bondage. Nearly all were eager to see something done to destroy the system." Thus even *American History* emphasizes the political and social meaning of Turner's act, not its psychological genesis in an allegedly questionable mind.

The textbooks' withdrawal of sympathy from Brown is also apparent in what they include and exclude about his life before Harpers Ferry. "In the 1840s he somehow got interested in helping black slaves," according to *American Adventures.* Brown's interest is no mystery: he learned it from his father, who was a trustee of Oberlin College, a center of abolitionist sentiment. If *Adventures* wanted, it could have related the well-known story about how young John made friends with a black boy during the War of 1812, which convinced him that blacks were not inferior. Instead, its sentence reads like a slur. Textbook authors make Brown's Pottawatomie killings seem equally unmotivated by neglecting to tell that the violence in Kansas had hitherto been perpetrated primarily by the pro-slavery side. Indeed, slavery sympathizers had previously killed six free-soil settlers. Several months after Pottawatomie, at Osawatomie, Kansas, Brown had helped thirty-five free-soil men defend themselves against several hundred marauding pro-slavery men from Missouri, thereby earning the nickname "Osawatomie John Brown." Not one textbook mentions what Brown did at Osawatomie, where he was the defender, but fourteen of eighteen tell what he did at Pottawatomie, where he was the attacker.[23]

Our textbooks also handicap Brown by not letting him speak for himself. Even his jailer let Brown put pen to paper! Twelve of the eighteen textbooks I studied do not provide even a phrase he spoke or wrote. Brown's words, which moved a nation, therefore cannot move most students today.

Textbook authors may avoid Brown's ideas because they are tinged with Christianity. Religion has been one of the great inspirations and explanations of human enterprise in this country. Yet textbooks, while they may mention religious organizations such as the Shakers or Christian Science, never treat religious ideas in any period seriously.[24] An in-depth portrayal of Mormonism, Christian Science, or the Methodism of the Great Awakening would be controversial. Mentioning atheism or Deism would be even worse. "Are you going to tell kids that Thomas Jefferson didn't believe in Jesus? Not me!" a textbook editor exclaimed to me. Treating religious ideas neutrally, nonreligiously, simply as factors in society, won't do, either, for that would likely offend some adherents. The textbooks' solution is to leave out religious ideas entirely.[25] Quoting John Brown's courtroom paraphrase of the Golden Rule—"whatsoever I would that men should do to me, I should do even so to them"—would violate the taboo.

Ideological contradiction is terribly important in history. Ideas have power. The ideas that motivated John Brown and the example he set lived on long after his body lay a-moldering in the grave. Yet American history textbooks give us no way to understand the role of ideas in our past.

Conceivably, textbook authors ignore John Brown's ideas because in their eyes his violent acts make him ineligible for sympathetic consideration. When we turn from Brown to Abraham Lincoln, we shift from one of the most controversial to one of the most venerated figures in American history. Textbooks describe Abraham Lincoln with sympathy, of course. Nonetheless, they also minimize his ideas, especially on the subject of race. In life Abraham Lincoln wrestled with the race question more openly than any other president except perhaps Thomas Jefferson, and, unlike Jefferson, Lincoln's actions sometimes matched his words. Most of our textbooks say nothing about Lincoln's internal debate. If they did show it, what teaching devices they would become! Students would see that speakers modify their ideas to appease and appeal to different audiences, so we cannot simply take their statements literally. If textbooks recognized Lincoln's racism, students would learn that racism not only affects Ku Klux Klan extremists but has been "normal" throughout our history. And as they watched Lincoln struggle with himself to apply America's democratic principles across the color line, students would see how ideas can develop and a person can grow.

In conversation, Lincoln, like most whites of his century, referred to blacks as "niggers." In the Lincoln-Douglas debates, he sometimes descended into explicit white supremacy, as we saw in the last chapter. Lincoln's ideas about race were more complicated than Douglas's, however. The day after Douglas declared for white supremacy in Chicago, saying the issues were "distinctly drawn," Lincoln replied and indeed drew the issue distinctly:

> I should like to know if taking this old Declaration of Independence, which declares that all men are equal upon principle, and making exceptions to it—where will it stop? If one man says it does not mean a Negro, why does not another say it does not mean some other man? If that Declaration is not . . . true, let us tear it out! [Cries of "no, no!"] Let us stick to it then, let us stand firmly by it then.[26]

No textbook quotes this passage, and every book but one leaves out Lincoln's thundering summation of what his debates with Douglas were really about: "That is the issue that will continue in this country when these poor tongues of Judge Douglas and myself shall be silent. It is the eternal struggle between these two principles—right and wrong—throughout the world."[27]

Lincoln's realization of the basic humanity of African Americans may have derived from his father, who moved the family to Indiana partly because he disliked the racial slavery that was sanctioned in Kentucky. Or it may stem from an experience Lincoln had on a steamboat trip in 1841, which he recalled years later when writing to his friend Josh Speed: "You may remember, as I well do, that from Louisville to the mouth of the Ohio there were on board ten or twelve slaves, shackled together with irons. That sight was continual torment to me, and I see something like it every time I touch the Ohio, or any other slave-border." Lincoln concluded that the memory still had "the power of making me miserable."[28] No textbook quotes this letter or anything like it.

As early as 1835, in his first term in the Illinois House of Representatives, Lincoln cast one of only five votes opposing a resolution that condemned abolitionists. Textbooks imply that Lincoln was nominated for president in 1860 because he was a moderate on slavery, but, in fact, Republicans chose Lincoln over front-runner William H. Seward partly because of Lincoln's "rock-solid antislavery beliefs," while Seward was considered a compromiser.[29]

As president, Lincoln understood the importance of symbolic leadership in improving race relations. For the first time the United States exchanged diplomats with Haiti and Liberia. In 1863 Lincoln desegregated the White House staff, which initiated a desegregation of the federal government that lasted until Woodrow Wilson. Lincoln opened the White House to black callers, notably Frederick Douglass. He also continued to wrestle with his own racism, asking aides to investigate the feasibility of deporting (euphemistically termed *colonizing*) African Americans to Africa or Latin America.

Most of the textbooks mention that Lincoln "personally" opposed slavery. Two even quote his 1864 letter: "If slavery isn't wrong, then nothing is wrong." [30] However, most textbook authors take pains to separate Lincoln from undue idealism about slavery. They venerate Lincoln mainly because he "saved the Union." By far their favorite statement of Lincoln's, quoted or paraphrased by fifteen of the eighteen books, is his letter of August 22, 1862, to Horace Greeley's *New York Tribune:*

> My paramount object in this struggle is to save the Union, and is not either to save or to destroy slavery. If I could save the Union without freeing *any* slave, I would do it; and if I could save it by freeing *all* the slaves, I would do it; and if I could save it by freeing some and leaving others alone, I would also do that. What I do about slavery and the colored race I do because I believe it helps to save this Union; and what I forbear, I forbear because I do not believe it would help to save the Union. . . .

By emphasizing this quote, most textbooks present a Lincoln who was morally indifferent to slavery and certainly did not care about black people. As *Pathways to the Present* puts it, "Lincoln came to regard ending slavery as one more strategy for ending the war." Ironically, this is also the Lincoln whom black nationalists present to African Americans to persuade them to stop thinking well of him. [31]

To present such a Lincoln, the textbooks have to remove all context. The very first thing they omit is the next point Lincoln made: ". . . I have here stated my purpose according to my view of *official* duty, and I intend no modification of my oft-expressed *personal* wish that all men, everywhere could be free." That says something quite different about slavery, of course. So all but three textbooks leave that part out.

Next, they remove the political context. Every historian knows that the fragment of Lincoln's letter to Greeley that most textbooks quote does not simply represent his intent regarding slavery. Lincoln wrote the letter to seek support for the war from residents of New York City, one of the most Democratic (and therefore white supremacist) cities in the North. He could never hope to win that support by claiming the war would end slavery. They would be against it on that ground. So he made the only appeal he could: support the war and it will hold the nation together. He was speaking not to Greeley, who wanted slavery to end, but to antiwar Democrats and antiblack Irish Americans, as well as to governors of the border states and the many other Northerners who opposed emancipating the slaves. Saving the Union had *never* been Lincoln's sole concern, as shown by his 1860 rejection of the eleventh-hour Crittenden Compromise, a constitutional amendment intended to preserve the Union by preserving slavery forever.[32] Not one author explains the political context or the intended audience for the Greeley letter. Nor does a single textbook quote Lincoln's encouragement that same summer to Unitarian ministers to "go home and try to bring the people to your views," because "we shall need all the antislavery feeling in the country, and more." If they did, students would understand that Lincoln's response to the issue of slavery in America was hardly indifference.

When textbooks discuss the Emancipation Proclamation, they explain Lincoln's actions in realpolitik terms. "By September 1862," says *Triumph of the American Nation*, "Lincoln had reluctantly decided that a war fought at least partly to free the slaves would win European support and lessen the danger of foreign intervention on the side of the Confederacy." To be sure, international and domestic political concerns did impinge on Abraham Lincoln, master politician that he was. But so did considerations of right and wrong. Political analysts then and now believe that Lincoln's September 1862 announcement of emancipation cost Republicans the control of Congress the following November, because Northern white public opinion would not evolve to favor black freedom for another year.[33] Textbook authors suppress the possibility that Lincoln acted at least in part because he thought it was right. From Indian wars to slavery to Vietnam, textbook authors not only sidestep putting questions of right and wrong to our past actions but even avoid acknowledging that Americans of the time did so.

Abraham Lincoln was one of the great masters of the English language. Perhaps more than any other president he invoked and manipulated powerful symbols in his speeches to move public opinion, often on the subject of race relations and slavery. Textbooks, in keeping with their habit of telling everything in the authorial monotone, dribble out Lincoln's words three and four at a time. The only complete speech or letter any of them provide is the Gettysburg Address, and only six of the eighteen textbooks dispense even that. Lincoln's three paragraphs at Gettysburg comprise one of the most important speeches ever given in America and take up only a fourth of a page in the textbooks that include them. Nonetheless, five books do not even mention the speech, while five others provide only the last sentence or phrase from it: "government of the people, by the people, for the people." Silliest of all is the new edition of *The American Pageant*, which devotes an entire page to the address but uses most of it to show the manuscript in Lincoln's handwriting, so much reduced to fit on the page that it is rendered illegible![34] *Pageant* provides more words *about* the Address than are in the original—and fails to include a single phrase that Lincoln wrote.

The words, however, are important, and it is important to get students to think about them. Lincoln understood that fighting a war for freedom was ideologically more satisfying than fighting simply to preserve a morally neutral Union. To save the Union, it was necessary to find rationales for the war other than "to save the Union." At Gettysburg he provided one.

Lincoln was a fine lawyer who knew full well that the United States was conceived in slavery, for the Constitution specifically treats slavery in at least five places. Nevertheless he began, "Four score and seven years ago, our fathers brought forth on this continent a new nation, conceived in liberty and dedicated to the proposition that all men are created equal." Thus Lincoln wrapped the Union cause in the rhetoric of the Declaration of Independence, which emphasized freedom even while many of its signers were slave owners.[35] In so doing, Lincoln was at the same time using the Declaration to redefine the Union cause, suggesting that it ultimately implied equal rights for all Americans, regardless of race.

"Now we are engaged in a great civil war," Lincoln continued, "testing whether that nation or any nation, so conceived and so dedicated, can long endure." Again, Lincoln knew better: by 1863 other nations had joined us in democracy. For that matter, every European nation and most American nations had outlawed slavery. How did our Civil War test whether *they* could endure? Here Lincoln was wrapping the Union cause in the old "last best hope of mankind" cloak, a secular version of the idea of a special covenant between the United States and God.[36] Although bad history, such rhetoric makes for great speeches. The president thus appealed to the antiwar Democrats of the North to support the war effort for the good of all mankind.

After invoking a third powerful symbol—"the brave men, living and dead, who struggled here"—Lincoln closed by identifying the cause for which so many had died: "that this nation, under God, shall have a new birth of free-dom." To what freedom did he refer? Black freedom, of course. As Lincoln well knew, the war itself was undermining slavery, for what began as a war to save the Union increasingly had become a war for black freedom. Citizens at the time understood Lincoln perfectly. Indeed, throughout this period Americans pur-chased copies of political speeches, read them, discussed issues, and voted at rates that now seem impossibly high. The *Chicago Times*, a Democratic newspa-per, denounced the address precisely because of "the proposition that all men are created equal." The Union dead, claimed the *Times*, "were men possessing too much self-respect to declare that Negroes were their equals, or were entitled to equal privileges." [37]

Textbooks need not explain Lincoln's words at Gettysburg as I have done. The Gettysburg Address is rich enough to survive various analyses.[38] But of the six books that do reprint the speech, four merely put it in a box by itself in a

The strange career of the log cabin in which Abraham Lincoln was born symbolizes in a way what textbooks have done to Lincoln. The actual cabin fell into disrepair probably be-fore Lincoln became president. According to research by D. T. Pitcaithley, the new cabin, a hoax built in 1894, was leased to two amusement park owners, went to Coney Island, where it got commingled with the birthplace cabin of Jefferson Davis (another hoax), and was finally shrunk to fit inside a marble pantheon in Kentucky, where, reassembled, it still stands. The cabin also became a children's toy: Lincoln Logs, invented by Frank Lloyd Wright's son John in 1920, came with instructions on how to build both Lincoln's log cabin and Uncle Tom's cabin! The cabin still makes its archetypal appearance in our textbooks, signifying the rags-to-riches legend of Abraham Lincoln's upward mobility. No wonder one college student could only say of him, in a much-repeated blooper, "He was born in a log cabin which he built with his own hands."

corner of the page. *Pathways to the Present* offers a rather empty summation afterward. Only *Life and Liberty* asks intelligent questions about it.[39] As a result, I have yet to meet a high school graduate who has devoted any time to thinking about the Gettysburg Address.

Even worse is textbook treatment of Lincoln's Second Inaugural. In this towering speech, one of the masterpieces of American oratory, Lincoln specifically identified differences over slavery as the primary cause of the Civil War, then in its fourth bloody year.[40]

> If we shall suppose that American slavery is one of those offenses which, in the providence of God, must needs come, but which, having continued through his appointed time, he now wills to remove, and that he gives to both North and South this terrible war, as the woe due to those by whom the offense came, shall we discern therein any departure from those divine attributes which the believers in a living God always ascribe to him?

Lincoln continued in this vein by invoking the doctrine of predestination, a more vital element of the nation's idea system then than now:

> Fondly do we hope—fervently do we pray—that this mighty scourge of war may speedily pass away. Yet, if God wills that it continue until all the wealth piled by the bondman's two hundred and fifty years of unrequited toil shall be sunk, and until every drop of blood drawn with the lash shall be paid by another drawn with the sword, as was said three thousand years ago, so still it must be said, "The judgments of the Lord are true and righteous altogether."

This last is an astonishing sentence. Its length alone astounds. Politicians don't talk like that nowadays. When students read this passage aloud, slowly and deliberately, they do not fail to perceive it as a searing indictment of America's sins against black people. The Civil War was by far the most devastating experience in our nation's history. Yet we had it coming, Lincoln says here. And in his rhetorical context, sin or crime, not mere tragedy, is the fitting and proper term. Indeed, this indictment of U.S. race relations echoes John Brown's last note: "I, John Brown, am now quite certain that the crimes of this guilty land will never be purged away, but with Blood."[41]

Lincoln's Second Inaugural made such an impact on Americans that when the president was shot, a month later, farmers in New York and Ohio greeted his funeral train with placards bearing its phrases. But only *The United States—A History of the Republic* includes any of the material quoted above.[42] Seven other textbooks restrict their quotation to the speech's final phrase, about binding up the nation's wounds "with malice toward none." Ten ignore the speech altogether.

Like Helen Keller's concern about the injustice of social class, Lincoln's concern about the crime of racism may appear unseemly to textbook authors. Must we remember Lincoln for *that?* Let's leave it out! Such an approach to Lincoln might be called the Walt Disney interpretation: Disney's exhibit at the 1964 New York World's Fair featured an animated sculpture of Lincoln that spoke for several minutes, choosing his words carefully to say nothing about slavery.

Having disconnected Abraham Lincoln from considerations of right and wrong, several textbooks present the Civil War the same way. In reality, U.S. soldiers, who began fighting to save the Union and not much more, ended by fighting for all the vague but portentous ideas in the Gettysburg Address. From 1862 on, Union armies sang "Battle Cry of Freedom," composed by George Root in the summer of that year:

> *We will welcome to our numbers the loyal true and brave,*
> *Shouting the battle cry of freedom.*
> *And although he may be poor, not a man shall be a slave,*
> *Shouting the battle cry of freedom.*[43]

Triumph of the American Nation includes this evocative photograph of the crew of the USS *Hunchback* in the Civil War. Such racial integration disappeared during the nadir of race relations in the United States, from 1890–1940.

Surely no one can sing these lines even today without perceiving that both free-dom *and* the preservation of the Union were war aims of the United States and without feeling some of the power of that potent combination. This power is what textbooks omit: they give students no inkling that ideas *matter.*

The actions of African Americans played a big role in challenging white racism. Slaves fled to Union lines. After they were allowed to fight, the contri-butions of black troops to the war effort made it harder for whites to deny that blacks were fully human.[44] A Union captain wrote to his wife, "A great many [whites] have the idea that the entire Negro race are vastly their inferiors—a few weeks of calm unprejudiced life here would disabuse them, I think—I have a more elevated opinion of their abilities than I ever had before."[45] Unlike historians of a few decades ago, today's textbook authors realize that trying to present the war without the actions of African Americans makes for bad history. All eighteen textbooks at least mention that more than 180,000 blacks fought in the Union army and navy. Several of the textbooks include an illus-tration of African American soldiers and describe the unequal pay they received until late in the war.[46] *Discovering American History* mentions that Union soldiers trapped behind Confederate lines found slaves to be "of invaluable assistance." Only *The United States—A History of the Republic*, however, takes the next step by pointing out how the existence and success of black troops decreased white racism.[47]

The antiracist repercussions of the Civil War were particularly apparent in the border states. Lincoln's Emancipation Proclamation applied only to the Confederacy. It left slavery untouched in Unionist Delaware, Maryland, Ken-tucky, and Missouri. But the war did not. The status of planters became am-biguous: owning black people was no longer what a young white man aspired to do or what a young white woman aspired to accomplish by marriage. Maryland was a slave state with considerable support for the Confederacy at the onset of the war. But Maryland held for the Union and sent thousands of soldiers to defend Washington. What happened next provides a "positive" example of the effects of cognitive dissonance: for Maryland whites to fight a war against slave owners while allowing slavery within their own state created a tension that de-

Opposite: This is the October 15, 1864, centerfold of *Harper's* magazine, which throughout the nineteenth century was the mouthpiece of the Republican Party. The words are from the Democratic platform. The illustrations, by young Thomas Nast, show shortcomings in the Democratic plan. One could hardly imagine a political party today seeking white votes on the basis of such racial idealism.

The Democratic platform began innocuously enough: "We will adhere with unswerving fidelity to the UNION under the CONSTITUTION as the ONLY solid foundation of our STRENGTH, SECURITY, and HAPPINESS as a PEOPLE." But Nast's illustration was a knockout: he shows slave catchers and dogs pursuing hapless runaways into a swamp. He jolts the reader to exclaim, What about them? These are people, too!

manded resolution. In 1864 the increasingly persuasive abolitionists in Maryland brought the issue to a vote. The tally went narrowly against emancipation until the large number of absentee ballots were counted. By an enormous margin, these ballots were for freedom. Who cast most absentee ballots in 1864 in Maryland? Soldiers and sailors, of course. Just as these soldiers marched into battle with "John Brown's Body" upon their lips, so their minds had changed to favor the freedom that their actions were forging.[48]

As noted in the previous chapter, songs such as "Nigger Doodle Dandy" reflect the racist tone of the Democrats' presidential campaign in 1864. How did Republicans counter? In part, they sought white votes by being antiracist. The Republican campaign, boosted by military victories in the fall of 1864, proved effective. The Democrats' overt appeals to racism failed, and antiracist Republicans triumphed almost everywhere. One New York Republican wrote, "The change of opinion on this slavery question . . . is a great and historic fact. Who could have predicted . . . this great and blessed revolution?"[49] People around the world supported the Union because of its ideology. Forty thousand Canadians alone, some of them black, came south to volunteer for the Union cause. "Ideas are more important than battles," said abolitionist senator Charles Sumner, speaking as the war wound down.[50]

Illustrating "PUBLIC LIBERTY and PRIVATE RIGHT," Nast shows the New York City draft riot of 1863: white thugs are exercising their "right" to beat and kill African Americans, including a child held upside down.

Ideas made the opposite impact in the Confederacy. Ideological contradictions afflicted the slave system even before the war began. John Brown knew that masters secretly feared that their slaves might revolt, even as they assured abolitionists that slaves really liked slavery. One reason his Harpers Ferry raid prompted such an outcry in the South was that slave owners feared their slaves might join him. Yet their condemnations of Brown and the "Black Republicans" who financed him did not persuade Northern moderates but only pushed them toward the abolitionist camp. After all, if Brown was truly dangerous, as slave owners claimed, then slavery was truly unjust. Happy slaves would never revolt.

White Southerners founded the Confederacy on the ideology of white supremacy. According to Alexander Stephens, vice president of the Confederacy: "Our new government's foundations are laid, its cornerstone rests, upon the great truth that the Negro is not equal to the white man, that slavery—subordination to the superior race—is his natural and normal condition." Confederate soldiers on their way to Antietam and Gettysburg, their two main forays into Union states, put this ideology into practice: they seized scores of free black people in Maryland and Pennsylvania and sent them south into slavery. Confederates maltreated black Union troops when they captured them.[51] Throughout the war, points out historian Paul Escott, "the protection of slavery had been and still remained the central core of Confederate purpose."[52] Textbooks downplay all this, probably because they do not want to offend white Southerners today.

The last chapter showed that concern for states' rights did not motivate secession. Moreover, as the war continued, the Confederacy began to deny states' rights within the new nation. As early as December 1862, President Jefferson Davis denounced states' rights as destructive to the Confederacy. The mountainous counties in western Virginia bolted to the Union. Confederate troops had to occupy east Tennessee to keep it from emulating West Virginia. Winn Parish, Louisiana, refused to secede from the Union. Winston County, Alabama, declared itself the Free State of Winston. Unionist farmers and woodsmen in Jones County, Mississippi, declared the Free State of Jones. Every Confederate state except South Carolina supplied a regiment or at least a company of white soldiers to the Union army, as well as many black recruits. Armed guerrilla actions plagued every Confederate state. (With the exception of Missouri, and the 1863 New York City draft riots, few Union states were afflicted with such problems.) It became dangerous for Confederates to travel in parts of Alabama, Florida, North Carolina, Tennessee, and Texas. The war was fought not just between North and South but between Unionists and Confederates within the Confederacy (and Missouri).[53] By February 1864, President Davis despaired: "Public meetings of treasonable character, in the name of state sovereignty, are being held." Thus states' rights as an ideology was contradictory and could not mobilize the white South for the long haul.

Every recent textbook tells how the issue of states' rights interfered with the Confederate cause. Otherwise, however, they ignore the role of ideas in the South. The racial ideas of the Confederacy proved even less serviceable to the war effort. According to Confederate ideology, blacks liked slavery; nevertheless, to avert revolts and runaways, the Confederate states passed the "twenty nigger law," exempting from military conscription one white man as overseer for every twenty slaves. Throughout the war, Confederates withheld as much as a third of their fighting forces from the front lines and scattered them throughout areas with large slave populations to prevent slave uprisings.[54] When the United States allowed African Americans to enlist, Confederates were forced by their ideology to assert that it would not work—blacks would hardly fight like white men. The undeniable bravery of the 54th Massachusetts and other black regiments disproved the idea of black inferiority. Then came the incongruity of truly beastly behavior by Southern whites toward captured black soldiers, such as the infamous Fort Pillow massacre by troops under Nathan Bedford Forrest, who crucified black prisoners on tent frames and then burned them alive, all in the name of preserving white civilization.[55]

After the fall of Vicksburg, President Davis proposed to arm slaves to fight for the Confederacy, promising them freedom to win their cooperation. But if servitude was the best condition for the slave, protested supporters of slavery, how could freedom be a reward? Black behavior proved that slaves *did* value freedom: several textbooks show how slavery broke down when Union armies came near. But authors miss the ideological confusion that slaves' defections caused among their former owners. Contradiction piled upon contradiction. To win foreign recognition, other Confederate leaders proposed to abolish slavery altogether. Some newspaper editors concurred. "Although slavery is one of the principles that we started to fight for," said the *Jackson Mississippian*, if it must be jettisoned to achieve our "separate nationality, away with it!" A month before Appomattox, the Confederate Congress passed a measure to enroll black troops, showing how the war had elevated even slave owners' estimations of black abilities and also revealing complete ideological disarray. What, after all, would the new black soldiers be fighting *for*? Slavery? Secession? What, for that matter, would white Southern troops be fighting for, once blacks were also armed? As Howell Cobb of Georgia said, "If slaves will make good soldiers our whole theory of slavery is wrong."[56]

In part, owing to these contradictions, some Confederate soldiers switched sides, beginning as early as 1862. When Sherman made his famous march to the sea from Atlanta to Savannah, his army actually grew in number, because thousands of white Southerners volunteered along the way. Meanwhile, almost two-thirds of the Confederate army opposing Sherman disappeared through desertion.[57] Eighteen thousand slaves also joined Sherman, so many that the army had to turn some away. Compare these facts with the portrait common in our textbooks of Sherman's marauders looting their way through a united South.

The increasing ideological confusion in the Confederate states, coupled with the increasing ideological strength of the United States, helps explain the Union victory. "Even with all the hardships," Carleton Beals has noted, "the South up to the very end still had great resources and manpower." Many nations and people have continued to fight with far inferior means and weapons. Beals thinks that the Confederacy's ideological contradictions were its gravest liabilities, ultimately causing its defeat. He shows how the Confederate army was disbanding by the spring of 1865 in Texas and other states, even in the absence of Union approaches. On the home front, too, as Jefferson Davis put it, "The zeal of the people is failing." [58]

Why are textbooks silent regarding ideas or ideologies as a weakness of the Confederacy?[59] The Civil War was about something, after all, and that something even influenced its outcome. Textbooks should tell us what it was.[60]

This silence has a history. Throughout the twentieth century, textbooks presented the Civil War as a struggle between "virtually identical peoples." This is all part of the unspoken agreement, reached during the nadir of race relations in the United States (1890–1940), that whites in the South were as American as whites in the North.[61] White Northerners and white Southerners reconciled on the backs of African Americans in those years, while the abolitionists became the bad guys.

As the nadir set in, Confederate Col. John S. Mosby, "Gray Ghost of the Confederacy," grew frustrated at the obfuscation that historians were throwing up as to what the war had been about. "The South went to war on account of slavery," he wrote in 1907, seeking historical accuracy. He cited South Carolina's secession proclamation and noted scornfully, "South Carolina ought to know what was the cause for her seceding." By the 1920s the Grand Army of the Republic, the organization of Union veterans, complained that American history textbooks presented the Civil War with "no suggestion" that the Union cause was right. Apparently the United Daughters of the Confederacy carried more weight with publishers.[62] Beyond influencing the tone of textbooks to portray the Confederate cause sympathetically, the UDC was even able to erect a statue to the Confederate dead in *Wisconsin*, claiming they "died to repel unconstitutional invasion, to protect the rights reserved to the people, to perpetuate the sovereignty of the states."[63] Not a word about slavery or even disunion.

To this day, history textbooks still present Union and Confederate sympathizers as equally idealistic. The North fought to hold the Union together, while the Southern states fought, according to *The American Way*, "for the preservation of their rights and freedom to decide for themselves." Nobody fought to preserve racial slavery; nobody fought to end it. As one result, unlike the Nazi swastika, which lies disgraced, even in the North whites still proudly display the Stars and Bars of the Confederacy on den walls, license plates, T-shirts, and high school logos. Even some (white) Northerners vaguely regret the defeat of the "lost cause." It is as if racism against blacks could be remembered with nostalgia.[64] In this sense, long after Appomattox, the Confederacy finally won.

Five days after Appomattox, President Lincoln was murdered. His martyrdom pushed Union ideology one step further. Even whites who had opposed emancipation now joined to call Lincoln the great emancipator.[65] Under Republican leadership, the nation entered Reconstruction, a period of continuing ideological conflict.

At first Confederates tried to maintain prewar conditions through new laws, modeled after their slave codes and antebellum restrictions on free blacks. Mississippi was the first state to pass these draconian "Black Codes." They did not work, however. The Civil War had changed American ideology. The new antiracism forged in its flames would dominate Northern thinking for a decade. The *Chicago Tribune*, the most important organ of the Republican Party in the Midwest, responded angrily: "We tell the white men of Mississippi that the men of the North will convert the state of Mississippi into a frog pond before they will allow any such laws to disgrace one foot of soil in which the bones of our soldiers sleep and over which the flag of freedom waves."[66] Thus black civil rights again became the central issue in the congressional elections of 1866. "Support Congress and You Support the Negro," said the Democrats in a campaign broadside featuring a disgusting caricature of an African American. "Sustain the President and You Protect the White Man."[67] Northern voters did not buy it. They returned "radical" Republicans to Congress in a thunderous repudiation of President Andrew Johnson's accommodation of the ex-Confederates. Even more than in 1864, when Republicans swept Congress in 1866, antiracism became the policy of the nation, agreed to by most of its voters. Despite Johnson's opposition, Congress and the states passed the Fourteenth Amendment, making all persons citizens and guaranteeing them "the equal protection of the laws." The passage, on behalf of blacks, of this shining jewel of our Constitution shows how idealistic were the officeholders of the Republican Party, particularly when we consider that similar legislation on behalf of women cannot be passed today.[68]

During Reconstruction a surprising variety of people went to the new civilian "front lines" and worked among the newly freed African Americans in the South. Many were black Northerners, including several graduates of Oberlin College. This passage from a letter by Edmonia Highgate, a black woman who went south to teach school, describes her life in Lafayette Parish, Louisiana.

The majority of my pupils come from plantations, three, four and even eight miles distant. So anxious are they to learn that they walk these distances so early in the morning as never to be tardy.

There has been much opposition to the School. Twice I have been shot at in my room. My night school scholars have been shot but none killed. A week ago an aged freedman just across the way was shot so badly as to break his arm and leg. The rebels here threatened to burn down the school and house in which I board yet they have not materially harmed us. The nearest military protection is 200 miles distant at New Orleans.[69]

Some Union soldiers stayed in the South when they were demobilized. Some Northern Republican would-be politicians moved south to organize their party in a region where it had not been a factor before the war. Some went

The white woman at left, whom textbooks would call a "carpetbagger," could hardly expect to grow rich teaching school near Vicksburg, where this illustration was done. This woman risked her life to bring basic literacy to African American children and adults during Reconstruction.

hoping to win office by election or appointment. Many abolitionists continued their commitment by working in the Freedman's Bureau and private organizations to help blacks obtain full civil and political rights. In terms of party affiliation, almost all of these persons were Republicans; otherwise, they were a diverse group. Still, all but one of the eighteen textbooks routinely use the disgraceful old tag *carpetbaggers*, without quotation marks and often without noting its bias, to describe Northern white Republicans who lived in the South during Reconstruction.[70]

Many whites who were born in the South supported Reconstruction. Every Southern state boasted Unionists, some of whom had volunteered for the Union army. Most of them now became Republicans. Some former Confederates, including even Gen. James Longstreet, second in command under Lee at Gettysburg, also became Republicans because they had grown convinced that equality for blacks was morally right. Robert Flournoy, a Mississippi planter, had raised a company of Confederate soldiers but then resigned his commission and returned home because "there was a conflict in my conscience." During the war he was once arrested for encouraging blacks to flee to Union lines. During Reconstruction he helped organize the Republican Party, published a newspaper, *Equal Rights*, and argued for desegregating the University of Mississippi and the new state's public school system.[71] Republican policies, including free public education, never before available in the South to children of either race, convinced some poor whites to vote for the party. Many former Whigs became Republicans rather than join their old nemesis, the Democrats. Some white Southerners became Republicans because they were convinced that black suffrage was an accomplished fact; they preferred winning political power with blacks on their side to losing. Others became Republicans to make connections or win contracts from the new Republican state governments. Of the 113 white Republican congressmen from the South during Reconstruction, 53 were Southerners, many of them from wealthy families.[72] In sum, this is another diverse group, amounting to between one-fourth and one-third of the white population and in some counties a majority. Nevertheless, all but one textbook still routinely apply the disgraceful old tag *scalawags* to Southern white Republicans.[73]

Carpetbaggers and *scalawags* are terms coined by white Southern Democrats to defame their opponents as illegitimate. At the time, newspapers in Mississippi, at least, used *Republicans* far more often than *carpetbaggers* or *scalawags*. *Carpetbagger* implies that the dregs of Northern society, carrying all their belongings in a carpetbag, had come down to make their fortunes off the "prostrate [white] south." *Scalawag* means "scoundrel." They became the terms of choice long after Reconstruction, during the nadir of race relations, when white Americans, North as well as South, found it hard to believe that white Northerners would have gone south to help blacks without ulterior motives. If authors explained when and why the terms became popular, students would learn something important about Reconstruction, the nadir, and the writing of history. The closest they come is this sentence from *The Americans*: "Although the terms *scalawag* and *carpetbagger* were negative labels imposed by political enemies, historians still use the terms when referring to the two groups." Like all the other books, *The Americans* then uses the words as if they were proper historical labels, with no quotation marks.

Consider this phrase from *Pathways to the Present* listing the victims of Klan violence: "carpetbaggers, scalawags, freedmen who had become prosperous—even those who had merely learned to read." Why not simply say "Republicans—black and white"? Or this from *The American Tradition:* "Despite southern white claims to the contrary, the Radical regimes were not dominated by blacks, but by scalawags and carpetbaggers." In reality, "scalawags" *were* Southern whites, of course, but this sentence writes them out of the white South, just as die-hard Confederates were wont to do. Moreover, referring to perfectly legal governments as "regimes" is a way of delegitimizing them, a technique *Tradition* applies to no other administration, not even the 1836 Republic of Texas or the 1893 Dole pineapple takeover in Hawaii.

To be sure, newer editions of American history textbooks no longer denounce Northerners who participated in Southern politics and society as "dishonest adventurers whose only thought was to feather their own nests at the expense of their fellows," as *Rise of the American Nation* put it in 1961. Again, the civil rights movement has allowed us to rethink our history. Having watched Northerners, black and white, go south to help blacks win civil rights in the 1960s, today's textbook authors display more sympathy for Northerners who worked with Southern blacks during Reconstruction.[74] Here is the paragraph on "carpetbaggers" from *Rise's* successor, *Holt American Nation*, published in 2003:

> The arrival of northern Republicans—both whites and African Americans—eager to participate in the state conventions increased resentment among many white southerners. They called these northern Republicans

carpetbaggers. The newcomers, they joked, were "needy adventurers" of the "lowest class" who could carry everything they owned in a carpet-bag—a type of cheap suitcase.

And here is the paragraph on "scalawags":

> Former Confederates heaped even greater scorn on southern whites who had backed the Union cause and now supported Reconstruction. They called these whites **scalawags,** or scoundrels. They viewed them as "southern renegades, betrayers of their race and country."

The new treatment distances the author from the derogatory terms, putting them in the mouths of "many white southerners," but the terms themselves are never discredited. Instead, they are to be learned, which is why they are bolded. And textbooks still invoke greed to "explain" whites who believed blacks should have civil and political rights. Of course, authors might use the notion of private gain to disparage every textbook hero from Christopher Columbus and the Pilgrims through George Washington to Jackie Robinson. They don't, though. Textbooks attribute selfish motives only to characters with whom they have little sympathy, such as the idealists in Reconstruction. The negatives then stick in the mind, cemented by the catchy pejoratives *carpetbaggers* and *scalawags,* while the qualifying phrases—*many white southerners*—are likely to be forgotten.

Everyone who supported black rights in the South during Reconstruction did so at personal risk. At the beginning of Reconstruction, simply to walk to school to teach could be life-threatening. Toward the end of the era, there were communities in which simply to vote Republican was life-threatening. While some Reconstructionists undoubtedly achieved economic gain, it was a dangerous way to make a buck. Textbooks need to show the risk, and the racial idealism that prompted most of the people who took it.[75]

Instead, most textbooks deprive us of our racial idealists, from Highgate and Flournoy, whom they omit, through Brown, whom they make fanatic, to Lincoln, whose idealism they flatten. In the course of events, Lincoln would come to accomplish on a national scale what Brown tried to accomplish at Harpers Ferry: helping African Americans mobilize to fight slavery. Finally, like John Brown, Abraham Lincoln became a martyr and a hero. Seven million Americans, almost one-third of the entire Union population, stood to watch his funeral train pass.[76] African Americans mourned with particular intensity.

In Vicksburg, Mississippi, these African Americans gathered at the courthouse to hear the news of Lincoln's death confirmed, to express their grief, and perhaps to seek protection in the face of an uncertain future.

Gideon Welles, secretary of the navy, walked the streets of Washington at dawn an hour before the president breathed his last and described the scene: "The colored people especially—and there were at this time more of them, perhaps, than of whites—were overwhelmed with grief." Welles went on to tell how all day long "on the avenue in front of the White House were several hundred black people, mostly women and children, weeping for their loss," a crowd that "did not appear to diminish through the whole of that cold, wet day." In their grief African Americans were neither misguided nor childlike. When the hour came for dealing with slavery, as Lincoln had surmised, he had done his duty and it had cost his life.[77] Abraham Lincoln, racism and all, was the blacks' legitimate hero, as earlier John Brown had been. In a sense, Brown and Lincoln were even killed for the same deed: arming black people for their own liberation. People around the world mourned the passing of both men.

But when I ask my (white) college students on the first day of class who their heroes are in American history, only one or two in a hundred pick Lincoln.[78] Even those who choose Lincoln know only that he was "really great"— they don't know why. Their ignorance makes sense—after all, textbooks present Abraham Lincoln almost devoid of content. No students choose John Brown. Not one has ever named a white abolitionist, a Reconstruction Republican, or a white civil rights martyr. Yet these same students feel sympathy with America's struggle to improve race relations. Among their more popular choices are African Americans, from Sojourner Truth and Frederick Douglass to Rosa Parks and Malcolm X.

While John Brown was on trial, the abolitionist Wendell Phillips spoke of Brown's place in history. Phillips foresaw that slavery was a cause whose time was passing, and he asked "the American people" of the future, when slavery was long dead in "the civilization of the twentieth century," this question: "When that day comes, what will be thought of these first martyrs, who teach us how to live and how to die?"[79] Phillips meant the question rhetorically. He never dreamed that Americans would take no pleasure in those who had helped lead the nation to abolish slavery, or that textbooks would label Brown's small band misguided if not fanatic and Brown himself possibly mad.[80]

Antiracism is one of America's great gifts to the world. Its relevance extends far beyond race relations. Antiracism led to "a new birth of freedom" after the Civil War, and not only for African Americans. Twice, once in each century, the movement for black rights triggered the movement for women's rights. Twice it reinvigorated our democratic spirit, which had been atrophying. Throughout the world, from South Africa to Northern Ireland, movements of oppressed people continue to use tactics and words borrowed from our abolitionist and civil rights movements. The clandestine early meetings of anticommunists in East Germany were marked by singing "We Shall Overcome." Iranians used nonviolent methods borrowed from Thoreau and Martin Luther King Jr., to overthrow their hated shah. On Ho Chi Minh's desk in Hanoi on the day he died lay a biography of John Brown. Among the heroes whose ideas inspired the students in Tiananmen Square and whose words spilled from their lips was Abraham Lincoln.[81] Yet we in America, whose antiracist idealists are admired around the globe, seem to have lost these men and women as heroes. Our textbooks need to present them in such a way that we might again value our own idealism.

7.

THE LAND OF OPPORTUNITY

Labor is prior to, and independent of, capital. Capital is only the fruit of labor, and could never have existed if labor had not first existed. Labor is the superior of capital, and deserves much the higher consideration. —ABRAHAM LINCOLN[1]

I had once believed that we were all masters of our fate—that we could mold our lives into any form we pleased. . . . I had overcome deafness and blindness sufficiently to be happy, and I supposed that anyone could come out victorious if he threw himself valiantly into life's struggle. But as I went more and more about the country I learned that I had spoken with assurance on a subject I knew little about. . . . I learned that the power to rise in the world is not within the reach of everyone. —HELEN KELLER[2]

Ten men in our country could buy the whole world and ten million can't buy enough to eat. —WILL ROGERS, 1931

The history of a nation is, unfortunately, too easily written as the history of its dominant class. —KWAME NKRUMAH[3]

HIGH SCHOOL STUDENTS have eyes, ears, and television sets (all too many have their own TV sets), so they know a lot about relative privilege in America. They measure their family's social position against that of other families, and their community's position against other communities. Middle-class students, especially, know little about how the American class structure works, however, and nothing at all about how it has changed over time. These students do not leave high school merely ignorant of the workings of the class structure; they come out as terrible sociologists. "Why are people poor?" I have asked first-year college students. Or, if their own class position is one of relative privilege, "Why is your family well-off?" The answers I've received, to characterize them charitably, are half-formed and naïve. The students blame the poor for not being successful.[4] They have no understanding of the ways that opportunity is not equal in America and no notion that social structure pushes people around, influencing the ideas they hold and the lives they fashion.

High school history textbooks can take some of the credit for this state of affairs. Some textbooks do cover certain high points of labor history, such as the 1894 Pullman strike near Chicago that President Cleveland broke with federal troops, or the 1911 Triangle Shirtwaist fire that killed 146 women in New York City, but the most recent event mentioned in most books is the Taft-Hartley Act of sixty years ago. No book mentions any of the major strikes that labor lost in the late twentieth century, such as the 1985 Hormel meatpackers' strike in Austin, Minnesota, or the 1991 Caterpillar strike in Decatur, Illinois—defeats that signify labor's diminished power today.[5] Nor do most textbooks describe any continuing issues facing labor, such as the growth of multinational corporations and their exporting of jobs overseas. With such omissions, textbook authors can construe labor history as something that happened long ago, like slavery, and that, like slavery, was corrected long ago. It

This photograph of a sweatshop in New York's Chinatown, taken in the early 1990s, illustrates that the working class still works, in America, sometimes under conditions not so different from a century ago, and often in the same locations.

logically follows that unions now appear anachronistic. The idea that they might be necessary for workers to have a voice in the workplace goes unstated.

These books' poor treatment of labor history is magnificent compared to their treatment of social class. *Nothing* that textbooks discuss—not even strikes—is ever anchored in any analysis of social class.[6] This amounts to delivering the footnotes instead of the lecture! Half of the eighteen high school American history textbooks I examined contain no index listing at all for *social class, social stratification, class structure, income distribution, inequality*, or any conceivably related topic. Not one book lists *upper class* or *lower class.* Three list *middle class*, but only to assure students that America is a middle-class country. "Except for slaves, most of the colonists were members of the 'middling ranks,' " says *Land of Promise*, and nails home the point that we are a middle-class country by asking students to "describe three 'middle-class' values that united free Americans of all classes." Several of the textbooks note the explosion of middle-class suburbs after World War II. Talking about the middle class is hardly equivalent to discussing social stratification, however. On the contrary, as Gregory Mantsios has pointed out, "such references appear to be acceptable precisely because they mute class differences."[7]

Stressing how middle-class we all are is increasingly problematic today, because the proportion of households earning between 75 percent and 125 percent of the median income has fallen steadily since 1967. The Reagan-Bush administrations accelerated this shrinkage of the middle class, and most families who left its ranks fell rather than rose.[8] As late as 1970, family incomes in the United States were only slightly less equal than in Canada. By 2000, inequality here was much greater than Canada's; the United States was becoming more like Mexico, a very stratified society.[9] The Bush II administration, with its tax cuts aimed openly at the wealthy, continued to increase the gap between the haves and have-nots. This is the kind of historical trend one would think history books would take as appropriate subject matter, but only five of the eighteen books in my sample provide any analysis of social stratification in the United States. Even these fragmentary analyses are set mostly in colonial America. Boorstin and Kelley, unusual in actually including *social class* in its index, lists only *social classes in 1790* and *social classes in early America.* These turn out to be two references to the same paragraph, which tells us that England "was a land of rigid social classes," while here in America "social classes were much more fluid." "One great difference between colonial and European society was that the colonists had more social mobility," echoes *The American Tradition.* Never mind that the most violent class conflicts in American history—Bacon's Rebellion and Shays's Rebellion—took place in and just after colonial times. Textbooks still say that colonial society was relatively classless and marked by upward mobility.

And things have only gotten rosier since. "By 1815," *The Challenge of Freedom* assures us, two classes had withered away and "America was a country of middle class people and of middle class goals." This book returns repeatedly, every fifty years or so, to the theme of how open opportunity is in America. The stress on upward mobility is striking. There is almost nothing in any of these textbooks about class inequalities or barriers of any kind to social mobility. "What conditions made it possible for poor white immigrants to become richer in the colonies?" *Land of Promise* asks. "What conditions made/make it difficult?" goes unasked. Boorstin and Kelley close their sole discussion of social class (in 1790, described above) with the happy sentence, "As the careers of American Presidents would soon show, here a person might rise by hard work, intelligence, skill, and perhaps a little luck, from the lowest positions to the highest."

If only that were so! Social class is probably the single most important variable in society. From womb to tomb, it correlates with almost all other social characteristics of people that we can measure. Affluent expectant mothers are more likely to get prenatal care, receive current medical advice, and enjoy general health, fitness, and nutrition. Many poor and working-class mothers-to-be first contact the medical profession in the last month, sometimes the last hours, of their pregnancies. Rich babies come out healthier and weighing more than poor babies. The infants go home to very different situations. Poor babies are more likely to have high levels of poisonous lead in their environments and their bodies. Rich babies get more time and verbal interaction with their parents and higher quality day care when not with their parents. When they enter kindergarten, and through the twelve years that follow, rich children benefit from suburban schools that spend two to three times as much money per student as schools in inner cities or impoverished rural areas. Poor children are taught in classes that are often 50 percent larger than the classes of affluent children. Differences such as these help account for the higher school-dropout rate among poor children.

Even when poor children are fortunate enough to attend the same school as rich children, they encounter teachers who expect only children of affluent families to know the right answers. Social science research shows that teachers are often surprised and even distressed when poor children excel. Teachers and counselors believe they can predict who is "college material." Since many working-class children give off the wrong signals, even in first grade, they end up in the "general education" track in high school.[10] "If you are the child of low-income parents, the chances are good that you will receive limited and often careless attention from adults in your high school," in the words of Theodore Sizer's bestselling study of American high schools, *Horace's Compromise.* "If you are the child of upper-middle-income parents, the chances are good that you will receive substantial and careful attention."[11] Researcher Reba Page has provided vivid accounts of how high school American history courses use rote learning to turn off lower-class students.[12] Thus schools have put into practice Woodrow Wilson's recommendation: "We want one class of persons to have a liberal education, and we want another class of persons, a very much larger class of necessity in every society, to forgo the privilege of a liberal education and fit themselves to perform specific difficult manual tasks."[13]

As if this unequal home and school life were not enough, rich teenagers then enroll in the Princeton Review or other coaching sessions for the Scholastic Aptitude Test. Even without coaching, affluent children are advantaged because their background is similar to that of the test makers, so they are comfortable with the vocabulary and subtle subcultural assumptions of the test. To no one's surprise, social class correlates strongly with SAT scores.

All these are among the reasons that social class predicts the rate of college attendance and the type of college chosen more effectively than does any other factor, including intellectual ability, however measured. After college, most affluent children get white-collar jobs, most working-class children get blue-collar jobs, and the class differences continue. As adults, rich people are more likely to have hired an attorney and to be a member of formal organizations that increase their civic power. Poor people are more likely to watch TV. Because affluent families can save some money while poor families must spend what they make, wealth differences are ten times larger than income differences. Therefore most poor and working-class families cannot accumulate the down payment required to buy a house, which in turn shuts them out from our most important tax shelter, the write-off of home mortgage interest. Working-class parents cannot afford to live in elite subdivisions or hire high-quality day care, so the process of educational inequality replicates itself in the next generation. Finally, affluent Americans also have longer life expectancies than lower- and working-class people, the largest single cause of which is better access to health care.[14] Echoing the results of Helen Keller's study of blindness, research has determined that poor health is not distributed randomly about the social structure but is concentrated in the lower class. Social Security then becomes a huge transfer system, using monies contributed by all Americans to pay benefits disproportionately to longer-lived affluent Americans.

Ultimately, social class determines how people think about social class. When asked if poverty in America is the fault of the poor or the fault of the system, 57 percent of business leaders blamed the poor; just 9 percent blamed the system. Labor leaders showed sharply reversed choices: only 15 percent said the poor were at fault while 56 percent blamed the system. (Some people replied "don't know" or chose a middle position.) The largest single difference between our two main political parties lies in how their members think about social class: 55 percent of Republicans blamed the poor for their poverty, while only 13 percent blamed the system for it; 68 percent of Democrats, on the other hand, blamed the system, while only 5 percent blamed the poor.[15]

Few of these statements are news, I know, which is why I have not bothered to document most of them, but the majority of high school students do not know or understand these ideas. Moreover, the processes have changed over time, for the class structure in America today is not the same as it was in 1890, let alone in colonial America. Yet in the most recent *American Pageant*, for example, social class goes unmentioned in the twentieth century. Many teachers compound the problem by avoiding talking about social class in the twenty-first. A study of history and social studies teachers "revealed that they had a much broader knowledge of the economy, both academically and experientially, than they admitted in class." Teachers "expressed fear that students might find out about the injustices and inadequacies of their economic and political institutions."[16] By never blaming the system, American history courses thus present Republican history.

Historically, social class is intertwined with all kinds of events and processes in our past. Our governing system was established by rich men, following theories that emphasized government as a bulwark of the propertied class. Although rich himself, James Madison worried about social inequality and wrote *The Federalist* #10 to explain how the proposed government would not succumb to the influence of the affluent. Madison did not fully succeed, according to Edward Pessen, who examined the social-class backgrounds of all American presidents through Reagan. Pessen found that more than 40 percent hailed from the upper class, mostly from the upper fringes of that elite group, and another 15 percent originated in families located between the upper and upper-

Beer has been one of the few products (pickup trucks, some patent medicines, and false-teeth cleansers are others) that advertisers try to sell with working-class images. Advertisers use upper-middle-class imagery to sell most items, from wine to nylons to toilet-bowl cleansers. Signs of social class cover these two models, from footwear to headgear. Note who has the newspaper, briefcase, lunch box, and, in a final statement, the cans and the bottles.

middle classes. More than 25 percent came from a solid upper-middle-class background, leaving just six presidents, or 15 percent, to come from the middle and lower-middle classes and just one, Andrew Johnson, representing any part of the lower class. One recent president, Bill Clinton, also comes from a working-class background, for a total of two. For good reason, Pessen titled his book *The Log Cabin Myth.*[17] Clearly Boorstin and Kelley never read Pessen, or they could not have claimed that the careers of our presidents demonstrate how persons can rise "from the lowest positions to the highest." In fact, most Americans die in the same social class in which they were born, sociologists have shown, and those who are mobile usually rise or fall just a single social class.

Social class buys life even in the midst of danger. While it was sad when the great ship *Titanic* went down, as the old song refrain goes, it was saddest for the lower class: among women, only 4 of 143 first-class passengers were lost, while 15 of 93 second-class passengers drowned, along with 81 of 179 third-class women and girls. The crew ordered third-class passengers to remain below deck, holding some there at gunpoint.[18] More recently, social class played a major role in determining who fought in the Vietnam War: despite the "universal" draft, sons of the affluent won educational and medical deferments through most of the conflict. The all-volunteer army that fights in Iraq relies even more on lower-class recruits, who sign up as one way out of poverty.[19] Textbooks and teachers ignore all this.

Teachers may avoid social class out of a laudable desire not to embarrass their charges. If so, their concern is misguided. When my students from nonaffluent backgrounds learn about the class system, they find the experience liberating. Once they see the social processes that have helped keep their families poor, they can let go of their negative self-image about being poor. If to understand is to pardon, for working-class children to understand how stratification works is to pardon *themselves* and their families. Knowledge of the social-class system also reduces the tendency of Americans from other social classes to blame the victim for being poor. Pedagogically, stratification provides a gripping learning experience. Students are fascinated to discover how the upper class wields disproportionate power relating to everything from energy bills in Congress to zoning decisions in small towns.

Consider a white ninth-grade student taking American history in a predominantly middle-class town in Vermont. Her father tapes Sheetrock, earning an income that in slow construction seasons leaves the family quite poor. Her mother helps out by driving a school bus part-time, in addition to taking care of her two younger siblings. The girl lives with her family in a small house, a winterized former summer cabin, while most of her classmates live in large suburban homes. How is this girl to understand her poverty? Since history textbooks present the American past as four hundred years of progress and portray our society as a land of opportunity in which folks get what they deserve and deserve what they get, the failures of working-class Americans to transcend their class origin inevitably get laid at their own doorsteps.

Within the white working-class community the girl will probably find few resources—teachers, church parishioners, family members—who can tell her of heroes or struggles among people of her background, for, except in pockets of continuing class conflict, the working class usually forgets its own history. More than any other group, white working-class students believe that they deserve their low status. A subculture of shame results. This negative self-image is foremost among what Richard Sennett and Jonathan Cobb have called "the hidden injuries of class."[20] Two students of mine provided a demonstration: they drove around Burlington, Vermont, in a big, nearly new, shiny black luxury car and then in a battered ten-year-old subcompact. In each vehicle, when they reached a stoplight and it turned green, they waited until they were honked at before driving on. Motorists averaged less than seven seconds to honk at them in the subcompact, but in the luxury car the students enjoyed 13.2 seconds before anyone honked. Besides providing a good reason to buy an expensive car, this experiment shows how Americans unconsciously grant respect to the educated and successful. Since motorists of all social stations honked at the subcompact more readily, working-class drivers were in a sense disrespecting themselves while deferring to their betters. The biting quip "If you're so smart, why aren't you rich?" conveys the injury done to the self-image of the poor when the idea that America is a meritocracy goes unchallenged in school.

Part of the problem is that American history textbooks describe American education itself as meritocratic. A huge body of research confirms that education is dominated by the class structure and operates to replicate that structure in the next generation.[21] Meanwhile, history textbooks blithely tell of such federal largesse to education as the Elementary and Secondary Education Act, passed under President Lyndon Johnson. Not one textbook offers any data on or analysis of inequality within educational institutions. None mentions how school districts in low-income areas labor under financial constraints so shocking that Jonathan Kozol calls them "savage inequalities."[22] No textbook ever suggests that students might research the history of their own school and the population it serves. The only textbooks that relate education to the class system at all see it as a remedy! Schooling "was a key to upward mobility in postwar America," in the words of *The Challenge of Freedom*. It was also key to continued inequality.[23]

The tendency of teachers and textbooks to avoid social class as if it were a dirty little secret only reinforces the reluctance of working-class families to talk about it. Paul Cowan has told of interviewing the children of Italian immigrant workers involved in the famous 1912 Lawrence, Massachusetts, mill strike. He spoke with the daughter of one of the Lawrence workers who testified at a Washington congressional hearing investigating the strike. The worker, Camella Teoli, then thirteen years old, had been scalped by a cotton-twisting machine just before the strike and had been hospitalized for several months. Her testimony "became front-page news all over America." But Teoli's daughter, interviewed in 1976 after her mother's death, could not help Cowan. Her mother had told her nothing of the incident, nothing of her trip to Washington, nothing about her impact on America's conscience—even though almost every day, the daughter "had combed her mother's hair into a bun that disguised the bald spot."[24] A professional of working-class origin told me a similar story about being ashamed of her uncle "for being a steelworker." A certain defensiveness is built into working-class culture; even its successful acts of working-class resistance, like the Lawrence strike, necessarily presuppose lower status and income, hence connote a certain inferiority. If the larger community is so good, as textbooks tell us it is, then celebrating or even passing on the memory of conflict with it seems somehow disloyal.

Textbooks do present immigrant history. Around the turn of the century immigrants dominated the American urban working class, even in cities as distant from seacoasts as Des Moines and Louisville. When more than 70 percent of the white population was native stock, less than 10 percent of the urban working class was.[25] But when textbooks tell the immigrant story, they emphasize Joseph Pulitzer, Andrew Carnegie, and their ilk—immigrants who made supergood. Several textbooks apply the phrases *rags to riches* or *land of opportunity* to the immigrant experience. Such legendary successes were achieved, to be sure, but they were the exceptions, not the rule. Ninety-five percent of the executives and financiers in America around the turn of the century came from upper-class or upper-middle-class backgrounds. Fewer than 3 percent started as poor immigrants or farm children. Throughout the nineteenth century, just 2 percent of American industrialists came from working-class origins.[26] By concentrating on the inspiring exceptions, textbooks present immigrant history as another heartening confirmation of America as the land of unparalleled opportunity.

Again and again, textbooks emphasize how America has differed from Europe in having less class stratification and more economic and social mobility. This is another aspect of the archetype of American exceptionalism: our society has been uniquely fair. It would never occur to historians in, say, France or Australia, to claim that their society was exceptionally equalitarian. Does this treatment of the United States prepare students for reality? It certainly does not accurately describe our country today. Social scientists have on many occasions compared the degree of economic equality in the United States with that in other industrial nations. Depending on the measure used, the United States has ranked sixth of six, seventh of seven, ninth of twelve, thirteenth of thirteen, or fourteenth of fourteen.[27] In the United States the richest fifth of the population earns twelve times as much income as the poorest fifth, one of the highest ratios in the industrialized world; in Great Britain the ratio is seven to one, in Japan just four to one.[28] In 1965 the average chief executive officer in the United States made 26 times what the average worker made. By 2004, the CEO made 431 times an average worker's pay. Meanwhile, Japanese CEOs continue to make about 26 times as much as their average workers, and it is hard to claim that the leadership of GM and Ford is that much better than Toyota's and Honda's.[29] The Jeffersonian conceit of a nation of independent farmers and merchants is also long gone: only one working American in thirteen is self-employed, compared to one in eight in Western Europe.[30] Thus, not only do we have far fewer independent entrepreneurs compared to two hundred years ago, we have fewer compared to Europe today.

Since textbooks claim that colonial America was radically less stratified than Europe, they should tell their readers when inequality set in. It surely was not a recent development. By 1910 the top 1 percent of the U.S. population received more than a third of all personal income, while the bottom fifth got less than one-eighth.[31] This level of inequality was on a par with that in Germany or Great Britain.[32] If textbooks acknowledged inequality, then they could describe the changes in our class structure over time, which would introduce their students to fascinating historical debate.[33]

For example, some historians argue that wealth in colonial society was more equally distributed than it is today and that economic inequality increased during the presidency of Andrew Jackson—a period known, ironically, as the age of the common man. Others believe that the flowering of the large corporation in the late nineteenth century made the class structure more rigid. Walter Dean Burnham has argued that the Republican presidential victory in 1896 (McKinley over Bryan) brought about a sweeping political realignment that changed "a fairly democratic regime into a rather broadly based oligarchy," so by the 1920s, business controlled public policy.[34] Clearly the gap between rich and poor, like the distance between blacks and whites, was greater at the end of the Progressive Era in 1920 than at its beginning around 1890.[35] The story is not all one of increasing stratification, for between the Depression and the end of World War II, income and wealth in America gradually became more equal. Distributions of income then remained reasonably constant until President Reagan took office in 1981, when inequality began to grow.[36] Still other scholars think that little change has occurred since the Revolution. Lee Soltow, for example, finds "surprising inequality of wealth and income" in America in 1798. At least for Boston, Stephan Thernstrom concludes that inequalities in life chances owing to social class show an eerie continuity.[37] All this is part of American history. But it is not part of American history as taught in high school.

To social scientists, the level of inequality is a portentous thing to know about a society. When we rank countries by this variable, we find Scandinavian nations at the top, the most equal, and agricultural societies like Colombia and

Zimbabwe near the bottom. The policies of the Reagan and first Bush administrations, which openly favored the rich, abetted a secular trend already in motion, causing inequality to increase measurably between 1981 and 1992. For the United States to move perceptibly toward Colombia in social inequality is a development of no small import.[38] Surely high school students would be interested to learn that in 1950 physicians made two and a half times what unionized industrial workers made but now make five times as much. Surely they need to understand that top managers of clothing firms, who used to earn 50 times what their American employees made, now make 1,500 times what their Bangladeshi workers earn. Surely it is wrong for our history textbooks and teachers to withhold the historical information that might prompt and inform discussion of these trends.

Why might they commit such a blunder? First and foremost, publisher censorship of textbook authors. "You always run the risk, if you talk about social class, of being labeled Marxist," the editor for social studies and history at one of the biggest publishing houses told me. This editor communicates the taboo, formally or subtly, to every writer she works with, and she implied that most other editors do, too.

Publisher pressure derives in part from textbook adoption boards and committees in states and school districts. These are subject in turn to pressure from organized groups and individuals who appear before them. Perhaps the most robust such lobby is still Educational Research Analysts, led until 2004 by Mel Gabler of Texas. Gabler's stable of right-wing critics regards even alleging that a textbook contains some class analysis as a devastating criticism. As one writer has put it, "Formulating issues in terms of class is unacceptable, perhaps even un-American."[39] Fear of not winning adoption in Texas is a prime source of publisher angst and might help explain why *Life and Liberty* limits its social-class analysis to colonial times in *England.* By contrast, "the colonies were places of great opportunity," even back then. Some Texans cannot easily be placated, however. Deborah L. Brezina, a Gabler ally, wrote that *Life and Liberty* describes America "as an unjust society," unfair to lower economic groups, and therefore should not be approved.[40] Such pressure is hardly new. Harold Rugg's *Introduction to Problems of American Culture* and his popular history textbook, written during the Depression, included some class analysis. In the early 1940s, according to Frances FitzGerald, the National Association of Manufacturers attacked Rugg's books, partly for this feature, and "brought to an end" social and economic analysis in American history textbooks.[41]

More often the influence of the upper class is less direct. The most potent rationale for class privilege in American history has been social Darwinism, an archetype that still has great power in American culture. The notion that people rise and fall in a survival of the fittest may not conform to the data on intergenerational mobility in the United States, but that has hardly caused the archetype to fade away from American education, particularly from American history classes.[42] Facts that do not fit with the archetype, such as the entire literature of social stratification, simply get left out.

Textbook authors may not even need pressure from publishers, the right wing, the upper class, or cultural archetypes to avoid social stratification. As part of the process of heroification, textbook authors treat America itself as a hero, indeed as *the* hero of their books, so they remove its warts. Even to report the facts of income and wealth distribution might seem critical of America the hero, for it is difficult to come up with a theory of social justice that can explain why 1 percent of the population controls almost 40 percent of the wealth. Could the other 99 percent of us be *that* lazy or otherwise undeserving? To go on to include some of the mechanisms—unequal schooling and the like—by which the upper class stays upper would clearly involve criticism of our beloved nation.

For any or all of these reasons, textbooks minimize social stratification. They then do something less comprehensible: they fail to explain the benefits of free enterprise. Writing about an earlier generation of textbooks, Frances FitzGerald pointed out that the books ignored "the virtues as well as the vices of their own economic system."[43] Teachers might mention free enterprise with respect, but seldom do the words become more than a slogan.[44] This omission is strange, for capitalism has its advantages, after all. Former basketball star Michael Jordan, Chrysler executive Lee Iacocca, and ice-cream makers Ben and Jerry all got rich by supplying goods and services that people desired. To be sure, much social stratification cannot be justified so neatly, because it results from the abuse of wealth and power by those who have these advantages to shut out those who do not. As a social and economic order, the capitalist system offers much to criticize but also much to praise. America *is* a land of opportunity for many people. And for all the distortions capitalism imposes upon it, democracy also benefits from the separation of power between public and private spheres. Our history textbooks fail to teach these benefits.

Publishers or those who influence them have evidently concluded that what American society needs to stay strong is citizens who assent to its social structure and economic system without thought. As a consequence, today's textbooks defend our economic system mindlessly, with insupportable pieties about its unique lack of stratification; thus they produce alumni of American history courses unable to criticize or defend our system of social stratification knowledgeably.

But isn't it nice simply to believe that America is equal? Maybe the "land of opportunity" archetype is an empowering myth—maybe believing in it might even help make it come true. For if students *think* the sky is the limit, they may reach for the sky, while if they don't, they won't.

The analogy of gender points to the problem with this line of thought. How could high school girls understand their place in American history if their textbooks told them that, from colonial America to the present, women have had equal opportunity for upward mobility and political participation? How could they then explain why no woman has been president? Girls would have to infer, perhaps unconsciously, that it has been their own gender's fault, a conclusion that is hardly empowering.

Textbooks do tell how women were denied the right to vote in many states until 1920 and faced other barriers to upward mobility. Textbooks also tell of barriers confronting racial minorities. The final question *Land of Promise* asks students following its "Social Mobility" section is "What social barriers prevented blacks, Indians, and women from competing on an equal basis with white male colonists?" After its passage extolling upward mobility, *The Challenge of Freedom* notes, "Not all people, however, enjoyed equal rights or an equal chance to improve their way of life," and goes on to address the issues of sexism and racism. But neither here nor anywhere else do *Promise* or *Challenge* (or most other textbooks) hint that opportunity might not be equal today for white Americans of the lower and working classes.[45] Perhaps as a result, even business leaders and Republicans, the respondents statistically most likely to engage in what sociologists call "blaming the victim," blame the social system rather than African Americans for black poverty and blame the system rather than women for the latter's unequal achievement in the workplace. In sum, affluent Americans, like their textbooks, are willing to credit racial discrimination as the cause of poverty among blacks and Indians and sex discrimination as the cause of women's inequality but don't see class discrimination as the cause of poverty in general.[46]

More than math or science, more even than American literature, courses in American history hold the promise of telling high school students how they and their parents, their communities, and their society came to be as they are. One way things are unequal is by social class. Although poor and working-class children usually cannot identify the cause of their alienation, history often turns them off because it justifies rather than explains the present. When these students react by dropping out, intellectually if not physically, their poor school performance helps convince them as well as their peers in the faster tracks that the system is meritocratic and that they themselves lack merit. In the end, the absence of social-class analysis in American history courses amounts to one more way that education in America is rigged against the working class.

8.

WATCHING BIG BROTHER

WHAT TEXTBOOKS TEACH ABOUT
THE FEDERAL GOVERNMENT

The historian must have no country. —JOHN QUINCY ADAMS[1]

What did you learn in school today, dear little boy of mine?
I learned our government must be strong.
It's always right and never wrong. . . .
That's what I learned in school. —"WHAT DID YOU LEARN
IN SCHOOL TODAY?," TOM PAXTON, 1963[2]

We have to face the unpleasant as well as the affirmative side of the human story,
including our own story as a nation, our own stories of our peoples. We have got to
have the ugly facts in order to protect us from the official view of reality.

—BILL MOYERS[3]

As long as you are convinced you have never done anything, you can never do
anything. —MALCOLM X[4]

To study foreign affairs without putting ourselves into others' shoes is to deal in illusion
and to prepare students for a lifelong misunderstanding of our place in the world.

—PAUL GAGNON[5]

OME TRADITIONAL HISTORIANS, critics of the new emphasis on social and cultural history, believe that American history textbooks have been seduced from their central narrative, which they see as the story of the American state. Methinks they protest too much. The expanded treatments that textbooks now give to women, slavery, modes of transportation, developments in popular music, and other topics not directly related to the state have yet to produce a new core narrative. Therefore, they appear as unnecessary diversions that only interrupt the basic narrative that the textbooks still tell: the history of the American government. Two of the twelve textbooks in my initial sample were "inquiry" textbooks, mostly assembled from primary sources. They no longer made the story of the state quite so central.[6] The ten narrative textbooks in that sample and all current textbooks continue to pay overwhelming attention to the actions of the executive branch of the federal government. They still demarcate U.S. history as a series of presidential administrations.

Thus, for instance, *Land of Promise* grants each president a biographical vignette, even William Henry Harrison (who served for one month), but never mentions arguably our greatest composer, Charles Ives; our most influential architect, Frank Lloyd Wright; or our most prominent non-Indian humanitarian on behalf of Indians, Helen Hunt Jackson. Although textbook authors include more social history than they used to, they still regard the actions and words of the state as incomparably more important than what the American people were doing, listening to, sleeping in, living through, or thinking about. Particularly for the centuries before the Woodrow Wilson administration, this stress on the state is inappropriate, because the federal executive was not nearly as important then as now.

What story do textbooks tell about our government? First, they imply that the state we live in today is the state created in 1789. Textbook authors overlook the possibility that the balance of powers set forth in the Constitution, granting some power to each branch of the federal government, some to the states, and reserving some for individuals, has been decisively altered over the last two hundred years. The federal government they picture is still the people's servant, manageable and tractable. Paradoxically, textbooks then underplay the role of nongovernmental institutions or private citizens in bringing about improvements in the environment, race relations, education, and other social issues. In short, textbook authors portray a heroic state, and, like their other heroes, this one is pretty much without blemishes. Such an approach converts textbooks into anti–citizenship manuals—handbooks for acquiescence.

Perhaps the best way to show textbooks' sycophancy is by examining how authors treat the government when its actions have been least defensible. Let us begin with considerations relating to U.S. foreign policy.

College courses in political science generally take one of two approaches when analyzing U.S. actions abroad. Some professors and textbooks are quite critical of what might be called the American colossus. In this "American century" (1917–2017?), the United States has been the most powerful nation on earth and has typically acted to maintain its hegemony. This view holds that we Americans abandoned our revolutionary ideology long ago, if indeed we ever held one, and now typically act to repress the legitimate attempts at self-determination of other nations and peoples.

More common is the realpolitik view. George Kennan, who for almost half a century was an architect of and commentator on U.S. foreign policy, provided a succinct statement of this approach in 1948. As head of the Policy Planning Staff of the State Department, Kennan wrote in a now famous memorandum:

> We have about 50% of the world's wealth but only 6.3% of its population. In this situation, we cannot fail to be the object of envy and resentment. Our real test in the coming period is to devise a pattern of relationships which will permit us to maintain this position of disparity. We need not deceive ourselves that we can afford today the luxury of altruism and world benefaction—unreal objectives such as human rights, the raising of living standards, and democratization.[7]

Under this view, the historian or political scientist proceeds by identifying American national interests as articulated by policy makers in the past as well as by historians today. Then s/he analyzes our acts and policies to assess the degree to which they furthered these interests.

High school American history textbooks do not, of course, adopt or even hint at the American colossus view. Unfortunately, they also omit the realpolitik approach. Instead, they take a strikingly different tack. They see our policies as part of a morality play in which the United States typically acts on behalf of human rights, democracy, and "the American way." When Americans have done wrong, according to this view, it has been because others misunderstood us, or perhaps because we misunderstood the situation. But always our motives were good. This approach might be called the "international good guy" view.

Textbooks do not indulge in any direct discussion of what "good" is or might mean. In Frances FitzGerald's phrase, textbooks present the United

States as "a kind of Salvation Army to the rest of the world."[8] In so doing, they echo the nation our leaders like to present to its citizens: the supremely moral, disinterested peacekeeper, the supremely responsible world citizen. "Other countries look to their own interests," said President John F. Kennedy in 1961, pridefully invoking what he termed our "obligations" around the globe. "Only the United States—and we are only six percent of the world's population— bears this kind of burden."[9] Today this "peacekeeping burden" has gotten out of hand: the United States now spends more on its armed forces than all other nations combined and has them stationed in 144 countries. But under the international good guy interpretation fostered by Kennedy and our textbook authors, these actions become symbols of our altruism rather than our hegemony. Since at least the 1920s, textbook authors have also claimed that the United States is more generous than any other nation in the world in providing foreign aid.[10] The myth was untrue then; it is likewise untrue now. Today at least twenty European and Arab nations devote much larger proportions of their gross domestic product (GDP) or total governmental expenditures to foreign aid than does the United States.[11]

The desire to emphasize our humanitarian dealings with the world influences what textbook authors choose to include and omit. All but one of my original twelve textbooks contained at least a paragraph on the Peace Corps, and the tone of these treatments was adoring. "The Peace Corps made friends for America everywhere," gushed *Life and Liberty*. Most recent textbooks agree: "a huge success" claims *The Americans*. Only one book admits any problems. "Curing the ills of needy people was not so simple," Boorstin and Kelley note. "Intelligent young Americans with high ideals seldom had enough of the knowledge or the skills required."

At least the Peace Corps means well. More important and often less affable, American exports are our multinational corporations. One multinational alone, International Telephone and Telegraph (ITT), which took the lead in prompting our government to destabilize the socialist government of Salvador Allende, had more impact on Chile than all the Peace Corps workers America ever sent to Latin America. The same might be said of Union Carbide in India and United Fruit in Guatemala. By influencing U.S. government policies, other American-based multinationals have had even more profound effects on other nations.[12] At times the corporations' influence has been constructive. For example, when President Gerald Ford was trying to persuade Congress to support U.S. military intervention on behalf of the UNITA rebels in Angola's civil

Textbook authors select images to reinforce the idea that our country's main role in the world is to bring about good. This photograph from *The Americans* is captioned "A Peace Corps volunteer gives a ride to a Nigerian girl." I have no quarrel with the Peace Corps, but students should realize that its main impact has been on the intellectual development of its own volunteers.

war, Gulf Oil lobbied against intervention. Gulf was happily producing oil in partnership with Angola's Marxist government when it found its refineries coming under fire from American arms in the hands of UNITA. At other times, multinationals have persuaded our government to intervene when only their corporate interest, not our national interest, was at stake.

All this is a matter of grave potential concern to students, who after graduation may get sent to fight in a foreign country, partly because U.S. policy has been unduly influenced by some Delaware corporation, Texas construction company, or New York bank. Or students may find their jobs eliminated by multinationals that move factories or computer programming to Third World countries whose citizens must work for almost nothing.[13] Social scientists used to describe the world as stratified into a wealthy industrialized center and a poor colonialized periphery; some now hold that multinationals and faster modes of transportation and communication have made management the new center, workers at home and abroad the new periphery. Even if students are not personally affected, they will have to deal with the multinationalization of the world. As multinational corporations such as Wal-Mart and Mitsubishi come to have budgets larger than those of most governments, national economies are becoming obsolete. Robert Reich, secretary of labor in the Clinton administration, has pointed out, "The very idea of an American economy is becoming meaningless, as are the notions of an American corporation, American capital, American products, and American technology."[14] Multinationals may represent a threat to national autonomy, affecting not only small nations but also the United States.

When Americans try to think through the issues raised by the complex interweaving of our economic and political interests, they will not be helped by what they learned in their American history courses. Most history textbooks do not even mention multinationals. The topic doesn't fit their "international good guy" approach. Among my original twelve textbooks, only *American Adventures* even listed *multinationals* in its index, and its treatment consisted of a single sentence: "These investments [in Europe after World War I] led to the development of multinational corporations—large companies with interests in several countries." Even this lone statement was inaccurate: European multinationals date back centuries, and American multinationals have played an important role in our history since at least 1900.

Among the six new books, just two books even mention the term, and both pair it with "benefit." *Pathways to the Present* supplies these two sentences:

> Multinationals benefit consumers and workers around the world by providing new products and jobs and by introducing advanced technologies and production methods. On the other hand, these powerful big businesses sometimes skirt the law by using their economic clout to unduly influence politicians or by devising dishonest ways to keep profits growing.

That's not adequate. Often multinationals bribe the elites of poor countries like Equatorial Guinea, Kazakhstan, and Nigeria. IBM, Monsanto, Schering-Plough, and many other companies have had executives or corporate policies in one country or another found to be corrupt. In Equatorial Guinea, for example, oil companies pay millions of dollars to the regime's leaders for the privilege of taking the country's oil—supporting their children in luxury when they study abroad, leasing buildings from them, and simply paying bribes. Meanwhile, three-fourths of Equatorial Guinea's population suffers from malnutrition. Why do our oil companies do business this way? Because they pay royalties of only about 10 percent for taking Equatorial Guinea's oil—far less than they would pay in a justly-run nation.[15] In the process, these companies comprise an antidemocratic force that helps to solidify the control of a rapacious elite on the country. This is exactly the opposite of what U.S. influence should accomplish, according to either the realpolitik or "international good guy" model. Eventually, as in Iran, our entwinement with regimes like Guinea's may come back to haunt us.

The undue impact of multinationals on governments isn't limited to foreign countries. Textbooks need to discuss their influence on U.S. foreign policy, beginning perhaps with the administration of Woodrow Wilson. Pressure from First National Bank of New York helped prompt Wilson's intervention in Haiti, for example. After Russia's new communist government nationalized all petroleum assets, Standard Oil of New Jersey was "the major impetus" behind the U.S. invasion of Russia in 1918, according to historian Barry Weisberg.[16] Textbooks mystify these circumstances, however. The closest they come to telling the story of economic influences on our foreign policy is in passages such as this, from the current *American Pageant:*

> Hoping to head off trouble, Washington urged Wall Street bankers to pump dollars into the financial vacuums in Honduras and Haiti to keep out foreign funds. The United States, under the Monroe Doctrine, would not permit foreign nations to intervene, and consequently felt obligated to put its money where its mouth was to prevent economic and political instability.

Evidently even our financial interventions were humanitarian! The authors of *Pageant* could use a shot of the realism supplied by former Marine Corps Gen. Smedley D. Butler, whose 1931 statement has become famous:

I helped make Mexico safe for American oil interests in 1914. I helped make Haiti and Cuba a decent place for the National City Bank boys to collect revenue in. I helped purify Nicaragua for the international banking house of Brown Brothers. . . . I brought light to the Dominican Republic for American sugar interests in 1916. I helped make Honduras "right" for American fruit companies in 1903. Looking back on it, I might have given Al Capone a few hints.[17]

Business influence on U.S. foreign policy did not start with Woodrow Wilson's administration. John A. Hobson, in his 1903 book, *Imperialism*, described "a constantly growing tendency" of the wealthy class "to use their political power as citizens of this State to interfere with the political condition of those States where they have an industrial stake."[18] Nor did such influence end with Wilson. Jonathan Kwitny's fine book *Endless Enemies* cites various distortions of U.S. foreign policy owing to specific economic interests of individual corporations and/or to misconceived ideological interests of U.S. foreign policy planners. Kwitny points out that during the entire period from 1953 to 1977, the people in charge of U.S. foreign policy were all on the Rockefeller family payroll. Dean Rusk and Henry Kissinger, who ran our foreign policy from 1961 to 1977, were dependent on Rockefeller payments for their very solvency.[19] Nonetheless, no textbook ever mentions the influence of multinationals on U.S. policy. This is the case not necessarily because textbook authors are afraid of offending multinationals, but because they never discuss *any* influence on U.S. policy. Rather, they present our governmental policies as rational humanitarian responses to trying situations, and they do not seek to penetrate the surface of the government's own explanations of its actions.

Having ignored *why* the federal government acts as it does, textbooks proceed to ignore much of *what* the government does. Textbook authors portray the U.S. government's actions as agreeable and nice, even when U.S. government officials have admitted motives and intentions of a quite different nature. Among the less savory examples are various attempts by U.S. officials and agencies to assassinate leaders or bring down governments of other countries. The United States has indulged in activities of this sort at least since the Wilson administration, which hired two Japanese-Mexicans to try to poison Pancho Villa.[20] I surveyed all eighteen textbooks to see how they treated six more recent U.S. attempts to subvert foreign governments. To ensure that the events were adequately covered in the historical literature, I examined only incidents that occurred before 1973, well before any of these textbooks went to press. The episodes are:

1. Our assistance to the shah's faction in Iran in deposing Prime Minister Mossadegh and returning the shah to the throne in 1953;
2. Our role in bringing down the elected government of Guatemala in 1954;
3. Our rigging of the 1957 election in Lebanon, which entrenched the Christians on top and led to the Muslim revolt and civil war the next year;
4. Our involvement in the assassination of Patrice Lumumba of Zaire in 1961;
5. Our repeated attempts to murder Premier Fidel Castro of Cuba and bring down his government by terror and sabotage; and
6. Our role in bringing down the elected government of Chile in 1973.

The U.S. government calls actions such as these "state-sponsored terrorism" when other countries do them to us. We would be indignant to learn of Cuban or Libyan attempts to influence our politics or destabilize our economy. Our government expressed outrage at Iraq's Saddam Hussein for trying to arrange the assassination of former President George H. W. Bush when he visited Kuwait in 1993 and retaliated with a bombing attack on Baghdad, yet the United States has repeatedly orchestrated similar assassination attempts.

Our review begins auspiciously. Eight of the twelve textbooks I reviewed for the first edition of *Lies* omitted all mention of the CIA coup that put Shah Mohammad Reza Pahlevi in power in Iran in 1953. All six new books do tell of our overthrow of Mossadegh. *The American Pageant* provides this account:

> The government of Iran, supposedly influenced by the Kremlin, began to resist the power of the gigantic Western companies that controlled Iranian petroleum. In response, the . . . CIA helped to engineer a coup in 1953 that installed the youthful shah of Iran, Mohammed Reza Pahlevi, as a kind of dictator. Though successful in the short run in securing Iranian oil for the West, the American intervention left a bitter legacy of resentment among many Iranians.

These sentences do give students some means for understanding why Iranians took over the American embassy in 1979, imprisoning its occupants for more than a year.

Iran's continuing hostility to U.S. policies in the Middle East may explain why textbooks now cover our provocative actions there more fully. Unfortunately, other than about Iran, textbooks have not improved in their treatment of our foreign adventures. In Guatemala, in 1944, college students, urban workers, and members of Guatemala's middle class joined to overthrow a dictator and set up a democratic government. During the next ten years, elected governments extended the vote to American Indians, to the poor (largely synonymous), and to women; ended forced labor on coffee plantations; and enacted other reforms. All this came to an end in 1954, when the CIA threatened the government of Jacobo Arbenz with an armed invasion. Arbenz had antagonized the United Fruit Company by proposing land reform and planning a highway and railroad that might break their trade monopoly. The United States chose an obscure army colonel as the new president, and when Arbenz panicked and sought asylum in the Mexican embassy, we flew our man to the capital aboard the U.S. ambassador's private plane. The result was a repressive junta that treated its Indian majority brutally for another forty years.

Four of six recent textbooks do mention this event. *The American Journey* provides a representative treatment:

> The Eisenhower administration also faced Communist challenges in Latin America. In 1954 the Central Intelligence Agency helped overthrow the government of Jacobo Arbenz in Guatemala, which some American leaders feared was leaning toward communism.

Here *Journey* offers anticommunism as the sole motive for U.S. policies. Bear in mind that this incident took place at the height of McCarthyism, when, as commentator Lewis Lapham has pointed out, the United States saw communism everywhere: "When the duly elected Guatemalan president, Jacobo Arbenz, began to talk too much like a democrat, the United States accused him of communism." [21] Fifty years later *The American Journey* maintains the U.S. government's McCarthyist rhetoric. So do other textbooks, if they mention Guatemala at all.

Not one textbook includes a word about how the United States helped the Christians in Lebanon fix the 1957 parliamentary election in that then tenuously balanced country. The next year, denied a fair share of power by electoral means, the Muslims took to armed combat, and President Eisenhower sent in the marines on the Christians' behalf. Eight of eighteen books discuss that 1958 intervention. *Land of Promise* offers the fullest treatment:

Next, chaos broke out in Lebanon, and the Lebanese President, Camille Chamoun, fearing a leftist coup, asked for American help. Although reluctant to interfere, in July 1958 Eisenhower sent 15,000 United States marines into Lebanon. Order was soon restored, and the marines were withdrawn.

This is standard textbook rhetoric: chaos seems always to be breaking out or about to break out, and Americans intervene only "reluctantly." Other than communism, "chaos" is what textbooks usually offer to explain the actions of the other side. The recent edition of *American Pageant* relies on the older explanation, communism:

> [B]oth Egyptian and communist plottings threatened to engulf Western-oriented Lebanon. After its president had called for aid under the Eisenhower Doctrine, the United States boldly landed several thousand troops and helped restore order without taking a single life.

But communism was never a significant factor in Lebanon, and in other countries it often offers no better explanation than chaos. Kwinty points out that the United States has often behaved so badly in the Third World that some governments and independence movements saw no alternative but to turn to the USSR.[22] Since textbook authors are unwilling to criticize the U.S. government, they present opponents of the United States that are not intelligible. This only misleads and mystifies students. Only by disclosing our actions can textbooks provide readers with rational accounts of our adversaries.

Promise goes on to tell the happy results of our intervention: "Although there was no immediate Communist threat to Lebanon, Eisenhower demonstrated that the United States could react quickly. As a result, tensions in the region receded." In reality, the civil war in Lebanon broke out again in 1975, with mounting destruction in Beirut and throughout the nation. In 1983 a whole lot of chaos broke out, so President Reagan sent in our marines again. A truck bomb then killed 241 marines in their barracks, prompting Reagan to withdraw the rest. Several textbooks tell of this event, but not one offers students anything of substance about the continuity of conflict in Lebanon or our role in causing it. In 2006, "chaos" broke out in Lebanon once more in the form of a miniwar between the Arab nationalist organization Hezbollah and

Israel. Textbooks' shallow discussions of Lebanon's past provide no help to students seeking to understand this new conflict.

Zaire or *the Congo* appears in the index of just two older textbooks, *Triumph of the American Nation* and the 1991 edition of *American Pageant*. Neither book mentions that the CIA urged the assassination of Patrice Lumumba in 1961.[23] *Pageant* offered an accurate account of the beginning of the strife: "The African Congo received its independence from Belgium in 1960 and immediately exploded into violence. The United Nations sent in a peacekeeping force, to which Washington contributed much money but no manpower." There *Pageant* stops. The account in *Triumph of the American Nation* mentioned Lumumba by name: "A new crisis developed in 1961 when Patrice Lumumba, leader of the pro-Communist faction, was assassinated." *Triumph* says nothing about U.S. involvement with the assassination and concludes with the happiest of endings: "By the late 1960s, most scars of the civil war seemed healed. The Congo (Zaire) became one of the most prosperous African nations." Would that it were! The CIA helped bring to power Joseph Mobutu, a former army sergeant. By the end of the 1960s, *Triumph* to the contrary, Zaire under Mobutu had become one of the most wretched African nations, economically and politically. In the first edition of this book, I predicted "in 1994, Zaire is ripe for a 'new' crisis to develop." Indeed, soon civil war did erupt in Zaire, forcing Mobutu to flee in 1997. Various parts of the country have faced continued strife since then, killing almost four million residents. Today's students and authors have no basis to understand this new outbreak of "chaos," however, because not one recent book even mentions Congo/Zaire.

Nor does any textbook, old or new, mention our repeated attempts to assassinate Premier Fidel Castro of Cuba.[24] The federal government had tried to kill Castro eight times by 1965, according to testimony before the U.S. Senate; by 1975 Castro had thwarted twenty-four attempts, according to Cuba. These undertakings ranged from a botched effort to get Castro to light an exploding cigar to a contract with the Mafia to murder him. After the Bay of Pigs invasion failed, President John F. Kennedy launched Operation Mongoose, "a vast covert program" to destabilize Cuba, in the words of Pierre Salinger, Kennedy's press secretary. Salinger also has written that JFK even planned to invade Cuba with U.S. armed forces until forestalled by the Cuban missile crisis.[25] No textbook tells about Operation Mongoose.

Authors' silence about our attempts to assassinate Castro undermines their treatments of the assassination of JFK. Since Kennedy probably ordered several of the earlier attempts on Castro's life personally, including the Mafia contract, Kennedy's own assassination might be explained as a revenge slaying. Of course, Lee Harvey Oswald may have killed Kennedy on his own, and Jack Ruby may have killed Oswald on *his* own. Because no textbook tells how Kennedy tried to kill Castro, however, none can logically suggest a Cuban or Mafia connection in discussing Kennedy's death.[26] Instead, authors limit themselves to vague statements like this, from *Pathways to the Present*: "Some investigations support the theory that Oswald was involved in a larger conspiracy, and that he was killed in order to protect others who had helped plan Kennedy's murder."

Undaunted by its failures in Cuba, the CIA turned its attention farther south. Only six of eighteen textbooks even mention Chile. "President Nixon helped the Chilean army overthrow Chile's elected government because he did not like its radical socialist policies," *Life and Liberty* says bluntly. This single sentence, which is all that *Life and Liberty* offers, lies buried in a section about President Carter's human rights record, but it is the best account in any textbook. Two recent books, *The American Journey* and *Holt American Nation*, echo *Life and Liberty* less bluntly. Three books leave the matter of America's involvement—which is not in question at all—up in the air. The other twelve leave it out entirely.

Why leave our involvement open to question? Historians know that the CIA had earlier joined with ITT to try to defeat Allende in the 1970 elections. Failing this, the United States sought to disrupt the Chilean economy and bring down Allende's government. The United States blocked international loans to Chile, subsidized opposition newspapers, labor unions, and political parties, denied spare parts to industries, paid for and fomented a nationwide truckers' strike that paralyzed the Chilean economy, and trained and financed the military that staged the bloody coup in 1973 in which Allende was killed. The next year, CIA Director William Colby testified that "a secret high-level intelligence committee led by Kissinger himself had authorized CIA expenditures of over eight million dollars during the period 1970–73 to 'destabilize' the government of President Allende."[27] Secretary of State Kissinger himself later explained, "I don't see why we have to let a country go Marxist just because its people are irresponsible."[28] Since the Chilean people's "irresponsibility" consisted of voting for Allende, here Kissinger openly says that the United States should not and will not respect the electoral process or sovereignty of another country if the results do not please us.[29]

Do textbooks need to include all government skullduggery? Certainly not. I am *not* arguing in favor of what Paul Gagnon calls "relentless mentioning."[30]

Textbooks do need to analyze at least *some* of our interventions in depth, however, for they raise important issues. To defend these acts on moral grounds is not easy. The acts diminish U.S. foreign policy to the level of Mafia thuggery, strip the United States of its claim to lawful conduct, and reduce our prestige around the world. To be sure, covert violence may be defensible on realpolitik grounds as an appropriate way to deal with international problems. It can be argued that the United States *should be* destabilizing governments in other countries, assassinating leaders unfriendly to us, and fighting undeclared unpublicized wars. The six cloak-and-dagger operations recounted here do not support this view, however. In Cuba, for instance, the CIA's "pointless sabotage operations," in Rhodri Jeffreys-Jones's words, "only increased Castro's popularity." Even when they succeed, these covert acts provide only a short-term fix, keeping people who worry us out of power for a time, but identifying the United States with repressive, undemocratic, unpopular regimes, hence undermining our long-term interests.[31] The historian Ronald Kessler relates that a CIA officer responsible for engineering Arbenz's downfall in Guatemala agreed later that overthrowing elected leaders is a shortsighted policy.[32] "Was it desirable to trade Mossadegh for the Ayatollah Khomeini?" asks the historian Charles Ameringer about our "success" in Iran. Covert action always risks blowback—retaliation from abroad that we cannot effectively counter because our initial acts were taken without support from the American people. When covert attacks fail, like the Bay of Pigs landing in 1961, they leave the U.S. government with no viable next step short of embarrassed withdrawal or overt military intervention. If instead of covert action we had had a public debate about how to handle Mossadegh or Castro, we might have avoided Khomeini or the Bay of Pigs debacle. Unless we become more open to nationalist governments that embody the dreams of their people, Robert F. Smith believes we will face "crisis after crisis."[33]

This debate cannot take place in American history courses, however, because most textbooks do not let on about what our government has done. Except for Iran, most of the eighteen textbooks I surveyed leave out all six incidents. When authors do treat one or two, they often imply that our actions were based on humanitarian motives. Thus, textbook authors portray the United States basically as an idealistic actor, responding generously to other nations' social and economic woes. Robert Leckie has referred to "the myth of 'the most peace-loving nation in the world'" and noted that it persists "in American folklore." It also persists in our history textbooks.[34]

These interventions raise another issue: Are they compatible with democracy? Covert violent operations against foreign nations, individuals, and political parties violate the openness on which our own democracy relies. Inevitably, covert international interference leads to domestic lying. U.S. citizens cannot possibly critique government policies if they do not know of them. Thus, covert violent actions usually flout the popular will. These actions also threaten our long-standing separation of powers, which textbooks so justly laud in their chapters on the Constitution. Covert actions are always undertaken by the executive branch, which typically lies to the legislative branch about what it has done and plans to do, thus preventing Congress from playing its constitutionally intended role.

The U.S. government lied about most of the six examples of foreign intervention just described. On the same day in 1961 that our Cuban exiles were landing at the Bay of Pigs in their hapless attempt to overthrow Fidel Castro, Secretary of State Dean Rusk said, "The American people are entitled to know whether we are intervening in Cuba or intend to do so in the future. The answer to that question is no." Among the dead three days later were four American pilots. When asked about Chile in his Senate confirmation hearings for U.S. secretary of state in 1973, Henry Kissinger replied, "The CIA had nothing to do with the [Chilean] coup, to the best of my knowledge and belief, and I only put in that qualification in case some madman appears down there who, without instruction, talked to somebody." Later statements by CIA Director William Colby and Kissinger himself directly contradicted this testimony. The U.S. Senate Intelligence Committee eventually denounced our campaign against the Allende government.[35]

President Eisenhower used national security as his excuse when he was caught in an obvious lie: he denied that the United States was flying over Soviet airspace, only to have captured airman Gary Powers admit the truth on Russian television. Much later, the public learned that Powers had been just the tip of the iceberg: in the 1950s we had at least thirty-one flights downed over the USSR, with more than 170 men aboard. For decades our government lied to the families of the lost men and never made substantial representation to the USSR to get them back, because the flights were illegal and were supposed to be secret.[36] Similarly, during the Vietnam War the government kept our bombing of Laos secret for years, later citing national security as its excuse. This did not fool Laotians, who knew full well we were bombing them, but did fool Americans. Often presidents and their advisors keep actions covert not for reasons of tactics abroad, but because they suspect the actions would not be popular with Congress or with the American people.

Over and over, presidents have chosen not to risk their popularity by waging the campaign required to persuade Americans to support their secret military policies.[37] Our Constitution provides that Congress must declare war. Back in 1918 Woodrow Wilson tried to keep our intervention in Russia hidden from Congress and the American people. Helen Keller helped get out the truth: "Our governments are not honest. They do not openly declare war against Russia and proclaim the reasons," she wrote to a New York newspaper in 1919. "They are fighting the Russian people half-secretly and in the dark with the lie of democracy on their lips."[38] Ultimately, Wilson failed to keep his invasion secret, but he was able to keep it hidden from American history textbooks. Therein lies the problem: textbooks cannot report accurately on the six foreign interventions described in this chapter without mentioning that the U.S. government covered them up.

The sole piece of criminal government activity that most textbooks treat is the series of related scandals called Watergate. In its impact on the public, the Watergate break-in stood out. In the early 1970s Congress and the American people learned that President Nixon had helped cover up a string of illegal acts, including robberies of the Democratic National Committee and the office of Lewis Fielding, a psychiatrist. Nixon also tried with some success to use the Internal Revenue Service, the FBI, the CIA, and various regulatory agencies to inspire fear in the hearts of his "enemies list" of people who had dared to oppose his policies or his reelection. In telling of Watergate, textbooks blame Richard Nixon, as they should.[39] But they go no deeper. Faced with this undeniable instance of governmental wrongdoing, they manage to retain their uniformly rosy view of the government. In the representative words of *Pathways to the Present*:

> Many Americans lost a great deal of faith and trust in their government. However, the scandal also proved the strength of the nation's constitutional system, especially its balance of powers. When members of the executive branch violated the law instead of enforcing it, the judicial and legislative branches of government stepped in and stopped them.

Getting rid of Richard Nixon did not solve the problem, however, because the problem is structural, stemming from the vastly increased power of the federal executive bureaucracy. Indeed, in some ways the Iran-Contra scandal of the Reagan and first Bush administrations, a web of secret legal and illegal acts involving the president, vice president, cabinet members, special operatives such as Oliver North, and government officials in Israel, Iran, Brunei, and elsewhere, showed an executive branch more out of control than Nixon's.[40] Textbooks' failure to put Watergate into this perspective is part of their authors' apparent program to whitewash the federal government so that schoolchildren will respect it. Since the structural problem in the government has not gone away, it is likely that students will again, in their adult lives, face an out-of-control federal executive pursuing criminal clandestine foreign and domestic policies—indeed, some have argued that the Bush II administration's post-9/11 behavior amounts to just that.[41] To the extent that their understanding of the government comes from their American history courses, students will be shocked by these events and unprepared to think about them.

"Our country . . . may she always be in the right," toasted Stephen Decatur in 1816, "but our country, right or wrong!" Educators and textbook authors seem to want to inculcate the next generation into blind allegiance to our country. Going a step beyond Decatur, textbook analyses fail to assess our actions abroad according to either a standard of right and wrong *or* realpolitik. Instead, textbooks merely assume that the government tried to do the right thing. Citizens who embrace the textbook view would presumably support *any* intervention, armed or otherwise, and *any* policy, protective of our legitimate national interests or not, because they would be persuaded that all our policies and interventions are on behalf of humanitarian aims. They could never credit our enemies with equal humanity.

This "international good guy" approach is educationally dysfunctional if we seek citizens who are able to think rationally about American foreign policy.[42] To the citizen raised on textbook platitudes, George Kennan's realpolitik may be painful to contemplate. Under the thrall of the America-the-good archetype, we expect more from our country. But Kennan describes how nations actually behave. We would not risk the decline of democracy and the end of Western civilization if we simply let students see a realistic description and analysis of our foreign policies. Doing so would also help close the embarrassing gap between what high school textbooks say about American foreign policy and how their big brothers, college textbooks in political science courses, treat the subject.

When high school history textbooks turn to the internal affairs of the U.S.

government, the books again part company with political scientists. A large chunk of introductory political science course work is devoted to analyzing the various forces that influence our government's domestic policies. High school American history textbooks simply credit the government for most of what gets done. This is not surprising, for when authors idealize the federal government, perforce they also distort the real dynamic between the governed and the government. It is particularly upsetting to watch this happen in the field of civil rights, where the courageous acts of thousands of citizens in the 1960s entreated and even forced the government to act.

Between 1960 and 1968 the civil rights movement repeatedly appealed to the federal government for protection and for implementation of federal law, including the Fourteenth Amendment and other laws passed during Reconstruction. Especially during the Kennedy administration, governmental response was woefully inadequate. In Mississippi, movement offices displayed this bitter rejoinder:

> THERE'S A STREET IN ITTA BENA CALLED FREEDOM.
> THERE'S A TOWN IN MISSISSIPPI CALLED LIBERTY.
> THERE'S A DEPARTMENT IN WASHINGTON CALLED JUSTICE.

The Federal Bureau of Investigation's response to the movement's call was particularly important, since the FBI is the premier national law enforcement agency. The bureau had a long and unfortunate history of antagonism toward African Americans. J. Edgar Hoover and the agency that became the FBI got their start investigating alleged communists during the Woodrow Wilson administration. Although the last four years of that administration saw more antiblack race riots than any other time in our history, Wilson had agents focus on gathering intelligence on African Americans, not on white Americans who were violating blacks' civil rights. Hoover explained the antiblack race riot of 1919 in Washington, D.C., as due to "the numerous assaults committed by Negroes upon white women." In that year the agency institutionalized its surveillance of black organizations, not white organizations like the Ku Klux Klan. In the bureau's early years, there were a few black agents, but by the 1930s Hoover had weeded out all but two. By the early 1960s the FBI had not a single black officer, although Hoover tried to claim it did by counting his chauffeurs.[43] FBI agents in the South were mostly white Southerners who cared what their white Southern neighbors thought of them and were themselves white supremacists. And although this next complaint is reminiscent of the diner who protested that the soup was terrible and there wasn't enough of it, the bureau had far too few agents in the South. In Mississippi it had no office at all and relied for its initial reports on local sheriffs and police chiefs, often precisely the people from whom the civil rights movement sought protection.

Even in the 1960s Hoover remained an avowed white supremacist who thought the 1954 Supreme Court decision outlawing racial segregation in *Brown v. Board of Education* was a terrible error. He helped Kentucky prosecute a Caucasian civil rights leader, Carl Braden, for selling a house in a white neighborhood to a black family. In August 1963 Hoover initiated a campaign to destroy Martin Luther King Jr., and the civil rights movement. With the approval of Attorney General Robert F. Kennedy, he tapped the telephones of King's associates, bugged King's hotel rooms, and made tape recordings of King's conversations with and about women. The FBI then passed on the lurid details, including photographs, transcripts, and tapes, to Senator Strom Thurmond and other white supremacists, reporters, labor leaders, foundation administrators, and, of course, the president. In 1964 a high FBI administrator sent a tape recording of King having sex, along with an anonymous note suggesting that King kill himself, to the office of King's organization, the Southern Christian Leadership Conference (SCLC). The FBI must have known that the incident might not actually persuade King to commit suicide; the bureau's intention was apparently to get Coretta Scott King to divorce her husband or to blackmail King into abandoning the civil rights movement.[44] The FBI tried to sabotage receptions in King's honor when he traveled to Europe to claim the Nobel Peace Prize. Hoover called King "the most notorious liar in the country" and tried to prove that the SCLC was infested with communists. King wasn't the only target: Hoover also passed on disinformation about the Mississippi Summer Project; other civil rights organizations such as CORE (Congress of Racial Equality) and SNCC (Student Nonviolent Coordinating Committee); and other civil rights leaders, including Jesse Jackson.[45]

At the same time the FBI refused to pass on to King information about death threats to him.[46] The FBI knew these threats were serious, for civil rights workers were indeed being killed. In Mississippi alone, civil rights workers endured more than a thousand arrests at the hands of local officials, thirty-five shooting incidents, and six murders. The FBI repeatedly claimed, however, that protecting civil rights workers from violence was not its job.[47] In 1962 SNCC sued Robert F. Kennedy and J. Edgar Hoover to force them to protect civil rights demonstrators. Desperate to get the federal government to enforce the law in the

Deep South, Mississippi civil rights workers Amzie Moore and Robert Moses hit upon the 1964 "Freedom Summer" idea: bring a thousand Northern college students, most of them white, to Mississippi to work among blacks for civil rights. Even this helped little: white supremacists bombed thirty homes and burned thirty-seven black churches in the summer of 1964 alone.[48] After the national outcry prompted by the murders of James Chaney, Andrew Goodman, and Michael Schwerner in Philadelphia, Mississippi, however, the FBI finally opened an office in Jackson. Later that summer, at the 1964 Democratic national convention in Atlantic City, the FBI tapped the phones of the Mississippi Freedom Democratic Party and Martin Luther King Jr.; in so doing, the bureau was complying with a request from President Lyndon Johnson.[49]

Because I lived and did research in Mississippi, I have concentrated on acts of the federal government and the civil rights movement in that state, but the FBI's attack on black and interracial organizations was national in scope. For example, after Congress passed the 1964 Civil Rights Bill, a bowling alley in Orangeburg, South Carolina, refused to obey the law. Students from the nearby black state college demonstrated against the facility. State troopers fired on the demonstrators, killing three and wounding twenty-eight, many of them shot in the balls of their feet as they ran away and threw themselves on the ground to avoid the gunfire. The FBI responded not by helping to identify which officers fired in what became known as "the Orangeburg Massacre," but by falsifying information about the students to help the troopers with their defense.[50] In California, Chicago, and elsewhere in the North, the bureau tried to eliminate the breakfast programs of the Black Panther organization, spread false rumors about venereal disease and encounters with prostitutes to break up Panther marriages, helped escalate conflict between other black groups and the Panthers, and helped Chicago police raid the apartment of Panther leader Fred Hampton and kill him in his bed in 1969.[51] The FBI warned black leader Stokely Carmichael's mother of a fictitious Black Panther plot to murder her son, prompting Carmichael to flee the United States.[52] It is even possible that the FBI or the CIA was involved in the murder of Martin Luther King Jr. "Raoul" in Montreal, who supplied King's convicted killer, James Earl Ray, with the alias "Eric Gault," may have had CIA connections.[53] Certainly Ray, a country boy with no income, could never have traveled to Montreal, arranged a false identity, and flown to London and Lisbon without help. Despite or because of these incongruities, the FBI has never shown any interest in uncovering the conspiracy that killed King. Instead, shortly after King's death in 1968, the

FBI twice broke into SNCC offices. Years later the bureau tried to prevent King's birthday from becoming a national holiday.[54]

The FBI investigated black faculty members at colleges and universities from Virginia to Montana to California. In 1970 Hoover approved the automatic investigation of "all black student unions and similar organizations organized to project the demands of black students." The institution at which I taught, Tougaloo College, was a special target: at one point agents in Jackson even proposed to "neutralize" the entire college, in part because its students had sponsored "out-of-state militant Negro speakers, voter-registration drives, and African cultural seminars and lectures . . . [and] condemned various publicized injustices to the civil rights of Negroes in Mississippi." Obviously high crimes and misdemeanors![55]

The FBI's conduct and the federal leadership that tolerated it and sometimes requested it are part of the legacy of the 1960s, alongside such positive achievements as the 1964 Civil Rights Act and the 1965 Voting Rights Act. As historian Kenneth O'Reilly put it, "When the FBI stood against black people, so did the government."[56] How do American history textbooks treat this legacy? They simply leave out everything bad the government ever did. They omit not only the FBI's campaign against the civil rights movement, but also its break-ins and undercover investigations of church groups, organizations promoting changes in U.S. policy in Latin America, and the U.S. Supreme Court.[57] Textbooks don't even want to say anything bad about *state* governments: all sixteen narrative textbooks in my sample include part of Martin Luther King's "I Have a Dream" speech, but fifteen of them censor his negative comments about the governments of Alabama and Mississippi.

Not only do textbooks fail to blame the federal government for its opposition to the civil rights movement, many actually credit the government, almost single-handedly, for the advances made during the period. In so doing, textbooks follow what we might call the Hollywood approach to civil rights. To date Hollywood's main feature film on the movement is Alan Parker's *Mississippi Burning*.[58] In that movie, the three civil rights workers get killed in the first five minutes; for the rest of its two hours the movie portrays not a single civil rights worker or black Mississippian over the age of twelve with whom the viewer could possibly identify. Instead, Parker concocts two fictional white FBI agents who play out the hoary "good cop/bad cop" formula and in the process double-handedly solve the murders. In reality—that is, in the real story on which the movie is based—supporters of the civil rights movement, including Michael Schwerner's widow, Rita, and every white northern friend the movement could muster, pressured Congress and the executive branch of the federal government to force the FBI to open a Mississippi office and make bringing the murderers to justice a priority. Meanwhile, Hoover tapped Schwerner's father's telephone to see if he might be a communist. Everyone in eastern Mississippi knew for weeks who had committed the murder and that the Neshoba County deputy sheriff was involved. No innovative police work was required; the FBI finally apprehended the conspirators after bribing one of them with $30,000 to testify against the others.[59]

The twelve textbooks I studied for the first edition of this book offered a Parkerlike analysis of the entire civil rights movement. Like the arrests of the Mississippi Klansmen, advances in civil rights were simply the result of good government. Federal initiative in itself "explained" such milestones as the Civil Rights Act of 1964 and the Voting Rights Act of 1965. John F. Kennedy proposed them, Lyndon Baines Johnson passed them through Congress, and thus we have them today. Or, in the immortal passive voice of *American History*, "Another civil rights measure, the Voting Rights Act, was passed." Several textbooks even reversed the time order, putting the bills first, the civil rights movement later. *Challenge of Freedom* provided a typical treatment:

> President Kennedy and his administration responded to the call for racial equality. In June 1963 the President asked for congressional action on far-reaching equal rights laws. Following the President's example, thousands of Americans became involved in the equal rights movement as well. In August 1963 more than 200,000 people took part in a march in Washington, D.C.

This account reverses leader and led. In reality, Kennedy initially tried to stop the march and sent his vice president to Norway to keep him away from it because he felt Lyndon Johnson was too pro–civil rights. Even Arthur Schlesinger Jr., a Kennedy partisan, has dryly noted that "the best spirit of Kennedy was largely absent from the racial deliberations of his presidency."[60]

The damage is not localized to the unfounded boost textbooks give to Kennedy's reputation. The greater danger comes from removing what scholars call "agency" from African Americans. When describing the attack on segregation that culminated in the 1954 Supreme Court decision, the bestselling old book, *Triumph of the American Nation*, and one of the bestselling current books, *The*

American Pageant, make no mention that African Americans were the plaintiffs and attorneys in *Brown v. Board of Education* or that prior cases also brought by the NAACP prepared the way. The latest *Pageant* actually claims that the Kennedys—Jack and Robert—prodded SNCC and other civil rights groups to register blacks to vote. All prodding went the other way around! Today many young African Americans think that desegregation was something the federal government imposed on the black community. They have no idea it was something the black community forced on the federal government.[61] Meanwhile, many young white Americans can reasonably infer that the federal government has been nice enough to blacks. Crediting the federal government for actions instigated by African Americans and their white allies surely disempowers African American students today, and surely helps them feel that they "have never done anything," as Malcolm X put it.

Fortunately, the six recent textbooks do show some improvement. All six tell how attempts by African Americans in Selma, Alabama, to vote led to attacks by white police. All six note that the resulting march from Selma to Montgomery, led by Martin Luther King Jr., prodded LBJ and Congress to pass the 1965 Voting Rights Act. Three of the six current textbooks—*Pathways to the Present, The Americans*, and *American Journey*—show that African Americans forced the federal government to move on civil rights more generally, although they claim that President Kennedy personally favored them.[62] Along with *American Adventures* and *Discovering American History*, these new books do show the basic dynamics of the civil rights movement: African Americans, often with white allies, challenged an unjust law or practice in a nonviolent way, which then incited whites to respond barbarically to defend "civilization," in turn appalling the nation and convincing some people to change the law or practice. These books celebrate the courage of the civil rights volunteers. But only *Discovering American History*, published in 1974, tells how the movement directly challenged the mores of segregation, with the result that some civil rights workers were killed or beaten by white racists simply for holding hands as an interracial couple or eating together in a restaurant.

Textbooks treat the environmental movement similarly, telling how "Congress passed" the laws setting up the Environmental Protection Agency while giving little or no attention to the environmental crusade. Students are again left to infer that the government typically does the right thing on its own, and new books are no better than old ones in this regard. Many teachers don't help; a study of twelve randomly selected teachers of twelfth-grade American government courses found that about the only way the teachers suggested that individuals could influence local or national governments was through voting.[63]

Textbook authors seem to believe that Americans can be loyal to their government only so long as they believe it has never done anything bad. Textbooks therefore present a U.S. government that deserves students' allegiance, not their criticism. "We live in the greatest country in the world," wrote James F. Delong, an associate of the right-wing textbook critic Mel Gabler, in his critique of *American Adventures.* "Any book billing itself as a story of this country should certainly get that heritage and pride across." *American Adventures,* in conveying the basic dynamic of the civil rights movement, implies that the U.S. government was not doing all it should for civil rights. Perhaps as a result, *Adventures* failed Delong's patriotism test: "I will not, I can not endorse it for use in our schools."[64]

The textbooks' sycophantic presentations of the federal government may help win adoptions, but they don't win students' attention. It is boring to read about all the good things the government did on its own, with no dramatic struggles. Moreover, most adult Americans no longer trust the government as credulously as they did in the 1950s. From the Vietnam War to Watergate to Iran-Contragate to Clinton's sex life to the mythical weapons of mass destruction that allegedly caused George W. Bush to invade Iraq, revelation after revelation of misconduct and deceit in the federal executive branch shattered the trust of the American people, as confirmed in poll after opinion poll. In 1964, 64 percent of Americans still trusted the government to "do the right thing"; thirty years later this proportion had dwindled to just 19 percent. Textbook authors, since they are unwilling to say bad things about the government, come across as the last innocents in America. Their trust is poignant. They present students with a benign government whose statements should be believed. This is hardly the opinion of their parents, who, according to opinion polls, remain deeply skeptical of what leaders in the federal government tell them. To encounter so little material in school about the bad things the government has done, especially when parents and the daily newspaper tell a different story, "makes all education suspect," according to education researcher Donald Barr.[65]

Nor can the textbook authors' servile approach to the government teach students to be effective citizens. Just as the story of Columbus-the-wise has as its flip side the archetype of the superstitious unruly crew, so the archetype of a wise and good government implies that the correct role for us citizens is to follow its leadership. Without pushing the point too far, it does seem that many nondemocratic states, from the Third Reich to the Central African Empire to the Democratic People's Republic of (North) Korea, have had citizens who gave their governments too much rather than too little allegiance. The United States, on the other hand, has been blessed with dissenters. Some of these dissenters have had to flee the country. Since 1776, Canada has provided a refuge for Americans who disagreed with policies of the U.S. government, from Tories who fled harassment during and after the Revolution, to free blacks who sought haven from the *Dred Scott* ruling, to young men of draftable age who opposed the Vietnam War. No textbook mentions this Canadian role, because no textbook portrays a U.S. government that might ever merit such principled opposition.[66]

Certainly many political scientists and historians in the United States suggest that governmental actions are a greater threat to democracy than citizen disloyalty. Many worry that the dominance of the executive branch has eroded the checks and balances built into the Constitution. Some analysts also believe that the might of the federal government vis-à-vis state governments has made a mockery of federalism. From the Woodrow Wilson administration until now, the federal executive has grown ever stronger and now looms as by far our nation's largest employer. In the last fifty years, the power of the CIA, the National Security Council, and other covert agencies has grown to become, in some eyes, a fearsome fourth branch of government. Threats to democracy abound when officials in the FBI, the CIA, the State Department, and other institutions of government determine not only our policies but also what the people and the Congress need to know about them.[67]

By downplaying covert and illegal acts by the government, textbook authors narcotize students from thinking about such issues as the increasing dominance and secrecy of the executive branch. By taking the government's side, textbooks encourage students to conclude that criticism is incompatible with citizenship. And by presenting government actions in a vacuum, rather than as responses to such institutions as multinational corporations and civil rights organizations, textbooks mystify the creative tension between the people and their leaders. All this encourages students to throw up their hands in the belief that the government determines everything anyway, so why bother, especially if its actions are usually so benign. Thus, our American history textbooks minimize the potential power of the people and, despite their best patriotic efforts, take a stance that is overtly antidemocratic.

9.

SEE NO EVIL

CHOOSING NOT TO LOOK AT THE WAR IN VIETNAM

If we do not speak of it, others will surely rewrite the script. Each of the body bags, all of the mass graves will be reopened and their contents abracadabraed into a noble cause. —GEORGE SWIERS, VIETNAM VETERAN[1]

We have destroyed their two most cherished institutions: the family and the village. We have destroyed their land and their crops. . . . We have corrupted their women and children and killed their men. —MARTIN LUTHER KING JR.[2]

Without censorship, things can get terribly confused in the public mind.
—GEN. WILLIAM WESTMORELAND[3]

He is a lover of his country who rebukes and does not excuse its sins.
—FREDERICK DOUGLASS[4]

AS WE COLLEGE PROFESSORS get older, we grow ever more astonished at what our undergraduates don't know about the recent past. I first became aware of this phenomenon as the 1970s inexorably became the 1980s. Lecturing on the Vietnam War, I increasingly got blank looks. One in four, then one in two, and in the 1990s four in five first-year college students did not know the meaning of the four-letter words *hawk* and *dove*. On the first day of class in 1989 I gave my students a quiz including the open-ended question, "Who fought in the war in Vietnam?" Almost a fourth of my students said the combatants were North and South Korea! I was stunned—to me this resembled answering "1957" to the question "When did the War of 1812 begin?" In fact, many recent high school graduates know more about the War of 1812 than about the Vietnam War.[5]

It makes little sense and surely does no good to blame the students. It can hardly be their fault. If our civic memories begin when we are about ten years old, then the last students to have any memory of the Vietnam War graduated from high school in the spring of 1983. The war is unknown territory to *the parents* of most high school students today. So are the women's movement, Watergate, and the Iran hostage crisis. Students need information about the Vietnam War from their high school American history courses.

In the textbooks of the 1980s they did not get much. Since the war ended in 1975, even the earliest of these books had the benefit of hindsight in teaching about the conflict that has often been called "America's longest war," as well as the advantage of their authors' personal knowledge of the event. They squander these advantages.

Comparing coverage of the Vietnam War and the War of 1812 in my original twelve textbooks illuminates the problem. The War of 1812 took place almost two centuries ago and killed maybe two thousand Americans. Nevertheless, the high school history books in my original sample devoted the same quantitative coverage—nine pages—to the War of 1812 and the Vietnam War. One might argue, I suppose, that the War of 1812 was so much more important than the Vietnam War that it deserves as much space, even though it took place so long ago. Our textbooks made no such claim; most authors didn't know what to make of the War of 1812 and claimed no particular importance for it.

Since the War of 1812 lasted only half as long as the Vietnam War, authors treated it in far more detail. They enjoyed the luxury of telling about individual battles and heroes. *Land of Promise,* for instance, devoted three paragraphs to a naval battle off Put-in-Bay Island in Lake Erie, which works out to one paragraph per hour of battle. Vietnam got no such coverage.

Scant space was only part of the problem. Nine gripping analytic pages on the Vietnam War might prove more than adequate.[6] We must ask what kind of coverage textbooks provided.

In the original edition of *Lies,* I did not set out my own account of the war and then critique authors for presenting an analysis different from my own. Instead, to avoid the charge of subjectivity, I focused on the photographs the textbooks supplied. The Vietnam War was distinguished by a series of images that seared themselves into the public consciousness. I identified seven of these images: five famous photos (such as the little girl running naked toward the camera as she fled a napalm attack, and the bodies piled in the ditch at the My Lai massacre) and two generic images of the war's destructiveness. Photographs have been part of the record of war in the United States since Matthew Brady's famous images of the Civil War. In Vietnam, television images joined still photos to shape the perceptions and sensibility of the American people. Even including our two recent wars in Iraq, Vietnam is still our most photographed and televised war.

I asked dozens of adults old enough to have lived during the war to tell me what visual images they remember; the list of images they supplied shows remarkable overlap. A short list includes these five specific images:

1. A Buddhist monk sitting at a Saigon intersection immolating himself to protest the South Vietnamese government;
2. The little girl running naked down Highway 1, fleeing a napalm attack;
3. The national police chief executing a terrified man, a member of the Vietcong, with a pistol shot to the side of his head;
4. The bodies in the ditch after the My Lai massacre; and
5. Americans evacuating from a Saigon rooftop by helicopter while desperate Vietnamese try to climb aboard.

The list also included two generic images: B-52s with bombs streaming below them into the pockmarked countryside of Vietnam, and a ruined city such as

Quang Duc, the first Buddhist monk to set himself on fire to protest the policies of the Ngo Dinh Diem regime that the United States supported in South Vietnam, shocked the South Vietnamese and the American people. Before the war ended, several other Vietnamese and at least one American followed Quang Duc's example.

This little girl, Kim Phuc, ran screaming down Highway 1, fleeing from an accidental napalm attack on her village by South Vietnamese airplanes. She had stripped off her burning clothing as she ran. The television footage and still photographs of her flight were among the most searing of the war. The photograph violates two textbook taboos at once: no textbook ever shows anyone naked, and none shows such suffering, even in time of war.

Hué, nothing but rubble in view, as American and South Vietnamese troops move in to retake it after the Tet offensive.[7]

Merely reading these short descriptions prompts most older Americans to remember the images in sharp detail. The emotions that accompanied them come back vividly as well. Of course, since the main American involvement in the war took place from 1965 to 1973, Americans must be well over forty to recall these images today. Young people have little chance to see or recall these images unless their history books provide them.

In 1995 the twelve textbooks in my original sample failed miserably. One book, *The American Pageant*, included one of these pictures: the police chief shooting the terrified man.[8] No other textbook reproduced any of them. *The American Adventures* contained an image of our bombing Vietnam, but the photograph showed B-52s and bombs from below and gave no sense of any damage on the ground. Thus, there remained huge room for improvement.

The seven cited images are important examples of the primary materials of the Vietnam War. Hawks (people who were pro-war) might claim that these images exaggerate the aspects of the war they portray. However, these images have additional claims to historical significance: they actually *made* history, prompt-

Nguyen Ngoc Loan, the national police chief of South Vietnam, casually shot this man, a member of the Vietcong, on a street in Saigon on February 1, 1968, as an American photographer and television crew looked on. This photograph helped persuade many Americans that their side was not morally superior to the communists.[10] The image is so haunting that, forty years later, I have only to cock my fingers like a gun and people who were old enough to read newspapers or watch television in 1968 immediately recall the event and can describe it in some detail.

ing news stories and changing the way viewers around the world understood the conflict. Several of these photographs remain "among the most well-known images in the world even now [1991]," according to Patrick Hagopian, who studied the ways America memorialized the Vietnam War.[9] Leaving them out shortchanges today's readers. As a student of mine wrote, "To show a photograph of one naked girl crying after she has been napalmed changes the entire meaning of that war to a high school student."

In Vietnam the United States dropped three times as many explosives as it dropped in all theaters of World War II, even including our nuclear bombing of Hiroshima and Nagasaki, so textbook authors had many images of bomb damage to choose from. On the ground, after the Tet offensive, in which Vietcong and North Vietnamese troops captured cities and towns all over South Vietnam, American and South Vietnamese troops shelled Hué, Ben Tre, Quang Tri, and other cities before moving in to retake them. Nonetheless, not one textbook showed any damage done by our side.

That was then. Chapter 11 shows how the Vietnam War was still considered

Left: In the My Lai massacre American combat troops murdered women, old men, and children. Ronald Haeberle's photographs, including this one, which ran in *Life* magazine, seared the massacre into the nation's consciousness and still affect our culture.[11] Most Hollywood movies made about Vietnam include My Lai imagery; *Platoon* offers a particularly vivid example.

Right: On April, 29, 1975, this American helicopter evacuated people from a Saigon rooftop. The next day Saigon fell, and the long American (and Vietnamese) nightmare came to an end. More than half of all Americans alive today were younger than ten or not yet born when this photograph was taken. Thus, most Americans know the war only from movies and textbooks. On January 14, 2007, the *Washington Post* devoted half a page to this image, with the caption: "Iraq Endgame: Will It Look Like This?"

recent in the 1980s and early 1990s, and textbooks always slight the recent past, no matter how important it was. How do they do today, now that the war has receded into the distant past for most Americans?

Two "legacy textbooks"—Boorstin and Kelley and *The American Pageant*—descended from books originally published half a century ago, still aimlessly give the War of 1812 about as much space as the Vietnam War. Neither includes even one of the important images of the Vietnam War. *Pageant* actually moved backward: it dropped its photo of the police chief executing the Vietcong man.

The three "really new" books, along with *Holt American Nation* (distantly descended from Todd and Curti, *Triumph of the American Nation*), provide much more coverage. *The Americans* gives the war more than thirty-four pages. Still, a certain softness inhibits its treatment. Although *The Americans* includes twenty-one illustrations of the war, only one—the monk immolating himself—comes from my list of seven. Not one of twenty-one photos shows any damage the United States inflicted upon Vietnam. *Pathways to the Present* also includes the immolation image, and it and *American Journey* show the evacuation from the rooftop near our embassy. *Journey* also provides a generic rubble photo. *Holt* shows a landscape pockmarked by B-52 craters. Among all six books, that's it.

Of course, the authors and editors of textbooks choose among thousands of images of the Vietnam War. They might make different selections and still do justice to the war. But at the very least they must show atrocities against the Vietnamese civilian population, for these were a frequent and even inevitable part of this war without front lines, in which our armed forces had only the foggiest notion as to who was ally or opponent. Indeed, attacks on civilians were U.S. policy, as shown by Gen. William C. Westmoreland's characterization of civilian casualties: "It does deprive the enemy of the population, doesn't it?"[12] We evaluated our progress by body counts and drew free-fire zones in which the entire civilian population was treated as the enemy. Such a strategy inevitably led to war crimes. Any photograph of an American soldier setting fire to a Vietnamese *hootch* (house), a common sight during the war, would get this point across, but no textbook shows such an act.[13] *American Journey* includes a shot of marines climbing "a mound of rubble that was once a tower of the fortress of Hué." Readers might be able to infer that our munitions reduced the fortress to rubble, so that photograph qualifies as the only illustration of *any* destruction, even of legitimate targets, clearly caused by our side, to be found in any textbook. Today's textbooks seem to be supplying precisely the censorship that Gen. William Westmoreland wished for (in the quote at the head of the chapter), while he was in command. Unfortunately, censorship is the cause, not the remedy, of confusion about the war.

My Lai was not a minor event, unworthy of inclusion in a nation's history, but was important precisely because it was emblematic of much of what went wrong with the entire war in Vietnam. My Lai was the most famous instance of what John Kerry, formerly of Vietnam Veterans Against the War, now U.S. senator, called "not isolated incidents but crimes committed on a day-to-day basis with the full awareness of officers at all levels of command." Appearing before the Senate Foreign Relations Committee in April 1971, Kerry said, "Over one hundred and fifty honorably discharged and many very highly decorated veterans testified to war crimes committed in Southeast Asia." He went on to retell how American troops "had personally raped, cut off ears, cut off heads, taped wires from portable telephones to human genitals and turned up the power, cut off limbs, blown up bodies, randomly shot at civilians, razed villages in fashion reminiscent of Genghis Khan, shot cattle and dogs for fun, poisoned food stocks, and generally ravaged the countryside of South Vietnam." All this was "in addition to the normal ravage of war," as Kerry pointed out in his testimony.[14]

Only *Discovering American History*, the oldest textbook in my sample, treats the My Lai massacre as anything but an isolated incident. *The Americans* has a perfectly adequate paragraph on My Lai, far better than any other new book, but it never mentions that attacks on civilians were a general problem. In addition to leaving students ignorant of the history of the war, textbook silence on this matter also makes the antiwar movement incomprehensible.

Two textbook authors, James West Davidson and Mark H. Lytle, are on record elsewhere as knowing of the importance of My Lai. "The American strategy had atrocity built into it," Lytle said to me. Davidson and Lytle devote most of a chapter to the My Lai massacre in their book *After the Fact.* There they tell how news of the massacre stunned the United States. "One thing was certain," they write, "the encounter became a defining moment in the public's perception of the war."[15] Plainly they do not think high school students need to know about it, however, for their high school history textbook, *The United States—A History of the Republic*, like ten other textbooks in my sample, never mentions My Lai.[16]

If textbooks omit the important photographs of the Vietnam War, what images *do* they include? Uncontroversial shots, for the most part—servicemen

The only photograph of troops in *Triumph of the American Nation* shows them happily surrounding President Johnson when he visited the American base at Cam Ranh Bay during the war.

on patrol, walking through swamps, or jumping from helicopters. Ten books show refugees or damage caused by the *other* side, but since such damage was usually less extensive than that caused by our bombardment, the pictures are not very dramatic.

This is an outrage, and there is no excuse for it. Joy Hakim shows we can do better in her textbook *A History of US*, intended for about fifth grade. She includes the police chief shooting the terrified man, another image of a guard threatening a Vietnamese POW with a knife, a photograph of a town destroyed by "our side," and the most famous image of the My Lai massacre. Surprisingly, Hakim also gives her readers the image of the little girl running naked down Highway 1. This is surprising because textbook publishers typically follow the rule of "no nudity"; as one editor told me, "in elementary books *cows* don't have udders." Yet her series has been a bestseller—perhaps because it also reads better than most standard textbooks.

What about their prose? Sadly, most textbook authors also leave out all the memorable quotations of the era. No textbook quotes the trademark cadences of Martin Luther King Jr., the first major leader to come out against the war, reproduced at the head of this chapter.[17] Even more famous was the dissent of Muhammad Ali, then heavyweight boxing champion of the world. Ali refused induction into the military, for which his title was stripped from him, and said, "No Vietcong ever called me 'nigger.'" All eighteen textbooks leave out that line, too. After the Tet offensive, a U.S. army officer involved in retaking Ben Tre said, "It became necessary to destroy the town to save it." For millions of Americans, this statement summarized America's impact on Vietnam. No textbook supplies it.[18] Nor does any textbook quote John Kerry's plea for immediate withdrawal: "How do you ask a man to be the last man to die for a mistake?"[19] Most books also exclude the antiwar songs, the chants—"Hell, no; we won't go!" and "Hey, hey, LBJ, how many kids did you kill today?"—and, above all, the emotions. Indeed, the entire antiwar movement becomes unintelligible in many textbooks, because they do not allow it to speak for itself. Virtually the only people who do get quoted are Presidents Johnson and Nixon and Secretary of State Henry Kissinger.[20]

Three new books do better. The new *Pageant* and *We Americans* include the chants from the opposition. They as well as *Pathways to the Present* give more space to the antiwar movement and to the dirty underside of the war than did older texts. The improvement may reflect that, with the passage of time, the Vietnam War is no longer very recent or very controversial, as we shall see below. Authors may be coming to treat the war more forthrightly, as they now treat slavery, now that the Cold War, like formal segregation against African Americans, has ended.

However, their coverage is jerky, perhaps reflecting the multiple authors who probably wrote it. Chapter 12 explains that the authors listed on the covers of high school American history textbooks often did not write them, especially in their later editions. Two competing books show this problem in their treatment of Vietnam.

Because some of the enemy lived amidst the civilian population, it was difficult for U.S. troops to discern friend from foe. A woman selling soft drinks to U.S. soldiers might be a Vietcong spy. A boy standing on the corner might be ready to throw a grenade.

—*The Americans*

American troops . . . never could be sure who was a friend and who was an enemy. The Vietnamese woman selling soft drinks by the roadside might be a Viet Cong ally, counting government soldiers as they passed. A child peddling candy might be concealing a live grenade.

—*Pathways to the Present*

It is hardly likely that independent authors wrote these two passages. Did Gerald Danzer (or one of his "coauthors") copy and modify from *Pathways*? Did Alan Winkler (or one of his "coauthors") copy and modify from *The Americans*? If so, one should charge the other with plagiarism. No one ever does, however—not about high school textbooks—because everyone in the publishing industry knows that their "authors" did not really write them. Probably the publishers of *Pathways* and *The Americans* happened to hire the same freelancer to write or update both books. Still other unnamed clerks add photos and write captions and teaching suggestions.

Using different unnamed authors for different chapters, different features, and different updates is not only misleading, since school systems choose textbooks partly because they think distinguished historians wrote them. It also makes textbooks less coherent. Often different paragraphs in the core narrative contradict each other. To present contrasting viewpoints would be fine, but that is not what textbooks do. Instead, their treatments of the war amount to one thing after another, displaying little overall organization and no point of view or interpretation. They cannot be organized, because they were written by what amount to disorganized sequential committees that never met. That's why Frances FitzGerald, who, in addition to *America Revised* wrote *Fire in the Lake*, a fine book about Vietnam, called the textbooks she reviewed in 1979 "neither hawkish nor dovish on the war—they are simply evasive." She went on to say, "Since it is really quite hard to discuss the war and evade all the major issues, their Vietnam sections make remarkable reading."[21]

To some degree, defining the issues is a matter of interpretation, and I would not want to fault textbooks for holding a different interpretation from my own. Perhaps we can agree that any reasonable treatment of the Vietnam War would discuss at least these six questions:

Why did the United States fight in Vietnam?
What was the war like before the United States entered it? How did we change it?
How did the war change the United States?
Why did an antiwar movement become so strong in the United States? What were its criticisms of the war in Vietnam? Were they right?
Why did the United States lose the war?
What lesson(s) should we take from the experience?

Simply to list these questions is to recognize that each of them is still controversial. Take the first. Some people still argue that the United States fought in Vietnam to secure access to the country's valuable natural resources. The "international good guy" approach noted in the last chapter would claim that we fought to bring democracy to Vietnam's people. Perhaps more common are analyses of our internal politics: Democratic Presidents Kennedy and Johnson, having seen how Republicans castigated Truman for "losing" China, did not want to be seen as "losing" Vietnam. One realpolitik approach stresses the domino theory: while we know now that Vietnam's communists are antagonists of China, we didn't then, and some leaders believed that if Vietnam "fell" to the communists, so would Thailand, Malaysia, Indonesia, and the Philippines. Yet another view is that America felt its prestige was on the line, so it did not want a defeat in Vietnam, lest Pax Americana be threatened in Africa, South America, or elsewhere in the world.[22] Some conspiracy theorists go even further and claim that big business fomented the war to help the economy. Other historians take a longer view, arguing that our intervention in Vietnam derives from a cultural pattern of racism and imperialism that began with the first Indian war in

Virginia in 1622, continued in the nineteenth century with "Manifest Destiny," and is now winding down in the "American century." They point out that GIs in Vietnam collected and displayed Vietnamese ears just as British colonists in North America collected and displayed Indian scalps.[23] A final view might be that there was no clear cause and certainly no clear purpose, that we blundered into the war because no subsequent administration had the courage to undo our 1946 mistake of opposing a popular independence movement. "The fundamental blunder with respect to Indochina was made after 1945," wrote Secretary of State John Foster Dulles, when "our Government allowed itself to be persuaded" by the French and British "to restore France's colonial position in Indochina."[24]

Perhaps the seeds of America's tragic involvement with Vietnam were sown at Versailles in 1918, when Woodrow Wilson failed to hear Ho Chi Minh's plea for his country's independence. Perhaps they germinated when FDR's policy of not helping the French recolonize Southeast Asia after World War II terminated with his death. Since textbooks rarely suggest that the events of one period caused events of the next, unsurprisingly, none of the textbooks I surveyed looks before the 1950s to explain the Vietnam War.

Within the 1950s and 1960s, the historical evidence for some of these conflicting interpretations is much weaker than for others, although I will not choose sides here.[25] Textbook authors need not choose sides, either. They could present several interpretations, along with an overview of the historical support for each, and invite students to come to their own conclusions. Such challenges are not the textbook authors' style, however. They seem compelled to present the "right" answer to all questions, even unresolved controversies.

So which interpretation do they choose? None of the above! Most textbooks simply dodge the issue. Here is a representative analysis, from *American Adventures*: "Later in the 1950s, war broke out in South Vietnam. This time the United States gave aid to the South Vietnamese government." "War broke out"—what could be simpler? *Adventures* devotes four pages to discussing why we got into the War of 1812 but just these two sentences to why we fought in Vietnam. Newer textbooks simply rely on anticommunism to explain U.S. involvement.

Teachers are unlikely to make up for the deficiencies in their textbooks' treatment of the war. According to Linda McNeil, most teachers particularly don't want to teach about Vietnam. "Their memories of the Vietnam War era made them wish to avoid topics on which the students were likely to disagree with their views or that would make the students 'cynical' about American institutions." Therefore, in the 1980s, the average teacher granted the Vietnam War 0 to 4.5 *minutes* in the entire school year. Coverage has not increased much since then; many college students report that their high school history courses wound down about the time of the Korean War.[26]

Neither our textbooks nor most teachers help students think critically about the Vietnam War and marshall historical evidence to support their conclusions. Never do they raise questions like "Was the war right? Was it ethical?" Some books appear to raise moral issues but veer away. For example, *Challenge of Freedom* asks, "Why did the United States use so much military power in South Vietnam?" Attempting to answer this question could get interesting: Because our antagonists weren't white? Because they couldn't strike at the United States? Because we had it available? Because the United States has a history of imperialism vis-à-vis "primitive" peoples from our Indian wars through the Philippine-American War of 1899–1913 to Vietnam? Because, like most other nations, we behave not by standards of morality but of realpolitik? The answer that *Challenge* suggests to teachers, however, shows that the authors don't really want students to think about why we intervened and certainly not about whether we should have done so, but merely to regurgitate President Johnson's stated rationale for so much bombing, which the book has previously supplied: "To show the Vietcong and their ally, North Vietnam, that they could not win the war." This answer is mystifying, since the Vietcong and North Vietnam *did* win the war; moreover, the authors' claim to know Johnson's motivation arrives without evidence. In the rhetorical climate created by this textbook, for a teacher to raise a moral question would come across as a violation of classroom norms.

Similarly, Boorstin and Kelley mostly ask regurgitation items like "Identify Dean Rusk," occasionally interspersed with "Critical Thinking" questions like "How did the Tonkin Gulf incident lead to our increased involvement in Vietnam?" In fact, on August 2, 1964, a U.S. destroyer, *Maddox*, was cruising the Tonkin Gulf four miles from islands belonging to North Vietnam. At the same time, smaller U.S. boats were ferrying South Vietnamese commandos to attack some of those islands. Three North Vietnamese patrol boats fired torpedos at *Maddox*, missing; the destroyer crippled two of them and sank the third. North Vietnam protested to the International Control Commission. The next day, as the smaller U.S. boats ferried South Vietnamese commandos to attack mainland targets this time, *Maddox* returned, thought it was again attacked, and fired in all directions. Soon it became fairly clear that the attacks were phantoms caused by weather and misinterpretations of sonar. Nevertheless, President Johnson professed outrage and sent what came to be called the "Gulf of Tonkin Resolution" to Congress, where it passed overwhelmingly. This resolution authorized the president to do whatever he wanted in Vietnam, and he used it immediately to begin bombing North Vietnam. Real "critical thinking" might lead students to conclude that the question has it backward: our increased involvement in Vietnam led to the Tonkin Gulf incident, especially since the second attack on *Maddox*, upon which "our increased involvement in Vietnam" was predicated, never happened. (As Johnson confided to an aide at the time, "Those dumb stupid sailors were just shooting at flying fish."[27]) Unfortunately, except for the old *Discovering American History*, published in 1974, all high school history textbooks I surveyed shy away from actually prompting students to think critically about the Vietnam War.

Ironically, students could probably get away with critical thinking without upsetting their parents. At least 70 percent of Americans now consider the Vietnam War to have been morally wrong as well as tactically inept.[28] That's quite a consensus. Nevertheless, the strident arguments about the military records of George W. Bush and John Kerry in the 2004 presidential campaign showed that the war can still be controversial. Fear of controversy may be why Florida's Disney World, in its "American Adventure" exhibit, a twenty-nine-minute history of the United States, completely, if awkwardly, leaves out the Vietnam War. And it may explain why history textbooks omit the images and the issues that might trouble students—or their parents—today.

Mystifying the Vietnam War has left students unable to understand much public discourse since then. Politicians across the political spectrum invoked "the lessons of Vietnam" as they debated intervening in Angola, Lebanon, Kuwait, Somalia, Bosnia, and, most recently, Iraq. Bumper stickers reading EL SALVADOR IS SPANISH FOR VIETNAM helped block sending U.S. troops to that nation. John Dumbrell and David Ryan's *Vietnam in Iraq* and Robert Brigham's *Is Iraq Another Vietnam?* draw specific parallels between those two seemingly endless wars.[29] In 2006 Henry Kissinger used his perverse misreading of our Vietnam debacle— he blames Congress for pulling out—to advise George W. Bush to "stay the course" in Iraq.[30] "The lessons of Vietnam" have also been used to inform or mislead discussions about secrecy, the press, how the federal government operates, and even whether the military should admit gays. High school graduates have a right to enough knowledge about the Vietnam War to participate intelligently in such debates. After all, they are the people who will be called upon to fight in our next (and our ongoing) war—whether it resembles Vietnam or not.[31]

IO.

DOWN THE MEMORY HOLE:

THE DISAPPEARANCE OF THE RECENT PAST

We see things not as they are but as we are. —ANAÏS NIN

Patriotism can flourish only where racism and nationalism are given no quarter. We should never mistake patriotism for nationalism. A patriot is one who loves his homeland. A nationalist is one who scorns the homelands of others. —JOHANNES RAU[1]

Of course the people do not want war. . . . But, after all, it is the leaders of the country who determine the policy, and it is always a simple matter to drag the people along, whether it is a democracy, a fascist dictatorship, a parliament, or a communist dictatorship. Voice or no voice, the people can always be brought to the bidding of the leaders. That is easy. All you have to do is tell them that they are being attacked and denounce the pacifists for lack of patriotism. —GERMAN FIELD MARSHALL
HERMANN GOERING, NUREMBERG, APRIL 18, 1946[2]

When information which properly belongs to the public is systematically withheld by those in power, the people soon become ignorant of their own affairs, distrustful of those who manage them, and—eventually—incapable of determining their own destinies. —RICHARD M. NIXON[3]

MANY AFRICAN SOCIETIES divide humans into three categories: those still alive on the earth, the *sasha*, and the *zamani*. The recently departed whose time on earth overlapped with people still here are the *sasha*, the living-dead. They are not wholly dead, for they still live in the memories of the living, who can call them to mind, create their likeness in art, and bring them to life in anecdote. When the last person to know an ancestor dies, that ancestor leaves the *sasha* for the *zamani*, the dead. As generalized ancestors, the *zamani* are not forgotten but revered. Many, like George Washington or Clara Barton, can be recalled by name. But they are not living-dead. There is a difference.[4]

Because we lack these Kiswahili terms, we rarely think about this distinction systematically, but we also make it. Consider how we read an account of an event we lived through, especially one in which we ourselves took part, whether a sporting event or the Iraq War. We read partly in a spirit of criticism, assessing what the authors got wrong as well as agreeing with and perhaps learning from what they got right. When we study the more distant past, we may also read critically, but now our primary mode is ingestive. Especially if we are reading for the first time about an event, we have little ground on which to stand and criticize what we read.

Authors of American history textbooks appear all too aware of the *sasha*—of the fact that teachers, parents, and textbook adoption board members were alive in the recent past. They seem uncomfortable with it. Revering the *zamani*—generalized ancestors—is more their style. By definition, the world of the *sasha* is controversial, because readers bring to it their own knowledge and understanding, so they may not agree with what is written. Therefore, the less said about the recent past, the better.

I examined how the ten narrative American histories in my original sample covered the five decades leading up to the 1980s. (I excluded the 1980s because some of the older textbooks came out in that decade, so they could not be expected to cover it fully.) On average, the textbooks give forty-seven pages to the 1930s, forty-four to the 1940s, and fewer than thirty-five pages to each later decade. Even the turbulent decade of the 1960s—including the civil rights movement, most of the Vietnam War, and the murders of Martin Luther King Jr., Medgar Evers, Malcolm X, and John and Robert Kennedy—got fewer than thirty-five pages.[5]

Textbooks in 2006–07 show quite a different approach. Now the 1960s are no longer recent history, so textbooks can give them the emphasis they should always have received, fifty-five pages. (That total is greater than for any other decade of the twentieth century.) But today's texts, published between 2000 and 2007, give short shrift to the new recent past, the 1980s, 1990s, and 2000s.[6] Now they devote forty-nine pages to the 1930s and forty-seven to the 1940s, but fewer than twenty to the 1980s and 1990s (even tossing in the first years of the new millennium). Yet these were important decades in which the United States twice attacked Iraq, went through the second presidential impeachment trial in history, saw its closest and most disputed election in more than a century, and endured the terrorist strikes of 9/11/2001.

Each of these matters is still contentious, however. Some parents are Democrats, some Republicans, so what authors say about the impeachment and trial of Bill Clinton will likely offend half the community. An increasing proportion of Americans believe the Iraq War to be a bad idea, but if authors say that, they will alienate some important people, perhaps including school board members. Homosexuality is even more taboo as a subject of discussion or learning in American high schools. Affirmative action leads to angry debates. The women's movement can still be a minefield, even though it peaked in the 1970s. Every school district includes parents who strongly affirm traditional sex roles and others who do not. So let's not say much about feminism today; let's leave it in the 1970s. Thus authors tiptoe through the *sasha* with extreme caution, evading all the main issues, all the "why" questions.

Textbook authors are not solely responsible for the slighting of the recent past in high school history courses. Many teachers also lack courage or simply run out of time. Even if textbooks gave the *sasha* the space it deserves, most students would have to read about it on their own, because most teachers never get near the end of the textbook. In her yearlong American history course, fifth-grade teacher Chris Zajac, subject of Tracy Kidder's *Among Schoolchildren*, never gets past Reconstruction![7] Time is not the only problem. Like publishers, teachers do not want to risk offending parents. The result is a treatment of the recent past along the line suggested by Thumper's mom: "If you can't say somethin' nice, don't say nothin' at all."

One excuse authors and publishers sometimes give for their compressed and bland accounts of the recent past in American history textbooks is precisely that it is so recent. We don't know how historians will view the period once they have achieved the detachment that historical perspective will bring, so the less said, the better.

For topics in the *zamani*, textbook authors do indeed use historical perspective as a shield. By writing in an omniscient boring tone about events in the *zamani*, authors imply that a single historic truth exists, upon which historians have agreed and which they now teach and students should now memorize. Such writing implies that our historical perspective grows ever more accurate with the passage of time, blessing today's textbook authors with cumulative historical insight. They cannot use historical perspective to defend their treatment of events in the *sasha*, however. Without historical perspective, textbook authors appear naked: no particular qualification gives them the right to narrate recent events with the same Olympian detachment and absolute certainty with which they declaim on events in the *zamani*. As well, textbooks are tertiary sources, supposed to be based on secondary sources, and these books and articles have mostly not yet been written about the very recent past.

As usually thought about, historical perspective does implicitly justify neglecting the *sasha*. Historians tell us how we are too close to recent events to be able to step back and view them in context. As new material becomes available in archives, they claim, or as the consequences of actions become clearer over time, we can reach more "objective" assessments. The passage of time does not in itself provide perspective, however. Information is lost as well as gained over time. Therefore, the claim of inadequate historical perspective cannot excuse ignoring the *sasha*.

At this point we might usefully recall three changes in perspective noted in earlier chapters. Woodrow Wilson enjoys a dramatically more positive ranking now than he did in 1920. His elevated reputation did not derive from the discovery of fresh information on his administration but from the ideological needs of the late 1940s and early 1950s. In those years white historians would hardly fault Wilson for segregating the federal government, because no consensus held that racial segregation was wrong. The foremost public issue of that postwar era was not race relations but the containment of communism. During the Cold War our government operated as it did under Wilson, with semideclared wars, executive deception of Congress, and suppression of civil liberties in the name of anticommunism. Wilson's policies, controversial and unpopular in 1920, had become ordinary by the 1950s. Statesmen and historians of the 1950s rejected and even trivialized isolationism. Interested in pushing the United Nations, then thoroughly under U.S. influence, they appreciated Wilson's efforts on behalf of the League of Nations. Historian Gordon Levin Jr. put it neatly: "Ultimately, in the post–World War II period, Wilsonian values would have their complete triumph in the bipartisan Cold War consensus."[8] Thus, Wilson's improved evaluation in today's textbooks can be attributed largely to the fact that the ideological needs of the 1950s, when Wilson was in the *zamani*, were different from those of the 1920s, when he was passing into the *sasha*.

Changing times can also change our view of the more distant past. Bartolomé de Las Casas and other writers and priests noted the Spaniards' mistreatment and enslavement of the Caribbean Indians while Columbus was still in the *sasha*. Later, however, Columbus was lionized as a daring man of science who disproved the flat-earth notion and opened a new hemisphere to progress. This nineteenth-century Columbus appealed to a nation concluding three hundred years of triumphant warfare over Indian nations. But by 1992 many Columbus celebrations drew countercelebrations, often mounted by Native Americans; now Columbus the exploiter began receiving equal billing with Columbus the explorer. The "new" Columbus, closer to the Columbus of the *sasha*, appealed to a nation that had to get along with dozens of former colonies of European powers, now new nations, often governed by people of color. By 2007, as we have seen, even our textbooks began to record disastrous as well as beneficial consequences of the Columbian Exchange. The contrast between the 1892 and 1992 celebrations of Columbus's first voyage again shows the effect of different vantage points. As Anaïs Nin put it, we see things as *we* are, and "we" changed between 1892 and 1992.

The Confederate myth of Reconstruction first permeated the historical literature during the nadir of race relations, from 1890 to 1940, and hung on in textbooks until the 1960s. Reconstruction regimes came to be portrayed as illegitimate and corrupt examples of "Negro domination." Now historians have returned to the view of Reconstruction put forth in earlier histories, written while Republican governments still administered the Southern states. Eric Foner hails the change as owed to "objective scholarship and modern experience," a turn of phrase that concisely links the two key causes. Objective scholarship does exist in history, which is why I risk words like *truth* and *lies*. Unfortunately, the passage of time does not in itself foster objective scholarship. Mere chronological distance did not promote a more accurate depiction of Reconstruction. Because the facts about Reconstruction simply did not suit the "modern experience" of the nadir period, they lay mute during the early decades of the twentieth century, overlooked by most historians. Not until the civil rights movement altered "modern experience" could the facts speak to us.[9] Historical perspective is thus not a by-product of the passage of time. A more accurate view derives from Leon Festinger's theory of cognitive dissonance, which suggests that the social practices of the period when history is written largely determine that history's perspective on the past.[10] Objective scholarship must be linked with a modern experience that permits it to prevail.

In writing about the recent past, then, textbook authors may not be disadvantaged by any lack of historical perspective. On the contrary, the recency of events confers three potential benefits upon them. First, since the authors themselves lived through the events, they were exposed to a wealth of information from television, journalism, and conversations with others about the issues of the day. Second, multiple points of view are available, each backed by evidence, more or less convincing. Third, authors are free to do research themselves— consult newspapers, interview recent history-makers, and share their interpretations with scholars in disciplines like political science, who are studying these issues. Armed with this information, textbook authors could then develop a story line about the recent past that would be interesting as well as informative. That's what I tried to do while writing this chapter.[11] I concluded that among the most important issues of the past decade were the terrorist attacks of 9/11/2001, our response in Afghanistan, and our (second) war against Iraq. Far more than the Clinton impeachment, for example, these three events promise to impact our lives in the future. What do textbooks say about them? What *should* they say?

About 9/11, surely students—like other Americans—seek answers to four questions. First, what happened? Second, why were we attacked? Third, how did we allow it to happen? Questions two and three lead logically to the fourth query, Will it happen again?

Perhaps because it is the easiest task, textbooks do tell what happened on September 11, 2001—at great length. *Holt American Nation* and *The Americans*, for example, devote five full pages to what happened at the World Trade Center and the Pentagon. They make mistakes; *Holt* claims, for instance, "For the first time since the War of 1812, a foreign enemy had attacked the American homeland." This will come as news to the residents of Columbus, New Mexico, where Pancho Villa State Park maintains the memory of Mexico's 1916 attack that killed two dozen Americans and left the town a smoldering ruin. There is also a lot of slack in these accounts—wasted words that could be far better employed. At one point *Holt* tells us, for example: "The collapse of the massive buildings killed or trapped thousands of people still inside or near the towers, including hundreds of firefighters, police officers, and other rescuers." A page later it repeats: "About 2,500 people were killed by the attack on the World Trade Center. This number included more than 300 firefighters and many other rescue workers who were on the scene."

Telling what happened answers the least important of the four questions, because today's high school students already know what happened. (In three or four years, however, students too young to remember will need these descriptions.) What about the "why" question, which today's students do need to contemplate? In its teacher's edition, *Holt* makes clear that "why" is not something teachers should address: "Tell students that in this section they will learn about the attacks of September 11, 2001, their economic and social consequences, and the response by Americans and the U.S. government." *Pathways to the Present* and Boorstin and Kelley also ignore the "why" question. *The Americans* blurs any causal investigation by adding in terrorist acts by the Irish Republican Army, Peru's Shining Path movement, and Japan's religious cult, Aum Shinrikyo.[12] Only *Pageant* tells why the United States was attacked:

> Bin Laden was known to harbor venomous resentment toward the United States for its economic embargo against Saddam Hussein's Iraq, its growing military presence in the Middle East (especially on the sacred soil of the Arabian Peninsula), and its support for Israel's hostility toward Palestinian nationalism. Bin Laden also fed on worldwide resentment of America's enormous economic, military, and cultural power.

The first sentence accurately summarizes the "Declaration of the World Islamic Front for Jihad against the Jews and the Crusaders" that Osama bin Laden, leader of al Qaeda, which was responsible for the 9/11 attacks, issued in 1998.[13] The second sentence is also accurate and useful.

Unfortunately, other than *Pageant*'s two sentences, today's textbooks leave students defenseless against the misinterpretations deliberately spread by our government. Nine days after the attacks, President George W. Bush gave Congress his answer to the "why" question:

> Americans are asking, why do they hate us? They hate what we see right here in this chamber—a democratically elected government. Their leaders are self-appointed. They hate our freedoms—our freedom of religion, our freedom of speech, our freedom to vote and assemble and disagree with each other.[14]

What a happy thought: they hate us because we are good!

Bush repeated variants on that paragraph throughout the next year. Perhaps because it is so consoling, his interpretation took hold widely. The first and perhaps leading book interpreting the terrorist attacks for young people, *Understanding September 11th*, by *Time* reporter Mitch Frank, made a similar claim specifically for the World Trade Center:

The Twin Towers were meant to symbolize peace. Shortly after they were finished in 1973, the architect who designed them, Minoru Yamasaki, said, "World trade means world peace. The World Trade Center is a living symbol of man's dedication to world peace. It should become a representation of man's belief in humanity, his need for individual dignity, his beliefs in the cooperation of men, and through cooperation, his ability to find greatness." The terrorists were striking at all of this.[15]

Of course, this is nonsense. If on September 10, 2001, Frank had asked a hundred visitors to the World Trade Center what the buildings symbolized to them, none would have replied, "world peace," "individual dignity," or "the cooperation of men."[16] The building housed stockbrokers and investment bankers, after all. As the editors of *American Heritage* put it in 2005, in an essay commending efforts to restore and display the architectural model of the Twin Towers, they were "internationally recognizable symbols of American economic might."[17]

The notion that terrorists attacked us because of our values, our freedoms, or our dedication to world peace is self-serving but shallow and inaccurate. Such thinking might be termed nationalist but is hardly patriotic, to follow the distinction made by Johannes Rau at the head of this chapter. Nationalism does not encourage us to critique our country and seek its betterment. Therefore, nationalism serves us only in the short run. In the long run, our nation needs citizens who question its policies rather than blindly saluting them. Indeed, knowledgeable Americans pointed this out to journalist James Fallows, who summarized in *Atlantic Monthly:* "The soldiers, spies, academics, and diplomats I have interviewed are unanimous in saying that 'They hate us for who we are' is dangerous claptrap." Fallows himself called the idea that they hate us for who we are "lazily self-justifying and self-deluding." Michael Scheuer, first chief of the CIA's bin Laden unit, agreed:

Bin Laden has been precise in telling America the reasons he is waging war on us. None of the reasons have anything to do with our freedom, liberty, and democracy, but have everything to do with U.S. policies and actions in the Muslim world.

In November 2004, confirmation of this view came from an interesting source: a Pentagon report that pointed out "Muslims do not 'hate our freedom,' but rather they hate our policies." If we took this sentence seriously, we might question or change our policies in the Middle East. Bush's analysis—and most textbooks' avoidance of *any* analysis—stifles such thought.[18]

Textbooks find it hard to question our foreign policy because from beginning to end they typically assume the America as "international good guy" model we noted in Chapter 8. Consider the first page of *Pathways to the Present*, for example, which introduces history as a "theme" (along with geography, economics, etc.). Here is every word it supplies students about "history as a theme":

> Fighting for Freedom and Democracy: Throughout the nation's history, Americans have risked their lives to protect their freedoms and to fight for democracy both at home and abroad. Use the American Pathways feature on pages 410–411 to help you trace specific events in the struggle to protect and defend these cherished ideas.

Turning to these pages as instructed reveals the same heading and the same prose, accompanied by images from the Revolutionary War, Civil War, World War I, World War II, and the iconic shot of firemen raising the U.S. flag in front of the ruins of the World Trade Center after 9/11/2001. Conspicuously absent are images from our centuries of warfare against Native Americans, the Mexican War, Philippines War, or any other conflict that cannot be shoehorned into the classification "to fight for democracy both at home and abroad." Our longest war—Vietnam—rates not even a mention. To be sure, some of our military engagements—our 1999 intervention in Serbia-Kosovo, perhaps, or World War II—might fit under the "international good guy" rubric. Others— the Seminole Wars, the Philippines War—cannot. When authors blandly treat our military history under the heading "Fighting for Freedom and Democracy," they merely signal students that they will not be presenting a serious analysis.

In the middle of *A History of the United States*, right after describing the end of our war against Vietnam, Boorstin and Kelley send students a similar signal: "Still a superpower, the United States could not avoid some responsibility for keeping peace in the world. Since the American Revolution, the nation had served as a beacon of hope for people who wanted to govern themselves." Apparently students are not supposed to have noticed that the United States had just spent a decade making war, not "keeping peace," precisely to deny the Vietnamese the ability "to govern themselves." Such "analysis" makes it hard to understand why anyone would attack a peacekeeper, "a beacon of hope."

The very last paragraph in Appleby, Brinkley, and McPherson's *The American Journey* provides the most egregious example of all:

> The United States spent the last decade of the twentieth century trying to increase the peace and prosperity of the world. Many Americans still believed that their nation should serve as an example to the world. As President Clinton explained in his 1997 State of the Union address: "America must continue to be an unrelenting force for peace—from the Middle East to Haiti . . ."

Now, really. This is hardly "telling the truth about history," the title of Appleby's 1995 book on historiography. Such a passage may amount to mere pandering to the right, and if so, it seems to have worked. In 2004, the Thomas B. Fordham Institute, a conservative think tank in Washington, D.C., released *A Consumer's Guide to High School History Textbooks* by Diane Ravitch, Chester Finn, and others, rating six American history textbooks. *Journey* won highest ranking: "Analysis overall seems to be fair, measured, and reasonable." [19] But surely neither Ravitch nor Finn would claim in a lecture on American foreign policy, "The United States spent the last decade of the twentieth century trying to increase the peace and prosperity of the world." It's not even clear that the nation *should* have this agenda. Like all nations, the United States seeks first to increase its own prosperity and influence in the world.

Carrying a 2000 copyright date, *Journey* is the oldest of the six new textbooks I studied for this book, so we cannot know for sure what its authors might have said when the United States—no longer "trying to increase the peace and prosperity of the world"—preemptively attacked Iraq three years later. But would they have been astonished at behavior so at odds with their assessment of our national character? Surely not; after all, the United States had been at war somewhere almost every one of the sixty years before their book came out. To close a textbook with that paragraph is to confuse justification with fact, to present ideology instead of analysis. Again, such words do not help students comprehend why others might attack such a selfless, innocent nation.

Presenting a nation without sin—one that has always conducted its Middle Eastern policies evenhandedly and with best intentions toward both Palestinians and Israelis, for example—merely leaves students ignorant, unable to understand why others are upset with us. Such presentations also fuel students' ethnocentrism—the belief that ours is the finest society in the world and all other nations should be like us. Americans are already more ethnocentric than any other people, partly because the immense economic, military, and cultural strengths of the United States encourage us to believe that our nation is not only the most powerful but also the best on the planet. Any history course that further increases this already robust ethnocentrism only decreases students' ability to learn from other cultures.

Besides being crippled by their "international good guy" assumption, textbook authors operate at a second disadvantage. Our wars with Iraq have a history. Chapter 8 pointed out how textbooks have done a woeful job of discussing the history of U.S. interventions in the Middle East. The United States helped Saddam Hussein seize power in the first place. In 1963, Iraq's Shi'ite prime minister, Gen. Abdul Karim Qassem, "began to threaten U.S. and British influence," in the words of journalists Anthony Lappé and Stephen Marshall. The CIA masterminded Qassem's overthrow; in return, Hussein and his Ba'ath Party welcomed Western oil companies at first. A few years later, however, Hussein nationalized the Iraqi oil industry. Nevertheless, since an old principle of war and diplomacy holds "the enemy of my enemy is my friend," the United States supported Hussein when he invaded Iran in 1980. In 1982, President Reagan removed Iraq from the list of known terrorist countries so we could supply Hussein with military equipment and other aid for his war with Iran. During the rest of the 1980s, the United States sold Iraq military helicopters, computers, scientific instruments, chemicals, and other goods for Iraq's missile, chemical, biological, and nuclear weapons programs, according to reporter John King. The CIA and the Defense Intelligence Agency supplied Iraq with information to help its forces use chemical weapons on Iranian troops. Although such weapons have long been outlawed, the United States then blocked UN Security Council resolutions condemning Iraq's use of them. Even after the war with Iran ended and we knew Hussein was using these weapons on his own people, we continued to send weapons-grade anthrax, cyanide, and other chemical and biological weapons to Iraq. No textbook acknowledges our linkages with Hussein in the past.[20]

Even more important to understanding 9/11 were our actions in Iran. Chapter 8 tells of our repeated interventions on behalf of the shah, interventions that explain that country's enmity toward us today. The Iranian Revolution that overthrew the shah is key to the subsequent history of the Middle East. Since most textbooks don't portray our role in Iran honestly, they are handicapped when they try to explain what happened next, so students cannot use history to understand what happens today. Just as we supported the shah in Iran in the 1970s, we cast our lot today with repressive regimes in Saudi Arabia, Kuwait, Egypt, Uzbekistan, and elsewhere, which prompts most Arabs and many other Muslims to consider the United States "a great hypocrite," in the words of historian Scott Appleby. We preach democracy while supporting dictatorships.[21]

Also crucial to any understanding of the Middle East and terrorism is our tilt toward Israel. The United States is adamant that Iran must not have nuclear weapons. President Bush used Iraq's alleged attempt to obtain nuclear weapons to legitimize our preemptive war upon that country. Yet we have never even admonished Israel verbally for possessing nuclear weapons, which we have known about for decades.[22] On the contrary, from its formation in 1948 to today, regardless of its nuclear weapons or other policies, the United States has always provided Israel critical financial and military support.

Having passed on the "why were we attacked" question, most textbooks also ignore query three: How did we allow it to happen? Authors do not want to criticize the U.S. government, but the blame is bipartisan. In its eight years in office, the Clinton administration took few steps to improve our security against terrorist attacks. In particular, the Immigration and Naturalization Service has been notoriously incompetent for years—unable to create useful lists of people who should not be let in to the United States, incompetent at tracking people once they overstay student or work visas, not even willing to seek people who fail to show up for court hearings related to immigration violations. The Bush administration did even less to make us secure, but authors say nothing about the president's failure to act on the warnings he had before 9/11/2001. In 2000, the Clinton administration had staged rescue exercises simulating a plane being crashed into the Pentagon, showing that they were aware of the possibility. "At least three months before 9/11," according to Lappé and Marshall, "German agents warned the CIA that 'Middle Eastern terrorists were planning to hijack commercial aircraft to use as weapons to attack important symbols of American culture.'" The CIA did not even relay that warning to airline companies. Agents within the FBI sent memos to their superiors about suspicious Arabs training to fly commercial jets in U.S. flying schools, to no avail. George W. Bush received a briefing titled "Bin Laden Determined to Strike in U.S." more than a month before the attacks, but took no action.[23]

Prompted by the families of 9/11 victims, Congress was inspired by these issues to call for a commission to investigate the failure of intelligence, defense, and law enforcement agencies to cooperate, investigate, and forestall the terrorists. *The Americans* makes George Bush the instigator of the resulting 9/11 Commission. In reality he opposed it, and after public opinion forced him to agree to it, his administration cooperated only grudgingly. All the other books omit the commission entirely.

Will it happen again? The books do not say, of course, nor can they, but their tone is upbeat. "The President also moved quickly to combat terrorism at home," says *Pathways to the Present*. "Less than a month after the 9/11 attacks, Bush created the Office of Homeland Security." Then follow three long encouraging paragraphs about this governmental reorganization—paragraphs that contain not a word of critique or query. To be sure, *Pathways* went to press before the federal government's pathetic response to Hurricane Katrina revealed that the Bush administration had actually downsized and downgraded FEMA—the Federal Emergency Management Agency—while merging it into Homeland Security, in the process drastically curtailing our national ability to cope with disasters. But authors did have available to them widespread and expert questioning of our preparedness against terrorist materials coming in through our ports, the waiver program that made it especially easy for Saudi Arabians to get visas, and other problems that Homeland Security had not addressed. Cheerful prose will reassure students only until the next attack. Then they will feel cheated.

The initial U.S. response to 9/11 was to attack the Taliban government in Afghanistan in October 2001. Like Hussein, this fundamentalist Muslim regime had initially been supported by our CIA because they opposed the previous communist regime in Afghanistan, which was backed by the Soviet Union. In the 1980s the CIA not only supplied Afghan Muslim fundamentalists with American advisors and anticraft missiles but also helped recruit Muslims from other countries to fight alongside the Afghans. Unfortunately, after coming to power these extremists sheltered Osama bin Laden and his training camps that produced the terrorists who attacked the World Trade Center and the Pentagon. After the 9/11/2001 attacks and in response to U.S. demands, the Taliban government offered to hand bin Laden over to a third nation. The United States declined the offer, calling it inadequate.[24] Instead, within a month, we began bombing Taliban forces on behalf of the Northern Alliance, enemies of the Taliban. With our aid the Alliance won a quick victory. As Afghans, members of the Alliance were able to differentiate between Taliban supporters and other

Afghans. However, distracted by preparations for its upcoming war on Iraq, the Bush administration then lost focus on capturing Osama bin Laden and on securing Afghanistan as a neutral or favorable state. Those mistakes in early 2002 still haunted the United States five years later, as bin Laden remained at large and the Afghan government had little control over much of Afghanistan.[25]

Only one textbook, *Pageant*, tells that the United States had supported the Islamic fundamentalists in their battle against Afghanistan's communist gov-

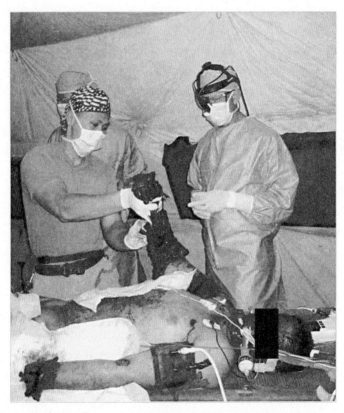

The United States seems to go to war ever more easily, partly because most of us do not really know war's human costs. Our ignorance has several causes. In Iraq, our body armor, medical care, etc., have been much better than previously. As a result, the ratio of combat deaths to wounded is far lower—about 1 to 9, while in Vietnam it was 1 to 3. It is splendid that fewer soldiers are dying. Since many more are wounded, however, some severely, like this man at Walter Reed Army Medical Center, deaths no longer tell the full story. The death toll shrinks further because many war services, like driving and guarding truck convoys, have been contracted out to private companies, whose losses are omitted from official statistics. Iraqi deaths—far more numerous than our own—also don't figure in the totals. Yet the death toll forms our main knowledge of a war's cost, since most of us make no personal sacrifice.

ernment. *Pageant* joins other books in stating, inaccurately, that the Taliban flatly refused to hand over bin Laden. Otherwise, however, most textbooks give a compact and reasonably accurate account of how the United States with the Northern Alliance brought down the Taliban government. They do note that Osama bin Laden got away. Perhaps we should not be surprised that their accounts are accurate: our intervention in Afghanistan was justified and effective, at least at first.[26]

Historically, the next event is the war the United States launched against Iraq in March 2003. However, while chronological, our attack on Iraq was not obviously logical. To be sure, the Bush administration initially claimed a connection between the 9/11 terrorists and Saddam Hussein. Two days after we attacked, explaining why, President Bush gave three reasons: "to disarm Iraq of weapons of mass destruction, to end Saddam Hussein's support for terrorism, and to free the Iraqi people." Similarly, Vice President Dick Cheney called Iraq "the geographic base of the terrorists who have had us under assault for many years, but most especially on 9/11." Even at the time, the linkage claim made no sense. Iraq had no connection with the 9/11 attacks on the United States; Osama bin Laden had nothing but contempt for Saddam Hussein's secular and brutal dictatorship; and Hussein, in turn, had no interest in letting terrorists organize in his police state of a nation.[27]

Nor did the "weapons of mass destruction" claim make sense, for Bush's aggressive diplomacy had persuaded Hussein to let UN weapons inspectors back into Iraq the previous November, and they had found no evidence of such weapons. Hussein's government had also submitted a report the next month describing (truthfully, it turned out) how Iraq had dismantled its WMD programs in the 1990s. The inspectors begged Bush to let them finish their inspections, but Bush ordered the UN out of Iraq so the invasion could proceed. After our initial military victory, thorough search confirmed that no weapons of mass destruction existed in Iraq. Information suppressed at the time has since made clear that British Prime Minister Tony Blair as well as President Bush knew before the invasion that Iraq had no WMD, or should have known.[28] Moreover, even if Iraq's alleged WMD programs had made the progress claimed by the Bush administration, they would still have lagged far behind those of the other two nations Bush denounced as part of the "Axis of Evil," Iran and North Korea. Logically, then, we should have attacked those countries first. Instead, we attacked Iraq—precisely because it *was* the weakest target.[29] Among its other problems, our attack on Iraq thus encouraged Iran and North Korea—along with any other nation wanting to forestall a possible U.S. attack in the future—to *get* nuclear and other weapons of mass destruction. Clearly we attacked Iraq not because it had WMD but because it *did not*.

President Bush's third stated reason for attacking Iraq, "to free the Iraqi people," is another example of the "international good guy" school of U.S. foreign policy. Without doubt, under Hussein the people of Iraq—especially its Shi'ite majority and Kurdish minority—suffered. As a result, substantial segments of Iraqi society initially, and correctly, briefly viewed our troops as liberators. As a cause of our intervention, however, Hussein's oppression never figured prominently. If a people's suffering prompted American intervention, we would have sent troops first to Darfur, in southern Sudan, where the Arab-dominated government was killing or allowing its civilian allies to kill hundreds of thousands of black Africans; or to Zimbabwe, whose dictator, Robert Mugabe, grew more repressive with each passing year. The "international good guy" interpretation did provide rhetorical cover for the invasion, however, and did convince some Democrats to vote for the resolution awarding the president war powers.

If the government's stated reasons for attacking Iraq won't scan, what does explain this military adventure? Surely a huge unstated cause is this: President Bush and his associates hoped to gain from it, politically and economically. Everyone knew that Hussein's armed forces, which the United States had easily defeated in the Persian Gulf War in 1991, were now far weaker. Before the Gulf War, Iraq had 4,280 tanks; it ended that war with 580.[30] Iraq's armed forces were further crippled by the "no fly zone" imposed by the United States and its allies since 1991, which meant U.S. planes would control Iraqi airspace from the beginning of any hostilities. So politicians knew it would be dangerous politically to oppose a war that we would win in a few weeks. Indeed, in November 2004, electoral fallout from the seemingly successful war and the capture of Saddam Hussein helped President Bush win reelection and his party control of Congress. Economics played an even more obvious role. Many of the Bush family's friends have long been involved in the construction of the oil industry and armed forces projects. In April 2003, the Bush administration put the international community on notice that U.S. companies and government agencies, not those of other nations, would rebuild Iraq. To no one's surprise, Vice President Cheney's former firm, Halliburton, has gotten more government money for this rebuilding than any other company—and has been charged with more fraud and malfeasance. Meanwhile, Cheney continues to receive $150,000 a year in deferred compensation from Halliburton and has stock options worth more than $18 million in it. Conversely, to help ensure Cheney's reelection and that of his allies, Halliburton funneled more than half a million dollars to the Republican Party.[31]

The Bush family has historic ties to the oil industry, and early in Bush's presidency, Vice President Cheney convened a secret energy task force comprised mainly of oil industry insiders. In 2003 a political insider, Tom Foley, former speaker of the house, bluntly assailed the good guy interpretation of U.S. foreign policy, implicitly offering a far less flattering picture of a U.S. administration waging war on behalf of private oil firms: "Our belief is that we are not self-interested. For example, our perception is that we didn't go to war against Iraq to dominate the oil market, and we're very offended if anyone suggests such a thing. We always excuse ourselves from self-interested motives."[32] If anyone still doubted that oil played a key role, in 2007 Dow Jones announced that Iraq's puppet parliament was considering a law "which the U.S. government has been helping to craft" that would give giant Western oil companies thirty-year contracts to extract Iraqi oil. Moreover, 75 percent of the profits in the early years would go to the foreign companies, compared to an average of 10 percent in other oil-producing countries.[33]

No textbook suggests that reasons such as these played any part in our decision to go to war, our selection of Iraq as target, or such tactical matters—now widely understood to be blunders—as the choice to sideline entities such as France, Germany, and the United Nations from participating in the rebuilding and reorganization of Iraq. Textbooks never do. Even though several textbooks note the boost in the polls that Americans gave George H. W. Bush after America's quick victory in the Persian Gulf War, authors never suggest domestic politics as an explanation for war.[34] Instead, they choose to believe the reasons officials supply for their actions, rather than peering beneath the surface. Note the perspective adopted in the first sentence of the account of the Iraq War in *The Americans,* for example: "In 2003, Bush expanded the war on terrorism to Iraq." As we have seen, attacking Iraq had nothing to do with "the war on terrorism." Soon enough, even Bush had to admit there was no connection.[35] Nevertheless, the president and vice president continued making their now contradicted statements linking Iraq and the 9/11 terrorist attacks. Political scientists Amy Gershkoff and Shana Kushner have shown that this imaginary connection was the primary wellspring of public support for the war, which shows the truth of Herman Goering's statement that to get people to back a war, "all you have to do is tell them that they are being attacked" and denounce opponents for their lack of patriotism. When textbooks like *The Americans* repeat the fictional tie between terrorism and Hussein's Iraq, they promote support for this misguided war among our young.[36]

Whatever its reasons for going to war in Iraq, after its initial victory the Bush administration forgot the basic rule of any successful occupation: decapitate the occupied society, then rule it through the structures already in place on the local level. After all, Saddam Hussein used more than half a million troops and policemen to keep Iraq quiet. At the insistence of Secretary of Defense Donald Rumsfeld, who overruled Pentagon brass, we went in with far fewer troops, almost none of whom spoke Arabic. So we had no alternative but to use the Iraqi military to cordon off ammunition dumps, direct traffic, accompany our forces on patrol, and do other useful jobs. Instead, against the advice of U.S. officials with Iraq experience like Gen. Jay Garner, we simply declared the Iraqi military illegal. Moreover, we did so without bothering to have it come in and disarm, instantly creating an illegal armed force outside our control. Occupying Iraq is not rocket science. All we had to do was emulate most successful occupations of the last five hundred years. How did Germany govern France in the 1940s, for instance? Through the French police, local leadership, and the imposed Vichy government. The course we chose showed incompetence of a high order.[37]

From the standpoint of realpolitik, the war against Iraq was a poor idea from the start. The United States had Saddam Hussein in a box. His caving in to the UN's demand to readmit WMD inspectors exemplified his dilemma: he ruled his nation by force, yet could hardly mobilize significant force vis-à-vis the UN and the United States. Moreover, Iraq was a secular Arab state, if not a democratic one. By 2004, experts on the Middle East, army commanders, and CIA officials were telling journalist Fallows that our choice to attack Iraq "hampered the campaign in Afghanistan before fighting began and wound it down prematurely, along the way losing the chance to capture Osama bin Laden." It also distracted our attention from the true sources—in Saudi Arabia, Egypt, and Pakistan—of the 9/11/2001 terrorist attacks and from the gaping holes in our domestic security apparatus. It "overused and wore out" the army, Fallows continues, "without committing enough troops for a successful occupation." Worst of all, it created new terrorists. Four months after attacking Iraq, President Bush dared Muslim extremists to "attack us there. My answer is, bring them on."[38] The extremists responded. Al Qaeda, which had no presence in Iraq under Hussein, found Iraq under Bush fertile ground for recruits.

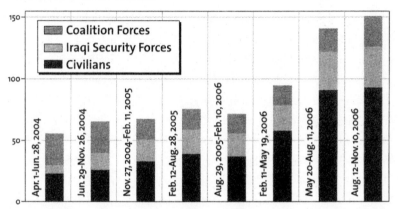

Sources: Government Accountability Office (Attacks); Brookings Institution (Bombings); Department of Defense (Sectarian Violence, Casualties)

This graph shows Iraq's steady slide toward statelessness. Of course statelessness was likely after the United States disbanded Iraq's government and armed forces.

To be sure, the war did not look as misguided or mishandled in 2004 as in 2007, so it is hardly fair for me to suggest that textbook authors should have known then what is obvious now. However, for the most part I have summarized criticisms levied by journalists, historians, and former government officials between 2002 and 2004, before four of these books had gone to press. Certainly by 2007, almost all historians and policy analysts—as well as a majority of American citizens—concluded that the decision to wage war on Iraq was a mistake. Today, Iraq, instead of being a secular (if undemocratic) state, is moving toward statelessness, which breeds terrorism, or toward fundamentalist Shi'ite control with expanded Iranian influence. Iran, unlike Iraq, has sponsored terrorist groups in the Middle East, so its enhanced power resulting from our intervention is hardly in our interest. Our military presence as occupier generates ever-increasing resentment among Muslims everywhere, which in turn helps terrorists solicit new members. Owing to internal sabotage, Iraq hardly exports any oil and suffers shortages of its own, so the war has hardly helped the world cope with its energy shortfall. American prestige abroad has sunk to a new low, owing partly to the illegal and inhumane methods we have used against "detainees" suspected of being terrorists. All these problems, too, were predictable from the start. Indeed, the CIA warned the Bush administration of the likely negative outcomes of our invasion, but Bush and Cheney paid no heed.

For that matter, back in April 1999, an operation of the U.S. government under the Clinton administration, a series of war games known as Desert Crossing, predicted most of them. Still earlier, a paper by Ivan Eland, director of defense policy studies at the Cato Institute, asked, "Does U.S. Intervention Overseas Breed Terrorism? The Historical Record," and answered affirmatively.[39]

Yet only one textbook—again it is *Pageant*—suggests the war was a mistake. It does so by reprinting President George H. W. Bush's rationale for *not* toppling Hussein after the Persian Gulf War:

> Trying to eliminate Saddam . . . would have incurred incalculable human and political costs. . . . Going in and occupying Iraq, thus unilaterally exceeding the United Nations' mandate, would have destroyed the precedent of international response to aggression that we hoped to establish. Had we gone this invasion route, the United States could conceivably still be an occupying power in a bitterly hostile land. It would have been a dramatically different—and perhaps barren—outcome.

As the authors note, the paragraph makes "sobering reading in the context of his son's subsequent invasion of Iraq." To suggest that the other five textbooks support administration policy would be too strong, however. Probably their authors would claim they neither support nor decry administration policy. But since they mostly adopt the administration's terms, and since they start from the "international good guy" point of view, authors do come across as supportive, on the whole. In addition, given that the quagmire in Iraq—like any failed enterprise—was not in America's best interest, even a neutral assessment seems inappropriate.

Even more than earlier chapters, the last pages of U.S. history textbooks come across as "just one damn thing after another" (a line variously attributed to Henry Ford, Winston Churchill, Harry Truman, historian H.A.L. Fisher, Voltaire, and anonymous). Notwithstanding the names of famous historians with imposing personalities on their title pages, the books' final chapters seem especially devoid of a point of view. I suspect this is because no one writes them—at least no one hired to have a point of view. Chapter 12 tells how publishers often farm out history textbooks, especially after their first editions, to be written by underlings. Many of these clerks and freelance writers are not qualified to have a point of view—some have no background in history at all, not even a BA. Nor can they afford the time, as I could while writing this chapter, to review the literature and develop a sense of its most cogent positions. They are hired simply to summarize what happened in the recent past, and summarize they do. The product that results has even less style and is even more boring than the rest of these ponderous volumes. No wonder teachers skip the last chapters!

Nevertheless, the notion that history courses should slight the *sasha* for the distant *zamani* is perverse. Giving short shrift to the *sasha*, the way most textbooks do, or avoiding the recent past altogether, the way most teachers do, does not meet students' needs. Authors may work on the assumption that covering recent events thoroughly is unnecessary because students already know about them. Since textbook authors tend to be old, however, what is *sasha* for them is *zamani* to their students. Students need information about the recent past to understand ongoing developments. Yet high school juniors have almost no personal memory of the Clinton administration, to say nothing of anything earlier, like the women's movement. Soon the disputed Florida election results of 2000, so recent to many of us, will be ancient history to high school students. Moreover, when textbooks and teachers downplay the *sasha*, they make it hard for students to draw connections between the study of the past and the issues they are sure to face in the future, which can only encourage students to consider all history irrelevant.

"The past is never dead," wrote William Faulkner. "It's not even past." Unquestionably this is truest about the *sasha*. The *sasha* is perhaps our most important past, because it is not dead but living-dead. Its theft by textbooks and teachers is the most wicked crime schools perpetrate on high school students, depriving them of perspective about the issues that most affect them. The semi-remembered factoids students carry with them about the Battle of Put-in-Bay or Silent Cal Coolidge do little to help them understand the world into which they move at graduation. That world is still working out sex roles. That world faces nations such as Pakistan, Iran, and North Korea with growing capabilities to make nuclear bombs. That world is marked by growing social and economic inequality within and between nations, which among other things underlies our inability to keep out illegal immigrants. Leaving out the recent past ensures that students will take away little from their history courses that they can apply to that world.

11.

PROGRESS IS OUR MOST IMPORTANT PRODUCT

God has not been preparing the English speaking and Teutonic peoples for a thousand years for nothing. . . . He has given us the spirit of progress to overwhelm the forces of reaction throughout the earth. He has made us adept in government that we may administer government among savage and senile people. . . . And of all our race He has marked the American people as His chosen nation to finally lead in the redemption of the world. —SENATOR ALBERT J. BEVERIDGE, 1900[1]

Americans see history as a straight line and themselves standing at the cutting edge of it as representatives for all mankind. —FRANCES FITZGERALD[2]

The study of economic growth is too serious to be left to the economists.
—E. J. MISHAN[3]

It is becoming increasingly apparent that we shall not have the benefits of this world for much longer. The imminent and expected destruction of the life cycle of world ecology can only be prevented by a radical shift in outlook from our present naïve conception of this world as a testing ground to a more mature view of the universe as a comprehensive matrix of life forms. Making this shift in viewpoint is essentially religious, not economic or political. —VINE DELORIA JR.[4]

STEADFAST READER, we are about to do something no high school American history class has ever accomplished in the annals of American education: reach the end of the textbook. What final words do American history courses impart to their students?

The American Tradition assures students "that the American tradition remains strong—strong enough to meet the many challenges that lie ahead." "If these values are those on which most Americans can agree," says *The American Adventure,* "the American adventure will surely continue." "Most Americans remained optimistic about the nation's future. They were convinced that their free institutions, their great natural wealth, and the genius of the American people would enable the U.S. to continue to be—as it always has been—THE LAND OF PROMISE," *Land of Promise* concludes.

Even most textbooks that don't end with their titles close with the same vapid cheer. "The American spirit surged with vitality as the nation headed toward the close of the twentieth century," the authors of *The American Pageant* assured us in 1991, ignoring opinion polls that suggest the opposite. Fifteen years later, "The American spirit pulsed with vitality in the early twenty-first century," they write, but now "grave problems continued to plague the Republic." *Life and Liberty* climbs farther out on this hollow limb: "America will have a great role to play in these future events. What this nation does depends on the people in it." Can't argue with that! "Problems lie ahead, certainly," predicts *American Adventures*. "But so do opportunities." The American people "need only the will and the commitment to meet the new challenges of the future," according to *Triumph of the American Nation*. In short, all we must do to prepare for the morrow is keep our collective chin up. Or as *Holt American Nation* put it in 2003, "Americans faced the future with hope and determination." [5]

Back in 1995, *Lies My Teacher Told Me* poked fun at textbooks for such endings. Obviously *Lies* had little influence on textbook publishers.

Well, why not end happily? might be one response. We don't want to depress high school students. After all, it's not really history anyway—we cannot know for sure what's going to come next. So let's end on an upbeat.

Indeed, just as we don't know with precision what went on thousands of years ago, we cannot know with precision what will happen next. Precisely for this reason, the endings of these books provide another site where authors might appropriately provoke intellectual curiosity. Can students apply ideas they have learned from these huge American history textbooks? After all, as Shakespeare said, "the past is prologue." If we understand what has caused what in the past, we may be able to predict what will happen next and even adopt national policies informed by our knowledge. Surely helping students learn to do so is the key reason for teaching history in the first place. If history textbooks supplied tools for projection or examples of causation in the past that might (or might not) continue into the future, they would encourage students to think about what they have just spent a year learning. What a thrilling way to end a history textbook!

According to *American History*, *Westward the Course of Empire Takes Its Way* has been reproduced in more American histories than any other picture by Currier and Ives. Stereotypically contrasting "primitive" Native hunters and fishers with bustling white settlers, the picture suggests that progress doomed the Indian, so we need not look closely today at the process of dispossession.

But no, the lack of intellectual excitement in these books is *most* pronounced at their ends. All is well, the authors soothe us. Just keep on keepin' on. No need to ponder whether the nation or all humankind are on the right path. No need to think at all. Not only is this boring pedagogy, it's bad history. Nevertheless, endings like these are customary.

As usual, such content-free unanimity signals that a social archetype lurks nearby. This one, the archetype of progress, bursts forth in full flower on the textbooks' last pages but has been germinating from their opening chapters.

For centuries, Americans viewed their own history as a demonstration of the idea of progress. As Thomas Jefferson put it:

> Let the philosophical observer commence a journey from the savages of the Rocky Mountains eastwards towards our seacoast. These he would observe in the earliest stage of association, living under no law but that of nature. . . . He would next find those on our frontiers in the pastoral state, raising domestic animals to supply the defects of hunting, . . . and so in his progress he would meet the gradual shades of improving man until he would reach his, as yet, most improved state in our seaport towns. This, in fact, is equivalent to a survey, in time, of the progress of man from the

infancy of creation to the present day. And where this progress will stop no one can say.[6]

The idea of progress dominated American culture in the nineteenth century and was still being celebrated in Chicago at the Century of Progress Exposition in 1933. As recently as the 1950s, more was still assumed to be better. Every midwestern town displayed civic pride in signs marking the city limits: WELCOME TO DECATUR, ILLINOIS, POP. 65,000 AND GROWING. Growth meant progress, and progress provided meaning, in some basic but unthinking way. In Washington the secretary of commerce routinely celebrated when our nation hit each new milestone—170,000,000, 185,000,000, etc.—on his "population clock."[7] We boasted that America's marvelous economic system had given the United States "72 percent of the world's automobiles, 61 percent of the world's telephones, and 92 percent of the world's bathtubs," and all this with only 6 percent of the world's population.[8] The future looked brighter yet: most Americans believed their children would inherit a better planet and enjoy fuller lives.

This is the America in which most textbook authors grew up and the America they still try to sell to students today. Perhaps textbooks do not question the notion that bigger is better because the idea of progress conforms with the way Americans like to think about education: ameliorative, leading step by step to opportunity for individuals and progress for the whole society. The ideology of progress also provides hope for the future. Certainly most Americans want to believe that their society has been, on balance, a boon and not a curse to mankind and to the planet.[9] History textbooks go even further to imply that simply by participating in society, Americans contribute to a nation that is constantly progressing and remains the hope of the world. As Boorstin and Kelley put it,

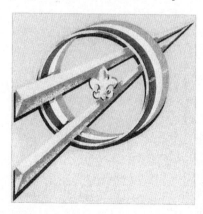

In the 1950s a graphics firm redesigned the symbol for Explorer Scouting to be more "up to date." The new symbol's onward and upward thrust perfectly represents the archetype of progress.

near the end of *A History of the United States*, "Americans—makers of something out of nothing—have delivered a new way of life to far corners of the world." Thus, the idea of American exceptionalism—the United States as the best country in the world—which starts in our textbooks with the Pilgrims, gets projected into the future.

Faith in progress has played various functions in society and in American history textbooks. The faith has promoted the status quo in the most literal sense, for it proclaims that to progress we must simply do more of the same. This belief has been particularly useful to the upper class, because Americans could be persuaded to ignore the injustice of social class if they thought the economic pie kept getting bigger for all. The idea of progress also fits in with social Darwinism, which implies that the lower class is lower owing to its own fault. Progress as an ideology has been intrinsically antirevolutionary: because things are getting better all the time, everyone should believe in the system. Portraying America so optimistically also helps textbooks withstand attacks by ultrapatriotic critics in Texas and other textbook adoption states.

Internationally, referring to have-not countries as "developing nations" has helped the "developed nations" avoid facing the injustice of worldwide stratification. In reality "development" has been making Third World nations poorer, compared to the First World. Per capita income in the First World was five times that in the Third World in 1850, ten times in 1960, and fourteen times by 1970. It's tricky to measure these ratios, partly because a dollar buys more in the Third World than in the First, but per capita income in the First World is now twenty to sixty times that in the Third World.[10] The vocabulary of progress remains relentlessly hopeful, however, with regard to the "undeveloped." As economist E. J. Mishan put it, "Complacency is suffused over the globe, by referring to these destitute and sometimes desperate countries by the fatuous nomenclature of 'developing nations.'"[11] In the nineteenth century, progress provided an equally splendid rationale for imperialism. Europeans and Americans saw themselves as performing governmental services for and utilizing the natural resources of natives in distant lands, who were too backward to do it themselves.

Gradually the archetype of progress has been losing its grip. In the last quarter-century the intellectual community in the United States has largely abandoned the idea. Opinion polls show that the general public, too, has been losing its faith that the future is automatically getting better. Reporting this new climate of opinion, the editors of a 1982 symposium entitled "Progress and Its Discontents" put it this way: "Future historians will probably record that from the mid-twentieth century on, it was difficult for anyone to retain faith in the idea of inevitable and continuing progress."[12]

Probably not even textbook authors still believe that bigger is necessarily better. No one celebrates higher populations.[13] Today, rather than boast of our consumption, we are more likely to lament our waste, as in this passage by Donella H. Meadows, coauthor of *The Limits to Growth:* "In terms of spoiling the environment and using world resources, we are the world's most irresponsible and dangerous citizens." Each American born in the 1970s will throw out ten thousand no-return bottles and almost twenty thousand cans while generating 126 tons of garbage and 9.8 tons of particulate air pollution. And that's just the tip of the trashberg, because every ton of waste at the consumer end has also required five tons at the manufacturing stage and even more at the site of initial resource extraction.[14]

In some ways, bigger still seems to equal better. When we compare ourselves to others around us, having more seems to bring happiness, for earning a lot of money or driving an expensive car implies that one is a more valued member of society. Sociologists routinely find positive correlations between income and happiness. Over time, however, and in an absolute sense, more may not mean happier. Americans believed themselves to be less happy in 1970 than in 1957, and still less happy by 1998, yet they used much more energy and raw materials per capita in 1998.[15]

The 1973 oil crisis precipitated the new climate of opinion, for it showed America's vulnerability to economic and even geological factors over which we have little control. The new pessimism was exemplified by the enormous popularity of that year's ecocidal bestseller, *The Limits to Growth.*[16] Writing the next year, Robert Heilbroner noted the new pessimism: "There is a question in the air . . . 'Is there hope for man?' "[17] Robert Nisbet, who thinks that the idea of progress "has done more good over a 2500-year period . . . than any other single idea in Western history,"[18] nonetheless agrees that the idea is in twilight. This change did not take place all at once. Intellectuals had been challenging the idea of progress for some time, dating back to *The Decline of the West,* published during World War I, in which Oswald Spengler suggested that Western civilization was beginning a profound and inevitable downturn.[19] The war itself, the Great Depression, Stalinism, the Holocaust, and World War II shook Western belief in progress at its foundations.

Developments in social theory further undermined the idea of progress by making social Darwinism intellectually obsolete. Modern anthropologists no longer believe that our society is "ahead of" or "fitter than" so-called "primitive" societies. They realize that our society is more complex than its predecessors but do not rank our religions higher than "primitive" religions or consider our kinship system superior. Even our technology, though assuredly more advanced, may not be better in that it may not meet human needs over the long term.[20]

Another key justification for our belief in progress had come from biological theory. Biologists used to see natural evolution as the survival of the fittest. By 1973 a much more complex view of the development of organisms had swept the field. "Life is not a tale of progress," according to Stephen Jay Gould. "It is, rather, a story of intricate branching and wandering, with momentary survivors adapting to changing local environments, not approaching cosmic or engineering perfection."[21]

Since textbooks do not discuss ideas, it is no surprise that they fail to address the changes in American thinking resulting from World War I, World War II, the Holocaust, or Stalinism, let alone from developments in anthropological or biological theory. By 1973, however, another problem with progress was becoming apparent: the downside risks of our increasing dominance over nature. Environmental problems have grown more ominous every year.

In the 1980s and 1990s, most books at least mentioned the energy crises caused by the oil embargo of 1973 and the Iran-Iraq War in 1980. No worries, however: textbook authors implied that both crises found immediate solutions. "As a result" of the 1973 embargo, *Triumph of the American Nation* told us, "Nixon announced a program to make the United States independent of all foreign countries for its energy requirements by the early 1980s." Ten pages later, in response to gas rationing in 1979, "Carter set forth another energy plan, calling for a massive program to develop synthetic fuels. The long-range goal of the plan was to cut importation of oil in half." No mention in 1979 of Nixon's 1973 plan, which had failed so abjectly that our dependence on foreign oil had spiraled upward, not downward.[22] No mention that Congress never even passed most of Carter's 1979 plan, inadequate as it was. Virtually all the textbooks adopted this trouble-free approach. "By the end of the Carter administration, the energy crisis had eased off," *Land of Promise* reassured its readers. "Americans were building and buying smaller cars." "People gradually began to use less gasoline and conserve energy," echoes *The American Tradition*.

If only it were that simple! Between 1950 and 1975 world fuel consumption doubled, oil and gas consumption tripled, and the use of electricity grew almost sevenfold.[23] Since then things have only grown worse. Meanwhile, world oil production has reached a plateau, as M. K. Hubbert predicted it would decades ago. In 1994 I wrote, "If our sources of energy are not infinite, which seems likely since we live on a finite planet, then at some point we will run up against shortages." By 2007 these shortages have begun to manifest themselves, and the dislocations will prove enormous. A century ago farming in America was energy self-sufficient: livestock provided the fertilizer and tillage power, farm families did the work of planting and weeding, wood heated the house, wind pumped the water, and photosynthesis grew the crops. Today American farming relies on enormous amounts of oil, not only for tractors and trucks and air-conditioning, but also for fertilizers and herbicides. Given these circumstances, most social and natural scientists concluded from the 1973 energy crisis that we cannot blithely maintain our economic growth forever. "Anyone having the slightest familiarity with the physics of heat, energy, and matter," wrote Mishan in 1977, "will realize that, in terms of historical time, the end of economic growth, as we currently experience it, cannot be that far off." [24] This is largely because of the awesome power of compound interest. Economic growth at 3 percent, a conventional standard, means that the economy doubles every quarter-century, typically doubling society's use of raw materials, expenditures of energy, and generation of waste.

The energy crises of 1973 and 1979 pointed to the difficulty that capitalism, a marvelous system of production, was never designed to accommodate shortage. For demand to exceed supply is supposed to be *good* for capitalism, leading to increased production and often to lower costs. Oil, however, is not really produced but extracted. In a way it is rationed by the oil companies and OPEC from an unknown but finite pool. Thus, the oil companies, which we habitually perceive as competing capitalist producers, might more accurately be viewed as keepers of the commons.

America has seen commons problems before. Imagine a colonial New England town in which each household kept a cow. Every morning, a family member would take the cow to the common town pasture, where it would join other cows and graze all day under the supervision of a cowherd paid by the town. An affluent family might benefit from buying a second cow; any excess milk and butter they could sell to cowless sailors and merchants. Expansion of this sort could go on only for a finite period, however, before the common pasture was hopelessly overgrazed. What was in the short-term interest of the individual family was not in the long-term interest of the community. If we compare contemporary oil companies with cow-holding colonial families, we see that new forms of governmental regulations, analogous to the regulated use of the commons, may be necessary to assure there will be a commons—in this case, an oil pool—for our children.[25]

The commons issue affects our society in other ways. Fishing and shellfishing are in crisis. A catch of 20 million bushels of crabs and oysters in Chesapeake Bay in 1892 and 3.5 million in 1982 fell to just 166,000 bushels in 1992. Fisherfolk responded the way people usually do when their standard of living is imperiled: work harder. This meant redoubling their efforts to take more of the few crabs and oysters still out there. Although this tactic may benefit an individual family, it cannot but wreak disaster on the commons. By 2006, scientists estimated that one-fifth of the fishing and oystering fleet in the bay would reap about the same harvest, with much less ecological damage. The problem of the bay is amplified in the oceans by the use of increasingly sophisticated fishing technology. A report in *Science* in 2006 predicted that 90 percent of all species of fish and shellfish that now feed people may be gone by 2048. Twenty-nine percent of those species have already collapsed, meaning that their harvests were already less than one-tenth what they had been. The United Nations is struggling to develop a global system "to manage and repropagate the fish that are still left." Since international waters are involved, however, negotiations may not succeed until after many species have been made extinct.[26]

Because the economy has become global, the commons now encompasses the entire planet. If we consider that around the world humans owned ten times as many cars in 1990 as in 1950, no sane observer would predict that such a proportional increase could or should continue for another forty years.[27] According to Jared Diamond, in 2005 the average American consumed thirty-two times as much of the world's largesse and produced thirty-two times as much pollution as the average Third World citizen.[28] Our continued economic development coexists in some tension with a corollary of the archetype of progress: the notion that America's cause is the cause of all humankind. Thus, our economic leadership is very different from our political leadership. Politically, we can hope other nations will put in place our forms of democracy and respect for civil liberties. Economically, we can only hope other nations will *never* achieve our standard of living, for if they did, the earth would become a desert. Economically, we are the bane, not the hope of the world. Since the planet is finite, as we expand our economy we make it *less* likely that less developed nations can expand theirs. Today, increasing demand for fuel for Chinese vehicles is already creating a worldwide oil shortage.

Almost every day brings new reasons for ecological concern, from deforestation at the equator to ozone holes at the poles. Cancer rates climb and we don't know why.[29] We have no way even to measure the full extent of human impact on the earth. The average sperm count in healthy human males around the world has dropped by nearly 50 percent over the past fifty years. If environmentally caused, this is no laughing matter, for sperm have only to decline in a straight line for another fifty years and we will have wiped out humankind without even knowing how we did it.[30] We were similarly unaware for years that killing mosquitoes with DDT was wiping out birds of prey around the globe. Our increasing power makes it increasingly possible that humankind will make the planet uninhabitable by accident. Indeed, we almost have, on several occasions. In the early 1990s, for example, nations around the planet agreed to stop production of many CFCs (chlorofluorocarbons) that damaged the ozone in the upper atmosphere. In 2006 *Washington Post* writer Joel Achenbach noted, "Scientists are haunted by the realization that if CFCs had been made with a slightly different type of chemistry, they'd have destroyed much of the ozone layer over the entire planet."[31] We were simply lucky.

All these considerations imply that more of the same economic development and nation-state governance that brought us this far may not guide us to a livable planet in the long run. We do not simply face an energy crisis that might be solved if we only develop a low-cost form of energy that does not pollute or cause global warming. On the contrary, if we had cheaper energy, imagine the havoc we might cause! Scientists have already envisioned how we could happily use it to decrease the salinity of the seas, increase our arable land, and in other ways make our planet nicer for us—in the short run. Instead, we must start treating the earth as if we plan to stay here. At some point in the future, perhaps before readers of today's high school textbooks pass their fiftieth birthdays, industrialized nations, including the United States, may have to move toward steady-state economies in their consumption of energy and raw materials. Thus, our oil crisis can best be viewed as a wake-up call to change our ways.

Getting to zero economic growth involves another form of the problem of the commons, however, for no country wants to be first to achieve a no-growth economy, just as no individual family finds it in its interest to stop with one cow. A new international mechanism may be required, one hard even to envision today. Heilbroner is pessimistic: "No substantial voluntary diminution of growth, much less a planned reorganization of society, is today even remotely imaginable."[32] If, tomorrow, citizens must imagine diminished growth, we cannot rest easily, knowing that most high school history courses do nothing whatever to prepare Americans of the future to think imaginatively about the problem. Continued unthinking allegiance to the idea of progress in our textbooks can only be a deterrent, blinding students to the need for change, thus making change that much more difficult. David Donald characterizes the "incurable optimism" of American history courses as "not merely irrelevant but dangerous."[33] In this sense, our environmental crisis is an *educational* problem to which American history courses contribute.

Edward O. Wilson divides those who write on environmental issues into two camps: environmentalists and exceptionalists.[34] Most scholars and writers, including Wilson, are of the former persuasion. On the other side stand a relative handful of political scientists, economists, and natural scientists, several associated with right-wing think tanks, who have mounted important counterarguments to the doomsaying environmentalists. In 1994 I pointed to Julian Simon, Herman Kahn, and some others who compared their world to the world of our ancestors and argued that although modern societies have more power to harm the planet, they also have more power to set the environment right. After all, environmental damage has been undone on occasion. Some American rivers that were deemed hopelessly polluted forty years ago are now fit for fish and human swimmers. Human activity has reforested South Korea.[35] Hence, the exceptionalists claimed, modern technology may exempt us from environmental pressures. They noted that recovery time after natural disasters such as earthquakes or man-made disasters such as World War II has become much shorter today than in the nineteenth century, owing in part to the ability of our large bureaucratic organizations to mobilize information and coordinate enormous undertakings. Human life expectancy, one measure of the quality of life, continues to lengthen. Herbert London, who titled his book *Why Are They Lying to Our Children?* because he believes that teachers and textbooks overemphasize the perils of economic growth, pointed out that more food was available in 1990 than twenty years earlier.[36] Simon pointed out how most short-term predictions of shortages in everything from whale oil in the last century to silver in the 1990s have been confuted by new technological developments.[37] To be sure, higher prices will eventually make it profitable to use extraordinary measures—steam pressure and the like—to extract more oil.

In 1994 I faulted textbooks for not supplying students with *either* side of this debate and then encouraging them to think about it. Not only did the books ignore the looming problems, they also did not present the adaptive capacities of modern society. Authors should have shown trends in the past that suggest we face catastrophe and other trends that suggest solutions. Doing so would encourage students to use evidence from history to reach their own conclusions. Instead, authors assured us that everything will come out right in the end, so we need not worry much about where we are going.[38] Their endorsement of progress was as shallow as General Electric's, a company that claims, "Progress is our most important product," but whose ecological irresponsibility has repeatedly earned it a place on *Fortune*'s list of the ten worst corporate environmental offenders.[39]

No longer do I suggest this evenhanded approach. Even though Simon is right and capitalism *is* supple, in at least two ways our current crisis is new and cannot be solved by capitalism alone. First, we face a permanent energy shortage, only beginning with an oil shortage. Such a shortage leads toward oligopoly—a "natural" cartel, not a forced cartel such as John D. Rockefeller achieved with Standard Oil around 1900—and cartels are not good capitalism. If a handful of companies controlled the manufacture of skis, so they could get together and charge whatever they wanted, someone might start another company not bound by their agreement or develop new, cheaper materials for skis or invent the snowboard—or we the public could stop buying skis. But if a handful of companies or countries control the oil industry, no new producer can break in. Moreover, no alternative can easily be developed for petroleum in transportation.

Second, our use of oil (and all other fossil fuels) has a serious worldwide impact: global warming. As everyone now knows, except some high school history textbook authors, this warming melts the polar ice caps, causing sea levels to rise. Oceans rose one foot in the last century. The most conservative estimate, embraced by the George W. Bush administration, predicts they will rise another three feet in this century. Around the world—from Miami to Venice to much of Bangladesh—hundreds of millions of people live close enough to sea level that this rise will endanger their lives and occupations. The resulting dislocation will constitute the biggest crisis mankind has faced since the beginning of recorded history. And this is the most pleasant estimate. If the Greenland ice sheet melts, the oceans may rise twenty-three feet. Scientist James Lovelock in 1970 famously invented the "Gaia hypothesis," the idea that the earth acts as a homeostatic system. Recently Lovelock has pointed out that as the earth's equilibrium gets disturbed, some disequilibrium processes may cause even faster warming. As the polar ice caps melt, for example, they no longer reflect the sun's rays, so the earth absorbs still more heat. Lovelock predicts the death of billions of people before equilibrium is established once more. Global warming also increases other weather problems: the average windspeeds of hurricanes have doubled in the past thirty years, and they are also more frequent.[40]

That's not all. Evidence shows that carbon dioxide, a normal result of burning oil or coal, also makes the oceans more acidic. Scientists warn that, by the end of this century, this acidity could decimate coral reefs and kill off creatures that undergird the sea's food chain. "It's the single most profound environmental change I've learned about in my entire career," said Thomas Lovejoy, author of *Climate Change and Biodiversity*. "What we're doing in the next decade will affect our oceans for millions of years," said Ken Caldeira, oceanographer at Stanford University.[41]

In addition to our energy and global-warming crises, we face other severe problems. Thousands of species face imminent extinction. One list of likely candidates includes a third of all amphibians, a fourth of the world's mammals, and an eighth of its birds. Wilson thinks the foregoing is optimistic and believes two thirds of all species will perish before the end of the century. Nuclear proliferation poses another threat. In 1945 only one country—the United States—had the know-how and economic means to build nuclear weapons. Since then, Great Britain, the USSR, France, China, India, Pakistan, Israel, South Africa, and apparently North Korea have joined the nuclear club. If Pakistan and North Korea can do it, clearly almost every nation on earth—and some private organizations, including terrorist groups—has the capability. The United States came uncomfortably close to using nuclear weapons in Vietnam in 1969, and India and Pakistan came uncomfortably close to using them against each other in 2002.[42]

In the long run, just keeping to the old paths regarding all these new problems is unlikely to work. "From the mere fact that humanity has survived to the present, no hope for the future can be salvaged," Mishan noted. "The human race can perish only once."[43] If the arguments in this new edition of this chapter seem skewed to favor the environmentalists, perhaps the potential downside risk if they are right, as well as the ominous developments since the first edition, make this bias appropriate. After all, history reveals many previously vital societies, from the Mayans and Easter Island to Haiti and the Canaries, that irreparably damaged their ecosystems.[44] "Considering the beauty of the land," Christopher Columbus wrote on first seeing Haiti, "there must be gain to be got." Columbus and the Spanish transformed the island biologically by introducing diseases, plants, and livestock. The pigs, hunting dogs, cows, and horses propagated quickly, causing tremendous environmental damage. By 1550 the "thousands upon thousands of pigs" in the Americas had all descended from the eight pigs that Columbus brought over in 1493. "Although these islands had been, since God made the earth, prosperous and full of people lacking nothing they needed," a Spanish settler wrote in 1518, after the Europeans' arrival "they were laid waste, inhabited only by wild animals and birds."[45] Later, sugarcane monoculture replaced gardening in the name of quick profit, thereby impoverishing the soil. More recently, population pressure has caused Haitians and Dominicans to farm the island's steep hillsides, resulting in erosion of the topsoil. Today this island ecosystem that formerly supported a large population in relative equilibrium is in far worse condition than when Columbus first saw it. This sad story may be a prophecy for the future, now that modern technology has the power to make of the entire earth a Haiti.

Not one textbook brings up the whale oil lesson, the Haiti lesson, or any other inference from the past that might bear on the question of progress and the environment. In sum, although this issue may be the most important of our time, no hint of its seriousness seeps into our history textbooks. To my surprise, today's textbooks have actually gotten worse than their predecessors about the environment. Except for two passages in *Pageant* and one in *Journey*, they say nothing about environmental issues since the Carter presidency. The 1970 invention of Earth Day, 1973 Arab oil embargo, and 1979 Iran hostage crisis are the environmental events that get into our textbooks, along with the establishment of the Environmental Protection Agency during the Nixon administration. Fifteen more years have passed since these events took place. Since authors take no note of underlying trends but only of flashy events, they see no history to report in the interval. Putting the energy crisis that much further back in time, however, implies that it's old news. Moreover, the textbooks imply that it has pretty much been fixed. "With the help of the [National Energy] act," *The Americans* assures us in a typical passage, "U.S. dependence on foreign oil had eased slightly by 1979." If so, 1979 was unusual, because in 1975, before Carter became president, the United States imported 35 percent of its petroleum, while in 2005 we imported 58 percent.

To expect textbooks published around 1990 to treat global warming might not be fair. In *Atlantic Monthly* in 2006, Gregg Easterbrook noted that it had not been proven:

> Fifteen years ago, a thoughtful person looking at global-warming studies might have focused on the uncertainty; at that time the National Academy of Sciences itself emphasized uncertainty. Today a thoughtful person who looks at recent science, including recent National Academy of Sciences statements, must deduce there is a danger.

Easterbrook described himself as "skeptical," then "gradually persuaded by the evidence. Inuits living in the Arctic strongly agree; they warn that the entire ecosystem there is in collapse. Every year between 1997 and 2005 was one of the ten hottest ever recorded; 2005 set a record." [46]

So how do today's textbooks treat what may be the most important single issue of our time? Here is every word on the subject in all six textbooks, except for a passage at the very end of *Pageant* that we will analyze at the end of this chapter:

> At the outset of the 21st century, developments like global warming served dramatic notice that planet earth was the biggest ecological system of them all—one that did not recognize national boundaries. Yet while Americans took pride in the efforts they had made to clean up their own turf, who were they, having long since consumed much of their own timberlands, to tell the Brazilians that they should not cut down the Amazon rain forest?
>
> —*The American Pageant*

> Although no one is sure what causes global warming, a United Nations report warned that air pollution could be a factor.
>
> —*The American Journey*

Here *Pageant* implies that Third World countries form the bulk of the problem, although the United States contributes almost 25 percent of all CO_2 emissions, far more than any other nation. *Journey* hedges: air pollution *"could be a factor."* And four books never mention the subject. [47]

Why are textbook treatments of environmental issues so feeble? If authors revised their closing pages to jettison the unthinking devotion to progress, their final chapters would sit in uneasy dissonance with earlier chapters. Their tone throughout might have to change. From their titles on, American history textbooks are celebratory, and the idea of progress legitimates the celebration. Textbook authors present our nation as getting ever better in all areas, from race relations to transportation. The traditional portrayal of Reconstruction as a period of Yankee usurpation and Negro debauchery fits with the upward curve of progress, for if relations were bad in Reconstruction, perhaps not as bad as in slavery but surely worse than what came later, then we can imagine that race relations have gradually been getting better. However, the facts about Reconstruction compel us to acknowledge that in many ways race relations in this country have yet to return to the point reached in, say, 1870. In that year, to take a small but symbolic example, A. T. Morgan, a white state senator from Hinds County, Mississippi, married Carrie Highgate, a black woman from New York, *and was reelected.*[48] Today this probably could not happen, not in Hinds County, Mississippi, or in many counties throughout the United States. Nonetheless, the archetype of progress prompts many white Americans to conclude that black Americans have no legitimate claim on our attention today because the problem of race relations has surely been ameliorated.[49]

A. T. Morgan's marriage is hard for us to make sense of, because Americans have so internalized the cultural archetype of progress that by now we have a built-in tendency to assume that we are more tolerant, more sophisticated, more, well, *progressive* than we were in the past. Even a trivial illustration—Abraham Lincoln's beard—can teach us otherwise. In 1860 a clean-shaven Lincoln won the presidency; in 1864, with a beard, he was reelected. Could that happen nowadays? Today many institutions, from investment banking firms to Brigham Young University, are closed to white males with facial hair. No white presidential candidate or successful Supreme Court nominee has ventured even a mustache since Tom Dewey in 1948. Beards may not in themselves be signs of progress, although mine has subtly improved my thinking, but we have reached an arresting state of intolerance when the huge Disney corporation, founded by a man with a mustache, will not allow any employee to wear one. On a more profound note, consider that Lincoln was also the last American president who was not a member of a Christian denomination when taking office. Americans may not be becoming more tolerant; we may only think we are. Thus, the ideology of progress amounts to a chronological form of ethnocentrism.

Not only does the siren song of progress lull us into thinking that every-

The United States was founded in a spirit of dominion over nature. "My family, I believe, have cut down more trees in America than any other name!" boasted John Adams. Benjamin Lincoln, a Revolutionary War general, spoke for most Americans of his day when he observed in 1792, "Civilization directs us to remove as fast as possible that natural growth from the lands." The Adams-Lincoln mode of thought did make possible America's rapid expansion to the Pacific, the Chicago school of architecture, and Henry Ford's assembly line. Our growing environmental awareness casts a colder light on these accomplishments, however. Since 1950 more than 25 percent of the remaining forests on the planet have been cut down. Recognizing that trees are the lungs of the planet, few people still think that this represents progress.

thing now is more "advanced," it also tempts us to conclude that societies long ago were more primitive than they may have been. Progress underlies the various unilinear evolutionary schemes into which our society used to classify peoples and cultures: savagery-barbarism-civilization, for example, or gathering-hunting-horticultural-agricultural-industrial. Under the influence of these schemes, scholars completely misconceived "primitive" humans as living lives that, as Hobbes put it, were "nasty, brutish, and short." Only "higher" cultures were conceived of as having sufficient leisure to develop art, literature, or religion.

Anthropologists have long known better. "Despite the theories traditionally taught in high school social studies," pointed out anthropologist Peter Farb, "the truth is, the more primitive the society, the more leisured its way of life."[50] Thus "primitive" cultures were hardly "nasty." As to "brutish," we might recall the comparison of the peaceful Arawaks on Haiti and the Spanish conquistadors who subdued them. "Short" is also problematic. Before encountering the diseases brought by Europeans and Africans, many people in Australia, the Pacific islands, and the Americas probably enjoyed remarkable longevity, particularly when compared with European and African city dwellers. "They live a long life and rarely fall sick," observed Giovanni da Verrazano, after whom the Verrazano Narrows and bridge in New York City are named.[51] "The Indians be of lusty and healthful bodies not experimentally knowing the Catalogue of those health-wasting diseases which are incident to other Countries," according to a very early New England colonist, who apparently ignored the recently introduced European diseases that were then laying waste the Native Americans. He reported that the Indians lived to "three-score, four-score, some a hundred years, before the world's universal summoner cites them to the craving Grave."[52] In Maryland, another early settler marveled that many Indians were great-grandfathers, while in England few people survived to become grandparents.[53] The first Europeans to meet Australian aborigines noted a range of ages that implied a goodly number lived to be seventy. For that matter, Psalm 90 in the Bible implies that thousands of years ago most people in the Middle East lived to be seventy: "The years of our lives are three score and ten, and if by reason of strength they be four score, yet is their labor sorrow . . ."[54]

Besides fostering ignorance of past societies, belief in progress makes students oblivious to merit in present-day societies other than our own. To conclude that other cultures have achieved little about which we need to know is a natural side effect of believing our society the most progressive. Anthropology professors despair of the severe ethnocentrism shown by many first-year college students. William A. Haviland, author of a popular anthropology textbook, says that in his experience the possibility that "some of the things that we aspire to today—equal treatment of men and women, to cite but one example—have in fact been achieved by some other peoples simply has never occurred to the average beginning undergraduate."[55] Few high schools offer anthropology courses, and fewer than one American in ten ever takes a college anthropology course, so we can hardly count on anthropology to reduce ethnocentrism. High school history and social studies courses could help open students to ideas from other cultures. That does not happen, however, because the idea of progress saturates these courses from Columbus to their final words. Therefore, they can only promote, not diminish, ethnocentrism. Yet ethnocentric faith in progress in Western culture has had disastrous consequences. People who believed in their society as the vanguard of the future, the most progressive on earth, have been all too likely to indulge in such excessive cruelties as the Pequot massacre, Stalin's purges, the Holocaust, or the Great Leap Forward.

Rather than assuming that our ways must be best, textbook authors would do well to challenge students to think about practices from the American way of birth to the American way of death. Some elements of modern medicine, for instance, are inarguably more effective and based on far better theory than previous medicines. On the other hand, our "scientific" antigravity way of birth, which dominated delivery rooms in the United States from about 1930 to at least 1970, shows the influence of the idea of progress at its most laughable. The analogy for childbirth was an operation: the doctor anesthetized the mother and removed the anesthetized infant like a gall bladder.[56] Even as late as 1992, only half of all women who gave birth in U.S. hospitals breast-fed their babies, even though we now know, as "primitive" societies never forgot, that human milk, not bovine milk or "formula," is designed for human babies.[57] If history textbooks relinquished their blind devotion to the archetype of progress, they could invite readers to assess technologies as to which have truly been progressive. Defining *progress* would itself become problematic. Alternative forms of social organization, made possible or perhaps even necessary by technological and economic developments, could also be considered. Today's children may see the decline of the nation-state, for instance, because the problem of the planetary commons may force planetary decision-making or because growing tribalism may fragment many nations from within.[58] The closing chapters of history textbooks might become inquiry exercises, directing students toward facts and readings on both sides of such issues. Surely such an approach would prepare students for their six decades of life after high school better than today's mindlessly upbeat textbook endings.

Thoughtfulness about such matters as the quality of life is often touted as a goal of education in the humanities, but history textbooks sweep such topics under the brightly colored rug of progress. Textbooks manifest no real worries even about the environmental downside of our economic and scientific institutions. Instead, they stress the fortunate adequacy of our government's reaction. Textbook authors seem much happier telling of the governmental response—mainly the creation of the Environmental Protection Agency—than discussing any continuing environmental problems. By far the most serious treatment of our future in any of the new textbooks is this passage on the next to last page of *The American Pageant:*

Environmental worries clouded the country's future. Coal-fired electrical generating plants helped form acid rain and probably contributed to the greenhouse effect, an ominous warming of the planet's temperature. The unsolved problem of radioactive waste disposal hampered the development of nuclear power plants. The planet was being drained of oil. . . .

By the early twenty-first century, the once-lonely cries for alternative fuel sources had given way to mainstream public fascination with solar power and windmills, methane fuel, electric "hybrid" cars, and the pursuit of an affordable hydrogen fuel cell. Energy conservation remained another crucial but elusive strategy—much-heralded at the politician's rostrum, but too rarely embodied in public policy. . . .

Although hardly a wake-up call, at least those words raise the issues and do not imply that they are nothing to worry about.

Unfortunately, on the next page—its last page—*Pageant* blandly reassures: "In facing those challenges, the world's oldest republic had an extraordinary tradition of resilience and resourcefulness to draw on." Many students are not so easily reassured. According to a 1993 survey, children are much more concerned about the environment than are their parents.[59] In the late 1980s about one high school senior in three thought that nuclear or biological annihilation will probably be the fate of all mankind within their lifetimes.[60] "I have talked with my friends about this," a student of mine wrote in her class journal. "We all agree that we feel as if we are not going to finish our adult lives." A survey of high school seniors in 1999 found that almost half believed the "best years of the United States were behind us."[61] These students had all taken American history courses, but the textbooks' regimen of positive thinking does not seem to have rubbed off on them. Students know when they are being conned. They sense that underneath the mindless optimism is a defensiveness that rings hollow. Or maybe they simply never reached the cheerful endings of their textbooks.

Probably the principal effect of the textbook whitewash of environmental issues in favor of the idea of progress is to persuade high school students that American history courses are not appropriate places to bring up the future course of American history.[62] What is perhaps the key issue of the day will have to be discussed in other classes—maybe science or health—even though it is foremost a social rather than biological or health issue. Meanwhile, back in history class, there are more bland, data-free assurances that things are getting better.

E. J. Mishan has suggested that feeding students rosy tales of automatic progress helps keep them passive, for it presents the future as a process over which they have no control.[63] I don't believe this is why textbooks end as they do, however. Their upbeat endings may best be understood as ploys by publishers who hope that nationalist optimism will get their books adopted. Moreover, they know that Republicans have descended from the party of Nixon—when they passed the Environmental Protection Act—to the party of George W. Bush, where big business, especially oil, directs our environmental and energy policies. In today's political climate publishers may worry that to suggest that global warming or energy shortages are real threats may be taken as partisan Democratic history. Hence, they may lose adoptions.

Such happy endings in our history books really amount to concessions of defeat, however. By implying that no real questions about our future need be asked and no real thinking about trends in our history need be done, textbook authors concede implicitly that our history has no serious bearing on our future. We can hardly fault students for concluding that the study of history is irrelevant to their futures.

12.

WHY IS HISTORY
TAUGHT LIKE THIS?

I do not know if there is any other field of knowledge which suffers so badly as history from the sheer blind repetitions that occur year after year, and from book to book.
—HERBERT BUTTERFIELD[1]

There is no other country in the world where there is such a large gap between the sophisticated understanding of some professional historians and the basic education given by teachers. —MARC FERRO[2]

When you're publishing a book, if there's something that is controversial, it's better to take it out. —HOLT, RINEHART AND WINSTON REPRESENTATIVE[3]

They hired somebody. I don't remember the man's name.
—BROOKS MATHER KELLEY, COAUTHOR,
A HISTORY OF THE UNITED STATES, EXPLAINING
WHO REALLY WROTE ITS LAST CHAPTER[4]

Here's $3,000 for a freelance writer, and our editorial staff will take it from there. . . . They pick things up pretty quickly, and in a couple of days, they're up on the Civil War.

—VETERAN EDITOR OF HIGH SCHOOL HISTORY TEXTBOOKS[5]

ELEVEN CHAPTERS HAVE SHOWN that textbooks supply irrelevant and even erroneous details, while omitting pivotal questions and facts in their treatments of issues ranging from Columbus's second voyage to the possibility of impending ecocide. We have also seen that history textbooks offer students no practice in applying their understanding of the past to present concerns, hence no basis for thinking rationally about anything in the future. Reality gets lost as authors stray further and further from the primary sources and even the secondary literature. Textbooks rarely present the various sides of historical controversies and almost never reveal to students the evidence on which each side bases its position. The textbooks are unscholarly in other ways. Of the eighteen I studied, only the two oldest, published back in the 1970s, contain any footnotes.[6] Ten textbooks even deny students a bibliography.

Despite heavy criticisms by scholars,[7] new editions of the old texts come out year after year, largely unchanged. Year after year, clones appear, allegedly by new authors but with nearly identical covers, titles, and contents. What explains such appalling uniformity?

The textbooks must be satisfying somebody.

Publishers produce textbooks with several audiences in mind. One is their intended readers: students. Their characteristics, as publishers perceive them, particularly affect reading level and page layout, and we will return to this point. Historians and professors of education are another audience, perhaps two audiences. Teachers comprise another, and their characteristics and wants we will also review. Conceptions of the general public also enter publishers' thinking, since public opinion influences adoption committees and since parents represent a potential interest group that publishers seek *not* to arouse.

Some members of the public have not been shy about what they want textbooks to do. In 1925 the American Legion declaimed that the ideal textbook:

must inspire the children with patriotism . . .

must be careful to tell the truth optimistically . . .

must dwell on failure only for its value as a moral lesson, must speak chiefly of success . . .

must give each State and Section full space and value for the achievements of each.[8]

By contrast, in 1986 Shirley Engle and Anna Ochoa, longtime luminaries of social studies education, voiced very different recommendations for textbooks. From their vantage point, the ideal textbook should:

confront students with important questions and problems for which answers are not readily available;

be highly selective;

be organized around an important problem in society that is to be studied in depth;

utilize . . . data from a variety of sources such as history, the social sciences, litera-ture, journalism, and from students' first-hand experiences.[9]

Today's textbooks hew closely to the American Legion line and disregard the recommendations of Engle and Ochoa. Why?

Is the secondary literature in history to blame? We can hardly expect text-book authors to return to primary sources and dig out facts that are truly ob-scure. A few decades back, the secondary literature in history was quite biased. Until World War II, history, much more than the other social sciences, was overtly anti-Semitic and antiblack. According to Peter Novick, whose book *That Noble Dream* is the best recent account of the history profession, looking at every white college and university in America, exactly *one* black was *ever* employed to teach history before 1945.[10] Most historians were males from privileged white families. They wrote with blinders on. Arthur Schlesinger Jr. found himself able to write an entire book on the presidency of Andrew Jackson without ever mentioning perhaps the foremost issue Jackson dealt with as president: the re-moval of American Indians from the Southeast. What's more, Schlesinger's book won the Pulitzer Prize![11]

These days, however, the secondary literature in American history is much more comprehensive. Indeed, every chapter of this book has been based on commonly available research. Competent historians will find nothing new here. The information is all there, in the secondary literature, but has not made its way into our textbooks, educational media, or teacher-training programs, and therefore hasn't reached our schools.[12] As a consequence, according to compara-tive historian Marc Ferro, the United States has wound up with the largest gap of any country in the world between what historians know and what the rest of us are taught.[13]

Could these omissions be a question of professional judgment? Textbook authors cannot include every event. The past is immense. No book claims to be complete. Decisions must be made. What is important? What is appropriate for a given age level? Perhaps teachers should devote no time at all to Helen Keller, no matter how heroic she was.

But when we look at what textbooks do include—when we contemplate the minute details, some of them false, that they foist upon us about Columbus, for example—we have to think again. Constraints of time and space cannot be causing textbooks to leave out any discussion of what Columbus did with the

Americas or how Europe came to dominate the world, since these issues are among the most vital in all the broad sweep of the past.

Perhaps an upper-class conspiracy is to blame. Perhaps we are all dupes, manipulated by elite white male capitalists who orchestrate how history is written as part of their scheme to perpetuate their own power and privilege at the expense of the rest of us. Certainly high school history textbooks are so similar that they *look* as if they might all have been produced by the same executive committee of the bourgeoisie. In *1984*, George Orwell was clear about who determines the way history is written: "Who controls the present controls the past." [14]

The symbolic representation of a society's past is particularly important in stratified societies. The United States is stratified, of course, by social class, by race, and by gender. Some sociologists think that social inequality motivates people, prompting harder work and more innovative performance. It does, but stratificaton is also intrinsically unfair, because those with more money, status, and influence use their advantage to get still more, for themselves and their children. In a society marked by inequality, people who have endured less-than-equal opportunities may become restive. Members of favored groups may become ashamed of the unfairness, unable to defend it to the oppressed or even to themselves. To maintain a stratified system, it is terribly important to control how people *think* about that system. Marx advanced this analysis under the rubric *false consciousness*. How people think about the past is an important part of their consciousness. If members of the elite come to think that their privilege was historically justified and earned, it will be hard to persuade them to yield opportunity to others. If members of deprived groups come to think that their deprivaton is their own fault, then there will be no need to use force or violence to keep them in their places.

"Textbooks offer an obvious means of realizing hegemony in education," according to William L. Griffen and John Marciano, who analyzed textbook treatment of the Vietnam War.

> By hegemony we refer specifically to the influence that dominant classes or groups exercise by virtue of their control of ideological institutions, such as schools, that shape perception on such vital issues as the Vietnam War. . . . Within history texts, for example, the omission of crucial facts and viewpoints limits profoundly the ways in which students come to view history events. Further, through their one-dimensionality textbooks shield

students from intellectual encounters with their world that would sharpen their critical abilities.[15]

Here, in polite academic language, Griffen and Marciano tell us that controlling elements of our society keep crucial facts from us to keep us ignorant and stupid.

Most scholars of education share this perspective, often referred to as "critical theory."[16] Jonathan Kozol is of this school when he writes, "School is in business to produce reliable people."[17] Paulo Freire of Brazil puts it this way: "It would be extremely naïve to expect the dominant classes to develop a type of education that would enable subordinate classes to perceive social injustices critically."[18] Henry Giroux, Freire's leading disciple in the United States, maintains, "The dominant culture actively functions to suppress the development of a critical historical consciousness among the populace."[19] David Tyack and Elisabeth Hansot tell us when this all started: between 1890 and 1920 businessmen came to have by far a greater impact on public education than any other occupational group or stratum.[20] Some writers on education even conclude that upper-class control makes real improvement impossible. In a critique of educational reform initiatives, Henry M. Levin stated, "The educational system will always be applied toward serving the role of cultural transmission and preserving the status quo."[21] "The public schools we have today are what the powerful and the considerable have made of them," wrote Walter Karp. "They will not be redeemed by trifling reforms."[22]

These education writers take their cue from an even weightier school of thought in social science, the power elite theorists. This school has shown that an upper class does exist in America, and its members can be found at elegant private clubs, gatherings of the Trilateral Commission, and board meetings of the directors of the multinational corporations. Rich capitalists control the major TV networks, most newspapers, and all textbook-publishing companies, and thus possess immense power to frame the way we talk and think about current events. And on occasion they use it. ExxonMobil, for example, by some measures the world's largest corporation, gave $6 million over the last decade to the National Science Teachers Association, chump change to Exxon but a bonanza to the teachers. As a result, NSTA initially refused fifty thousand free copies of Al Gore's video about global warming, *An Inconvenient Truth*—which was the Motion Picture Academy winner for "Best Documentary"—citing "unnecessary risk upon the capital campaign" if they accepted. NSTA does distribute a video by the American Petroleum Institute that a *Washington Post* reporter calls "a shameless pitch for oil dependence." So money corrupts.[23]

Nevertheless, it is inappropriate to lay this particular bundle on the doorstep of the upper class. To blame the power elite for what is taught in a rural Vermont school or an inner-city classroom is too easy. If the elite is so dominant, why hasn't it also censored the books and articles that expose its influence in education? Paradoxically, critical theory cannot explain its own popularity. Any upper class worth its salt—so dominant and so monolithic that it determines how American history is taught in almost every American classroom—must also have the power to marginalize those social scientists who expose it. But the upper class has hardly kept critical theory out of education. On the contrary, critical theorists dominate scholarship in the field. Their books get prominently published and well reviewed; education professors assign them to thousands of students every year.

The upper class controls publishing, to be sure, but its control does not extend to content, at least not if the books in question make money. Robert Heilbroner has pointed out that no matter what is done in America, members of the upper class usually have a hand in it, but their participation does not mean that they directed the action, nor that it was in their class's interest.[24] Many of the books that criticize American education are published by companies that also put out the textbooks they criticize. One of the glories of capitalism is that somewhere there are publishers who will publish almost *any* book, so long as they stand to make a profit from it. If the upper class forces the omission of "crucial facts and viewpoints," then why has it failed to censor the entire marvelous secondary literature in American history—which occasionally even breaks into prime-time public television in series like *Eyes on the Prize*, an account of the civil rights movement. The upper class seems to be falling down on the job.

The elite has also apparently lost control of the landscape. Across America, new, more accurate historical markers and monuments are going up. In Alabama and Illinois, for example, new markers give tourists a good sense of the "Trail of Tears" of the Cherokees and Choctaws. A new monument in Duluth, Minnesota, tells of the tragic day in the nadir of race relations when whites lynched three black circus workers. American Indians have created new museums, such as the Pequot Museum in Connecticut that tells the full story of the tribe, including their partial annihilation by the Pilgrims, their survival through the nadir, and their successful new casino. The Museum of the Confederacy in

Richmond, Virginia, mounted its first-ever exhibit on slavery, which included chains, torture devices, and a resulting book that did not minimize the inhumanity of the institution.[25] Perhaps we must conclude, mixing a metaphor, that the power elite did not have its thumb in every pie.

Interestingly, the upper class may not even control what is taught in its "own" history classrooms. Graduates of elite "prep" schools are more likely than public school graduates to have encountered high school history teachers who challenged them and diverged from rote use of textbooks. Such teachers' success in teaching "subversively" in the belly of the upper class should hearten us to believe that it can be done anywhere.[26] On the other hand, if textbooks are devised by the upper class to manipulate youngsters to support the status quo, they hardly seem to be succeeding. Instead of revering Columbus et al., students wind up detesting history. Evidence suggests that history textbooks and courses make little impact in increasing trust in the United States or inducing good citizenship, however these are measured.[27]

In sum, power elite theories seem to explain everything but may explain nothing. They may credit the upper class with more power, unity, and conscious self-interest than it has. Indeed, regarding its alleged influence on American history textbooks, the upper class may be a scapegoat. Blaming the power elite is comforting. Power elite theory offers tidy explanations: educational institutions cannot reform because to do so is not in that class's interest, so the upper class prevents change. Accordingly, power elite theory may create a world more satisfying and more coherent in evil than the real world with which we are all complicit. Power elite theories thus absolve the rest of us from seeing that all of us participate in the process of cultural distortion. This line of thought not only excuses us from responsibility for the sorry state of American history as currently taught, it also frees us from the responsibility for changing it. What's the use? Any action we might take would be inconsequential by definition.

Upper-class control may not be necessary to explain textbook misrepresentation, however. Special pressures in the world of textbook publishing may account to some extent for the uniformity and dullness of American history textbooks. Almost half the states have textbook adoption boards. Some of these boards function explicitly as censors, making sure that books not only meet criteria for length, coverage, and reading level, but also that they avoid topics and treatments that might offend some parents. States without such boards are not necessarily freer of censorship, for their screening usually takes place on the local level, where concern about giving offense can be even more immediate. Moreover, states without textbook boards constitute smaller markets, since publishers must win approval at the individual district or school level. Therefore, states without boards have less influence on publishers, who orient their best efforts toward the large states with adoption boards. California and Texas, in particular, directly affect publishers and textbooks because they are large markets with statewide adoption and active lobbying groups. Schools and districts in nonadoption states must choose among books designed for the larger markets.[28]

Textbook adoption processes are complex.[29] Some states, such as Tennessee, accept almost every book that meets certain basic criteria for binding, reading level, and subject matter. Tennessee schools then select from among perhaps a dozen books, usually making district-wide decisions.[30] At the other extreme, Alabama used to adopt just one book per subject for the entire state. State textbook boards are usually small committees whose members have been appointed by the governor or the state commissioner of education. They are volunteers who may be teachers, lawyers, parents, or other concerned citizens. The daily work of the textbook board is typically performed by a small staff that begins by circulating specifications that tell publishers the grade levels, physical requirements (size, binding, and the like), and guidelines as to content for all subjects in which they next plan to adopt textbooks. Publishers respond by sending books and ancillary materials. Meanwhile the board, with input from the person(s) who appointed them and sometimes with staff input as well, sets up rating committees in each subject area—for instance, high school American history. The staff holds orientation meetings for these rating committees, explains the forms used for rating the textbooks, and then sends the books to the raters.

Usually one formal meeting is set up for publishers' representatives to address the rating committees. Large states may hold several meetings in different parts of the state. At these meetings the representatives emphasize the ways in which their books excel. For the most part representatives push form, not content: they tout special features of layout, art work, "skills building," and ancillary material such as videos and exams.

Rating committees face a Herculean task. Remember that the recent books I examined average 1,150 pages. In a single summer, raters cannot even read all the books, let alone compare them meaningfully. Raters also wrestle with an average of seventy-three different rating criteria that they are supposed to apply to each book—an Augean stable. Since they have time only to flip through most books, they look for easy readability, newness, a stunning color cover, appealing design, color illustrations, and ancillaries such as audiovisual materials, ready-made teaching aids, and test questions. Ancillaries can be critical. Many teachers, especially those with little background, depend on them. Publishers supply complete lecture outlines, little stories to add color to the basic narrative, and websites with "animated maps" and "infographics," to quote a McDougal-Littell brochure. Test questions are especially important. Many teachers have neither time nor knowledge to make up their own unit tests, having 120 students in four sections of the course. Thus, a discussion group of teachers of advanced-placement U.S. history courses was notified in fall 2006 that some teacher somewhere had posted questions and answers from the test bank that accompanies *The American Pageant*. "To say the least this is quite distressing," wrote a teacher in alarm. "I have e-mailed the teacher in question and asked him to remove the links ASAP." [31]

Unfortunately, marketing textbooks is like marketing fishing lures: the point is to catch fishermen, not fish. Thus, many adopted textbooks are flashy to catch the eye of adoption committees but dull when read by students. *The American Journey*, the new seventh-grade textbook by Joyce Appleby, Alan Brinkley, and James McPherson, exemplifies the problem. It is disjointed to the point of incoherence. Perhaps in response to the alleged short attention spans of today's students, the layout department at McGraw-Hill has run amok. Consider what should be a compact, interesting chapter: "World War II." This chapter begins with a star in a box containing a paragraph titled "Why It's Important." Another star in a box introduces five "Chapter Themes." A theme, we learn in the beginning of the book under the heading "How Can I Remember Everything?" is "a concept, or main idea, that happens again and again throughout history." Whether a concept or idea "happens" is dubious, as is whether such themes as "continuity and change" can help anyone remember anything. As we read the first section, "Road to War," for example, how does it help us to know that it fits under the theme "continuity and change"? What doesn't?

Then, highlighted by a star in a rectangle titled "History and Art," comes the title "Embarkation, San Francisco, California," for a painting by Barse Miller. It is captioned, "World War II American soldiers believed they were fighting for what President Roosevelt called the Four Freedoms: freedom of speech and expression, freedom of worship, freedom from want, and freedom from fear." As a historical statement, that caption is questionable, showing none of the sophistication one of the authors, James McPherson, brought to his

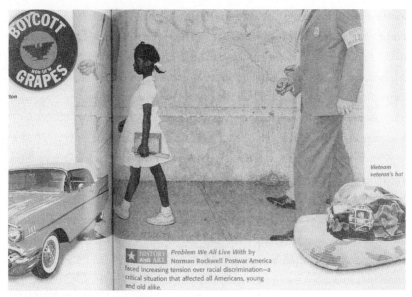

'ton

Vietnam veteran's hat

★ HISTORY AND ART *Problem We All Live With* by Norman Rockwell Postwar America faced increasing tension over racial discrimination—a critical situation that affected all Americans, young and old alike.

Even the graphics get ruined by the busyness of modern textbooks. On the next page after World War II in *The American Journey,* we see Norman Rockwell's famous painting *The Problem We All Live With,* showing a black girl dressed in her Sunday best for her first day of school, with federal marshals walking before and after her. Only we don't see it well. The illustration is overlaid by an ad for a 1957 Chevrolet, a button for the United Farm Workers grape boycott, and a hat. Its power is further vitiated by the unfortunate layout: the designer has moved it into the crease between pages to make room for the caption "Vietnam veteran's hat." (Showing their own attention deficit disorder, the authors give us another "Vietnam veteran's hat" with the same caption, superimposed over another image, a hundred pages later.) This placement cuts out much of the forward marshal and makes the girl appear to be marching into the page crease.

book *For Cause and Comrades: Why Men Fought in the Civil War.* The next page brings a time line of the 1930s with only four events on it: Japan invades Manchuria, Hitler becomes chancellor of Germany, Italy invades Ethiopia, and Germany seizes Czechoslovakia. At the risk of suggesting more cluttering, plenty of room remains for more entries, such as Kristallnacht, the 1938 event that launched Germany's pogrom against the Jews.

Then comes a heading, "Section I," in a little golden egg, and "Road to War." Still the chapter does not start; first we have a summary headed "Read to Discover . . ." followed by three topics. (I would call them *themes,* except that term has already been usurped.) Then we have five "Terms to Learn." They are followed by a heading, "The Storyteller," which introduces a paragraph by William Shirer about a Nazi rally. At last, after a photograph of the book jacket of

Mein Kampf, we finally begin the narrative text about World War II. In all, about 55 percent of the World War II chapter is *not* the narrative text, but interruptions to it. Some of these sidebars and boxes offer excerpts from original sources or useful vignettes. Others are less than useful "Activities" and "Terms to Learn." Overall, they distract. Since the narrative text comprises less than half of the whole, often it looks lost on the page, becoming just one more interruption.

Could this jumble be necessary? Millions of middle-schoolers have read Harry Potter books voluntarily. Yet each book contains hundreds of pairs of facing text pages with no illustrations, no sidebars—nothing but the main story. Cluttering every page with "Multimedia Activities," "The Storyteller," and "Terms to Learn" seems aimed at textbook adoption committees rather than actual readers. The narrative *looks* more readable than Harry Potter but is actually far *less* readable.

Moving beyond style, what content do adopters want to see? First off, they look for nice treatments of events and people important to their own state. In New Hampshire, woe to the textbook that speaks honestly about Franklin W. Pierce, famed fourteenth president of these United States. He was perhaps our second-worst president ever, as he presided over near civil war in Kansas, had his diplomats gather to produce the embarrassing Ostend Manifesto (which threatened to take Cuba; eventually the U.S. State Department had to disavow the document), and was drunk much of the time. But he was the only president New Hampshire ever produced. Likewise, the Alamo lies deep in the heart of (Anglo) Texans; woe to any textbook that might point out that love of slavery motivated Anglos to fight there for "freedom." Some local demands make for more inclusive history: California's legislature recently debated a bill to require textbooks to include the internment of Japanese Americans during World War II.[32]

Usually adopters find the details they seek. Most textbook editors start their careers in publishing as sales representatives. They are not historians, but they know their market. They make sure their books include whatever is likely to be of concern. Everything gets mentioned. Lynne Cheney, former director of the National Endowment for the Humanities, decried the result: "Textbooks come to seem like glossaries of historical events—compendiums of topics."[33] In recent years, even more has to get mentioned, owing to the multiple-choice tests that many states have concocted to comply with the No Child Left Behind Act. Teachers will always teach to a test, especially a high-stakes test that results in students not getting diplomas or schools being placed on probation. Multiple-choice exams almost have to test "twig history"—tiny factoids like "When did the War of 1812 begin?"[34] No Child Left Behind does not require multiple-choice tests in history. Indeed, it does not require *any* tests in history. Teachers have learned to their sorrow, however, that the only thing worse than a multiple-choice test in history is *no* test in history, for then a school district de-emphasizes history entirely, focusing instead on those subjects that are tested. There is an answer to this conundrum, however, and some states have found it: develop a test—or portfolio or other instrument—worth teaching to. In the meantime, however, NCLB and the statewide exams it has spawned provide one more reason for textbooks to grow longer and teachers to use them haplessly.

In some states the next step is hearings, at which the public is invited to comment on books under consideration by the rating committees. In Texas and California, at least, these hearings are occasions at which organized groups attack or promote one or more of the selections, often contending that a book fails to meet a requirement found within the regulations or specifications. Although publishers lament the procedure, critics, particularly in Texas, have unearthed and forced publishers to correct hundreds of errors, from misspellings to major blunders. Since adoption committees do try to please constituents, those who complain at hearings often make a difference, for better and sometimes for worse.

Adoption states used to pressure publishers overtly to espouse certain points of view. For years any textbook sold in Dixie had to call the Civil War "the War between the States." Earlier editions of *The American Pageant* used the even more pro-Confederate term "the War for Southern Independence." This is simply bad history. Between 1861 and 1865 while it was going on, the Civil War was called "the Civil War," "the Rebellion," or "the Great Rebellion"— hence "rebels." But *Pageant* did "exceptionally well" in Southern states, so who cares? Only after the civil rights movement did *Pageant* revert to "the Civil War."[35] Alabama law used to require that schools avoid "textbooks containing anything partisan, prejudicial, or inimical to the interests of the [white] people of the State" or that would "cast a reflection on their past history."[36] Texas still requires that "textbooks shall not contain material which serves to undermine authority."[37] Such standards are astounding in their breadth and might force drastic cuts in almost every chapter of every textbook, except that authors have already omitted most unpleasantries and controversies.

Many states have rewritten their textbook specifications to strike such blatant content requirements. Since at least 1970 Mississippi's regulations, for example, have consisted of a series of clichés with which no reasonable textbook author or critic could disagree. Publishers might be forgiven if they believe that the spirit of the old regulations still survives, however, for the initial rejection of *Mississippi: Conflict and Change* proves that it does. I was senior author of the book, a revisionist state history text finally published by Pantheon Books in 1974. I say "finally" because Pantheon brought it out only after eleven other publishers refused. The problem wasn't with the quality of the manuscript, which won the Lillian Smith Award for best Southern nonfiction that year. The problem was that trade publishers said they could not publish a textbook, while textbook publishers said they could not publish a book so unlikely to be adopted. Some publishers even feared that Mississippi might retaliate against their textbooks in other subjects. Textbook publishers proved partly right—the textbook board refused to allow our book. It contained too much "black history," included a photograph of a lynching, and gave too much attention to the recent past, according to the white majority on the rating committee. My coauthors and I, joined by three school systems that wanted to adopt the book, sued the state in a First Amendment challenge, *Loewen et al. v. Turnipseed et al.*, and in 1980 got the book on the state's approved list.

Despite the value of *Turnipseed* as a precedent, publishers still fear right-wing criticism. And with reason. In 2006 Florida passed a law that states, "The history of the United States shall be taught as genuine history and shall not follow the revisionist or postmodernist viewpoints of relative truth. . . . American history shall be viewed as factual, not as constructed." This law is meant as a shot across the bow of "liberal" professors who "interpret" the past rather than "telling it like it was." Its authors have no understanding that *any* telling of history requires choices as to what is included and what is left out and is therefore by definition an interpretation.

Another force for uniform, conservative textbooks comes from publishing houses themselves. "There's a great deal of copying," Carolyn Jackson, who has probably edited more American history textbooks than any other single individual, told me. In the 1980s every house coveted the success of *Triumph of the American Nation*, which held a quarter to a third of the market. So most textbooks resembled *Triumph*. Indeed, they still do. Although adequate scholarship exists in the secondary literature to support such ventures intellectually, not a single left-wing or right-wing American history textbook has ever appeared from a mainstream publisher. Neither has a textbook emphasizing African American, Latino, labor, or feminist history as the entry point to general American history.[38] Such books might sell dozens of thousands of copies a year and make thousands of dollars in profit. At the least, they would command niches in the marketplace all their own. Publishers might do fine without Texas.[39] Nonetheless, no publishing house can see such possibilities. All are blinded by the golden prospect of putting out the next *Triumph* and making millions of dollars. One editor characterized a prospective book, perhaps unfairly, as too focused on "the mistreatment of blacks" in American history. "We couldn't have that as our only American history," he continued. "So we broke the contract." The manuscript was never published. "We didn't want a book with an ax to grind," the editor concluded. Of course, one person's point of view is another's ax to grind, so textbooks end up without axes *or* points of view.

Thus, textbook uniformity cannot be attributed exclusively to overt state censors. Even in the formerly communist countries of Eastern Europe, censorship was largely effected by authors, editors, and publishers, not by state censors, and was "ultimately a matter of . . . sensitivity to the ideological atmosphere."[40] It is not too different here: textbook publishers rarely do anything that they *imagine* might risk state disapproval. Therefore, they never stray far from the traditional textbooks in form, tone, and content. Indeed, when Scott, Foresman merely replaced *Macbeth* with *Hamlet* in their literature reader, educators and editors considered the change so radical that Hillel Black devoted three pages to the event in his book on textbook publishing, *The American Schoolbook*.[41] In American history, even more than in literature, publishers strive for a "balanced" approach to offend no one.

Publishers would undoubtedly think twice before including a hard-hitting account of Columbus, for example. In Chapter 2, I used *genocide* to refer to the destruction of the Arawaks in the Caribbean. When scholars used the same term in applying for a grant for a television series on Columbus from the National Endowment for the Humanities, the endowment rejected them.[42] Lynne Cheney said that the word was a problem. The entire project, *1492: Clash of Visions*, was too pro-Indian for the endowment. "It's okay to talk about the barbarism of the Indians, but not about the barbarism of the Europeans," complained the series producer.[43]

For publishers to avoid giving offense is getting increasingly difficult, however. A dizzying array of critics—creationists, the radical right, civil liberties groups, racial minorities, feminists, and even professional historians—have entered the fray. No longer do textbooks get denounced only as integrationist or liberal.[44] Now they are also attacked as colonialist, Eurocentric, or East Coast–centric. Publishers must feel a bit flustered as they delete a passage modestly critical of American policy to please right-wing critics in one state, only to find they have offended left-wing critics in another. Including a photograph of Henry Cisneros may please Hispanics but risk denunciation by New Englanders demanding an image of John Adams.

Although publishers want to think of themselves as moral beings, they also want to make money. "We want to do well *while* doing good," the president of Random House, the parent company of Pantheon, said to me as he inquired into the commercial prospects of our Mississippi textbook.[45] Thoughts of the bottom line narrow the range of thought publishers tolerate in textbooks. Publishers risk over half a million dollars in production costs with every new textbook. Understandably, this scares them.

What about the authors? Since every bad paragraph had to have an author, surely authors lie at the heart of the process. It's not always clear who the real authors are, however. The names on the cover of a textbook are rarely those of the people who really wrote it.[46] Lewis Todd and Merle Curti may have written the first draft of *Rise of the American Nation* back in 1949, but by the time its tenth edition came out in 1991, now titled *Triumph of the American Nation*, Curti was ninety-five and in a nursing home and Todd was dead. The people listed as authors on some other textbooks have even less to do with them. Some teachers and historians merely rent their names to publishers, supplying occasional advice in return for a fraction of the usual royalties, while minions in the bowels of the publishing houses do the work of organizing and writing the textbooks. Often these anonymous clerks have only a BA in English, according to an editor at McGraw-Hill.[47]

An executive at Prentice Hall told me that Daniel Boorstin "controls every word that goes into his book," which does not claim that he wrote it but does imply substantial author involvement. We will see later that even this claim cannot be substantiated. Prentice Hall relies on Davidson and Lytle to keep *A History of the Republic* current in historical content, according to the publisher. Even these modest claims are suspect, however. Mark Lytle admitted that he and his coauthor play only "a kind of authentication role" regarding new editions. The publisher initiates the new material, and it is "too late to make any major changes once it reaches us."

In 2006, as I was studying the six new textbooks for this revised edition of

Lies My Teacher Told Me, one topic I focused on was their treatments of the recent past, especially of our two Iraq wars and the attacks of 9/11/2001 on the World Trade Center and the Pentagon. To my astonishment, I found that for paragraph after paragraph, two books—*America: Pathways to the Present*, by Andrew Cayton, Elisabeth Perry, Linda Reed, and Allan Winkler, and *A History of the United States*, by Daniel Boorstin and Brooks Mather Kelley—were identical, or nearly identical. Here, for example, are the first paragraphs of their discussion of the disputed Florida election between Bush and Gore in 2000.

On election night, the votes in several states were too close to call; neither candidate had captured the 270 electoral votes needed to win the presidency. One undecided state, Florida, could give either candidate enough electoral votes to win the presidency. Because the vote there was so close, state law required a recount of the ballots. Florida became a battleground for the presidency as lawyers, politicians, and the media swarmed there to monitor the recount.

—*America: Pathways to the Present*

On election night the votes in several states were too close to call and neither candidate captured the 270 electoral votes needed to win. One undecided state, Florida, would give either candidate the electoral votes needed to win. A recount of the votes there was ordered by law, due to the close results which slightly favored Bush. Florida became a battleground for the presidency as lawyers and the media swarmed there to monitor the recount.

—*A History of the United States*

Both books choose the same image to represent the destruction of the World Trade Center on 9/11/2001: three men in firemen's hats raising the American flag, reminiscent of the famous photo of the marines on Iwo Jima. Both give the photo the same caption: "Rescue workers raise the American flag amidst the rubble of the fallen World Trade Center towers," although Boorstin and Kelley append the date. The rest of their treatments of the 9/11 attacks are equally similar. In *Pathways*, "the impact of the fully fueled jets caused both towers to burst into flames," while in *A History*, "the impact of the fully fueled jets caused the twin towers to burst into flames."

So it goes, page after page. The books describe our war in Afghanistan in identical sentences, too. Both contain a section titled *Department of Homeland*

Security, although *Pathways* drops *Department of.* In both books, these sections begin, "The President also moved quickly to combat terrorism at home." They continue:

> Less than a month after the 9/11 attacks, Bush created the Office of Homeland Security, to be headed by Pennsylvania Governor Tom Ridge. Ridge took office amidst a new wave of mysterious attacks. Anthrax spores, which can be deadly if inhaled, began turning up in letters. . . .
> —*Pathways to the Present*

> Less than a month after the 9/11 attacks, Bush created the Office of Homeland Security, with Pennsylvania Governor Tom Ridge in charge.
> Ridge took office amidst a new wave of mysterious attacks. Anthrax spores, which can be deadly if inhaled, began turning up in letters. . . .
> —*A History of the United States*

What is happening here?

Do we imagine that Boorstin and Kelley cribbed from Cayton, Perry, Reed, and Winkler? Daniel J. Boorstin was a famous historian, former Librarian of Congress, and the author of more than twenty books. According to his obituary in the *Manchester Guardian*, his "learning and diligence were legendary." But he was in his eighty-ninth and final year when this textbook was being written. Maybe the fault lies with his coauthor. Brooks Mather Kelley formerly served as Yale University archivist and curator of historical manuscripts, so he must know about proper scholarship and attribution.

Or maybe Cayton, Perry, Reed, and Winkler cribbed from Boorstin and Kelley? They are less famous than Boorstin, but all are tenured professors and hold doctorates in history, so all have been exposed to proper scholarly etiquette. One of them, Allan Winkler, "Distinguished Professor of History" at Miami University in Ohio, specializes in recent history, especially the history of the home front during World War II. So maybe *he* wrote the passages in question and Boorstin and Mather pilfered them.

If these were real books, historians would hold their collective breaths, waiting to see whether Kelley (and Boorstin's estate) sues Cayton et al., or vice versa. These identical passages are far longer and more flagrant, after all, than the copying that got Stephen Ambrose and Doris Kearns Goodwin into so much hot water a few years ago. One of Ambrose's sins, for example, was quoting primary sources as if he had found them, rather than double-quoting them because he had read them in a secondary source. Nothing so subtle is going on here. For page after page, topic after topic, these textbooks sport paragraphs that are interchangeable.

I asked Kelley what he thought had taken place. He said he had nothing to do with the 2005 revision: "Dan Boorstin did that one." (Kelley claimed to have had more to do with the "classic edition," which also carries a 2005 copyright, has the same cover, lists for the same price, and appears to be the same book.) I asked who wrote the material on the recent past. "They hired somebody," he replied. "I don't remember the man's name. Dan then looked over it and, I'm sure, rewrote it in his inimitable fashion." When he learned that the passages are the same as those in another history textbook, he was taken aback. "That's terrible!" he exclaimed. "I wonder if they hired one of the same people who wrote *that* book." Asked for his reaction to the duplication, Kelley replied, "I'm extremely distressed."[48]

At first Allan Winkler claimed authorship of the last chapter of *Pathways to the Present*: "I wrote most of that. Then the editors played with it." After I told him that paragraph after paragraph are the same or nearly the same as those in Boorstin and Kelley, he hastened to deny that he had copied from them: "I have never even opened the Boorstin and Kelley book." He then backed away from the claim of authorship. "It's possible that somebody in-house wrote that for both books, which would appall me." Asked for his reaction to the duplication, Winkler replied, "I find that profoundly disturbing. Lord!"[49]

Thus, neither set of authors copied from the other. That's because neither wrote *anything*. Prentice Hall published both textbooks, and both new chapters were written by a nameless person known only to its editorial staff. The tiny differences between the two probably came about in the copyediting process. Prentice Hall's bargain-basement thinking does draw back the curtain on the sordid process of textbook construction, however.

I asked Winkler what he thought of the treatment of the recent past that had been published under his name. "Well, let me get it off the shelf," he replied. He then admitted that he had not read it. Nor had Kelley read the last chapter of *A History*, and he had already given up on his claim that Boorstin had done so.

Superficially, these acts by Boorstin, Kelly, Winkler, et al., recall those busy undergraduates who buy term papers off the Web, slap their names on them, and hand them in as their own. Both sets of "authors" take credit for the work of others, who remain nameless but do get paid. A key difference, however, is that the cheating students usually at least *read* the material, even though they didn't write it. These textbook authors have never even bothered to read the words that go out over their names. Boorstin, Kelley, and Winkler may be crediting Saddam Hussein with having nuclear weapons. They may have misidentified Osama bin Laden as a Jewish rabbi. If so, they'll be the last to know.

These passages are not mere revisions of earlier material that the putative authors actually wrote. This is brand-new history. Moreover, final chapters surely rank among the most important in the books. They cover important, hotly contested, ongoing issues. Unlike the War of 1812, or even World War II, there can be no doubt about their relevance to the present. If the people listed as authors of these textbooks never wrote *these* passages, what *did* they write? And if they did not even *read* these passages, what did they read? Surely not the small and not-so-small changes in interpretations that have swept through the treatment of American Indians, for example, as a result of the new scholarship of the past three decades.

It's not just these two books that suffer from anonymous writing. Editors tell me that recent chapters of American history textbooks are "typically" written by freelance writers. Nor is it just the final chapters. Judith Conaway, who has ghostwritten elementary-level textbooks in several fields, wrote, "It is absolutely the standard practice in the textbook publishing industry to assign ALL the writing to freelancers. Then you rent a name to go on the cover." Since *Rise/ Triumph of the American Nation* by Todd and Curti sold so well in the 1970s and 1980s, the publisher wanted to keep it in print. In 1994, having finally become embarrassed by the fact that Todd was dead and Curti was in a nursing home, Holt, Rinehart and Winston moved their names into the title and engaged Paul Boyer to "write" what was now called *Todd and Curti's The American Nation*. Ironically, Boyer had become "Merle Curti Professor of History" at Wisconsin. Asked if he substantially rewrote the book at that point, Boyer would not say. Instead, he replied, "I really would like to know more of your motive before discussing details of my career." I identified myself as a member of the Organization of American Historians and the American Historical Association, explained that I was the author of *Lies My Teacher Told Me*, and noted that *Lies* would be coming out in a new edition. Although he had heard of *Lies*, he still would not reveal who had written *Todd and Curti's The American Nation*, referring me to an editor at Holt. In 1998 "his" book came out again, now titled *The American Nation*. In 2003 it was again renamed, to *Holt American Nation*, which does carry a certain honesty, since the publisher, not the author, surely does write most of it. To the *New York Times*, Boyer excused the practice with the quip, "Textbooks are hardly the same as the *Iliad* or *Beowulf*." Interviewed by the *Times*, Brooks Mather Kelley said, "Frankly, many of these textbooks, unlike ours, were not written by the authors who were once involved with them." His use of "unlike ours" was staggering, since I had just caught Boorstin and him red-handed. Moreover, two days later his claim that he and Boorstin had written earlier editions of their book was contradicted by James Goodwin, who revealed that about fifteen years earlier, he had revised and written several chapters of it. "I did it for the money," he said, "ten thousand dollars for a few months of part-time work." [50]

The editor quoted at the head of the chapter implies no one is the loser from this practice, because the freelancers "pick things up pretty quickly, and in a couple of days, they're up on the Civil War." Historians who have spent decades researching that war may not agree that it can be mastered in two days, however. Hiring neophyte stand-ins to do authors' work may help explain the sometimes astonishing mistakes that textbooks commit. A notorious example was the claim in a 1990-era textbook, "President Truman easily settled the Korean War by dropping the atomic bomb." [51] Truman's action certainly came as a surprise to Dwight Eisenhower, who campaigned for the presidency in 1952 with the slogan, "I will go to Korea." Similar errors dot history textbooks from start to finish. Boorstin and Kelley tell us, for instance, that one reason Columbus sailed to the Americas from the Canary Islands, rather than from Spain, was that "the Canaries were on the same latitude as Japan, so if he went due west he thought he would arrive where he wanted to be." Actually Seville, Spain's leading port at the time, lies precisely at the midpoint of Honshu, Japan's largest island. The Canaries lie far to the south, as a glance at a globe reveals. To take another example, *The American Journey* claims that "Maggie Lena" "was the first American woman to serve as a bank president," leaving out Maggie Walker's last name. One of *Journey*'s three putative authors is James McPherson, specialist in Civil War African American history. He would never have written—or even read—that passage and allowed such a mistake to stand.

The anonymous author of the last chapter of *The American Pageant* didn't have to be a specialist to avoid the following egregious error about the 2004 election:

On election day, Bush nailed down a decisive victory. His three-pronged strategy of emphasizing taxes, terror, and moral values paid off handsomely. He posted the first popular vote majority in more than a decade, 60,639,281 to Kerry's 57,355,978, with a commanding advantage in the Electoral College, 286 to 252.

Commanding advantage indeed! The mere switch of Ohio's 20 electoral votes, which Kerry almost won, would have given Kerry 272 and the victory, to Bush's 266. Does not the author recall the suspense on election night, along with the claims of voting irregularities in Ohio during the next week? Moreover, in percentage terms, Bush got 51.2 percent of the Bush-Kerry total, while in 1996 Clinton got 54.7 percent of the Clinton-Dole total. To spin the election to produce a "handsome" mandate where none occurred may be good politics, but it's bad history.[52]

Updating does not just require adding a new chapter at the end, to handle the new happenings since the book last came out. New facts are discovered about older events, from new information about the events of the 1990s all the way back to new discoveries in archaeology that influence our understanding of the first people in our hemisphere. Throughout the book, the process of updating also suffers from the absence of oversight—by the alleged authors or anyone else. Consider the sabotage of Pan American Airlines flight 103, which exploded over Lockerbie, Scotland, in 1988. In 1989, 1992, and 1995, Boorstin and Kelley had sound company when they wrote "there were many indications that the Iranians had ordered the bombing." For their book to make this claim in its 2005 edition implies that the authors were not convinced by the conviction of a Libyan in 2001, missed Libya's payment of more than two billion dollars to victims of the disaster in 2002, and did not credit Libya's admission of guilt in 2003.[53] Of course, the anonymous authors and updaters, being anonymous, do not risk their reputations by such errors.

Even authors who *do* write their books write only the core narrative, which is gradually becoming an ever smaller proportion of the whole. Authors have nothing to do with the countless boxes, teaching aids, questions, photo captions, and "activities" that now often take up more space than the narrative itself. Perhaps that is why this material is frequently so mindless. Consider this suggestion after the chapter about the coming of the Civil War in *Holt American Nation*: "Homework: Have each student obtain and read *John Brown's Body* by Stephen Vincent Benét and write a two-paragraph response to the poem." This assignment is so absurd as to prompt the conclusion that no one is home intellectually at Holt, Rinehart and Winston. The task does follow an account of John Brown's 1859 takeover of the armory at Harpers Ferry. But *John Brown's Body* is not even about that takeover. Rather, it is the poet's evocation of selected aspects of the Civil War and of the society that resulted from it. Moreover, the poem is nearly four hundred pages long. "Have each student obtain and read" it, indeed—most adults have never read a four-hundred-page poem in their lives, and if one did, how does one respond to it in two paragraphs?[54]

Other questions are mindlessly huge. *The Americans*, for example, asks: "How has location influenced the history of your city or town?" Now, that's quite a question. A PhD dissertation might make a good stab at answering it. Quite an assignment for someone just starting a course in American history. Next it asks, "How have the characteristics and concerns of your region changed over the last generation?" Again, quite a question. If we think about answering it for the South, we realize how formidable the question is. Yet the South is America's most defined region. To define the "characteristics and concerns of the Midwest" would be still harder, let alone assess how they have changed. What could these authors have in mind? Nothing, I submit. Someone decided that the page would look better with questions on it; someone else supplied them; but they aren't meant to be answered. Unfortunately, questions like these encourage students to conclude that idle speculation amounts to a form of learning.

When questions aren't mindless, often they are mind-numbing. Several books have the annoying habit of ending every photo caption with a question. Consider this question in *The American Journey* under a photo showing Hitler at a Nazi rally: "What group especially suffered from the Nazis?" Three inches above the photo, the text tells of Hitler's "extreme anti-Semitism." If "groups" had been asked in the plural, the question becomes more interesting, with additional possible answers such as the Rom people, socialists, homosexuals, and others. All *Journey* wants, however, is for students to mutter "Jews." *The Americans* dots its margins with questions headed "Main Idea." Next to a paragraph telling why women organized the National Organization for Women, for example, is the question "What prompted women to establish NOW?" All students need to do is rewrite the paragraph in their own hand, and lo! they are studying history!

Even when the question is interesting, too often the desired answer is self-evident, hence boring. *Holt American Nation* provides the quotation reprinted in

Chapter 6 from the *Chicago Tribune* responding to Mississippi's "Black Codes": "The men of the North will convert the State of Mississippi into a frog pond before they will allow such laws to disgrace one foot of soil in which the bones of our soldiers sleep and over which the flag of freedom waves." That quotation is arresting and important. *Holt* then asks: "Identifying Bias: How does the writer reveal his opinion of the Black Codes?" Although not perfect, that question might lead students to draw interesting observations. The quote shows the extent to which the war had become identified with the cause of black freedom, for example—at least among Republicans, the *Tribune* being an important organ of the Republican Party. It then links the intense emotional attachment to "our" war dead to the cause of antiracism. "Into a frog pond" deserves analysis, too, as a piece of rhetoric that at once disrespects the state of Mississippi and proclaims Northern power over it. The answer in the teacher's edition, however, makes clear that no actual thought is envisioned: "By writing that northern men will turn Mississippi into a frog pond before allowing the state to impose the Black Codes." This merely repeats the quotation, turning the assignment into another exercise of rote repetition.

Although we can hope the authors had nothing to do with such silly teaching suggestions, their names are on the books and they should be held responsible for what is inside their covers.

Ironically, once in a while the material added by publishers' clerks conflicts with and enhances the base narrative. In *American Journey*, someone added "My Lai Massacre" and its date to the map "The Vietnam War," even though the text never mentions the event. Exactly what students are to make of this map notation is unclear.

In interviews with me, publishing executives blamed adoption boards, school administrators, or parents, whom they feel they have to please, for the distortions and lies of omission that mar U.S. history textbooks. Parents, whether black militants or Texas conservatives, blame publishers. Teachers blame administrators who make them use distasteful books or the publishers who produced them. But authors blame no one. They claim credit for their books. Several authors told me that they suffered no editorial interference. Indeed, authors of three different textbooks told me that their editors never offered *a single* content suggestion. "That book doesn't have fifty words in it that were changed by the editor!" exclaimed one author. "They were so respectful of my judgment, they were obsequious," said another. "I kept waiting for them to say no, but they never did." [55]

If authors claim to have written the textbooks as they wanted, then maybe they are to blame for their books. Sometimes they don't know any better. I asked John Garraty, author of *American History*, why he omitted the plague in New England that devastated Indian societies before the Pilgrims came. "I didn't know about it" was his straightforward reply. To his credit, soon afterword Garraty learned about the Columbian Exchange and made it the first entry in his *1001 Things Everyone Should Know About American History*.[56]

Sometimes authors do know better. As previously mentioned, in *After the Fact*, a book aimed at college history majors, James Davidson and Mark Lytle do a splendid job telling of the Indian plagues, demonstrating that they understand their geopolitical significance, their devastating impact on Indian culture and religion, and their effect on estimates of the precontact Indian population. In *After the Fact*, looking down from the Olympian heights of academe, Davidson and Lytle even write, "Textbooks have finally begun to take note of these large-scale epidemics." Meanwhile, their own high school history textbooks leave them out.[57]

How are we to understand this kind of behavior? Authors know that even if their textbook is good, it won't really count toward tenure and promotion at most universities. "*Real scholars* don't write textbooks" is a saying in academia.[58] If the textbook is bad, the authors won't get chastised by the profession because professional historians do not read high school textbooks.[59] The *American Historical Review, Journal of American History*, and *Reviews in American History* do not review high school textbooks. Thus, the authors' academic reputations are not really on the line.[60]

Adoption boards loom in the textbook authors' minds to a degree, especially when publishers bring them up. Authors rarely have personal knowledge of the adoption process—I am an unfortunate exception. Editors may invoke students' parents as well as adoption boards in cautioning authors not to give offense. "I wanted a text that could be used in every state," one author told me. She relied on her publisher for guidance about what would and would not accomplish this aim. Mark Lytle characterized his own textbook as "a McDonald's version of history—if it has any flavor, people won't buy it." He based this conclusion on his publisher's "survey of what the market wanted."[61]

On the other hand, publishers know that "students, parents, teachers want to see themselves represented in the texts," as one editor said to me, and occasionally influence authors to make their books *less* traditional. Michael Kammen tells of a publisher who tried to persuade the two authors of an American history textbook to give more space to Native Americans. Thomas Bailey's publisher pressed him to include more women and African Americans in *The American Pageant*.[62]

Regardless of the direction of the input, publishers are in charge. "They didn't want famous people, because we'd be more tractable," Mark Lytle told me, explaining why a major publisher had sought out him and James Davidson, relative unknowns. Two widely published authors told me that publishers tore up textbook contracts with them because they didn't like the political slant of their manuscripts. "We have arguments," one editor told me bluntly. "We usually win."

Very different conditions apply to secondary works in history, where the intended readership typically *includes* professional historians. Authors of book-length secondary works know that publishers and journal editors hire professional historians to evaluate manuscripts, so they write for other historians from the beginning. Writers also know that other historians will review their monographs after publication, and their reputation will be made or broken by those reviews in the historical journals.

With such different readerships, it is natural for secondary works and textbooks to be very different from each other. Textbook authors need not concern themselves unduly with what actually happened in history, since publishers use patriotism, rather than scholarship, to sell their books. This emphasis should hardly be surprising: the requirement to take American history originated as part of a nationalist flag-waving campaign early in this century.[63] Publishers start the pitch on their outside covers, where nationalist titles such as *The Challenge of Freedom* and *Land of Promise* are paired with traditional patriotic icons: eagles, Independence Hall, the Stars and Stripes, and the Statue of Liberty. Four of the six new books in my sample display the American flag on their covers; the other two use red, white, and blue for their titles and authors.[64] Publishers market the books as tools for helping students to "discover" our "common beliefs" and "appreciate our heritage." No publisher tries to sell a textbook with the claim that it is more accurate than its competitors.

Textbook authors also bear their student readers in mind, to a degree. From my own experience I know that imagining what one's readers need is an important part of the process of writing a history textbook. Some textbook authors are high school teachers, but most are college professors who know only a few high school or junior high school students personally. Interviews with textbook authors revealed that their imagining of what students need is a strange process.

Something about the enterprise of writing a high school American history text-book converts historians into patriots. One author told me that she was the single parent of an eleven-year-old girl when she started work on her textbook. She "wanted to write a book that Samantha would be proud of." I empathized with this desire and told of my own single parenting of a daughter about the same age. Further conversation made clear, however, that this author did not simply mean a book her daughter would respect and enjoy. Rather, she wanted a book that would make her daughter feel good about *America*, a very different thing.[65]

Other textbook authors have shared similar comments with me. They want to produce good citizens, by which they mean people who take pride in their country. Somehow authors feel they must strap on the burden of transmitting and defending Western civilization. Sometimes there was almost a touch of desperation in their comments—sort of an *après moi le déluge*. Authors can feel that they get only one shot at these children; if they do not reach them now, America's future might be jeopardized. In turn, this leads to a feeling of self-importance—that one is on the front line of our society, helping the United States continue to grow strong. Not only textbook authors feel this way: historians and history teachers commonly cite their role in building good citizens to justify what they do. In "A Proud Word for History," Allan Nevins waxes euphoric over "school texts that told of Plymouth Rock, Valley Forge, and the Alamo." He lauds history's role in making a nation strong. "Developing in the young such traits as character, morals, ethics, and good citizenship," according to Richard Gross, former president of the National Council for the Social Studies, "are the reasons for studying history and the social sciences."[66] When we were writing our Mississippi history my coauthors and I felt the same way—that we might improve our state and its citizens by imparting knowledge and changing attitudes in its next generation.

When the authors of American history textbooks have their chance to address the next generation at large, however, even those who in their monographs and private conversations are critical of some aspects of our society seem to want only to maintain America rather than change it. One textbook author, Carol Berkin, began her interview with me by saying, "As a historian, I am a feminist socialist."[67] My jaw dropped, because her textbook displays no hint of feminism or socialism. Surely, a feminist author would write a textbook that would help readers understand why no woman has ever been president or even vice president of the United States. Surely, a socialist author would write a textbook that would enable readers to understand why children of working-class families rarely become president or vice president, the mythical Abraham Lincoln to the contrary.[68]

If textbooks are overstuffed, overlong, often wrong, mindless, boring, and all alike, why do teachers use them? In one sense, teachers are responsible for the miseducation in our history classrooms. After all, the distortions and omissions exposed in the first ten chapters of this book are lies our teachers tell us. If enough teachers complained about American history textbooks, wouldn't publishers change them? Teachers also play a substantial role in adopting the textbooks: in most states, textbook rating committees are made up mainly of teachers, from whom publishers have faced no groundswell of opposition. On the contrary, many teachers like the textbooks as they are. According to researchers K. K. Wong and T. Loveless, most teachers believe that history textbooks are good and getting better.[69]

Could it be that they just don't know the truth? Many history teachers don't know much history: a national survey of 257 teachers in 1990 revealed that 13 percent had never taken a single college history course, and only 40 percent held a BA or MA in history or a field with "some history" in it, like sociology or political science.[70] Furthermore, a study of Indiana teachers revealed that fewer than one in five stay current by reading books or articles in American history. An audience of high school history teachers at a 1992 conference on Christopher Columbus and the Age of Exploitation gasped aloud to learn that people before Columbus knew the world to be round. These teachers were mortified to realize that for years they had been disseminating false information. Of course, teachers cannot teach what they do not know.

Most teachers do not like controversy. A study some years ago found that 92 percent of teachers did not initiate discussion of controversial issues, 89 percent didn't discuss controversial issues when students brought them up, and 79 percent didn't believe they should. Among the topics that teachers felt children were interested in discussing but that most teachers believed should not be discussed in the classroom were the Vietnam War, politics, race relations, nuclear war, religion, and family problems such as divorce.[71]

Many teachers are frightened of controversy because they have not experienced it themselves in an academic setting and do not know how to handle it. "Most social studies teachers in U.S. schools are ill prepared by their own schooling to deal with uncertainty," according to Shirley Engle. "They are in over their heads the minute that pat answers no longer suffice." Inertia is also built into the system: many teachers teach as they were taught. Even many college history professors who well know that history is full of controversy and dispute become old-fashioned transmitters of knowledge in their own classrooms.[72]

Since textbooks employ a rhetoric of certainty, it is hard for teachers to introduce either controversy or uncertainty into the classroom without deviating from the usual standards of discourse. Teachers rarely say "I don't know" in class and rarely discuss how one might then find the answer. "I don't know" violates a norm. The teacher, like the textbook, is *supposed* to know. Students, for their part, are supposed to learn what teachers and textbook authors already know.[73]

It is hard for teachers to teach open-endedly. They are afraid not to be in control of the answer, afraid of losing their authority over the class. To avoid exposing gaps in their knowledge, teachers allow their students to make "very little use of the school's extensive resources," according to researcher Linda McNeil, who completed three studies of high school social studies classes between 1975 and 1981.[74] Who knows where inquiry might lead or how to manage it? John Goodlad found that less than 1 percent of instructional time involved class discussions requiring "reasoning or perhaps an opinion from students."[75] Instead of discussion and research, teachers emphasize "simplistic teacher-controlled information." Teachers' "patterns of knowledge control were, according to their own statements in taped interviews, rooted in their desire for classroom control," according to McNeil.[76] They end up adopting the same omniscient tone as their textbooks. As a result, teachers present a boring, overly ordered way of thinking, much less interesting than the way people really think. Summarizing McNeil's research, Albert Shanker, himself an advocate for teachers, noted that the same teachers who are "vital, broad-minded, and immensely knowledgeable in private conversations" nonetheless come across as "narrow, dull, and rigid in the classroom."[77]

David Jenness has pointed out that professional historical organizations for at least a century have repeatedly exhorted teachers not to teach history as fact memorization. "Stir up the minds of the pupils," cried the American Historical Association in 1893; avoid stressing "dates, names, and specific events," historians urged in 1934; leaders of the profession have made similar appeals in almost every decade in between and since.[78] Nevertheless, teachers continue to present factoids for students to memorize. Like textbook authors, teachers can be lazy. Teaching is stressful. Bad textbooks make life easier. They make lesson plans easy to organize. Moreover, we have seen how publishers furnish lavish packages that include videos for classroom viewing, teachers' manuals with suggestions on how to introduce each topic, and examinations ready to duplicate and gradable by machine. Textbooks also offer teachers the security of knowing they are covering the waterfront, so their students won't be disadvantaged on statewide or nationwide standardized tests.

For all these reasons, national surveys have confirmed that teachers use textbooks more than 70 percent of the time.[79] Moreover, most teachers prefer textbooks that are similar to the books they are already using, a big reason that the "inquiry textbook" movement never caught on in the late 1970s. "Teachers often prefer the errors they are familiar with," Tyson-Bernstein even claims, "to unfamiliar but correct information"—another reason that errors get preserved and passed on to new generations.[80]

Laziness is not exactly a fair charge, however. When are teachers supposed to find time to do research so they can develop their own course outlines and readings? They already work a fifty-five-hour week. Most teachers are far too busy teaching, grading, policing, handing out announcements, advising, comforting, hall monitoring, cafeteria quieting, and then running their own households to go off and research topics they do not even know to question. After hours, they are often required to supervise extracurricular activities, to say nothing of grading papers and planning lessons.[81] During the academic year most school districts allow teachers just two to four days of "in-service training." Summers offer time to retool but no money, and we can hardly expect teachers to subsidize the rest of us by going two months with no income to learn American history on their own.

Some of the foregoing pressures affect teachers of *any* subject. But certain additional constraints affect teachers in American history. Like the authors of history textbooks, history teachers can get themselves into a mind-set wherein they feel defensive about the United States, especially in front of minority students. Like authors, teachers can feel that they are supposed to defend and endorse America. Even African American teachers may feel vaguely threatened by criticism of America, threatened lest they be attacked, too. Teachers naturally identify with the material they teach. Since the textbooks are defensively boosterish about America, teachers who use them run the risk of becoming defensively boosterish, too. Compare the happier state of the English teacher, who can hardly teach, say, Langston Hughes's mildly subversive poem "Freedom Train" without becoming mildly subversive. Similarly, it is hard to teach *Holt American Nation* without becoming mildly boring.

Social studies and history teachers often get less respect from colleagues than faculty in other disciplines. When asked what subject might be dropped, elementary school teachers mentioned social studies more often than any other academic area.[82] Especially in the Midwest and South, high school principals often assign history to coaches, who have to teach something, after all, since there aren't enough physical education classes to go around. Assigning American history classes to teachers for whom history lies outside their field of competence—which is the case for 60 percent of U.S. history teachers, according to a nationwide study—obviously implies the subject is not important or that "anyone can teach it." History teachers also have higher class loads than teachers of any other academic subject.[83]

Students, too, consider history singularly unimportant. According to recent research on student attitudes toward social studies, "Most students in the United States, at all grade levels, found social studies to be one of the least interesting, most irrelevant subjects in the school curriculum."[84] Many teachers sense what students think of their subject matter. All too many respond by giving up inside—not trying to be creative, making only minimal demands, simply staying ahead of their students in the book. Students, in turn, respond "with minimal classroom effort," and the cycle continues.[85]

Relying on textbooks makes it easier for students as well as teachers to put forth minimal effort. Textbooks' innumerable lists—of main ideas, key terms, people to remember, dates, skill activities, matching, fill in the blanks, and review identifications—which appear to be the bane of students' existence, actually have positive functions. These lists make the course content look rigorous and factual, so teachers and students can imagine they are learning something. They make the teacher appear knowledgeable, whereas freer discussion might expose gaps in his/her information or intelligence. And they give students a sense of fairness about grading: performance on "objective" exams seeking recall of specific factoids is easy to measure. Thus, lists reduce uncertainty by conveying to students exactly what they need to know.[86] Fragmenting history into unconnected "facts" also guarantees, however, that students will not be able to relate many of these terms to their own lives and will retain almost none of them after the six-weeks' grading period.[87]

In some ways the two inquiry textbooks in my sample are better than the sixteen narrative textbooks. Both inquiry books, *The American Adventure* and *Discovering American History*, suggest ways students can use primary materials while examining them for distortions. *The American Adventure* directly challenges ethnocentrism in its teachers' guide, a topic never mentioned in any of the other textbooks or their supplementary teaching guides. Research suggests that the inquiry approach leads to higher student interest in contemporary political issues.[88] However, inquiry textbooks require much more active teaching. Classes can't just plow through them. Teachers must supplement them with additional information, leave out parts of the book, choose which exercises to assign, and work in concert with their school librarians. Perhaps it is because inquiry textbooks do not rely on rote learning that teachers and school administrations soon abandoned them. The inquiry approach was too much work.[89]

If teachers seem locked into the traditional narrative textbooks, why don't teachers teach *against* them, at least occasionally? Again, teaching against the book is hard. We have already noted the logistical problems of time and workload. Resources are also a problem. Where do teachers find a point of leverage? If a state historical museum or university is nearby, that can help. But how do teachers know when they do not know something? How do they know when their book is wrong or misleading? Moreover, students have been trained to believe what they read in print. How can teachers compete with the expertise of established authors backed by powerful publishers?

Teaching against a textbook can also be scary. Textbooks offer security. Teachers can hide behind them when principals, parents, or students challenge them to defend their work. Teaching against the textbook might be construed as critical of the school system, supervisor, principal, or department head who selected it. Teachers could get in trouble for doing that. Or so they imagine.[90]

A student of mine who was practice-teaching in an elementary school decided to introduce her students to what she had learned from my course about the Pilgrims, the plagues, and Thanksgiving. The professor of education who supervised her field placement vetoed her plan. "Telling the kids this information, going against their traditions, is like telling them there's no Santa Claus." He was also concerned that the information might "cause a big controversy with the families." With the approval of the classroom teacher, my student persevered, however. While she received no parental complaints, it is true that she risked being perceived as hostile or negative by some parents, administrators, and even fellow teachers.

Teachers *do* get fired, after all. I have interviewed several high school teachers and librarians who have been fired or threatened with dismissal for minor acts of independence such as making material available that some parents consider controversial. Teachers have been fired for teaching *Brave New World* in Baltimore, *One Flew Over the Cuckoo's Nest* in Idaho, and almost everything else in between.[91] Knowing this, many teachers anticipate that powerful forces will pounce upon them and doubt that anyone will come to their defense, so they relax into what Kenneth Carlson called the "security of self-censorship."[92] I am convinced, though, that most teachers enjoy substantial freedom in practice. "Most teachers have little control over school policy or curriculum," wrote Tracy Kidder in *Among Schoolchildren*, "but most have a great deal of autonomy inside their classrooms." In *Who Controls Our Schools?* Michael W. Kirst agreed: "Teachers have in effect a pocket veto on what is taught. An old tradition in American public schools is that once the door of the classroom shuts nobody checks on what a teacher actually does."[93] Nonetheless, even teachers who have little real cause to fear for their jobs typically avoid unnecessary risks.

Perhaps I have been too pessimistic here about teachers. Everywhere I have traveled to speak about the problems with textbooks, I have encountered teachers hungry for accurate historical information. I have met many imaginative teachers who make American history come alive—who bring in controversies and primary-source material and challenge students to think. Despite these heroic exceptions in schools all over America, however, the majority of social studies and history teachers are part of the problem, not part of the solution.

Let us cast our net even wider. Are all of us involved? The myths in our history are not limited to our schooling, after all. These cultural lies have been woven into the fabric of our entire society. From the flat-earth advertisements on Columbus Day weekend to the racist distortion of Reconstruction in *Gone With the Wind*, our society lies to itself about its past. Questioning these lies can seem anti-American. Textbooks may reflect these lies only because we want them to. Textbooks may also avoid controversy because we want them to: at least half of the respondents in national public opinion polls routinely agree that "books that contain dangerous ideas should be banned from public school libraries."[94] And when the National Assessment for Educational Progress sent its social studies assessment instruments to lay reviewers "to help insure that [they] would be acceptable to the general public," the public replied, "references to specific minority groups should be eliminated whenever possible"; "extreme care" should be used in wording any references to the FBI, the president, labor unions, and some other organizations; and "exercises which show national heroes in an uncomplimentary fashion though factually accurate are offensive."[95]

John Williamson, the president of a major textbook publishing company, employed this line to defend publishers: "In the thirties, the treatment of females and of black people clearly mirrored the attitudes of society. All females were portrayed in homemaker roles. . . . Blacks were not portrayed at all." Williamson went on to admit that recent improvements in the treatment of women and blacks have not been owed to publishers, "much as we would like the credit." As in the past, "textbooks mirror our society and contain what that society considers acceptable." Williamson concluded that all this was as it should be—parents, teachers, and members of the community *should* have the right to pressure publishers to present history as they want it presented.[96]

Williamson has a point. However, when publishers hide behind "society," their argument invokes a chicken-and-egg problematic, for if textbooks varied more, pressure groups in society would have more alternatives for which to lobby. Moreover, Williamson has conceded the major point: that history textbooks stand in a very different relationship to the discipline of history than most textbooks do to their respective fields. "Society" determines what goes into history textbooks. By contrast, the mathematics profession determines what goes into math textbooks and, creationist pressure notwithstanding, the biology profession determines what goes into biology textbooks. To be sure, mathematics and biology textbooks are products of the same complex organizations and delicate adoption procedures as American history textbooks. To be sure, math and biology books also err. But only about history and social studies do writers actually ask, "Can textbooks have scholarly integrity?"[97] Only in history is accuracy so political.

Consider the example of black soldiers in the Civil War. Even in the 1930s the facts about their contribution were plain for all to see in the primary sources and even the textbooks of the Civil War and Reconstruction eras. Depression-era textbooks omitted those facts, not because they were unknown but because including important acts by African Americans did not "mirror the attitudes of [white] society" during the nadir of race relations. Thus, to understand how textbooks in the 1930s presented the Civil War, we do not look at the history of the 1860s, but at the society of the 1930s. Likewise, to understand how textbooks today present the Civil War, the Pilgrims, or Columbus, we do not look at the 1860s, 1620s, or 1490s, but at our time. What distortions of history does *our* society cause? We must not fool ourselves that the process of distorting history has magically stopped. We must not congratulate ourselves that our society now treats everyone fairly and manifests attitudes that allow accurate interpretations of the past. We must not pretend that, unlike all previous generations, we write true history. Authors of high school history textbooks often don't even try, as we have seen. When parents and teachers do not demand from publishers and schools the same effort to present accurate history that we expect in other disciplines, we become part of the problem.

For that matter, many history textbooks published in the present are not really products of our time at all. Chapter 5 told of the nadir of American race relations, between 1890 and 1940. In that period, not only did we slide backward in race relations, we also developed a deeply biased understanding of what was then our recent past—Reconstruction (1866–77), the confused period that followed (1877–90), and the nadir itself. Chapter 6 showed how John Brown went insane after 1890, but Brown's sanity was not the only casualty of the nadir. Interpretations concocted during the nadir still affect what textbooks say today about the Grant administration, Woodrow Wilson, and even Christopher Columbus. In the nadir, African Americans seemed so "obviously" inferior that most whites could not imagine that President Grant, the "Stalwarts," and most Republican officeholders in the South had really cared about racial equality. Logically, it followed that they must have had some other motivation—most likely, greed or power. Therefore, a textbook like *The American Pageant* in 2006 emphasizes corruption and minimizes idealism to discredit Republican behavior in the 1870s and 1880s. How can the nadir still distort a textbook published in 2006? For one thing, *Pageant*'s interpretation of Grant was not written in 2006. It dates to 1956, long before the civil rights movement had any influence on American history textbooks. Interpretations in 1956 were still based on ideas set in the nadir, and *Pageant*'s author, Thomas Bailey, earned his PhD in 1927, in the heart of that period. Interpretations of Columbus in the 1980s derived from the celebrations of 1892; Chapter 2 showed how new textbooks were influenced by the more complex remembrances of 1992. Thus *when* a book is written—or, rather, when its interpretation of an event was set in our culture—determines *what* is written.

Some people feel that we should sanitize history to protect students from unpleasantries, at least until they are eighteen or so. Children have to grow up soon enough as it is, these people say; let them enjoy childhood. Why confront our young people with issues even adults cannot resolve? Must we tell all the grisly details about what Columbus did on Haiti, for example, to fifth graders?[98] Sissela Bok wrote a whole book about, and mostly against, lying; but she seems to agree that lying to children is okay and compares it to sheltering them from harsh weather.[99]

Certainly age-graded censorship is the one form of censorship that almost everyone believes is appropriate: fifth graders should not see violent pornography, for instance. Some fifth or even twelfth graders who encounter illustrations of Spaniards cutting off Indians' hands or Indians committing suicide might have nightmares about Columbus. Withholding pornography is not a precise analogy to whitewashing history, however. When we fail to present students with the truth about, say, Columbus, we end up presenting a lie instead—at least a lie of serious omission. I doubt that shielding children from horror and violence is really the cause of textbook omissions and distortions. Books *do* include violence, after all, so long as it isn't by "us." For instance, *American History* describes John Brown's actions at Pottawatomie, Kansas, in 1856:

> When Brown learned of the [Lawrence] attack, he led a party of seven men. . . . In the dead of night they entered the cabins of three unsuspecting families. For no apparent reason they murdered five people. They split open their skulls with heavy, razor-sharp swords. They even cut off the hand of one of their victims.

Telling of skulls split open and providing minutiae like the heft and sharpness of the swords prompt us to feel revulsion toward Brown. Certainly the author does not provide these details to shield students from unpleasantries.

If textbooks are going to include severed hands, those of the Arawaks cut off by Columbus are much more historically significant. Columbus's severings were systematic and helped depopulate Haiti. *American History*, having omitted these atrocities, cannot claim to present Pottawatomie evenhandedly.

Violence aside, what about shielding children from other untoward realities of our society? How should social studies classes teach young people about the police, for instance? Should the approach be Officer Friendly? Or should children receive a Marxist interpretation of how the power structure uses the police as its first line of control in urban ghettoes? Does the approach we choose depend on whether we teach in the suburbs or the inner city? If a more complex analysis of the police is more useful than Officer Friendly for inner-city children, does that mean we should teach about slavery in a different way in the suburbs than we would in the inner city?

In 1992, Los Angeles exploded in a violent race riot, triggered by a white suburban jury's acquittal of four police officers who had been videotaped beating a black traffic offender, Rodney King. Almost every child in America saw this most famous of all home videotapes. Therefore, almost every child in America learned that Officer Friendly is not the whole story. We do not protect children from controversy by offering only an Officer Friendly analysis in school. All we do is make school irrelevant to the major issues of the day. Rock songs bought by thirteen-year-olds deal with AIDS, nuclear war, and global warming. Rap songs discuss racism, sexism, drug use—and American history. We can be sure that our children already know about and think about these and other issues, whether we like it or not. Indeed, attempts by parents to preserve some nonexistent childhood innocence through avoidance are likely to heighten rather than reduce anxiety.[100] Lying and omission are not the right ways. There is a way to teach truth to a child at any age level.

Because history is more personal than geology or even American literature, more about "us," there is an additional reason not to present it honestly: don't we want our children to be optimists? Maybe textbooks that emphasize how wonderful, fair, and progressive our society has been give some students a basis for idealism. It may be empowering for children to believe that simply by living we all contribute to a constantly improving society. Maybe later, when students grow up and learn more, they will be motivated to change the system to make it resemble the ideal. Maybe stressing fairness as a basic American value provides a fulcrum from which students can criticize society when they discover, perhaps in college history courses, how it has often been unfair. This all may be an instance of Emily Dickinson's couplet "The Truth must dazzle gradually/Or every man be blind." [101]

Since fewer than one American in six ever takes an American history course after leaving high school, it is not clear just when the next generation will get dazzled by the truth in American history. Another problem with this line of thinking is that the truth may then dazzle students with the sudden realization that their teachers have been lying to them. A student of mine wrote of having been "taught the story of George Washington receiving a hatchet for his birthday and proceeding to chop down his father's favorite cherry tree." To her horror this student later discovered that "a story I had held sacred in my memory for so long had been a lie." She ended up "feeling bitter and betrayed by my earlier teachers who had to lie to build up George Washington's image, causing me to question all that I had previously learned." This student's alienation pales besides that of African Americans when they confront another truth about the

Founding Fathers: "When I first learned that Washington and Jefferson had slaves, I was devastated," historian Mark Lloyd told me. "I didn't want to have anything more to do with them." [102] Selling Washington as a hero to Native Americans will eventually founder on a similar rock when they learn what he did to the Iroquois.

It is hard to believe that adults keep children ignorant in order to preserve their idealism. More likely, adults keep children ignorant so they *won't* be idealistic. Many adults fear children and worry that respect for authority is all that keeps them from running amok. So they teach them to respect authorities whom adults themselves do not respect. In the late 1970s, survey researchers gave parents a series of statements and asked whether they believed them and wanted their children to believe them. One statement stood out: "People in authority know best." Parents replied in these proportions:

13 percent—"believe and want children to believe"

56 percent—"have doubts but still want to teach to children"

30 percent—"don't believe and don't want to pass on to children"

Thus, 56 percent of parents wanted their children *not* to doubt authority figures, even though the parents themselves doubted. [103]

Some adults simply do not trust children to think. For several decades sociologists have documented Americans' distrust of the next generation. Parents may feel undermined when children get tools of information and inquiry not available to adults and use them in ways that seem to threaten adult-held values. Many parents want children to concentrate on the three R's, not on multicultural history. [104] Shirley Engle has described "a strident minority [of teachers and parents] who do not really believe in democracy and do not really believe that kids should be taught to think." [105] Perhaps adults' biggest reason for lying is that they fear our history—fear that it *isn't* so wonderful and that if children were to learn what has really gone on, they would lose all respect for our society. Thus, when Edward Ruzzo tried in 1964 to cover up Warren G. Harding's embarrassing love letters to a married woman, he used the rationale "that anything damaging to the image of an American President should be suppressed to protect the younger generation." As Judge Ruzzo put it, there are too many juvenile delinquents as it is. [106]

Ironically, only people who themselves have been raised on shallow feel-good history could harbor such doubts. Harding may not have been much of a role model, but other Americans—Tom Paine, Thoreau, Lincoln, Helen Hunt Jackson, Martin Luther King, and, yes, John Brown, Helen Keller, and Woodrow Wilson, too—are still celebrated by lovers of freedom everywhere. Yet publishers, authors, teachers, and parents seem afraid to expose children to the blazing idealism of these leaders at their best. Today many aspects of American life, from the premises of our legal system to elements of our popular culture, inspire other societies. If Russia can abandon boosterish history, as it seems to have done, surely America can, too.[107] "We do not need a bodyguard of lies," points out Paul Gagnon. "We can afford to present ourselves in the totality of our acts."[108]

Textbook authors seem not to share Gagnon's confidence, however. There is a certain contradiction in the logic of those who write nationalist textbooks. On the one hand, they describe a country without repression, without real conflict. On the other hand, they obviously believe that we need to lie to students to instill in them love of country. But if the country is so wonderful, why must we lie?

Ironically, our lying only diminishes us. Bernice Reagon, founder of the singing group Sweet Honey in the Rock, has pointed out that other countries are impressed when we send spokespeople abroad who, like herself, are willing to criticize the United States. Surely, this is part of what democracy is about. Surely, in a democracy a historian's duty is to tell the truth. Surely, in a democracy students need to develop informed reasons to criticize as well as take pride in their country. Maybe somewhere along the line we gave up on democracy?

Lying to children is a slippery slope. Once we have started sliding down it, how and when do we stop? Who decides when to lie? Which lies to tell? To what age group? As soon as we loosen the anchor of fact, of historical evidence, our history textboat is free to blow here and there, pointing first in one direction, then in another. If we obscure or omit facts because they make Columbus look bad, why not omit those that make the United States look bad? Or the Mormon Church? Or the state of Mississippi? *This* is the politicization of history. How do we decide what to teach in an American history course once authors have decided not to value the truth? If our history courses aren't based on fact anyway, why not tell one story to whites, another to blacks? Isn't Scott, Foresman already doing something like that when it puts out a "Lone Star" edition of *Land of Promise*, tailoring the facts of history to suit (white) Texans?

Philosopher Martin Heidegger once defined truth as "that which makes a people certain, clear, and strong," and publishers of American history textbooks apparently intend to do just that, avoiding topics that superficially might seem to divide Americans. Before we abandon the old "correspondence to fact" sense of truth in favor of Heidegger's more useful definition, however, we may want to recall that he gave it in the service of Adolf Hitler. Moreover, we need to consider the meaning of *a people*. Does *a people* mean only European Americans? Perhaps openly facing topics that seem divisive might actually unify Americans *across* racial, ethnic, and other lines.[109] After all, if the textbooks aren't true, they leave us with no grounds for defending the courses based on them when students charge that American history is a waste of time. Why should children believe what they learn in American history if their textbooks are full of distortions and lies? Why should they bother to learn it?

Luckily, as the next chapter tells, they don't.

13.

WHAT IS THE RESULT OF TEACHING HISTORY LIKE THIS?

William Jennings Bryan: "I do not think about things that I don't think about."
Clarence Darrow: "Do you ever think about things you do think about?"

—SCOPES TRIAL TRANSCRIPT[1]

Learning social studies is, to no small extent, whether in elementary school or the university, learning to be stupid.

—JULES HENRY[2]

Yeah, I cut class, I got a D
'Cause history meant nothin' to me.

—JUNGLE BROTHERS[3]

The truth shall make us free.
The truth shall make us free.
The truth shall make us free some day.
Oh, deep in my heart, I do believe,
The truth shall make us free some day.

—VERSE OF "WE SHALL OVERCOME"

ALL OVER AMERICA, high school students sit in social studies and American history classes, look at their textbooks, write answers to the questions at the end of each chapter, and take quizzes and examinations that test factual recall. When I was subjected to this regimen, I never defined any of the terms at the end of the chapter until the sixth week of each six-week grading period. Then the teacher and I would negotiate what proportion of the terms I had to define correctly to get an *A-* (usually something like 85 percent) and I would madly write out definitions through the last two days of class. Three years later, when my sister took American history, she developed a more effective technique. She handed in the work on time, writing real definitions to the first two and last two terms, but for the thirty or forty in the middle she free-associated whatever nonsense she wanted. "Hawley-Smoot Tariff: I have no idea, Mr. DeMoulin," was one entry. "Blue Eagle: FDR's pet bird who got very sad when he died" was another. Today students use the Internet: "At my school we divided up the list and then posted our part on the Internet. Then you could download the terms, change the style, print them out, and hand them in." Educational theorists call such acts "day-to-day resistance"—a phrase that comes from theorizing about slavery—but I did not know that then. I am still envious that I never thought of such marvelous labor-saving ploys.[4]

Of course, fooling the teacher is of little consequence. Quite possibly my sister's teacher even knew of the ruse and joked about it with his colleagues, the way masters chuckled that their slaves were so stupid they had to be told every evening to bring in the hoes or they would leave them out in the night dew. Some social studies and history teachers try to win student cooperation by telling them, when introducing a topic, not to worry, they won't have to learn much about it. Students happily acquiesce.[5] Students also invest a great deal of creative energy in getting teachers to waste time and relax requirements.[6] Teachers acquiesce partly because, as with much day-to-day resistance during slavery, yielding does not really threaten the system. Day-to-day school resistance also provides students a form of psychic distance, a sense that although the system may have commanded their pens, it has not won real cooperation from their minds.

How could it? Who wants to learn useless minutiae? Every chapter of *The American Journey*, for example, ends with two to six pages of "Assessment and Activities," mostly stressing twigs. For example, the final chapter has a "Time Line Activity" that asks students to "place the following events in chronological order."

- Serbs, Croats, and Bosnian Muslims sign peace agreement to end civil war
- Soviet Union dissolves
- Bill Clinton is elected to first term as president
- Geraldine Ferraro is first woman from a major party to run for vice president
- Iraq invades Kuwait

- Sandra Day O'Connor named to Supreme Court
- Ronald Reagan is reelected president

I defy readers to put these seven events in the correct order without looking them up. Certainly I can't do it, and I bet Joyce Appleby, Alan Brinkley, and James McPherson, whose names are on the cover of the book, can't either. Even if they can, what have they accomplished? There is no important causal or logical connection among most of the events, so there is no reason to remember which came first. This activity merely asks students to memorize the order of unrelated occurrences. Even though some items seem connected—O'Connor and Reagan, for example—on closer examination it is not enough to know that he appointed her; one must also remember whether he did so in his first or second term.

Study after study shows that students successfully resist learning "facts" like these.[7] Indeed, they resist all too well. When two-thirds of American seventeen-year-olds cannot place the Civil War in the right half-century, or 22 percent of my students reply that the Vietnam War was fought between North and South *Korea*, we must salute young people for more than mere ignorance.[8] This is resistance raised to a high level. Students are simply not learning even those details of American history that educated citizens *should* know. Still less do they learn what *caused* the major developments in our past. Therefore, they cannot apply lessons from the past to current issues.

Unfortunately, students are left with no resources to understand, accept, or rebut historical referents used in arguments by candidates for office, sociology professors, or newspaper journalists. If knowledge is power, ignorance cannot be bliss.

Emotion is the glue that causes history to stick. We remember where we were when we heard of the attack on the World Trade Center because it affected us emotionally. American history is a heartrending subject. When students read real voices from our past, the emotions do not fail to move them. Recall Las Casas's passionate denunciations of the Spanish treatment of Indians: "What we committed in the Indies stands out among the most unpardonable offenses ever committed against God and mankind." Consider the famous final words of William Jennings Bryan to the 1896 Democratic national convention: "You shall not press down upon the brow of labor this crown of thorns. You shall not crucify mankind upon a cross of gold." Or Helen Keller's attack on the

Brooklyn Eagle: "Socially blind and deaf, it defends an intolerable system." Or Franklin D. Roosevelt's words in the depression, assuring us we had "nothing to fear but fear itself." Events and images also call forth strong feelings. The saga of Elizabeth Blackwell in medical school, the liberation of Nazi death camp inmates by American (and Russian and British) soldiers, the ultimate success of Jonas Salk in finding a vaccine that would kill polio—these are stirring stories. As textbook critic Mrs. W. K. Haralson writes, "There is no way the glowing, throbbing events of history can be presented fairly, accurately, and factually without involving emotion."[9]

Earlier chapters have shown, however, that American history textbooks and courses are neither dispassionate nor passionate. All textbook authors and many teachers seem not to have thought deeply about just what in our past might be worthy of passion or even serious contemplation. No *real* emotion seeps into these books, not even real pride.[10] Instead, heroic exceptions to the contrary, most American history courses and textbooks operate in a gray emotional land-scape of pious duty in which the United States has a good history, so studying it is good for students. "They don't think of history as drama," one teacher told me. "They all tell me they hate history, because it's dead facts, and boring."

Another way to cause history to stick is to present it so that it touches students' lives. To show students how racism affects African Americans, a teacher in Iowa discriminated by eye color among members of her all-white class of third graders for two days. The film *A Class Divided* shows how vividly these students remembered the lesson fifteen years later.[11] In contrast, material from U.S. history textbooks is rarely retained for fifteen weeks after the end of the school year. By stressing the distant past, textbooks discourage students from seeking to learn history from their families or community, which again disconnects school from the other parts of students' lives.

"Children, like most adults, do not readily retain isolated, incoherent, and meaningless data," claim two Canadian educators.[12] Surely they are right, and since textbooks provide almost no causal skeleton, surely that lack of coherence helps to explain why students forget most of the mass of detail they "learn" in their history courses. Not all students forget it equally, however. Caste minority children—Native Americans, African Americans, and Hispanics—do worse in all subjects, compared to white or Asian American children, but the gap is larg-est in social studies. That is because the way American history is taught particu-larly alienates students of color and children from impoverished families.

Feel-good history for affluent white males inevitably amounts to feel-bad history for everyone else. A student of mine, who was practice-teaching in Swanton, Vermont, a town with a considerable American Indian population, noticed an Abenaki fifth grader obviously tuning out when he brought up the subject of Thanksgiving. Talking with the child brought forth the following reaction: "My father told me the real truth about that day and not to listen to any white man scum like you!" Yet Thanksgiving seems reasonably benign compared to, say, Columbus Day. Throughout the school year, in a thousand little ways, American history offends many students. Unlike the Abenaki youngster, most have-not students do not consciously take offense and do not rebel but are nonetheless subtly put off. It hurts children's self-image to swallow what their history books teach about the exceptional fairness of America. Black students consider American history, as usually taught, "white" and assimilative, so they resist learning it. This explains why research shows a larger performance differential between poor and rich students, or black and white students, in history than in other school subjects.[13] Girls also dislike social studies and history even more than boys, probably because women and women's concerns and perceptions still go underrepresented in history classes.[14]

Afrocentric history arose partly in response to this problem. Arthur M. Schlesinger Jr., denounced Afrocentrism as "psychotherapy" for blacks—a one-sided misguided attempt to make African Americans feel good about themselves.[15] Unfortunately, the Eurocentric history in our textbooks amounts to psychotherapy for whites. Since historians like Schlesinger have not addressed Eurocentrism, they do not come into the discussion with clean hands. To be sure, the answer to Eurocentric textbooks is not one-sided Afrocentric history, the kind that has Africans inventing everything good and whites inventing slavery and oppression. Surely, we do not really want a generation of African Americans raised on antiwhite Afrocentric history, but just as surely, we cannot afford another generation of white Americans raised on complacent celebratory Eurocentric history. Even if they don't learn much history from their textbooks, students are affected by the book's slant. Educator Martha Toppin found unanimous agreement with this proposition among ninety high school students: "If Africa had had a history worth learning about, we would have had it last year in Western Civilization."[16] The message that Eurocentric history sends to non-European Americans is: your ancestors have not done much of importance. It is easy for European Americans and non-European Americans to take a step further and conclude that non-European Americans are not important today.

From the beginning, when textbooks call Columbus's 1492 voyage "a miracle" and proclaim, "Soon the grateful captain wades ashore and gives thanks to God," they make the Christian deity God and put Him [*sic*] on the white side. Omitting the Arawaks' perspective on Haiti continues the process of "otherizing" nonwhites in this first diorama from our history. If the "we" in a textbook included American Indians, African Americans, Latinos, women, and all social classes, the book would read differently, just as whites *talk* differently (and more humanely) in the presence of people of color. Surely it is possible to write accurate multicultural history that spreads the discomfort around, rather than distorting history to help only affluent white children feel comfortable about their past. Maybe we can even write and teach an American history that children of the nonelite would *want* to study.

Equally as worrisome is the impact of American history courses on white affluent children. This grave result can best be shown by what I call the "Vietnam exercise." Throughout the Vietnam War, pollsters were constantly asking the American people whether they wanted to bring our troops home. At first, only a small fraction of Americans favored withdrawal. Toward the end of the war, a large majority wanted us to pull out.

Not only did Gallup, Roper, the National Opinion Research Center, and other organizations ask Americans about the war, they also usually inquired about background variables—sex, education, region, and the like—so they could find out which kinds of people were most hawkish (pro-war), which most dovish. Over ten years I have asked more than a thousand college undergraduates and several hundred others their beliefs about what kind of adults, by educational level, supported the war in Vietnam. I ask audiences to fill out Table 1, trying to replicate the results of the January 1971 national Gallup survey on the war. By January 1971, as I tell audiences, the national mood was overwhelmingly dove: 73 percent favored withdrawal. (I excluded "don't knows.")

TABLE 1

In January 1971 the Gallup Poll asked: "A proposal has been made in Congress to require the U.S. government to bring home all U.S. troops before the end of this year. Would you like to have your congressman vote for or against this proposal?"

Estimate the results, by education, by filling out this table:

ADULTS WITH:	COLLEGE EDUCATION	HIGH SCHOOL EDUCATION	GRADE SCHOOL EDUCATION	TOTAL ADULTS
% FOR withdrawal of U.S. troops (Doves)				73%
% AGAINST withdrawal of U.S. troops (Hawks)				27%
Totals	100%	100%	100%	100%

Most recent high school graduates are not able even to construct a simple table or interpret a graph. Accordingly, I teach audiences how the table must balance—how, if grade school–educated adults, for instance, were more dovish than others, hence supported withdrawal by more than 73 percent, some other group must be less dovish than 73 percent for the entire population to balance out at 73 percent doves. If you wish to be an active reader, you might fill out the table yourself before reading further.

By an overwhelming margin—almost 10 to 1—audiences believe that college-educated persons were more dovish. Table 2 shows a typical response.

TABLE 2

ADULTS WITH:	COLLEGE EDUCATION	HIGH SCHOOL EDUCATION	GRADE SCHOOL EDUCATION	TOTAL ADULTS
% FOR with-drawal of U.S. troops (Doves)	90%	75%	60%	73%
% AGAINST withdrawal of U.S. troops (Hawks)	10%	25%	40%	27%
Totals	100%	100%	100%	100%

I then ask audiences to assume that their tables are correct—that the results of the survey correspond to what they guessed—and to state at least two reasonable hypotheses to explain these results. Their most common responses:

Educated people are more informed and critical, hence more able to sift through misinformation and conclude that the Vietnam War was not in our best interests, politically or morally.

Educated people are more tolerant. There were elements of racism and ethnocentrism in our conduct of the war; educated people are less likely to accept such prejudice.

Less-educated people, being of lower occupational status, were more likely to be employed in a war-related industry or in the armed forces themselves, hence had self-interest in being pro-war.

There is nothing surprising here. Most people feel that schooling is a good thing and enables us to sift facts, weigh evidence, and think rationally. An educated people has been said to be a bulwark of democracy.

However, the truth is quite different. Educated people disproportionately supported the Vietnam War. Table 3 shows the actual outcome of the January 1971 poll:

TABLE 3

ADULTS WITH:	COLLEGE EDUCATION	HIGH SCHOOL EDUCATION	GRADE SCHOOL EDUCATION	TOTAL ADULTS
% FOR withdrawal of U.S. troops (Doves)	60%	75%	80%	73%
% AGAINST withdrawal of U.S. troops (Hawks)	40%	25%	20%	27%
Totals	100%	100%	100%	100%

These results surprise even some professional social scientists. Twice as high a proportion of college-educated adults, 40 percent, were hawks, compared to only 20 percent of adults with grade school educations. And this poll was no isolated phenomenon. Similar results were registered again and again, in surveys by Harris, NORC, and others. Back in 1965, when only 24 percent of the nation agreed that the United States "made a mistake" in sending troops to Vietnam, 28 percent of the grade school–educated felt so. Later, when less than half of the college-educated adults favored pullout, among the grade school–educated 61 percent did. Throughout our long involvement in Southeast Asia, on issues related to Vietnam, Thailand, Cambodia, or Laos, the grade school–educated were *always* the most dovish, the college-educated the most hawkish.

Today most Americans agree that the Vietnam War was a mistake, politically and morally; so do most political analysts, including such men as Robert McNamara and Clark Clifford, who waged the war.[17] If we concur with this now conventional wisdom, then we must concede that the more educated a person was, the more likely s/he was to be wrong about the war.

Why did educated Americans support the war? When my audiences learn that educated people were more hawkish, they scurry about concocting new explanations. Since they are still locked into their presumption that educated people are more intelligent and have more goodwill than the less educated, their theories have to strain to explain why less-educated Americans were right. The most popular revamped theory asserts that since working-class young men bore the real cost of the war, "naturally" they and their families opposed it. This explanation seems reasonable, for it does credit the working class with opposing the war and with a certain brute rationality. But it reduces the thinking of the working class to a crude personal cost-benefit analysis, implicitly denying that the less educated might take society as a whole into consideration. Thus, this hypothesis diminishes the position of the working class—which was more correct than that of the educated, after all—to a mere reflex based on self-interest. It is also wrong. Human nature doesn't work that way. Research has shown that people of whatever educational level who expect to go to war tend to *support* that war, because people rarely don't believe in something they plan to do. Working-class young men who enlisted or looked forward to being drafted could not easily influence their destinies to avoid Vietnam, but they could change their attitudes about the war to be more positive. Thus, cognitive dissonance helps explain why young men of draft age supported the war more than older men, and why men supported the war more than women. While less-educated families with sons in the Vietnam conflict often formed pockets of support for the war, such pockets were exceptions to the dovishness that pervaded the less-educated segments of our populace.[18]

By now my audiences are keen to learn why educated Americans were more hawkish. Two social processes, each tied to schooling, can account for educated Americans' support of the Vietnam War. The first can be summarized by the term *allegiance*. Educated adults tend to be successful and earn high incomes— partly because schooling leads to better jobs and higher incomes, but mainly because high parental incomes lead to more education for their offspring. Also, parents transmit affluence and education directly to their children. Successful Americans do not usually lay their success at their parents' doorstep, however. They usually explain their accomplishments as owing to their own individual characteristics, so they see American society as meritocratic. They achieved their own success; other people must be getting their just desserts. Believing that American society is open to individual input, the educated well-to-do tend to agree with society's decisions and feel they had a hand in forming them. They identify more with our society and its policies. We can use the term *vested interest* here, so long as we realize we are referring to an ideological interest or need, a need to come to terms with the privilege with which one has been blessed, not simple economic self-interest. In this sense, educated successful people have a vested interest in believing that the society that helped them be educated and successful is fair. As a result, those in the upper third of our educational and income structure are more likely to show allegiance to society, while those in the lower third are more likely to be critical of it.

The other process causing educated adults to be more likely to support the Vietnam War can be summarized under the rubric *socialization*. Sociologists have long agreed that schools are important socializing agents in our society. *Socializing* in this context does not mean hobnobbing around a punch bowl but refers to the process of learning and internalizing the basic social rules—language, norms, etiquette—necessary for an individual to function in society. Socialization is not primarily cognitive. We are not persuaded rationally not to pee in the living room; we are *required* not to. We then internalize and obey this rule even when no authority figure lurks to enforce it. Teachers may try to convince themselves that education's main function is to promote inquiry, not iconography, but in fact the socialization function of schooling remains dominant at least through high school and hardly disappears in college. Education as socialization tells people what to think and how to act and requires them to conform. Education as socialization influences students simply to accept the rightness of our society. American history textbooks overtly tell us to be proud of America. The more schooling, the more socialization, and the more likely the individual will conclude that America is good.

Both the allegiance and socialization processes cause the educated to believe that what America does is right. Public opinion polls show the nonthinking results. In late spring 1966, just before the United States began bombing Hanoi and Haiphong in North Vietnam, Americans split 50-50 as to whether we should bomb these targets. After the bombing began, 85 percent favored the bombing while only 15 percent opposed. The sudden shift was the result, not the cause, of the government's decision to bomb. The same allegiance and socialization processes operated again when policy changed in the opposite direction. In 1968, war sentiment was waning; but 51 percent of Americans opposed a bombing halt, partly because the United States was still bombing North Vietnam. A month later, after President Johnson announced a bombing halt, 71 percent favored the halt. Thus, 23 percent of our citizens changed their minds within a month, mirroring the shift in government policy. This swaying of thought by policy affects attitudes on issues ranging from our space program to environmental policy and shows the so-called "silent majority" to be an unthinking majority as well. Educated people are overrepresented among these straws in the wind.[19]

We like to think of education as a mix of thoughtful learning processes.

Allegiance and socialization, however, are intrinsic to the role of schooling in our society or any hierarchical society. Socialist leaders such as Fidel Castro and Mao Tse-tung vastly extended schooling in Cuba and China in part because they knew that an educated people is a socialized populace and a bulwark of allegiance. Education works the same way here: it encourages students not to think about society but merely to trust that it is good. To the degree that American history in particular is celebratory, it offers no way to understand any problem—such as the Vietnam War, poverty, inequality, international haves and have-nots, environmental degradation, or changing sex roles—that has historical roots. Therefore, we might expect that the *more* traditional schooling in history that Americans have, the *less* they will understand Vietnam or any other historically based problem. This is why educated people were more hawkish on the Vietnam War.

Some people have suggested that the Vietnam War was idiosyncratic. For six long years, they point out, it was a Republican war, and Republicans are on average more educated than Democrats; *that* is why more educated Americans were hawks. Such thinking founders on several grounds. First, more than any other war in our history, Vietnam was a bipartisan war. John Kennedy, Democrat, sent in the first soldiers; Lyndon Johnson, Democrat, sent in the most. Second, more-educated Americans were pro-war when those Democratic administrations waged it, compared to less-educated Americans. Finally, not just the Vietnam War shows more support by the educated. About the Iraq War, surveys by the Pew Trust found the same pattern. In August 2004, for example, two-thirds of all Americans who graduated from college favored keeping troops in Iraq "long enough to bring stability," while 61 percent with less than a high school degree favored "a quick pullout."[20]

Table 2 supplies an additional example of nonthinking by the educated and affluent: they are wrong about who supported the war. By a 9 to 1 margin, the hundreds of educated people who have filled out Table 1 believed that educated Americans were more dovish. Thus, the Vietnam exercise suggests two errors by the elite. The first error that educated people made was being excessively hawkish back in 1966, 1968, or 1971. The second error they made was in filling out Table 1.

Why have my audiences been so wrong in remembering or deducing who opposed the Vietnam War? One reason is that Americans like to believe that schooling is a good thing. Most Americans tend automatically to equate *educated* with *informed* or *tolerant*.[21] Traditional purveyors of social studies and American history seize upon precisely this belief to rationalize their enterprise, claiming that history courses lead to a more enlightened citizenry. Respondents to my Vietnam exercise who thrash about claiming that it worked only for that war or only because less-educated respondents feared having to fight are still trying to preserve their belief in the mantra that education makes us wise. The Vietnam exercise suggests the opposite is more likely true.

Audiences would not be so easily fooled if they would only recall that educated people were and are more likely to be Republicans, while high school dropouts are more likely to be Democrats. Hawkish right-wing Republicans, including the core supporters of Barry Goldwater in 1964, of Ronald Reagan in 1980, and of groups like the John Birch Society, come disproportionately from the most educated and affluent segments of our society, particularly dentists and physicians. So we should not be surprised that education correlates with hawkishness. At the other end of the social-status spectrum, although most African Americans, like most whites, initially supported U.S. intervention in Vietnam, blacks were always more questioning and more dovish than whites, and African American leaders—Muhammad Ali, Martin Luther King Jr., and Malcolm X—were prominent among the early opponents of the war.[22]

American history textbooks help perpetrate the archetype of the blindly patriotic hard hat by omitting or understating progressive elements in the working class. Textbooks do not reveal that CIO unions and some working-class fraternal associations were open to all when many chambers of commerce and country clubs were still white-only. Few textbooks tell of organized labor's role in the civil rights movement, including the 1963 March on Washington. Nevertheless, many members of my audiences are aware that educated Americans are likely to be Republicans, hard-liners on defense, and right-wing extremists. Some members of my audiences know about Goldwater voters, Muhammad Ali's induction refusal, Birchers and education, or labor unions and the war—information that would have helped them fill in the blanks in Table 1 correctly. Somehow, though, they never think to apply such knowledge. Most people fill out the table in a daze without ever using what they know. Their education and their position in society cause them not to think.[23]

Such nonthinking occurs most commonly when society is the subject. "One of the major duties of an American citizen is to analyze issues and interpret events intelligently," *Discovering American History* exhorts students. Our textbooks fail miserably at this task. The Vietnam exercise shows how bad the situation really is. Sociology professors are amazed and depressed at the level of thinking about society displayed each fall, especially by white upper-middle-class students in their first-year classes. These students cannot use the past to illuminate the present and have no inkling of causation in history, so they cannot think coherently about social life. Extending the terminology of Jules Henry, we might use "social stupidity" to describe the illogical intellectual process and conclusions that result.

Social stupidity continues in the twenty-first century. In 2005, for example, the Pew Research Center found that 62 percent of Republicans agreed with the statement, "Poor people today have it easy because they can get government benefits without doing anything in return." Twenty-seven percent of Democrats also agreed. Such responses can only come from people who have neither had a conversation with a poor person nor imagined their economic and social reality—yet somehow imagine they know enough to hold an opinion. Educated people are more likely to venture such ill-informed opinions.[24]

Education does not have this impact in other areas of study. People who have taken more mathematics courses are more proficient at math than those who have not. The same holds true for English, foreign languages, and almost every other subject. Only in history is stupidity the result of more, not less, schooling. Why do educated people often display particularly nonsensical reasoning about the social world? For some, it is in their ideological interest. Members of the upper- and upper-middle classes are comforted by a view of society that emphasizes schooling as the solution to intolerance, poverty, even war. Such a rosy view of education and its effects lets them avoid considering the need to make major changes in other institutions. To the degree that this view permeates our society, students automatically think well of education and expect the educated to have seen through the Vietnam War.

Moreover, thinking well of education reinforces the ideology we might call American individualism. It leaves intact the archetypal image of a society marked by or at least striving toward equality of opportunity. Yet precisely to the extent that students believe that equality of opportunity exists, they are encouraged to blame the uneducated for being poor, just as my audiences blame them for being hawks on the war in Vietnam. Americans who are not poor find American individualism a satisfying ideology, for it explains their success in life by laying it at their own doorstep. This enables them to feel proud of their success, even if it is modest, rather than somehow ashamed of it. Crediting success to their position in social structure threatens those good feelings. It is much more gratifying to believe that their educational attainments and occupational successes result from ambition and hard work—that their privilege has been earned. To a considerable degree, working-class and lower-class Americans also adopt this prevailing ethic about society and schooling. Often working-class adults in dead-end jobs blame themselves, focusing on their own earlier failure to excel in school, and feel they are inferior in some basic way.[25]

Students also have short-term reasons for accepting what teachers and textbooks tell them about the social world in their history and social studies classes, of course. They are going to be tested on it. It is in the students' interest just to learn the material. Arguing takes more energy, doesn't help one's grade, and even violates classroom norms. Moreover, there is a feeling of accomplishment derived from learning something, even something as useless and mindless as the answers to the identification questions that occupy the last two pages of each chapter in most history textbooks. Students can feel frustrated by the ambiguity of real history, the debates among historians, or the challenge of applying ideas from the past to their own lives. They may resist changes in the curriculum, especially if these involve more work or work less clearly structured than simply "doing the terms." After years of rote education, students can become habituated to it and inexperienced and ineffectual at any other kind of learning.[26]

In the long run, however, "learning" history this way is not really satisfying. Most history textbooks and many high school history teachers give students no reason to love or appreciate the subject. The abysmal ratings that students give to their history courses provide a warning flag,[27] and we cannot respond merely by exhorting students to like history more. But all this does not mean the sorry state of learning in most history classrooms cannot be changed. Students will start learning history when they see the point of doing so, when it seems interesting and important to them, and when they believe history might relate to their lives and futures. Students will start finding history interesting when their teachers and textbooks stop lying to them.

AFTERWORD

THE FUTURE LIES AHEAD—
AND WHAT TO DO ABOUT THEM

One does not collect facts he does not need, hang on to them, and then stumble across the propitious moment to use them. One is first perplexed by a problem and then makes use of facts to achieve a solution. —CHARLES SELLERS[1]

Once you have learned how to ask questions—relevant and appropriate and substantial questions—you have learned how to learn and no one can keep you from learning whatever you want or need to know.

—NEIL POSTMAN AND CHARLES WEINGARTNER[2]

Do not try to satisfy your vanity by teaching a great many things. Awaken people's curiosity. It is enough to open minds; do not overload them.

—ANATOLE FRANCE[3]

The future of mankind lies waiting for those who will come to understand their lives and take up their responsibilities to all living things. —VINE DELORIA JR.[4]

IF THE AUTHORS OF American history textbooks took notice of the points made in the first eleven chapters of this book, then textbooks would be far less likely to present, and teachers to teach, distorted and indefensibly incomplete accounts of our past. *Lies My Teacher Told Me* is itself incomplete, however. It says little about Hispanic history, for example. Yet our textbooks are so Anglocentric that they might be considered Protestant history.[5] What about women's history and the history of gender in America, two different but related topics? *Lies* mentions both subjects from time to time but makes no thorough critique of how textbooks present women's history and gender issues.[6] And what about the next lie? The next historical marker, commemorative statue, museum exhibit, feature film set in the American past, television miniseries, or historical novel will probably pass on more misinformation. At the least, it will present its topic incompletely and partially. What is to be done about these future lies?

The answer is not to expand *Lies My Teacher Told Me* to cover every distortion and error in history as traditionally taught, to say nothing of the future lies yet to be developed. That approach would make me the arbitrator—I who surely still unknowingly accept all manner of hoary legends as historical fact.[7] Instead, the answer is for all of us to become, in Postman and Weingartner's vulgar term, "crap detectors"[8]—independent learners who can sift through arguments and evidence and make reasoned judgments. Then we will have learned how to learn, as Postman and Weingartner put it, and neither a one-sided textbook nor a one-sided critique of textbooks will be able to confuse us.

To succeed, schools must help us learn how to ask questions about our society and its history and how to figure out answers for ourselves. At this crucial task most American history textbooks and courses fail miserably.

Part of the problem is with form. Because they try to cover so many things, textbooks, at least as currently incarnated, *cannot* effectively acquaint students with issues and controversies and thereby with historical argument, with its attendant skills of using logic and marshaling evidence to persuade. Mentioning is part of the problem. Even when textbooks discredit the myths that clog our historical arteries, students don't retain the tiny rebuttals in their history textbooks.[9] They forget the untoward fact that contradicts the myth, for it doesn't fit with the powerful archetype. History textbooks and teachers must make special efforts and take enough time to teach effectively against these archetypes. Mircea Eliade has referred to "the inability of collective memory to retain historical events except insofar as it transforms them into archetypes."[10] Truth, to be retained, must be given the same mythic significance that we have given our lies.

For this reason, I find myself tongue-tied when teachers ask what textbook I recommend. Perhaps no traditional textbook can be written that will empower rather than bore us with history.

What, then, is to be done?

The portrait of lying painted in the last two chapters as a vertically integrated industry, including textbook boards, publishers, authors, teachers, stu-

UNION ARMY
PASSES ROCKY SPRINGS

—————— • ♦ • ——————

Upon the occupation of Willow Springs on May 3, 1863, Union Gen. J. A. McClernand sent patrols up the Jackson road. These groups rode through Rocky Springs, where they encountered no resistance beyond the icy stares of the people who gathered at the side of the road to watch.

On May 5, Gen. P. J. Osterhaus' division stopped briefly at Rocky Springs, while en route to Big Sand Creek. The next day, Gen. A. P. Hovey's division arrived and spent the night. From May 7, when Gen. U. S. Grant began his drive toward the Southern Railroad of Mississippi until May 16 when Gen. H. Ewing's brigade passed through hurrying to overtake the army, the Yankees were never far away. During this period 45,000 blueclad invaders and uncounted wagons had passed along this road.

Throughout the United States, roadside markers, monuments, forts, ships, and museums distort history. My book *Lies Across America* critiqued one hundred such sites. This marker, which I critiqued in the first edition of *Lies My Teacher Told Me*, inspired that book. Like many Civil War monuments and roadside markers across the South, it misrepresented Southerners as united in support of the Confederacy. In reality, in 1863, support from black residents in southwest Mississippi—and from some whites as well—enabled Grant to abandon his supply lines and attack Vicksburg from the south and east. Despite this roadside marker's words, "the people" Grant's forces encountered were mostly African Americans who responded to "the blueclad invaders" by supplying them with food, showing them the best roads to Jackson, and telling them exactly where the Confederates were.

By 2000, perhaps because of this book, the marker had been removed. The Mississippi Department of Archives and History does not admit to knowing what happened to it, but it no longer stands in southwest Mississippi. A marvelous teaching device would be for a class to examine roadside markers and monuments in their own community, deciding which is least accurate. Then students could propose a corrective marker to stand next to the biased commemoration; they might even help raise money to erect it. In the process, they might stumble upon some of the forces that influence historical memory, especially when it is on the landscape.

dents, and the public, may appear bleak. It follows, however, that intervention can occur at any point in the cycle. The next few paragraphs are directed particularly toward teachers, who can intervene even in the absence of transformed textbooks. Those of us not in the classroom can play a role in changing how history is taught by supporting teachers who put innovative approaches into practice.

The first critical change must be in the form: we must introduce fewer topics and examine them more thoroughly. There is no way to get students to explore and bring primary and secondary sources to bear on the thousands of topics that now clutter history textbooks. Rather than having students memorize the names Amerigo Vespucci, Giovanni Verrazano, Ponce de Leon, Hernando de Soto, etc., and a phrase telling what each allegedly did, teachers can help students focus on the larger picture—the effects of Columbus's 1493 expedition upon Haiti and Spain, and then on all the Americas, Europe, the Islamic world, and Africa. So many details connect with major issues such as this that I suspect students will come away remembering more particulars than if they had merely regurgitated factoids. Certainly, students will recall the projects they worked on and the issues they worked through themselves. Many educators have already put into effect teaching methods that deviate from the deadening "learn the textbook" routine and provide models for other teachers.[11]

Covering fewer topics will enable classes to delve into historical controversies. Doing so is an absolute requirement if students are to learn that history is not just answers. The answers one gets depend partly upon the questions one asks, and the questions one asks depend partly upon one's purpose and one's place in the social structure. Perhaps not everyone in the classroom will come to the same conclusion. Teachers need to put themselves in the position that for students to disagree with their interpretation is okay, so long as students back up their disagreement with serious historical work: argumentation based on evidence. People have a right to their own opinions, but not to their own facts. Evidence must be located, not created, and opinions not backed by evidence cannot be given much weight. Students who research both sides will discover which issues and questions facts will resolve, and which differences involve basic values and assumptions. The students' positions must then be respected. This does not imply that teachers should concede the floor or accede to the now fashionable opinion that all points of view are equally appropriate and none is to be "privileged" with the label "true."[12]

Teachers do not have to know everything to facilitate independent student learning. They can act as informed reference librarians, directing children to books, maps, and people who can answer their questions about history. Resources already exist that can help teachers teach history creatively, using primary materials.[13]

Perhaps the best resources are right at hand. Students can interview their own family members, diverse people in the community, leaders of local institutions, and older citizens.[14] Some history classes have compiled oral histories of how the depression affected their town or how desegregation affected their school. Students in a Mississippi high school published a book, *Minds Stayed on*

Freedom, about the civil rights movement in their community.[15] Students in a Massachusetts school "became" historical figures and published their work.[16] For students to create knowledge is exciting and empowering, even if the product merely gets placed in the school library. Students might also suggest a new historical marker for their school or community. Often the most important events go unrecorded on the landscape, while markers commemorate the nineteenth-century site of the First Presbyterian Church. What events at a high school were important enough to be noted on a marker? Which graduates "should" be commemorated? Which made history, and is a broader definition of "making history" needed? Do the names of local streets or buildings honor people whose acts we are now trying to rectify? Mississippi's Ross Barnett Reservoir, for example, pays tribute to the racist governor who tried to keep African Americans out of the University of Mississippi. Who should be honored? Why? How? Raising these questions leads students to important issues; if their answers are controversial, so much the better.

Teaching history backward from the present also grips students' attention. The teacher presents current statistics on high school seniors' life chances, analyzed by race, sex, social class, and region—their prospects for various levels of educational achievement, divorce, incarceration, death by violence; their life expectancy, frequency of voting, etc. Then students are challenged to discuss events and processes in the past that cause these differences.

Teachers can also encourage their students to critique their textbook. Each student can pick on a topic s/he thinks is badly handled, or the entire class can work together on a common problem. Chapter 5 told of an Illinois teacher who upset her sixth graders by telling them that most presidents before Lincoln were slave owners. After her students convinced themselves that she was right, they were outraged with their textbook, which devoted many pages to Washington, Jefferson, Madison, Jackson, and the rest without a word about their owning slaves. They wound up sending a letter to the putative author and the publisher. The author never replied, but someone at the publisher sent a bland reply that thanked them for providing "useful feedback on our product," assured them "we are always striving to improve our product," and concluded by pointing out that the textbook included several pages on the civil rights movement. "What does this have to do with our critique?" exclaimed the students. Presumably the answer to their question was "It's 'black,' isn't it?!" Such an encounter amounts to a win-win situation. If the students receive an intelligent reply that takes their point seriously, then they have helped to improve the book in its next edition. If they get a boilerplate reply like these Illinois sixth graders, then they realize no one is at home intellectually in this publishing enterprise, so they had better read critically from here on.

Even if teachers do not challenge textbook doctrine, students and the rest of us are potential sources of change. African American students have actively pressured several urban school systems for new history curricula. Two white sixth-grade girls in Springfield, Illinois, who did a National History Day project on the 1908 riot that tried to make that town an all-white "sundown town," followed their project up by spurring the city to create a "race riot walking tour" as apology and remembrance. Two Native American high school students spurred the state of Minnesota to eliminate the word *squaw*, a derogatory term for female American Indians, as a formal name on the landscape. And all across America, confronted with teachers who still simply teach from the textbook, students have challenged them with ideas from *Lies My Teacher Told Me*. As one student put it: "I've been using your book to heckle my teacher from the back of the room."

Whether dealing with bad textbooks, watching historical movies, or visiting museum exhibits, students—and the rest of us—must learn how to deal with sources. This process entails putting five questions to each work.[17]

First, when and why was it written (or painted, etc.)? Locate the intended audience in the social structure. Consider what the speaker was trying to accomplish with them. This is part of what sociologists call the *sociology of knowledge* approach. English professors call it *contextualization*: learning about the social context of the text. As we have seen, historians call it *historiography*: studying the writing of history. Historiography—the concept and the term—can be taught to students as young as fourth grade, and it helps make them critical readers and critical thinkers.[18]

A second question, also part of historiography, is to ask whose viewpoint is presented. Where is the speaker, writer, etc., located in the social structure? What interests, material or ideological, does the statement serve? Whose viewpoints are omitted? Students might then attempt to rewrite the story from a different viewpoint, thus learning that history is inevitably partial.

Third, is the account believable? Does each acting group behave reasonably—as we might, given the same situation and socialization? This approach also requires examining the work for internal contradictions. Does it cohere? Do some of its assertions contradict others? If textbooks emphasize the United

States as a generally helpful presence in Latin America, for example, how do they explain anti-Yankee sentiment in the region?

Fourth, is the account backed up by other sources? Or do other authors contradict it? This question sends us to the secondary historical and social science literature. Even a cursory encounter with research on social class in other countries, for instance, is enough to refute the glowing textbook accounts of America as a land of unparalleled opportunity.

Finally, after reading the words or seeing the image, how is one supposed to feel about the America that has been presented? This analysis also includes examining the authors' choice of words and images. "Most of the words we use in history and everyday speech are like mental depth charges," James Axtell has written. "As they descend [through our consciousness] and detonate, their resonant power is unleashed, showering our understanding with fragments of accumulated meaning and association."[19]

Readers who keep these five questions in mind will have learned how to learn history.

Teachers and students are not the only fulcrums for change. New factors make transformed textbooks possible. In California, Texas, and other states, right-wing conservatives still influence textbook adoptions, but so now do many others. Beginning in 1985, for instance, Texas forced some publishers to treat evolution more honestly, avoid such stereotypical terms as *go on the warpath*, when referring to Native Americans, and add *white* before *Southerners* where appropriate.[20] The ensuing standoffs between black nationalists, feminists, right-wingers, First Amendment groups, etc., allow authors and publishers new room to maneuver.

Consumers of education—students, teachers, parents, and interested citizens—are beginning to demand textbooks with real flavor, history that can even upset the stomach. According to Michael Wallace, Americans are ready for it. People generally "are angry at having been conned and are curious to know more," he claims. "Witness the triumph of *Roots* in a culture once seemingly mired in the pieties of *Gone With the Wind*."[21] For that matter, the success of the first edition of *Lies My Teacher Told Me* provides additional evidence.

It is about time. For history is central to our ongoing understanding of ourselves and our society. We need to produce Americans of all social-class and racial backgrounds and of both genders who command the power of history— the ability to use one's understanding of the past to inspire and legitimize one's actions in the present. Then the past will seriously inform Americans as individuals and as a nation, instead of serving as a source of weary clichés. Products of successful American history courses know basic social facts about the United States and understand the historical processes that have shaped these facts. They can locate themselves in the social structure, and they know some of the societal and ideological forces that have influenced their lives. Such Americans are ready to become citizens, because they understand how to effect change in our society. They know how to check out historical assertions and are suspicious of archetypal "truths." They can rebut the charge that history is irrelevant, because they realize ways that the past influences the present, including their own present.

Thomas Jefferson surely had it right when he urged the teaching of political history so that Americans might learn "how to judge for themselves what will secure or endanger their freedom."[22] Citizens who are their own historians, willing to identify lies and distortions and able to use sources to determine what really went on in the past, become a formidable force for democracy. Hugh Trevor-Roper, the dean of British historians, has written, "A nation that has lost sight of its history, or is discouraged from the study of it by the desiccating professionalism [or unprofessionalism!] of its historians, is intellectually and perhaps politically amputated. But that history must be true history in the fullest sense." After the eleven years of research and writing that went into the first edition of this book,[23] and thirteen more years of study since, my own quest to know what truly happened in our American past has only begun. After reading all this way, so has yours. Bon voyage to us both!

NOTES

INTRODUCTION TO THE
SECOND EDITION

1. Student, email via AOL.com, 1996.

2. Tomi Evans, email, 10/2005.

3. Via Erik Bailey, emial, 11/2005.

4. Dudley Lewis, "Teaching the Truth," *San Francisco Examiner & Chronicle*, 11/26/1995. Lewis was the first commentator to pair Howard Zinn's *People's History* and *Lies*. He was far from the last. Our books are very different, partly because our politics differ, but we are equally critical of the smug boring textbooks that still dominate American history on the high school level.

5. Mary Mackey, "Don't Know Much About History . . . ," *San Francisco Chronicle*, 2/12/1995.

6. "Joan" at independentreader.com (1995); website has since changed hands.

7. Others have done better, but they're dead!

8. Several readers have taken me to task for including almost nothing about women's history. To be sure, in the Afterword I took myself to task for this omission and explained it by noting that the job had already been done. A note to that chapter directs readers to six different critiques of history textbooks' treatment of women; I could not bring myself to do again what others had done so well. I must admit, however, that I have yet to meet a single person who read one of these critiques because of my suggestion, so perhaps I should have addressed the topic myself.

9. When I did this on a panel with Herbert Kohl and Howard Zinn in Boston, Zinn suggested, "Maybe you should have called your book *Lies 70 Percent of My Teachers Told Me*."

10. Please, before you quit, buy at least *one* book from the club!

11. Polite would be nice, though.

INTRODUCTION: SOMETHING
HAS GONE VERY WRONG

1. Billings, whose real name was Henry Wheeler Shaw, coined this phrase probably between 1850 and 1885.

2. James Baldwin, "A Talk to Teachers," *Saturday Review*, 12/21/1963, reprinted in Rick Simonson and Scott Walker, eds., *Multi-cultural Literacy* (St. Paul, MN: Graywolf Press, 1988), 11.

3. Gen. Petro G. Grigorenko, quoted in Robert Slusser, "History and the Democratic Opposition," in Rudolf L. Tökés, ed., *Dissent in the USSR* (Baltimore: Johns Hopkins University Press, 1975), 329–53.

4. I use the term *history* as encompassing social studies, as do most researchers and students. When the distinction is important, I will make it. Robert Reinhold, Harris poll, reported in *New York Times*, 7/3/1971, and quoted in Herbert Aptheker, *The Unfolding Drama* (New York:

International, 1978), 146; Terry Borton, *The Weekly Reader National Survey on Education* (Middletown, CT: Field Publications, 1985), 14, 16; Mark Schug, Robert Todd, and R. Beery, "Why Kids Don't Like Social Studies," *Social Education* 48 (May 1984): 382–87; Albert Shanker, "The 'Efficient' Diploma Mill," paid column in *New York Times*, 2/14/1988; Joan M. Shaughnessy and Thomas M. Haladyna, "Research on Student Attitudes Toward Social Studies," *Social Education* 49 (November 1985): 692–95. National grade averages in *1992 ACT Assessment Results, Summary Report, Mississippi* (Iowa City: ACT, 1993), 7.

5. Diane Ravitch and Chester E. Finn Jr., *What Do Our 17-Year-Olds Know?* (New York: Harper and Row, 1987); National Geographic Society, *Geography: An International Gallup Survey* (Washington, D.C.: National Geographic Society, 1988). Since the first edition of *Lies My Teacher Told Me*, these studies continue to come out. Recent examples include Elizabeth McPike, *Education for Democracy* (Washington, D.C.: Albert Shanker Institute, 2000); a study of 556 students at fifty-five elite colleges and universities commissioned by the American Council of Trustees and Alumni, summarized by the Associated Press—"Students Ignorant of History," *USA Today*, 6/29/2000; the 2001 National Assessment of Educational Progress in History, summarized by Diane Ravitch, "Should We Be Alarmed by the Results of the Latest U.S. History Test? (Yes)," History News Network, hnn.us/articles/1526.html, 10/19/2003; Sheldon M. Stern, *Effective State Standards for U.S. History* (Washington, D.C.: Thomas B. Fordham Institute, 2003); and Joe Williams, "Duh! 81% of kids fail test," *New York Daily News*, nydailynews.com/front/story/308139p

263646c.html, 5/10/2005. In addition to pointing out that graduates know little history, McPike also claims they are not nationalist enough, having been taught too many bad things about our past. I disagree.

6. James Green, "Everyone His/Her Own Historian?" *Radical Historians Newsletter* 80 (5/99): 3, reviewing and quoting Roy Rosenzweig and David Thelen, *The Presence of the Past* (New York: Columbia University Press, 1998).

7. Richard L. Sawyer, "College Student Profiles: Norms for the ACT Assessment, 1980–81" (Iowa City: ACT, 1980). Sawyer finds larger differences by race and income in social studies than in English, mathematics, and the natural sciences.

8. Years ago Mills discerned that Americans feel a need to locate themselves in the social structure in order to understand the forces that shape their society and themselves. See C. Wright Mills, *The Sociological Imagination* (New York: Oxford University Press, 1959), 3–20.

9. Paul Goldstein, *Changing the American Schoolbook* (Lexington, MA: D. C. Heath, 1978). Goldstein says textbooks are the organizing principle for more than 75 percent of classroom time. In history, the proportion is even higher.

10. One of the "new new" books, *We Americans*, also has ancient antecedents but changed authors and was radically revised around 1990.

11. ———, "Ask an Alum," *Vermont Quarterly* (Fall 2005): 53.

12. Ravitch and Finn, *What Do Our 17-Year-Olds Know?* 49.

13. Mel Gabler's right-wing textbook critics and I concur that textbooks are boring. Mrs. W. Kelley Haralson writes, "The censoring of emotionalism from history texts during the last half century

has resulted in history textbooks which are boring to students." "Objections [to *The American Adventure*]" (Longview, TX: Educational Research Analysts, n.d.), 4. We part company in our proposed solutions, however, for the only emotion that Gabler and his allies seem to want to add is pride.

14. "It's a Great Country," sung with pride by a high school choir from Webster Groves, Missouri, in a CBS News video, *Sixteen in Webster Groves* (NY: Carousel Films, 1966).

15. In the aftermath of the Vietnam War, Harcourt Brace renamed this last one *Triumph of the American Nation*. This is the Rambo approach to history: we may have lost the war in Southeast Asia, but we'll win it on the book jackets!

16. James Axtell, "Europeans, Indians, and the Age of Discovery in American History Textbooks," *American Historical Review* 92 (1987): 627. Essays such as Axtell's, which review college-level textbooks, rarely appear in history journals. Almost never are high school textbooks reviewed.

17. Twelve were in my first sample for the first edition of this book, six in my second, for this revision. Two books, *Discovering American History* and *The American Adventure*, are "inquiry textbooks," composed of maps, illustrations, and extracts from primary sources such as diaries and laws, all woven together by an overarching narrative. Briefly popular in the mid-1970s, these books were meant to invite students to "do" history themselves. *The American Way, Land of Promise, The United States—A History of the Republic, American History,* and *The American Tradition* are traditional high school narrative history textbooks in my earlier sample. *American Adventures, Life and Liberty,* and *The Challenge of Freedom,* also in my original sample, were

intended for junior high students but were often used by "slow" senior high classes. *Triumph of the American Nation* and *The American Pageant* were often used in "advanced placement" high school history courses. The newer six books included a descendant of *Triumph of the American Nation* retitled *Holt American Nation,* the newest *Pageant, A History of the United States* by Daniel Boorstin and Brooks Mather Kelley, *The Americans,* now listing Gerald Danzer and four other authors, *Pathways to the Present,* listing four authors, and a seventh-grade book, *The American Journey,* which I included because a McGraw-Hill representative urged me to, impressed with the three outstanding historians listed as its authors. Sales figures are trade secrets, but the five current high school textbooks I examined are probably the biggest sellers and probably account for more than three-fourths of all American history textbook sales.

CHAPTER 1: HANDICAPPED BY HISTORY: THE PROCESS OF HERO-MAKING

1. James Baldwin, "A Talk to Teachers," *Saturday Review,* 12/21/1963, reprinted in Rick Simonson and Scott Walker, eds., *Multi-cultural Literacy* (St. Paul, MN: Graywolf Press, 1988), 9.

2. W. E. B. DuBois, *Black Reconstruction* (Cleveland: World Meridian, 1964 [1935]), 722.

3. Charles V. Willie, quoted in David J. Garrow, *Bearing the Cross* (New York: William Morrow, 1986), 625.

4. The phrase, of course, refers to his father's wealth and Senate seat.

5. *Helen Keller* (New York: McGraw-Hill Films, 1969).

6. Helen Keller, "Onward, Comrades," address at the Rand School of So-

cial Science, New York, 12/31/1920, reprinted in Philip S. Foner, ed., *Helen Keller: Her Socialist Years* (New York: International Publishers, 1967), 107.

7. Quoted in Jonathan Kozol, *The Night Is Dark and I Am Far from Home* (New York: Simon & Schuster, 1990 [1975]), 101.

8. Foner, ed., *Helen Keller: Her Socialist Years,* 26.

9. Joseph P. Lash, *Helen and Teacher* (New York: Delacorte, 1980), 454; Dennis Wepman, *Helen Keller* (New York: Chelsea House, 1987), 69; Foner, ed., *Helen Keller: Her Socialist Years,* 17–18. The United States did not allow Flynn to receive the letter.

10. Jonathan Kozol brought this suppression to my attention in an address at the University of Wyoming in 1975.

Nazi leaders also knew about her radicalism: in 1933 they burned Keller's books because of their socialist content and banned her from their libraries. We overlook her socialist content, thus learning no more than the German public about her ideas. See Irving Wallace, David Wallechinsky, and Amy Wallace, *Significa* (New York: Dutton, 1983), 1–2.

11. N. Gordon Levin Jr., *Woodrow Wilson and World Politics: America's Response to War and Revolution* (New York: Oxford University Press, 1968), 67. Everett M. Dirksen, "Use of U.S. Armed Forces in Foreign Countries," *Congressional Record,* June 23, 1969, 16840–43.

12. Robert J. Maddox, *The Unknown War with Russia* (San Rafael, CA: Presidio Press, 1977), 137.

13. Hans Schmidt, *The United States Occupation of Haiti, 1915–1934* (New Brunswick, NJ: Rutgers University Press, 1971), 86.

14. Ibid., 66, 74.

15. Walter Karp, *The Politics of War*

(New York: Harper and Row, 1979), 158–67.

16. Piero Gleijesus, "The Other Americas," *Washington Post Book World,* 12/27/1992, 5.

17. "Reports Unlawful Killing of Haitians by Our Marines," *New York Times,* 10/14/1920, 1ff. Also see Schmidt, *The United States Occupation of Haiti.*

18. *Addresses of President Wilson.* 66th Congress, Senate Document 120 (Washington, D.C.: Government Printing Office, 1919), 133.

19. Jean Lacouture, *Ho Chi Minh* (New York: Random House, 1968), 24, 265.

20. Rayford W. Logan, *The Betrayal of the Negro* (New York: Collier, 1965 [1954]), 360–70; Nancy J. Weiss, "Wilson Draws the Color Line," in Arthur Mann, ed., *The Progressive Era* (Hinsdale, IL: Dryden, 1975), 144; Harvey Wasserman, *America Born and Reborn* (New York: Macmillan, 1983), 131; Kathleen Wolgemuth, "Woodrow Wilson and Federal Segregation," *Journal of Negro History* 44 (1959): 158–73; and Morton Sosna, "The South in the Saddle," *Wisconsin Magazine of History* 54 (Fall 1970): 30–49.

21. Colored Advisory Committee of the Republican National Committee, "Address to the Colored Voters," October 6, 1916, reprinted in Herbert Aptheker, ed., *A Documentary History of the Negro People in the United States, 1910–1932* (Secaucus, NJ: Citadel, 1973), 140; Nancy Weiss, "The Negro and the New Freedom," *Political Science Quarterly* 84, 1 (March 1969): 66; Theodore Kornweibel Jr., *"Seeing Red": Federal Campaigns Against Black Militancy, 1919–1925* (Bloomington: Indiana University Press, 1998).

22. Wyn C. Wade, *The Fiery Cross* (New York: Simon & Schuster, 1987), 115–51.

23. Ibid., 135–37.

24. Ibid., 138.

25. Lerone Bennett, Jr., *Before the Mayflower* (Baltimore: Penguin, 1966 [1962]), 292–94. Bennett counts twenty-six major race riots in 1919 alone, including riots in Omaha; Knoxville; Longview, Texas; Chicago; Phillips County, Arkansas; and Washington, D.C. Also see Herbert Shapiro, *White Violence and Black Response* (Amherst: University of Massachusetts Press, 1988), 123–54.

26. *Addresses of President Wilson*, 108–99.

27. William Bruce Wheeler and Susan D. Becker, *Discovering the American Past*, vol. 2 (Boston: Houghton Mifflin, 1990), 127, "Revive Spirit of 76," *NY Times*, 7/14/1921.

28. Ronald Schaffer, *Americans in the Great War* (New York: Oxford University Press, 1991), quoted in Garry Wills, "The Presbyterian Nietzsche," *New York Review of Books*, 1/16/1992, 6.

29. Karp, *The Politics of War*, 326–28; Charles D. Ameringer, *U.S. Foreign Intelligence* (Lexington, MA: D. C. Heath, 1990), 109. Ironically, after the war Wilson agreed with Debs on the power of economic interests: "Is there any man here . . . who does not know that the seed of war in the modern world is industrial and commercial rivalry?" (speech in Saint Louis, 9/5/1919; *Addresses of President Wilson*, 41).

30. Ameringer, *U.S. Foreign Intelligence*, 109.

31. Ibid. Ameringer points out that Wilson's attacks on civil liberties had become a political liability and Attorney General Palmer a pathetic joke by the fall of 1920.

32. The seventh-grade textbook *American Journey* does tell of her in two places, each time saying "according to popular legend."

33. Michael H. Frisch, *A Shared Authority* (Albany: State University of New York Press, 1990), 39–47.

34. In Arthur M. Schlesinger's 1962 poll of seventy-five "leading historians," Wilson came in fourth, ahead of Thomas Jefferson (Kenneth S. Davis, "Not So Common Man," *New York Review of Books*, December 4, 1986, 29). Eight hundred and forty-six professors of American history rated Wilson sixth, after FDR and the four gentlemen already on Mount Rushmore (Robert K. Murray and Tim Blessing, "The Presidential Performance Study," *Journal of American History* 70 [December 1983]: 535–55). See also George Hornby, ed., *Great Americana Scrap Book* (New York: Crown, 1985), 121.

35. Thomas A. Bailey, *Probing America's Past*, vol. 2 (Lexington, MA: D. C. Heath, 1973), 575.

36. Michael Kammen, *Mystic Chords of Memory* (New York: Alfred A. Knopf, 1991), 701.

37. Quoted in Marjory Kline, "Social Influences in Textbook Publishing," in *Educational Forum* 48, no. 2 (1984): 230.

38. Bessie Pierce, *Public Opinion and the Teaching of History in the United States* (New York: Alfred A. Knopf, 1926), 332.

39. Charles Dickens, *American Notes*, Chapter 3, in The Complete Works of Charles Dickens, dickens-literature.com/American_Notes/3.html, 11/2006; Elisabeth Gitler, *The Imprisoned Guest* (New York: Farrar, Straus, & Giroux, 2001); "Laura Dewey Bridgman" at Wikipedia, 11/2006; Helen Keller, *Midstream: My Later Life* (New York: Greenwood, 1968 [1929]), 156.

40. Levin, *Woodrow Wilson and World Politics*, 1. Since Wilson's was the only Democratic administration in the first third of the twentieth century, it was natural that many of Franklin Roosevelt's

statesmen, including FDR himself, had received their foreign policy experience under Wilson.

41. Quoted in Kozol, *The Night Is Dark and I Am Far from Home*, 101.

42. Kammen, *Mystic Chords of Memory*, 639.

43. See also Arthur Levine, *When Dreams and Heroes Died* (San Francisco: Jossey-Bass, 1980), and Frisch, *A Shared Authority*.

44. Quoted in Claudia Bushman, "America Discovers Columbus" (Costa Mesa, CA: American Studies Association Annual Meeting, 1992), 9.

CHAPTER 2:
1493: THE TRUE IMPORTANCE
OF CHRISTOPHER COLUMBUS

1. Kirkpatrick Sale, *The Conquest of Paradise* (New York: Alfred A. Knopf, 1990), 5.

2. Samuel D. Marble, *Before Columbus* (Cranbury, NJ: Barnes, 1989), 25.

3. Bartolomé de Las Casas, *History of the Indies*, translated by Andrée M. Collard (New York: Harper and Row, 1971), 289.

4. David Quinn, *England and the Discovery of America, 1481–1620* (New York: Alfred A. Knopf, 1974), 5–105; Robert Blow, *Abroad in America* (New York: Continuum, 1990), 17; Jack Forbes, *Black Africans and Native Americans* (Oxford: Basil Blackwell, 1988), 20.

5. Angus Calder, *Revolutionary Empire* (New York: Dutton, 1981), 5.

6. A. H. Lybyer, "The Ottoman Turks and the Routes of Oriental Trade," *English Historical Review* 30, no. 120 (10/1915): 577–88. Turkey may have shut out Portuguese and Spanish merchants from the trade for a time, however, owing to warfare between Turkey and Spain/Portugal.

7. Ibid.

8. William H. McNeill, *The Age of Gunpowder Empires* (Washington, D.C.: American Historical Association, 1989).

9. Some textbooks use the term *Native Americans*, some use *American Indians*, and some use both. Since about 1975 some Native Americans have rejected the term *American Indian*. Others, including the American Indian Movement, have chosen to stick with it. Because Native people use both terms, so will I.

10. Letter to the king and queen of Spain, 7/1503, in *Select Letters of Christopher Columbus*, translated and edited by R. H. Major (New York: Corinth, 1961 [1847]), 196.

11. Columbus renamed the island now occupied by Haiti and the Dominican Republic *Hispaniola*, "Little Spain." I call the island *Haiti* because, as a term, *Hispaniola* is less well known by the public than *Haiti*, and because *Haiti* was the aboriginal term, although confusion remains as to whether *Haiti* referred to the entire island or the highlands. See Las Casas, *History of the Indies*, 44.

12. Michele de Cuneo, 1495 letter referring to 1/20/1494, quoted in Sale, *Conquest of Paradise*, 143.

13. The Requirement has been widely reprinted. This translation is from "500 Years of Indigenous and Popular Resistance Campaign" (np: Guatemala Committee for Peasant Unity, 1990).

14. Alfred W. Crosby, *Ecological Imperialism: The Biological Expansion of Europe, 900–1900* (New York: Cambridge University Press, 1976), 71–93.

15. bell hooks makes this point in "Columbus: Gone but Not Forgotten," *Z*, December 1992, 26.

16. Sale, *The Conquest of Paradise*, 71–72.

17. Constance Irwin, *Fair Gods and*

Stone Faces (New York: St. Martin's, 1963), 193–211, 217, 241; Cyrus Gordon, *Before Columbus* (New York: Crown, 1971), 119–25; Geoffrey Ashe et al., *The Quest for America* (London: Pall Mall, 1971), 78–79.

18. Richard Eaton, *Islamic History as Global History* (Washington, D.C.: American Historical Association, 1990), 17; on *caravel*, Smithsonian Institution "Seeds of Change" exhibit (Washington, D.C.: National Museum of Natural History, 1991).

19. *The American Adventure* points out "the magnetic compass had come from China," and "from the Arabs came an instrument called the astrolabe." *Holt American Nation* credits the Chinese for the compass and the Persians or Indians for the lateen sail. Otherwise, all eighteen textbooks present the Portuguese achievements as unprecedented.

20. Stephen C. Jett, "Diffusion vs. Independent Development," in Carroll Riley et al., eds., *Man Across the Sea* (Austin: University of Texas Press, 1971), 7.

21. An entry-level list of sources for these alleged predecessors of Columbus begins with the enormous bibliography by John L. Sorenson and Martin H. Raish, *Pre-Columbian Contact with the Americas Across the Oceans* (Provo, UT: Research Press, 1990), hereafter "Sorenson and Raish." See also:

For Indonesia: Stephen C. Jett. "The Development and Distribution of the Blowgun," *Annals of the Association of American Geographers* (Davis: University of California, December 1970). Similar manufacture of paper: Paul Tolstoy, "Paper Route," *Natural History*, 6/1991, 6–14; and *Feats and Wisdom of the Ancients* (Alexandria, VA: Time-Life, 1990), 122. Also see Carroll Riley et al., eds., *Man Across the Sea*, especially the article by Jett,

and Sorenson and Raish, entries H255, M109, and S57.

For Japanese: Betty J. Meggers, "Did Japanese Fishermen Really Reach Ecuador 5000 Years Ago?" *Early Man 2* (1980): 15–19, and Ashe et al., *The Quest for America*, 239–59. Also see *Feats and Wisdom of the Ancients*, 124.

For Crees, Navajos, and Inuits: William Fitzhugh, "Crossroads of Continents: Review and Prospect," in William Fitzhugh and V. Chaussonet, eds., *Proceedings of the Crossroads Symposium* (Washington, D.C.: Smithsonian Institution Press, 1988). See also Ian Stevenson, *Twenty Cases Suggestive of Reincarnation* (Charlottesville: University of Virginia Press, 1974), 218–19.

For Chinese: Joseph Needham and Lu Gwei-Djen, *Trans-Pacific Echoes and Resonances* (Singapore: World Scientific, 1985). Also see *Feats and Wisdom of the Ancients*, 121; Stevenson, *Twenty Cases Suggestive of Reincarnation*, 218–19; Irwin, *Fair Gods and Stone Faces*, 249–51; Paul Shao, *The Origins of Ancient American Culture* (Ames: Iowa State University Press, 1983); and Sorenson and Raish, entries L228, 231, 238–41 et al.

For Afro-Phoenicians: Alexander von Wuthenau, *The Art of Terracotta Pottery in Pre-Columbian Central and South America* (New York: Crown, 1970), and *Unexpected Faces in Ancient America* (New York: Crown, 1975). Also see Ivan Van Sertima, *They Came Before Columbus* (New York: Random House, 1976); Thor Heyerdahl, "The Bearded Gods Speak," in Ashe et al., *The Quest for America*, 199–238; *Feats and Wisdom of the Ancients*, 123; Irwin, *Fair Gods and Stone Faces*, 67–71, 89–96, 122–45, 176–86; J. A. Rogers, *100 Amazing Facts About the Negro* (St. Petersburg, FL: Helga Rogers, 1970), 21–22; and Sorenson and Raish, entries J13–17, G71 et al. Kenneth Feder attacks Van Sertima's evidence in *Frauds, Myths, and Mysteries* (Mountain View, CA: Mayfield, 1990), 75–77.

For Celts: Barry Fell, *America B.C.* (New York: Quadrangle, 1976), and Barry Fell, *Saga America* (New York: Times Books, 1980).

For Irish: Ashe et al., *The Quest for America*, 24–48. Ashe concludes that the evidence for Irish voyages is weak.

For Norse: Erik Wahlgren, *The Vikings and America* (New York: Thames and Hudson, 1986).

For West Africans: Marble, *Before Columbus*, 22–25. See also Van Sertima, *They Came Before Columbus*; Arthur E. Morgan, *Nowhere Was Somewhere* (Chapel Hill: University of North Carolina Press, 1946), 198; Michael Anderson Bradley, *Dawn Voyage* (Toronto: Summer Hill Press, 1987); Pathe Diagne, "*Du Centenaire de la Decouverte du Nouveau Monde par Bakari II, en 1312, et Christopher Colomb, en 1492*" (Dakar: privately printed, 1990); and Sorenson and Raish, entry H344.

For Polynesians: Heather Whipps, "Chicken Bones Suggest Polynesians Found Americas Before Columbus," Live Science website, 6/4/2007, livescience.com/history/070604_polynesian_chicken.html.

For Portuguese: Marble, *Before Columbus*, 25. See also Van Sertima, *They Came Before Columbus*: Morgan, *Nowhere Was Somewhere*, 197; Ashe et al., *The Quest for America*, 265–66; Quinn, *England and the Discovery of America*, 41–43, 85–86; and H. Y. Oldham, "A Pre-Columbian Discovery of America," *Geographical Journal* 3 (1895): 221–33.

For Basques: Forbes, *Black Africans and Native Americans*, 20.

For Bristol fishers: Quinn, *England and the Discovery of America*, 5–105. Also see A. A. Ruddock, "John Day of Bristol," *Geographical Journal* 132 (1966): 225–33; Blow, *Abroad in America*, 17; G. R. Crone, *The Discovery of America* (New York: Weybright and Talley, 1960), 157–58; and Carl Sauer, *Sixteenth-Century North America* (Berkeley and Los Angeles: University of California Press, 1971), 6.

22. Charles H. Hapgood, *Maps of the Ancient Sea Kings* (New York: Chilton, 1966). Hapgood argues for the Turkish map, which he believes contains details unknown to European explorers in 1513, hence could not be fraudulent. *Current Anthropology* 21, no. 1 (February 1980) contains arguments for and against coins as evidence of Roman visits.

23. Forbes, *Black Africans and Native Americans*, 7–14; William Fitzhugh, personal communication, November 16, 1993; Van Sertima, *They Came Before Columbus*, Chapter 12. See also Alice B. Kehoe, "Small Boats Upon the North Atlantic," in Riley et al., *Man Across the Sea*, 276.

24. James West Davidson and Mark H. Lytle, *After the Fact* (New York: McGraw-Hill, 1992).

25. Forbes, *Black Africans and Native Americans*, 19. Morgan Llywelyn, "The Norse Discovery of the New World," *Early Man* 2, no. 4 (1980): 3–6; Marshall McKusick and Erik Wahlgren, "Viking in America—Fact and Fiction," *Early Man* 2, no. 4 (1980): 7–9. Unlike most authorities, Sale, *The Conquest of Paradise*, 374, is unsure that Columbus reached Iceland. The Norse findings were known in Europe, according to James Duff, *The Truth about Columbus* (London: Jarrolds, 1937), 9–13.

26. Van Sertima, *They Came Before Columbus*, 30. See also Irwin, *Fair Gods and Stone Faces*, 126.

27. Von Wuthenau, *The Art of Terracotta Pottery in Pre-Columbian Central and South America*, 50.

28. Jose Maria Melgar quoted in Jacquest Soustelle, *The Olmecs* (Garden City: Doubleday, 1984), 9. Gabriel Haslip-Viera, Bernard Ortiz de Montellano, and Warren Barbour summarize the case against African contact in "Robbing Native American Cultures," *Current Anthropology* 38 #3 (6/1997), 419–31.

29. Note 21 includes pro and con sources for Afro-Phoenician contact.

30. Quoted by Jan Carew, *Fulcrums of Change* (Trenton, NJ: Africa World Press, 1988), 13.

31. For example, "Acknowledge Your Own History" by Jungle Brothers.

32. Phoenicians and Egyptians did not keep track of "races" in today's terms and ranged (as they do today) from light to dark.

33. A controversy rages over what impact these alleged newcomers had. Older Eurocentric theories credited white visitors to the Americas with the ideas that led to Olmec and Mayan civilizations. Pierre Honore, *In Quest of the White God* (New York: Putnam, 1964), is a late example. A few authors believe the black visitors to be the source of many Olmec skills and ideas. See Irving Wallace, David Wallechinsky, and Amy Wallace, *Significa* (New York: Dutton, 1983), 58. Most Mesoamericanists believe the Olmecs developed entirely on their own. For an early statement of this criticism, see Gregory Mason, *Columbus Came Late* (New York: Century, 1931). A fourth view holds that the Afro-Phoenician contact might have triggered a flowering of Olmec society. This view retains the potential for genius in both hemispheres.

34. *Adventure* is an "inquiry textbook," composed of maps, illustrations, and extracts from primary sources such as diaries and laws, linked by narrative passages. Questions of this sort are the bane of inquiry books. Wrestling with them would require abundant library materials, curricular time, and teaching savvy.

35. Marble, *Before Columbus*, 25.

36. De Soto's only geopolitical significance was smallpox, which he left among the Indians, and which left their populations much reduced even by the time La Salle floated down the Mississippi 140 years later. Among the books I reviewed only *Life and Liberty* mentions this plague, giving it just five words.

37. After I published this imagined classroom exchange in *The Truth About Columbus* (New York: New Press, 1992), I read an account of the African American novelist Ishmael Reed's bringing up similar material, learned from the historian J. A. Rogers, in his fourth-grade history class. His teacher dismissed his ideas in "a lengthy outburst," Reed reports. See "The Forbidden Books of Youth," *New York Times Book Review*, June 6, 1993, 26–28.

38. Diagne, "*Du Centenaire de la Decouverte du Nouveau Monde par Bakari II, en 1312, et Christopher Colomb, en 1492*," 2–3; Van Sertima, *They Came Before Columbus*, 6. Forbes, *Black Africans and Native Americans*, 13–14, cites Las Casas as evidence that Columbus knew of American trade from West Africa.

39. Van Sertima, *They Came Before Columbus*, 21, 26. Regarding African diseases in the Americas, see Sorenson and Raish, entry H344, and Richard Hoeppli, "Parasitic Diseases in Africa and the Western Hemisphere," in *Acta Tropica*, Supplementum 10 (Basel: Verlag für Recht und Gesellschaft, n.d.), 54–59. Forbes, *Black Africans and Native Americans*, cautions that *black* and *Negro* might be misleading terms, for Europeans often applied them to any dark person of low status. Forbes believes that Balboa saw blacks, but thinks these blacks might have come somehow from

Haiti. Since African slaves were brought to Haiti only in 1505, they would have had to escape from Haiti to Panama with Indians in order to have preceded Balboa, who arrived in Panama in 1510. Regarding black oral tradition in Mexico, see Gonzalo Aguirre Beltran, *La población negra de México* (Mexico City: Fondo de Cultura Económica, 1989); and John G. Jackson, *Man, God, and Civilization* (New Hyde Park, NY: University Books, 1972), 283.

40. Riley et al., *Man Across the Sea,* especially Alice B. Kehoe, "Small Boats upon the North Atlantic," 275–92. Even Marc Stengel leaves out Brendan from his lively and sympathetic summary, "The Diffusionists Have Landed," *Atlantic Monthly,* 1/2000, 35–48.

41. The three small fragments of knowledge about Columbus's background are described in Lorenzo Camusso, *The Voyages of Columbus* (New York: Dorset, 1991), 9–10. See also Sale, *The Conquest of Paradise,* 51–52.

42. Las Casas, *History of the Indies,* 21.

43. Sale, *The Conquest of Paradise,* 23–26.

44. Ibid., 344; J. B. Russell, *Inventing the Flat Earth* (New York: Praeger, 1991).

45. By 2003 the descendant textbook *Holt American Nation* dropped the mutiny altogether.

46. Sale, *The Conquest of Paradise,* 171, 185, 204–14, 362; John Hebert, ed., *1492: An Ongoing Voyage* (Washington, D.C.: Library of Congress, 1992), 100.

47. Hans Koning, *Columbus, His Enterprise* (New York: Monthly Review Press, 1976), 39–40; Sale, *The Conquest of Paradise,* 238.

48. Pietro Barozzi, "Navigation and Ships in the Age of Columbus," *Italian Journal* 5, no. 4 (1990): 38–41.

49. Samuel Eliot Morison, *The Great Explorers* (New York: Oxford University Press, 1978), 397–98. Elsewhere Morison gives talk of revolt a bit more credence, but Koning, *Columbus, His Enterprise,* 50, pooh-poohs the mutiny. The best source for the trip, Columbus's journal, now lost but summarized by Bartolomé de Las Casas, offers this account: "Here [10/10] the men could bear no more and complained of the length of the voyage. But the Admiral encouraged them in the best way he could, giving them hope of the advantage they might gain from it [riches]. He added that however much they might complain, having come so far, he had nothing to do but go to the Indies, and he would go on until he found them." Sale, *The Conquest of Paradise,* 60, believes the story has little historical credibility. Indeed, by October 9, they were following large flocks of birds, which they believed (correctly) would take them toward land, making an October 10 mutiny threat quite unlikely.

50. Bill Bigelow, "Once Upon a Genocide . . . ," in *Rethinking Schools* 5, no. 1 (October–November 1990): 7–8.

51. Salvador de Madariaga, *Christopher Columbus* (New York: Frederick Ungar, 1967 [1940]), 203–4.

52. *The Journal of Christopher Columbus,* translated by Cecil Jane (New York: Bonanza, 1989), 171.

53. Ibid., 23.

54. *The Log of Christopher Columbus's First Voyage to America in the Year 1492,* as copied out in brief by Las Casas (Hamden, CT: Linnet, 1989), unpaginated.

55. Sale, *The Conquest of Paradise,* 122.

56. Philip Klass, "Wells, Welles, and the Martians," *New York Times Book Review,* October 30, 1988. Ironically, in Wells's story, the aliens are finally done in by microbes, while, in reality, disease wiped out the Natives. "Amazon tribe faces 'annihilation'," BBC, 5/17/2005, news.bbc.co

.uk/go/pr/fr/2/hi/americas/4554221.stm, 11/2006.

57. Quoted in Michael Paiewonsky, *The Conquest of Eden, 1493–1515* (Chicago: Academy, 1991), 109. I have slightly modified the translation based on a translation in Juan Friede and Benjamin Keen, *Bartolomé de Las Casas in History* (De Kalb: Northern Illinois Press, 1971), 312.

58. Sale, *The Conquest of Paradise*, 153–54.

59. Cuneo, quoted in Sale, *The Conquest of Paradise*, 138. See also Howard Zinn, *A People's History of the United States* (New York: Harper and Row, 1980), 4.

60. 1496 letter, quoted in Eric Williams, *Documents of West Indian History*, (Port-of-Spain, Trinidad: PNM, 1963), 1:57.

61. Ferdinand Columbus, *The Life of the Admiral Christopher Columbus* (New Brunswick, NJ: Rutgers University Press, 1959), 149–50.

62. Maria Norlander-Martinez, "Christopher Columbus: The Man, the Myth, and the Slave Trade," *Adventures of the Incredible Librarian*, 4/1990, 17; Troy Floyd, *The Columbus Dynasty in the Caribbean* (Albuquerque: University of New Mexico Press, 1973), 29.

63. One book, *The Americans*, does much better. It includes the quotation about subjugating the island with fifty men, quotes Las Casas, and tells the story of the 1493 voyage and the subjugation of the Natives that followed.

64. James Axtell, "Europeans, Indians, and the Age of Discovery in American History Textbooks," *American Historical Review* 92 (1987): 621–32; Sale, *The Conquest of Paradise*, 156.

65. De Cordoba letter in Williams, *Documents of West Indian History*, 1:94.

66. Smallpox, usually the big killer, probably did not appear on the island until after 1516.

67. Benjamin Keen, "Black Legend," in *The Christopher Columbus Encyclopedia* (New York: Simon & Schuster, 1991). Las Casas cited by Sale, *The Conquest of Paradise*, 160–61. See also Alfred W. Crosby Jr., *The Columbian Exchange: Biological and Cultural Consequences of 1492* (Westport, CT: Greenwood, 1972), 45.

68. Regarding Isabella, see J. Leitch Wright Jr., *The Only Land They Knew* (New York: Free Press, 1981), 128; Forbes, *Black Africans and Native Americans*, 28; Morison, *The Great Explorers*, 78. Warren Lowes, *Indian Giver* (Penticton, British Columbia: Theytus, 1986), 32, says *Labrador* means "place to get cheap labor." Regarding the Natchez, see James W. Loewen and Charles Sallis, *Mississippi: Conflict and Change* (New York: Pantheon, 1980), 40.

69. Letter by Michele de Cuneo quoted in Paiewonsky, *The Conquest of Eden*, 50.

70. Letter by Columbus quoted in Williams, *Documents of West Indian History*, 1:36–37.

71. Ronald Sanders, *Lost Tribes and Promised Lands: The Origins of American Racism* (Boston: Little, Brown, 1978), 131, also quoting and paraphrasing Peter Martyr, *De Orbe Novo* (1516).

72. Las Casas, *History of the Indies*, quoted in Williams, *Documents of West Indian History*, 1:67. See also Sanders, *Lost Tribes and Promised Lands*, 131, also quoting and paraphrasing Las Casas.

73. Norlander-Martinez, "Christopher Columbus: The Man, the Myth, and the Slave Trade," 17; Sale, *The Conquest of Paradise*, 156; Sanders, *Lost Tribes and Promised Lands*, 169; Eduardo Galeano, *Memory of Fire* (New York: Pantheon, 1988), 72; Floyd, *The Columbus Dynasty in the Caribbean*, 75, 222. Diego Columbus was almost killed in this revolt, according to J. A. Rogers, *Your History* (Baltimore: Black

Classic Press, 1983 [1940]), 71. Nicholas de Ovando may have imported Africans as slaves even before 1505.

74. This turn of phrase is Bill Bigelow's.

75. Official statement, June 8, 1989, quoted in *Five Hundred* (magazine of the Columbus Quincentenary Jubilee Commission), 10/1989, 9.

76. Jeffrey Hart, "Discovering Columbus," *National Review*, 10/15/1990, 56–57.

77. Sale, *The Conquest of Paradise*, 129.

78. Quoted in Sanders, *Lost Tribes and Promised Lands*, 290.

79. Koning, *Columbus, His Enterprise*, 86.

80. Marcel Dunan, ed., *Larousse Encyclopedia of Modern History* (New York: Crescent, 1987), 40.

81. Crosby, *The Columbian Exchange*, 11–12. See also Calder, *Revolutionary Empire*, 13–14; Dunan, ed., *Larousse Encyclopedia of Modern History*, 40, 67; Crone, *Discovery of America*, 184.

82. Morgan, *Nowhere Was Somewhere*; Marble, *Before Columbus*, 73–75; Calder, *Revolutionary Empire*, 13. Lowes, *Indian Giver*, 82, regarding Montaigne. Also Sanders, *Lost Tribes and Promised Lands*, 208–9. The direct influence of the anthropologist L. H. Morgan on Marx and Engels is described by Bruce Johansen, *Forgotten Founders: How the American Indian Helped Shape Democracy* (Cambridge, MA: Harvard Common Press, 1982), 122–23. Sale, *The Conquest of Paradise*. See also Crone, *Discovery of America*, 184.

83. Quoted by Peter Farb, *Man's Rise to Civilization* (New York: Avon, 1969), 296. *The Tempest* shows Shakespeare's own fascination: he modeled its Native character, Caliban, after the Carib Indians, who were cannibals, according to what the Arawaks had told Columbus.

84. For that matter, Europe *isn't* a continent, unless the word is defined Eurocentrically! Europe is a peninsula; the division between Europe and Asia is arbitrary, unlike the divisions between other continents.

85. Leon Festinger, *A Theory of Cognitive Dissonance* (Evanston, IL: Row, Peterson, 1957).

86. Crosby, *The Columbian Exchange*, 124–25 and Chapter 5; William Langer, "American Foods and Europe's Population Growth, 1750–1850," *Journal of Social History* 8 (winter 1975): 51–66; Jack Weatherford, *Indian Givers* (New York: Fawcett, 1988), 65–71; "Seeds of Change" exhibit (Washington, D.C.: National Museum of Natural History, 1991).

87. Crosby, *The Columbian Exchange*, 124–25; Lowes, *Indian Giver*, 59–60; Weatherford, *Indian Givers*, 65–71; Boyce Rensberger, "Did Syphilis Sail to Europe with Columbus and His Crew?" *Burlington Free Press*, 7/31/1992, 3D.

88. See also Williams, *Documents of West Indian History*, I:xxxi. Karl Marx and Fredrich Engels, "Communist Manifesto," in Robert C. Tucker, ed., *The Marx-Engels Reader* (New York: Norton, 1978), 474. Weatherford, *Indian Givers*, 43, 58, argues that long-staple American cotton, more useful for making cloth than Old World varieties, prompted the industrial revolution; he also considers the early production of coins in Bolivia and sugar in the Caribbean to amount to proto-factories that spurred the industrial revolution in Europe.

89. Weatherford, *Indian Givers*, 12, 15–17. Dunan, ed., *Larousse Encyclopedia of Modern History*, 69, and Sale, *The Conquest of Paradise*, 236, regarding inflation. Marx and Engels, "Communist Manifesto."

90. Herman J. Viola and Carolyn

Margolis, eds., *Seeds of Change* (Washington, D.C.: Smithsonian Institution Press, 1991), 186–207.

91. Michael Wallace, "The Politics of Public History," in Jo Blatti, ed., *Past Meets Present* (Washington, D.C.: Smithsonian Institution Press, 1987), 41–42. See also Garry Wills, "Goodbye, Columbus," *New York Review of Books*, November 22, 1990, 6–10. Interestingly, in response to the Columbus quincentenary the United Nations voted to declare the 1990s "the Decade to Eradicate Colonialism." Only the United States dissented. Even Spain and other Western European former colonial powers abstained out of respect for the new global reality. See John Yewell, "To Growing Numbers, Columbus No Hero," *St. Paul Pioneer Press*, 10/11/1990.

92. *Johnson v. M'Intosh*; see Robert K. Faulkner, *The Jurisprudence of John Marshall* (Princeton, NJ: Princeton University Press, 1968), 53; and Bruce A. Wagman, "Advancing Tribal Sovereign Immunity as a Pathway to Power," *University of San Francisco Law Review* 27, no. 2 (Winter 1993): 419–20.

93. Roy Preiswerk and Dominique Perrot, *Ethnocentrism and History* (New York: NOK, 1988), 245–46.

94. Columbus quoted in Sale, *The Conquest of Paradise*, 116; see also 201.

95. John Burns, "Canada Tries to Make Restitution to Its Own," *New York Times*, 9/1/1988.

96. Virgil Vogel, *This Country Was Ours* (New York: Harper and Row, 1972), 38, re Cartier. Weatherford, *Indian Givers*, 30, re Drake. Regarding Lewis and Clark, one textbook, *American History*, gives full credit to their Indian guides. Romeo B. Garrett, *Famous First Facts About the Negro* (New York: Arno, 1972), 68–69, re Henson as first at Pole. Some claim Peary's expedition never reached the Pole; if it did, we cannot now

determine which person did so first. Interestingly, Peary and Henson both fathered sons during the expedition. In 1987 these men, now eighty years old, participated in a reunion with Peary's and Henson's "legitimate" descendants. For the first time, the men's mothers' role in the expedition was recognized. See "Discoverers' Sons Arrive for Reunion," *Burlington Free Press*, 5/1/1987; also Susan A. Kaplan's introduction to Matthew Henson, *A Black Explorer at the North Pole* (Lincoln: University of Nebraska Press, 1989). A good short account of Henson appears in Wallace, Wallechinsky, and Wallace, *Significa*, 17–18. For a view of how Peary took advantage of the Inuits, including a charge of "scientific criminality," see Michael T. Kaufman, "A Museum's Eskimo Skeletons and Its Own," *New York Times*, 8/21/1993, I, 24.

97. Sale, *The Conquest of Paradise*, 238.

98. Las Casas, oral history collected from Tainos, in Williams, *Documents of West Indian History*, 1:17, 92–93.

99. Las Casas quoted in J. H. Elliot, *The Old World and the New* (New York: Cambridge University Press, 1970), 48; Las Casas, *History of the Indies*, 289; John Wilford, *The Mysterious History of Columbus* (New York: Alfred A. Knopf, 1991), 40. Las Casas is justly criticized for suggesting that African slaves be brought in to replace Indian slaves. However, he recanted this proposal and concluded "that black slavery was as unjust as Indian slavery" (*History of the Indies*, 257).

CHAPTER 3: THE TRUTH ABOUT
THE FIRST THANKSGIVING

1. Michael Dorris, "Why I'm Not Thankful for Thanksgiving" (New York: Council on Interracial Books for Children *Bulletin* 9, no. 7, 1978): 7.

2. Francis Jennings, *The Invasion of*

America: Indians, Colonialism, and the Cant of Conquest (Chapel Hill: University of North Carolina Press, 1975), 15.

3. Howard Simpson, *Invisible Armies: The Impact of Disease on American History* (Indianapolis: Bobbs-Merrill, 1980), 2.

4. Col. Thomas Aspinwall, quoted in Jennings, *The Invasion of America*, 175.

5. Kathleen Teltsch, "Scholars and Descendants Uncover Hidden Legacy of Jews in Southwest," *New York Times*, 11/11/1990, A30; "Hidden Jews of the Southwest," *Groundrock* (Spring 1992). Michael Carroll, "The Debate over a Crypto-Jewish Presence in New Mexico," *Sociology of Religion*, 63 #1 (Spring, 2002), 1–19, argues that whether these early Spaniards were crypto-Jews is contested.

6. Alfred W. Crosby Jr., *The Columbian Exchange: Biological and Cultural Consequences of 1492* (Westport, CT: Greenwood, 1972), 83. Our cowboy culture's Spanish origin explains why it is so similar to the gaucho tradition of Argentina.

7. The new *Pageant* has also increased its treatment of Spanish rule.

8. James Axtell, "Europeans, Indians, and the Age of Discovery in American History Textbooks," *American Historical Review* 92 (1987): 630.

9. The passage is basically accurate, although the winter of 1620–21 was not particularly harsh and probably did not surprise the British, and Indians did not assist them until spring.

10. William Langer, "The Black Death," *Scientific American*, February 1964.

11. Ibid.; see also William H. McNeill, *Plagues and Peoples* (Garden City, NY: Doubleday, 1976), 166–85.

12. William H. McNeill, "Disease in History," lecture at the University of Vermont, 10/18/1988. I use *microbe* and later *germ* in their larger meaning, including viral as well as bacterial pathogens.

13. Crosby, *The Columbian Exchange*, 34. Although people do get pneumonia or other illnesses after exposure to the elements, they do not get sick *from* the cold but *in* the cold, because their bodily defenses are weakened. Pneumonia and other pathogens do not lurk in icy lakes and snowy hillsides but dwell on and within us, where it is warm.

14. Peter Farb, *Man's Rise to Civilization* (New York: Avon, 1969), 42–43; Hubbert McCulloch Schnurrenberger, *Diseases Transmitted from Animals to Man* (Springfield, IL: Charles C. Thomas, 1975); see also Alfred W. Crosby Jr., *Ecological Imperialism: The Biological Expansion of Europe, 900–1900* (New York: Cambridge University Press, 1976), 31. Andeans did have llamas; the Andes may be too high and cold to promote disease among llamas or people, however, as is implied by the fact that European and African epidemics after 1492 were less devastating there than elsewhere.

15. McNeill, "Disease in History"; Crosby, *The Columbian Exchange*, 37; Henry Dobyns, *Their Number Become Thinned* (Knoxville: University of Tennessee Press, 1983).

16. Crosby, *Ecological Imperialism*, 38–39, argues that smallpox epidemics can repeatedly wipe out most of the population among such groups each time they recur, perhaps every generation.

17. McNeill, *Plagues and Peoples*, 201.

18. Gregory Mason, *Columbus Came Late* (New York: Century, 1931), 269–70.

19. Farb, *Man's Rise to Civilization*, 268. See also Jennings, *The Invasion of America*, 86; Crosby, *Ecological Imperialism*, 210.

20. Feenie Ziner, *Squanto* (Hamden, CT: Linnet Books, 1988), 141. See also Jennings, *The Invasion of America*, 48–52; Robert Loeb Jr., *Meet the Real Pilgrims* (Garden City, NY: Doubleday, 1979), 23, 87; and Warren Lowes, *Indian Giver* (Penticton, British Columbia: Theytus, 1986), 51. It

wasn't only the Pilgrims: Queen Isabella boasted that she took only two baths in her life, at birth and before her marriage, according to Jay Stuller, "Cleanliness," *Smithsonian* 21 (February 1991): 126–35.

21. Simpson, *Invisible Armies*, 2; Crosby, *The Columbian Exchange*, 37.

22. Neal Salisbury, "Red Puritans: The 'Praying Indians' of Massachusetts Bay and John Eliot," in Bruce A. Glasrud and Alan M. Smith, eds., *Race Relations in British North America, 1607–1783* (Chicago: Nelson-Hall, 1982), 44; and Neal Salisbury, "Squanto: Last of the Patuxets," in David Sweet and Gary Nash, eds., *Struggle and Survival in Colonial America* (Berkeley and Los Angeles: University of California Press, 1981), 231–37. Dobyns agrees that the 1617 plague was bubonic but believes it swept up the Atlantic seaboard all the way from Florida; see *Their Number Become Thinned*. William Bradford, *Of Plimoth Plantation*, rendered by Valerian Paget (New York: McBride, 1909), 258, implies that the Indians knew that smallpox was not the epidemic that laid waste to them in 1617, for in describing a 1634 outbreak of smallpox, Bradford stated, "They fear it worse than the plague." William Cronon, *Changes in the Land* (New York: Hill and Wang, 1983), 87, votes for chicken pox.

23. Excluding other plagues in the Americas, of course. Cushman is quoted in Charles M. Segal and David C. Stineback, *Puritans, Indians, and Manifest Destiny* (New York: Putnam's, 1977), 54–55.

24. Simpson, *Invisible Armies*, 6.

25. Quoted in Ibid., 7.

26. Cushman, quoted in Segal and Stineback, *Puritans, Indians, and Manifest Destiny*, 54–55; William S. Willis, "Division and Rule: Red, White, and Black in the Southeast," in Leonard Dinnerstein and Kenneth Jackson, eds., *American Vistas,*

1607–1877 (New York: Oxford University Press, 1975), 66.

27. Particularly the remnants of the once-hostile Massachusetts, reduced in number from 4,500 to 750, converted, according to James Axtell, *The European and the Indian* (New York: Oxford University Press, 1981), 252, 370; see also James W. Davidson and Mark H. Lytle, *After the Fact* (New York: McGraw-Hill, 1992), iii.

28. Bradford, *Of Plimoth Plantation*, 93; cf. Peter Hulme, *Colonial Encounters* (London: Methuen, 1986), 147–48.

29. John Winthrop to Simonds D'Ewes, 7/21/1634, *Publications of the Colonial Society of Massachusetts 1900–02*, 7 (12/1905) 71, at books.google.com/books.

30. Karen Ordahl Kupperman, *Settling with the Indians* (London: J. M. Dent, 1980), 186; cf. Simpson, *Invisible Armies*, 8.

31. Tee Loftin Snell, *America's Beginnings* (Washington, D.C.: National Geographic, 1974), 73, 77.

32. Crosby, *Ecological Imperialism*, 50–51.

33. Ibid., 202–15.

34. Simpson, *Invisible Armies*, 35.

35. Dobyns, *Their Number Become Thinned*.

36. David Quummen, "Columbus and Submuloc," *Outside*, June 1990, 31–34. Cf. Crosby, *The Columbian Exchange*, 49; McNeill, *Plagues and Peoples*, 205–7.

37. James Brooke, "For an Amazon Indian Tribe, Civilization Brings Mostly Disease and Death," *New York Times*, 12/24/1989. Violent uprooting of Native cultures continues as well; see Amnesty International, *Human Rights Violations Against the Indigenous Peoples of the Americas* (New York: Amnesty International, 1992). Charles Darwin, *Voyage of the Beagle*, quoted in Crosby, *Ecological Imperialism*, vii. As Darwin knew, the same sad processes have recurred wherever Europeans, Asians, or Africans encountered isolated peoples,

from Australia to Easter Island, Hawaii to Siberia. Thus, for example, the population of the Marquesan Islands in the South Pacific sank from one hundred thousand at first contact to twenty-five hundred in 1955. See Thor Heyerdahl, *Aku-Aku* (Chicago: Rand McNally, 1958), 352.

38. Langer, "The Black Death," 5; see also McNeill, *Plagues and Peoples*.

39. Farb, *Man's Rise to Civilization*, 294–95.

40. Colin McEvedy, *The Penguin Atlas of North American History* (New York: Viking, 1988), 3. McEvedy is a clinical psychiatrist.

41. Jennings, *The Invasion of America*, 16.

42. Bradford, *Of Plimoth Plantation*, 258.

43. Hurtado, *Indian Survival on the California Frontier* (New Haven: Yale University Press, 1988), I.

44. Sources estimating precontact populations in this range include P. M. Ashburn, *The Ranks of Death* (Philadelphia: Porcupine, 1980 [1947]); Woodrow Borah, "The Historical Demography of Aboriginal and Colonial America," in William Denevan, ed., *The Native Population of the Americas in 1492* (Madison: University of Wisconsin Press, 1976), 13–34; Sherburne Cook and Woodrow Borah, *Essays in Population History: Mexico and the Caribbean*, vol. I (Berkeley and Los Angeles: University of California Press, 1971); Crosby, *The Columbian Exchange*; Jared Diamond, "The Arrow of Disease," *Discover*, October 1992, 64–73; Dobyns, *Their Number Become Thinned*, 42; Jennings, *Invasion of America*, 16–30; Simpson, *Invisible Armies*; David Stannard, *American Holocaust* (New York: Oxford University Press, 1992), 11–24; and Russell Thornton, *American Indian Holocaust and Survival: A Pop-*

ulation History Since 1492 (Norman: University of Oklahoma Press, 1987) and "The Native American Holocaust," *Winds of Change* 4, no. 4 (Autumn 1989): 23–28. For a review of the population literature, see Melissa Meyer and Russell Thornton, "Indians and the Numbers Game," in Colin Calloway, ed., *New Directions in American Indian History* (Norman: University of Oklahoma Press, 1988), Ch. I.

45. A paragraph in *The American Pageant* does tell of the 90 percent toll throughout the hemisphere but leaves out any mention of the plague at Plymouth.

46. Quoted in Ziner, *Squanto*, 147.

47. J. W. Barber, *Interesting Events in the History of the United States* (New Haven: Barber, 1829), 30. Barber does not cite the authority he quotes.

48. Even though "Virginia" then included most of New Jersey, the *Mayflower* nonetheless landed hundreds of miles northeast. Historians who support the "on purpose" theory include George F. Willison, *Saints and Strangers* (New York: Reynal and Hitchcock, 1945); Lincoln Kinnicutt, "The Settlement at Plymouth Contemplated Before 1620," *Publications of the American Historical Association* (1920): 211–21; and Neal Salisbury, *Manitou and Providence* (New York: Oxford University Press, 1982), 109, 270. Leon Clark Hills, *History and Genealogy of the Mayflower Planters* (Baltimore: Genealogical Publ. Co., 1975), and Francis R. Stoddard, *The Truth about the Pilgrims* (New York: Society of Mayflower Descendants, 1952), 19–20, support the "Dutch bribe" theory, based on primary source material by Nathanial Morton. Historians at Plimoth Plantation support the theories of pilot error or storm.

49. Ziner, *Squanto*, 147; Kinnicutt, "The Settlement at Plymouth Contemplated Before 1620"; Almon W. Lauber,

Indian Slavery in Colonial Times Within the Present Limits of the United States (Williamstown, MA: Corner House, 1970 [1913]), 156–59; Stoddard, *The Truth about the Pilgrims*, 16.

50. The *Mayflower* sailed south for half a day, until encountering "dangerous shoals," according to several of our textbooks. Then the captain and the Pilgrim leadership insisted on returning to Provincetown and eventually New Plymouth. Conspiracy theorists take this to be a charade to dissuade the majority from insisting on Virginia. See Willison, *Saints and Strangers*, 145, 466; Kinnicutt, "The Settlement at Plymouth Contemplated Before 1620"; and Salisbury, *Manitou and Providence*, 109, 270.

51. Willison, *Saints and Strangers*, 421–22.

52. Speech in Sioux Falls, 9/8/1919, in *Addresses of President Wilson*, (Washington, D.C.: Government Printing Office, 1919), 86.

53. T. H. Breen, "Right Man, Wrong Place," *New York Review of Books*, 11/20/1986, 50.

54. Written by Robert Beverley in 1705 and quoted in Wesley Frank Craven, *The Legend of the Founding Fathers* (Westport, CT: Greenwood, 1983 [1956]), 5–8.

55. Axtell, *The European and the Indian*, 292–95.

56. J. Leitch Wright Jr., *The Only Land They Knew* (New York: Free Press, 1981), 78.

57. Kupperman, *Settling with the Indians*, 173; James Truslow Adams, *The March of Democracy* (New York: Scribner's, 1933), 1:12.

58. I encountered most of these students in New England, but many of them came from suburbs of Philadelphia, Washington, D.C., and New Jersey. I suspect that replies from the rest of the United States would be similar, except perhaps the Far West.

59. Gary Nash, *Red, White, and Black* (Englewood Cliffs, NJ: Prentice Hall, 1974), 139, describes the same process in Pennsylvania.

60. Emmanuel Altham letter quoted in Sydney V. James, ed., *Three Visitors to Early Plymouth* (Plymouth: Plimoth Plantation, 1963), 29.

61. Could there be a fairy tale parallel to this Pilgrim incident? Like Goldilocks, the Pilgrims broke-and-entered, trespassed, vandalized, and stole, and like Goldilocks, educators forgive them because they are Aryan. The Goldilocks tale makes her victims less than human, and the shadowy way our histories represent Indians makes the Pilgrims' victims also less than human. My thanks to Toni Cade Bambara for this analysis of Goldilocks.

62. Kupperman, *Settling with the Indians*, 125.

63. All five had names other than Squanto or Tisquantum, but Indians sometimes went by different names in different tribes. Squanto's biographer, Feenie Ziner, believes he was one of the five. Ferdinando Gorges stated in 1658 that Squanto was among those abducted in 1605 and lived with him in England for three years, which convinced Kinnicutt ("The Settlement at Plymouth Contemplated Before 1620," 212–13) but not historians at Plimoth Plantation or Neal Salisbury (*Manitou and Providence*, 265–66), although Salisbury seems more positive in "Squanto: Last of the Patuxets." See also Lauber, *Indian Slavery in Colonial Times*, 156–59.

64. Simpson, *Invisible Armies*, 6.

65. One textbook, the latest edition of Boorstin and Kelley, does summarize the enslavement and the destruction of Squanto's village.

66. William Bradford, *Of Plimouth Plantation*, 99. See also, inter alia, Salisbury, "Squanto: Last of the Patuxets," 228–46.

67. Robert Moore, *Stereotypes, Distortions, and Omissions in U.S. History Textbooks* (New York: CIBC, 1977), 19.

68. Robert M. Bartlett, *The Pilgrim Way* (Philadelphia: Pilgrim Press, 1971), 265; and Loeb, *Meet the Real Pilgrims*, 65.

69. Charles Hudson et al., "The Tristan de Luna Expeditions, 1559–61," in Jerald T. Milanich and Susan Milbrath, eds., *First Encounters* (Gainesville: University of Florida Press, 1989), 119–34, supplies a vivid illustration of European dependence on Indians for food. They tell of the little-known second Spanish expedition (after de Soto) into what is now the southeastern United States. Because the Indians retreated from them and burned their own crops, the Europeans almost starved.

70. Bessie L. Pierce, *Public Opinion and the Teaching of History in the United States* (New York: Alfred A. Knopf, 1926), 113–14. See also Alice B. Kehoe, " 'In fourteen hundred and ninety two, Columbus sailed . . . ': The Primacy of the National Myth in U.S. Schools," in Peter Stone and Robert MacKenzie, eds., *The Excluded Past* (London: Unwin Hyman, 1990), 207.

71. Mircea Eliade, *Myth and Reality* (New York: Harper and Row, 1963), 18–19.

72. Robert N. Bellah, "Civil Religion in America," *Daedalus* (Winter 1967): 1–21. See Hugh Brogan, *The Pelican History of the U.S.A.* (Harmondsworth, England: Penguin, 1986), 37, regarding Plymouth Rock. See also Michael Kammen, *Mystic Chords of Memory* (New York: Alfred A. Knopf, 1991), 207–10.

73. Valerian Paget, introduction to *Bradford's History of the Plymouth Settlement, 1608–1650* (New York: McBride, 1909), xvii.

74. Dorris, "Why I'm Not Thankful for Thanksgiving," 9. The addition is mine, in the interest of accuracy.

75. Plimoth Plantation, "The American Thanksgiving Tradition, or How Thanksgiving Stole the Pilgrims" (Plymouth, MA: n.d., photocopy); Stoddard, *The Truth about the Pilgrims*, 13. Jeremy D. Bangs, "Thanksgiving on the Net: Roast Bull with Cranberry Sauce Part I," Society of Mayflower Descendants in the Commonwealth of Pennsylvania Web page, sail1620.org/discover_feature_thanksgiving_on_the_net_roast_bull_with_cranberry_sauce_part_l.shtml, 1/2007.

76. Reginald Horsman, *Race and Manifest Destiny* (Cambridge: Harvard University Press, 1981), 5.

77. Arlene Hirshfelder and Jane Califf, "Celebration or Mourning? It's All in the Point of View" (New York: Council on Interracial Books for Children *Bulletin* 10, no. 6, 1979), 9.

78. Frank James, "Frank James' Speech" (New York: Council on Interracial Books for Children *Bulletin* 10, no. 6, 1979), 13.

79. Willison, *Saints and Strangers*; Salisbury, *Manitou and Providence*, 114–17; Wright, *The Only Land They Knew*, 220. Salisbury, *Manitou and Providence*, 120–25, tells of the militaristic and coercive nature of Plymouth's dealings with the Indians, however, right from the first.

CHAPTER 4: RED EYES

1. James Axtell, "Europeans, Indians, and the Age of Discovery in American History Textbooks," *American Historical Review* 92 (1987): 629–30.

2. Francis Jennings, *The Invasion of America* (Chapel Hill: University of North Carolina Press, 1975), vii.

3. Friedrich Nietzsche, *Beyond Good and Evil* (New York: MacMillan, 1907), 86.

4. Rupert Costo, "There Is Not One Indian Child Who Has Not Come Home in Shame and Tears," in Miriam Wasserman, *Demystifying School* (New York: Praeger, 1974), 192–93.

5. Thomas Bailey, "The Mythmakers of American History," *Journal of American History* (1968): 18.

6. Quoted in Calvin Martin, ed., *The American Indian and the Problem of History* (New York: Oxford University Press, 1987), 102.

7. Axtell, "Europeans, Indians, and the Age of Discovery," 621–32.

8. Sol Tax, foreword to Virgil Vogel, ed., *This Country Was Ours* (New York: Harper and Row, 1972), xxii.

9. The exceptions are *Pathways to the Present*, just one and a half pages of 1,088 or 0.1 percent; *Discovering American History*, 2 of 831 or 0.2 percent; *The American Pageant* (1991), 4 of 1,077 or 0.4 percent; *Pageant* (2006), 4 of 1,162 or 0.3 percent; and Boorstin and Kelley, 4 of 1,056 or 0.2 percent. My edition to *Pathways to the Present*, while covering American history from the beginning, emphasizes the modern era; another edition might treat American Indian cultures at greater length.

10. I will use the terms *tribe* and *nation* interchangeably, because some Native American leaders argue that *nation* is a European construct, implying more emphasis on the state than they feel applies to most Indian societies. As explained in the previous chapter, I also use *Native American* and *American Indian* synonymously. The textbooks I surveyed also walk this linguistic minefield. Interestingly, those that use *Native American* are not necessarily more up-to-date in their interpretations. I call Native individuals by their Native names, after introducing them by their Native names and the names more familiar to non-Native readers.

11. Robin McKie, "Diamonds Tell Tale of Comet That Killed Off the Cavemen," *The Observer*, 5/20/2007; observer.guardian.co.uk/, 5/20/2007.

12. Although refusing to give up the usual "knows all" textbook tone, one other book, *The United States—A History of the Republic* by James Davidson and Mark Lytle, does tell of controversy and uncertainty in archaeology.

13. John N. Wilford, "New Mexico Cave Yields Clues to Early Man," *New York Times*, May 5, 1991, describes research by Richard MacNeish suggesting 35,000 BP there. David Stannard, *American Holocaust* (New York: Oxford University Press, 1992), 10, suggests 32,000 to 70,000 BP. Sharon Begley offers a useful popular summary in "The First Americans," in *Newsweek*'s special issue *When Worlds Collide* (Fall/Winter 1991), 15–20. Cf. Andrew Murr, "Who Got Here First?" *Newsweek*, 11/15/99; Marc Stengel, "The Diffusionists Have Landed," *Atlantic Monthly* 1/1/2000, 35–48, theatlantic.com/issues/2000/01/001stengel.htm; Steve Olson, "The Genetic Archaeology of Race," *Atlantic Monthly*, 4/2001, 70–71; and Steve Olson, "First Americans More Diverse than Once Thought, Study Finds," *Washington Post*, 7/31/2001.

14. According to Robert F. Spencer, Jesse D. Jennings et al., *The Native Americans* (New York: Harper and Row, 1977), 8, most archaeologists believe in the small-gene-pool theory.

15. Since people arrived in Australia long before 12,000 BP and could not have walked there, we cannot be sure that Indians did not get here by boat. Archaeology reveals no boats from this era, but then they would not have been built from stone or have lasted in wood.

16. *American Journey* even suggests "that the Inuit were the last migrants to

cross the land bridge into North America." Presumably, these famed kayakers carried their boats on their shoulders!

17. To be sure, when lower sea level provided an isthmus across the Bering Strait, North and South America were not totally surrounded by water, so there is no reason that the first settlers—or Boorstin, Kelley, or Garraty—should have concluded that they were. In an age that accords continent status to Europe, however, which is far from surrounded by water, this is a nitpick and not the point our authors were making.

18. Again, absence of evidence is not evidence of absence. Not nearly enough archaeology has been done in Alaska or Canada, and almost none in the now-flooded coastal routes that might have been most auspicious for early human migration.

19. Llamas were the only draft animal in the Americas, and Diamond explains why they were not really suitable.

20. Díaz quoted in *Sources in American History* (Orlando, FL: Harcourt Brace Jovanovich, 1986). Population from Robert F. Spencer and Jesse D. Jennings, *The Native Americans*, 480.

21. Quoted in Costo and Henry, *Textbooks and the American Indian*.

22. In *The Cunning of History* (New York: Harper, 1987), 91, a rumination on the Nazi holocaust, Richard L. Rubenstein emphasizes that "the Holocaust bears witness to *the advance of civilization*."

23. Christmas is an example of syncretism in European culture, combining elements from the Jewish religion, like the idea of a Messiah, and Northern European "pagan" observances, like the winter solstice and the emphasis on plants that are green in winter (holly, ivy, evergreen tree, mistletoe). Corn culture among the Iroquois and other Eastern nations is an example of syncretism in American culture, combining corn from Mexico and Peru with ideas already present in the Northeast.

24. Pertti Pelto, *The Snowmobile Revolution* (Menlo Park, CA: Cummings, 1973).

25. Fred Anderson, review of *The Skulking Way of War, Journal of American History* 79, no. 3 (December 1992): 1134.

26. Robert Utley, *The Indian Frontier of the American West* (Albuquerque: University of New Mexico Press, 1984), 12.

27. This admixture of peoples in Native societies makes it hard to identify physical types on reservations today. "Creek" or "Lumbee" is cultural, not physical. J. Leitch Wright Jr., *The Only Land They Knew* (New York: Free Press, 1981), 230. More powerful centralized governments were also forced upon indigenous people by European powers so they would have conflict partners with whom to deal.

28. Gary Nash, *Red, White, and Black* (Englewood Cliffs, NJ: Prentice Hall, 1974), 257; James Axtell, *The European and the Indian* (New York: Oxford University Press, 1981), 257.

29. On Ireland, see Allen Barton, *Communities in Disaster* (Garden City, NY: Doubleday, 1970), 11–12. The large-scale nations in Mexico and Peru, like nations in Europe, waged large-scale war. In some areas within the present United States, notably the Northwest, tribal warfare was sometimes brutal before European influence.

30. Wright, *The Only Land They Knew*, 138; Patricia Galloway, "Choctaw Factionalism and Civil War, 1746–1750," *Journal of Mississippi History* 44, no. 4 (11/1982): 289–327; Joseph L. Peyser, "The Chickasaw Wars of 1736 and 1740," *Journal of Mississippi History* 44, no. 1 (1/1982): 1–25.

31. Six of eighteen books mention that survivors of the Pequot War or King Philip's War were sold into slavery, but they treat this as an isolated incident and do not otherwise mention the Indian slave trade.

32. Wright, *The Only Land They Knew*, 33, 130.

33. Peter N. Carroll and David Noble, *The Free and the Unfree* (New York: Penguin, 1988), 57.

34. Almon W. Lauber, *Indian Slavery in Colonial Times Within the Present Limits of the United States* (Williamstown, MA: Corner House, 1970 [1913]), 110.

35. Lauber, *Indian Slavery in Colonial Times*, 106. Nash, *Red, White, and Black*, 113, 119, offers somewhat different figures: 5,300 whites, presumably including indentures; 2,900 blacks; and 1,400 Indians.

36. J. A. Rogers, *Your History* (Baltimore: Black Classic Press, 1983 [1940]), 78. See also Frederick W. Hodge, ed., *Handbook of the Indians* (Bureau of American Ethnology *Bulletin*, vol. 30, part 2) (Washington, D.C.: Government Printing Office, 1906), 216.

37. On California, see Albert Hurtado, *Indian Survival on the California Frontier* (New Haven: Yale University Press, 1988), 75. On the Southwest, see Jack Forbes, *The Indian in America's Past* (Englewood Cliffs, NJ: Prentice Hall, 1964), 94–95. Cf. Alan Gallay, *The Indian Slave Trade* (New Haven: Yale University Press, 2002).

38. Wright, *The Only Land They Knew*, 81–83.

39. Henry Dobyns, *Their Number Become Thinned* (Knoxville: University of Tennessee Press, 1983), 332. He also points out that the plagues, by killing experts and reducing numbers generally, thus decreasing the division of labor, played a role in de-skilling Natives. See also Nash, *Red, White, and Black*, 97; Jennings, *The Invasion of America*, 41, 87; Anthony F. C. Wallace, *The Death and Rebirth of the Seneca* (New York: Alfred A. Knopf, 1970), 24–25; Neal Salisbury, *Manitou and Providence* (New York: Oxford, 1982), 56–57.

40. Utley, *The Indian Frontier of the American West*, 21. *Wasichu* in Lakota is also translated as "fat grabber," one who is greedy (Wendy Rose, "For Some, It's a Time of Mourning," *The New World* [Smithsonian Quincentenary Publication], no. 1 [Spring 1990]: 4). The Cherokee word for *white man* similarly translates as "people greedily grasping for land," according to Ray Fadden in a private communication, November 25, 1993.

41. *The Americans* does mention that Europeans "need to borrow from the peoples they sought to dominate," but gives nary an example.

42. D. W. Meinig, "A Geographical Transect of the Atlantic World, ca. 1750," in Eugene Genovese and Leonard Hochberg, eds., *Geographic Perspectives in History* (Oxford: Basil Blackwell, 1989), 197; Patricia Nelson Limerick, "The Case of the Premature Departure: The Trans-Mississippi West and American History Textbooks," *Journal of American History* 78, no. 4 (3/1992): 1381. The textbook view can be contrasted with that shown in the feature movie *Koyaanisqatsii*, which is filmed from a Hopi viewpoint and portrays western canyons serenely but is disquieted by the canyons of New York City.

43. Ronald Sanders, *Lost Tribes and Promised Lands: The Origins of American Racism* (Boston: Little, Brown, 1978), 373–74.

44. Helen H. Tanner, "The Glaize in 1792: A Composite Indian Community," *Ethnohistory* 25, no. 1 (Winter 1978): 15–39.

45. Hurtado, *Indian Survival on the California Frontier*, 47–49.

46. Nash, *Red, White, and Black*, 60.

47. Quoted in Peter Farb, *Man's Rise to Civilization* (New York: Dutton, 1978), 313.

48. Benjamin Franklin, quoted in Bruce Johansen, *Forgotten Founders: How the American Indian Helped Shape Democracy* (Cambridge, MA: Harvard Common Press, 1982), 92–93. Farb, *Man's Rise to Civilization*, 313; Frederick Turner, *Beyond Geography* (New York: Viking, 1980), 244; Nash, *Red, White, and Black*, 317–18; and James Axtell, "The White Indians" in *The Invasion Within* (New York: Oxford University Press, 1985), 302–27, agree that many more whites became Indian than vice versa.

49. Turner, *Beyond Geography*, 241; Karen Ordahl Kupperman, *Settling with the Indians* (London: J. M. Dent, 1980), 156. See also Axtell, "The White Indians," and *The European and the Indian*, 160–76.

50. Franklin quoted in Jose Barreiro, ed., *Indian Roots of American Democracy* (Ithaca, NY: Cornell University American Indian Program, 1988), 43; Vogel, ed., *This Country Was Ours*, 257–59. Not all Indian societies were equalitarian: the Natchez in Mississippi and the Aztecs in Mexico showed a rigid hierarchy.

51. Cadwallader Colden quoted in Vogel, ed., *This Country Was Ours*, 259.

52. Alvin Josephy, Jr., *The Indian Heritage of America* (New York: Alfred A. Knopf, 1973), 35; William Brandon, *New Worlds for Old* (Athens: Ohio University Press, 1986), 3–26; Michel de Montaigne, "On Cannibals," in Thomas Christensen and Carol Christensen, eds., *The Discovery of America and Other Myths* (San Francisco: Chronicle Books, 1992), 110–15.

53. Quoted in Bruce Johansen and Roberto Maestas, *Wasichu: The Continuing Indian Wars* (New York: Monthly Review Press, 1979), 35.

54. Jack Weatherford, *Indian Givers* (New York: Fawcett, 1988), Ch. 8; Johansen, *Forgotten Founders*; Barreiro, ed., *Indian Roots of American Democracy*, 29–31. See also Bruce A. Burton, "Squanto's Legacy: The Origin of the Town Meeting," *Northeast Indian Quarterly* 6, no. 4 (Winter 1989): 4–9; Donald A. Grinde Jr., "Iroquoian Political Concept and the Genesis of American Government," *Northeast Indian Quarterly* 6, no. 4 (Winter 1989): 10–21; and Robert W. Venables, "The Founding Fathers," *Northeast Indian Quarterly* 6, no. 4 (Winter 1989): 30–55. While this was partly flattery, in this and other documents of that time, Congress repeatedly used symbols and ideas from the Iroquois League. Not only Franklin but also Thomas Jefferson and Thomas Paine knew and respected Indian political philosophy and organization. Nevertheless, Elizabeth Tooker denies this influence in "The U.S. Constitution and the Iroquois League," *Ethnohistory* 35, no. 4 (Fall 1988): 305–36. But see "Commentary" on Tooker in *Ethnohistory* 37, no. 3 (Summer 1990). In *The Disuniting of America* (New York: Norton, 1992), 127, Arthur Schlesinger Jr., makes the Eurocentric claim that Europe was "also the source— the *unique* source—of those liberating ideas of individual liberty . . . ," but he offers no evidence, only assertion, for this claim. Apparently he does not know of Europe's astonishment not only at Native American liberty but also at religious freedom in China and Turkey. Marco Polo reported that of all the fabulous things he saw during his twenty-seven-year trip to "Cathay," none amazed him more than its religious freedom: Jews, Christians, Muslims, and Buddhists worshipped freely and participated in civil society without

handicap. When Spain expelled its Jews in 1492, Turkey took them in and allowed them to worship.

55. John Mohawk, "The Indian Way Is a Thinking Tradition," in Barreiro, ed., *Indian Roots of American Democracy*, 16.

56. James Axtell, "The Indian in American History, the Colonial Period," in *The Impact of Indian History on the Teaching of United States History* (Chicago: Newberry Library, 1984), 20–23; Barreiro, ed., *Indian Roots of American Democracy*, 40–41; Bernard Sheehan, "The Ideology of the Revolution and the American Indian," in Francis Jennings, ed., *The American Indian and the American Revolution* (Chicago: Newberry Library, 1983), 12–23; and Stewart Holbrook, *Dreamers of the American Dream* (Garden City, NY: Doubleday, 1957), 137–45, regarding New York State.

57. Weatherford, *Indian Givers*, Ch. 6.

58. Wright, *The Only Land They Knew*, 264.

59. Alfred Crosby Jr., "Demographics and Ecology" (paper presented at Smithsonian Institution Seminar, Washington, D.C.: September 1990), 4. Andean Indians practiced the only agriculture known to produce more topsoil than it depleted. We have yet to unlock all the secrets of Mexican and Guatemalan agriculture, which seem to have combined floating gardens, canals, and fisheries.

60. Vogel, ed., *This Country Was Ours*, 268.

61. Ibid., 266–67.

62. Faith Davis Ruffins, colloquium at the National Museum of American History (Washington, D.C.: April 25, 1991), regarding patent medicine images. See also the treatment of *American Indian Medicine* by Virgil J. Vogel (Norman: University of Oklahoma Press, 1990). Bruce Johansen, *Forgotten Founders*, 117; Warren Lowes, *Indian Giver* (Penticton, British

Columbia: Theytus Books, 1986), 51; William B. Newell, "Contributions of the American Indian to Modern Civilization," *Akwesasne Notes* (Late Spring 1987): 14–15; Lewis Hanke, *The Spanish Struggle for Justice in the Conquest of America* (Philadelphia: University of Pennsylvania Press, 1949), 90, regarding political and ideological influences.

63. Costo and Henry, *Textbooks and the American Indian*, 22.

64. Vine Deloria, an American Indian writer, does this in *God Is Red* (Golden, CO: North American Press, 1992 [1973]).

65. In Calvin Martin, ed., *The American Indian and the Problem of History* (New York: Oxford University Press, 1987), 21.

66. Quoted in Lee Clark Mitchell, *Witnesses to a Vanishing America* (Princeton, NJ: Princeton University Press, 1981), 260. See also Richard Drinnon, *Facing West* (Minneapolis: University of Minnesota Press, 1980), 539.

67. James Merrell, *The Indians' New World* (Chapel Hill: University of North Carolina Press, 1989), 193–95.

68. Drinnon, *Facing West*, xvii–xix. In his well-known novel *Rabbit Boss* (New York: Vintage, 1989 [1973]), which tells of the Washo Indians of California in the nineteenth and early twentieth centuries, Thomas Sanchez supplies a vivid portrayal of what happens to a people denied equal rights before the law.

69. David Horowitz, *The First Frontier* (New York: Simon & Schuster, 1978), 14; Stephen Aron, "Lessons in Conquest (Princeton, NJ: Princeton University, 1993, typescript), 15; Wiley Sword, *President Washington's Indian War* (Norman: University of Oklahoma Press, 1985), 191–97. An exception is *Land of Promise*, which offers a subheading, "150 Years of

Warfare," preceding a competent treatment of Indian wars in general and King Philip's War in particular.

70. Jennings, *The Invasion of America*, 146.

71. From the inside jacket of *Missouri!* (New York: Bantam, 1984). Ross was the pen name of Noel B. Gerson, who wrote 325 in all.

72. Joe Feagin, *Racial and Ethnic Relations* (Englewood Cliffs: NJ: Prentice-Hall, 1984), 181. John D. Unruh, *The Plains Indians* (Urbana: University of Illinois Press, 1979).

73. Quoted in Kupperman, *Settling with the Indians*, 185. See also Jennings, *The Invasion of America*, 220.

74. Bradford, *Of Plimoth Plantation*, rendered by Valerian Paget (New York: McBride, 1909), 284–87. Underhill quoted in Jennings, *The Invasion of America*, 223, and Segal and Stineback, *Puritans, Indians, and Manifest Destiny*, 106. Indians quickly adjusted to European warfare and raised their level of violence accordingly. The Pequots were not quite destroyed; a few still live on and near a tiny reservation of a few acres in Connecticut, where they own a huge casino.

75. Peter A. Thomas, "Cultural Change on the Southern New England Frontier, 1630–1655," in Fitzhugh, ed., *Cultures in Contact*, 155.

76. Nash, *Red, White, and Black*, 126. But see Jennings's lower figures, *The Invasion of America*, 324.

77. To make this claim, I include lives lost on both sides, since Wampanoags and Narragansetts are now U.S. citizens. Including only colonial deaths, King Philip's War was nevertheless more deadly than the French and Indian War, the War of 1812, or the Spanish-American War. See also Stephen Saunders Webb, as paraphrased by Pauline Maier, "Second Thoughts on Our First Century," *New York Times Book Review*, 8/7/1985.

78. Weatherford, *Indian Givers*, 225.

79. Jan Carew, *Fulcrums of Change* (Trenton, NJ: Africa World Press, 1988), 55. Carolyn Stefanco-Schill, "Guale Indian Revolt," *Southern Exposure* 12, no. 6 (11/1984): 4–9.

80. Dorothy V. Jones, *License for Empire* (Chicago: University of Chicago Press, 1982), 125.

81. The novel *Okla Hannali* by R. A. Lafferty (Garden City, NY: Doubleday, 1972), 136–42, 186–89, treats the Civil War within Indian Territory.

82. Irving Wallace, David Wallechinsky, and Amy Wallace, *Significa* (New York: Dutton, 1983), 326. Cf. James W. Loewen, *Lies Across America* (New York: New Press, 1999), 385–89.

83. Even today, this remains true: people have the right to hunt, fish, and walk across private rural land, unless it is posted, and posting developed relatively recently.

84. Carleton Beals, *American Earth* (Philadelphia: Lippincott, 1939), 327–30; Steven Hahn, "Hunting, Fishing, and Foraging," *Radical History Review* 26 (1982): 37–64; Peter A. Thomas, "Cultural Change on the Southern New England Frontier, 1630–1655," in Fitzhugh, ed., *Cultures in Contact*, 151.

85. See, for example, Pierre Berton, *The Invasion of Canada, 1812–1813* (Toronto: McClelland and Stewart, 1980), 27. The seven battles do not include Tippecanoe, which predated a formal declaration of war against England.

86. The transformed character of our Indian wars after 1815 was revealed by the next war in the Northwest, the Black Hawk War of 1832. Although it nearly destroyed the Sac and Fox nations, it was insignificant compared to the battles in

that theater during the War of 1812. See also Brian Dippie, *The Vanishing American* (Middletown, CT: Wesleyan University Press, 1982), 7–8.

87. Johansen, *Forgotten Founders*, 118. See also Frances FitzGerald, *America Revised* (New York: Vintage, 1980), 90–93.

88. Before 1815, according to William Clark (of Lewis and Clark fame), "the tribes nearest our settlements were a formidable and terrible enemy; since then their power has been broken . . . and themselves sunk into objects of pity." Quoted in Dippie, *The Vanishing American*, 7–9.

89. Fergus M. Bordewich, review of David Roberts's *Once They Moved Like the Wind*, in *Smithsonian*, 3/1994, 128.

90. Carleton Beals, *American Earth*, 63–64. See also Reginald Horsman, *Race and Manifest Destiny* (Cambridge: Harvard University Press, 1981), 1, 3, 190–95.

91. Kupperman, *Settling with the Indians*, 188; and Dippie, *The Vanishing American*, 7–9.

92. Nash, *Red, White, and Black*, 63; Jennings, *Empire of Fortune*, 63; Horsman, *Race and Manifest Destiny*, 32–36. Cf. Leon Festinger, *A Theory of Cognitive Dissonance* (Evanston, IL: Row, Peterson, 1957).

93. William Gilmore Simms quoted in Mitchell, *Witnesses to a Vanishing America*, 255. See also Vogel, ed., *This Country Was Ours*, 286. Francis A. Walker, message to his department, 1871.

94. John Toland, *Adolf Hitler* (Garden City, NY: Doubleday, 1976), 702.

95. Edward H. Carr, *What Is History?* (New York: Random House, 1961), 167.

96. Gordon Craig, "History as a Humanistic Discipline," in Paul Gagnon, ed., *Historical Literacy* (New York: Macmillan, 1989), 134.

97. Jennings, *The Invasion of America*, 144.

98. Ronald Satz, *American Indian Policy in the Jacksonian Era* (Lincoln: University of Nebraska Press, 1975), 143.

99. Francis Drake seems to have had something like this in mind for British North America in 1573, but he never brought his plans to fruition. See Sanders, *Lost Tribes and Promised Lands*, 218–19.

100. Over time, Lumbees and Seminoles became more racist. Lumbees kept a nearby "blacker" triracial group out of their schools; Seminoles omitted "black Seminoles" from their presentation of tribal history at the National Museum of the American Indian.

101. J. F. Fausz, "Patterns of Anglo-Indian Aggression and Accommodation Along the Mid-Atlantic Coast, 1584–1634," in William Fitzhugh, ed., *Cultures in Contact* (Washington, D.C.: Smithsonian Institution, 1985), 234–35; Adolph Dial and David Eliades, *The Only Land I Know* (San Francisco: Indian Historian Press, 1975), 2–13. See also Turner, *Beyond Geography*, 241–42. *Challenge of Freedom* does tell about the likelihood that descendants of the lost colony can be found today among the Lumbee. Peter Hulme, *Colonial Encounters* (London: Methuen, 1986), 143, agrees that the lost colony probably became Croatoan Indians. *Holt American Nation* does suggest that the Lost Colony might have been absorbed into a nearby American Indian tribe but does not otherwise treat possible bi- or triracial societies.

102. Robert Beverly, *The History and Present State of Virginia* (Chapel Hill: University of North Carolina Press, 1947 [1705]), 38.

103. Lauber, *Indian Slavery in Colonial Times*; Lonn Taylor, "American Encounters," (address at the Smithsonian Institution, Washington, D.C., 4/29/1993).

104. Thomas, "Cultural Change on

the Southern New England Frontier, 1630–1655," in Fitzhugh, ed., *Cultures in Contact*, 141. In their very first years in Virginia, the British encouraged intermarriage to promote alliances with nearby Indians, even offering a bribe to any white Virginian who would marry an Indian, but this offer lasted briefly, and few colonists took advantage of it.

105. Wright, *The Only Land They Knew*, 235; Nash, *Red, White, and Black*; Axtell, "The White Indians."

106. Francis Jennings, *Empire of Fortune* (New York: Norton, 1988), 479. See also Charles J. Kappler, *Indian Treaties 1778–1883* (New York: Interland, 1972 [1904]), 5.

107. Satz, *American Indian Policy in the Jacksonian Era*, 216–18.

108. Pearce, *The Savages of America*.

109. S. Blancke and C.J.P. Slow Turtle, "The Teaching of the Past of the Native Peoples of North America in U.S. Schools," in Peter Stone and Robert MacKenzie, eds., *The Excluded Past* (London: Unwin Hyman, 1990), 123.

110. Reginald Horsman, "American Indian Policy and the Origins of Manifest Destiny," in Francis Prucha, ed., *The Indian in American History* (New York: Holt, Rinehart and Winston, 1971), 22.

111. Drinnon, *Facing West*, 85.

112. Nash, *Red, White, and Black*, 285. Cf. Evon Vogt, "Acculturation of American Indians," in Prucha, ed., *The Indian in American History*, 99–107; and Axtell, *The European and the Indian*, 168.

113. Hurtado, *Indian Survival on the California Frontier*, 122.

114. Chief Seattle, "Our People Are Ebbing Away," in Wayne Moquin with Charles Van Doren, *Great Documents in American Indian History* (New York: Praeger, 1973), 80–83. Today's Manhattanite who summers in Vermont would surely understand Indian patterns of movement.

115. Ruellen Ottery, "Treatment of Native Americans Under the Jurisdiction of the Plymouth Colony" (Johnson, VT, 1984, typescript), 8–9; Jennings, *The Invasion of America*, 144–45. Alden Vaughan, *New England Frontier* (New York: Norton, 1979), claims Indians did fine in New England courts, although his book has been attacked by the new scholarship.

116. David A. Nichols, *Lincoln and the Indians* (Columbia: University of Missouri Press, 1978), 189–90.

117. Inmuttooyahlatlat quoted in Robert C. Baron, ed., *Soul of America* (Golden, CO: Fulcrum, 1989), 289.

118. Farb, *Man's Rise to Civilization*, 317.

119. Charles M. Segal and David C. Stineback, *Puritans, Indians, and Manifest Destiny* (New York: Putnam, 1977), 48. Turner, *Beyond Geography*, 215–16, also says Indian-white relations and whites' "unjustified and blasphemous" land claims, in Williams's view, were the key cause of his banishment.

120. Prucha, ed., *The Indian in American History*, 7.

121. Satz, *American Indian Policy in the Jacksonian Era*, 25.

122. Blancke and Slow Turtle, "The Teaching of the Past of the Native Peoples of North America in U.S. Schools," 121.

123. This point is implied by Dean A. Crawford, David L. Peterson, and Virgil Wurr, "Why They Remain Indians," in Vogel, ed., *This Country Was Ours*, 282–84. See also Robert Berkhover, *The White Man's Indian* (New York: Alfred A. Knopf, 1978), 192–93.

124. Christopher Vecsey, "Envision Ourselves Darkly, Imagine Ourselves Richly," in Martin, ed., *The American Indian*

and the *Problem of History*, 126. Jennings makes a similar argument in *The Ambiguous Iroquois Empire* (New York: Norton, 1984), 482.

CHAPTER 5: "GONE WITH THE WIND": THE INVISIBILITY OF RACISM IN AMERICAN HISTORY TEXTBOOKS

1. Maya Angelou, "On the Pulse of Morning," poem written for the Clinton inauguration, January 20, 1993.

2. Ken Burns, "Mystic Chords of Memory" (speech delivered at the University of Vermont, Burlington, September 12, 1991).

3. W.E.B. DuBois, *Black Reconstruction* (Cleveland: World Meridian, 1964 [1935]), 722.

4. Warren Beck and Myles Clowers, *Understanding American History Through Fiction* (New York: McGraw-Hill, 1975), I:ix.

5. Herbert Aptheker, *Essays in the History of the American Negro* (New York: International, 1964 [1945]), 17; Irving J. Sloan, *Blacks in America, 1492–1970* (Dobbs Ferry, NY: Oceana, 1971), I. Blacks were also probably among the Spanish slave masters, according to J. A. Rogers, *Your History* (Baltimore: Black Classic Press, 1983 [1940]), 73. I follow my usage in Chapter 2, but the Spanish called Haiti "Santo Domingo."

6. Two new textbooks—*The Americans* and *Pathways to the Present*—structure their accounts of early America as a three-way encounter among these culture areas, which makes for effective pedagogy and accurate history. However, they never develop the idea of three-way race relations.

7. Filibuster information in John and Claire Whitecomb, *Oh Say Can You See?* (New York: Morrow, 1987), 116. On Republicans, see Richard H. Sewell, *Ballots for Freedom* (New York: Oxford University Press, 1976), 292. On parties, see Thomas Byrne Edsall, *Chain Reaction* (New York: Norton, 1991), and "Willie Horton's Message," *New York Review of Books,* 2/13/1992, 7–11.

8. Minstrelsy was an important mass entertainment from 1850 to 1930 and the dominant form from about 1875 to World War I. *Gone With the Wind* was the largest grossing film ever in constant dollars. When first shown on television, it also won the highest ratings accorded an entertainment program up to that time. Admittedly, it is first a romance, but its larger social setting is primarily about race. *Time,* 2/14/1977, tells of the popularity of *Roots.* For general discussions of black stereotyping in mass media see Michael Rogin, "Making America Home," *Journal of American History* 79, no. 3 (12/1992): 1071–73; Donald J. Bogle, *Toms, Coons, Mulattoes, Mammies, and Bucks* (New York: Bantam, 1974); and James W. Loewen, "Black Image in White Vermont: The Origin, Meaning, and Abolition of Kake Walk," in Robert V. Daniels, ed., *Bicentennial History of the University of Vermont* (Boston: University Press of New England, 1991).

An early draft of this paragraph cited racial content I remembered from an early full-length animated movie, *Fantasia.* When I rented the video to check my memory, I found no race relations. Then I learned from Ariel Dorfman (*The Empire's Old Clothes* [New York: Pantheon, 1983], 120) that the Disney company had eliminated all the segments containing racial stereotypes from the video rerelease.

9. 1993 exhibition: "The Cotton Gin and Its Bittersweet Harvest" at the Old State Capitol Museum in Jackson, MS.

10. The Alamo and the Seminoles will be discussed later in the chapter. The foremost reason why white Missourians

drove the Mormons out of Missouri into Illinois in the 1830s was the suspicion that they were not "sound" on slavery. Indeed, they were not: Mormons admitted black males to the priesthood and invited free Negroes to join them in Missouri. In response to this pressure, Mormons not only fled Missouri but changed their attitudes and policies to resemble those of most white Americans in the 1840s, concluding that blacks were inferior and should not become full members. They did not reverse this policy until 1978. See Ray West Jr., *Kingdom of the Saints* (New York: Viking, 1957), 45–49, 88; Forrest G. Wood, *The Arrogance of Faith* (New York: Alfred A. Knopf, 1990), 96–97; and Newell Bringhurst, *Saints, Slaves, and Blacks* (Westport, CT: Greenwood, 1981).

11. Studs Terkel, *Race: How Blacks and Whites Think and Feel About the American Obsession* (New York: New Press, 1992).

12. Samuel Eliot Morison and Henry Steele Commager, *The Growth of the American Republic* (New York: Oxford University Press, 1950), 521. In Andrew Rooney and Perry Wolf's film *Black History: Lost, Stolen or Strayed?* (Santa Monica, CA: BFA, 1968), Bill Cosby points out that this textbook was written by two northern Pulitzer Prize–winning historians.

13. Nancy Bauer's *The American Way* says little about slavery as experienced by slaves, but she does mention slave revolts and the underground railroad. *Discovering American History* tells about slavery, using primary sources, but these are all by whites and contain little about slavery from the slaves' point of view. Considering the many slave narratives, it is surprising that *Discovering* excludes black sources.

There is nothing "cutting edge" in any of the books' coverage of slavery. Twenty years ago historians developed the "slave community" interpretation to emphasize how African Americans experienced the institution; no textbook shows any familiarity with that school. Nor do any authors describe the controversies among competing slavery "schools." For a compact discussion of these interpretations, see James W. Loewen, "Slave Narratives and Sociology," *Contemporary Sociology* 11, no. 4 (7/1982): 380–84, reviewing works by Blassingame, Escott, Genovese, Gutman, and Rawick.

14. Whether slavery was profitable in the nineteenth century spurred a minor historical tempest a few years back. Although it eroded Southern soil, and although the Southern economy grew increasingly dependent on the North, evidence indicates planters did find slavery profitable. See, inter alia, Herbert Aptheker, *And Why Not Every Man?* (New York: International, 1961), 191–92.

15. James Currie, review of *The South and Politics of Slavery, Journal of Mississippi History* 41 (1979): 389; see also William Cooper, Jr., *The South and the Politics of Slavery, 1828–56* (Baton Rouge: Louisiana State University Press, 1978).

16. Roger Thompson, "Slavery, Sectionalism, and Secession," *Australian Journal of American Studies* 1, no. 2 (7/1981): 3, 5; William R. Brock, *Parties and Political Conscience* (Millwood, NY: KTO Press, 1979).

17. Joseph R. Conlin, ed., *Morrow Book of Quotations in American History* (New York: Morrow, 1984), 38.

18. Frank Owsley, a historian with Confederate sympathies, championed reasons for war other than slavery. When it was fought, however, virtually everyone, including Abraham Lincoln, Oliver Wendell Holmes, and Ulysses S. Grant on the Union side and Jefferson Davis and Alex-

ander H. Stephens, president and vice president of the Confederacy, thought the war was caused by slavery. See Daniel Aaron, *The Unwritten War* (New York: Oxford University Press, 1973), 28, 180.

19. *Pageant* does supply a short quote from this document, but it is so vague that few readers will understand it.

20. Bessie L. Pierce, *Public Opinion and the Teaching of History in the United States* (New York: Alfred A. Knopf, 1926), 66–70. Nor was the North a great incubator of progressive textbooks in those decades.

21. Frances FitzGerald, *America Revised* (New York: Vintage, 1980), tells how history textbooks changed their treatment of slavery and Reconstruction in the 1970s. Hillel Black describes the former influence of white segregationist Southerners and the new black influence in Northern urban school districts, resulting from the civil rights and Black Power movements, in *The American Schoolbook* (New York: Morrow, 1967), Chapter 8. "Liberating Our Past," *Southern Exposure*, 11/1984, 2–3, tells of the influence of the civil rights movement. The new treatments of slavery are closer to most of those written at the time and to the primary sources.

22. Interviews at Williamsburg; Sloan, *Blacks in America, 1492–1970*, 2; Howard Zinn, *The Politics of History* (Boston: Beacon, 1970), 67.

23. Horton is quoted by Robert Moore in *Stereotypes, Distortions, and Omissions in U.S. History Textbooks* (New York: Council on Interracial Books for Children, 1977), 17.

24. *Before Freedom Came*, which was also a book, edited by E.D.C. Campbell Jr. (Richmond, VA: Museum of the Confederacy, 1991).

25. Quoted in Felix Okoye, *The American Image of Africa: Myth and Reality* (Buffalo: Black Academy Press, 1971), 37. Here Montesquieu presages Festinger's idea of cognitive dissonance. See Leon Festinger, *A Theory of Cognitive Dissonance* (Evanston, IL: Row, Peterson, 1957).

26. Okoye, *The American Image of Africa*.

27. Margaret Mitchell, *Gone With the Wind* (New York: Avon, 1964 [1936]), 645.

28. In reporting the survey, a journalist added dryly, "The Bible also ranked high."

29. I also searched under *white racism, white supremacy*, and various other headings, to no avail.

30. On Ecuador, see Ivan Van Sertima, *They Came Before Columbus* (New York: Random House, 1976), 30. On blacks' influence among the Seminoles, see Daniel F. Littlefield, Jr., *Africans and Creeks* (Westport, CT: Greenwood, 1979). On Elliot's Iowa eye-color experiment, see the PBS *Frontline* documentary, *A Class Divided* (video, Yale University Films. Alexandria, Virginia: PBS, 1986). On the Arctic, see "Discoverers' Sons Arrive for Reunion," *Burlington Free Press*, May 1, 1987; Susan A. Kaplan, introduction to Matthew Henson, *A Black Explorer at the North Pole* (Lincoln: University of Nebraska Press, 1989); and Irving Wallace, David Wallechinsky, and Amy Wallace, *Significa* (New York: Dutton, 1983), 17–18. Note that *The American Adventure* blithely assumes assimilation to white society as the goal.

31. That racism has varied is a problem for black rhetors who seek to make it always the overwhelming force of history, which, of course, reduces our ability to recognize other factors.

32. James W. Loewen and Charles

Sallis, *Mississippi: Conflict and Change* (New York: Pantheon, 1980), 141.

33. FitzGerald, *America Revised*, 158. Matthew Downey makes the same point in "Speaking of Textbooks: Putting Pressure on the Publishers," *History Teacher* 14 (1980): 68.

34. David Lowenthal, *The Past Is a Foreign Country* (Cambridge: Cambridge University Press, 1988), 343.

35. Richard R. Beeman, *Patrick Henry* (New York: McGraw-Hill, 1974), 182; Henry quoted in J. Franklin Jameson, *The American Revolution Considered as a Social Movement* (Boston: Beacon Press, 1965), 23.

36. *The American Adventure*, an inquiry textbook partly assembled from primary sources, includes more of the letter from which the quoted sentence was drawn. Henry went on to write, "Let us transmit to our descendants, together with our slaves, a pity for their unhappy lot, and an abhorrence of slavery." His biographer, Richard R. Beeman, treats Henry's view of slavery drily: "If it was not hypocrisy, then it was at least self-deception on a grand scale." See *Patrick Henry* (New York: McGraw-Hill, 1974), 97.

37. Paul Finkelman, "Jefferson and Slavery," in Peter S. Onuf, ed., *Jeffersonian Legacies* (Charlottesville: University Press of Virginia, 1993), 181–221, is an extensive analysis of Jefferson's slaveholding and the difference it made on his thought.

38. Paul Finkelman, "Treason Against the Hopes of the World: Thomas Jefferson and the Problem of Slavery" (Washington, D.C.: National Museum of American History colloquium, March 23, 1993); Roger Kennedy, *Mr. Lincoln's Ancient Egypt* (Washington, D.C.: National Museum of American History, 1991, typescript), 93; Ronald Takaki, *A Different Mirror* (Boston: Little, Brown, 1993), 69. William W. Freehling also treats Jefferson's ambivalence about slavery in *The Road to Disunion* (New York: Oxford University Press, 1990), 123–31, 136.

39. Patronizing compliments like this are surely intended to woo African American and liberal white members of textbook adoption committees. Or perhaps publishers imagine that such praise helps white students think less badly of African Americans today. Showing how the Revolution decreased white racism would be more legitimate historically, however, and probably more relevant to reducing bigotry today.

40. Bruce Glasrud and Alan Smith, *Race Relations in British North America, 1607–1783* (Chicago: Nelson-Hall, 1982), 330.

41. George Imlay, quoted in Okoye, *The American Image of Africa*, 55. See also Glasrud and Smith, *Race Relations in British North America*, 278–330.

42. Aptheker, *Essays in the History of the American Negro*, 76.

43. Quoted in Jameson, *The American Revolution Considered as a Social Movement*, 23.

44. Regarding the impact of the Revolution on slavery, see Glasrud and Smith, *Race Relations in British North America*, 278; Richard H. Sewell, *Ballots for Freedom* (New York: Oxford University Press, 1976), 3; Dwight Dumond, *Antislavery* (New York: Norton, 1966 [1961]), 27–34; Arthur Zilversmit, *The First Emancipation* (Chicago: University of Chicago Press, 1967); and Paul Finkelman, *An Imperfect Union* (Chapel Hill: University of North Carolina Press, 1981). Virginia data from Finkelman, "Jefferson and Slavery," 187.

45. Finkelman, "Treason Against the Hopes of the World."

46. David Walker, quoted in Okoye,

The American Image of Africa, 45–46. Even as he attacked Jefferson, Walker also quoted with approval from the Declaration of Independence.

47. Once he realized Napoleon was serious about occupying "Louisiana," Jefferson did revise his tilt toward France to a neutral position. See John Chester Miller, *The Wolf by the Ears* (New York: Free Press, 1977), 134–37.

48. Piero Gleijesus "The Limits of Sympathy," *Journal of Latin American Studies* 24, no. 3 (October 1992): 486, 500; Roger Kennedy, *Orders from France* (New York: Alfred A. Knopf, 1989), 140–45, 152–57.

49. Gleijesus, "The Limits of Sympathy," 504; the Ostend Manifesto quoted in Dumond, *Antislavery*, 361. See also Robert May, *The Southern Dream of a Caribbean Empire, 1854–1861* (Baton Rouge: Louisiana State University Press, 1973).

50. Henry Sterks, *The Free Negro in Antebellum Louisiana* (Rutherford, NJ: Fairleigh Dickenson University Press, 1972), 301–4.

51. William S. Willis, "Division and Rule: Red, White, and Black in the Southeast," in Leonard Dinnerstein and Kenneth Jackson, eds., *American Vistas, 1607–1877* (New York: Oxford University Press, 1975), 61–64; see also Littlefield, *Africans and Creeks*, 10–100, and Theda Perdue, "Red and Black in the Southern Appalachians," *Southern Exposure* 12, no. 6 (November 1984): 19.

52. Sloan, *Blacks in America*, 9; Littlefield, *Africans and Creeks*, 72–80.

53. William C. Sturtevant, "Creek Into Seminole," in Eleanor Burke Leacock and Nancy O. Lurie, eds., *North American Indians in Historical Perspective* (Prospect Heights, IL: Waveland, 1988 [1971]), 92–128.

54. J. Leitch Wright Jr., *The Only Land They Knew* (New York: Free Press, 1981), 277; William Loren Katz, *Teachers' Guide to American Negro History* (Chicago: Quadrangle, 1971), 34, 63. See also Scott Thybony, "Against All Odds, Black Seminole Won Their Freedom," *Smithsonian Magazine* 22, no. 5 (8/1991): 90–100; and Littlefield, *Africans and Creeks*, 85–90.

55. Reginald Horsman, "American Indian Policy and the Origins of Manifest Destiny," in Francis Prucha, ed., *The Indian in American History* (New York: Holt, Rinehart and Winston, 1971), 28. Almost every textbook mentions slavery as an issue in Texas, but most bury it within other "rights" Mexicans denied Anglos. On free blacks see Moore, *Stereotypes, Distortions, and Omissions in U.S. History Textbooks*, 24. Readers may also enjoy a brilliant historical novel by R. A. Lafferty, *Okla Hannali* (Garden City, NY: Doubleday, 1972), 100, which declares: "however it be falsified (and the falsification remains one of the classic things), there was only one issue there: slavery."

56. Thomas David Schoonover, *Dollars Over Dominion* (Baton Rouge: Louisiana State University Press, 1978), 41, 78.

57. Patricia N. Limerick, *The Legacy of Conquest* (New York: Norton, 1987), 92–93.

58. The debates were also the first events in American public life to be transcribed verbatim, allowing much fuller and more accurate news coverage.

59. Amazingly, the two inquiry texts gloss over the debates. *The American Adventure* includes only a paragraph of questions, *Discovering American History* only a paragraph of descriptive prose (though it does quote from Lincoln's "House Divided" speech). When treating actions, inquiry texts can have a difficult time in-

corporating primary sources, which by nature are usually words rather than deeds. Here the action consists of words—yet the textbooks ignore them!

60. Paul M. Angle, *Created Equal? The Complete Lincoln-Douglas Debates of 1858* (Chicago: University of Chicago Press, 1958). See also Gustave Koerner, *Memoirs*, 2:58–60, quoted in Angle, *The American Reader* (New York: Rand McNally, 1958), 297.

61. Angle, *Created Equal?* 22–23.

62. Quoted in Paul D. Escott, *Slavery Remembered* (Chapel Hill: University of North Carolina Press, 1979), 153.

63. The exceptions are *The American Pageant*, *The American Way*, and *Discovering American History*. *American Pageant* is a patch job by David Kennedy on Thomas Bailey's original, which dates to 1956! Where Bailey embraced Margaret Mitchell— "The moonlight-and-magnolia Old South of ante-bellum days had gone with the wind"—after "days" Kennedy adds "largely imaginary in any case." Despite such new material, the result is still a dated and racist interpretation of "Reconstruction by the Sword," emphasizing its "drastic legislation" and completely downplaying the considerable acceptance Republican policies won among many Southern whites. *The American Way* paints "Radical" Republicans as opportunists who "sent northerners to the South to make sure the Blacks remembered to vote for the party that freed them." (Blacks needed no such aid, of course; many voted Republican through the 1950s!) *The American Way* also claims that "The Radicals felt that it was not enough to give Blacks the same rights as Whites," so they "managed to pass the Fourteenth Amendment"—but that amendment gave blacks exactly the same rights as whites! In all, *American Way*'s treatment is amateurish.

Even sparser is the coverage in *Discovering American History*, an inquiry text: it devotes just two pages to all of Congressional Reconstruction, and most of that space is used to reprint the texts of the Fourteenth and Fifteenth Amendments. *Discovering American History* is the only text to avoid the terms *carpetbagger* and *scalawag*, but then again it avoids Reconstruction almost entirely.

64. Perhaps Bauer was influenced by Margaret Mitchell's portrait of African Americans who lazed about as soon as slavery ended and white supervision relaxed. Writings and recollections by newly freed people offer no support for this portrait, however. See Escott, *Slavery Remembered*, which offers valuable information about Reconstruction remembered. See also studies of individual locales and statewide analyses, such as Roberta Sue Alexander, *North Carolina Faces the Freedmen* (Durham: Duke University Press, 1985).

65. George C. Rable, *But There Was No Peace* (Athens: University of Georgia Press, 1984), 1.

66. Morgan Kousser, "The Voting Rights Act and the Two Reconstructions" (Washington, D.C.: Brookings Institution, October 19, 1990); DuBois, *Black Reconstruction*, 681.

67. Eric Foner, *Reconstruction* (New York: Harper & Row, 1988), as reviewed by C. Vann Woodward in "Unfinished Business," *New York Review of Books*, 5/12/1988, referring to statistics gathered by Albion W. Tourgée. See also Alexander, *North Carolina Faces the Freedmen*.

68. Gen. O. O. Howard quoted in Robert Moore, *Reconstruction: The Promise and Betrayal of Democracy* (New York: CIBC, 1983), 17.

69. Gunnar Myrdal, *An American Dilemma* (New York: McGraw-Hill, 1964 [1944]), lxxv–lxxvi.

70. Rayford W. Logan, *The Betrayal of the Negro* (New York: Macmillan, 1970 [1954]). See also Foner, *Reconstruction*, 604.

71. FitzGerald, *America Revised*, 157.

72. In *Minority Education and Caste* (New York: Academic Press, 1978), anthropologist John Ogbu uses stigma to explain why members of oppressed minorities typically fare better outside their home societies.

73. Michael L. Cooper, *Playing America's Game* (New York: Lodestar, 1993), 10; Gordon Morgan, "Emancipation Bowl" (Fayetteville: University of Arkansas Department of Sociology, n.d., typescript).

74. Robert Azug and Stephen Maizlish, eds., *New Perspectives on Race and Slavery in America* (Lexington: University Press of Kentucky, 1986), 118–21, 125; Loewen and Sallis, *Mississippi: Conflict and Change*, 241.

75. Wallace, Wallechinsky, and Wallace, *Significa*, 26–27, "Man in the Zoo."

76. On the cultural meaning of minstrelsy, see Robert Toll, *Blacking Up* (New York: Oxford University Press, 1974), 57, and the introduction to Ike Simond, *Old Slack's Reminiscence and Pocket History of the Colored Profession* (Bowling Green, OH: Popular Press, 1974), xxv; Joseph Boskin, *Sambo* (New York: Oxford University Press, 1986), 129; Myrdal, *An American Dilemma*, 989; and Loewen, "Black Image in White Vermont."

77. For Cleveland, see Stanley Hirshson, *Farewell to the Bloody Shirt* (Chicago: Quadrangle, 1968), 239–45. For Democrats, see Kousser, "The Voting Rights Act and the Two Reconstructions," 12. For Harding see Wyn Craig Wade, *The Fiery Cross* (New York: Simon & Schuster, 1987), 165. Harding's induction merely showed the legitimacy of the KKK; his administration was not as racist as Wilson's, although it did not undo Wilson's segregative policies. For *Rice v. Gong Lum*, see James W. Loewen, *The Mississippi Chinese: Between Black and White* (Prospect Heights, IL: Waveland Press, 1988), 66–68. For Tulsa, see Wallace, Wallechinsky, and Wallace, *Significa*, 60–61. As I was writing this chapter in 1992, Los Angeles erupted in what many reporters called "the worst race riot of the century." Perhaps, having been weaned on our history textbooks, they didn't know of the savage riots of the nadir.

78. See James W. Loewen, *Sundown Towns: A Hidden Dimension of American Racism* (New York: New Press, 2005), especially Ch. 3.

79. Americans who did not experience segregation, which ended in the South in about 1970, may consider these words melodramatic. American history textbooks do not help today's students feel the reality of the period. Please see the last field study of segregation, Loewen, *The Mississippi Chinese*, 45–48, 51, and 131–34.

80. In *The Mississippi Chinese*, 48, I show that black economic success in itself affronted white Southerners and was hard to maintain without legal rights.

81. See Stanley Lieberson, *A Piece of the Pie: Blacks and White Immigrants Since 1880* (Berkeley: University of California Press, 1980). Herbert Gutman in *The Black Family in Slavery and Freedom* (New York: Vintage, 1977) notes that black family instability cannot be traced back to slavery or Reconstruction. Edmund S. Morgan in "Negrophobia," *New York Review of Books*, 6/16/1988, 27–29, summarizing research by Roger Lane, reports that in Philadelphia by the 1890s, blacks turned to criminal occupations at much higher rates than whites owing to their exclusion

from virtually all industrial occupations. See also Vernon Burton, *In My Father's House Are Many Mansions* (Chapel Hill: University of North Carolina Press, 1985). On "tangle of pathology," see Lee Rainwater, ed., *The Moynihan Report and the Politics of Controversy* (Cambridge, MA: MIT Press, 1967).

82. "Racial Division Taking Root in Young America, People for Finds," People for the American Way *Forum* 2, no. 1 (3/1992): 1.

83. Richard Cohen, "Generation of Bigots," *Washington Post*, 7/23/1993; Marttila & Kiley, Inc., *Highlights from an Anti-Defamation League Survey on Racial Attitudes in America* (New York: Anti-Defamation League, 1993), 21.

CHAPTER 6: JOHN BROWN AND ABRAHAM LINCOLN: THE INVISIBILITY OF ANTIRACISM IN AMERICAN HISTORY TEXTBOOKS

1. Frances FitzGerald, *America Revised* (New York: Vintage, 1980), 151.

2. John Brown quoted by Henry David Thoreau in "A Plea for Captain John Brown," in Richard Scheidenhelm, ed., *The Response to John Brown* (Belmont, CA: Wadsworth, 1972), 58.

3. Ibid., 57.

4. Said to Rev. M. D. Conway and Rev. William Henry Channing and quoted in Carl Sandburg, *Abraham Lincoln* (New York: Harcourt, Brace and World, 1954), 315.

5. FitzGerald, *America Revised*, 151. Paul Gagnon points out that textbooks similarly underplay the worldwide impact of the American Revolution in *Democracy's Half-Told Story* (New York: American Federation of Teachers, 1989), 46–47.

6. Many textbook authors do describe the acts of William Lloyd Garrison, Theodore Weld, and sometimes other abolitionists, but without their words and ideas and without much sympathy. Black abolitionists—Sojourner Truth, Harriet Tubman, and Frederick Douglass—emerge with more life. *American Adventures* is exceptional in its warm and extended treatment of Thaddeus Stevens, and *Discovering American History*, an inquiry text, quotes enough Garrison that students can get a sense of the man's position.

7. Sara Robinson, *Kansas: Its Interior and Exterior Life*, Ch. 16, "The Attack upon Lawrence," kancoll.org/books/robinson/r_chap16.htm; Marvin Stottelmire, "John Brown: Madman or Martyr?" *Brown Quarterly* 3, no. 3 (Winter 2000), brownvboard.org/brwnqurt/03-3/03-3a.htm#cap1, 9/2006; Louis A. DeCaro, Jr., *John Brown—The Cost of Freedom* (New York: International, 2007), 41–42.

8. Slaves who refused to take part were left alone.

9. Hannah Geffert and Jean Libby, "Regional Involvement in John Brown's Raid on Harpers Ferry," in T. M. McCarthy and J. Stauffer, eds., *Prophets of Protest* (New York: New Press, 2006), 173–75; Jean Libby, ed., *John Brown Mysteries* (Missoula, MT: Pictorial Histories Publishing, 1999), 16–21, 25, 29–35.

10. Of course, Wise wanted to find Brown sane so he could hang him, just as Brown's defenders wanted to argue him insane so he could be spared. The best evidence as to Brown's state of mind is provided by his own letters, statements, and interviews, which show no trace of insanity. See also the discussion by Stephen B. Oates, *To Purge This Land With Blood* (New York: Harper and Row, 1970), 329–34. Wise's "Message to the Virginia Legislature, December 5, 1859," is reprinted in

Scheidenhelm, ed., *The Response to John Brown*, 132–53; his evaluation of Brown is on page 143. Wise is additionally quoted by Henry David Thoreau in "A Plea for Captain John Brown," on page 51 of same.

11. As Brown pointed out in his last speech in court, each "joined me of his own accord." This was true even of his sons.

12. Letter to Judge Daniel R. Tilden, 11/28/1959, quoted in Barrie Stavis, *John Brown: The Sword and the Word* (New York: A. S. Barnes, 1970), 164.

13. John Brown, "Last Words in Court," in Scheidenhelm, ed., *The Response to John Brown*, 36–37.

14. Thoreau, "A Plea for Captain John Brown," in Scheidenhelm, ed., *The Response to John Brown*, 53.

15. George Templeton Strong quoted in Daniel Aaron, *The Unwritten War* (New York: Oxford University Press, 1973), 24.

16. Letter quoted in William J. Schafer, ed., *The Truman Nelson Reader* (Amherst: University of Massachusetts Press, 1989), 250.

17. Stavis, *John Brown: The Sword and the Word*, 14, 167; Richard Warch and Jonathan Fanton, eds., *John Brown* (Englewood Cliffs, NJ: Prentice Hall, 1973), 142.

18. The melody thus made a full circle, because it began as the Methodist hymn, "Say Brothers, Will You Meet on Canaan's Happy Shore." Leon Litwack describes the Boston scene in *Been in the Storm So Long* (New York: Alfred A. Knopf, 1979), 77–78. Hollywood finally portrayed the 54th Massachusetts in *Glory* in 1990.

19. John Spencer Bassett, *A Short History of the United States* (New York: Macmillan, 1923), 502.

20. The treatment of Harpers Ferry in the current *Holt American Nation* finally gets beyond this language and does not question Brown's sanity.

21. See Benjamin Quarles, *The Black Abolitionists* (New York: Oxford University Press, 1969), 244.

22. *Pathways* simply never mentions that Brown was religious.

23. See Oates, *To Purge This Land With Blood*, for a full account of Brown's acts.

24. *The American Pageant* comes the closest, with substantial treatment of religions as social institutions and some discussion of their ideas. Otherwise, I agree with Robert Bryan's assessment, *History, Pseudo-History, Anti-History: How Public School Textbooks Treat Religion* (Washington, D.C.: Learn, Inc., 1984), 3, that after the Pilgrims, Christianity has no historical presence in American history textbooks. See also Paul Gagnon, *Democracy's Untold Story: What World History Textbooks Neglect* (Washington, D.C.: American Federation of Teachers, 1987); Charles C. Haynes, *Religion in American History* (Alexandria, VA: Association for Supervision and Curriculum Development, 1990); and William F. Jasper, "America's Textbooks Are Censored in Favor of the Left," in Lisa Orr, ed., *Censorship: Opposing Viewpoints* (San Diego: Greenhaven, 1990), 154–59.

25. Right-wing textbook critics are rightly incensed by this; as one of Mel Gabler's reviewers put it, criticizing *Life and Liberty*, "Obviously, the Publishers are not threatened by admitting the Arapaho were religious—so why not the notable [non-Indian] Americans past and present?" (untitled critique by Deborah L. Brezina [n.p., typescript distributed by Mel Gabler's Educational Research Analysts, 1993], 7). Unfortunately, Gabler's reviewers want only positive things said about religion, and mainly about their religion, Christianity; thus they attack an-

other textbook for mentioning that Benjamin Franklin was a Deist.

26. Paul M. Angle, *Created Equal? The Complete Lincoln-Douglas Debates of 1858* (Chicago: University of Chicago Press, 1958), 41.

27. The new edition of *The American Pageant* includes a well-chosen paragraph in which Lincoln agrees with Douglas that whites should be superior socially, but argues that blacks should have equal rights.

28. Richard Current, *The Lincoln Nobody Knows* (Westport, CT: Greenwood Press, 1980 [1958]), 216.

29. Richard H. Sewell, *A House Divided* (Baltimore: Johns Hopkins University Press, 1988), 74–75.

30. *American Adventures* and *American History* quote from Lincoln's letter to Albert Hodges, April 4, 1864. See Herbert Aptheker, *And Why Not Every Man?* (New York: International, 1961), 249, for the entire text.

31. See, for example, Jehuti El-Mali Amen-Ra, *Shattering the Myth of the Man Who Freed the Slaves* (Silver Spring, MD: Fourth Dynasty Publishing, 1990), 21. Amen-Ra, an "Afrikan" nationalist from Baltimore, edits Lincoln's letter just as textbook authors do, to discredit him.

32. Proposed by the border states, this compromise would have reversed *Dred Scott* and restored the Missouri Compromise line while guaranteeing slavery forever south of it. Lincoln could not abide the latter idea and instructed Republican congressmen not to support it. Without Republican support, it narrowly failed in both houses. Several new textbooks do provide Lincoln's opposition to the Crittenden Compromise.

33. V. J. Voegeli, *Free but Not Equal* (Chicago: University of Chicago Press, 1967), 62–63, 128–50.

34. *Pageant* provides a blowup of the last half of the last sentence, which therefore can be made out, with difficulty.

35. Later that year he would establish Thanksgiving Day, to identify another set of Founding Fathers with the United States.

36. Lest this analysis makes Lincoln appear too ethnocentric, note that some Europeans, including Tocqueville, and many Americans in the nineteenth century believed that the United States indeed exemplified the future. See Abbott Gleason, "Republic of Humbug," *American Quarterly* 44, no. 1 (3/1992): 1–20; and G. D. Lillibridge, *Beacon of Freedom* (Philadelphia: University of Pennsylvania Press, 1955).

37. Quoted in M. Hirsh Goldberg, *The Book of Lies* (New York: Morrow, 1990), 79–80.

38. Intellectuals still debate its implications for our present age. See, inter alia, Clarence Thomas, "The Modern Civil Rights Movement" (Winston-Salem, NC: The Tocqueville Forum, 4/18/1988); Garry Wills, *Lincoln at Gettysburg* (New York: Simon & Schuster, 1992); Robert Lowell as described in Allan Nevins, ed., *Lincoln and the Gettysburg Address* (Urbana: University of Illinois Press, 1964), 88–89; Robert Bellah, "Civil Religion in America," *Daedalus* (Winter 1967): 1–21; Willmoore Kendall, "Equality: Commitment or Ideal?" *Intercollegiate Review* (Fall 1989): 25–33; and Harry V. Jaffa, "Inventing the Gettysburg Address," *Intercollegiate Review* (Fall 1992): 51–56.

39. *Triumph of the American Nation* does ask two questions but buries them inside two pages of "Reviewing Important Terms," "Practicing Critical Thinking Skills," and so on at the end of the unit.

40. With the same reasoning, Paul Gagnon agrees that "all texts should reprint the [Second Inaugural] in its en-

tirety" in *Democracy's Half-Told Story*, 70–71.

41. Cf. Voegeli, *Free but Not Equal*, 138.

42. *Pathways to the Present* does include a different sentence that mentions slavery.

43. Lyrics quoted in James M. McPherson, *Battle Cry of Freedom* (New York: Oxford University Press, 1988), vi.

44. See Carleton Beals, *War Within a War* (Philadelphia: Chilton, 1965), 145–50.

45. Quoted in James M. McPherson, "Wartime," *New York Review of Books*, March 12, 1990, 33. Black soldiers caused "a revolution in thinking" in the Union army, according to Litwack, *Been in the Storm So Long*, 100.

46. *The American Adventure, Challenge of Freedom, Discovering American History*, and *Life and Liberty* treat the topic of black soldiers particularly well.

47. A particularly astute reader might be able to infer that result from the treatment in *The American Journey*.

48. Bill Evans points out (personal communication, 12/1993) that another factor encouraging border-state abolitionism was the absence from the polls of some slavery sympathizers fighting in the Confederate Army.

49. As quoted by McPherson, *Battle Cry of Freedom*, 688 (his ellipses).

50. Hugh L. Keenleyside, *Canada and the United States* (New York: Knopf, 1952), 115; Aptheker, *Essays in the History of the American Negro*, 159; Charles Sumner, speech, 6/1/1865.

51. Only *The American Adventure*, an inquiry text, includes this quote. *The American Pageant* includes an equally telling passage by abolitionist James Russell Lowell on the South's reasons for seceding. Otherwise, although misinformation on the South's raison d'etre is rampant throughout the United States and could

be countered by this quote, no text includes it. See McPherson, *Battle Cry of Freedom*, 649; Reid Mitchell, "The Creation of Confederate Loyalties," in Robert Azug and Stephen Maizlish, eds., *New Perspectives on Race and Slavery in America* (Lexington: University Press of Kentucky, 1986), 101–2.

52. Paul Escott, *After Secession* (Baton Rouge: Louisiana State University Press, 1978), 254.

53. James W. Loewen and Charles Sallis, eds., *Mississippi: Conflict and Change* (New York: Pantheon, 1980), 129–31; Beals, *War Within a War*; Mitchell, "The Creation of Confederate Loyalties," 93–108.

54. Beals, *War Within a War*, 12, 142; see also Stavis, *John Brown: The Sword and the Word*, 100–101.

55. John Cimprich and Robert C. Mainfort Jr., "The Fort Pillow Massacre: A Statistical Note," *Journal of American History*, 76 #2 (12/89), 832–37; Brian S. Wills, *A Battle from the Start* (NY: Harper, 1993), 77–78, 178, 186–93, 215; David Ndilei, *Extinguish the Flames of Racial Prejudice* (Gainesville, FL: I.E.F. Publications, 1996), 40, 91, 131, 157–58; John L. Jordan, "Was There a Massacre at Fort Pillow?" *Tennessee Historical Quarterly*, 6 (1947); Nathan Bedford Forrest, 4/15/64 dispatch, from *War of the Rebellion: Official Records*, v.32 pt. 1 (DC: GPO, 1891), 609–10; Richard Nelson Current, *Lincoln's Loyalists* (NY: Oxford University Press, 1992), 139–43; Richard L. Fuchs, *An Unerring Fire: The Massacre at Fort Pillow* (Rutherford, NJ: Fairleigh Dickinson University Press, 1994), 23, 116–17, 144–46; James McPherson, *Battle Cry of Freedom* (NY: Oxford University Press, 1988), 565–66, 793–95; McPherson, *The Negro's Civil War* (NY: Pantheon, 1965), 186–7; Joseph T. Glatthaar, *Forged*

in Battle: The Civil War Alliance of Black Soldiers and White Officers (NY: Free Press, 1990), 133–34.

56. Escott, *After Secession*, 198; McPherson, *Battle Cry of Freedom*, 833–35; Beals, *War Within a War*, 147.

57. Stavis, *John Brown: The Sword and the Word*, 101–2; see also McPherson, *Battle Cry of Freedom*, 832–38; Joseph T. Glatthaar, *The March to the Sea and Beyond* (Baton Rouge: Louisiana State University Press, 1995). Until the last year of the war, Union desertion rates were almost as high as Confederate, but Union deserters almost never joined the Confederate army.

58. Beals, *War Within a War*, 73. See also Gabor Boritt, ed., *Why the Confederacy Lost* (New York: Oxford University Press, 1992).

59. One old book from my original sample, *The American Adventure*, quoted original sources on the evolution of Union war aims and asked, "How would such attitudes affect the conduct and outcome of the war?"

60. *American History*, its author apparently unfamiliar with the literature about division within the South, even claims as an advantage for the Confederates that "their whole way of life [was] at stake. This added to their determination and helped make up for the shortage of men and supplies." Of course, ideas were not the sole cause of Union victory. Many textbooks mention the North's considerable advantages in population, industry, and railroads. Some textbooks note the naval blockade of the South, coupled with the region's inadequate internal transportation. Several recognize that the Union's government and financing were already in place. On the other hand, some textbooks point out that the Confederates had the advantage of fighting on their home turf with shorter supply lines; a few note that they also had initial sympathy from the governments of Britain and France. Beyond these factors, idiosyncratic considerations—what historians like to call historical contingency—were at work. The South had better generals at first. Lincoln was a far better president than Davis. McClellan was indecisive. Two of the South's most capable generals, Albert Sidney Johnston and Stonewall Jackson, were killed early in the war. Certain officers did or did not bring their troops to bear in time in certain battles. Lee's plans at Antietam fell into Union hands. And so on. Thus, there was no inevitability to the outcome, and I do not claim that textbooks err by not saying that the Union won for ideological reasons. I do suggest that since American history textbooks rarely discuss causation at all, they are unlikely to treat causes of the Union victory very well, and, indeed, five textbooks give *no* reasons! Since textbooks discuss ideas even less often, they are unlikely to treat ideas as causes in the Civil War. *The American Adventure* does so with intelligence.

61. David Lowenthal, *The Past Is a Foreign Country* (Cambridge: Cambridge University Press, 1988), 345; see also Peter Novick, *That Noble Dream* (Cambridge: Cambridge University Press, 1988), 74–80.

62. Bessie L. Pierce, *Public Opinion and the Teaching of History in the United States* (New York: Alfred A. Knopf, 1926), 146–70; see also Lowenthal, *The Past Is a Foreign Country*, 345; John S. Mosby, letter to Sam Chapman, 7/4/1907, at Gilder Lehrman Institute of American History, gilderlehrman.org/collection/docs_current.html.

63. Michael Kammen, *Mystic Chords of*

Memory (New York: Alfred A. Knopf, 1991), 118.

64. Mark Halton offers an interesting discussion of the resurgence of the Confederate flag in the 1950s and its symbolic opposition to the civil rights movement in "Time to Furl the Confederate Flag," *Christian Century* 105, no. 17 (5/18/1988): 494–96. "Embattled Emblem," an exhibit at the Museum of the Confederacy on the history of the Army of Northern Virginia flag from Reconstruction to the 1990s, similarly credits its resurgence to white opposition to civil rights. The white South is slowly giving up its identification with the Confederacy. In 1983 even the University of Mississippi, once a citadel of resistance to racial change, dropped the Confederate flag as its official emblem. In 2001, Georgia removed the Confederate flag from its state flag, and in 2004 voters supported the new design.

65. Carl Sandburg, *Abraham Lincoln: The War Years* (New York: Harcourt, Brace, 1939), 4:347–49.

66. Loewen and Sallis, eds., *Mississippi: Conflict and Change*, 145–47. John Hope Franklin suggested renaming "Presidential Reconstruction" "Confederate Reconstruction."

67. American Social History Project, *Who Built America?* (New York: Pantheon, 1989), 482.

68. Eric Foner, *Reconstruction* (New York: Harper and Row, 1988), 267.

69. Edmonia Highgate quoted in Robert Moore, *Reconstruction: The Promise and Betrayal of Democracy* (New York: CIBC, 1983), 17.

70. The exception, *Discovering American History*, doesn't mention Southern Republicans at all and hardly covers Reconstruction.

71. William C. Harris, "A Reconsideration of the Mississippi Scalawag," *Journal of Mississippi History* 37, no. 1 (2/1970): 11–13.

72. Ibid., 3–42; C. Vann Woodward, "Unfinished Business," *New York Review of Books*, May 12, 1988.

73. Again, *Discovering American History* is the exception because it doesn't mention Southern Republicans at all and hardly covers Reconstruction. Ironically, most Northern whites who went south for economic gain were Democrats.

74. The editors, "Liberating Our Past," *Southern Exposure* 12, no. 6 (11/1984): 2.

75. See LaWanda Cox and John Cox, "Negro Suffrage and Republican Politics: The Problem of Motivation in Reconstruction Historiography," *Journal of Southern History* 33 (August 1967): 317–26; Richard Curry, ed., *Radicalism, Racism, and Party Realignment* (Baltimore: Johns Hopkins University Press, 1969).

76. McPherson, *Battle Cry of Freedom*, 853. The population of the Union was twenty-two million. In "The Reconstruction of Abraham Lincoln," Ch. 5 of David Middleton and Derek Edwards, eds., *Collective Remembering* (London: Sage, 1991), Barry Schwartz analyzes the funeral as a crucial step in Lincoln's iconolatry.

77. Sandburg, *Abraham Lincoln: The War Years*, 4:296, 373–80; John T. Morse Jr., ed., *The Diary of Gideon Welles* (Boston: Houghton Mifflin, 1911), 2:288–90.

78. Among white respondents Lincoln usually comes in first in opinion polls as the "greatest president" or "greatest American," partly because whites like such personal traits as his humanitarianism, populist touch, and empathy, according to Barry Schwartz in "Abraham

Lincoln in the Black Community of Memory" (Washington, D.C.: National Museum of American History colloquium, 8/24/1993).

79. "The Lesson of the Hour," in Warch and Fanton, *John Brown*, 108.

80. I must note an important exception: *American Adventures*, which is aimed at younger or "slower" readers, devotes two of its two- to three-page chapters to abolitionists William Lloyd Garrison and Thaddeus Stevens and presents them with unusual flair.

81. On Brown and Ho Chi Minh, see Truman Nelson, *The Truman Nelson Reader* (Amherst: University of Massachusetts Press, 1989), 285; on South Africa and Northern Ireland, see Peter Maas, "Generations of Torment," *New York Times Magazine*, 6/10/1988, 32; 1988 PBS documentary, *We Shall Overcome*.

CHAPTER 7: THE LAND OF OPPORTUNITY

1. Abraham Lincoln quoted in Carl Sandburg, *Abraham Lincoln* (New York: Harcourt, Brace, 1954), 271.

2. Helen Keller, *Midstream: My Later Life* (New York: Greenwood, 1968 [1929]), 156.

3. Kwame Nkrumah, *Consciencism* (New York: Monthly Review Press, 1964), 63.

4. Similarly, Cynthia S. Sunal and Perry D. Phillips tell how their students aged six to eighteen "seemed unable to explain inequalities." See "Rural Students' Development of the Conception of Economic Inequality" (New Orleans: American Educational Research Association, 1988, abstract, ERIC ED299069).

5. Two recent books do mention the air traffic controllers' strike broken by President Reagan, but as part of the Reagan presidency rather than labor history.

6. Jean Anyon, "Ideology and United States History Textbooks," *Harvard Educational Review* 49, no. 3 (8/1979): 373. Anyon claims that high school history textbooks always concentrate on "the same three strikes": the 1877 railroad strike, 1892 Homestead steel strike, and 1894 Pullman strike. Each was "especially violent," she writes, and labor lost all three; hence to emphasize them is "to cast doubt on striking as a valid course of action." However, if textbooks emphasized successful strikes, Anyon could then charge them with minimizing the seriousness of the struggle labor faced. Conversely, some appallingly violent instances of class conflict go unmentioned by most textbooks.

7. Gregory Mantsios, "Class in America: Myths and Realities," in Paula S. Rothernberg, ed., *Racism and Sexism: An Integrated Study* (New York: St. Martin's, 1988), 56. The 2003 *Holt American Nation* does treat "The New Working Class" around 1900 and in other eras contains some discussion of poverty.

8. Ibid., 60; Kevin Phillips, *The Politics of Rich and Poor* (New York: Random House, 1990); Robert Heilbroner, "Lifting the Silent Depression," *New York Review of Books*, 10/24/1991, 6; and Sylvia Nasar, "The Rich Get Richer," *New York Times*, 8/16/1992. Stephen J. Rose, *Social Stratification in the United States* (New York: New Press, 2007), is a posterbook that shows graphically the shrinkage of the middle class between 1979 and 2004.

9. "Income Disparity Since World War II—The Gini Index," in "Gini coefficient," en.wikipedia.org/wiki/Gini_coefficient, 9/2006.

10. Jere Brophy and Thomas Good summarize some of the vast literature on social class, teacher expectation, and tracking in *Teacher-Student Relationships* (New York: Holt, 1974), esp. 7–171. Ray Rist

observed similar tracking and differential teacher expectation by social class within first-grade classes in black schools, as summarized in Edsel Erickson et al., "The Educability of Dominant Groups," *Phi Delta Kappan* (December 1972): 320. Dale Harvey and Gerald Slatin showed that teachers willingly categorize children by social class on the basis of photographs and hold higher expectations for middle- and upper-class children; see "The Relationship Between Child's SES and Teacher Expectations," *Social Forces* 54, no. 1 (1975): 140–59. See also Richard H. DeLone, *Small Futures* (New York: Harcourt Brace Jovanovich, 1979).

11. Sizer quoted in Walter Karp, "Why Johnny Can't Think," *Harper's*, 6/1985, 73.

12. Reba Page, "The Lower-Track Students' View of Curriculum," (Washington, D.C.: American Education Research Association, 1987).

13. Woodrow Wilson quoted in Lewis H. Lapham, "Notebook," *Harper's*, 7/1991, 10.

14. The difference is dramatically documented in the film *Health Care: Your Money or Your Life* (New York: Downtown Community TV Center, c. 1977), which compares two publicly funded neighboring hospitals in New York City, one caring mostly for poor people, the other for a more affluent clientele.

15. Survey data from about 1979 reported in Sidney Verba and Gary Orren, *Equality in America* (Cambridge: Harvard University Press, 1985), 72–75. Other surveys, before and after, report similar results.

16. Linda McNeil, "Defensive Teaching and Classroom Control," in Michael W. Apple and Lois Weis, eds., *Ideology and Practice in Schooling* (Philadelphia: Temple University Press, 1983), 116.

17. Edward Pessen, *The Log Cabin Myth* (New Haven: Yale University Press, 1984).

18. August Hollingshead and Frederick C. Redlich, *Social Class and Mental Illness* (New York: Wiley, 1958), 6. Traditional sex roles, here favoring women, caused the death rate among men to be much higher in all classes.

19. Lawrence M. Baskir and William Strauss, *Chance and Circumstance* (New York: Random House, 1986).

20. Richard Sennett and Jonathan Cobb, *The Hidden Injuries of Class* (New York: Alfred A. Knopf, 1972).

21. Citing only literature from the 1970s, see, inter alia, Joel Spring, *Education and the Rise of the Corporate State* (Boston: Beacon, 1972); Ray Rist, *The Urban School: A Factory for Failure* (Cambridge: MIT Press, 1973); Samuel Bowles and Herbert Gintis, *Schooling in Capitalist America* (New York: Basic Books, 1976); Joel Spring, *The Sorting Machine* (New York: David McKay, 1976); James Rosenbaum, *Making Inequality* (New York: Wiley, 1976); Paul Willis, *Learning to Labor* (Farnborough, Eng.: Saxon House, Teakfield Ltd., 1977); and Jerome Karabel and A. H. Halsey, eds., *Power and Ideology in Education* (New York: Oxford University Press, 1977).

22. Jonathan Kozol, *Savage Inequalities* (New York: Crown, 1991).

23. The inquiry textbook *The American Adventure* comes closest to analyzing education and social class among the eighteen books I surveyed.

24. Cowan's work is described and quoted in Herbert Gutman, *Power and Culture* (New York: Pantheon, 1987), 396–97.

25. Gutman, *Power and Culture*, 386–90.

26. William Miller, "American Historians and the Business Elite," in Miller,

ed., *Men in Business* (New York: Harper and Row, 1962), 326–28, summarizing his own research and work by Reinhard Bendix and F. W. Howton. See also David Montgomery, *Beyond Equality* (New York: Vintage, 1967), 15. Some other studies showed marginally higher proportions, not materially different, except for scattered pockets of opportunity, including Paterson, NJ.

27. Verba and Orren, *Equality in America*, 10. See also Paul Gagnon, *Democracy's Half-Told Story* (New York: American Federation of Teachers, 1989), 84–85; "Income Disparity Since World War II," op cit.

28. Mantsios, "Class in America," 59; Isaac Shapiro and Robert Greenstein, *The Widening Gulf* (Washington, D.C.: Center on Budget and Policy Priorities, 1999).

29. "Index," *Harper's*, May 1990, 19, citing data from the United Automobile Workers; Jeanne Sahadi, "CEO Pay: Sky High Gets Even Higher," CNNMoney .com, 8/30/2005; money/cnn.com/ 2005/08/26/news/economy/ceo_ pay/.

30. "Index," *Harper's*, January 1993, 19, citing the Organization for Economic Cooperation and Development.

31. David Tyack and Elisabeth Hansot, "Conflict and Consensus in American Public Education," *Daedalus* 110, no. 2 (Summer 1981): 11–12.

32. Jeffrey Williamson and Lindert, *American Inequality: A Macroeconomic History* (New York: Academic Press, 1980), Chapter 3. Seymour Martin Lipset, *The First New Nation* (New York: Basic Books, 1963), 324–26, holds that wealth was less equal in Great Britain, although income was not.

33. *The American Pageant* (2006) stands out by noting that "many nations boasted more equitable distributions of wealth."

This book also reveals that "the gap between rich and poor even widened somewhat in the 1980s." Unfortunately, *The American Pageant* also says that 80 percent of the workforce in the 1990s worked in white-collar jobs, double the actual proportion.

34. Walter Dean Burnham, "The Changing Shape of the American Political University," *American Political Science Review* 59 (1965): 23–25.

35. Barry Schwartz, "The Reconstruction of Abraham Lincoln," in David Middleton and Derek Edwards, eds., *Collective Remembering* (London: Sage, 1991).

36. Williamson and Lindert, *American Inequality*, 41–42, 49–51; Robert E. Gallman, "Trends in the Size Distribution of Wealth in the Nineteenth Century," in Lee Soltow, ed., *Six Papers on the Size Distribution of Wealth and Income* (New York: National Bureau of Economic Research, 1969), 6–7.

37. Lee Soltow, *Distribution of Wealth and Income in the United States in 1798* (Pittsburgh: University of Pittsburgh Press, 1989), 252; Stephan Thernstrom, *The Other Bostonians* (Cambridge: Harvard University Press, 1973), Chapters 5, 9.

38. See Alan Macrobert, "The Unfairness of It All," *Vermont Vanguard Press*, September 30, 1984, 12–13; Alfie Kohn, *You Know What They Say . . .* (New York: HarperCollins, 1990), 38–39; Heilbroner, "Lifting the Silent Depression," 6; Sheldon Danziger and Peter Gottschalk, *Uneven Tides* (New York: Sage, 1993).

39. Mantsios, "Class in America," 56.

40. Deborah L. Brezina, "Critique of *Life and Liberty*" (np, n.d., typescript, distributed by Mel Gabler's Educational Research Analysts, 1993), 2.

41. Frances FitzGerald, *America Revised* (New York: Vintage, 1979), 108–9.

42. David Tyack and Elisabeth Hansot, "Conflict and Consensus in American Public Education," *Daedalus* 110, no. 2 (Summer 1981): 1–25, found that economic inequality is typically justified by the twin notions of meritocracy and equality of opportunity.

43. FitzGerald, *America Revised*, 109. The Gablers and their allies repeatedly make the same criticism; see Brezina, "Critique of *Life and Liberty*," 2.

44. McNeil, "Defensive Teaching and Classroom Control," 125.

45. A paragraph titled "A Permanent Class of Poor Workers" in *The American Way* and another in *The American Pageant* are exceptions.

46. Survey data from Verba and Orren, *Equality in America*, 72–75.

CHAPTER 8: WATCHING BIG BROTHER: WHAT TEXTBOOKS TEACH ABOUT THE FEDERAL GOVERNMENT

1. Said regarding the writing of the history of the Mexican War; quoted by Edward Pessen, "JQA . . . ," in the Organization of American Historians newsletter, 2/1988.

2. Lyrics from Tom Paxton's "That's What I Learned in School," Cherry Lane Music Publishing Co., Inc., all rights reserved, used by permission, copyright 1962, 1990.

3. "An Interview with Bill Moyers," in *Facing History and Ourselves News*, c. 1991, 4.

4. Malcolm X quoted in Gil Noble's film *El Hajj Malik el Shabazz (Malcolm X)* (Carlsbad, CA: CRM Films, 1965).

5. Paul Gagnon, "Why Study History?" *Atlantic*, 11/1988, 63.

6. Unfortunately, the inquiry textbooks have gone out of print.

7. George Kennan quoted in Sheila D. Collins, "From the Bottom Up and the Outside In," *CALC Report* 15, no. 3 (3/1990): 9–10.

8. Frances FitzGerald, *America Revised* (New York: Vintage, 1980), 129.

9. Quoted in James Oliver Robertson, *American Myth, American Reality* (New York: Hill and Wang, 1980), 272.

10. Bessie L. Pierce, *Civic Attitudes in American School Textbooks* (Chicago: University of Chicago Press, 1930), 110–11.

11. Ruth Leger Sivard, *World Military and Social Expenditures, 1985* (Washington, D.C.: World Priorities, 1985), 35–37; Curt Tarnoff and Larry Nowels, "Foreign Aid: An Introductory Overview of U.S. Programs and Policy," Washington, D.C., Library of Congress Congressional Research Service, 2004; David Wallechinsky "Is America Still No. 1?" *Parade* (1/14/2007) 4. Moreover, most foreign aid goes to just four or five countries, always including Israel and Egypt, and is more military than social or educational in nature.

12. Interviews with high-level managers of multinational corporations in Larry Adelman's video, *Controlling Interest: The World of the Multinational Corporation* (San Francisco: California Newsreel, 1978), show their influence particularly over U.S. policy in Chile.

13. With the end of communism in Eastern Europe, *Second World* no longer has its old meaning. *Third World* was always ethnocentric, implying *our* world was first. Because terms like *LDCs*—less developed countries—raise problems of their own, and since *Third World* was the term used in the period, I will use it here.

14. Robert Reich quoted in Robert Heilbroner, "The Worst Is Yet to Come," *New York Times*, 2/14/1993, 25.

15. "Corporate Crime and Abuse," Center for Corporate Policy website,

corporatepolicy.org/issues/FCPA.htm, 1/2007; "Kuwait of Africa?" *60 Minutes*, 7/18/2004, CBS News website, cbs news.com/stories/2003/11/14/60 minutes; Katy Shaw, "Making a Killing: Corporations, Conflict and Poverty in Equatorial Guinea," War on Want annual conference 2005, War on Want website, waronwant.org/download.php?id=299, 10/2006; Eduardo Cue, "Dictator and Diplomat," *U.S. News & World Report*, 9/17/2006, usnews.com/usnews/news/articles/060917/25oil.htm, 1/2006; John Vidal, "Oil Rich, Dirt Poor," *The Guardian*, 8/26/2004, guardian.co.uk/print/0,,5001814-114321,00.html, 1/2007; Justin Blum, "U.S. Oil Firms Entwined in Equatorial Guinea Deals," *Washington Post*, 9/7/2004, washington post.com/ac2/wp-dyn/A1101-2004Sep6 . . . , 1/2007.

16. Barry Weisberg, *Beyond Repair* (Boston: Beacon Press, 1971), 79. Allied urging and Wilson's anticommunism may have been larger factors.

17. Gen. Smedley D. Butler, quoted in a *New York Times* interview, 8/21/1931, reprinted in Joseph R. Conlin, ed., *The Morrow Book of Quotations in American History* (New York: Morrow, 1984), 58.

18. John A. Hobson, quoted in Lloyd C. Gardner, *Safe for Democracy* (New York: Oxford University Press, 1984), 11.

19. Jonathan Kwitny, *Endless Enemies* (New York: Congdon and Weed, 1984), 178.

20. Charles Harriss III and Louis Sadler, *The Border and the Revolution* (Silver City, NM: High-Lonesome Books, 1988), Chapter I.

21. Lewis H. Lapham, *America's Century Series Transcript* (San Francisco: KQED, 1989), 48; Greg Grandin, "Your Americanism and Mine: Americanism and Anti-Americanism in the Americas," *American*

Historical Review Forum, 10/2006, history cooperative.org/journals/ahr/111.4/grandin.html (11/2006), 1.

22. Kwitny, *Endless Enemies*, 389. Andrew Kopkind also makes this point in "One-and-a-Half (Strangled) Cheers for the USSR," *Village Voice*, 2/4/1980.

23. According to evidence from the Church Committee of the U.S. Senate, summarized in Satish Kumar, *The CIA and the Third World* (New Delhi: Vikas, 1981), 86–90, Allen Dulles, director of the CIA, instructed the CIA in Zaire that "removal" of Lumumba "should be a high priority of our covert action." CIA headquarters then sent toxic substances to its operatives in Zaire with which to assassinate Lumumba while he was in UN custody. Charles Ameringer describes President Eisenhower's indirect ordering of Lumumba's assassination on 8/18/1960, in *U.S. Foreign Intelligence* (Lexington, MA: D. C. Heath, 1990), 291. In the end, Congolese, not CIA agents, killed Lumumba after he left UN custody, so although the CIA approved of the murder, had been trying to accomplish it itself, and had prior knowledge of the plan to transfer Lumumba to the site where he would be killed, the United States could deny any direct involvement in his demise. See also Ellen Ray et al., eds., *Dirty Work 2* (Secaucus, NJ: Lyle Stuart, 1979), 15–19, 185–92, and 202–11; Victor Marchetti and John D. Marks, *The CIA and the Cult of Intelligence* (New York: Dell, 1974), 131–32; and Kevin Reilly, *The West and the World* (New York: Harper and Row, 1989), 412–15.

24. *Holt American Nation* does say that the United States wanted to "remove" Castro.

25. Pierre Salinger, "Gaps in the Cuban Missile Crisis Story," *New York Times*, 2/5/1989. See also Lapham, *America's*

Century Series Transcript, 51; Ameringer, U.S. Foreign Intelligence, 285–95; Rhodri Jeffreys-Jones, The CIA and American Democracy (New Haven: Yale University Press, 1989), 131–40.

26. Philip Agee and Louis Wolf, Dirty Work (Secaucus, NJ: Lyle Stuart, 1978), 270–71. Lee Harvey Oswald, Kennedy's alleged assassin, may only coincidentally have tried to go to Cuba. We do not know; distrust of the official Warren Commission explanation fuels speculation to this day. Many Americans found Oliver Stone's film JFK persuasive, even though the conspiracy it concocts seems to include Vice President Johnson, the Pentagon brass, the CIA, the military-industrial complex, the Mafia, and the Mormon Tabernacle Choir. Textbooks bear some responsibility for the public gullibility, because they do a poor job of discussing Kennedy's murder. Half-blindly trust the Warren Commission conclusion that Oswald was the lone and idiosyncratically motivated killer. The others cast doubt on the Warren Commission but leave completely vague who else might have been involved. According to historian Jeffreys-Jones, The CIA and American Democracy, 140, Attorney General Robert Kennedy did not want the public to know about JFK's Operation Mongoose or contracts with the Mafia; secrecy on these points helped make the Warren report incomplete about both Castro and the Mafia. LBJ thought Castro probably had JFK killed in retaliation for JFK's attempts on his life, but no textbook raises the possibility. See Nathan Miller, Spying for America (New York: Paragon, 1989), 375. In 1978 the House Select Committee on Assassinations concluded the Mafia probably did it, since both Oswald and his slayer, Jack Ruby, had mob ties, but no textbook raises the possibility. See G. R. Blakey, "Mur-

dered by the Mob?" Washington Post, 11/7/1993.

27. Christopher Cerf and Victor Navasky, The Experts Speak (New York: Pantheon, 1984), 145; Ameringer, U.S. Foreign Intelligence, 261–64.

28. Kissinger, quoted in Thomas G. Paterson, J. G. Clifford, and K. J. Hagen, American Foreign Policy: A History Since 1900 (Lexington, MA: D. C. Heath, 1983), 589.

29. My thanks to David Shiman for some of the ideas and wording of these paragraphs on Chile, parts of which originally appeared as "U.S. in the Third World: Challenging the Textbook Myth," by David Shiman and James W. Loewen, Chapter 11 of T. M. Thomas et al., eds., Global Images of Peace: Transforming the War System (Kottayam, India: Prakasam Publications, 1985), reprinted in this country as Global Images of Peace and Education (Ann Arbor: Prakken, 1987). David also suggested the term international good guy and the book's title.

30. Gagnon, "Why Study History?" 60.

31. George W. Ball, "JFK's Big Moment," New York Review of Books, 2/13/1992, 16–20; Jeffreys-Jones, The CIA and American Democracy, 131; Ameringer, U.S. Foreign Intelligence, 250, 268.

32. Ronald Kessler, Inside the CIA (New York: Pocket Books, 1992), 41; see also George W. Ball, "JFK's Big Moment," 16; Marchetti and Marks, The CIA and the Cult of Intelligence, 350–54.

33. Robert F. Smith, The United States and Revolutionary Nationalism in Mexico, 1916–1932 (Chicago: University of Chicago Press, 1972), xiii; see also Ameringer, U.S. Foreign Intelligence, 268.

34. Robert Leckie, The Wars of America (New York: Harper and Row, 1968), 12.

35. Nicolas Shumway, "Someone to

Be Stopped in Chile," *New York Times Book Review*, 5/9/1993, 19; *Oversight of U.S. Government Intelligence Functions: Hearings Before the Committee on Government Operations*, U.S. Senate, 94th Congress, Second Session (Washington, D.C.: U.S. Government Printing Office, 1976).

36. Thomas W. Lippman, "138 Reported Missing in U.S. Spy Flights," *Washington Post*, March 5, 1993; Thomas Powers, "Notes from Underground," *New York Review of Books*, 6/21/2001, 51.

37. Mark Danner, "How the Foreign Policy Machine Broke Down," *New York Times Magazine*, 3/7/1993, 33–34.

38. Helen Keller, letter to *New York Call*, November 10, 1919, in Philip S. Foner, ed., *Helen Keller: Her Socialist Years* (New York: International Publishers, 1967), 100.

39. One book, *Life and Liberty*, over-blames Nixon, stating in two different places, "Evidence uncovered later showed that Nixon did know about the burglary before it happened." No evidence has yet shown this.

40. Richard Rubenstein, *The Cunning of History* (New York: Harper & Row, 1987), 82.

41. Peter Kornbluh, "Back Into the Loop," *Washington Post*, 8/22/1993, C2; Fritz Schwartz, *Unchecked and Unbalanced* (New York: New Press, 2007).

42. Theodore Draper makes this point in "American Hubris: From Truman to the Persian Gulf," *New York Review of Books*, 7/16/1987, 40–48.

43. Kenneth O'Reilly, *"Racial Matters"* (New York: Free Press, 1989), 9, 12–13, 17, and 96–99; Ameringer, *U.S. Foreign Intelligence*, 109.

44. O'Reilly, *"Racial Matters,"* 43, 126, 144, and 355; David J. Garrow, *The FBI and Martin Luther King Jr.* (New York: Penguin, 1981), 125–26, 161–64; Taylor

Branch, *Parting the Waters* (New York: Simon & Schuster, 1988), 861; Ameringer, *U.S. Foreign Intelligence*, 322–23; Frank J. Donner, *The Age of Surveillance* (New York: Alfred A. Knopf, 1980), 214–19; Athan Theoharis and John Stuart Cox, *The Boss* (Philadelphia: Temple University Press, 1988), 354–57. The media, in those days respecting a barrier between private and public lives, generally refused to use the material.

45. Ameringer, *U.S. Foreign Intelligence*, 323; Branch, *Parting the Waters*, 835–65; O'Reilly, *"Racial Matters,"* 140, 186; Garrow, *The FBI and Martin Luther King Jr.*, 130–31; Donner, *The Age of Surveillance*, 217.

46. Branch, *Parting the Waters*, 692.

47. O'Reilly, *"Racial Matters,"* 357.

48. James W. Loewen and Charles Sallis, eds., *Mississippi: Conflict and Change* (New York: Pantheon, 1980), 265–83.

49. O'Reilly, *"Racial Matters,"* 186.

50. Ibid., 256; Arlie Schardt, "Civil Rights: Too Much, Too Late," in Pat Watters and Stephen Gillers, *Investigating the FBI* (New York: Ballantine, 1973), 167–79.

51. Adam Hochschild, "His Life as a Panther," *New York Times Book Review*, January 31, 1993; O'Reilly, *"Racial Matters,"* 302–16; Donner, *The Age of Surveillance*, 220–32.

52. Donner, *The Age of Surveillance*, 220.

53. This Raoul, last name apparently Maora, is not to be conflated with the "Raoul" who masterminded the entire assassination, according to Ray, but who cannot be found and was likely fictitious.

54. Donner, *The Age of Surveillance*, 214–19; John Edginton and John Sergeant, "The Murder of Martin Luther King Jr.," *Covert Action Information Bulletin*, no. 34 (Summer 1990): 21–27; Theoha-

ris and Cox, *The Boss*, 439. See also Ameringer, *U.S. Foreign Intelligence*, 322; John
Elliff, "Aspects of Federal Civil Rights
Enforcement," in *Law in American History*,
vol. 5 of *Perspectives in American History*
(Cambridge: Harvard University Press,
1971), 643–47.

55. O'Reilly, *"Racial Matters,"* 336–37.
Division administrators toned down the
Jackson agents, reminding them to focus
on the Tougaloo Political Action Committee, "since Tougaloo College, per se, is
not a counterintelligence target." See also
Donner, *The Age of Surveillance*, 219–20.
Donner says the FBI forced the departure
from Mississippi of Muhammad Kenyatta, a prominent black nationalist in
Jackson. In internal memos, FBI agents
took credit for setting up Kenyatta on the
charge of attempting to steal a television
set from Tougaloo College. Actually, Kenyatta hastened his own departure by getting caught while doing just that.

56. O'Reilly, *"Racial Matters,"* 337.

57. Ross Gelbspan, *Break-ins, Death
Threats, and the FBI* (Boston: South End
Press, 1991).

58. Danny Glover's *Freedom Song*, although more accurate, is almost unknown.

59. Seth Cagin and Philip Dray, *We
Are Not Afraid* (New York: Bantam Books,
1991), describes the murders and the
FBI's reluctant but eventually effective police work.

60. Arthur Schlesinger Jr., quoted in
Branch, *Parting the Waters*, 918–19.

61. See Beverly Kraft, "Some Lack
Knowledge About Evers," *Jackson Clarion
Ledger*, January 20, 1994, 1A.

62. To a degree, Boorstin and Kelley
also provide this analysis, but their overall
treatment is muddled and might lead students to conclude the very opposite.

63. Patrick Ferguson, "Promoting

Political Participation: Teachers' Attitudes
and Instructional Practices" (San Francisco: American Educational Research
Association, 1989).

64. Critique by James F. Delong
(Hoover, AL: 1986, typescript, distributed by Mel Gabler's Educational Research Analysts, 1993).

65. Donald Barr, *Who Pushed Humpty
Dumpty? Dilemmas in American Education To-
day* (New York: Atheneum, 1972), 308;
Lewis Lapham, *Pretensions to Empire* (New
York: New Press, 2006), 24.

66. Michigan State Board of Education, *1982–83 Michigan Social Studies Textbook Report* (Lansing, MI: Michigan State
Board of Education, 1984).

67. Rubenstein, *The Cunning of History*,
80–82; Clarence Lusane, *Pipe Dream Blues*
(Boston: South End Press, 1991), 4,
116–22, and 200–201.

CHAPTER 9: SEE NO EVIL:
CHOOSING NOT TO LOOK
AT THE WAR IN VIETNAM

1. George Swiers, quoted in William
Appleman Williams et al., eds., *America in
Vietnam* (New York: Norton, 1989), ix.

2. Martin Luther King Jr., "Beyond
Vietnam" (New York: Riverside Church
sermon, 4/4/1967).

3. Gen. William C. Westmoreland
quoted at Brainy Quote, brainyquote
.com, 5/2007; Antiwar, antiwar.com/
quotes.php, 5/2007; and elsewhere.

4. Frederick Douglass quoted on in-
side cover of Robert Moore, *Reconstruction:
The Promise and Betrayal of Democracy* (New
York: Council on Interracial Books for
Children, 1983).

5. Student ignorance is no accident.
According to the historian Michael Kammen, writing in *Mystic Chords of Memory*
(New York: Alfred A. Knopf, 1991),
661–62, President Ford wanted us to for-

get Vietnam. President Reagan slashed the National Archives budget and kept documents "secret" longer, to interfere with our producing and knowing the history of the recent past. In *A Shared Authority* (Albany: State University of New York Press, 1990), 16–18, Michael Frisch cites an astounding classroom incident in which a student thinks the United States *won* the Vietnam War. In an interesting analysis, he argues against mere failure of her memory and agrees with Kammen that our political leaders, presumably influencing our popular culture, habitually refer to a need to put the war "behind us" to avoid discussing it.

6. Indeed, one inquiry textbook, *Discovering American History*, gives less than two pages to the entire war. But *Discovering American History* focuses its coverage on causes and results, precisely what the traditional narrative textbooks botch, and thus provides a more coherent and memorable account of the war than the much longer accounts in other books.

7. Lewis H. Lapham's analysis of the importance of "a sequence of brutal images" reinforces the foregoing. He describes just three, including the first, third, and seventh of those I list. See *America's Century Series Transcript* (San Francisco: KQED, 1989), 57–58.

8. *Pageant* also includes a confusing image of an American punching a Vietnamese, probably to keep him off a helicopter evacuating South Vietnam.

9. Hagopian specifically refers to the naked napalmed girl and the My Lai massacre victims and cites another student of photojournalism who adds the monk's immolation and the police chief's shooting of the Vietcong suspect. See "Vietnam Veterans and the Right to the Past" (Baltimore: American Studies Association, 1991), 14.

10. Michael Delli Carpini, "Vietnam and the Press," 125–56, in D. Michael Shafer, ed., *The Legacy* (Boston: Beacon, 1990), 142.

11. "The Massacre at Mylai," *Life*, December 5, 1969, 36–42; Kammen, *Mystic Chords of Memory*, 647; James Davidson and Mark Lytle, *After the Fact* (New York: McGraw-Hill, 1992), 2: 379–82.

12. Gen. William C. Westmoreland, quoted in Murray Kempton, "Heart of Darkness," *New York Review of Books*, 11/24/1988, 26.

13. *Holt* does show GIs retreating from a Cambodian village that is in flames, but the photo does not indicate who burned the village.

14. John Kerry, "Winter Soldier Investigation," testimony to U.S. Senate Foreign Relations Committee, 4/1971, reprinted in Williams et al., eds., *America in Vietnam*, 295. In 2006, news stories confirmed that My Lai stood for a class of crimes. See "Declassified Papers Show U.S. Atrocities in Vietnam Went Far Beyond My Lai," *Los Angeles Times*, (8/6/06), at History News Network, hnn.us/roundup/entries/28956.html.

15. Davidson and Lytle, *After the Fact*, 2:356–83, quote from 2:371.

16. Davidson continues to churn out American histories, with and without Lytle. His most recent effort, *The American Nation*, appeared in 2005; I do not review it here because it is marketed primarily to middle schools. It continues his policy of never mentioning My Lai or anything like it. *After the Fact* thus stands as its own rebuke of the level of scholarly responsibility in the new book.

17. *We Americans* does supply two other sentences by King that mention the sacrifices black soldiers were making in Vietnam while they could not enjoy equal rights at home.

18. One textbook, *The Challenge of Freedom*, does offer this rather pallid paraphrase of the Ben Tre quote: "Other doves believed that the war was harming South Vietnam. These people said that there was not much sense in destroying the country to save it from communism."

19. John Kerry testimony reprinted in Williams et al., eds., *America in Vietnam*, 295.

20. George W. Chilcoat shows how the songs of the Vietnam War era—from "Where Have All the Flowers Gone?" and "Give Peace a Chance" on the antiwar side to the pro-war "Okie from Muskogee" and "Ballad of the Green Berets"—provide students with a fascinating introduction to its issues in "The Images of Vietnam: A Popular Music Approach," *Social Education* 49 (1985): 601–3.

21. Frances FitzGerald, *America Revised* (New York: Vintage, 1980), 126.

22. In "Falling Dominoes," *New York Review of Books*, 10/27/1983, 19, Theodore Draper points out that under this rhetoric, the size, location, and importance of the country and of the actual threat facing it or us was beside the point, for such an argument would rationalize intervention anywhere in the world.

23. See Richard Drinnon, *Facing West* (Minneapolis: University of Minnesota Press, 1980), and Richard Slotkin, *Regeneration Through Violence* (Middletown, CT: Wesleyan University Press, 1973).

24. John Foster Dulles, quoted in Williams et al., eds., *America in Vietnam*, 167.

25. Frances FitzGerald, *Fire in the Lake* (Boston: Atlantic-Little, Brown, 1972), offers insight into why the United States intervened; Stanley Karnow, *Vietnam* (New York: Viking, 1983), describes how the escalation occurred.

26. Linda McNeil, "Defensive Teaching and Classroom Control," in Michael W. Apple and Lois Weis, eds., *Ideology and Practice in Schooling* (Philadelphia: Temple University Press, 1983), 116, 126–27; see also David Jenness, *Making Sense of Social Studies* (New York: Macmillan, 1990), 270–75; and Jim DeFrongo, "How Sociologists Can Help Prevent War" (Storrs, CT: n.d., typescript). The Vietnam War is similarly minimized in the museum aircraft carrier *Intrepid* in New York City. The museum's film and slide shows simply omit *Intrepid*'s role in that war. According to the board of retired admirals that vets the museum's interpretive programs by order of the navy, Vietnam is too "political." See James W. Loewen, *Lies Across America* (New York: New Press, 1999), 404–7.

27. Karnow, *Vietnam*, 365–76.

28. Gallup poll, November 1986; Roper poll, 8/1984.

29. See Dick Cluster, ed., *They Should Have Served That Cup of Coffee* (Boston: South End Press, 1979), 149–79; John Dumbrell and David Ryan, *Vietnam in Iraq* (Taylor & Francis, 2006); Robert Brigham, *Is Iraq Another Vietnam?* (Washington, D.C.: Public Affairs, 2006).

30. Kissinger's claim is perverse for two reasons. First, he negotiated our pullout and knows full well that all he achieved was a face-saving "decent interval" between that pullout and the final Vietnamese offensive. Second, "stay the course" for whom? He also knows that the parade of generals in charge of the South Vietnam "government" offered no meaningful leader or ideology to the Vietnamese people.

31. Kammen, *Mystic Chords of Memory*, 639.

CHAPTER 10: DOWN THE MEMORY HOLE: THE DISAPPEARANCE OF THE RECENT PAST

1. Quoted by Daniel Barenboim, "Germans, Jews, and Music," *New York Review of Books*, 3/29/2001, 50.

2. Goering, quoted by U.S. Army Capt. Gustave Gilbert in *Nuremberg Diary* (Cambridge, MA: Da Capo, 1995 [1947?]); cf. pinkfreud-ga, "Answer," 7/26/2003, at answers.google.com/answers/main?cmd=threadview&id=235519, 5/2007.

3. 1972 presidential proclamation to strengthen the Freedom of Information Act, quoted in Tim Weiner, "The Cold War Freezer Keeps Historians Out," *New York Times*, May 23, 1993.

4. John Mbiti, *African Religions and Philosophy* (Oxford: Heinemann, 1990).

5. I used the qualifier *narrative* textbooks in the previous paragraph because the examination revealed a striking difference between the two "inquiry" textbooks and narrative books. *Discovering American History* and *The American Adventure*, which consist largely of maps, illustrations, and extracts from primary sources, do not downplay the *sasha*. Indeed, their attention to the recent past reflects their authors' intention of making history relevant to current events and issues. Therefore, despite the fact that both of the books were published before the 1970s ended, they give more space to the 1960s and 1970s than do the sixteen narrative textbooks. Unfortunately, inquiry textbooks have long since gone out of favor and print; so far as I know, none remains on the market.

6. I put *2007* in quotation marks because publishers lie on their copyright page; I owned the "2007" book since early 2006, and it contains no information more recent than mid-2005.

7. Tracy Kidder, *Among Schoolchildren* (New York: Harper Perennial, 1990).

8. Gordon Levin Jr., *Woodrow Wilson and World Politics: America's Response to War and Revolution* (New York: Oxford University Press, 1968), 260. Cf. Arthur S. Link, untitled essay in J. J. Huthmacher and W. I. Susman, eds., *Wilson's Diplomacy: An International Symposium* (Cambridge: Schenkman, 1973), 9.

9. Eric Foner provides a capsule account of the changes in Reconstruction historiography in *Reconstruction* (New York: Harper & Row, 1988), xix–xxiii and 609–11.

10. Leon Festinger, *A Theory of Cognitive Dissonance* (Evanston, IL: Row, Peterson, 1957).

11. Well, I didn't interview any recent history-makers.

12. *The American Journey* went to press before the terrorists struck.

13. Warren Bass, a staff member of the 9/11 Commission, summarized bin Laden in "Incendiary," *Washington Post Book World*, 1/14/2007.

14. George W. Bush, "Address to Joint Session of Congress," 9/20/2001, whitehouse.gov/news/releases/2001/09/20010920-8.html.

15. Mitch Frank, *Understanding September 11th* (New York: Viking, 2002), 16; Mitch Frank, "Restoring the World Trade Center," *American Heritage*, 2/2005, 9.

16. Their construction did rely upon "the cooperation of men," but then so does any large-scale enterprise, including the terrorists' attack.

17. Frank, "Restoring the World Trade Center," 2/2005, 9.

18. James Fallows's *Atlantic* articles are summarized in his *Blind into Baghdad* (New York: Random House Vintage, 2006); Michael Scheuer is quoted in Jason Burke, "Will the Real al-Qaida Please Stand

Up?" *The Guardian*, 3/11/2006, books .guardian.co.uk/review/story/0,, 1726185,00.html (May 2007); Pentagon report, 11/2004, quoted in Thom Shanker, "U.S. Failing to Persuade Muslims, Panel Says," *International Herald Tribune*, 11/25/2004.

19. Diane Ravitch, Chester Finn, et al., *A Consumer's Guide to High School History Textbooks* (Washington, D.C.: Thomas B. Fordham Institute, 2004).

20. Anthony Lappé and Stephen Marshall, *True Lies* (New York: Penguin Plume, 2004), 125–26; Gerald D. McKnight, "How the Warren Commission Failed the Nation and Why," excerpted on History News Network, 11/28/05, hnn .us/articles/16615.html; John King, "Arming Iraq and the Path to War," *U.N. Observer and International Report*, 3/31/2003, unobserver.com/index.php?pagina =layout5.php&id=815&blz=1.

21. R. Scott Appleby, "History in the Fundamentalist Imagination," *Journal of American History*, 9/2002, 511.

22. Federation of American Scientists, "Nuclear Weapons," fas.org/nuke/ guide/israel/nuke/, 1/2007.

23. Gerald Posner, *Why America Slept* (New York: Random House, 2003), 121, 152, 157, 169; Lappé and Marshall, *True Lies*, 52–53.

24. Some observers think the Taliban may only have been stalling.

25. Mahmood Mamdani, "Good Muslim, Bad Muslim," in Eric Hershberg and Kevin Moore, eds., *Critical Views of September 11* (New York: New Press, 2002), 52; Seymour Hersh, *Chain of Command* (New York: Harper Perennial, 2005), 151.

26. There is a darker side to our work in Afghanistan. The CIA largely financed the war against the USSR through the drug trade, as it had its wars in Nicaragua and Southeast Asia. This prompted Afghanistan and neighboring parts of Pakistan to become the world's largest producers of heroin and opium. Following principles in the Koran, the Taliban in 2000 largely ended Afghanistan's drug production. Today, under the government we installed in 2002, the most important crop in Afghanistan is again the opium poppy. Also, the United States has imprisoned hundreds of alleged "enemy combatants" from the war in Afghanistan for years now, and may simply hold them until they die, without trial and even without letting them see family members or legal counsel. This is precisely the behavior we lament when Third World countries do it to our citizens.

27. Cheney and Bush, quoted in Staughton Lynd and Carl Mirra, "I Am a Revisionist Historian," History News Network, hnn.us/articles/22700.html 31306.

28. Colin Brown and Andy McSmith, "Diplomat's Suppressed Document Lays Bare the Lies Behind Iraq War," *The Independent*, 12/15/2006, news.independent .co.uk/uk/politics/article2076137.

29. Carl M. Cannon, "Untruth and Consequences," *Atlantic*, 1/2007 the atlantic.com/doc/200701/cannon-lying, 1/2007; Eric Alterman, "Liar, 'Liar,'" *Nation*, 12/11/2006, 9.

30. Lappé and Marshall, *True Lies*, 146.

31. David E. Sanger, "Bush Aide Says US, Not UN, Will Rebuild Iraq," *New York Times*, 4/5/2003; "Houston: We Have a Problem," CorpWatch, 2004, corp watch.org/article.php?id=11322,2/2007; Frances Fox Piven, *The War at Home* (New York: New Press, 2006), 17–18.

32. Lappé and Marshall, *True Lies*, 120; cf. Linda McQuaig, "Iraq's Oil," ZNet 9/27/2004, at netscape.com/

viewstory/2006/10/21/iraqs-oil, 10/2006.

33. "Western Companies May Get 75% of Iraqi Oil Profits," Dow Jones Newswires, 1/8/2007, Market Watch website, marketwatch.com/news/story/western-companies–may-get-75/story.

34. Michael Billig, *Banal Nationalism* (London: Sage, 1995), 1.

35. See The Memory Hole, thememoryhole.org/war/no-saddam-qaeda.htm 2/2007, for transcript of 1/31/2003 press conference, and Think Progress, thinkprogress.org/2006/08/21/bush-on-911/, 2/2007, for video of Bush saying "nothing" in response to question asking what evidence linked September 11 and Iraq. Later the 9/11 Commission found "no evidence of an operational link between Iraq and Al Qaeda," according to Seymour Hersh, *Chain of Command* (New York: Harper Perennial, 2005), 210–11. See also Lynd and Mirra, "I Am a Revisionist Historian."

36. Amy Gerkshoff and Shana Kushner, "Shaping Public Opinion: The 9/11–Iraq Connection in the Bush Administration's Rhetoric," *Perspectives on Politics* 3 no. 3 (9/2005), 525.

37. Fallows, *Blind Into Baghdad*, 155–63; cf. Thomas E. Ricks, *Fiasco* (New York: Penguin, 2006), and Nancy Trejos and K. I. Ibrahim, "A Call to Hussein-Era Soldiers," *Washington Post*, 12/17/2006.

38. Fallows, *Blind Into Baghdad*, 146; Bush quoted, 167.

39. National Security Archive Electronic Briefing Book No. 207, gwu.edu/~nsarchiv/NSAEBB/NSAEBB207/index.htm, 12/2007; Ivan Eland, "Does U.S. Intervention Overseas Breed Terrorism? The Historical Record" (Washington, D.C.: Cato Institute, 1998); Walter Pincus, "Before War, CIA Warned of Negative Outcomes," *Washington Post*, 6/3/2007.

CHAPTER 11:
PROGRESS IS OUR MOST
IMPORTANT PRODUCT

1. Senator Albert J. Beveridge, speech in the U.S. Senate, January 9, 1900, *Congressional Record, 56th Congress* 33 (Washington, D.C.: U.S. Government Printing Office, 1900).

2. Frances FitzGerald, *Fire in the Lake* (Boston: Atlantic-Little, Brown, 1972), 8.

3. E. J. Mishan, *The Economic Growth Debate* (London: George Allen and Unwin, 1977), 12.

4. Vine Deloria Jr., *God Is Red* (New York: Dell, 1983 [1973]), 290.

5. Two new textbooks, *Pathways to the Present* and Boorstin and Kelley, end not with a bang but a whimper—the same whimper:

In May 2003, Bush signed another tax cut into law, this one for $350 billion. The President insisted that this "bold package of tax relief" would add a million jobs in the first year and boost the stock market. Critics charged that the tax cuts would create huge budget deficits far into the future.

—*Pathways*

However, in May 2003 Bush signed another tax cut into law, this one for $350 billion. The President insisted that the bold package of tax relief would add jobs and boost the stock market. Critics charged that the tax cuts might create huge deficits for many years into the future.

—Boorstin and Kelley

Chapter 12 explains how neither of these passages was written by the listed authors, but by a clerk or freelancer hired by the publisher. Apparently this person, entrusted with ending both books, was not paid enough to produce a real ending, so the chapter simply stops after this last detail.

6. Thomas Jefferson quoted in Robert Nisbet, *History of the Idea of Progress* (New York: Basic Books, 1980), 198.

7. Jules Henry, *Culture Against Man* (New York: Random House, 1963), 16–17. Crawford Young quotes Indian leader Jawaharlal Nehru and sociologist Orlando Patterson, pointing out that Third World countries also bought into progress. See "Ideas of Progress in the Third World," in Gabriel Almond et al., eds., *Progress and Its Discontents* (Berkeley and Los Angeles: University of California Press, 1982), 83.

8. According to the Advertising Council's citizenship manual, *Good Citizen*, quoted in Stuart Little, "The Freedom Train" (Bloomington: Indiana University, c. 1990, typescript), 11.

9. Edward H. Carr, *What Is History?* (New York: Random House, 1961), 158, 166; see also Almond et al., eds., *Progress and Its Discontents*, xi. Some Americans have a contrary need to believe our society has been, on balance, a curse to humankind. Such thinking has alternative psychological and cultural payoffs, allowing believers to imagine themselves wiser, "lefter," or more critical than their peers.

10. Carr, *What Is History?*, 116; L. S. Stavrianos, *Global Rift* (New York: Morrow, 1981), 38. In *Why Are They Lying to Our Children?* (New York: Stein and Day, 1984), 124, Herbert London argues that the gap between rich and poor nations is not widening. See also: Cliff DuRand, "Mexico-U.S. Migration: We Fly, They Walk," talk at Morgan State University,

11/16/2005, at World Prout Assembly website, worldproutassembly.org/archives/2006/01/mexicous_migrat.html, 11/2006; Giovanni Arrighi, "The African Crisis," *New Left Review* 15, 5/2002, newleftreview.org/?page=article&view=2387, 11/2006.

11. Mishan, *The Economic Growth Debate*, 116.

12. Almond et al., eds., *Progress and Its Discontents*, xi.

13. The Reagan and Bush administrations still maintained through the 1980s that there was no population crisis, even in the Third World, because larger populations created more opportunity for capitalist development. These statements were intended to appeal to antiabortion groups at home, however, not as serious analyses of the social structures of disadvantaged nations, whose leaders ridiculed the American position.

14. Donella H. Meadows, "A Look at the Future," in Robin Clarke, ed., *Notes for the Future* (New York: Universe Books, 1976), 63; Donella H. Meadows, correspondence, 11/15/1993.

15. General Social Survey, "If you were to consider your life in general these days, how happy or unhappy would you say you are, on the whole. . . . " webapp .icpsr.umich.edu/GSS/, 11/2006.

16. Donella H. Meadows et al., *The Limits to Growth* (New York: Universe Books, 1972, 2d ed., 1974).

17. Robert L. Heilbroner, *An Inquiry into the Human Prospect* (New York: Norton, 1974), 13.

18. Nisbet, *History of the Idea of Progress*, 8.

19. Oswald Spengler, *The Decline of the West* (New York: Modern Library, 1965).

20. Colin Turnbull, *The Human Cycle* (New York: Simon & Schuster, 1983), 21.

21. Stephen Jay Gould, *Hen's Teeth and Horse's Toes* (New York: Norton, 1983).

22. Oil imports in 1980 were 63 percent greater than in 1973, according to the *Statistical Abstract of the United States: 1993* (Washington, D.C.: Bureau of the Census, 1993).

23. Mike Feinsilber and William B. Mead, *American Averages* (Garden City, NY: Doubleday, 1980), 277; see also Matthew Wald, "After 20 Years, America's Foot Is Still on the Gas," *New York Times*, 10/17/1993.

24. Mishan, *The Economic Growth Debate*, 53. See also Warren Johnson, *The Future Is Not What It Used to Be* (New York: Dodd, Mead, 1985), 22–24.

25. See Garrett Hardin, "The Tragedy of the Commons," *Science* 162 (1968): 1243–48; and Garrett Hardin and John Baden, eds., *Managing the Commons* (San Francisco: W. H. Freeman, 1977).

26. B. D. Ayres Jr., "Hard Times for Chesapeake's Oyster Harvest," *New York Times*, October 15, 1993; David E. Pitt, "U.N. Talks Combat Threat to Fishery," *New York Times*, 7/25/1993; Pitt, "Despite Gaps, Data Leave Little Doubt That Fish Are in Peril," *New York Times*, August 3, 1993; Elizabeth Weise, "90% of the Ocean's Edible Species May Be Gone By 2048, Study Finds," *USA Today*, 11/3/2006; Juliet Eilperin, "U.S. Attempting to Reshape Fishing Rules," *Washington Post*, October 8, 2006; Chesapeake Research Consortium. "Managed Fisheries of the Chesapeake Bay," chesapeake.org/FEP-ManagedFisheries.pdf, 11/2006.

27. Noel Perrin, "Who Needs the World When You Have Cable?" *New York Times Book Review*, April 26, 1992.

28. Natural History Museum: "Seeds of Change" (exhibit, Smithsonian Institution, Washington, D.C., 1992); Richard A. Falk, *This Endangered Planet* (New York: Random House, 1971), 139; Jared Diamond, talk at Politics and Prose (Washington, D.C.) 1/18/2006.

29. See Barry Weisberg, *Beyond Repair* (Boston: Beacon, 1971), 9.

30. "Sperm Counts Drop Over 50 Years," *Facts on File* 52, no. 2706 (10/1/1992): 743(1); Michael Castleman, "The Sperm Crisis," *Mother Earth News*, no. 83 (9/1983): 176–77. The best guess as to the cause of the sperm-count drop may be disposable diapers that are too tight and overheat the testicles. See, inter alia, Andrea Braslavsky, "Could Disposable Diapers Lead to Infertility?" at AT&T Worldnet, dailynews.att.net, 9/28/2000. That's a relief!

31. Joel Achenbach, "The Tempest," *Washington Post Magazine*, 5/28/2006, 24.

32. Heilbroner, *An Inquiry into the Human Prospect*, 133.

33. David Donald, quoted by Paul Gagnon, "Why Study History?" *Atlantic*, 11/1988, 46.

34. Edward O. Wilson, "Is Humanity Suicidal?" *New York Times Magazine*, 5/30/1993, 24–29.

35. Clyde Haberman, "South Korea Goes from Wasteland to Woodland," *New York Times*, 7/7/1985, 6E.

36. London, *Why Are They Lying to Our Children?* 53. London must not have read the endings of American history textbooks!

37. John Tierney, "Betting the Planet," *New York Times Magazine*, 12/2/1990, 52–53, 75–81.

38. Jane Newitt makes this point in *The Treatment of Limits-to-Growth Issues in U.S. High School Textbooks* (Croton-on-Hudson, NY: Hudson Institute, 1982), 13. She also criticized textbooks for bias in favor of the limits-to-growth side of the debate, which I cannot confirm; the text-

books I examined do not really treat environmental issues as a serious matter.

39. Faye Rice, "Who Scores Best on the Environment?" *Fortune* (7/26/1993): 122. See also Debra Chasnoff's film on General Electric, *Deadly Deception* (Boston: Infact, 1990). General Electric's newer corporate mantra is "We Bring Good Things to Life."

40. Mike Tidwell, talk at Politics and Prose (Washington, D.C.): 8/30/2006; Bill McKibben, "How Close to Catastrophe?" *New York Review of Books,* 11/16/2006.

41. Juliet Eilperin, "Growing Acidity of Oceans May Kill Corals," *Washington Post,* 7/5/2006.

42. "The Red List," iucnredlist.org, as reported by Sam Cage, "16,000 Species Said to Face Extinction" Associated Press, 05/01/2006, cnn.netscape.cnn .com/news/story.jsp; Jeremy Rifkin, "The Risks of Too Much City," *Washington Post,* 12/17/2006; William Burr and Jeffrey Kimball, eds., "Nixon White House Considered Nuclear Options Against North Vietnam, Declassified Documents Reveal," National Security Archive Electronic Briefing Book No. 195, gwu.edu/~nsarchiv/NSAEBB/NSAEBB195/index .htm (7/31/2006).

43. Mishan, *The Economic Growth Debate,* Ch. 8.

44. On the Mayans, see Allen Chen, "Unraveling Another Mayan Mystery," *Discover,* 6/1987, 40–49; for the Canaries, see Alfred W. Crosby Jr., *Ecological Imperialism* (New York: Cambridge University Press, 1986), 80, 94–97.

45. Alfred W. Crosby Jr., "Demographics and Ecology," 1990, typescript, citing Las Casas; John Varner and Jeanette Varner, *Dogs of the Conquest* (Norman: University of Oklahoma Press, 1983), 19–20; Spanish letter quoted in Kirkpatrick

Sale, *The Conquest of Paradise* (New York: Alfred A. Knopf, 1990), 165.

46. Gregg Easterbrook, reply to letters about his "Some Convenient Truths," *Atlantic Monthly,* 11/2006, 21; Gretel Ehrlich, "Last Days of the Ice Hunters?" *National Geographic,* 1/2006, 80, 84; Eugene Linden, "Why You Can't Ignore the Changing Climate," *Parade,* 6/25/2006, 4.

47. *The Americans* includes a two-page section, "The Conservation Controversy," buried on pages 1122–23 in the midst of a two-page treatment of a mishmash of topics *after* the last chapter of the book. It seems fair to predict that no student will ever reach this section.

48. Lerone Bennett, *Black Power U.S.A.* (Baltimore: Penguin, 1969), 345–46.

49. But see Jonathan Kozol, *Savage Inequalities* (New York: Crown, 1991), 3.

50. Peter Farb, *Man's Rise to Civilization* (New York: Avon, 1969), 49–50.

51. Verrazano quoted in Neal Salisbury, *Manitou and Providence* (New York: Oxford University Press, 1982), 26.

52. Quoted in Russell Thornton, *American Indian Holocaust and Survival* (Norman: University of Oklahoma Press, 1987), 39.

53. Karen Ordahl Kupperman, *Settling with the Indians* (London: J. M. Dent, 1980), 58.

54. Psalm 90, verse 10. See also S. Boyd Eaton et al., *The Paleolithic Prescription* (New York: Harper and Row, 1988); and Marshall Sahlins, *Stone Age Economics* (Chicago: Aldine and Atherton, 1972).

There are statistical issues here, one being that average life expectancy at birth can be quite low if 40 percent of all newborns die in their first year, so a better measure is life expectancy at age one or age ten. Measuring life expectancy before European and African diseases is also not easy when those diseases accompanied and even antedated first contact. On the other hand, information from archaeology summarized by Jared Diamond in "The Worst Mistake in the History of the Human Race," *Discover*, 5/1987, 64–66, suggests the early European settlers quoted above may have been too optimistic in their assessments of Indian longevity.

55. William A. Haviland, "Cleansing Young Minds, or What Should We Be Doing in the Introductory Course to Anthropology?" (paper presented at the annual meeting of the American Anthropology Association, New Orleans, 1990), 3.

56. Special instruments were developed for the operation, and the whole thing was done not only against the forces of nature but also uphill, against the force of gravity. We might contrast Las Casas's description of birthing on Haiti before the arrival of Europeans: "Pregnant women work to the last minute and give birth almost painlessly; up the next day, they bathe in the river and are as clean and healthy as before giving birth." (*History of the Indies* [New York: Harper and Row, 1971], 64).

57. "Harper's Index," *Harper's*, 2/1993, 15, citing Ross Labs. Many hospitals still separate mothers and infants except for feeding time, even though scientific studies—which seem to be the only point of leverage for changing birthing practices—show that randomly selected neonatals raised with more parental contact have higher IQs. See Feinsilber and Mead, *American Averages*, 227–28.

58. Philip D. Curtin, *The Rise and Fall of the Plantation Complex* (Cambridge: Cambridge University Press, 1990), esp. 35, gives an interesting analysis of the rise of the nation-state as a necessary response to the military might of neighboring nation-

states. Curtin argues that in other ways nation-states were not necessarily advantageous for their citizens. If the need to control nuclear weapons leads to an era of relative peace in the next century, that may remove a primary reason for the power of the nation-state.

59. Ruth Bond, "In the Ozone, a Child Shall Lead Them," *New York Times*, 1/10,/1993.

60. Daniel Evan Weiss, *The Great Divide* (New York: Poseidon, 1991), 136.

61. National Association of Secretaries of State New Millennium Survey, 1999, stateofthevote.org/New%20Mill%20Survey%20Update.pdf, 12/2006.

62. See Catherine Cornbleth, Geneva Gay, and K. G. Dueck, "Pluralism and Unity," in Howard Mehlinger and O. L. Davis, eds., *The Social Studies* (Chicago: University of Chicago Press/NSSE Yearbook, 1981), 174.

63. E. J. Mishan, *Pornography, Psychedelics, and Technology* (London: George Allen and Unwin, 1980), 25, 150–51. See also Jonathan Kozol, *The Night Is Dark and I Am Far from Home* (Boston: Houghton Mifflin, 1975), 40.

CHAPTER 12: WHY IS HISTORY TAUGHT LIKE THIS?

1. Herbert Butterfield, quoted in Stephen Vaughn, ed., *The Vital Past* (Athens: University of Georgia Press, 1985), 222.

2. Marc Ferro, *The Use and Abuse of History* (Boston: Routledge and Kegan Paul, 1981), 225.

3. Quoted in Joan DelFattore, *What Johnny Shouldn't Read* (New Haven: Yale University Press, 1992), 120.

4. Brooks Mather Kelley, interview, 7/2006.

5. Textbook editor, interview, 7/2006.

6. *The American Adventure* has fewer than

one note per chapter. *Discovering American History* has no footnotes but does furnish marginal notes giving sources for its longer quotations.

7. Robert Moore, *Stereotypes, Distortions and Omissions in U.S. History Textbooks* (New York: Council on Interracial Books for Children, 1977); Frances FitzGerald, *America Revised* (New York: Vintage, 1980); Gerald Horne, ed., *Thinking and Rethinking U.S. History* (New York: Council on Interracial Books for Children, 1988); Diane Ravitch and Chester E. Finn Jr., *What Do Our 17-Year-Olds Know?* (New York: Harper and Row, 1987), which did not single out textbooks but had harsh words for what students don't know about history; Harriet Tyson-Bernstein, *A Conspiracy of Good Intentions: American's Textbook Fiasco* (Washington, D.C.: Council for Basic Education, 1988); Paul Gagnon, *Democracy's Half-Told Story* (New York: American Federation of Teachers, 1989); Chester E. Finn Jr. and Diane Ravitch, *The Mad, Mad World of Textbook Adoption* (Washington D.C.: Thomas B. Fordham Institute, 2004). Other critics have lambasted U.S. history textbooks from specialized viewpoints; for instance, the *1982–83 Michigan Social Studies Textbook Report* (Lansing: Michigan State Board of Education, 1984) found seven textbooks deficient in their treatment of Canadian-U.S. relations.

On the other hand, O. L. Davis Jr., et al., reviewed fifteen junior high and sixteen high school history textbooks in *Looking at History* (Washington, D.C.: People for the American Way, 1986). "Most of the thirty-one texts were good," they concluded; "some were excellent." Nathan Glazer and Reed Ueda's brief examination of six textbooks, *Ethnic Groups in History Textbooks* (Washington, D.C.: Ethics and Public Policy Center, 1983), offers a mixed evaluation of praise and blame. So does Gilbert Sewall's study of eleven textbooks, four on the high school level, *American History Textbooks: An Assessment of Quality* (New York: Columbia University Teachers College, 1987).

8. Quoted in Bessie L. Pierce, *Public Opinion and the Teaching of History in the United States* (New York: Alfred A. Knopf, 1926), 329–30.

9. Shirley Engle and Anna Ochoa, "A Curriculum for Democratic Citizenship," *Social Education* (11/1986): 515.

10. Peter Novick, *That Noble Dream* (Cambridge: Cambridge University Press, 1988), 172–73.

11. Arthur Schlesinger Jr., *The Age of Jackson* (Boston: Little, Brown, 1945); James O'Brien, personal communication, 11/12/1993.

12. Teacher-training programs now often assign *Lies My Teacher Told Me*; partly as a result of the ensuing discussions, American history in high schools is beginning to be better taught.

13. Ferro, *The Use and Abuse of History*, 225.

14. George Orwell, *1984* (New York: Harcourt, Brace, 1949), 35.

15. William L. Griffen and John Marciano, *Teaching the Vietnam War* (Montclair, NJ: Allanheld, Osmun, 1979), 163–72.

16. These writers include Michael Apple, Stanley Aronowitz, Kathleen Bennett, Samuel Bowles, Martin Carnoy, Herbert Gintis, Henry Giroux, Margaret LeCompte, Caroline Persell, Joel Spring, Kathleen Weiler, and many others.

17. Jonathan Kozol, *The Night Is Dark and I Am Far from Home* (New York: Simon & Schuster, 1990 [1975]), 99.

18. *The Politics of Education* (South Hadley, MA: Bergin and Garvey, 1985), 102.

19. Henry Giroux, *Ideology, Culture, and the Process of Schooling* (Philadelphia: Temple University Press, 1981), 47. Like some other critical theorists, Giroux goes on to specifically disclaim intentionality: "This is not meant to imply a conscious conspiracy on the part of an 'invisible' ruling elite." Except for the accurate but vague claim that the upper class sets the rhetoric of the age, which trickles down to influence how we all think about the past, these theorists never quite specify how the upper class influences what gets taught in a rural classroom in American history, for example. In the pages that follow, I suggest more specific forces that may be at work.

20. David Tyack and Elisabeth Hansot, "Conflict and Consensus in American Public Education," *Daedalus* 110, no. 2 (Summer 1981): 1, 12.

21. Henry M. Levin, "Educational Reform: Its Meaning?" in Martin Carnoy and Henry M. Levin, *The Limits of Educational Reform* (New York: McKay, 1976), 24.

22. Walter Karp, "Why Johnny Can't Think," *Harper's*, 6/1985, 73.

23. Among many sources on the power elite, see C. Wright Mills, *The Power Elite* (New York: Oxford University Press, 1956); Beth Mintz and Michael Schwartz, *The Power Structure of American Business* (Chicago: University of Chicago Press, 1985); G. William Domhoff, *Who Rules America Now?* (New York: Simon & Schuster, 1986); and Laurie David, "Science à la Joe Camel," *Washington Post*, 11/26/2006.

24. Robert Heilbroner, "Who's Running This Show?" *New York Review of Books*, 1/4/1968, 18–21.

25. E.D.C. Campbell Jr., ed., *Before Freedom Came* (Richmond, VA: Museum of the Confederacy, 1991).

26. I use *subversive* in the sense of Neil Postman and Charles Weingartner, *Teaching as a Subversive Activity* (New York: Delacorte, 1969). Conspiratorial Marxists might claim that the rich, having denied a thoughtful presentation of American history to most Americans, want it for their own children. More sophisticated Marxists know that false consciousness, of which false history is a key ingredient, is equally important for those who run society: upper-class children, no less than sons and daughters of the working class, need to believe that our society is just and progressive. More likely explanations for the mildly subversive history teaching in prep schools may be that most prep school teachers graduated from prep schools and elite private colleges and are simply replicating the teaching style they experienced. Also, prep schools are more likely to hire history majors rather than education majors, resulting in teachers who are better prepared and feel more comfortable exploring issues in history with their students. Moreover, the smaller size of prep school classes—sometimes as few as five to ten pupils—facilitates individual research on issues and projects, while public high school classes range from twenty-five to forty students, according to Karp, "Why Johnny Can't Think," 70, 72, citing Ernest L. Boyer's *High School*.

27. Lee H. Ehman, "The American School in the Political Socialization Process," *Review of Educational Research* 50, no. 1 (Spring 1980): 99–119. In the first edition of *Lies*, I pointed out that voting is the one form of citizenship that the textbooks pushed, yet voting in America was down, especially among recent high school graduates, and I suggested that the sanctimonious tinge that social studies and history courses give to citizenship may help explain why. Recently, voting by young people (aged eighteen to twenty-

four) rose from fewer than 17 percent in 1986 to 24 percent (aged eighteen to twenty-nine) in 2006. Although more than three-fourths still do *not* vote, the increase is heartening. I don't hold the modest improvements in history textbooks responsible for it.

28. Roger Farr and Michael A. Tulley offer an overview of adoption procedures in "Do Adoption Committees Perpetuate Mediocre Textbooks?" *Phi Delta Kappan*, March 1985, 467–71. California adopts statewide only for grades 1–8. However, it has statewide guidelines for texts in the higher grades. Gilbert Sewall, *Social Studies Review*, no. 5 (Summer 1990): 2, says California controls 11 percent of the $1.7 billion textbook market. (In an earlier copy of this newsletter, no. 1:4, Sewall sets a lower figure, 10.2 percent, for California, but says the top four adoption states—California, Texas, Florida, and North Carolina—together make up more than a fourth of the market and exert "enormous leverage" on publishers.) Michael W. Kirst, *Who Controls Our Schools?* (New York: Freeman, 1984), 115–20, describes California adoption and its and Texas's influence on national texts. See also Michael W. Apple, "The Culture and Commerce of the Textbook," in Michael W. Apple and Linda K. Christian-Smith, eds., *The Politics of the Textbook* (New York: Routledge, 1991), Ch. 2.

29. For fuller treatments, see J. Dan Marshall, "With a Little Help from Some Friends: Publishers, Protesters, and Texas Textbook Decisions," in Apple and Christian-Smith, eds., *The Politics of the Textbook*, Ch. 4; Joan DelFattore, *What Johnny Shouldn't Read*; and Michael W. Apple, "The Political Economy of Text Publishing," *Educational Theory* 34, no. 4 (Fall 1984): 307–19.

30. In 1994 I wrote *two dozen*, but

publisher consolidation has narrowed the options.

31. Farr and Tulley, "Do Adoption Committees Perpetuate Mediocre Textbooks?" 470; Marshall, "With a Little Help from Some Friends," 62; Harriet Tyson-Bernstein, "Remarks to the AERA Textbook SIG" (San Francisco, March 1989), 10; Harriet Tyson-Bernstein and Arthur Woodward, "Nineteenth Century Policies for Twenty-first Century Practice," in Philip Altbach et al., eds., *Textbooks in American Society* (Albany: State University of New York Press, 1991), 94–97; interviews with publishing executives; AP-USHIST discussion list (ap-ushist@lyrics.collegeboard.com), 12/2006.

32. Tyson-Bernstein, "Remarks to the AERA Textbook SIG," 5.

33. Lynne Cheney, *Tyrannical Machines* (Washington, D.C.: National Endowment for the Humanities, 1990), 12.

34. Okay, it's a joke, but recall the right answer from Ch. 4: November, *1811*, at Tippecanoe.

35. Thomas A. Bailey, *The American Pageant Revisited: Recollections of a Stanford Historian* (Stanford, CA: Hoover Institution Press, 1982), 192.

36. Quoted in Pierce, *Public Opinion and the Teaching of History in the United States*, 39.

37. Marshall, "With a Little Help from Some Friends," 66.

38. Perhaps someone somewhere has produced an unusual textbook for general American history. The closest I know is Howard Zinn's *People's History of the United States* (New York: Harper and Row, 1980), sometimes called an *anti-textbook*. For other suggestions, see notes to the Afterword.

39. Ironically, the closest things to "niche" books publishers now produce are the separate editions of their textbook

packages that some still put out *for* Texas to accommodate its highly politicized adoption pressures. *Loewen v. Turnipseed* offers a precedent that might help minority plaintiffs open markets in big-city school districts under majority control, if alternative textbooks existed. The power of Texas is parallel to "The Myth of the Southern Box Office," described by Thomas R. Cripps in J. C. Curtis and L. J. Gould, eds., *The Black Experience in America* (Austin: University of Texas Press, 1970), 116–44. For decades Hollywood producers were afraid to offend Southern movie-theater owners, who, they thought, controlled one-third of the market. However, in recent years the situation in Texas has improved, as told in the Afterword.

40. Robert Darnton, "The Good Old Days," *New York Review of Books*, 5/16/1991, 47.

41. Hillel Black, *The American Schoolbook* (New York: Morrow, 1967), 49–52.

42. *Genocide* may be too harsh a term. The Spanish, who profited from Indian labor on Haiti, didn't want to wipe out the Arawaks. Many Indians died from diseases that the Spanish introduced unknowingly, like malaria, and from famine resulting from Spanish disruption of Indian gardening practices. Disease and forced famine have been factors in other genocides, however. In "Deconstructing the Columbus Myth," in John Yewell et al., eds., *Confronting Columbus* (Jefferson, NC: McFarland, 1992), 149–58, Ward Churchill argues that Europeans' treatment of Indians can be compared with the Nazi Holocaust against Jews and Gypsies. Working slaves to their deaths was typical at Auschwitz and in the gold mines in Haiti.

43. Barbara Gamarekian, "Grants Rejected; Scholars Grumble," *New York Times*, April 10, 1991; Karen J. Winkler, "Humanities Agency Caught in Controversy Over Columbus Grants," *Chronicle of Higher Education*, 3/13/1991, A8.

44. Robert Reinhold, "Class Struggle," *New York Times Magazine*, 9/29/1991, 26–29ff.

45. Robert Bernstein, conversation, 1973.

46. Black, *The American Schoolbook*, 39.

47. Harriet Tyson-Bernstein, "The Academy's Contribution to the Impoverishment of America's Textbooks," *Phi Delta Kappan* 70, no. 3 (11/1988): 197; Scriptor Pseudonymous, "The Ghost Behind the Classroom Door," *Today's Education*, 4/1978, 41–45, an account by a person who has never taught a class or earned a history degree, yet writes textbooks and ancillary material in history and many other subjects; interview, McGraw-Hill editor, 7/2006.

48. Brooks Mather Kelley, interview, 7/2006; cf. Diana Schemo, "Schoolbooks Are Given F's In Originality," *New York Times*, 7/13/2006.

49. Allan M. Winkler, interview, 7/2006.

50. Judith Conaway, interview, 7/2006; textbook editor, interview, 7/2006; Paul Boyer, brief interview, 7/2006; Schemo, "Schoolbooks Are Given F's In Originality"; James Goodman, "The Mystery of the Echoing Textbooks," *New York Times*, 7/7/2006. Ironically, Boyer's comparison is inapt: textbooks *are* the same as *The Iliad* or *Beowulf* in that no one knows for sure who wrote them.

51. M. P., "Texas Schoolbook Massacre: 5200 Errors Found in 10 History Books," *Publishers Weekly*, 3/2/1992, 11. Not all 5,200 were errors, and many errors were trivial or arguable.

52. As well, *Pageant*'s vote totals were wrong. According to CNN, Bush got 62,040,000 votes, Kerry 59,028,000.

53. Some observers do think Libya simply paid up to end the episode and resume normal relations with Western nations, but this is a minority position, and I doubt that Boorstin and Kelley meant to take it. Cf., "Pan Am Flight 103," Wikipedia, en.wikipedia.org/wiki/Pan_Am_Flight_103, 10/2006.

54. Momentarily, I concluded that the hireling deep in the bowels of Holt who proposed this preposterous project had heard of but never seen Benét's epic poem and imagined it to be a page long, like many other poems. But no, the title is italicized, not quoted, as befits a book-length poem, not a shorter one.

55. Interviews, 12/1987. Gilbert Sewall, "Social Studies Textbooks: A View from the Publishers," *Social Studies Review,* no. 5 (Summer 1990): 14, takes a darker view of publisher influence: "Schoolbook authors have little or no control over their product." Frances FitzGerald suggests I am wrong to believe the textbooks' authors; certainly the authors might be ashamed to confess to editorial interference if they had succumbed to it. Later in his interview with me, one textbook author detailed several editorial suggestions, contradicting his earlier statement. We can conclude, however, that these authors unquestionably judged their relationship with their publishers harmonious.

56. John Garraty, interview, 11/1987. Garraty, *1001 Things Everyone Should Know About American History* (New York: Doubleday, 1989), 3.

57. James Davidson and Mark Lytle, *After the Fact* (New York: McGraw-Hill, 1992), 106–11. *A History of the Republic* does mention one incident, smallpox in Mexico City, in sentence fragments so tiny that the mention does not even get into the index.

58. Tyson-Bernstein, "The Academy's Contribution to the Impoverishment of America's Textbooks," 194, and "Remarks to the AERA Textbook SIG," 9; Thomas Bailey, senior writer of one of the textbooks in my sample, wrote that a successful book, which *The American Pageant* surely has been, "would actually hurt me with some of my peers" (*The American Pageant Revisited*, 180). My home institution, the University of Vermont, separates "scholarship" from what it calls "pedagogical works" and discounts the latter. See Black, *The American Schoolbook*, 39; Sewall, "Social Studies Textbooks: A View from the Publishers," 14; and Matthew Downey, "Speaking of Textbooks," in David Elliott and Arthur Woodward, eds., *Textbooks and Schooling in the United States* (Chicago: University of Chicago Press NSSE Yearbook, 1981).

59. The *American Historical Review,* the principal journal of the American Historical Association; *Social Education,* the principal journal of the National Council for the Social Studies; and *Reviews in American History* do not review high school textbooks. In what it considers a major innovation, *The Journal of American History* recently began to review *college* textbooks. Most other history journals have no policy about reviewing textbooks, but I could locate only one review of any of the twelve books here studied, in *The History Teacher.*

60. Many authors do not get much credit for writing textbooks even from their own publishers. In Scott, Foresman's advertisements for *Land of Promise,* one cannot make out the authors' names without a magnifying glass. Prentice Hall's ads for *The United States—A History of the Republic* never mention the authors at all. Sometimes authors' names are not even listed on the book covers. For authors who didn't write "their" textbooks, this lack of credit or blame is perfectly fair.

61. Mark Lytle interview, 11/1993.

62. Michael Kammen, *Mystic Chords of Memory* (New York: Alfred A. Knopf, 1991), 258–59; Bailey, *The American Pageant Revisited*, 192–95.

63. Pierce, *Public Opinion and the Teaching of History in the United States*, 6, 10–11, and 56–62.

64. The two inquiry texts take a different tack. *Discovering American History* offers a collage of old photographs. While clearly celebrating our past, with prominent images of Abraham Lincoln and other great leaders, its arrangement also suggests that photographs can be materials of history and thus implies an inquiry approach. *The American Adventure* goes partway, showing black-and-white photographs of Lincoln, Indian houses, and other buildings and faces. However, a graphic designer merely arranged them to look good and surrounded them with the red, white, and blue.

65. What's wrong with that, some might ask. The next chapter, which describes the effects on students of this kind of history, suggests one answer.

66. See Vaughn, ed., *The Vital Past*, 46, 241.

67. Carol Berkin, interview, 10/1987.

68. Edward Pessen, *The Log Cabin Myth* (New Haven: Yale University Press, 1984), claims that Lincoln's family was at least as prosperous as his neighbors when he was growing up.

69. Kenneth Wong and Tom Loveless, "The Politics of Textbooks Policy," in Altbach, *Textbooks in American Society*, 33–34. Mary Haas, a teacher educator, also told me, "We have been given the kinds of textbooks that teachers want."

70. Charlotte Crabtree and David O'Shea, "Teachers' Academic Preparation in History," National Center for History in the Schools *Newsletter* I, no. 3 (11/1991): 4, 10.

71. Reported in Black, *The American Schoolbook*, 91–95. See also Jack L. Nelson and William B. Stanley, "Academic Freedom: Fifty Years Standing Still," *Social Education* 49 (1985): 663.

72. Shirley Engle, "Late Night Thoughts About the New Social Studies," *Social Education* 50, no. 1 (1/1986): 20–22. John Goodlad agrees in "A Study of Schooling," *Phi Delta Kappan*, March 1983, reprinted in James W. Noll, ed., *Taking Sides: Clashing Views on Controversial Educational Issues* (Guilford, CT: Dushkin, 1989), 145.

73. Seymour B. Sarason, *The Culture of the School and the Problem of Change* (Boston: Allyn and Bacon, 1971), 180–87.

74. Linda McNeil, "Defensive Teaching and Classroom Control," in Michael W. Apple and Lois Weis, eds., *Ideology and Practice in Schooling* (Philadelphia: Temple University Press, 1983), 116.

75. Goodlad, "A Study of Schooling," 145–47.

76. McNeil, "Defensive Teaching and Classroom Control," 115–16. High school teachers have some reason to fear conflict and loss of control. Within any classroom, teachers do have to establish authority. How can they then question authority? Students in conflict—with their teacher, each other, or their textbook—can seem out of control. Appearances may deceive, however: norms of conduct do govern most student behavior, even when that behavior looks chaotic to nonstudents. Thus, teachers usually have more control in classrooms than they realize. Nonetheless, classes *can* go out of control, and it is understandable that teachers want to manage their situations.

77. Albert Shanker, "The Efficient

Diploma Mill," advertisement in *New York Times*, 2/14/1988.

78. Admonitions from 1893 and 1934 quoted by David Jenness, *Making Sense of Social Studies* (New York: Macmillan, 1990), 262. See also Gagnon, *Democracy's Half-Told Story*, 17–19.

79. Paul Goldstein, *Changing the American Schoolbook* (Lexington, MA: D. C. Heath, 1978). In history, the proportion is even higher. See Kirst, *Who Controls Our Schools?* 115. J. Y. Cole and T. G. Sticht, eds., *The Textbook in American Society* (Washington, D.C.: Library of Congress, 1981), 9, hold that textbooks and similar instructional material structure 95 percent to 100 percent of classroom instruction and 90 percent of homework time. Matthew Downey and Linda Levstik question the conventional wisdom that textbooks dominate history instruction, however, holding that little reading of *any* kind takes place. See "Teaching and Learning History: The Research Base," *Social Education* 52, no. 9 (September 1988): 336–41, esp. 337. This pessimistic finding offers only ironic encouragement, however, and does not square with information from my students, most of whom report that their high school history classes spent much time doing the same things that mine did, like answering the boring exercises at the ends of each chapter.

80. Tyson-Bernstein, "Remarks to the AERA Textbook SIG," 10. Her assessment may be too harsh: in my experience teachers are anxious not to spread outright misinformation. Most teachers work hard to learn and pass on correct information, but then, these are the teachers who attend workshops, not a random sample.

81. Tracy Kidder, *Among Schoolchildren* (Boston: Houghton Mifflin, 1989), evokes the nearly impossible job teachers do. See also John Goodlad, *A Place Called School* (New York: McGraw-Hill, 1983).

82. Mark Schug, "Why Teach Social Studies?" *The Social Studies* 80, no. 2 (3/1989): 74. His sample was unfortunately only twenty-nine teachers.

83. Crabtree and O'Shea, "Teachers' Academic Preparation in History," 4, 10. Some of these teachers majored in a social science, however, which is useful preparation for teaching American history. Crabtree and O'Shea also report that one in twelve history teachers has a BA in physical education; probably most of these are coaches. See also Robert A. Rutter, "Profile of the Profession," *Social Education*, no. 58 (4/1986): 253.

84. Joan M. Shaughnessy and Thomas M. Haladyna, "Research on Student Attitudes Toward Social Studies," *Social Education* 49 (November 1985): 692–95. See Mark Schug et al., "Why Kids Don't Like Social Studies," *Social Education* 48 (5/1984): 382–87; and Goodlad, "A Study of Schooling."

85. McNeil, "Defensive Teaching and Classroom Control," 117.

86. Ibid., 124; Jenness, *Making Sense of Social Studies*, 264–65, 291.

87. So teachers *couldn't* fall back on these lists, we eliminated *all* questions at the ends of chapters from *Mississippi: Conflict and Change*.

88. Patrick Ferguson, "Promoting Political Participation: Teachers' Attitudes and Instructional Practices" (San Francisco: American Educational Research Association, 1989), 4–5. The new *Pageant* does use *Eurocentric* inside an interesting boxed discussion of various scholars' views of Europe's influence on the United States.

89. In two respects, the inquiry books stand out: they provide primary sources and give much fuller treatment to the re-

cent past. Inquiry textbooks in my sample committed their share of errors of fact and interpretation, however. Jenness faults these textbooks for failing to see that expertise is required *in order* to reason appropriately about some controversies (*Making Sense of Social Studies*, 292). In casually assigning questions requiring weeks of research for a thoughtful answer, inquiry textbooks verge on being anti-intellectual, because they imply they don't really expect such thoroughness from students or teachers.

90. In some states, teachers can be held accountable for teaching the concepts that are in the adopted textbooks. See Sue Dueitt, "Textbooks and the Military," in Cole and Sticht, eds., *The Textbook in American Society*, 36.

91. Robert M. O'Neil, *Classrooms in the Crossfire* (Bloomington: Indiana University Press, 1981), 9–12, 23. Every year, People for the American Way documents what it calls *Attacks on the Freedom to Learn* in an annual by that title (Washington, D.C.: People for the American Way, 1993 and prior years). Jonathan Kozol tells of his own firing in Boston for teaching poetry by Langston Hughes in *Death at an Early Age* (New York: New American Library, 1985).

92. Carlson, "Academic Freedom in Hard Times," 430.

93. Kidder, *Among Schoolchildren*, 52; Kirst, *Who Controls Our Schools?* 135; Linda Levstik, "The Research Base for Curriculum Choice: A Response," *Social Education*, no. 54 (11/1990): 443.

94. See, inter alia, Gallup poll, 10/1987, reported in Stamford, CT, *Advocate*, 12/26/1987, 1.

95. Jean Fair, ed., *National Assessment and Social Studies Evaluation* (Washington, D.C.: National Council for the Social Studies, 1975), 35.

96. John Williamson quoted in Cole and Sticht, eds., *The Textbook in American Society*, 39.

97. Raymond English, "Can Social Studies Textbooks Have Scholarly Integrity?" *Social Education* 50, no. 1 (1/1986): 46–48.

98. Donald Barr, *Who Pushed Humpty Dumpty? Dilemmas in American Education Today* (New York: Atheneum, 1972), 316–17, tells how publishers have even tamed the story of the three little pigs, so now piggies number one and number two don't die but somehow run faster than the wolf from their smashed houses to the third piggie's suburban brick ranch.

99. Sissela Bok, *Lying* (New York: Pantheon, 1978), 24. Bok admits, however, that while people weigh the advantages of lying in a "nuanced way" when they imagine "themselves in the position of choosing whether or not to deceive," everyone wants "to avoid being deceived by *others* as much as possible." The Boston Children's Museum took a different and more honest tack in an exhibit on death; see "Children Learn That 'Dying Isn't a Vacation,'" *New York Times*, 8/26/1984. For other discussions of presenting controversial material to children, see Black, *The American Schoolbook*, 91–95; Kirsten Lundberg, "Addressing a Child's Fears about Life in the Nuclear Age," *Boston Globe*, 3/9/1986; and Betty Reardan, John Anthony Scott, and Sam Totten, "Nuclear Weapons: Concepts, Issues and Controversies," *Social Education* 47 (11/1983): 473–522.

100. See Natalie Gittelson, "The Fear That Haunts Our Children," *McCall's*, 5/1982, 77 et passim, and David S. Greenwald and Steven J. Zeitlin, *No Reason to Talk About It: Families Confront the Nuclear Taboo* (New York: Norton, 1986).

101. See Edward A. Wynne, "The Case for Censorship to Protect the Young," in *Issues in Education* (Winter 1985).

102. Mark Lloyd, interview, 1991.

103. Yankelovich, Skelly, and White, reported in "A 'New Breed' Emerges," *Family Weekly,* 1/1/1978.

104. In an astounding retreat from history, Arthur Schlesinger Jr., agrees: "I will be satisfied if we can teach children to read, write, and calculate," in "Toward a Divisive Diversity," *Wall Street Journal,* 6/25/1991.

105. Engle, "Late Night Thoughts About the New Social Studies," 20.

106. Francis Russell, *The Shadow of Blooming Grove* (New York: McGraw-Hill, 1968), 656.

107. Paul Gagnon, "Why Study History?" *Atlantic* (11/1988), 51.

108. Paul Gagnon, *Democracy's Untold Story* (Washington, D.C.: American Federation of Teachers, 1987), 19.

109. Heidegger, quoted in Noam Chomsky, *The Noam Chomsky Reader* (New York: Pantheon, 1987), 60.

CHAPTER 13: WHAT IS THE RESULT
OF TEACHING HISTORY LIKE THIS?

1. *Scopes trial transcript,* excerpt at "Day 7" at law.umkc.edu/faculty/projects/ftrials/scopes/day7.htm, 9/2006.

2. Jules Henry, *Culture Against Man* (New York: Random House, 1963), 287.

3. Jungle Brothers, "Acknowledge Your Own History," c. 1989. This African American rap group calls history *HIS story*, meaning "the Man's."

4. Greg Murry, e-mail, 2/2001.

5. Linda McNeil, "Defensive Teaching and Classroom Control," in Michael W. Apple and Lois Weis, eds., *Ideology and Practice in Schooling* (Philadelphia: Temple University Press, 1983), 128–41.

6. Robert B. Everhart, "Classroom Management," in Apple and Weis, eds., *Ideology and Practice in Schooling,* Ch. 7.

7. Probably the most important studies decrying what high school graduates don't know about history and geography are by Diane Ravitch and Chester E. Finn Jr., *What Do Our 17-Year-Olds Know?* (New York: Harper and Row, 1987), and the National Geographic Society, *Geography: An International Gallup Survey* (Washington, D.C.: National Geographic Society, 1988). See also Allen Bragdon, *Can You Pass These Tests?* (New York: Harper and Row, 1987), 129–40, comparing 1976 and 1943 results. The National Assessment of Educational Progress also decried U.S. high school seniors' knowledge of American history in 1994 and 2001. In 2006, however, they saw a bit of progress: the proportion scoring "Advanced" and "Proficient" increased in twelve years from 12 percent to 14 percent. "U.S. History 2006" at nces.ed.govtnationsreportcard/pdf/main2006/2007474_1.pdf.

8. Ravitch and Finn, *What Do Our 17-Year-Olds Know?* 49.

9. W. K. Haralson, "Objections [to *The American Adventure*]" (Longview, TX: n.d., typescript, distributed by Mel Gabler's Educational Research Analysts, 1993), 4.

10. John Goodlad, *A Place Called School* (New York: McGraw-Hill, 1983), argues that "affect—either positive or negative—was virtually absent" from the classrooms he and his associates studied. *Flat* is the adjective he applies to what went on.

11. Washington, D.C.: PBS *Frontline* video, 1985.

12. A. B. Hodgetts and Paul Gallagher, *Teaching Canada for the '80s* (Toronto: Ontario Institute for Studies in Education, 1978), 20.

13. John Ogbu, "Racial Stratification and Education," in Gail E. Thomas, ed., *U.S. Race Relations in the 1980s and 1990s* (New York: Hemisphere, 1990), 27–30. See also Herbert Kohl, "I Won't Learn from You!" in *I Won't Learn from You and Other Thoughts on Creative Maladjustment* (New York: New Press, 1994), 1–32. National Assessment of Educational Progress, *Report 1: 1969–1970 Science* (Washington, D.C.: NAEP, 1970), shows only small black/nonblack differences in science. Jean Fair, ed., *National Assessment and Social Studies Evaluation* (Washington, D.C.: National Council for the Social Studies, 1975), 56, 63–64, 77–82, shows large black/nonblack differences in social studies. Richard L. Sawyer, *College Student Profiles: Norms for the ACT Assessment, 1980–81* (Iowa City: ACT, 1980), gives norms in four academic areas, English, math, social studies, and natural sciences, by income, race, and so on.

14. Jeffrey Fouts, "Female Students, Women Teachers, and Perceptions of the Social Studies Classroom," *Social Education* 54 (11/1990): 418–20.

15. Arthur M. Schlesinger Jr., "When Ethnic Studies Are Un-American," *Social Studies Review*, no. 5 (Summer 1990): 11–13.

16. Martha Toppin, "I Know Who's Going with Me," *Social Education* 44 (10/1980): 458.

17. On Clifford, see Tom Wicker, "An Unwinnable War," *New York Times*, 6/12/1991; on McNamara, see Jonathan Mirsky, "Reconsidering Vietnam," *New York Review of Books*, 10/10/1991, 44. The Gallup poll, 11/1986, found 71 percent agreement (excluding "don't knows") that "the Vietnam War was more than a mistake: it was fundamentally wrong and immoral." In August 1984, the Roper organization asked "whether what this country did was the right thing or the wrong thing—or somewhere in between: fighting the war in Vietnam." Sixty-five percent said "wrong thing"; since 17 percent answered "somewhere in between" and 5 percent didn't know, 83 percent of persons making a choice called it wrong. For such proportions of the U.S. public in the 1980s to say that the Vietnam War was wrong, considering that the United States fought it and Presidents Reagan and Bush still defended it, shows strong opposition and independence of thought.

18. William L. Lunch and Peter W. Sprelich, "American Public Opinion and the War in Vietnam," *Western Political Quarterly* 32 (1979): 33–34. Leon Festinger, *A Theory of Cognitive Dissonance* (Evanston, IL: Row, Peterson, 1957). Festinger's theory also explains why male college students during World War II, who knew they were going to fight, were more pro-war than skilled electricians and welders, who knew they were going to be deferred to work in war industries. Both groups were bringing their opinions into line with their anticipated future actions, which they could not easily change.

19. John Mueller, *Presidents and Public Opinion* (New York: Wiley, 1973), 70–74; Harris poll reported in *Boston Globe*, 7/14/1969, on support for the Apollo program; see also Samuel P. Huntington, *The Common Defense*, 235–39.

20. "Foreign Policy Attitudes Now Driven by 9/11 and Iraq," Pew Trust survey, 8/18/2004, pewtrusts.org/ideas/ideas, 10/2006.

21. College students particularly have this reason to err, for they have "chosen"

(under the influence of their parents and their class position) to get college educations. In line with the principles of cognitive dissonance, they are likely to agree that people benefit from being in college and conclude that education leads to tolerance and wisdom. Many Americans see schooling as a panacea for racial inequality, environmental problems, or poverty.

22. Richard F. Hamilton, *Restraining Myths* (Beverly Hills: Sage, 1975), 118, 159; Lunch and Sprelich, "American Public Opinion and the War in Vietnam," 35–36.

23. *The American Tradition* encourages this wrong thinking by including a photograph of hard-hat counterdemonstrators supporting Nixon on Vietnam. "Who comprised the 'silent majority'?" *Tradition* asks, implying that working-class Americans did. *Land of Promise* similarly claims that a backlash among less educated people against "students who were leading the peace movement" allowed Nixon to continue the war.

24. Pew Research Center spokesperson summarizing information from 2005 survey, phone interview, 5/7/2007.

25. Richard Sennett and Jonathan Cobb, *Hidden Injuries of Class* (New York: Alfred A. Knopf, 1972).

26. See Erich Fromm, *Escape from Freedom* (New York: Farrar and Rinehart, 1941).

27. Robert Reinhold, Harris poll, reported in *New York Times*, 7/3/1971, quoted in Herbert Aptheker, *The Unfolding Drama* (New York: International, 1978), 146; Terry Borton, *The Weekly Reader National Survey on Education* (Middletown, CT: Field Publications, 1985), 14, 16; Joan M. Shaughnessy and Thomas M. Haladyna, "Research on Student Attitudes Toward Social Studies," *Social Education* 49 (11/1985): 692–95; Mark Schug, Robert Todd, and R. Beery, "Why Kids Don't Like Social Studies," *Social Education* 48 (5/1984): 382–87.

AFTERWORD:
THE FUTURE LIES AHEAD—
AND WHAT TO DO ABOUT THEM

1. Charles Sellers, "Is History on the Way Out of the Schools and Do Historians Care?" *Social Education* 33 (5/1969), 511, paraphrasing S. Samuel Shermis.

2. Neil Postman and Charles Weingartner, *Teaching as a Subversive Activity* (New York: Delacorte, 1969), 23.

3. Anatole France quoted in Freeman Tilden, *Interpreting Our Heritage* (Chapel Hill: University of North Carolina Press, 1967), v.

4. Vine Deloria Jr., *God Is Red* (New York: Dell, 1973) 301.

5. Indeed, during the first five decades of the twentieth century, Catholic schools taught American history from Catholic books—textbooks written especially to emphasize Father Junipero Serra, for instance, the priest who helped found the mission system in California in the eighteenth century.

6. One reason I did not devote a chapter to these topics is that others have repeatedly done the job, among them Mary Kay Tetreault, "Integrating Women's History: The Case of United States History High School Textbooks," *The History Teacher* 19 (2/1986): 211–62; Glen Blankenship, "How to Test a Textbook for Sexism," *Social Education* 48 (4/1984): 282–83; Darrell F. Kirby and Nancy B. Julian, "Treatment of Women in High School U.S. History Textbooks," *Social Studies* 72 (9/1981): 203–7; a special issue of *Social Education* 51, no. 3 (3/1987); and earlier, J. W. Smith, *An Appraisal of the Treatment of Females in United States High School History Textbooks* (PhD diss., Indiana Uni-

versity, 1977), and Janice Law Trecker, "Women in U.S. History High School Textbooks," *Social Education* (March 1971): 249–60. Also thought-provoking is Patricia Higgins, "New Gender Perspectives in Anthropology," *Anthropology Notes* 11, no. 3 (Fall 1989): 1–3, 13–15. Two very readable books introduce women's history effectively: Ruth Warren, *A Pictorial History of Women in America* (New York: Crown, 1975), and Elizabeth Janeway, ed., *Women: Their Changing Roles* (New York: Times/Arno Press, 1973).

7. If you agree, email me at jloewen@uvm.edu and bring them to my attention. Please know that whatever omissions and distortions I have perpetuated here have been accidental; to paraphrase Ernst Borinski, long-time professor of sociology at Tougaloo College, "What I have not learned, I do not know." If my tone has been too certain, know, too, that my own conclusions, whether about the causes of the War of 1812 or the effects of the civil rights movement, are still in flux.

8. Postman and Weingartner, *Teaching as a Subversive Activity;* term used throughout.

9. Neither do their teachers: several teachers I have met who taught from *Triumph of the American Nation* never noticed that it mildly counters the flat-earth notion, and continued to teach the myth to their high school students. College professors, too, can miss facts that go against the archetypal grain. After I lectured on the Pilgrims and the plague at a university in Atlanta, a history professor came up to me, amazed to learn of the plague, and decried the monograph from which he had learned colonial history for leaving out such an important fact. We withdrew to his office so he could check sources to prove to himself I was right about the plague; he grew further amazed to find the plague story mentioned in precisely the book he had criticized for omitting it!

10. Mircea Eliade, *The Myth of the Eternal Return* (New York: Pantheon, 1954), 46.

11. For teachers, here are a few references to get you started. James Percoco, a fine high school history teacher, has written two books of tips: *A Passion for the Past* (New York: Heinemann, 1998) and *Divided We Stand* (New York: Heinemann, 2001). Some of his scores of suggestions won't work for you, but some will. David Kobrin only suggests a handful of ideas in *Beyond the Textbook* (New York: Heinemann, 1996), but he explores each in depth, showing pitfalls to avoid. Stephen Botein et al., *Experiments in History Teaching* (Cambridge: Harvard-Danforth Center for Teaching and Learning, 1977), presents classroom exercises and research projects developed by high school, college, and community teachers. Gary Smith et al., *Teaching About United States History* (Denver: Center for Teaching International Relations, 1988), and Clair Keller, "Using Creative Interviews to Personalize Decision-Making on the American Revolution," *Social Education* 43 (3/1979): 271, suggest various learning projects. John Anthony Scott proposes ways to teach history without using textbooks in "There Is Another Way," *AHA Perspectives* 29, no. 5 (5/1991): 20–22; cf. Gary Nash, "Response," 21, 23, of the same issue. *Rethinking Schools* (1001 E. Keefe Ave., Milwaukee, WI, 53212) provides a fascinating if sometimes irritating mixture of educational ideas of national significance and news of school policies in Milwaukee. *Rethinking* also sells back issues and reprints. Four other periodicals contain ideas especially useful for teachers of American history: *The History Teacher, Social Education* (Washington, D.C.: National Council for

the Social Studies), *The Radical Teacher*, and *Democracy and Education* (313 McCracken Hall, Ohio University, Athens, OH 45701). The National Council for History Education, Suite B2, 26915 Westwood Road, Westlake, OH, 44145, distributes Paul Gagnon's important book, *Democracy's Half-Told Story*, and other material intended to improve how American history is taught. James Davidson and Mark Lytle's *After the Fact* (New York: McGraw-Hill, 1992) suggests important historical issues to explore. The massive general catalog from Social Studies School Service (PO Box 802, Culver City, CA, 90232) lists compact textbooks for American history; their use would free class time for study of a few issues in depth.

Another suggestion is to use two textbooks. This raises many issues, as students question why they differ, thereby realizing that history is not just writing down "the truth" for students to "learn." Even two editions of the same textbook can play this role, but it is more interesting to use very different books. Within my sample, the inquiry texts, Allan O. Kownslar and Donald B. Frizzle, *Discovering American History* (New York: Holt, Rinehart and Winston, 1974), and Social Science Staff of the Educational Research Council of America, *The American Adventure* (Boston: Allyn and Bacon, 1975), provide the greatest contrast to the usual narrative textbooks, but they are both out of print. Students could use reserve copies at their school library, however. Joy Hakim's series, *A History of US* (New York: Oxford University Press, 2006 [1993]), reads well and should be in every classroom.

More interesting still is to compare a very different book with a standard textbook. Possibilities include Howard Zinn's *A People's History of the United States* (New York: Harper, 2005), a left-wing approach, and Clarence B. Carson, *A Basic History of the United States* (Wadley, AL: American Textbook Committee, 1986), from the right. Or histories emphasizing a particular group or theme can be used, such as those listed in note 13 below.

Other ideas are available at workshops, seminars, and summer institutes for history teachers run by the National Endowment for the Humanities and state endowments, universities, historical museums, and professional associations.

I also hope that the full citations provided in the endnotes the first time a source is cited in each chapter will prove as useful as a separate bibliography.

12. *Using Taking Sides in the Classroom* (Guilford, CT: Dushkin, 1996), a guide for teachers using Dushkin's popular series, suggests ways to help students develop critical thinking skills and manage conflicting points of view. It is out of print but is usually available on the web. Also see Bill Bigelow, ed., et al., *Rethinking Our Classrooms* (Milwaukee: Rethinking Schools, 2007).

13. *Jackdaws*, packets of copies of original historical materials, are published by Jackdaw Publications (jackdaw.com). Several textbook publishers put out teachers' kits that are more interesting than their textbooks. Teaching for Change (teachingforchange.org) puts out a useful and compact catalog of materials for history teachers. Social Studies School Service puts out *Multicultural Studies Catalog*, which groups teaching materials for women's history, Hispanic history, and so on. Accessible at any university library, the ERIC database reports thousands of teaching ideas indexed by keywords on CD-ROM and available on microfiche. Some articles are online at eric.ed.gov.

American literature usefully ties in with American history, so long as that literature is historically accurate. Thus, *Okla Hannali* by R. A. Lafferty offers a rich overview of the nineteenth century.

Anthro. Notes, a newsletter published by the National Museum of Natural History (Kaupp, Public Information Office, Dept. of Anthropology, Stop 112, Smithsonian Institution, Washington, D.C. 20560) and available at no cost to high school teachers, often treats pre-Columbian Native American societies. My own 1992 book, *Lies My Teacher Told Me About Christopher Columbus* (New York: New Press, thenewpress.com), is a poster-book intended for classroom use in early October; it introduces students to issues of historiography and textbook analysis as well as the Great Navigator. Beverly Slapin and Doris Seale, *Through Indian Eyes*, published by Oyate, contains useful poetry and essays by Michael Dorris and other Native writers, a checklist for evaluating books for their treatment of Indian issues, and an extensive resource list. For teachers, Gary Nash's *Red, White, and Black* (Englewood Cliffs, NJ: Prentice Hall, 1974) is a masterful overview of race relations in colonial America.

The Office of Elementary and Secondary Education at the Smithsonian Institution (A&I Building, Room 1163, MRC 402, Washington, D.C., 20560) distributes *Teaching the Constitution*, a summary of their 1987 "Symposium for Educators" by that title. It offers ways to use documents, projects to make the issues come alive today, and a bibliography of resources for classroom use. See also *Teaching About the Bill of Rights* (Bethesda, MD: Phi Alpha Delta Public Service Center, c. 1987).

Histories of black-white race relations, such as *African American History* by Langston Hughes and Milton Meltzer (New York: Scholastic, 1990) on the high

school level and *Before the Mayflower* by Lerone Bennett (Baltimore: Penguin, 1966 [1962]) and *From Slavery to Freedom* by John Hope Franklin (New York: Knopf, 2000) on the advanced high school level relate to many issues in American history. In 1994 the Anti-Defamation League (823 United Nations Plaza, New York, NY, 10017) put out a new edition of David Shiman's *The Prejudice Book*, with classroom exercises on issues of race and gender relations. Several books by James A. Banks have useful ideas, including *Teaching Strategies for Ethnic Studies* (Boston: Allyn and Bacon, 1987) and *Multiethnic Education: Theory and Practice* (Boston: Allyn and Bacon, 1994). See also Carl A. Grant and Christine Sleeter, *Turning On Learning* (Columbus, OH: Merrill, 1989). *We Shall Overcome*, PBS *Frontline* video (1-800-328-7271), tells something of the impact of American antiracism overseas.

The Association for Supervision and Curriculum Development (1250 N. Pitt St., Alexandria, VA, 22314-1453), concerned that textbooks ignore religious ideas in our past, publishes a collection of primary documents by Charles C. Haynes, *Religion in American History*. It lives up to its subtitle, "What to Teach and How."

The American Social History Project's *Who Built America?* (New York: Pantheon, 1989), also available in a gripping video version on CD-ROM for Apple equipment, from Voyager (1-800-446-2001), makes labor history come alive. *How Schools Are Teaching About Labor*, published periodically by the AFL-CIO (815 16th St. NW, Washington, D.C., 20006), supplies lesson plans and classroom materials. *Labor's Heritage*, a quarterly from the AFL-CIO (10000 New Hampshire Ave., Silver Spring, MD, 20903), has produced teachers' guides and posters on teaching history and using local sources. *Power in Our Hands*, by Bill Bigelow and Norman Diamond (New York: Monthly Review Press, 1988), contains interesting exercises to get students to think about social class.

On the federal government, Jonathan Kwitny's *Endless Enemies* (New York: Congdon and Weed, 1984) wins my nod for teachers, because he condemns our counterproductive repression of popular movements abroad from a nevertheless patriotic perspective. Lonnie Bunch and Michelle K. Smith explore ways citizens have obliged governments to act in *Protest and Patriotism* (Washington, D.C.: Smithsonian Office of Elementary and Secondary Education [A&I Building, Room 1163, MRC 402, Washington, D.C., 20560], n.d.). The Center for Social Studies Education (teachvietnam.net) puts out an extensive kit for teaching high school students about the Vietnam War. Brooke Workman, *Teaching the Sixties*, published in 1992 by the National Council of Teachers of English (ncte.org), is somewhat diffuse and affable but offers ways for students to learn about that turbulent decade. The 1960s are also emphasized in *Teaching Tolerance* 1, no. 1, available to teachers without charge from the Southern Poverty Law Center, 400 Washington Ave., Montgomery, AL, 36104, which also distributes the *Civil Rights Teaching Kit*. Finally, a novel by Marge Piercy, *Woman on the Edge of Time* (New York: Fawcett Crest, 1977), provides a fun way to get students to think about progress and the future.

In addition to these mostly print recommendations, ever-changing websites provide crucial information. Of course students will use the Web, but remember two rules: first, they must not stop there.

Books still exist, along with the census, old-timers to be interviewed, etc. Second, students should annotate every source, Web or not, with a sentence telling why it is credible (for the use made of it). Thousands of primary sources are available at the Library of Congress (loc.gov) and National Archives (archives.gov). Census data by county in very usable form is at the Fisher Library of the University of Virginia (fisher.lib.virginia.edu/collections/stats/listcensus/). Data for towns is at the U.S. Census (census.gov/prod/www/abs/decennial/index.htm). Teachers should sign up for h-high-s and other discussion lists (free) at h-net.org. When history makes news, it is summarized at History News Network (hnn.us/), which anyone can sign up for. Students need good vetted sites, arranged by topic area (e.g., women's history, Civil War, etc.). There are many, including besthistorysites.net. A host of video and film resources exist, from feature films such as *Glory* and *Missing* to PBS documentaries such as *The Civil War*, *Eyes on the Prize*, and *Remember My Lai* (PBS *Frontline*, 1-800-328-7271). As they use videos, teachers may want to consider the points in Linda Christensen's "Unlearning the Myths That Bind Us," *Rethinking Schools* 5, no. 4 (5/1991): 1, 15–16.

14. Glenn Whitman gets his students doing local history and explains how in *Dialogue with the Past* (Lanham, MD: Alta Mira, 2004).

15. Rural Organizing and Cultural Center, *Minds Stayed on Freedom* (Boulder, CO: Westview, 1992). See also C. L. Lord, *Teaching History with Community Resources* (New York: Teachers College Press, 1967).

16. Mark Hilgendorf, ed., *Forgotten Voices in American History* (available from

Milton Academy, 170 Centre St., Milton, MA, 02186).

17. Shirley Engle tells how some of these questions, based on work by Alfred North Whitehead, were the basis of an innovation in social studies teaching, the "Indiana experiment." See "Late Night Thoughts About the New Social Studies," *Social Education* 50, no. 1 (1/1986): 21.

18. We did this in Chapter 6 when considering Abraham Lincoln's Greeley letter.

19. James Axtell, "Forked Tongues: Moral Judgments in Indian History," *AHA Perspectives* 25, no. 2 (2/1987): 10.

20. Lee Jones, "Textbooks: A Change of View," *Austin Star-Telegram*, 10/20/1985.

21. Michael Wallace, "The Politics of Public History," in Jo Blatti, ed., *Past Meets Present* (Washington, D.C.: Smithsonian Institution Press, 1987), 42–43.

22. Quoted in Lewis H. Lapham, "Notebook," *Harper's*, 7/1991, 12.

23. Well, I also did other things.

APPENDIX

HERE, LISTED ALPHABETICALLY BY TITLE, are the twelve American history textbooks I surveyed in preparing *Lies My Teacher Told Me*, followed on the next page by the six books I studied for the second edition. Quoted material is taken from these editions unless otherwise noted in the text.

Social Science Staff of the Educational Research Council of America, *The American Adventure* (Boston: Allyn and Bacon, 1975).

Ira Peck, Steven Jantzen, and Daniel Rosen, *American Adventures* (Austin, TX: Steck-Vaughn, 1987).

John A. Garraty with Aaron Singer and Michael Gallagher, *American History* (New York: Harcourt Brace Jovanovich, 1982).

Thomas A. Bailey and David M. Kennedy, *The American Pageant* (Lexington, MA: D. C. Heath, 1991).

Robert Green, Laura L. Becker, and Robert E. Coviello, *The American Tradition* (Columbus, OH: Charles E. Merrill, 1984).

Nancy Bauer, *The American Way* (New York: Holt, Rinehart and Winston, 1979).

Robert Sobel, Roger LaRaus, Linda Ann De Leon, and Harry P. Morris, *The Challenge of Freedom* (Mission Hills, CA: Glencoe, 1990).

Allan O. Kownslar and Donald B. Frizzle, *Discovering American History* (New York: Holt, Rinehart and Winston, 1974).

Carol Berkin and Leonard Wood, *Land of Promise* (Glenview, IL: Scott, Foresman, 1983).

Philip Roden, Robynn Greer, Bruce Kraig, and Betty Bivins, *Life and Liberty* (Glenview, IL: Scott, Foresman, 1984).

Paul Lewis Todd and Merle Curti, *Triumph of the American Nation* (Orlando, FL: Harcourt Brace Jovanovich, 1986).

James West Davidson and Mark H. Lytle, *The United States—A History of the Republic* (Englewood Cliffs, NJ: Prentice Hall, 1981).

Joyce Appleby, Alan Brinkley, and James McPherson, *The American Journey* (New York: Glencoe McGraw-Hill, 2000).

David M. Kennedy, Lizabeth Cohen, and Thomas A. Bailey, *The American Pageant* (Boston: Houghton Mifflin, 2006).

Gerald A. Danzer et al., *The Americans* (Boston: McDougal Littell [Houghton Mifflin], 2007).

Andrew Cayton, Elisabeth Perry, Linda Reed, and Allan Winkler, *America: Pathways to the Present* (Needham, MA: Pearson Prentice Hall, 2005).

Daniel Boorstin and Brooks Mather Kelley, *A History of the United States* (Needham, MA: Pearson Prentice Hall, 2005.)

Paul Boyer, *Holt American Nation* (Austin, TX: Holt, Rinehart & Winston [Harcourt], 2003).

INDEX

Crosby, Alfred, 62, 77
Cuba, 59, 66, 150, 152; U.S. interventions in, 16, 17, 227, 230–31
cultural imperialism, 105–6
Cushman, Robert, 75, 76

da Gama, Vasco, 45, 46
Darrow, Clarence, 340
Davidson, James West, 41, 251, 315, 324, 325; *see also* United States, The—A History of the Republic
Davis, Jefferson, 194
de Alva, J. Klor, 72
Debs, Eugene V., 15, 22, 24
Decatur, Stephen, 235
Declaration of Independence, 109, 148, 183, 186
DeLeon, Linda Ann, 72
de Leon, Ponce, 104
Delong, James F., 242
Deloria, Vine, Jr., 280, 355
de Madariaga, Salvador, 53
Democratic Party, 209; in Civil War and Reconstruction, 155–57, 190–92, 197; as white-supremacist party, 21, 149, 153, 155–56
Dermer, Capt. Thomas, 81, 87
De Soto, Hernando, 45–46, 77, 107
Diamond, Jared, 37
Díaz, Bernal, 100
Discovering American History, 173, 352; comparatively good coverage by, 111, 132, 190, 241, 251, 257; as "inquiry" textbook, 132, 331
diseases, 72–74, 91, 422; *see also* plagues
Disney enterprises, 28, 189, 295
Dixon, Thomas, 21
Dobyns, Henry, 77–78
Dominican Republic, 16, 17
Donald, David, 290
Dorris, Michael, 70, 90, 93
Douglas, Stephen A., 153–54, 183
Douglass, Frederick, 29, 174, 177, 184, 203, 244
Dred Scott decision, 151, 167, 243
Du Bois, W. E. B., 11, 135
Dulles, John Foster, 255
Dumbrell, John, 257

economic growth, 284, 285
Educational Research Analysts, 215
Eisenhower, Dwight D., 228, 229, 233
Eliade, Mircea, 88–89, 356
Emancipation Proclamation, 185
Engle, Shirley, 302–3, 327, 337
environmental movement, 241

environmental problems, 286–94, 298–99
epidemics, *see* plagues
Erasmus, William, 65
Escott, Paul, 193–94
ethnocentrism, 88, 90, 297, 331
Europe, impact on, of conquests, 60–63
Evers, Medgar, 260
explorers before Columbus, 33, 38

Fallows, James, 266, 276
Farb, Peter, 131, 296
Fausz, J. F., 126
Federal Bureau of Investigation (FBI), 236–40, 243
Ferro, Marc, 301, 303
Festinger, Leon, 62, 263
FitzGerald, Frances, 146, 162, 172, 215, 221–22, 254, 280
flat-earth fable, 49–50, 327
Flournoy, Robert, 199, 201
Foner, Eric, 263
foreign aid, 90, 221–22
foreign policy: realpolitik approach to, 221, 235; and slavery, 150–51; under Woodrow Wilson, 15–19, 225, 226, 234; after World War II, 28, 221–24; *see also* Vietnam War; War of 1812
Forrest, Nathan Bedford, 195
Fort Pillow massacre, 195
Fourteenth Amendment, 197, 236
France, Anatole, 355
Frank, Mitch, 265–66
Franklin, Benjamin, 108, 109, 111, 119
Freire, Paulo, 305
French and Indian War, 117, 118, 129
Frisch, Michael, 24–25

Gabler, Mel, 215, 242
Gabler, Norma, 26
Gagnon, Paul, 219, 231, 338
Garison, William Lloyd, 179
Garraty, John A., 83, 324; *see also* American History
Geffert, Hannah, 176
Gettysburg Address, 185–88
Giroux, Henry, 305
Gleijesus, Piero, 18
Gone With the Wind (novel and movie), 135, 136, 144, 161, 332
Goodlad, John, 328
Goodman, Andrew, 179–80, 238
"Good Neighbor Policy," 17
Gorges, Ferdinando, 81, 87
Graff, Henry, 34
Grand Army of the Republic, 196
Grant, Ulysses S., 21